Proceedings

Technology of Object-Oriented Languages and Systems

TOOLS 30

Proceedings

Technology of Object-Oriented Languages and Systems

TOOLS 30

August 1-5, 1999

Santa Barbara, California

Edited by

Donald Firesmith, Richard Riehle, Gilda Pour, and Bertrand Meyer

Sponsored by

Interactive Software Engineering, Inc.

IEEE
COMPUTER
SOCIETY

Los Alamitos, California

Washington • Brussels • Tokyo

IEEE Computer Society Order Number PR00278
ISBN 0-7695-0278-4
ISBN 0-7695-0280-6 (microfiche)
Library of Congress Number: 99-63093
IEEE Order Plan Catalog Number PR00278

Additional copies may be ordered from:

IEEE Computer Society
Customer Service Center
10662 Los Vaqueros Circle
P.O. Box 3014
Los Alamitos, CA 90720-1314
Tel: + 1-714-821-8380
Fax: + 1-714-821-4641
cs.books@computer.org

IEEE Service Center
445 Hoes Lane
P.O. Box 1331
Piscataway, NJ 08855-1331
Tel: + 1-732-981-0060
Fax: + 1-732-981-9667
mis.custserv@computer.org

IEEE Computer Society
Watanabe Building
1-4-2 Minami-Aoyama
Minato-ku, Tokyo 107-0062
JAPAN
Tel: + 81-3-3408-3118
Fax: + 81-3-3408-3553
tokyo.ofc@computer.org

Editorial production by Frances M. Titsworth

Cover art production by Joseph Daigle/Studio Productions

Printed in the United States of America by The Printing House

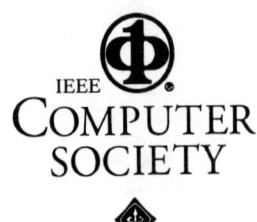

IEEE
COMPUTER
SOCIETY

TABLE OF CONTENTS

Technology of Object-Oriented Languages and Systems (TOOLS 30)

KEYNOTE PRESENTATIONS

TECHNICAL PAPERS

QUALITY

DATABASES

FRAMEWORKS2

METHODS2

TEACHING

JAVA2

TECHNOLOGY

METHODOLOGY

EXPERIENCE

PREFACE

On behalf of the TOOLS USA'99 program committee, welcome to the 30th TOOLS conference. The TOOLS conferences have always had an emphasis on quality, largely because of their long and close association with Eiffel and Design by Contract. This year, we wanted to further that emphasis by explicitly soliciting papers concerning quality, especially in the area of object-oriented testing. Thus, the theme this year is "Delivering Quality Software – The Road Ahead."

In spite of the name, the TOOLS USA '99 conference is truly international in scope. The program committee members come from eight countries, and the presenters of the technical papers come from eleven countries on four continents.

There were 97 technical paper submissions this year, an increase of 43% over the 68 that were submitted last year. Although each of these papers represented a significant investment by their authors, the program committee was committed to maintain the high quality of past conferences by being highly selective. In the end, we narrowed the selection to only 37 papers, thereby ensuring that the attendees and readers of these proceedings will find them packed with highly useful information.

Although the workload increased significantly, the program committee this year was only slightly larger than last year. Thus, each member of the committee was asked to review 8 to 10 papers in the short time we had between their submission and when the review results were sent to the authors. It is therefore my pleasure to thank and honor the other 22 members of the program committee: Nadia Adhami, Vasu Alagar, Jan Bosch, Benjamin Brosgol, Alistair Cockburn, Derek Coleman, Raimund K. Ege, Martin Griss, Brian Henderson-Sellers, Laura Hill, Stuart Kent, Reto Kramer, Qiaoyun Li (Liz), Robert Marcus, John McGregor, James McKim, Richard Mitchell, Michael Philippsen, Reinhold Plösch, Bran Selic, Frank Tip, and Jeffrey Voas. I would also like to thank the following additional people who helped the program committee members during the review process: PerOlof Bengtsson, Regis Brochu, Matthias Gimbel, Jilles van Gurp, Michael Mattsson, Andre van Meulebrouck, D. Muthiayen, Olga Ormandjieva, F. Pompeo, Mikael Svahnberg, Zhicheng Lance Wang, and Jim Willette.

Last, but not least, I would like to give special thanks to Karen Ouellette for her support in organizing the conference and setting up the program committee's web pages.

Donald Firesmith
TOOLS USA '99 Program Chair
Lante, USA

PROGRAM COMMITTEE

Chairperson: Donald Firesmith
Lante, USA

Nadia Adhami	Countrywide, USA
Vasu Alagar	Concordia University, Canada
Jan Bosch	University of Karlskrona/Ronneby, Sweden
Benjamin Brosgol	Aonix, USA
Alistair Cockburn	Humans and Technology, USA
Derek Coleman	Hewlett-Packard, USA
Raimund K. Ege	Florida International University, USA
Martin Griss	Hewlett-Packard Laboratories, USA
Brian Henderson-Sellers	University of Technology, Sydney, Australia
Laura Hill	Sun Microsystems, USA
Stuart Kent	University of Kent, UK
Reto Kramer	Cambridge Technology Partners, Switzerland
Qiaoyun Li	Sony Electronics Inc., USA
Robert Marcus	General Motors, USA
John McGregor	Software Architects, USA
James C. McKim	Rensselaer at Hartford, USA
Richard Mitchell	University of Brighton, UK
Michael Philippsen	University of Karlsruhe, Germany
Reinhold Plösch	Johannes Kepler University, Austria
Bran Selic	ObjecTime Limited, Canada
Frank Tip	IBM T.J. Watson Research Center, USA
Jeffrey Voas	RST Corporation, USA

Tutorials Chair:
Richard Riehle, AdaWorks, USA

Workshops & Panels Chair:
Gilda Pour, San Jose State University, USA

Eiffel Summit Chair:
Roger Osmond, Amalasoft, USA

Conference Series Chair:
Bertrand Meyer, Interactive Software Engineering, USA

Keynote Presentations

Tools for Component Documentation, Analysis and Testing

David L. Parnas
McMaster University, Canada

The best software components will be hard to use unless they are accompanied by precise accurate documentation. The talk describes some powerful notation for writing such documentation and tools that can be used to produce such documentation and check that it accurately describes the software.

David Lorge Parnas is the NSERC/Bell Industrial Research Chair in Software Engineering in the McMaster University Faculty of Engineering's Computing and Software Department where he is Director of the Software Engineering Programme. He is also an associate member of the Department of Electrical and Computer Engineering. He has been Professor at the University of Victoria, the Technische Hochschule Darmstadt, the University of North Carolina at Chapel Hill, Carnegie Mellon University and the University of Maryland. He has also held non-academic positions advising Philips Computer Industry (Apeldoorn), the United States Naval Research Laboratory in Washington, D.C., the IBM Federal Systems Division, and the Atomic Energy Control Board of Canada.

The Unity of Software and the Power of Roundtrip Engineering

Bertrand Meyer

Interactive Software Engineering, USA

Part of the initial progress in developing an engineering basis for software development was to identify the specific tasks at hand and highlight their differences. Although that step was probably inevitable, it has led to a somewhat skewed view of software engineering, which ignores the fundamental unity of software construction, and leads to unnecessary gaps, detrimental to quality and productivity. It is more fruitful to take advantage of the fundamental invariants of software development and view system engineering as a continuous, seamless and reversible process. The talk will show how that full roundtrip engineering is possible in practice, leading to far higher quality of both process and product.

Bertrand Meyer is president of Interactive Software Engineering and a pioneer of object technology through his books, in particular "Object-Oriented Software Construction" (whose second edition published by Prentice Hall received the Software Development Jolt Product Excellence Award 1997), "Reusable Software" and "Object Success". Active in both the business and academic scenes he has directed the development of widely used O-O tools and libraries totaling hundreds of thousands of lines, and taught O-O principles and modern software engineering worldwide. He is editor of the Object Technology column of IEEE Computer, the Eiffel column in the JOOP, the Prentice Hall O-O Series, and the Addison-Wesley Eiffel in Practice Series.

Life After the Object Wars

Don Box
DevelopMentor, USA

The object technology field has been fraught with format wars that have stifled wide spread adoption of any one particular technology. While language wars have existed since the beginning of time, the attention of most of the software industry has shifted from language debates to the component and distributed object battlefields. While it is difficult to predict which (if any) technology will dominate component software or distributed computing, a fair amount of common ground can be found if one is willing to "put down the sword" and view how each of the various camps solves the problems at hand. In that spirit, this talk will present a unified view of component software based on the common ideas shared by the dominant component technologies, identifying the best (and worst) aspects of the current state-of-the-practice in component development.

Don Box is a cofounder of DevelopMentor, a component software think tank that educates most of the industry on COM-related technologies. Don is the author of "Essential COM" and a coauthor of "Effective COM," both from Addison Wesley. Don is a contributing editor at Microsoft Systems Journal, where he writes the bimonthly "House of COM" column.

Programming Language Design and Software Quality

Tucker Taft
AverStar USA

When designing a programming language, one essential fact must be remembered: programmers are humans, with the human penchant for making mistakes. Are there ways that the design of a programming language can help overcome our human weaknesses, by allowing the implementation to catch, at compile-time, many of the kinds of mistakes we make, or failing that, at run-time? This talk will discuss some of the techniques that can be used during language design to make typical mistakes easier to detect, and thereby help programmers achieve a higher level of quality at an earlier stage in the life-cycle of an application. The talk will include examples from various recent programming language designs, including C++, Eiffel, Ada 95, and Java.

S. Tucker Taft is Technical Director of the AverStar, Inc. (formerly Intermetrics, Inc.) Distributed Information Technology Solutions (DITS) division. He is also chief architect for AverStar's Ada 95 technology, called "AdaMagic"™.

Mr. Taft graduated from Harvard College in 1975 with a bachelor's in Chemistry, Summa Cum Laude, and then worked four years for Harvard in the student computer center, managing the first Unix system that was installed outside of AT&T. Thereafter he worked one year as a private consultant, and then in 1980 joined Intermetrics. While at Intermetrics, he participated in the development of the Ada Integrated Environment for the Air Force, a commercial C cross-compiler, the Common APSE Interface Set (CAIS), and an Ada binding to SQL (SAME). From 1990 to 1995, Mr. Taft led the Ada 9X language design team, culminating in the February 1995 approval of Ada 95 as the first ISO standardized object-oriented programming language. More recently, Mr. Taft led the development of Intermetrics/Averstar's Ada 95 to Java byte-code compiler, called "AppletMagic"™.

Technical Papers

Quality

Performance Tuning Mobile Agent Workflow Applications

Sterling S. Foster
Dept. of Defense,
ssfoste@afterlife.ncsc.mil

Dana Moore
AT&T Laboratories
Dana.Moore@att.net

Michael J. Flester
RABA Technologies
Mike.Flester@raba.com

Bohdan A. Nebesh
Dept. of Defense
banebes@afterlife.ncsc.mil

Abstract

Workflow systems based on mobile software agents improve overall flexibility and adaptability. The design of such systems does however, require that some attention be paid to performance tuning. This paper describes a decentralized agent control and management strategy that prevents system flooding and maintains good overall system throughput. Control of the system is divided among the following three controlling entities: the Workflow Service Broker (WSB), Agent, and Agent Pool. The WSB maintains information about what services are available on the network. The Agent maintains its itinerary, current state, and travel log; this information is used in conjunction with the information from the WSB to direct routing of the Agent. The Agent Pool maintains information about the number of agents in the system, and the overall system load. We discuss the implementation of this control strategy in a workflow application called Autopilot, which is a heterogeneous text processing workflow system where the elements are of unknown complexity and size, and where the potential processing paths through the routing domain are initially unknown. We discuss performance tuning aspects of the system and offer conclusions on such issues as agent pooling, payload simplification, object reference vs. object movement, and service co-location.

1   Introduction

Workflow management systems (WFMS) are complex multi-stage processes. Examples of WFMS might be include medical claims processing, service activation processing for a telephone company, or purchase request approval. Typical extra-organizational WFMS applications include multi-party bid and offer systems in an auction system, or supplier chain inventory management system.

Automation of traditional WFMS succeed best when the logic for moving work forward is (largely) invariant, when the structure of the data (document) being processed is well-known *a priori*. For example, the amount requested might differ between two purchase requests, or the activation dates in a service request, however the field definitions in the documents themselves would not vary. WFMS which use Lotus Notes as undercarriage, for example, rely on a combination of rigid document definition, a user invoked store-and-forward (email) system, field validation scripting, and rigid document routing.

2   The Autopilot WFMS

In contrast, the design of Autopilot WFMS is based on several functional goals that are unlike traditional WFMS:

- No two documents entering the system should be considered alike in any way.
- The structure and content of documents are initially in an 'unknown' state.
- The overall system goal is to clarify, tag, and transform a given document.
- The system must allow for the addition or deletion of services while in operation.
- No rigid path through the system should be pre-defined.

These goals led us to consider design metaphors such as Mobile Agents, Places, and Workflow Service Brokers, as further documented in [3,4].

3   Autopilot: an Agent based Workflow Application

In order to create and study the practical implementation issues in a dynamic system with a large number of processing paths, a wide variety of payload sizes and complexity, we chose to apply an agent-based architecture to the problem of processing and disseminating incoming documents to appropriate users based on their interests. This is one of the problems being addressed by the Defense Advanced Research Projects Agency (DARPA) and the intelligence community TIPSTER Text Program [14]. TIPSTER is an effort to advance the state of the art in text processing technologies, specifically in the areas of: 1). Information Retrieval; 2). Message Understanding; and 3). Summarization. The resulting research system, Autopilot allowed us to study a number of questions in a highly distributed Java-language environment. Figure 1 depicts the use of mobile agents as the locus of control and processing in Autopilot.

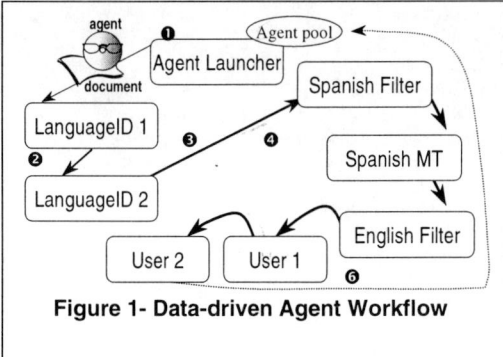

Figure 1- Data-driven Agent Workflow

(1). As a new document arrives at the system boundary, the Agent Launcher finds an available Agent from the Agent pool.

(2). The Agent consults a WSB that suggests the best (lowest cost) service available, in this case, the cheapest identifier Place, and then a second since the first Place could not identify the document.

(3). The document is identified as a Spanish language document. The Agent improves the document's state from 'UNKNOWN' to 'Spanish.'

(4).The Agent again consults a WSB to gain knowledge about how to further improve a Spanish document. It looks for Service Providers which have advertised an ability to process documents whose form is 'Spanish' and finds that the Spanish Machine Translation Service can translate a Spanish document to English. The Agent travels to the Spanish Translation Provider with the document and meta-data.

(5).The Agent consults a WSB and is directed to the nearest English Filter Place, which tells the Agent to give the document to users 1 and 2.

(6). The Agent will continue in this fashion until a state is reached in which no additional improvement can be done. Ultimately, the current state of the document will be set via one of the Service Providers, so that, when the Agent consults a WSB for a final time, a User Drop-off Place is its destination. When the Agent arrives at a drop-off point, it deposits documents of interest in the user's preferred directory. The document has been formatted for presentation in a browser. The document is also keyword indexed and archived. The Agent is recycled at the end of its mission, by traveling back to the Agent Launcher Place. The Agent Launcher Place voids the references to the Agent's data, and returns it to the Agent Pool. The Agent detects that is on its way back to the Launcher Place and scrubs its own payload, thereby avoiding serialization costs.

4 Agent Control and Management

The design abstractions in Autopilot with both functional and performance implications are Agents, Places, and Workflow Service Brokers (WSB). An Agent in AutoPilot can migrate from one address space to another while carrying its payload (data and meta-data.) A Place represents a network service that an Agent visits to satisfy processing needs. An Agent consults the WSB to determine which Place offers the best service at the lowest cost in terms of performance.

4.1 Optimizing Trader Services

The *Trader* functionality in Autopilot is provided by the WSB. Agents must consult WSBs to determine the next service to visit. The control logic in an Agent determines what the Agent needs at a given instance; conversely the *WSB* maintains information about what, if anything is currently available to satisfy the Agent's needs. Thus an Agent requiring a specific service consults the WSB to find any Place that fulfills its needs. Whenever possible, the agent prefers to arrange its itinerary to remain on the current physical machine.

Autopilot supports a multi-tiered hierarchy of WSBs, which substantially improves an Agent's access speed. One "master" WSB must exist at a well-known location, but the implementation encourages the establishment of local WSBs that hold information about Places available in a local domain. Local WSBs are used to ensure that Agents use local resources when available. The multi-tiered directory architecture operates as follows:

1. Any host is capable of hosting a local WSB if configured to do so.
2. Places, at start of execution, register with the most local WSB.
3. The WSB in each tier of AutoPilot reports the addition of new entries or the removal of existing entries to its parent. Ultimately the chain of reporting terminates in the well-known "master" WSB. The master contains, reasonably current, information of global scope. Local WSBs only know what is available in their domain.
4. If a request for a given service cannot be satisfied by a local WSB, the request is forwarded to its parent. Unresolved requests are forwarded until they are either resolved by some WSB in the hierarchy, or until the master WSB declares that no such service is available.
5. The WSB will invariably recommend Places on the local host over remote Places in order to minimize Agent travel; this improves overall system performance.
6. When Places of equal cost and quality exist only off-machine, the WSB uses a simple round-robin algorithm to decide which Place the Agent should visit. This has the added benefit of achieving some simple load balancing.

4.2 Using Agent Pooling to Improve System Concurrency

In traditional workflow management systems, processing flows exhibit minimal branching, and are to a great degree pre-planned. In such cases, it is feasible to develop an initial estimation of expected system performance, and understand to a large degree, strategies for system optimization. Further, a central control process handles the scheduling of distributed tasks to maintain overall system performance.

In contrast, AutoPilot uses autonomous mobile agents to handle the complex coordination and communication between a set of distributed Places. The main problem introduced by the autonomous and adaptive nature of mobile agents is the potential for processing congestion. At any given time, the overall system could potentially have a large number of Agents independently working on their assigned tasks. The tasks can vary in complexity and processing requirements resulting in an overall distributed system with non-deterministic behavior and congestion problems. Maintaining overall system throughput requires tracking and control mechanisms to manage the aggregation of autonomous agents. This section describes an agent pooling strategy we have deployed in AutoPilot to manage the consumption of distributed computing resources, and improve overall system performance.

In AutoPilot, a pool of Agents is created at system startup time and maintained throughout the processing. The Agents in the pool represent the available 'workers' that can be delegated tasks (documents to process) and released into the processing environment. The purpose of the pooling strategy is to prevent the overall system from becoming saturated with Agents requesting processing resources. In addition to managing the influx of Agents into a processing environment, the pooling strategy also has the benefit of improving performance. This is due to the fact that Agent creation is an expensive operations in terms of system resources. Therefore it is more efficient to generate a ready cache of Agents at system startup time and to store them in an idle state until needed. The process that manages the Agent pool has the following responsibilities:

1. Controlling the influx of Agents into the distributed processing environment. This control is maintained by limiting the number of Agents in the system to the maximum Agent pool size.
2. Handling tasking requests and assigning new tasks to available Agents in the pool. Tasks are ordered by priority to ensure that higher priority tasks are delegated first.
3. Monitoring Agents that have been assigned processing tasks and released into the processing environment. An important aspect of the monitoring responsibility includes requesting overdue Agents to return to the pool.
4. Creating new Agents to replenish the pool when the monitoring process determines that an Agent has failed or died.
5. Re-initializing Agents that have completed prior tasking and are returning to the pool. This process involves clearing the data and tasking portions of the Agent in preparation for re-use.

When a new task is received, a method is invoked to request an Agent. If available, an Agent is checked-out from the pool. However, if the pool has been depleted the request remains pending until the next Agent to complete processing has been returned to the available pool. Once an Agent has been retrieved from the pool, the following steps are required before dispatching the Agent:

1. A unique identification number (UID) is created and assigned to the Agent. UIDs are used by the pooling process to track Agents that have been released into the processing environment.
2. The Agent is assigned the new tasking. Appended onto the itinerary for each assigned task, are the instructions for the Agent to return to the pool after it has completed processing.
3. The Agent dispatch time is recorded and stored by the pooling process. The dispatch time along with information about task duration are used to estimate when the Agent can reasonably be expected to complete processing.

Once a dispatched Agent has completed processing the last step in the Agent's itinerary is to return to the process managing the pool. Upon returning to the pooling process the Agent invokes a method which re-initializes the Agent for future use.

4.3 Using Service Co-location to Increase System Performance

In mobile agent systems, the cost of travel can be quite high. The time spent in serializing data at the point of departure, and later deserializing it into object form at the new destination can far outweigh actual processing time by at least an order of magnitude. In Autopilot, all lightweight, high throughput services are replicated on each host in the system.

In certain cases, a service might require high amounts of underlying system resources or perhaps might use capabilities available only on a specific O/S, or finally, might use a service not persistently connected to the network. In these cases, the service is not co-located and the agent will need to move to the service. In general however, services whose processing cost is less than or equal to the cost of Agent movement are co-located which increases overall system performance. In addition, co-location adds redundancy and reliability to the system.

5 Analyzing and Tuning Performance

During the development of the AutoPilot workflow application several performance enhancements were added including: co-location of lightweight services, choosing a near optimal number of Agents to Place in the Agent Pool, simplifying the Agent payload, moving data instead of remotely referencing it, and minimizing off machine querying of the WSB. Each of these enhancements increased the overall performance of AutoPilot. Each performance enhancements was tested in a simple test environment prior to implementation. The test environment included the following Places:

Place	Service Provided
FilePickUp	creates a data object from a file and assigns it to an Agent from pool.
UpperCase	converts every character in the document to upper case
LowerCase	converts every character in the document to lower case
FileDropOff	writes a document to a file and sends the Agent back to pool
ID	randomly determines whether to send a document to Upper or Lower case Place first.

Two configurations were used to test the workflow. To simulate multi-step processing, each document was transformed between upper and lower case five times. In one configuration

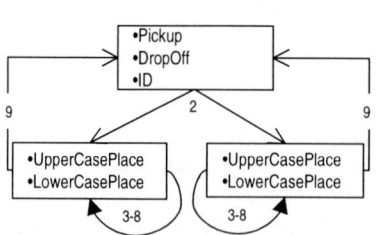

Figure 3a Co-located Test Configuration

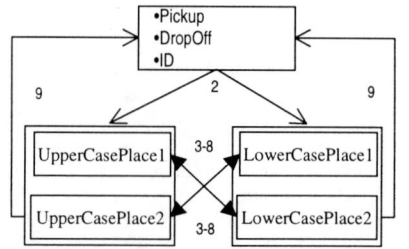

Figure 3b non Co-located Test Configuration

(depicted in Figure 3A) Places were co-located, with Agents being distributed between machines randomly by the ID Place. Once moved to a given machine, Agents traveled between the local LowerCasePlace and UpperCasePlace before returning to the DroppOffPlace, and being recycled into the Agent Pool. In the other configuration (depicted in Figure 3B) Places were not co-located; that is, agents were required to move between machines for each step of the multi-step processing. In this way, we were able to test the effects of a number of factors. In all tests, Agents processed 1000 documents of varying sizes in the range of 1 to 12 Kbytes by visiting nine Places. The test configuration consisted of three Sun Ultra 10 workstations connected with 100Mbit Ethernet, as depicted in Figure 3A-B.

5.1   Place Co-location

As previously mentioned, The cost associated with moving an Agent and its payload from one machine to another is significant, owing to the high cost of data serialization. Co-locating services whose processing cost is less than or equal to the cost of Agent movement can be shown to increase overall system performance. This assertion was verified running timing tests using the test

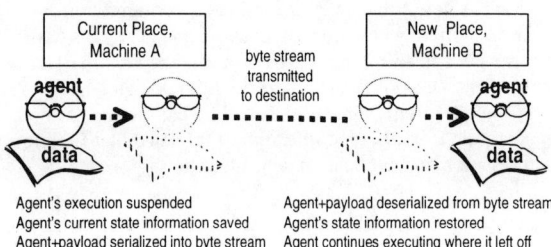

Agent's execution suspended | Agent+payload deserialized from byte stream
Agent's current state information saved | Agent's state information restored
Agent+payload serialized into byte stream | Agent continues executing where it left off

Figure 4 Agent movement between distributed Places

configuration shown in Figure 3. Each test was repeated 5 times and the results of the three mid-range results were averaged. The result is shown in the following exhibit:

Effects of Place Co-location	
❑ 3 SPARC Ultra-10, 512 MB RAM, 100 Mbit/s (fast) Ethernet. ❑ JVM Options: mx424m. JDK 1.1.8 ❑ Pool size =5 agents. ❑ 1000 documents with size 1K- 12K	Average results (seconds)
Places co-located. Agent and data move between Places	106.9
Places not Co-located. Agent and data move between Places	564.9

Table 1 - Co-Location of Lightweight services

The results of the various tests as summarized in Table 2 indicate that co-locating lightweight services when using Agent mobility can increase system performance significantly. In the interest of simplicity, this particular test suite used a consistent pool size. With larger pool sizes, we might expect to see narrowing of the differences in results.

5.2   Estimating the Effects of Agent Pool Size

One of the open research issues with the Agent pooling strategy is how to determine the optimum Agent pool size. Ideally, as the types of tasks and computing resources change over time the Agent pool should be adjusted accordingly to maintain overall system throughput. In the current AutoPilot implementation the Agent pool size is fixed at system startup time and remains constant throughout the processing. The pool size is determined by running a series of tests with varying Agent pool sizes on a representative collection of processing resources. The tests are designed around a worst-case tasking scenario to estimate the maximum number of Agents that can be handled in the system under demanding processing conditions. However, if the computing environment hosting the multi-agent application changes significantly the Agent pool size must be re-calculated to maintain optimum throughput.

By using the previously described test environment, we gathered results for increasing Agents pool sizes. In this suite of tests, the co-located configuration shown in Figure 3A was used, with Agents being distributed between machines randomly by the ID Place. Once moved to a given machine, Agents travelled between the local LowerCasePlace and UpperCasePlace a maximum of 5 times before returning to the DroppOffPlace, and being recycled into the Agent Pool.

Our results suggest that, at least for the test configuration, we achieved incrementally improving system concurrency and throughput as we added Agents to the Pool. Further, we observed that when the pool size was small (less than 20), the Pickup Place was often forced to wait for an agent to become available from the pool. For the larger pool sizes, an agent was always available, and in some test runs, some of the agents went unused. Although one might be tempted to derive a general rule from these results, it must be stated that finding a near-optimal pool size is very much situation and application dependent.

Effects of Agent Pool Size	
❑ 3 SPARC Ultra-10, 512 MB RAM, 100 Mbit/s (fast) Ethernet. ❑ JVM Options: mx424m. JDK 1.1.8 ❑ Places co-located. ❑ **Agent and data move between Places** ❑ **1000 documents with size 1K- 12K**	Average results (seconds)
Agent Pool Size = 1	328.4
Agent Pool Size = 5	107.1
Agent Pool Size = 10	88.7
Agent Pool Size = 25	84.0
Agent Pool Size = 50	85.1
Agent Pool Size = 100	85.3

Table 2 - Pool sizes may improve system concurrency

5.3   Remote references versus moving data

Several possibilities exist for how much the data ought to move in a WFMS. For example,
- The data might remain stationary and an Agent might carry only a remote reference to it and invoke a remote procedure to retrieve part of the data.
- An Agent might carry all or portions of the data to a number of services.
- The data might remain stationary and might include (or the Place containing the data might include) processing methods for visiting Agents.

It is the responsibility of the system designer to decide, based on the specific nature of the application, how much of the data to move, the circumstances under which data should move, and how best to optimise the data for serialization, for example simplifying the data representation, as discussed in the next section.

Additionally, it is important to remember that there are other issues, beyond the cost of serialization that should be considered. For example, in Java, there is no protection of remote references; a Java object's public methods are available to any other object that can obtain a reference to it.

5.4   Simplifying Payload

There is a considerable performance cost in both serializing complex data structures and in reconstructing the data structures. If Agents move often, then minimizing the cost can improve performance of the system.

As an example, consider the data structure depicted in the following exhibit:

```
// ...
public class ComplexReminder implements Serializable {
    private String _text = null;
    private String _type = null;

    private Date _eventDate;
    private Date _reminderDate;
//...
}
```

Exhibit 1 - Java Class representation

If a Java Vector containing several objects of this data structure were carried via a mobile agent across a network, the costs of marshalling and unmarshalling the Vector and its contents could be far higher than the cost of the invoked methods operating on the data at a remote location. Representing the same data in a less complex state, for example the XML DTD depicted in the next exhibit, can represent a considerable cost saving in the critical serialization operation.

```
<!--    Simplified Reminder DTD   -->
<!ELEMENT SimpleReminderData (SimpleReminder*)>
<!ELEMENT SimpleReminder (#PCDATA)>

<!ATTLIST SimpleReminder
        Text CDATA #REQUIRED
        Reminder-Type (Unknown |Appointment | Reminder) #REQUIRED
        Appointment-Date CDATA #IMPLIED
        Reminder-Date CDATA #IMPLIED
>
```

Exhibit 2 - XML representation

The results of experiments testing the effects of data representation is shown in the table below. The objects represented were rather simple. Our belief is that when object complexity rises, cost savings may even be more significant, and even if CPU (processing) costs far exceed I/O costs, the observation is nonetheless valid.

16

Effects of Data Simplification	
❏ 3 SPARC Ultra-10, 512 MB RAM, 100 Mbit/s (fast) Ethernet. ❏ JVM Options: mx424m. JDK 1.1.8 ❏ Pool size =5 agents. ❏ Places co-located. ❏ Agent and data move between Places ❏ 1000 documents with size 1K- 12K	Average results (seconds)
Agent with 100 element representation of XMLdata	182.6
Agent with 100 element Object representation of data	202.8

Table 3 - Effects of Data Representation

6   Conclusions

Controlling and tuning mobile agent implementations of workflow applications is challenging. To address the issues of Agent control and system performance in mobile-agent systems we have described three control mechanisms: the WSB, Agent and Agent Pool. This control strategy has been successfully used in the Autopilot workflow application, and is being used in the development of several other distributed workflow applications.

A number of valuable lessons were learned in the continued exploration of this control strategy, amongst them, the use of :
• Place co-location (especially for lightweight services) resulted in minimized Agent travel, which in turn increased system performance.
• Agent pooling minimized the formation of bottlenecks at slow processing Places by limiting the maximum number of Agents in the system at any given time.
• Local WSB's minimized off-machine travel to perform queries .
• Preferring local service over remote services minimized Agent movement and increased system performance.
• A "Flattened" Agent payload reduced the cost of serialization.
• The Itinerary stack increased flexibility and adaptability of the Agent without impacting system performance.

Although many open research items remain, the architecture as presented provides a strong foundation on which to build mobile agent based workflow applications.

References

[1] Clack, C., Farringdon, J., Lidwell, P., Yu, T. "An Adaptive Document Classification Agent," (Research Note, RN/96/45,) Dept. of Computer Science, University College London, 1996.
[2] Clack, C., Farringdon, J., Lidwell, P., Yu, T. "Autonomous Document Classification for Business," Proceedings of the First International Conference on Autonomous Agents, 1997, pp. 201-207.
[3] Foster, S., Moore, D, Nebesh, D., AutoPilot: Experiences Implementing a Distributed Data-Driven Agent Architecture. Proceedings of TOOLS-26 '98, August 3-7, 1998. IEEE Press. Piscataway, NJ
[4] Foster, S.; Moore, D.; Nebesh, D.; and Flester, M.; Control and Management in a Mobile Agent Workflow Architecture. Proceedings of the Third International Conference on Autonomous Agents, 1999, Workshop on Agent-based High Performance Computing, pp.6-14.
[5] Gamma, E., Helm, R., Johnson, R., Vlissides, J., Design Patterns: Elements of Reusable Object-Oriented Software, Addison-Wesley, 1995.
[6] Huhns, M., and Singh, M., "Workflow Agents," IEEE Internet Computing, Vol. 2, No. 3, 1998, July-August. Pp 94-96
[7] General Magic's Odyssey http://www.genmagic.com/html/agent_overview.html
[8] Java RMI API http://www.javasoft.com/products/jdk/1.1/docs/api/Package-java.rmi.html

[9] Merz, M., Liberman, M., Müller-Jones, Lamersdorf, W. "Interorganizational Workflow Management with Mobile Agents" *Hamburg University – Computer Science*

[10] ObjectSpace Voyager Core Technology http://www.objectspace.com/voyager/

[11] Object Management Group, "CORBA Services: Common Object Services Specification," November 1997.

[12] Otte, R., Patrick, P., Roy, M., Understanding CORBA, Prentice-Hall, 1996.

[13] Rus, D., Gray, R., Kotz, D., "Transportable Information Agents," Proceedings of the First International Conference on Autonomous Agents, 1997, pp. 228-236.

[14] The ODP Trader: Overview of Concepts, Models, and Services, http://amazon.postec.ac.kr/opd/summaries.html

[14] TIPSTER Program home page: http://www.tipster.org/

[15] White, Jim., "Telescript Technology: The Foundation for the Electronic Marketplace," General Magic White Paper, General Magic, Inc. , 1994.

[16] White, Jim. "Telescript Technology: Mobile Agents," http://www.genmagic.com/html/presentation.html, 1996.

Automatic Detection of Design Problems in Object-Oriented Reengineering

Oliver Ciupke

FZI Forschungszentrum Informatik

`ciupke@fzi.de`

Abstract

The evolution of software systems over many years often leads to unnecessarily complex and inflexible designs which in turn lead to a huge amount of effort for enhancements and maintenance. Thus, the reengineering of object-oriented software becomes more and more important as the number, age and size of such legacy systems grow. A key issue during reengineering is the identification and location of design problems which prevent the efficient further development of a system. Up to now this problem area has not been sufficiently supported, either by methods, or by tools.

In this paper, we present a technique for analyzing legacy code, specifying frequent design problems as queries and locating the occurrences of these problems in a model derived from source code. We present our experiences with a tool set which we implemented to support this task by automatically analyzing a given system and detecting the specified problems.

We applied our tools to check violations of a number of well-known design rules in existing source code taken from several case studies, both from industrial and academic fields. These experiments showed that the task of problem detection in reengineering can be automated to a large degree, and that the technique presented can be efficiently applied to real-world code.

Keywords: *Object-oriented reengineering, design problems, tool support for reengineering, model capture, problem detection*

1: Introduction

The evolution of software over many years often leads to unnecessarily complex and inflexible systems. It is hard to predict the effects of changes or even to determine what has to be changed and thus enhancements and maintenance of these systems are becoming more and more expensive. This is already true for many object-oriented systems. Sometimes they are first-generation oo systems when methods were less mature, sometimes only an object-oriented language was used but the developers were not trained in object-oriented design, but often the system is simply very large and the class structure itself is not as flexible and simple as it could be.

In order to allow further efficient evolution, the structure of such a system has to be improved. In order to do this, we need to find out which parts of the structure prohibit further enhancements to the system and what sort of problem we are facing. We want to know which classes, subsystems or methods have to be changed and what kind of changes we must make. We call this task *problem detection*. It is one phase in the life cycle of reengineering as defined by [4]. Problem detection is hard to do manually. Some of the reasons for this are:

- Programs which have to be reengineered tend to be very large.
- Systems are developed by different developers or teams. Design problems can affect several different subsystems and thus cannot be detected locally.
- It is often unclear *what* exactly to search for.

For all these reasons we need *automatic support* for the task of problem detection, i.e., tools which accept source code[1] as input and point to design fragments which are candidates for design problems. The result is a list of locations where problems have been found together with their classification. It can provide a starting point for reorganizing a system.

In this paper, we describe a method for the automatic detection of design problems in legacy code. We implemented tools to support this method and applied these to a set of case-studies. The following criteria are considered important for our method to fulfill:

- Method and tools work on the design level. In our opinion, the quality of the overall structure determines the flexibility of a system, i.e., how expensive it is to extend or maintain it.

  In the context of our reengineering work, we use the term "design" not only for the corresponding activity, but also for the "actual" structure, as we can observe it in a given system – even if it was never planned to be like it is.

- All of the required information is extracted from source code. We cannot rely on design documentation, since it often does not exist or is in most cases inconsistent. We cannot rely on information that has to be collected dynamically during run time either. First, there is no practically applicable method to ensure that all the necessary parts and paths of a program are executed. Second and even more important, many systems, especially the huge ones which need reengineering the most, simply cannot be run apart from the dedicated hardware or environment for which they are built.[2] Famous examples are systems in the telecommunications area and other embedded or real-time systems. Similarly, systems in the commercial area often need to have most of their data stored in databases to get meaningful program runs.

- To cope with large amounts of code, problem detections should run fully automatically. It may be necessary to check the results to determine their relevance, but this set of results should first be produced without any user intervention.

- A problem detection method should point us directly to the problems we are searching for. Software metrics, as a counter-example, only deliver numbers which require further interpretation. Only together with a set of thresholds can they point us towards potential problems.

- The approach (and associated tools) should be language independent (as much as possible). Since the design of a system is to some extent independent of the implementation language, this should be reflected in the chosen method as well. Nevertheless, it should be possible to add issues that are typical for a certain language.

- An approach to problem detection in reengineering should cover a wide range of possible problems.

---

[1] or a representation of it for languages such as Smalltalk
[2] And you hardly want to build your reengineering tools on that environment.

This paper is organized as follows. Section 2 describes our approach to automatic problem detection by querying design. Section 3 presents a tool set which implements the approach. Section 4 describes an experiment where we applied our tool set to detect violations of design guidelines in several case studies. Section 5 discusses related work and how our approach differs. Section 6 concludes.

The work described in this paper was done within the joint project FAMOOS which is funded by the European Commission as ESPRIT project 21975 within the software technologies domain. The goal of FAMOOS is the development of methods and tools for the reengineering of object-oriented legacy systems.

2: Automatic problem detection

We assume that legacy systems are given in the form of *source code* or an equivalent representation. In order to search for problems in the overall software structure, we must leave the concrete implementation behind and move towards a higher level of abstraction at which specifications of those problems are given. We do this by parsing the source code and producing high-level *design information*. What we then gain is a description of the *actual design* of the system, which often differs from what can be found in design documents produced in earlier phases of the development process.

To be able to express and interpret the information gathered from source-code, we have set up a *meta-model* for object-oriented systems. This meta-model defines the different entities and relations that may occur in the design of an object-oriented program. A model of a legacy system which conforms with the meta-model can be stored as graph, as entities and relations, or as predicates. This makes it possible to query and manipulate the model using different query languages.

2.1: Querying design

For detecting problems in the design of a system, we have to search for certain patterns representing those problems in the model built of the system. This means we have to be able to *specify* problems and to *query* the model about the existence of a specified problem. The result of such a query is a piece of design specifying the location of the problem in the system. Such a piece of design in a formal model is often referred to as a *design fragment*.

Several ways for specifying queries on a design model exist. A model can be understood as *typed graph* and the queries become algorithms working on this graph. A model can be specified by *sets and relations*. Queries then take the form of relational algebraic expressions. A model can also be expressed by logical propositions and be queried using *predicate calculus*, e.g., using a logic programming language.

The three above-mentioned approaches represent different viewpoints about the same meta-model. They are equivalently powerful[3] and the corresponding models and queries can be converted into each other. Each of them has its advantages in certain tasks and all three of them are used in our tools for different purposes. During the experiment described in the next section, we primarily used predicates implemented as Prolog clauses [7, 31], since we felt they were the easiest to map to the guidelines given in natural language. We will also concentrate on this way to query designs in the remainder of this paper.

---

[3]Given not full predicate calculus, but only horn-clauses are used and we only consider predicates concerning our (finite) meta-model.

```
% Base classes should not have knowledge about their descendants
knowsOfDerived (Class, DerivedClass) :-
    % Both Class and DerivedClass must be classes
    class (Class), class (DerivedClass),
    % DerivedClass is a direct or transitive descendant of Class
    trans (inheritsFrom, DerivedClass, Class),
    % The base class knows its heir
    knows (Class, DerivedClass).


% A class 'knows' another class, if
knows (Class1, Class2) :-
    % it inherits from that class, or
    class (Class1), class (Class2),
        inheritsFrom (Class1, Class2);
    % it has an attribute of that type, or
    hasAttribute (Class1, Attr), hasType(Attr, Class2);
    % it has a method which returns an object of that type, or
    hasMethod (Class1, Meth1), returns (Meth1, Class2);
    % it has a method which calls a method of that class, or
    hasMethod (Class1, Meth1), calls (Meth1, Meth2),
        hasMethod (Class2, Meth2);
    % it has a method containing a parameter with type of that class.
    hasType(Param, Class2).
```

Figure 1. Formalization of a design rule in Prolog

2.2: Example

Here we provide an example of how a design problem and a query which detects this problem may look like. We have chosen a problem related to a *design guideline*. If design guidelines (or heuristics) make a statement about good design, then a violation of such a guideline may indicate a design problem. The following is taken from [27]:

> "Derived classes must have knowledge of their base class by definition, but base classes should not know anything about their derived classes." (Heuristic 5.2)

If base classes depend on their descendants, then these descendants cannot be altered independently of their ancestors. But exactly this functionality is often needed during the evolution of an object-oriented system. So a violation of this guideline points to a spot in a software structure, where this structure is hard to change or maintain.

In order to be checked automatically, this rule must now be formalized. This can be done in different ways, e.g., using different query languages. An elegant formalization of this example can be done using Prolog, which we also used for many other queries in our prototypes. A base class would violate this heuristic, if it had knowledge of one of its direct or indirect heirs. *Knowing* a class means being dependent on the interface or the implementation of this class. In order to also consider the indirect heirs the transitive closure of the inheritance relation is also required. These two remarks lead us to the Prolog clause shown in Figure 1 which is satisfied by the entities setting up the design problem (for definition of **trans** see Appendix B).

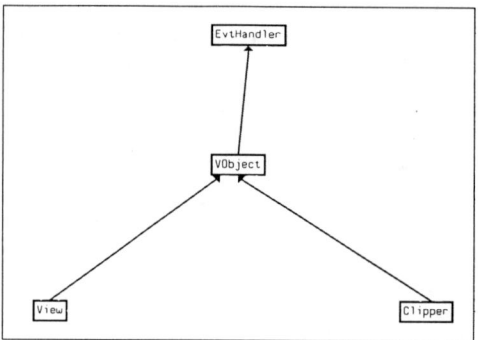

Figure 2. Visualization of a detected problem

In the 2.2 version of the object-oriented framework ET++ for example, the preceding Prolog query detected 23 violations. One of these is shown in Figure 2.[4] Boxes represent classes, dark arrows represent inheritance relationships, light arrows the existence of method calls between the methods of these classes. Here we even have two overlapping violations at once. The class "Clipper" inherits "VObject" directly and "EvtHandler" transitively. Both EvtlHandler and VObject contain calls to a method of Clipper. This means that changes to Clipper may require EvtlHandler and VObject to be changed as well. Both can be found at a high position in the inheritance hierarchy, where changes affect many other classes in turn. Actually, Figure 2 does not depict the full degree of complexity of this design fragment. In the complete graph of this ET++ version, each of the classes is connected to at least 50 other classes, VObject even to 376. What results is that we have found a design fragment that is resistant to change and difficult to maintain.

Possible reorganizations which could simplify this situation would be to introduce abstract base classes or migrating methods or attributes between classes. Which of the solutions is suitable depends on the overall structure and on the particular goals and requirements of the reengineering of a specific system.

ET++ does of course not resemble a typical example of a legacy system, since all in all it has a well designed structure. Nevertheless we used it here, because it is well-known in the object community and we wanted to show an example of a problem in a "real" object-oriented design.

3: Tool support

A tool set named GOOSE[5] intended for various reengineering tasks was developed at the Forschungszentrum Informatik in the framework of the FAMOOS project. It supports software structure visualization, metrics calculation, querying design and automatic reorganization. The structure of the tools relevant for the task of problem detection is shown in Figure 3. Boxes represent tools, ovals represent persistent data. Arrows denote the data

---

[4]The figure shows no methods, but only classes. To get a more abstract view, methods and relations between methods have been collapsed into their classes using our tool REVIEW to produce this visualization.

[5]The name originates from a preceding concept named "Moose" and the fact that it deals with graphs.

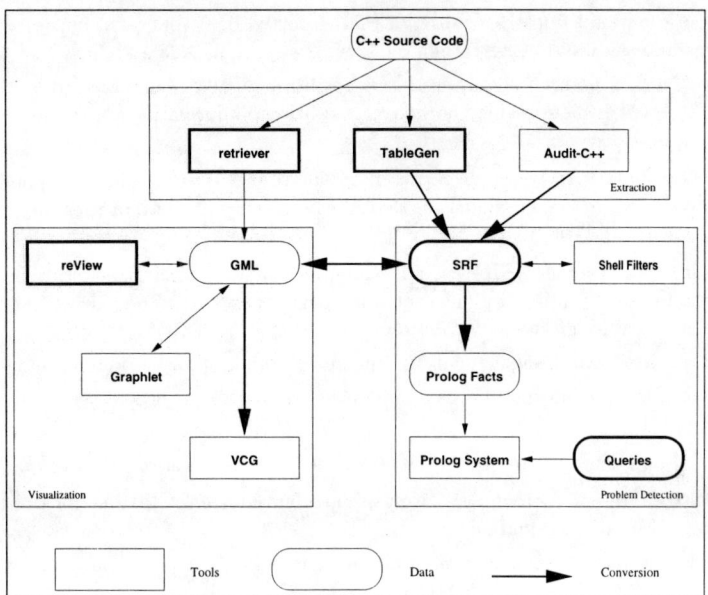

Figure 3. Overview of tool interaction

flow between tools or between different representations.

A large portion of the functionality was achieved by connecting already existing tools, rather than implementing them ourselves, e.g., for visualization and querying. Thickly highlighted borders or arrows in the picture are things we had to implement or define ourselves. Thick arrows represent conversions between different data formats, mostly implemented in the form of Perl scripts.

Detecting problems in a system is done as follows. First, the source code of the system is parsed. This can be done by different parsers depending on the environment. (See the upper grey box labeled "Extraction"). The system can now be visualized to provide a first view of the interdependencies. We use different publicly available visualization for this. If necessary, manipulations or simplifications can be made by hand (e.g., deleting undesired nodes) or done automatically (e.g., make common simplifications to generate a visualization on the class level). For the actual problem detection, the information is converted to Prolog facts. Queries formulated as Prolog rules examine this information and deliver the locations of problem candidates as result.

We now describe the individual tools and formats in more detail. The parsers for extracting design information from source code can be freely exchanged. So far we have made experiments with C++ and Chill [11]. Further extraction tools and parsers for Smalltalk, Ada and Java are available within the FAMOOS project.

retriever is an extraction tool which is connected to the API which comes with the UNIX version of the software development tool SNIFF+.

Audit: GOOSE can import tables produced by the commercial analysis tool AUDIT as well.

The information is mostly a subset of that exported by TABLEGEN, but we maintain this as an easy way to integrate other languages such as Ada and Java.

TableGen [19] is a parser built using the parser library FAST. Compared to RETRIEVER and AUDIT it is more stable and delivers additional information about function calls and variable accesses.

The different data formats we use to represent and exchange information correspond to the different ways to query design models as described in section 2.1. All of them are used for different tasks within GOOSE:

Simple relational format (SRF): SRF is an intermediate format to facilitate conversion of data formats required by different third party tools and to provide an easy-to-use interface to a design model for interactive querying.

GML (Graph Modeling Language)[6] is an upcoming standard for storing graph data.

Prolog facts: Design information can be converted to Prolog facts to query it with a Prolog system.

Several tools can query, manipulate or visualize the extracted design information:

Prolog system: In our current work, we use the environment ECLiPSe[7] for Constraint-Prolog to run deductional queries.

reView supports a large number of manipulations including a grouping (abstraction) functionality for graphs given in GML format.

Shell filters: Combinations of common shell filters like `grep, sort, comm, join, cut, wc, uniq` and `awk` are used together with the SRF format for ad-hoc queries, in order to filter noise or to merge data from different sources.

Graphlet is the tool we currently use most for visualizing design models. It supports both automatic and manual layout and allows editing graphs.[8]

VCG Supports fewer layout algorithms than Graphlet and does not allow the interactive manipulation of layouts, but is still used for some purposes.[9]

4: An experiment: checking guidelines in legacy systems

During our first experiment, we used guideline violations as specifications of problems to be searched for. A lot of material often given in the form of rules or heuristics exists in the literature about what *good* object-oriented design should look like. Every rule corresponds to a potential problem in an object-oriented design, where the rule has *not* been followed. Originally these guidelines were meant to be followed by a human developer when creating a new design, rather than as input for an automatic tool testing whether they are met in the actual design of a legacy system. Nevertheless, we examined whether such rules could be used to automatically detect problems.

First, we investigated how many of the guidelines found can be formalized within our model. Though these design guidelines cannot cover every possible design problem, they

---

[6] http://www.uni-passau.de/Graphlet/GML/index.html
[7] http://www.ie.utoronto.ca/EIL/ECLiPSe/eclipse.html
[8] http://www.uni-passau.de/Graphlet/
[9] http://www.cs.uni-sb.de:80/RW/users/sander/html/gsvcg1.html

can determine how well the task of problem detection is done by our approach. Secondly, we implemented the formalized guidelines as queries and applied them to several case studies, to demonstrate the practicability of both method and tools.

During our study, we encountered about 280 guidelines originating from various authors ([27, 15, 14, 18, 12, 30, 16, 13, 20, 33, 29, 8, 3, 23, 22] and several others). Many of these guidelines were equivalent or at least very similar to each other. Some were very implementation specific and thus too far away from what we considered to be a design rule. In the end, this left us a list of 59 rules which in our opinion best covered our area of interest for further examination [2].

4.1: Formal testability

Nearly all design guidelines were originally intended to give a human developer hints for designing a new system or new parts of a system. They are normally given in natural language and state what he or she should do or should avoid. For our purpose in contrast we wanted the rules to be checked on existing systems within a reengineering process and we wanted them to be checked automatically by a tool. Being able to implement such rules implies having an *exact formal definition* first. Thus we determined to what extent such formalizations can be made. *Testability* gives an idea of how precise an automatic search for the violation of a given guideline can be. We use a classification similar to [12].

The guidelines can be classified according to how close a formal definition according to our model can get to the original definition. We categorized guidelines into five classes of testability based on the relationship between two associated sets: the set V of design fragments violating the guideline and the set I of design fragments identified by the given formalization.

Exactly testable: $I = V$
An exact formalization can be given for this guideline.

Partially testable: $I \subset V$
Only a subset of the violating fragments can be found, but every fragment found violates the guideline.

Vaguely testable: $V \subset I$
Every violation is found, but some fragments found may not contain violations.

Symptomatically testable: I and V correlated, but neither $I \subset V$ nor $V \subset I$
These guidelines combine the disadvantages of the partially and vaguely testable ones.

Not testable: I is undefined.
We cannot give a satisfying formal definition for the guidelines in this class. The main characteristic of these guidelines is their lack of stringent demands. They may use information not extractable from source code, such as about dynamic behavior, or they may regard quantity and not include sharp limits to obey.

Table 1 shows the number of guidelines in each of the testability classes. Since the table is ordered from highly useful to (for our purpose) useless guidelines, one can see that 46% are exactly testable and nearly two thirds identify only actual violations. By setting thresholds to quantities or by slight changes to the definition, even more guidelines can be migrated into an other testability class and this way be turned into applicable rules.

Category	Quantity	Percentage
Exactly	27	46 %
Partially	10	17 %
Vaguely	1	2 %
Symptomatically	2	3 %
Not testable	19	32 %
Sum	59	100 %

Table 1. Size of the testability classes

4.2: Application to case studies

The rules implemented so far were applied to seven case studies written in C++: two versions of the well-known object-oriented framework ET++ [32], Rheingold, which is a development for a customer of our own group, and four industrial software systems or subsystems, named CS_4 to CS_7.[10] The systems run under different UNIX variants or under NT. To keep the results interpretable, we always measured only the systems themselves, i.e., without eventually underlying frameworks, such as the MFC.

The number of violations for a selection of the implemented rules in each case study is shown in Table 2. In the upper part, the table shows the sizes of the case studies in terms of lines of code, classes and methods. In the lower part, it shows the number of hits for each query.

As can be seen from the table, some of the queries do not report any violations at all (e.g., private methods). Others report huge numbers of violations for some of the systems (e.g., private attributes and unused inheritance). The reason for this is that many guidelines reflect a certain *style* of designing and programming. In some cases inheritance is only used for the sake of polymorphism, in others it is also used for the reuse of implementation. Thus, if we want to use the queries to point the reengineer to actual problems, we must make a selection according to the style of the given system.

4.3: Performance

By far most of the time for the whole analysis process was needed for parsing the source code to produce design information. Performance was measured for ET++-2.2 (40 kLOC). ET++ was not the biggest of our case studies in terms of lines of code, but needed the longest parsing times, though.[11] TABLEGEN needed 27 minutes for this task. The other parser used, RETRIEVER, needed only about two minutes, but this one does not deliver some of the information we need for some of the queries. (All measured on a Sun Ultra 1, Processor: Model 140 UltraSPARC, 64MB RAM).

Since parsing only has to take place once for every case study, the performance turned out to be fast enough, since further analysis work can always re-use already prepared design information. All other steps took less than half a minute. The problem detection itself running on ECLIPSE was amazingly fast. All queries returned their results immediately, or in at most 25 seconds in cases where a transitive closure was needed.

---

[10]Since these are subject to non disclosure agreements, we do not use their full names here.

[11]GOOSE was already being successfully used on a 5 MLOC system, but mainly for visualization purposes and less for automatic problem detection [28].

Case Study	ET++-2.2	ET++-3.a1	Rhein-gold	CS_4	CS_5	CS_6	CS_7
Size:							
Lines of Code	40167	48747	14165	68638	35180	53370	276000
Classes	352	543	136	87	17	53	806
Methods	3738	4981	607	1285	192	32	4536
Free Functions	425	323	63	37	4	130	n.k.
Query:							
A class should not contain more than six objects	8	12	2	19	0	1	92
Inheritance hierarchy too deep (> 6)	27	6	0	0	0	0	1
Avoid multiple inheritance	0	0	0	6	0	0	12
Inheriting the same class twice	0	0	0	0	0	0	1
Attributes should be private	224	402	260	12	15	29	560
Do not turn an operation into a class	103	197	23	10	7	3	172
Base classes should not have knowledge about derived classes	23	14	0	0	0	0	0
Divide large classes (> 12 methods)	96	118	15	39	3	0	91
Reduce number of arguments (> 4 args.)	0	0	0	0	0	0	0
Unused inheritance	293	421	22	14	10	0	425
Containment implies violation of use	154	249	7	58	0	7	591
Do not declare private methods	0	0	0	0	0	0	0

Table 2. Number of violations in different case-studies

5: Related work

CCEL [10] is a meta language in C++ to define rules for the entities of a C++ design. It is possible to check these rules for given C++ sources. CCEL defines an object-oriented meta-model, which only focuses on the *entities* of a design. Furthermore CCEL works exclusively with C++. A lot of the design rules we investigated in our work required a meta-model including relations. Thus our method deals with both entities and relations. It is also not restricted to one language.

Law-governed architecture [24, 25] is a general approach to ensure rules during software development. It distinguishes two kinds of rules: those concerning the development process and those concerning system structure. The approach observes the development of a *new system* and aims at the avoidance of problems there. It introduces mechanisms to detect design problems, but does not define rules for their detection. In contrast, our method examines already existing systems and we define queries to do that.

MeTHOOD [12] improves object-oriented designs at the level of a meta-model. As before, METHOOD can be applied during the design phase of *forward engineering*. A design model can be built using a special editor and can then be checked for the violation of rules.

GOOSE can extract the design model from source code and comes with a catalogue of formally defined rules. On the other hand, METHOOD is more general in the sense that it provides concepts for transforming designs and for resolving problems.

Object-oriented software metrics [6, 5] map pieces of design or implementation to a certain, normally *numerical value*. Most object-oriented metrics measure the different kinds of complexity of classes or the cohesion between classes [19].

If metrics are used for problem detection, their results must first be interpreted. For example one must add thresholds to finally get statements about what has to be considered as a problem. Up to now, this has been a difficult task. First, because of lack of experience in measuring large systems of real-world code; second, because the limits vary with the languages, programming style, details in the definition of a metric, etc. Furthermore, metrics can only detect problems related to magnitudes of values.

Our collection of queries for problem detections contains as well some which are based on quantities. GOOSE can also be (and has been) used for measuring software metrics. And of course, the number of occurrences of a certain problem in a system defines a metric, so both subjects are strongly related. But our main focus in the work presented here was on problems based on the more structural properties of a design, which are hard to define in terms of quantities and thus needed a different approach to automatic detection.

Software reflexion models [26] can be used to find *mismatches* between high-level designs and the corresponding source code. The approach requires the reference model, to which a system can be compared, to be given in advance. In our approach, arbitrary problems that can be formulated as queries can be detected with only the source code as a given.

Conceptual module querying [1] is a method for supporting queries about the relationships between fragments of source code. Conceptual module querying does not aim directly at the task of problem detection and thus only supports certain types of queries. Furthermore it focuses on program entities that basically belong to the level of source code. Our approach aims at as much as possible arbitrary reasoning about entities and relations of the design level.

Style checker: Several tools exist for checking rules in the given source code at the *implementation level*, e. g., searching for the improper use of references. The best known among these is probably LINT [9] which analyses C programs. GOOSE checks rules on the *design level* and is to a large extent language independent.

6: Summary and future work

Automatic problem detection reduces the effort of browsing through large amounts of code during the reengineering process. It can also assist developers in finding weak parts in the design of a piece of software, which they would otherwise not be aware of.

We presented an approach for detecting problems in the designs of object oriented systems. Problems are specified as queries on a design model. A problem can be detected using our method, if it can be formalized in terms of the query languages we used. In this way, we can provide a satisfying formalization for about two thirds of the guidelines we collected from literature.

Our method is supported by a tool set that we implemented with moderate effort, by connecting well-understood techniques and existing tools. The tools can cope with regular industrial code up for very large systems (MLOC) and proved to be fast enough to be practically applicable. These tools can check a catalogue of problem detections fully automatically and deliver results directly pointing the user to places in the source code which contain potential design problems. Applying our tools to a further programming language only required adding a parser (or extractor) for this language, which makes our approach highly language-independent.

The catalogue of queries as implemented so far is mainly constituted by design heuristics taken from the literature and some of them from our own experience. Our experiments showed that these give good hints about where to start reorganizing a system, but that legacy systems often suffer from further problems not addressed by such common rules. In the future, we want to collect such problems, to formalize them and to implement them as queries, as well.

The tools only run on certain platforms so far, require other software to be installed before, and require relatively highly skilled users. Hence, in the current phase of the FAMOOS project, a problem detection functionality is being built into the quality assurance and metrics tool AUDIT by the Sema Group. This will provide a solution that can be applicable in everyday software projects and for a large variety of environments.

References

[1] Elisa L. A. Baniassad and Gail C. Murphy. Conceptual module querying for software engineering. In *Proceedings of the 1998 International Conference on Software Engineering*, pages 64–73. IEEE Comput. Soc, Los Alamitos, CA, USA, 1998.

[2] Holger Bär and Oliver Ciupke. Exploiting design heuristics for automatic problem detection. In Stéphane Ducasse and Joachim Weisbrod, editors, *Proceedings of the ECOOP Workshop on Experiences in Object-Oriented Re-Engineering*, number 6/7/98 in FZI Report, June 1998.

[3] Grady Booch. *Object-Oriented Analysis and Design with Applications*. Benjamin Cummings, Redwood City, 2 edition, 1994.

[4] Eduardo Casais. Re-engineering object-oriented legacy systems. *Journal of Object-Oriented Programming*, pages 45–52, January 1998.

[5] S. R. Chidamber and C. F. Kemerer. A Metric Suite for Object-Oriented Design. *IEEE Transactions on Software Engineering*, 20(6):476–493, June 1994.

[6] Shyam R. Chidamber and Chris F. Kemerer. Towards a metrics suite for object oriented design. In *Proceedings OOPSLA '91, ACM SIGPLAN Notices*, pages 197–211, November 1991. Published as Proceedings OOPSLA '91, ACM SIGPLAN Notices, volume 26, number 11.

[7] W. F. Clocksin and C. S. Mellish. *Programming in Prolog*. Springer Verlag, Berlin and New York, 1981.

[8] Peter Coad and Edward Yourdon. *Object-Oriented Analysis*. Prentice Hall, London, 2 edition, 1991.

[9] Ian F. Darwin. *Checking C programs with* lint. O'Reilly & Associates, Inc., 981 Chestnut Street, Newton, MA 02164, USA, October 1998.

[10] Carolyn K. Duby, Scott Meyers, and Steven P. Reiss. CCEL: A metalanguage for C++. Technical Report CS-92-51, Department of Computer Science, Brown University, October 1992. Sun, 13 Jul 1997 18:30:16 GMT.

[11] Thomas Genßler and Oliver Ciupke. Toolgestützte Codeanalyse von Telekommunikationssoftware in Chill. Systemdokumentation und Projektbericht, Forschungszentrum Informatik, 1997.

[12] Thomas Grotehen and Klaus R. Dittrich. The MeTHOOD approach: Measures, transformation rules, and heuristics for object-oriented design. Technical Report ifi-97.09, University of Zürich, Switzerland, August 27, 1997.

[13] Walter L. Hürsch. Should superclasses be abstract? In Mario Tokoro and Remo Pareschi, editors, *Object-Oriented Programming, Proceedings of the 8th European Conference ECOOP'94*, volume 821 of *Lecture Notes in Computer Science*, pages 12–31, Bologna, Italy, 4—8 July 1994. Springer.

[14] Ralph E. Johnson and Brian Foote. Designing reuseable classes. *Journal of Object-Oriented Programming*, 1(2):22–35, June 1988.

[15] John Lakos. *Large-Scale C++ Software Design*. Addison-Wesley, 1996.

[16] Wilf LaLonde and John Pugh. Subclassing =/ subtyping =/ is-a. *Journal of Object-Oriented Programming*, 3(5):57–59,62, January 1991.

[17] K. J. Lieberherr and I. M. Holland. Assuring good style for object-oriented programming. *IEEE Software*, pages 38–48, September 1989.

[18] Karl J. Lieberherr, Ian Holland, and Arthur J. Riel. Object-oriented programming: An objective sense of style. In *Object-Oriented Programming Systems, Languages and Applications Conference*, in *Special Issue of SIGPLAN Notices*, number 11, pages 323–334, San Diego, CA, September 1988. A short version of this paper appears in *IEEE Computer Magazine*, June 1988, Open Channel section, pages 78-79.

[19] Radu Marinescu. The use of software metrics in the design of object oriented systems. Master's thesis, Universitatea Polytehnica din Timişoara, 1997.

[20] R. C. Martin. Object oriented design quality metrics. *Report on Object Analysis & Design*, September 1995.

[21] R. C. Martin. The Dependency Inversion Principle. *C++ Report*, 8(6):61–66, June 1996.

[22] Scott Meyers. *More Effective C++*. Addison-Wesley, 1996.

[23] Scott Meyers. *Effective C++*. Addison-Wesley, second edition, 1998.

[24] Naftaly H. Minsky. Law-governed regularities in object systems, part 1: An abstract model. *Theory and Practice of Object Sytems*, 2(4):283–301, 1996.

[25] Naftaly H. Minsky and Partha Pratim Pal. Law-governed regularities in object systems, part 2: A concrete implementation. *Theory and Practice of Object Sytems*, 3(2):87–101, 1997.

[26] Gail C. Murphy, David Notkin, and Kevin Sullivan. Software Reflexion Models: Bridging the Gap between Source and High-Level Models. In *Proceedings of SIGSOFT'95 Third ACM SIGSOFT Symposium on the Foundations of Software Engineering*, pages 18–28, October 1995.

[27] Arthur J. Riel. *Object-Oriented Design Heuristics*. Addison-Wesley, 1996.

[28] Fabian Ritzmann. Reverse Engineering of Large Scale Software Systems. Diplomarbeit, Universität Karlsruhe, June 1998.

[29] J. Rumbaugh, M. Blaha, W. Premerlani, F. Eddy, and W. Lorensen. *Object-Oriented Modeling and Design*. Prentice Hall, Englewood Cliffs, 1991.

[30] Ed Seidewitz. Controlling inheritance. *Journal of Object-Oriented Programming*, 08(08):36–42, 1996.

[31] Leon Sterling and Ehud Shapiro. *The Art of Prolog*. MIT Press, Cambridge, MA, 1986.

[32] A. Weinand, E. Gamma, and R. Marty. Design and implementation of ET++, a seamless object-oriented application framework. *Structured Programming*, 10(2):63–87, 1989.

[33] R. Wirfs-Brock and B. Wilkerson. Variables Limit Reusability. *Journal of Object-Oriented Programming*, pages 34–40, May/June 1989.

A: List of examined guidelines

The following table contains the names and references to all design guidelines we have examined so far. The reference column has to be interpreted as follows: references of the form $x.y$ can be found in [27] under the stated number; *Chapter x* can be found in [15] in the stated chapter; *Rule x* can be found in [14]; for other sources a reference to the literature is given. We used names that are close to the original description, but sometimes were not very clear out of this context. Please refer to the cited literature for definitions or more detailed descriptions.

Name	Reference
exactly testable	
All data should be hidden within its class	2.1
Classes should only use the public interface of other classes	2.7
Spin off non-related information into another class	2.10
No illegal dependencies	3.5
Remove unused components of a class	4.5
A class should not contain more than six objects	4.7
All data in a base class should be private	5.3
Depth of inheritance hierarchies	5.4, 5.5
All base classes should be abstract classes	5.6, 5.7
Avoid multiple inheritance	6.1, 6.2
Check for accidental multiple inheritance	6.3
Keep class data members private	Chapter 2
Avoid data with external linkage at file scope	Chapter 2
Declaration and definition constraints	Chapter 2
Avoid hiding a base-class function in a derived class	Chapter 9
Use virtual destructors with virtual methods	Chapter 9
A component should only include the header files it depends on	Chapter 3
Include the required header files directly	Chapter 3
Avoid granting long-distance friendship	Chapter 3
Cyclic dependencies only within components	Chapter 4&7
Eliminate explicit case analysis on object types	Rule 2, 5.12
The top of the class hierarchy should be abstract	Rule 6
Separate methods that do not communicate	Rule 11
Reduce implicit parameter passing	Rule 13
Law of Demeter—class form	[17]
Law of Demeter—object form	[17]
Define abstract interfaces to used classes	[21]
partially testable	
A class should not be dependent on its users	2.2
Implement a minimal public interface that all classes understand	2.4

Common-code private functions should be hidden within their class	2.5
Eliminate irrelevant classes	3.7, 3.8, 3.10
Do not turn an operation into a class	3.9
Base classes should not know anything about their derived classes	5.2
Avoid explicit case analysis on attribute values	5.13
Avoid global data	8.1
Subclasses should be specializations	Rule 8
Avoid inheritance to achieve code reuse	home-grown
vaguely testable	
Do not override a base class method with a NOP method	5.17
symptomatically testable	
Do not clutter the public interface of a class with useless things	2.6
A class should capture one and only one key abstraction	2.8
not testable	
Minimize the number of messages in the protocol of a class	2.3
Keep related data and behavior in one place	2.9
Only object roles requiring different behavior should be modeled as classes	2.11
Avoid centralized control	3.1–3.4
Minimize coupling between classes	4.1–4.4
Distribute system intelligence vertically within containment hierarchies	4.8
Constraints in the uses relation of contained objects	4.13, 4.14
Factor the commonality of classes	5.8, 5.10
Common attributes of classes should be placed in a class contained by each	5.9
Attribute values versus inheritance	5.15, 5.18
Recursion introduction	Rule 1
Reduce the number of arguments	Rule 3
Reduce the size of methods	Rule 4
Class hierarchies should be deep and narrow	Rule 5
Minimize accesses to variables	Rule 7
Split large classes	Rule 9
Factor implementation differences into subcomponents	Rule 10
Send messages to components instead to self	Rule 12
Avoid large subsystem interfaces	home-grown

B: Transitive closure with Prolog

We implemented a Prolog rule **trans** giving the transitive closure of any relation. Some of the syntax may be proprietary to ECLiPSe, the Prolog system we used.

```
% transitive closure of a relation named "Relation"
% trans (Relation, A, B) iff A Relation^+ B
trans (Relation, A, B) :- transRel (Relation, A, B, []).

transRel (Relation, A, B, _) :-
  Goal =.. [Relation, A, B, _], call (Goal).

transRel (Relation, A, C, AlreadySeen) :-
  Goal =.. [Relation, A, B, _], call (Goal),
  not member (B, AlreadySeen),
  transRel (Relation, B, C, [A|AlreadySeen]).
```

Evolution of a Small Object Oriented Manufacturing System

Thomas M. Morrisette
email: eiffelpgmr@excite.com

Abstract

Small software systems implemented for small organizations exhibit many of the same characteristics of large systems as they evolve. Developers who produce nontrivial small systems use essentially the same approaches to achieve quality as developers of large systems. Small systems face many of the same challenges before, during, and after implementation as large systems.

This paper traces the evolution of a small object oriented software system produced for a sunroom manufacturer from the original design and implementation through a decade of upgrades and ports to new operating systems. As with all such projects, it exhibits many common characteristics with other software projects. As with many projects, it has some issues that are rarely encountered by most developers.

Ten years' experience with and responsibility for the same project, through its entire history, have given the author an opportunity to review his successes and failures. The reader is invited to share the hard learned lessons.

1. Introduction

Starting in 1989, I led the implementation of a parts list generator for a sunroom manufacturer. On several occasions over the years, I've maintained and upgraded the program. This paper follows the evolution of the program from original problem through the solution and the expansion of the program to address other business requirements. Along the way, the paper examines a diverse set of software life cycle issues including object oriented design, supervising novice programmers, portability across operating systems, graphic user interfaces (GUI), parsers, documentation, and a couple of interesting optimization problems. It concludes with a look at what I think I did right and what I know I would do differently.

2. Project genesis

In 1989, the Pennsylvania Manufacturing Services Extension Center requested my assistance in salvaging a software project that was out of control. They were monitoring the project for Creative Structures, a Hellertown, Pennsylvania, sunroom manufacturer, and concluded that the original software consultants were overwhelmed with the complexity of the program they had contracted to write.

Creative Structures is a small but prestigious manufacturer of high-quality custom sunrooms. The company and its products have been featured in trade magazines and on the Discovery Channel program "Gimme Shelter." Dealers sell most of Creative Structures' sunrooms and install them at customer sites. Creative Structures ships unassembled kits to the dealers. Naturally, each job requires a parts list specifying exactly what to ship. This parts list identifies the precise size, shape, and quantity of each part in the shipment. The original process for generating parts list was tedious, difficult, and error prone, requiring many hours. As the product line and sales grew, Creative Structures implemented several spreadsheets, each performing some of the calculations. But the spreadsheets only worked as temporary stopgaps. Skilled staff still had to merge their results with each other and with many manually calculated parts. They were falling farther and farther behind.

Creative Structures needed a program that would accept high-level sunroom specifications as input and produce parts lists as output. Their vision went a lot farther, but the immediate, ever more desperate, requirement was for a parts list generator. The documentation was amazingly complete, by far the best I've ever seen from any client or user. Much of it was waiting the first day I visited Creative Structures. Much of the rest was available before we were ready for it. So where was the difficulty? Creative Structures' standard system for configuring sunrooms was very flexible. It included about one 125 different kinds of parts, not even counting the ten to fifteen different types of glass. All of these parts were available for use in a very wide range of designs, dimensions, configurations, and the like. Many of the parts varied in size and shape, often in fairly complex ways depending on the sunroom configuration and on neighboring parts. The first consulting team apparently got lost in implementing details, never developing a high-level architecture to pull them together. Experience had taught Creative Structures that partial solutions were inadequate. They needed a tool that could be quickly used by relatively unskilled staff to generate complete parts lists for any sunroom that fell within their wide ranging standard.

3. The Solution

I contracted with Creative Structures to write a parts list generator. We agreed that Creative Structures would specify the details of an old-fashioned character-oriented, teletype-style user interface. The program would produce the reports as text files so that they could be modified for custom jobs that deviated from the standard product line. Creative Structures was also responsible for documenting the user interface and program functionality.

4. The Model

The manufacturing industry's hierarchical bill of materials is the program's internal model for representing sunrooms. It represents products as lists of their components, and components as lists of their components, and so forth. Bills of material have numerous variants and many uses in manufacturing management and control. [3][7][10] Modern day programming theoreticians and practitioners will recognize that this model is an embodiment of the composite design pattern. [4] More specifically, we model a sunroom as a set of walls and the end posts that separate the walls, where we consider roofs as special types of walls and rafters as special types of posts. Similarly, walls comprise a set of bays and posts that separate the bays. Bays are sets of vertical components and horizontal dividers that separate them. The three sentences above provide a framework for almost the entire sunroom structure and for the portions of the software that model them. Within this framework, almost every calculation involves just a single part and the part that contains it. I discuss exceptions below, but this model localizes almost all of the many details.

The model also translates perfectly into the object oriented paradigm. It starts with a virtual part class, which is inherited by the complex piece class and by the piece part class. Parts, such as walls, bays, and various assemblies, which have subordinate parts inherit from the complex part class. The atomic parts, the ones displayed on the parts list, inherit from the virtual piece part class.

5. The Program

The original program executed four steps: (1) get input data to define the solar room configuration, (2) create the objects corresponding to the parts, (3) calculate any dimensions that were not provided in the input, and (4) print reports. Each step is briefly discussed below.

I required Creative Structures to specify a character-based user interface because at that time I had no experience with either X Window Systems or with any other graphic user interfaces (GUI). Creative Structures proposed an input protocol designed to minimize keystrokes. It included small, extremely concise codes to specify the components of each bay. These bay component codes specify customer choices, such as fixed glass, casement windows, awning windows, doors, fans, skylights, and so forth. When viewed as a formal language, the original encoding had one minor ambiguity, easily resolved by adding dashes to separate components. We still use these codes to describe bay contents today, even though the rest of input uses a modern GUI approach. It is simply much faster for someone familiar with the program to type in a small number of characters than to drag and drop each bay component.

For the most part, creating the model's objects was straightforward. Each object's constructor created the items beneath that object in the hierarchy. There were two major nontrivial issues that complicated the object creation process. First, the rules for defining the separators between bay components depended on the components on both sides. Fortunately, grouping the types of components into sets that required the same components reduced the number of cases enough to apply a brute force enumeration of all the possibilities. Other complications arose where parts did not conform to the model's assumption that calculations must be local to single pieces and their parents. For such pieces, the program could not instantiate the lowest level objects until after the calculations had been performed. The calculations determined the required number of pieces.

Within the model's framework, almost all of the calculations were also straightforward. But I needed Newton's Method for one of our several pitch (roof angle) calculations and dynamic programming for sill piece length calculations. Both of these are discussed in more detail below.

Generating part list reports requires very little code. The program simply traverses the hierarchical parts tree, putting each node (piece part) into a sorted list, then generates the report from the sorted list parts. Because the 1989 sorted list library class essentially implemented a slow bubble sort, the process appeared to halt for a while until the report was ready. But the delay was not a serious enough problem to justify reprogramming. Within several years, computers became much faster, and a heap-based priority queue class was added to the vendor's standard library. Changing a couple of lines of application code to use the heaps instead of the bubble sort made the calculations appear instantaneous.

The program also generates a classic indented bill-of-materials report showing the tree structure that the program builds internally. This report was an afterthought. Both the need for it and its effectiveness were completely unanticipated. When the client started receiving parts lists late in the implementation, he returned problem reports along the lines of "This greenhouse should have 17 widgets and you only report 15. Fix it." I didn't understand the details of the sunroom architecture well enough to know where to look for the cause of the discrepancy. I responded by implementing the indented bill of materials, printing it out, and giving it to the client to locate the problems more precisely. This worked very well. Suddenly, problem reports were detailed and specific enough for us to understand and make the appropriate corrections.

6. An Exception to the Model

Since this is a real-world problem and not an academic exercise, the conceptual model does not work perfectly. Not all calculations can be limited to a piece and its parent. The calculation that most violated the model boundaries applied to sills, ledgers, and eaves. Sills, for example, consist of wooden boards that run under the walls. The board lengths are bounded, currently at 13 feet, 6 inches. Each bay has a sill if and only if the bay does not have a door. Bays in the same wall can share sill pieces, as long as sharing does not make the sill piece too long. When a sill section is too long for a single board, the program must divide it into multiple sill pieces. The sill pieces of any sill section meet under the middle of posts between bays. For any given bay combination, the sill must be made with the smallest possible number of pieces subject to the maximum length constraint. As a secondary constraint, the pieces must be as equal to each other as possible. The program assigns responsibility for calculating sill piece lengths to the corresponding wall objects. This calculation requires a wall object to obtain and use the width of each of its bays that require sills. This violates the model's goal of limiting calculations to a single piece and its parent. But sill calculations break the model's locality principle even more. The configuration and length of the sill ends depend on whether or not there is a wall around the corner and upon whether the adjacent bay around the corner has a sill. So the walls have to learn whether there are adjacent walls at their corners and whether those walls have sills abutting their corners. The implementation permits two kinds of information sharing outside that permitted by the basic model: (1) corner posts "tell" walls the identity of the wall around the corner from them, and (2) walls will "tell" other walls if they have sills at their edges.

7. Three Calculation Problems

Even after the total length and possible cut locations are known for a sill, the question of cutting the sill pieces optimally is far from trivial. As walls get long, the potential number of ways to cut the sill pieces undergoes a combinatorial explosion, particularly if we can not assume that all of the bays are the same width. As with many real-world standards, the "as equal as possible" constraint is vague and imprecise. I solved this problem by writing a generic object oriented implementation of the dynamic programming algorithm invented by Richard Bellman [1], then extended to discrete problems and popularized by Bellman and Dreyfus [2]. My criterion for making the pieces as equal as possible is to minimize the sum of the squares of their lengths, but any other quantitative measure of "as equal as possible" would work with my implementation. Since the program's first installation, no problems have been reported with its division of sills into pieces.

Another incidental problem that required a relatively sophisticated solution was a roof-pitch variant that required finding a root x of the trigonometric equation

$$R = A \sin(x) + B / \cos(x) - C \tan(x)$$

In our problem space, $A \sin(x)$ is much bigger than the other two trigonometric terms, so $\sin(x)$ is close to R/A. Also, the angles are fairly small, so $\sin(x)$ is not too far from x's value in radians. The function is differentiable, and R/A is a first order approximation to the roots value in radians. The Newton Raphson method [9] is the obvious choice and indeed it converges in very few iterations.

Rafter length calculation had a subtlety that could have led the program into an endless loop if the analysis had been sloppy. Rafters are selected from a small set of predefined thicknesses. Each thickness has a length constraint and, optionally, a pitch constraint. The program uses the minimal thickness permitted by the rafter length. Although the situation may never have occurred in practice, I constructed a pathological example that would cause an infinite loop if the code were written without care. Given a particular sunroom configuration, a thicker rafter will be shorter than a thinner one. In the case in which a thin rafter just barely exceeds its maximum length constraint, the next thicker rafter will be shorter than the constraint for the thinner rafter. Rather than write code that would oscillate back and forth, the program calculates from thinnest to thickest, stopping with the first that passes all constraints. It also allows the user to specify a minimum thickness. The parts list will specify the minimum thickness greater than or equal to the user's entry that meets all constraints.

The vast majority of the implementation involved issues that neither violated the model nor required sophisticated algorithms. The development process consisted of working on one piece or assembly, learning all of the detailed rules and calculations for it, verifying that it fit into the conceptual model, implementing it, and starting all over again with the next piece or assembly until the project was finished. The main effect of the troublesome issues discussed in this section was to distract our attention and raise temporary concerns about whether our model was really sufficient for the project.

8. Environment and Evolution

The first version of the parts list program was implemented using Interactive Software Engineering's Eiffel 2.2 and 2.3 under UNIX V3.2 on a 20 MHz 80386 based IBM AT compatible. The target machine was a 16 MHz 80386 based IBM AT compatible running Xenix. The port amounted to nothing more than taking the C code and Makefile produced by the Eiffel compiler and running the build on the Xenix system. I did have to insert some spurious calls in the Eiffel code to prevent the compiler from performing some optimizations that moved code into other classes, making those classes' object code too big for the Xenix linker. Even with the slow compiler and primitive debugging tools, I never regretted using Eiffel. I developed the high-level analysis and designed the software architecture. I also wrote a small amount of the code. My employee, a recent computer science graduate with no object oriented background or industry experience, wrote the rest under my loose supervision.

The first complete parts list program was obsolete the day it was delivered. Creative Structure's manufacturing process is a moving target. During the time it took us to understand the requirements and implement the solution, the company made two significant revisions to their manufacturing process, requiring minor modifications to about two dozen classes. I attribute the ease of implementing those modifications to the appropriateness of our model and our implementation. We produced those changes as the deliverables of a completely separate contract. This time we worked with Creative Structures to write a complete set of specifications before we signed the contract and started the work. The project was completed in early 1991. For the first time in the company's history, generating parts lists was no longer a bottleneck. In addition, the new parts lists were more accurate than those constructed with the older manual process.

We ported the program from Xenix to Microsoft Windows 3.1 in 1995. Creative Structures' main reason for this upgrade was to eliminate dependence on the old computer, whose hard drive was starting to make strange noises. At the same time, we implemented about 30 very minor changes to reflect more revisions in Creative Structure's manufacturing process. The Eiffel programming environment shielded the project from the porting effort any significant operating system dependencies. Most of the actual work was converting from Eiffel 2 to Eiffel 3. The language upgrade did not require any individually significant changes, but it did require small changes in every single class. Luckily, an automated tool provided by the vendor made most of those changes. Although the program had run interactively since its first implementation, it still used a character-based user interface.

In 1997, I started a project to upgrade the program in several ways. First, I ported it from Windows 3.1 to Windows 95. Second, I converted from the old, modal, clumsy, character-oriented interface to a flexible, event driven, GUI based interface. I kept the small formal language for describing the contents of a single bay. It is simple to learn (at least for Creative Structures' staff who already know the product) and faster to use than GUI-based techniques. Third, I replaced the procedural logic that interpreted the bay description language with an object oriented parser [6] because the old code's intermixed parsing and processing was very hard to understand and upgrade for the next phases. Fourth, I loaded a lot of the static data from text files so that the client could modify it without reprogramming. Fifth, the program will be enhanced to produce cost analyses. Sixth, the program will be expanded to generate parts lists for a whole new class of Creative Structures sunrooms, octagonal ones that have forty-five degree angles between walls. And perhaps most significantly, by the time this paper is presented, the parts list will generate engineering drawings.

Generating parts lists has streamlined Creative Structure's post-sales operations. The parts lists provide the raw data for ordering parts, scheduling the manufacturing shop, and assembling shipments. But this package has a lot more to offer. Generating engineering drawings and quotes will streamline sales and marketing operations. From this project's perspective, the entire process and data flow from initial inquiry to final shipment can be summarized as follows:

1. Receive initial specs from a dealer.
2. Send engineering drawings and a quote to the dealer.
3. The dealer reviews the drawings with the customers
4. The customers revise the configuration to maximize features and minimize cost.
5. Receive modified specs from the dealer or jump to step 7.
6. Repeat steps 2 through 5.
7. Receive a firm order from the dealer.
8. Generate the parts list.
9. Manufacture and ship the sunroom.

Until the sale is firm, step 2 is the only one that Creative Structures controls. Unfortunately, it is often the bottleneck in the whole sales process. Not only is it expensive to produce engineering drawings manually, it also takes time. Creative Structures usually has several days backlog. At times, the queue has grown as long as a month. The effect on sales is disastrous. By automating the drawings and quotes, Creative Structures will be able to fax them back to the dealers within minutes after taking the specifications for standard sunrooms over the phone. Nonstandard sunrooms will still require manual intervention, but the engineer's starting point will be the program's engineering drawing loaded into a CAD program. In either case, the dealers can return to the customers with drawings and firm prices while they are still enthusiastic and emotionally committed. With streamlined procedures, Creative Structures expects to convert a much higher percentage of dealer inquiries to sales.

9. Lessons

What made this project possible? I think that the most important factor was the development of a clean conceptual model that divided the calculations recursively into disjoint smaller models. It enabled our small team to implement a solution where another consulting company had failed. Perhaps second in importance was the implementation tools and environment. The ISE Eiffel 2.3 development package included a very complete, integrated library of standard data structures for 1989. Reuse of ISE's libraries enabled the implementation of the model's architecture with very little application code. As a result, almost all of the application code focused on detailed application requirements within the context of the software architecture based on the model. The Eiffel libraries' thorough use of assertions to specify input requirements caught many problems immediately, minimizing the need for debugging. Eiffel also let me lock in semantics by writing preconditions, postconditions, and invariants for the classes that implemented the conceptual model. These factors more than compensated for that Eiffel generation's deficient debugging tools. Finally, the indented bill-of-materials report displayed the model in a format that domain experts could use to identify implementation problems precisely.

What made the project a success? The program quickly generated reports that were correct and complete for all standard sunrooms, where "standard" encompassed a very wide range of structures and components. Another important advantage to the client was having the reports in editable files so that only incremental work was required to modify reports for nonstandard sunrooms and only minimal edits were required when manufacturing procedures changed.

What would I do differently? First, I would analyze the issues more thoroughly before I turned the coding over to my junior programmer. I did not appreciate the incredible number of details or how interrelated they were. I would design at least one or two levels deeper before allowing coding to start. I would also supervise the implementation more carefully as it proceeded. My programmer was intelligent, hard working, and dedicated, but at that stage in her career, she did not have the experience required to understand the implications of high level abstractions and architectural issues. She did not use inheritance, polymorphism, and delegation nearly enough. The low-level code has far more conditional and procedural logic than it should. She violated the model's structure several places where the model was perfectly sufficient. She violated Yourdon and Constantine's [11] "tightly bound, loosely coupled" principles throughout, with especially detrimental effects from intermixing user input and parsing with application functionality. That she ultimately succeeded is a credit to the model, Eiffel and its development environment, and her perseverance. In retrospect, her job would have been much easier if I had designed not only the model for the hierarchical parts list, but also designed explicitly separate domain models for both the sunroom specifications and the input process that created it. It took a lot of work to add these later, when I implemented the graphic user interface and its editor with unlimited do, undo, and redo capabilities.

Another project deficiency, hardly unique, is the total lack of user documentation. In retrospect, it should have been obvious to me that the company owner would never make time to document properly how to use program. Once the program eliminated parts list generation as a critical issue, his attention was diverted by Creative Structures' next generation of critical issues. Even the thick book of detailed documentation that he developed for us got lost in the company for several years after he left. As the program was handed down from one staff member to another, numerous important features were completely forgotten.

10. Conclusions

The program is a major success. It has provided the foundation for Creative Structures' post-sales operations since 1991. It has been ported, modified, and enhanced repeatedly during that time. Now it is supporting the sales process too.

The model and the high-level implementation, with compiler enforced specs, were good enough to compensate, on this relatively small project, for inexperienced staff, essentially nonexistent project management, and never more than part-time effort from the single senior developer.

The total cost to the client for this custom system, from the initial feasibility meetings through all of the phases discussed in this paper, is under $30,000. Their sales support and part list generation is far ahead of the rest of their industry.

Could this functionality have been implemented without object oriented tools? Of course it could have. The Eiffel compiler translated the program to C, and the C compiler to machine language. In theory, any computer program could be written in machine language. But the object oriented language directly supported writing code at a level much closer to our conceptual model of the system.

Bibliography

[1]   Richard E. Bellman. *Dynamic Programming.* Princeton University Press, Princeton, NJ 1957.

[2]   Richard E. Bellman and Stuart E. Dreyfus. *Applied Dynamic Programming.* Princeton University Press, Princeton, NJ 1962.

[3]   Christopher D. Gray. *The Right Choice, A Complete Guide to Evaluating, Selecting, & Installing MRP II Software.* The Oliver Wight Companies, Essex Junction, VT 1985.

[4]   Eric Gamma, Richard Helm, Ralph Johnson and John Vlissides. *Design Patterns, Elements of Reusable Object Oriented Software.* Addison Wesley, Reading, MA 1995.

[5]   Bertrand Meyer. *Object Oriented Software Construction, First Edition.* Series in Computer Science, Prentice Hall, Englewood Cliffs, NJ 1988.

[6]   Bertrand Meyer ISE Technical Report TR44/LI Reusable Software: *The Base Object Oriented Component Libraries.* Interactive Software Engineering, Goleta, CA 1995.

[7]   Steven A. Melnyk and Joseph L. Carter. *Production Activity Control,* A Practical Guide Dow Jones Irwin, Homewood, IL 60430.

[8]   David Parnas. "On the Criteria to Be Used in Decomposing Systems into Modules" Communications of the ACM, vol. 15, no. 12, December 1972, pages 1053-1058.

[9]   James B. Scarborough. *Numerical Mathematical Analysis, Sixth Edition.* The Johns Hopkins Press, Baltimore, MD 1966.

[10] Thomas F. Wallace. *MRP II: Making It Happen.* The Oliver Wight Companies, Essex Junction, VT 1985.

[11] Edward Nash Yourdon and Larry L. Constantine. *Structured Design: Fundamentals of a Discipline of Computer Program and Systems Design* Prentice Hall, Englewood Cliffs, NJ, 1979.

Technical Papers

Databases

Implementing a Distributed Garbage Collector for OO Databases

Richard BIELAK, Jean-Pierre SARKIS
CAL FP (US), Inc.
610 Fifth Ave, Suite 616
New York, N.Y. 10020
richieb@calfp.com, sarkis@calfp.com

Abstract

In this paper we describe the implementation of a distributed garbage collector for group of object oriented database. We start by considering the issues that led to the choice of algorithm and why garbage collection in a database is more difficult than in memory. We describe the algorithm and how it was implemented in Eiffel, using PVM (Parallel Virtual Machine) and Versant ODBMS.

1: Introduction

One of the advantages of programming in object oriented languages such as Eiffel, Java or SmallTalk is the presence of automatic memory management, that is *garbage collection* (GC). GC frees the programmer from the tedious and error prone task of allocating and freeing memory.

Unfortunately the same cannot be said for most object oriented database systems. Although "garbage" can be easily created in the database as links between objects are changed during typical operations, no tools for automatic space cleanup are provided. Instead it is up to the application to reclaim the wasted space.

In our case we have to manage space in databases that are used by a large financial application (the Rainbow system [1]). Today our system uses four separate databases whose total size is over two Gigabytes and growing.

The system runs on a network of SUN UltraSparc machines running Solaris 2.6, with the database servers using Ultra2s. The database software is Versant version 5 and the collector was written in Eiffel.

1.1: Background

Our initial approach to handle the problem of database garbage collection was to use the simple techniques of in memory collectors. For example, one of our early collectors loaded all objects into memory and performed a standard mark and sweep algorithm. However, as the database grew this method stopped working because we all objects would not fit in memory.

The algorithm presented in this paper is similar to the garbage collector discussed Cook *et al.* [2]. We divide the objects to be collected into partition and perform garbage collection on each partition. In our case the partitions are entire databases.

We also handle the problem of cross partition references differently. In [2] the authors describe *remember sets*, sets of object pointers that identify which objects are referenced from other partitions. These sets are built and maintained while the database is in use. In our algorithm the equivalent of the *remember sets* are built during the collection process.

Finally, in [2] the authors describe an incremental collector that only removes garbage from one partition at a time and they concentrate on policies needed to pick a good partitions. In contrast our collector runs on all partitions in parallel and our partitions were picked for convenience of implementation.

Skubiszewski and Valduriez [3] present another algorithm for database garbage collection that uses multiple processes to perform its work. Their algorithm is based on a mark and sweep strategy. During the marking phase two processes execute - the cutting agent and the marking agent. The cutting agent identifies *GC-consistent* cuts within which collection can be performed safely. The third process, the sweeping agent, runs and deletes objects after a marking phase is done. With some assistance from the database server this collector can run while applications are using the database.

Our algorithm also uses many processes, but we only use them to speed up the collection process. Also, our collector does not require any specific support from the database server. On the other hand, applications cannot use the database while our collector is running.

Finally, our collector is being used on databases that are larger than the ones described in the papers [2, 3].

2: Organization of the database

In the Versant ODBMS it is possible to retrieve every object that has been stored, regardless of whether other objects reference it or not. This means that as far as the database system is concerned no objects are garbage. Instead the garbage is a byproduct of the application specific database organization.

Our databases are organized as follows. In each database there is a single object of type DATABASE_ROOT, from which all "live" objects can be reached. The database root object references a number of instances of a class PERSISTENT_ROOT. A PERSISTENT_ROOT is a named list of objects of a common type. Each item in this list can be an arbitrarily complex structure of objects that can reference objects within other roots and in other database.

An object is considered *reachable* if it is referenced by the database root, or if it is referenced by an attribute of another object that is already reachable. All objects that are reachable from a given object are called that object's *closure*.

Objects that can be reached from a DATABASE_ROOT are "live", all others are garbage. Notice, that the definition of "live" objects is made more complex by the presence of many databases, as it is possible that an object in a given database can only be reached from an object in another database.

3: Selecting a GC algorithm for databases

Garbage collection algorithms come in two basic flavors: *mark and sweep* collectors and *copy* collectors. A mark and sweep algorithm traverses the closure starting from the root object, and marks all the objects in closure as "live". Then all the objects are scanned again and the ones that are not marked are deleted.

A copy collector also traverses the closure starting from the specified root, but it copies the "live" objects elsewhere, so that the space that these objects occupied along with the remaining uncopied garbage objects can be released.

In addition to the simple mark and sweep and copy algorithms there are many other variations of collectors that are incremental in nature. We have not considered any of these, as incremental garbage collection presents some difficult problems in a database environment (for example preserving state between collector cycles).

3.1: Constraints

There are two important differences between garbage collection in memory and in a database. The first difference is that collection in a database requires I/O. Therefore it is important to choose an an algorithm that performs the least amount of I/O.

To complicate matters further, database I/O requires transactions and locks. Any object to be updated in a transaction must be locked first and the lock is not released until the enclosing transaction is committed. Since transactions imply additional I/O (writes to log files, etc), it is important to reduce the number of transaction, while keeping their size reasonable. Finally, deleting objects from a database is slow, especially if indices must be updated.

The second difference is that a database collector cannot keep all the objects in memory at once simply because databases contain too much data.

Given the above constrains we ruled out a mark and sweep collector, because such a collector would need to do too much I/O. First all the live objects would have to be read twice, once during the mark and once during the sweep phase. Then, if the marks were to be kept persistent the live objects would be written once. It is possible to avoid these writes if the marks can be kept in memory. Finally, all the garbage objects would be read once and deleted.

On the other hand, a copy collector only needs to read and write live objects. For example, if a database has M live objects and N garbage objects the number of I/Os required to perform the collection is show in the table below("PM" means persistent marks and "TM" transient marks):

	Mark and Sweep (PM)	Mark and Sweep (TM)	Copy
Reads:	2*M + N	2*M + N	M
Writes:	M	0	M
Deletes:	N	N	0
Total I/O:	3*M + 2*N	2*M + 2*N	2*M

In our initial analysis the percentage of garbage in our databases was about 50%, so we choose to implement a copy collector. J. E. Cook, *et al.* [2] also shows that a copy collector is more efficient if there is a lot of garbage present.

There was one additional advantage of using a copy collector. As the database in daily use are filled with objects, often they have to be extended and end up spanning several files. By copying all the objects into a clean database, we compact the storage into a single file which results in faster I/O.

A restriction that we have imposed in order to simplify the implementation was that our collector would be a *stop-the-world* collector. In other words, no access to the database would be allowed while the collection was in progress. So far this limitation has not proven to be a problem, because in the actual production use collection cycles are required about once a month and can be run over a weekend when the system is not in use.

4: Description of the Algorithm

4.1: System Environment

Versant ODBMS has a typical client/server architecture. The database files reside on one machine and are accessed through a group of server processes. Client application communicate with the server via the network. As a result database applications can be run on any computer that is part of the server's network and before using any databases the application must connect to its server.

Unlike other systems, instead of data pages, Versant passes objects between the client and the server. Furthermore, Versant supports object level locks, however the server is only a data server, any code associated with a persistent object is executed by the client

Within a group of related databases (a group being defined by the DBA) all the objects have unique object IDs (called LOID - for *Logical Object Identifiers*), even if the objects are stored in separate database. The object ID serves as a pointer that identifies an object and can be used for direct retrieval. The Versant LOID can be converted into a string representation that can be passed between programs and then converted back to a valid object pointer.

When one persistent object references another, the object ID of the referenced object is actually stored. In order to retrieve an object by object ID, the application must be connected to the database that contains the target object. If the object is not in any connected database the attempted retrieval will fail.

In normal operations object IDs must be unique. However, in the garbage collector we have to be able to copy objects into an empty database while keeping their object IDs. The Versant API [4] provides several calls that allow copy of objects from one database to another while preserving the object ID.

4.2: Process Architecture of the Collector

To reduce the amount of time needed for a garbage collection run we decided to split the work among separate processes running in parallel on different machines in our network. For each database a separate *copier* process executes. This process computes the closure of the database root and copies the live object to the target database.

While having multiple processes running at the same time reduces the time it takes to complete the garbage collection it does not solve the problem posed by references between databases. It is possible to have an object whose only references are in other databases and those objects would be considered garbage by a simple `copier` program.

Since the `copier` process connects only to its source and its target databases it can detect a reference to an object in another database. The question is what should be done when such a *dangling* reference is encountered.

The solution is to start another program that can determine which database the dangling references belong to. This *resolver* process is connected to all source databases, so that by retrieving the object it can see which database the object came from. While the `copiers` are running they pass the LOIDs of all the dangling references to the `resolver`. The `resolver` groups these by their source database, and then passes them to the appropriate `copier`. This way the externally referenced objects are counted as "live" and are copied.

4.3: Details of Communications

The `copier` and the `resolver` processes communicate by sending messages to each other. All messages sent between the collector processes are asynchronous. When a process needs to wait for more data it simply listens for the next message.

We defined the following types of messages:

- *register database copier*
  This is the first message sent by the `copier` process to the `resolver`. It contains the name of the source database that the sending `copier` is copying.

- *external references*
  This message contains a series of object IDs. When sent by the `copier` it has the references that fall outside the `copiers` source database. After sending this message the `copier` continues running. The `resolver` also sends this message when it forwards the reported external references to the right `copier`. However, the `resolver` only sends this message when explicitly asked by the `copier`.

- *ask for references*
  This message is sent by the `copier` when it has finished scanning the closure and is ready to process any external references.

- *finished*
  This message is sent by the `resolver` when it is finished distributing all references.

When the `resolver` starts, it connects to all the source databases and then waits for messages from the `copiers`. The processing is then driven by reception of messages.

For each `copier` process the `resolver` keeps an object of type DB_LOIDS_TABLE that contains this information:

- *task ID*
  This is the PVM [5] task ID, needed to send messages to the `copier`

- *copier is waiting flag*
  A boolean flag which is set to true if the `copier` is known to waiting for a message from the `resolver`.

- *hash table of object IDs*
  Table of LOIDs of objects that are stored in this `copier`'s database and are referenced from other databases. No matter how many times an object is referenced, its LOID occurs only once in this table.

The diagram below shows the outline of the communications between a `copier` and the `resolver`:

```
     COPIER                               RESOLVER

  [register_db]          ----------> verify the db is connected

  [external_refs]        ----------> process the references, adding them
                                     to the tables for the right copiers

     ... above message is repeated as often as needed ...


  [request_object_ids]   ----------> prepare message with object ids for
                                     this copier

check that refs          <---------- [external_refs]
are in closure, and
extend closure if needed

     ... above two message are repeated as needed ...

  [request_objects_ids] ----------->  when no more ref to send and
                                      other copiers done

  exit                   <---------- [finished]
```

5: Handling Messages in the Resolver

In this section we describe how the `resolver` handles each message it receives.

- *register database copier*
  When a database is registered by a `copier` process, a check is performed that a DB_LOIDS_TABLE instance for this database exists. If so the task ID of the `copier` is stored in this table. If not, the `resolver` aborts - since this error can only happens if the collector is wrongly configured.

- *external references*
  This message contains a list of LOIDs represented as strings. The `resolver` iterates over this list and for each LOID, it retrieves the object and determines which database it came from. Then, using the name of this database, it locates the appropriate DB_LOIDS_TABLE. If this is the first time this object has been retrieved it is inserted into the hash table of externally referenced objects.
  The final step of handling this message is to check if any of the `copiers` are waiting for more LOIDs. A check of all DB_LOIDS_TABLEs is made to see if there is a `copier` that has pending LOIDs but is waiting. If any are found an *external references*

message is build and sent.

- *ask for references*
  When this message is received the `resolver` finds the DB_LOIDS_TABLE for the requesting `copier`, it creates an *external references* message and sends it to the `copier`. In order not to overflow communication channels LOIDs are sent to `copiers` in small batches.
  If no LOIDs are waiting to be sent, the `copier` is marked as "waiting". If LOIDs are added to the table because external references were received from other `copiers` a message with the new LOIDs will be sent to the waiting copier.

The `resolver` terminates the collection process when it finds that all copiers are in the *waiting* state and all tables that contain LOIDs to be send are empty. At this point the `resolver` sends a *finish* message to all `copiers`.

5.1: Computing Closure and Copying

The `copier` process works in two phases. In the first phase the closure of the database root is computed and copied, and all the dangling references are forwarded to the `resolver`. In the second phase the `copier` waits for messages from the `resolver` with the LOIDS of objects referenced by the other databases and makes sure that these objects, along with their closures, are copied as well.

The closure computing algorithm is enclosed in one class, named CLOSURE_COMPUTOR. There are two structures that are created during the computation: a list of object IDs that are in the closure, and a hash table with the same object IDs. The hash table is used to quickly check if a given object ID under consideration is already in the closure.

Below is a code fragment (in Eiffel) showing the outline of the closure computing algorithm:

```
last_computed_closure: VSTR

closure_set: HASH_INTEGER_SET

closure_position: INTEGER

scan_objects is
    local
        done: BOOLEAN
    do
        from
        until done
        loop
            scan_one_object (last_computed_closure.i_th (closure_position))
            closure_position := closure_position + 1
            done := closure_position > last_computed_closure.count
        end
    end -- scan_objects
```

The last_computed_closure and closure_set are initialized to contain the object ID of the database root, and closure_position is set to one. When the scan_one_object routine traverses an object, it extends the list, last_computed_closure, with object IDs that are not yet in the closure yet. The closure_set hash table is used to quickly determine if an object ID is already in the closure, therefore any object ID added to the list is also added to the hash table.

The integer closure_position holds the index of the object in last_computed_closure that is being scanned for references. The algorithm terminates when the closure list stops growing - that is scan_one_object does not add any further item to the closure set. In this case closure_position will become larger then the number of items in last_computed_closure.

Termination of this algorithm is guaranteed, because every object in the closure is scanned only once and the database contains finitely many objects. Because closure_position increases each time through the loop, eventually it will become greater than any given number.

Shown below is the routine add_to_closure which is called from scan_one_object for each reference that is not yet in the closure list. The first line of this routine attempts to retrieve the object from the database. If the retrieval succeeds the new object ID is added to the closure list and to the hash table. In addition, a routine action_when_adding_to_closure is called. This routine can be redefined in a descendant of CLOSURE_COMPUTOR.

```
add_to_closure (pobject_id: INTEGER) is
    local
        obj_ptr: POINTER
        err: INTEGER
    do
        -- this call will retrieve the object
        obj_ptr := db_interface.o_locateobj (pobject_id, 0)
        if (obj_ptr /= default_pointer) then
            -- If object exists, then add it to closure
            last_computed_closure.extend_integer (pobject_id)
            closure_set.put (pobject_id)
            action_when_adding_to_closure (pobject_id)
                ...
        else
            -- can't get to it, call the action
            action_on_dangling_reference (pobject_id)
        end
    end
```

If the retrieval of the object fails, that means this object ID denotes an object in another database. In this case only the routine action_on_dangling_reference is called. Again, this routine can be redefined in a descendant class.

Finally CLOSURE_COMPUTER provides yet another customizable routine, called action_at_end_of_scan, that is called after the complete closure has been found.

The copier process does not use the CLOSURE_COMPUTER class directly, instead it uses a descendant class named CLOSURE_WITH_COPYING. There are two reasons for the existence of this class. First, to reduce the number of I/Os, since we want to read and write each object only once. Therefore, the objects must be copied into the target database during the closure computation. Second, when dangling references are found, messages have to be send to the `resolver` process.

CLOSURE_WITH_COPYING class inherits CLOSURE_COMPUTER and redefines the three routines: `action_when_adding_to_closure`, `action_on_dangling_reference` and `action_at_end_of_scan`. Briefly here is what these routines do:

- *action_when_adding_to_closure*
  in this routine objects in the closure are batched into groups and written to the target database.

- *action_on_dangling_reference*
  Object IDs are grouped into messages that are send to the `resolver` process. Because many different objects can reference the same object in another database, external references are checked so that duplicate object IDs are not sent in the same message.

- *action_on_end_of_scan*
  Any object IDs that were still waiting are packed into a message sent.

Since we cannot expect to keep all the objects in memory, once an object is scanned for references it is removed from memory. The only data that must be held for the entire run is the hash table of object IDs that are in the closure. We also keep the list of all object IDs that constitute closure, although keeping this list in memory in not absolutely necessary.

5.2: Tools Used

Our garbage collector is written in Eiffel. It turned out to be a rather small program, less than 2000 lines of Eiffel code, not including the interface libraries for the Versant database and PVM.

Because the Rainbow system is written in Eiffel and the the libraries for Versant and PVM were already written, it was easy just to use them.

There are few important features of the Versant DBMS that made writing the collector easier:

- The object IDs (LOIDs) have an external representation as strings. Therefore it is possible to pass LOIDs between separate processes. In other OODB systems object IDs are pointers that are valid only within a single address space.

- The Versant API provides the client with the ability to copy objects between databases and still retain the object IDs (as mentioned earlier).

- Versant API gives the programmer complete access to the database schema, that is, to the class definitions. Using this meta information it is easy to write generic code to examine any object, find the attributes that are references and extract their values.

We used Parallel Virtual Machine (PVM [5]) as the means for communication between the processes of the collector. PVM is a message passing software package designed for implementation of parallel programs. It has facilities for sending arbitrarily long message between processes, as well as various synchronization mechanisms. In our collector we only used the asynchronous message passing features of PVM. Each message sent by PVM can be assigned a type code, which makes dispatching to the right code at the receiver easy.

6: Performance in Actual Runs

In the production environment the collector is used on a group of four databases. Two of those databases, *static* and *front_office* are small, less than 200M, and two, *dynamic* and *accounts*, are large, 0.9 Gig and 1.2 Gig respectively.

We use three machines to run the collector. A server for the source databases, a server for the target database, and another machine to run the `resolver` and `copiers` for the smaller databases. All these machines are SUN UltraSparc2s running Solaris 2.6. The database servers also run the copiers for the large databases (one copier on each) and have very large swap spaces (over 1 Gig).

All the machines are connected to the same segment of a 100MB Ethernet network.

A typical execution of the garbage collector takes about 10 to 11 hours. This time is attributed mostly to the `copier` of the largest database. The table below shows the numbers of objects before and after a recent collection run:

Database	Before GC	After GC
Accounts	9,671,630	8,702,741
Dynamic	7,957,268	5,025,740
Front Office	28,741	7,549
Static	852,818	702,259
TOTAL	18,510,457	14,438,289

From the same run here is a summary of messages sent between the processes. The first column shows how many external references were found and sent to the `resolver` for each database, and the second number is the count of *external reference* messages that were sent to the `copiers`.

Database	Resolver Loids Rcved	Resolver Msg Sends
Accounts	0	0
Dynamic	4546	22
Front Office	6	1
Static	54,024	200

As you can see the objects in the *Static* are referenced most often from the other databases.

Before production use the collector is compiled in *finalized* mode. This means that all optimizations are applied and the code for all assertions is removed. In any case, the bottleneck in the execution of the collector does not seem to be the lack of CPU, but large amount of I/O and large use of memory, which leads to swapping.

To control the use of memory better each `copier` can be started with an argument specifying the initial size of the hash table needed for the closure computation. Because of the differences in sizes of the database this table should be sized properly. For example, the table for the *Accounts* must accommodate over 8 million objects. We found it is best to pick a size that is large enough to start with, so that no reallocation of the hash table is needed, should it fill up. For the *Accounts* database the table starts with about 12 million slots.

7: Conclusions and Future Work

The parallel garbage collector described in this paper was first used in the production environment late in 1998. Since then the collector has been run at least once a month to remove garbage from a group of large databases. For the moment the collector's performance is adequate, but as the database grows we will need to adjust the code.

Currently the limiting factor for the total running time of the collector is the size of the largest database. Therefore, one possible approach that will reduce the total runtime, is to make the algorithm more parallel. This could be implemented if we choose smaller partitions, instead of entire databases.

As we have been running the garbage collector regularly on our databases we found that in each run there is less garbage collected than in the past. As the ration of live objects to garbage objects changes the copy collector is becoming less efficient. Given the fact that database writes are more expensive than reads, as each write may require several I/Os (to write log files), at some point it should be faster to delete the garbage objects rather than copy the entire database. Therefore another possibility is to change the collector to delete the garbage objects instead of copying the live ones.

Acknowledgements

We would like to thank Jack Goldsmith and Jean-Francois Zubillaga for their helpful comments.

References

1. CALFP Bank Case History - http://www.sun.com/technical-computing/Software/Publications/CalFP.html, 1996.

2. J. E. Cook, A. L. Wolf, and B. G. Zorn, *Partition Selection Policies in Object Oriented Database Garbage Collection*, SIGMOD, 1994.

3. M. Skubiszewski and P. Valduriez, *Concurrent Garbage Collection in O2*, Proceedings of the 23rd VLDB Conference, 1997.

4. *Versant ODBMS 5.0 - C Reference Manual*, Versant Object Technology, 1997.

5. A. Geist, A. Beguelin, J. Dongarra, W. Jiang, R. Manchek, V. Sunderam, *PVM - A Users' Guide and Tutorial for Networked Parallel Computing*, MIT Press, 1994.

Persistent Object Synchronization with Active Relational Databases

Fábio A. M. Porto[1], Sérgio R. Carvalho[2], Maurício J. Vianna e Silva[3], Rubens N. Melo[4]
Departamento de Informática, Pontifícia Universidade Católica do Rio de Janeiro
Rua Marquês de São Vicente 225, Rio de Janeiro, RJ, 22453-900, Brazil
{porto[1], sergio[2], rubens[4]}@inf.puc-rio.br, mjvs@domain.com.br[3]

Abstract

One of the most common client/server architectures in enterprise systems today is the combination of object-oriented applications with active relational database systems. With this combination, developers have to overcome a difficult problem: the impedance mismatch between object orientation and the relational model. To date, there are several incomplete approaches for describing the integration of static and dynamic object aspects and active relational databases. An important issue missing from these approaches is the state synchronization between server tuples and client-cached objects. In a previous paper we proposed a technique for mapping the dynamic behavior of objects into active relational databases, using database triggers and stored-procedures. This paper extends our previous one with an architecture based on a replication strategy that maintains server tuples and client-cached objects synchronized with respect to state. This architecture automatically updates client-cached object versions when their corresponding server database tuples are updated.

Keywords: object orientation, active relational databases, state synchronization, data replication, object cache, stored procedures

1   Introduction

For more than a decade, business critical applications have been representing their information assets in relational database management systems (RDBMSs) [Duhl96]. More recently, advances in network technology, distributed programming and software architectures propose the organization of business applications in different tiers spread through various computers [Buschman+96, Aarsten+96, Hirschfeld96].

The combination of object-oriented applications with relational database systems within a client-server architecture is probably one of the most common choices for enterprise systems today [Delis+98]. Unfortunately, this combination has still many issues to overcome: the impedance between the Object Oriented (OO) model and the Relational model (RM) requires different approaches to deal with structural and behavioral clashes [Keller+96].

On the structural side, for example, object attributes may be stored in different database tables; also, object relationships such as inheritance have no counterpart in the relational world. On the behavioral side, which we address in this paper, state changes in application objects must be reflected on their persistent versions, and vice-versa.

Pattern languages have been proposed to bridge the existing gap between the two technologies [Brown+96a, Keller+96, Silva+97]. In [Porto+98], we discussed this issue with respect to object behavior. Our proposal allows the representation of object life cycles within active RDBMSs, implementing object behavior via database triggers and stored procedures. By encapsulating dynamic behavior into the RDBMS we simplified the client side of the application and reused all rule enforcement mechanisms provided by commercial database systems.

However, the action part of server rules can, in many cases, change the state of stored objects. The problem of representing these changes in the client side presents itself. The objective of this work, which extends the previous one, is to propose an architecture for the automatic update of client object versions from alterations performed on the database version of the object. We therefore continue to address behavioral OO/RM clashes, neglecting to consider structural mismatches.

In this work, client-server applications with persistent objects stored into RDBMSs can be perceived as instances of an environment with replicated object versions. Once a set of persistent objects is read into the client station, at least two versions of the same object exist: a persistent version, stored into the RDBMS, and an application version to be accessed by the user in the client machine.

The remainder of this paper is organized as follows. Section 2 describes the object synchronization problem in more detail. Section 3 presents the proposed object synchronization architecture. Section 4 shows the scenarios where data are updated and synchronized. Section 5 exemplifies the use of the architecture with a simple application scenario. Section 6 compares our solution with related work. Section 7 presents conclusions and future research.

2 The Synchronization Problem

Consider an application implemented with an OO programming language and an active RDBMS. The application runs on a PC type desktop and the RDBMS on a server machine. Clients start the application and request data from the RDBMS, thus loading the application business objects. Once data gets loaded into the client application, the user deals with it as an independent OO application. The relational implementation becomes entirely transparent [Keller+96].

Application objects become versions of the persistent relational data, cached at the client machine, or at the application layer environment. The reasons for creating such data versions are initially to offer OO semantics for the application data stored in a RDBMS, and secondly to increase overall performance by splitting the application between various collaborating environments.

Considering updating applications, object versions in each client and within a (possibly distributed) server can be modified by user actions in some client's environment, and by active behavior in the RDBMS, via pre-defined triggers and stored procedures [Widom+96, Porto+98]. Thus, in the presence of either application- side or database-side updates, object versions cached in client environments become out of date, so-called stale cached data [Franklin+97]. This happens for three main reasons:

In order to increase overall throughput, persistent application classes implement an optimistic concurrency control protocol [Gray+93], so data read from the RDBMS is not locked while being processed by the client;

User updates take place offline, over local data versions. This strategy greatly increases client execution performance and provides an improvement for overall RDBMS data concurrent access. Updates go to the RDBMSs only at the end of the transaction, during the commit processing;

Server logic, implemented as stored procedures and triggers, may update persistent data that might have been cached and asynchronously updated within the client environment.

With increasing numbers of application clients and application update rates, the lack of synchronization within object versions may turn out to be critical. Client data lag far behind their persistent versions. In such a scenario, a great number of transactions may have to be completely re-submitted.

Considering the above, update-intensive applications can benefit from a proposal that addresses the state synchronization between client-side and database-side objects, thus aiding in the resolution of the OO/RM impedance mismatch. In the next section we present such an architecture.

3   The Object Synchronization Architecture

Figure 1 shows the classes and relationships we propose. The ConcreteApplication, ConcretePersistentApplication and Transaction classes are structured in ways very similar to patterns proposed in [Keller+96, Keller98, Silva+97]. The service classes ApplicationLog, CopyManagerClient and CopyManagerServer provide our proposed functionality.

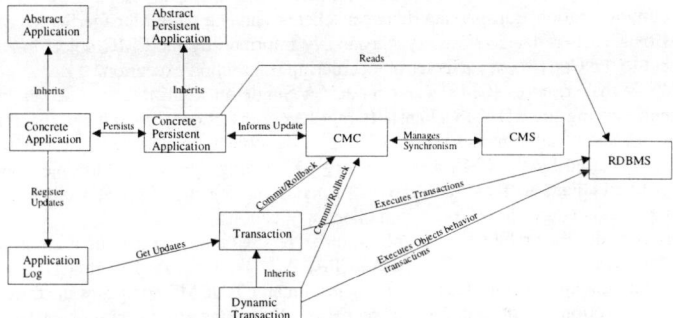

Figure 1 Object Synchronization Architecture Class Diagram

In the next paragraphs we shortly describe the participants in this architecture, their main responsibilities and collaborations. Section 4 presents the proposed synchronized behavior.

The AbstractApplication (AA) class generalizes the manipulation of application objects with persistent behavior. Each domain specific class modeling objects with persistent behavior extends this AA class. These ConcreteApplication (CA) classes model objects in application domains. Persistent read and write operations over CA class objects are passed to the corresponding ConcretePersistentApplication object, described below.

The AbstractPersistentApplication (APA) class provides a common persistent behavior for domain specific classes, including the special messages implementing the synchronization mechanisms between client objects and database tables. ConcretePersistentApplication (CPA) classes extend APA, modeling the persistent behavior of domain objects.

Each CPA is a Singleton [Gamma+95] responsible for the mappings between corresponding object views and relational tables. All communications involving object versions and RDBMS tables pass through one such CPA object, which acts as a broker. The kind of structural mappings1 that may be executed by a CPA class are those presented in [Keller+96]. They represent the main OO structural constructs, such as class, inheritance hierarchy, and association.

The Transaction class singleton controls client application transactions. The responsibilities of this singleton are: to generate transactions identifiers, to register new client transactions with the CMC object, to inform the CMC object of the success or failure of the corresponding transactions, and to apply updates over RDBMS data when a commit operation successfully concludes a client transaction.

The DynamicTransaction (DT) class extends the Transaction class with special behavior needed to process client transactions that execute stored-procedures, which in this work implement object behavior in the RDBMS. The DT object queries and updates data in the auxiliary tables used to inform the CMS object of updates executed by server procedures over persistent data.

The ApplicationLog (AL) class also models a Singleton. It registers the update operations executed by CA objects using a write-ahead policy [Gray+93]. Its object collaborates with the Transaction object during the commit processing, providing all the operations executed within the transaction's boundaries.

The CopyManagerClient (CMC) class models a Singleton responsible for the communication among all CPA objects and the Transaction object with the CopyManagerServer object. It provides communication transparency between clients and the CopyManagerServer object. All operations over cached data will be asynchronously informed by the CMC object in each client environment to the CopyManagerServer object, during transaction execution.

The CopyManagerServer (CMS) class models a Singleton multi-threaded server in a 3-tier environment, serving all RDBMS clients. It registers transactions running on client machines together with a list of table names corresponding to the objects loaded by the transactions. This data structure is used by the CMS as a directory for sending synchronization messages, which inform registered clients with cached versions of persistent objects, of updates committed by the RDBMS server procedures or by concurrent client applications.

We may consider the architecture as split in three tiers. Composing the client environment we have the following classes: AA, CA, APA, CPA, AL, Transaction, DynamicTransaction and CMC. In the middle tier runs the CMS server object and the RDBMS composes the third tier.

In the next section we describe a few scenarios illustrating the synchronized behavior we obtain with the architecture above.

4   Update Scenarios

The architecture presented in section 3 aims to reduce the time lag between a confirmed database update and the moment in which cached versions of the corresponding data have their attribute values synchronized. The database modifications are applied either by applications running on client machines and executing SQL statements through database connections, or by server procedures running on the database server machine.

This section integrates our synchronization architecture with the scenarios in which database data are modified. Our main concern is to present the scenario where server procedures update object data stored in the RDBMS. This is the case when we implement object behavior through database stored-procedures and triggers. We also discuss the modifications in database data executed by client applications. This scenario is divided in two parts: the process of loading and

---

[1] It is important to note that not all object views might be translated into tables. In special, non updateable views [Silberschatz+96, Elmasri+94] like the ones containing aggregated values do not map into tables modeled over the analytical data.

updating objects and the commit process. These scenarios are complemented with a fourth one that identifies and communicates registered clients of stale data.

In all four scenarios the main participants are the CMC and the CMS objects. They provide data structures and operations for supporting the synchronization process. We initiate the presentation of the update scenarios describing the responsibilities of these components.

The CMS object records, for each transaction in a client, a list of tables that have been accessed, and most importantly, have been updated during transaction execution.

The application successfully terminates a transaction by issuing the commit operation on the Transaction object. This event causes the staleness of cached versions being manipulated by other client environments. In order to synchronize data, the Transaction object informs the CMC object of the transaction's commit. The CMC object then passes the information to the CMS object through the InformCommit message. It's a function of the CMS object to inform registered clients that their data versions are out-of-date.

Once the CMC object, controlling a registered client transaction, receives a message about the existence of new versions of stored data, it notifies interested ConcretePersistentApplication objects. When all the clients have acknowledged the message, the CMS object destroys the object corresponding to the finished transaction.

4.1 Client side updates

Figure 2 and Figure 3 show scenarios where a ConcreteApplication object is updated. Object modifications are imposed by transaction operations. Transactions are initiated by calling the BeginTransaction( ) operation on the Transaction object. Each update operation over persistent ConcreteApplication objects informs the transaction object controlling its progress.

After having been associated to a transaction object, the ConcreteApplication object uses it in its communication with the CMC object. All information interchange references the transaction object, so that in the event of a commit, it becomes possible to identify which tables had their states changed during the transaction's processing.

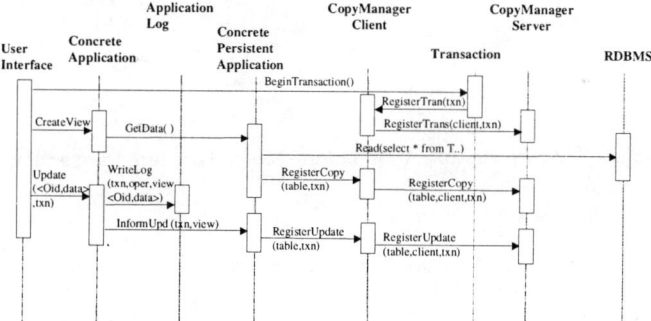

Figure 2 Object Synchronization Architecture Scenario – load and update Objects

Execution on the client side progresses with almost complete independence from the RDBMS side. Once an object is required, i.e. via an user interface request, the CPA object requests the proper tuples from the RDBMS and composes the object's view corresponding to the required ConcreteApplication object, for instantiation purposes. ConcreteApplication objects have a timestamp (ts) attribute. During instantiation, they receive the value of the oldest timestamp among its component tuples. This attribute will be used, during the RDBMS transaction commit, to validate the consistency of the cached version versus the RDBMS version.

An update in a ConcreteApplication object starts the synchronization process. This object informs its corresponding CPA object that an object has been updated. Considering the OO/RM mapping, the CPA object identifies the corresponding tables structurally associated with the updated object. Next, it informs the CMC object of the tables updated. Note that, if the object is composed by tuples in different relational tables, the CMC objects registers the update in all such tables. When the user decides to commit the transaction, it invokes the corresponding Transaction method. The commit process begins by identifying the update operations executed during the transaction, obtained by demanding the ApplicationLog object to provide the net effect of the operations executed during the period [Widom+96]. The CPA translates operations executed over objects into relational counterparts over tables. Once the set of operations is formulated, the Transaction object attempts to execute them within a single RDBMS transaction. During database updates, the corresponding client objects are locked, guaranteeing a consistent synchronization of views.

The Transaction object waits for the RDBMS's return from the commit operation. Following a successful return, it informs the CMC object of the transaction's commit. This object in turn informs participant clients of new database versions of data, of which they have stale versions. This is done by first informing the CMS object of the committed transaction, via the InformCommit message, with parameters identifying the client and the transaction that committed. The CMS object then invokes all clients registered for the updated objects.

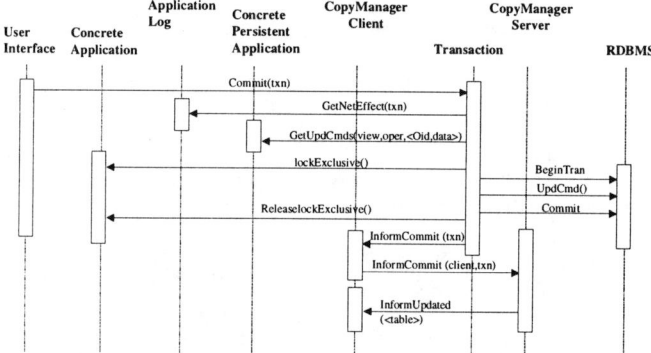

Figure 3 Object Synchronization Architecture Scenario - client transaction commit

4.2 Database side updates

Data may also be changed by RDBMS's server procedures. In particular, we propose the representation of client object behavior via triggers and stored procedures [Porto+98]. These server procedures may update, as part of their code, data cached in client environments.

Server procedures execute within the boundaries of a RDBMS transaction, controlled by the CPA object providing client object persistence. The CPA object uses a transaction object modeled by DynamicTransaction (DT) class to control transactions executing stored-procedures. The DT class extends the Transaction class overriding the operations for the creation and finalization of transactions.

To inform clients with cached object versions of updates executed by server code, we use three auxiliary tables: PersistentTable, UserTransactionTable and ProcedureUpdateTable. The PersistentTable is a meta-data table storing the table names and ids for the ones that have their states changed by server procedures. It serves two basic purposes: document tables representing objects with behavior stored in the RDBMS, and provide consistency for data stored in the ProcedureUpdate table.

The UserTransactionTable is updated by the DynamicTransaction object during begin (insert) and end (delete) of transactions implementing object behavior. Its data represent the collection of transaction operations, through the association of the database user identification and the client's transaction identification.

The ProcedureUpdateTable is updated by the server procedures implementing object behavior. Examples of possible modifications imposed by server procedures include deleting and inserting tuples in state tables, and the execution of pre- and post-conditions associated with a state transition. Each of these updated tables is registered in the auxiliary table together with the user-id and client transaction id.

Figure 4 presents the execution scenario for procedures and triggers implementing object behavior. The overridden methods of class DynamicTransaction are responsible for inserting and deleting user transaction information into the UserTransactionTable.

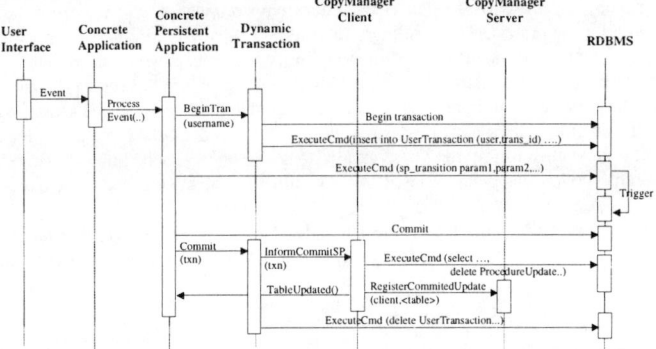

Figure 4 Server procedure's update scenario

After receiving a successful return code from the executed procedure, the CPA object commits the RDBMS transaction. It then terminates the client transaction by issuing the overridden DynamicTransaction Commit operation. The overridden operation controls the execution of a sequence of operations aiming to identify the tables updated during server processing and allowing for the initiation of the synchronization process. It also destroys the transaction object.

The CMC operation InformCommitSP, invoked by the Commit operation, executes in two steps: firstly it queries the ProcedureUpdateTable, finding out tables updated by server procedures, as shown by the query bellow.

"Select pt.table_name, timestamp From PersistentTables pt, ProcedureUpdate pu
Where pt.table_id = pu.table_id and pu.user = :username and
pu.trans_id = :trans_id"

Secondly it deletes the corresponding tuples in the ProcedureUpdateTable, deleting the registration of updated tables. Having recovered the execution control, the Commit operation deletes the tuple in the UserTransactionTable corresponding to the terminating transaction, deleting the transaction record.

Finally, it identifies the CPA objects associated with the updated tables and informs them of the RDBMS updates. To initiate the synchronization messages, the CMC object invokes the RegisterCommitedUpdate operation of the CMS object listing the tables that were updated during the execution of transactions.

4.3 Object level synchronization

The message sent by a CMC object to a CPA object informs that some data, corresponding to a view it controls, was changed. Considering that the granularity of the synchronization control exercised by CMC and CMS objects is a table, the CPA object is responsible for finding out if the change impacts some of the active objects under its scope. The CPA object invokes the GetObjects method of the corresponding ConcreteApplication object. The method returns a list containing the objects presently loaded at the client environment. Using its mapping rules, the CPA object queries the tables corresponding to its view. It uses the attributes composing the table primary key and the timestamp attribute value to identify the objects which need to be updated.

Basically, two sets of results are of interest. First, if no tuple is found for a primary key value, it means that the persistent version of the object has been deleted by some transaction. As a result, the version cached at the client must be destroyed. Second, if a database tuple exists for a primary key value but it presents a timestamp value greater then the one in cached object version, then the object persistent version has been updated. As a result, the object in cache must have its values updated.

Finally, with these queries the CPA object is able to identify the objects that had their states changed, lock them, update their versions and return a message to the user aborting the current transaction (see Figure 5).

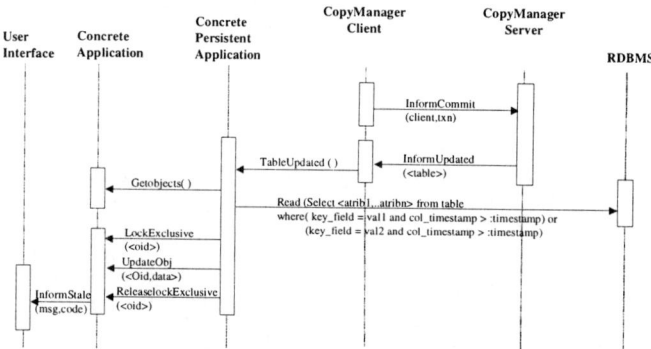

Figure 5 Object level synchronization

5   Related work

The problem of integrating OO applications with relational database systems has been the subject of various studies in the literature. [Keller+96] presents a relational access layer. We use this access layer as the basis for our work, and introduce a caching policy. Our proposal extends Keller's work with a treatment of the synchronization problem between client cached data and RDBMS server persistent data. The mapping rules implemented by the ConcretePersistenApplication class are those defined in [Keller+93]. In [Porto+98] we propose the modeling of object behavior through database stored-procedures and triggers. The patterns presented in [Silva+97] extend those in [Keller+96]. In this work we use their StrongLayering pattern.

There is also a great deal of work associated with the replication strategy. For example, [Gonçalves+98] presents a pattern language for implementing architectures supporting object replication with different policies. It is a more general approach then that found in the Observer pattern [Gamma+95]. In our proposal, the CMS object is responsible for informing registered CMC clients of committed changes in the RDBMS. In a way, the CMC/CMS objects present a behavior similar to that found in the subject/observer metaphor.

Another area of related work investigates RDBMSs extended to manage client cached data. [Franklin+97] presents a taxonomy for algorithms that maintain the consistency of cached data. With respect to this work, our proposed concurrency control strategy relates to detection based protocols with validity checks deferred until the commit, and change notification hints sent after commit. We extend their approach dealing with object-cache consistency, taking into account object data that has been updated by stored procedures and triggers.

6   Conclusions and Future Work

One of the most common choices for software development these days combines three important paradigms: OO programming, active RDBMS and client-server architectures. The first two paradigms are not orthogonal, offering different modeling perspectives. The third paradigm often involves a distributed architecture on top of which one can distribute parts of the application. Putting all this together is not easy. Much work has been done in the OO/RM mapping. In this area one of the main concerns is the problem of synchronizing client-side object state changes and database-side table updates.

In a previous paper [Porto+98], we proposed the relational integration of application object behavior through database triggers and stored procedures. We used the active mechanisms of the RDBMS to execute object transitions, verify pre-conditions and execute pos-conditions. The execution of RDBMS server procedures, however, presents us the inverse problem: once the database code updates persistent data, the application objects become out of date.

In this paper we propose a solution to this synchronization problem, encompassing both the application-to-database solution described in [Porto+98] and a new solution to the inverse database-to-application problem.

The architecture we propose considers applications developed using an OO programming language. Persistent application objects are stored in relational database systems with the active capability of running server procedures. This architecture makes no further assumptions; the classes and relationships we propose can be implemented in any OO language, and the object-relational mappings may follow any proposed pattern language.

Persistent objects are created and processed in the client OO environment, as part of a client transaction running an optimistic concurrency control protocol. At the time a client transaction is confirmed, the application tries to store the object into the relational database.

Processing in the client environment is almost completely independent from the RDBMS. The data requested from the database are loaded in the client environment without being locked by the server. Once the client environments run independently from the server, updates made by server procedures may interrupt an ongoing client transaction. Depending on the size of the client's transaction, it may be very painful for the client to cancel all that has been done.

Our architecture aims to diminish the impact on client transactions by informing, as earlier as possible, of updates committed by other transactions that change the values of client objects. Our main concern is to inform clients of updates caused by server procedures and triggers during the processing of object state transitions.

Our architecture implements a combination of a replication strategy with client/server optimistic concurrency controls, and patterns for solving the OO/RM impedance mismatch. This functionality may be summarized in three parts: the identification of updates over objects or tables, the registration of the updates and the broadcasting of the update message.

There are many opportunities for future work, examining alternative solutions to the problem. Our solution creates a RDBMS-like environment in the client. A possible alternative could be to use an OO DBMS in the client, simplifying part of the architecture. The control of updates by the CMS is done at table level; alternatively, we can control updates at the object granularity. Also, the communication between server RDBMSs and application components may be improved by eliminating the need to use auxiliary tables.

References

[Aarsten+96] A. Aarsten, D. Brugali, G. Menga, "Pattern for Three-Tier Client/Server Applications," In *Pattern Languages of Programs (PloP)*, Monticello, Illinois, 1996.

[Agarwal+95] S. Agarwal, C. Keene, and A. Keller, "Architecting Object Applications for High Performance with Relational Databases", In *OOPSLA Workshop on Object Database Behavior, Benchmarks, and Performance*, Austin, TX, October 1995.

[Brown+96a] K. Brown, and B. Whitenack, "Crossing Chasm: A Pattern Language for Object-RDBMS Integration", In J. Vlissides, J. Coplien, and N. Kerth (eds.), In *Pattern Languages of Program Design 2*, Addison-Wesley, 1996, pp. 227-238.

[Brown96b] K. Brown, "Crossing Chasm: The Architectural Patterns," In *Pattern Languages of Programs (PloP)*, Monticello, Illinois, 1996.

[Buschmann+96] F. Buschmann, R. Meunier, P. Sommerlad, and M. Stal, "Pattern-Oriented Software Architecture: A System of Patterns", John Wiley & Sons, 1996.

[Carey+91] M. Carey, W. Franklin, M. Livny, E. J. Shekita, "Data Caching tradeoffs in client-server DBMS architectures", In *Proceedings of the ACM SIGMOD Conference on Management of Data*, Minneapolis, MI, May, 1991, Pages 357-366.

[Delis+94] A. Delis, N. Roussopoulus, "Techniques for Update Handling in the Enhanced Client-Server DBMS', *IEEE Transactions on Knowledge and Data Engineering*, Vol. 10, No. 3, May/June 1988.

[Duhl96] J. Duhl, "Integrating Objects with Relational Data", In *Object-Magazine*, SIGS Publication, March 1996, pp. 89-90.

[Elmasri+94] R. Elmasri, S. Navathe, "Fundamentals of Database Systems", Addison-Wesley, second ed., 1994

[Franklin+97] M. Franklin, M. Carey, M. Livny, "Transactional Client-Server Cache Consistency: Alternatives and Performance", In *ACM Transactions on Database Systems*, vol.22, No.3, September 1997, Pages 315-363.

[Gamma+95] E. Gamma, R. Helm, R. Johnson, and J. Vlissides, "Design Patterns: Elements of Reusable Object-Oriented Software", Addison-Wesley, 1995.

[Gonçalves+98] T. Gonçalves, A Rito, "Passive Replicator: A Design Pattern for Object Replication", In *EuroPLoP 97*, Munich, Germany, July 1997.

[Gray+93] J. Gray; A. Reuter , "Transaction Processing: Concepts and Techniques", Morgan Kauffmann, 1993.

[Hanson+98] E. Hanson, I. Chen, R. Dastur, K. Engel, V. Ramaswamy, W. Tan, C. Xu, "A flexible and recoverable client/server database event notification system", In *The VLDB Journal*, 7:12-24, 1998.

[Hirschfeld96] R. Hirschfeld, "Three-Tier Distribution Architecture", In *Pattern Languages of Programs (PloP)*, Monticello, Illinois, 1996.

[Keating+95] G. Keating and J. Thomas, "The Winning Combination: Object/Relational Solutions", In *Object-Magazine*, SIGS Publication, September 1995, pp. 64-67.

[Keller+93] A. Keller, R. Jensen, and S. Agarwal, "Persistence Software: Bridging Object-Oriented Programming and Relational Databases", In *ACM SIGMOD*, May 1993.

[Keller+96] W. Keller and J. Coldewey, "Relational Database Access Layer", In *Pattern Languages of Programs (PloP)*, Monticello, Illinois, 1996.

[Keller98] W. Keller, "Object/Relational Access Layers – A Roadmap, Missing Links and More Patterns", In *Europlop98*, Bad Irsee, Germany, 1998.

[Porto+98] F. A. M. Porto, M. Vianna e Silva, S. R. Carvalho, "Object Life-Cycles in Active Relational Databases", In *TOOLS-USA*, Santa Barbara, CA, August 1998.

[Silva+97] M. Vianna e Silva, S. R. Carvalho, J. Kapson, "Patterns for Layered Object Oriented Applications", In *Proceedings Second European Conference on Pattern Languages of Program Design (EuroPLoP 97)*, Munich, Germany, July 1997, pp. 85-94.

[Silberschatz+96] A. Silberschatz, H. Korth, S. Sudarshan, "Database System Concepts', Mc Graw-Hill, third ed., 1996.

[Yourdon+95] E. Yourdon, K. Whitehead, J. Thomann, K. Oppel, P. Nevermann, "Mainstream Objects: An Analysis and Design Approach for Business", Prentice Hall, 1995.

[Widom+96] J. Widom, S. Ceri, "Active Database Systems: Triggers and Rules for Advanced Database", Addison Wesley, 1996.

Overview of the ROL2 Deductive Object-Oriented Database System

Mengchi Liu

Department of Computer Science, University of Regina

Regina, Saskatchewan, Canada S4S 0A2

mliu@cs.uregina.ca

Abstract

This paper presents an overview of ROL2, a novel deductive object-oriented database system developed at the University of Regina. ROL2 supports in a rule-based framework nearly all important object-oriented features such as object identity, complex objects, typing, information hiding, rule-based methods, encapsulation of such methods, overloading, late binding, polymorphism, class hierarchies, multiple structural and behavioral inheritance with overriding, blocking, and conflict handling. It is so far the only deductive system that supports all these features in a pure rule-based framework.

1 Introduction

Object-oriented databases and deductive databases are two important extensions of the traditional database technology. Object-oriented databases provide a better way to organize and manipulate structured objects. They integrate both structural and behavioral parts into a uniform framework. However, object-oriented databases lack declarative querying and logical foundations. Deductive databases offer logic-based inference and declarative querying with a firm logical foundation. But they lack the power of data modeling offered by object-oriented databases. Deductive object-oriented databases have been proposed as the natural next step to overcome these shortcomings.

In the past decade, a number of deductive object-oriented database languages have been proposed, such as O-logic [18], revised O-logic [13], IQL [1], LOGRES [7], Datalog^{meth} [2], CORAL++[22], F-logic [12], Rock & Roll [3], Datalog^{++} [10], and ROL [15, 16]. However, most of them are only structurally object-oriented. Important behaviorally object-oriented features such as methods and encapsulation common in object-oriented database systems such as GemStone [6], ONTOS [21], O$_2$ [21], Orion [14], Iris [9], ObjectStore [21], ODMG 2.0 [8] are not properly supported.

Several deductive object-oriented systems that are both structurally and behaviorally object-oriented, such as CORAL++ [22] and Rock & Roll [3], simply provide two kinds of incompatible languages: rule-based declarative language for deduction and query, and imperative language for data definitions and manipulations, and complex tasks. This method suffers various degrees of impedance mismatch.

In this paper, we present an overview of ROL2, a novel deductive object-oriented database system. It extends ROL [15, 16] with behaviorally object-oriented features such as rule-based methods and encapsulation so that it is now a real deductive object-oriented database system.

This paper is organized as follows. Section 2 focuses on schemas in ROL2. Section 3 discusses class hierarchy and multiple inheritance with overriding, blocking and conflict handling. Section 4 describes object creation and databases. Section 5 discusses queries and updates. Section 6 describes the architecture of the ROL2 implementation. Section 7 concludes the paper.

2 Schema

In ROL2, there is a separation of the notions of schema and instance. The schema of a database consists of a set of class definitions. A class definition describes the structure and behavior of a set of objects. The structural part of a class consists of a set of attribute definitions and default values of the attributes. The behavioral part of a class consists of a set of methods defined using rules. The instance consists of a set of objects together with their classes and attribute values. In this section, we describe classes, attribute definitions and default values, and methods,

2.1 Classes

ROL2 is a language that centers on objects and object properties. We do not distinguish between objects and values. Every physical and conceptual entity and relationship in the real world can be modeled as an object in ROL2. Objects sharing common structural and behavioral properties are classified into classes. A class has two aspects: it denotes a collection of objects and specifies the structural and behavioral properties for these objects. An object in the collection denoted by a class is an *instance* of the class.

Five kinds of classes are distinguished in ROL2: *value classes, oid classes, functor classes, tuple classes* and *set classes*. The following are examples of classes:

Value classes	integer, string, void, integer(0..100), string({'M', 'F'})
Oid classes	person, student, course, dept, supplier, part
Functor classes	family({person}) supplies(suppiler, part)
Set classes	{person}, {family({person})}
Tuple classes	(city → "Toronto", street → "Queens")

Value classes are the classes for primitive values. The collections which value classes denote are fixed. Oid classes are used to denote collections of oids (object identifiers) that represent real-world entities. Functor classes are used to denote collections of functor objects that represent relationships between real world entities. The collections which oid and functor classes denote are user-specified and vary from time to time through insertion and deletion operations. Set classes are used to denote collections of homogeneous sets. Tuple classes are used to denote collections of tuples. The collections which set and tuple classes denote depend on the collections which the component classes denote.

In addition, ROL2 supports two built-in classes *object* and *none*. The former denotes all objects while the latter has no instance at all.

2.2 Attribute Definitions

Objects may have attributes through which they are related to each other. The attribute applicable to all instances of a class must be declared on the class.

An attribute definition is an expression of the form:

$$c \; [[\text{public|private}] \; a \Rightarrow c' \; [\text{default } v]]$$

where c, c' are classes, a is an attribute and v is an object. It specifies that a is a partial mapping from the class c to the class c' such that if the value of the attribute a is not given for an object in the class, then the default value v is used automatically. Whatever in [ ] means that it can be omitted.

A number of attribute definitions for the same class $c[A_1]$ ..., $c[A_n]$ can be combined together into $c[A_1; ...; A_n]$. The following is an example:

```
person [birthyear ⇒integer(1900..2000) default 1970;
        gender ⇒char({'M', 'F'}) default 'F';
        spouse ⇒person;
        parents ⇒{person} ]
```

One of the key features of object-oriented paradigm is information hiding. That is, the access to attribute values can be controlled. In ROL2, we can use the access descriptor **private** to indicate that defined attribute cannot be accessed directly while its omission (i.e., default) or use of **public** indicates that the attribute can be accessed directly.

Consider the following example:

employee[name ⇒string;
        private salary ⇒integer]

For an instance of the class, the name attribute can be directly accessed while the salary attribute cannot.

2.3 Method Definitions

Objects can be queried and manipulated using methods. Methods in ROL2 are rule-based and are encapsulated in classes. A method consists of two parts: signature and implementation with the following form

$$c \ [[\text{public}|\text{private}] \ op(c_1, ..., c_n) \Rightarrow c_r \ \{ \ rule\_definitions \ \}]$$

where $op(c_1, .., c_n) \Rightarrow c_r$ is the n-ary signature which specifies the name op of the method, the argument classes $c_1, ..., c_n$ that the method takes, and the result class c_r. When c_r is void, we can simply omit it and use $op(c_1, ..., c_n)$ instead; when $n = 0$, we have to use $op() \Rightarrow c_r$ to differentiate it from attributes. For example age() ⇒integer(0..100) and ancestors() ⇒{person} are two 0-ary signatures while marry(person) is a unary signature. The rule definitions form the implementation of the method and have the form: $A :\!- L_1, ..., L_n$, where $A, L_1, ..., L_n$ are object expressions.

There are two kinds of rules in ROL2, one is query rule which returns a value and the other is update rule which updates the database and may or may not return any value. Query rules and update rules in ROL2 are evaluated differently. Query rules are evaluated bottom-up while update rules are top-down.

Consider the following rules for the class person:

ancestors() →⟨A⟩ :– parents →⟨A⟩
ancestors() →⟨A⟩ :– parents →⟨P⟩, P.ancestors() →⟨A⟩
marry(S) :– not spouse →S1, not S.spouse →S2,
                insert spouse →S, insert S.spouse →Self

The first two are query rules which say if A is a parent of the person, then A is an ancestor of the person and if P is a parent of the person and A is an ancestor of P, then A is an ancestor of the person. The last rule is an update rule which says if the person and S have no spouse, then make them the spouse of each other by using the update command insert and delete.

Note that the typical person for which the rules are defined is denoted by the variable Self and is omitted in some of these rules when it is obvious.

A number of methods for the same class $c[M_1]$ ..., $c[M_n]$ can be combined together in ROL2 into $c \ [M_1...M_n]$

Like object-oriented programming languages such as C++ and Java, ROL2 supports method overloading. That is, a method name can be used for several methods with different signatures in the same class.

Consider the following method signatures:

person[children() ⇒{person}   {children() →⟨C⟩:– C.parents →⟨Self⟩}
      children(person) ⇒{person}{children(P) →⟨C⟩:– C.parents →{Self, P}, Self ≠ P}]

Both methods have the same name children. The first one is a 0-ary method used to obtain the children of the person while the second is a unary one used to obtain the common children of two persons, one denoted by Self and the other by P. The name children is overloaded in these two methods.

Like attributes, the use of methods can also be controlled with the access descriptor public and private. The default is public while the use of private disallows the direct use and is mainly for intermediate methods.

2.4 Class Definitions

Based on the above discussion, a class has two kinds of information: attribute definitions with default values and method definitions. In ROL2, we have to encapsulate both kinds of information in a class definition.

A class definition has the following form:

$$\text{class } c \text{ [isa } c_1, ..., c_l] \ [\ A_1; ...; A_m, \ M_1 \ ... \ M_n \ ]$$

where c is the class to be defined, $c_1, ..., c_l$ with $l \geq 0$ are existing classes, $c[A_1, ..., A_m]$ is an attribute definition and $c[M_1 \ ... \ M_n]$ is a method definition of c with $m \geq 0, n \geq 0$. We discuss the meaning of isa in the next section.

Classes are defined in ROL2 using the insert command. For example, the class person discussed above can be defined in ROL2 as follows:

```
insert class person [
        birthyear ⇒integer(1900..2000) default 1970;
        gender ⇒char({'M', 'F'}) default 'F';
        spouse ⇒person;
        parents ⇒{person};
        age() ⇒integer(0..100) {age() →A :- birthyear →B, A = 1998 - B}
        ancestors() ⇒{person} {ancestors() →⟨A⟩:- parents →⟨A⟩;
                                ancestors() →⟨A⟩:- parents →⟨P⟩, P.ancestors() →⟨A⟩}
        children() ⇒{person} {children() →⟨C⟩:- C.parents →⟨Self⟩}
        divorce() {divorce() :- delete  spouse →S, delete  S.spouse →Self }
        marry(person) {marry(S) :- not  spouse →S1, not  S.spouse →S2,
                                insert  spouse →S, insert  S.spouse →Self}]
```

3 Class Hierarchy and Inheritance

In ROL2, we can organize classes into a class hierarchy with the two built-in classes object and none at the top and bottom respectively by using direct subclass/superclass definitions and take advantage of non-monotonic multiple structural and behavioral inheritance.

A subclass in ROL2 inherits all attribute definitions, default values, and methods of its direct superclasses and can introduce additional attribute definitions, default values, and methods local to itself. Besides, every instance of a subclass is a non-direct instance of its superclasses.

Consider the following class definition:

```
class employee isa person [
        salary⇒real default 1000.0;
        raise(real) {raise(R) :- delete  salary →S1, S2 = S1+S1*R, insert  salary →S2 }]
```

It says that employee is a subclass of person. Therefore, employee inherits all attribute definitions, default values, and methods from person. In addition, it also has its own attribute definition salary, with a default value, and method raise. Every instance of employee is a non-direct instance of person.

For direct subclasses of object, we can omit object in the class definition. For example, the class person can be defined in two different ways in ROL2:

```
class person isa object[...]
class person [...]
```

3.1 Inheritance with Overriding and Blocking

In ROL2, a subclass can also override or block attribute definition, default value and method inheritance from its superclasses.

Consider the following two class definitions:

class patient [treatedBy ⇒physician default smith]
class alcoholic isa patient [treatedBy ⇒psychologist]

The first one says patients are treated by physician with smith as the default physician. In this case, smith must be a physician at the time the class definition is added to the database. Otherwise the class definition is not well-typed. The second says alcoholics are patients but are treated by psychologist. However, psychologists usually are not physicians. The subclass alcoholic introduces a new definition for attribute treatedBy which overrides the attribute definition treatedBy and the corresponding default value inherited from patient.

The following example shows how to override default values without overriding attribute definitions.

class student isa person [
    birthyear default 1975;
    gender default 'M';
    takes ⇒{course};
    enroll(course) {enroll(C) :– insert takes →⟨C⟩}
    drop(course) {drop(C) :– delete takes →⟨C⟩}]

As a subclass of person, student inherits all attribute definitions, default values and methods of person. However, it has its own default values for birthyear and gender which override the inherited ones, its own attributes takes and methods enroll and drop.

The next example shows how to block attribute and method inheritance from a superclass:

class bachelor isa person [spouse ⇒none; marry(person) ⇒none; divorce() ⇒none]

The built-in class none is used here to block the inheritance of the corresponding attribute and methods (both signature and implementation) from person to bachelor and its subclasses if any.

As ROL2 supports method overloading, it is necessary to specify the complete signature for overriding and blocking. Besides, attribute definitions and their default values if any are bound together in terms of inheritance. That is, if a subclass inherits an attribute definition from one class, then it can only inherit the default value if any for the corresponding attribute from the same class. If the attribute definition is overridden or blocked, then the corresponding default value is also blocked.

3.2 Non-Monotonic Multiple Inheritance

ROL2 supports multiple inheritance. That is, a subclass can be a direct subclass of more than one superclass. Therefore, inheritance conflicts may happen.

Consider the following class definitions:

class employee [... room ⇒string]
class student [... room ⇒integer default 321]
class wstudent isa employee, student [...]

Here wstudent is a subclass of employee and student. It inherits attributes and methods from both employee and student and a conflict on the attribute room happens.

ROL2 provides four different ways for conflict resolution with user-specified priority as the default mechanism: (1) User-Specified Priority. (2) Overriding. (3) Inheritance Path Selection. (4) Explicit Renaming.

User-Specified Priority In ROL2, there is a built-in left-to-right ordering of superclasses in a class definition. If two or more superclasses have the attribute definitions and default values with the same name or methods with the same signature either directly defined or inherited, then the one found in the class appearing first in the list is inherited.

Continue with the previous example, wstudent automatically inherits attribute room from employee rather than student.

However, if two or more superclasses have methods with the same name but different signatures, then all of them are inherited by the subclass. In this case, the method name is just overloaded.

Overriding As ROL2 supports overriding, the inheritance conflicts may be resolved by using overriding.

Continue with the previous example. If we want the class wstudent to inherit the attribute definition and default value for room from student instead of employee without changing the order of superclasses, we can repeat the definition of student in wstudent as follows so that it overrides the inherited one from employee:

> class wstudent isa employee, student [room ⇒integer default 321]

However, this approach breaks the connection between the attribute room of student and the attribute room of wstudent so that any changes to the attribute definition or default value of room in student will not be reflected in wstudent. If this is a problem, then the following alternative should be used.

Inheritance Path Selection If a subclass needs to inherit one attribute definition, default value, or method from one superclass and another from a different superclass, then user-specified priority and overriding cannot meet these demands as discussed earlier. To solve this problem, ROL2 allows the user to specify the inheritance path to override user-specified priority using the from keyword.

Continue with the previous example of wstudent. Suppose that employee and student also have a method income with same signature but different implementations. If we want wstudent to inherit the attribute room and method income from student instead of employee, then we can use the following class definition:

> class wstudent isa employee, student [room, income() from student]

Note that with this class definition, wstudent inherits not only attribute definition but also default value of room from student. If the method income is overloaded in wstudent, only the 0-ary method is inherited with the above definition.

Explicit Renaming This alternative is used to avoid conflicts by renaming one or more conflicting attributes or methods so that they can be inherited under different names.

Continue with the example of wstudent. A working student may have two different rooms, one as a student and the other as an employee. The previous alternatives disallow this possibility. In this case, we can use explicit renaming as follows:

> class wstudent isa employee, student [employee.room as eroom; student.room as sroom]

As the room attribute from student and employee have different names in wstudent, there is no inheritance conflict.

4 Object Creation and Databases

In ROL2, the user can create new objects and assign their attribute values using the insert commands. Unlike other object-oriented systems, oid objects in ROL2 are created by the user rather than the system. They can only be a direct instance of one class and they have to be system-wide unique.

The following are object creation examples:

> insert person tom
> insert tom.birthyear →1930
> insert person pam.birthyear →1935

The first command creates a new oid object tom to be a direct instance of person. If tom is already an instance of some class, then the operation fails. If there are default attribute values for the class person, then tom gets these values. The second assigns 1930 as the value of the attribute birthyear of tom. If tom has a value for the attribute birthyear already, then this operation fails. Otherwise, the value is checked first with respect to the corresponding class definition. If it is well-typed with respect to the class definition, then it can be assigned to the object. The third command creates a new oid object pam and also assigns 1935 as the value of its birthyear attribute at the same time. In this case, if person has a default value for birthyear, the user provided value overrides it.

A ROL2 database is just a set of objects together with their direct classes and attribute values. The following is an example of a ROL2 database.

```
person    tom [birthyear →1930, spouse →pam]
person    pam[birthyear →1935, spouse →tom]
employee ann [spouse →jim]
employee jim [spouse →ann, salary →150 ]
employee bob [birthyear →1953, parents →{pam,tom}, salary →210]
student   sam [parents →{jim}]
student   pat [parents →{bob},salary→100]
wstudent joe [parents →{sam, pat}]
wstudent liz [birthyear →1970, parents →{bob}]
```

5   Queries and Updates

The ROL2 database can be queried and updated using the query and updates commands. In this section, we describe them using the examples.

5.1   Queries

The queries supported in ROL2 can be classified into two kinds: schema queries and object queries.

Schema Queries Schema queries are used to retrieve information about classes. Schema queries can be roughly classified into class queries, attribute definition queries, default value queries, method queries. Consider the following examples:

(1) query C isa object
(2) query C isa* object
(3) query person.spouse ⇒ _
(4) query person.A ⇒C
(5) query person.birthyear default 1975
(6) query person.A default V
(7) query person.age() ⇒C
(8) query person.age() {R}

The first query asks for each direct subclass of the built-in class object. The second asks for every subclass of object, that is, every user defined classes. The third asks whether the class person has an attribute spouse, where '_' is an anonymous variable. The fourth asks for each attribute definition of person. The fifth asks if the class person has default value 1975 for the attribute birthyear. The sixth asks for each default value and the corresponding attribute of the class person. The next query asks for the class of the result that the method age returns. The last asks for the implementation (i.e., rules) of the method age of person.

Object Queries Object queries are used to retrieve information about objects and to manipulate objects through method invocation. Object queries can be roughly classified into object class queries, object attribute queries, and method invocation. The following are several such examples:

(1) query person bob
(2) query C* bob
(3) query tom.birthyear →B
(4) query person O.birthyear →B
(5) query liz.M() →V
(6) query ann.marry(sam)

The first query asks whether the class person is the direct class of the oid bob. The second asks for each direct or non-direct classes that bob is an instance of. The third asks for the birth year of tom. The fourth asks for every direct instance of person and the person's birth year. The fifth invokes each 0-ary method that returns a value on liz. The last invokes the marry method to let ann and sam be married.

5.2 Updates

ROL2 provides two elementary update commands: insert and delete, with which complex update commands can be formed.

An update command in ROL2 is treated as a transaction which can either succeed or fail. If it fails, it has no effect on the database at all.

Update commands are used to define and manipulate databases. They can be classified loosely into two kinds: schema updates and object updates.

Schema Updates In ROL2, the user can insert, delete or modify class definitions using schema updates. Sections 2 and 3 have shown how to use the insert command for class definitions. The following examples show how to delete and modify class definitions:

(1) delete student.birthyear ⇒_
(2) delete person.gender default _
(3) delete student.enroll()
(4) delete student

The first command says delete the directly defined attribute birthyear from person. It fails if any of its instance has a value for this attribute. The second deletes the default value of gender from the class person. The operation fails if the class does not have the default value. The next one says delete the method enroll from student. The last says delete the class student. It fails if the class has any instance or subclass or is used in other class definitions.

Object Updates In ROL2, oid objects are system-wide unique that can be created or destroyed but cannot be modified. Their attribute values may change from time to time though method invocations or object updates. The insert and delete commands are used to create or destroy objects and to assign or delete their attribute values. The combination of insert and delete can be used to modify attribute values. Section 4 has shown how to use the insert command to create objects and assign their attribute values. The following are several further examples of object updates:

(1) delete bob.birthyear →_
(2) delete bob.parents →⟨pam⟩
(3) delete employee bob
(4) delete pat.salary →S1, S2 = S1 + 100, insert pat.salary →S2

The first command says delete the value of the attribute birthyear of bob. The second says delete pam from the Bob's parents set. The next command says delete bob from its direct class employee as well as all of its attribute values if any. The last says increase pat's salary by 100.

In ROL2, we can combine query and update commands to specify complex updates. The following are two such examples:

(1) query E.salary →S, S > 100, delete E
(2) query P.age() →A, A > 40, delete P.salary →S1, S2 = S1 + 100, insert P.salary →Z

6 Architecture of the ROL2 System

The ROL2 system is currently being developed as a single-user database management system at the University of Regina.

The architecture of the ROL2 system is shown as follows:

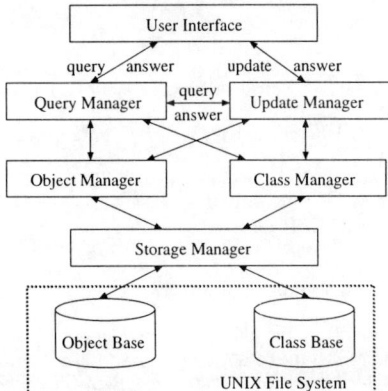

The system is organized into 4 layers. The first layer is the user interface. Three kinds of user interfaces are provided: textual user interface, graphic user interface, and web interface. They provide different kinds of environment for the user to query and update databases. They also perform syntactical analysis of the user query or update request, rewrite the request into standard form, send the possibly modified request to the query or update manager, and process the answers to the request from the lower layer according to the interface.

The second layer processes the query or update request. As an update may imply a query, the update manager may call the query manager before performing the update. Both the query and update managers interact with the object and class managers and have them actually handle simple queries and updates of objects and classes respectively. When we insert an object or add attribute values of an object, the update manager first asks the class manager to query the class definition associated with the object and determine whether or not the object or the attribute values of the object are well-typed. If so, it then asks the object manager to perform the insertion. Similarly, if we delete or modify part of a class definition, the update manager first asks the object manager to query the object base to check whether or not the objects will still be well-typed with respect to the class definition after the deletion or updates. If so, it then asks the class manager to perform the updates.

The storage manager provides rapid access to objects and classes stored on the disk.

7 Conclusion

We have described the ROL2 deductive object-oriented database system, which is an extension of the structurally object-oriented deductive system ROL. Unlike other approaches, ROL2 supports in a pure rule-based framework almost all important features that one may expect an object-oriented language to have.

We have partially implemented ROL2 on top of ROL. The prototype is available over the Internet from the Web page http://www.cs.uregina.ca/~mliu/ROL2. The ROL2 system runs on SUN, DEC, SGI workstations and IBM-PC compatible machines. The implementation of the complete ROL2 language as described in this paper, is still in progress and will be released as a new version.

The semantics for methods that update a database and their encapsulation in ROL2 has been investigated [17]. We are working on a more general semantics for ROL2. We are also extending ROL2 into a full-fledged database programming system by adding additional functionalities.

Acknowledgments This research was supported in part by the Natural Sciences and Engineering Research Council of Canada.

References

[1] S. Abiteboul and P. Kanellakis. Object Identity as a Query Language Primitive. In *Proceedings of SIGMOD 98*, pages 159–173.

[2] S. Abiteboul, G. Lausen, H. Uphoff, and E. Waller. Methods and Rules. In *Proceedings of SIGMOD 93*, pages 32–41.

[3] M. L. Barja, A. A. A. Fernandes, N. W. Paton, M. H. Williams, A. Dinn, and A. I. Abdelmoty. Design and implementation of ROCK & ROLL: a deductive object-oriented database system. *Information Systems*, 20(3):185–211, 1995.

[4] E. Bertino and D. Montesi. Towards a Logical Object-oriented Programming Language for Databases. In *Proceedings of EDBT 92*, pages 168–183, Springer-Verlag.

[5] A. Bonner and M. Kifer. Transaction Logic Programming. In *Proceedings of ICLP 93*, pages 257–279. MIT Press.

[6] P. Butterworth, A. Otis, and J. Stein. The Gemstone Object Database Management System. *Communications of the ACM*, 34(10):64–77, 1991.

[7] F. Cacace, S. Ceri, S. Crepi-Reghizzi, L. Tanca, and R. Zicari. Integrating Object-Oriented Data Modelling with a Rule-Based Programming Paradigm. In *Proceedings of SIGMOD 90*, pages 225–236.

[8] R. Cattell and D. Barry, editors. *The Object Database Standard: ODMG 2.0*. Morgan Kaufmann, 1997.

[9] D. H. Fishman, B. B., H. P. Cate, E. C. Chow, T. Connors, J. W. Davis, N. Derrett, C. G. Hoch, W. Kent, P. Lyngbaek, B. Mahbod, M. A. Neimat, T. A. Ryan, and M. C. Shan. Iris: An object-Oriented Database Management System. *ACM Trans. on Office Information Systems*, 5(1):48–69, 1987.

[10] H. Jamil. Implementing Abstract Objects with Inheritance in Datalog^{neg}. In *Proceedings of VLDB 97*, pages 46–65, Morgan Kaufmann Publishers, Inc.

[11] M. Kifer. Deductive and Object Data Language: A Quest for Integration. In T. W. Ling, A. O. Mendelzon, and L. Vieille, editors, *Proceedings of DOOD 95*, pages 187–212, Springer-Verlag LNCS 1013.

[12] M. Kifer, G. Lausen, and J. Wu. Logical Foundations of Object-Oriented and Frame-Based Languages. *Journal of ACM*, 42(4):741–843, 1995.

[13] M. Kifer and J. Wu. A Logic for Programming with Complex Objects. *J. Computer and System Sciences*, 47(1):77–120, 1993.

[14] W. Kim. *Introduction to Object-Oriented Databases*. The MIT Press, 1990.

[15] M. Liu. ROL: A Deductive Object Base Language. *Information Systems*, 21(5):431 – 457, 1996.

[16] M. Liu. An Overview of Rule-based Object Language. *Journal of Intelligent Information Systems*, 10(1):5–29, 1998.

[17] M. Liu. Incorporating Methods and Encapsulation into Deductive Object-Oriented Database Languages. In *Proceedings of DEXA 98*, pages 892–902, Springer-Verlag LNCS 1460.

[18] D. Maier. A logic for objects. Technical Report CS/E-86-012, Oregon Graduate Center, Beaverton, Oregon, 1986.

[19] C. Moss. *Prolog++*. Addison-Wesley, 1994.

[20] S. Naqvi and S. Tsur. *A Logical Language for Data and Knowledge Bases*. Computer Science Press, 1989.

[21] V. Soloviev. An Overview of Three Commercial Object-Oriented Database Management Systems: ONTOS, ObjectStore, O2. *SIGMOD Record*, 21(1):93–104, 1992.

[22] D. Srivastava, R. Ramakrishnan, D. Srivastava, and S. Sudarshan. CORAL++: Adding Object-Orientation to a Logic Database Language. In *Proceedings of VLDB 93*, pages 158–170, Morgan Kaufmann Publishers, Inc.

Technical Papers

Testing

Measuring the Effectiveness of Method Test Sequences Derived from Sequencing Constraints

F.J. Daniels
Bell Laboratories
fdaniels@lucent.com

K.C. Tai
North Carolina State University
kct@csc.ncsu.edu

Abstract

Intra-class testing refers to the testing of the interaction among methods and data structures encapsulated within a single class. Our approach to intra-class testing is to execute sequences of instance methods that are derived from sequencing constraints and evaluate their results for correctness. These constraints impose restrictions on method behaviors and can be derived from a formal or informal specification of a class. We present an empirical evaluation of different method sequence generation approaches, and analyze their effectiveness in detecting software faults. In addition, we define a number of coverage criteria based on method sequencing constraints for a class and examine the differences between them.

1. Introduction

Most of the work in intra-class testing has focused on specification-based testing techniques [7,10]. These techniques involve selecting sequences of methods that document the correct order in which the methods of classes can be invoked. In order to detect faults among the interacting methods, one can check whether a correct method sequence puts an object of a class into an inconsistent state. Our idea is to execute sequences of class methods that are derived from sequencing constraints, and to evaluate their results for correctness. These constraints impose restrictions on method behaviors and can be derived from a formal or informal specification of a class. This paper presents new method sequence generation approaches, and uses simulations to evaluate their effectiveness in detecting software faults. Focus is on issues involved in generating a set of method sequences for a class that are error sensitive yet practical.

2. Related work on intra-class testing

Kirani and Tsai [10] introduced a technique called message sequence specification that describes the correct order in which the methods of a class can be invoked by the methods in other client classes. The method sequence specification associated with an object specifies all sequences of messages that the object can receive while still providing correct behavior. Their strategy uses regular expressions to model the causal relationships between classes, where method names are used as the alphabet of the grammar. The grammar is then used to statically verify the program's implementation for improper method sequences. A runtime verification system identifies incorrect method invocations by checking for sequence consistency with respect to the sequence specification.

Doong and Frankl [7] developed a scheme for object-oriented (OO) testing using algebraic specifications. The idea is that the natural units to test are classes, and that in testing classes, one should focus on whether a sequence of messages puts an object of the class under test into the correct state. Each test case consists of a pair of sequences of messages, along with a tag indicating whether these sequences should result in objects that are in the same "abstract state". The authors developed A Set of Tools for Object-Oriented Testing (ASTOOT) that include: an interactive specification-based test case generation tool and a tool that automatically generates test drivers.

3. Method sequencing constraints

Current work uses method pre- and post-conditions to model a class' specification [12]. The pre-condition of a method is a set of requirements that must be met before the method is used, and the post-condition specifies the expected property resulting from the method. In our approach to testing, pre- and post-conditions are used to derive method sequencing constraints. These method sequencing constraint impose restrictions on method behaviors and are then used to guide the selection of method sequences during testing. The following notation follows the CSPE (Constraints on Succeeding and Proceeding Events) [14, 15], but it now has been adapted to method sequence selection.

Each method sequence constraint involves a constraint operator and two methods. These sequencing constraints allow us to derive always (a), possibly true (pT), possibly false (pF), and never (~) constraint operators. Let C represent a class and let M1 and M2 represent methods within class C. Then:

- a[M1; → M2] denotes that for an instance of class C, immediately after completion of method M1, invoking method M2 is *always valid*. Thus the post-condition of M1 implies the pre-condition of M2.

- p[M1; → M2] denotes that for an instance of class C, immediately after completion of method M1, invoking method M2 is *possibly valid*. Whether M2 can be invoked immediately after M1 depends on the input and the method sequence that precedes M1. Let K be the necessary and sufficient condition under which M1 can be immediately followed by M2. Thus, p[M1; →M2]K if and only if the conjunction of K and the post-condition of M1 implies the pre-condition of M2. To simplify our discussion, constraint p[M1; → M2]K is split into two constraints: possibly true constraint *pT[M1 ; → M2]K* and possibly false constraint *pF[M1; → M2](not K)*.

- ~[M1; → M2] denotes that for an instance of class C, immediately after completion of method M1, invoking method M2 is *never valid*. Thus post-condition M1 implies the negation of the pre-condition of M2.

3.1 Example Class Queue

To illustrate the method sequencing constraint notation, we use the unbound queue abstract data type [1] to model the class Queue. The queue object can be in either of three relevant states: 1) Empty, 2) Not Empty, and 3) Exception. Items can be enqueued in either the Empty or Non Empty state. However, if the state of the queue is Empty, items cannot be dequeued, the top item of the queue cannot be returned, and an exception is raised from the Exception State.

The class Queue implements five methods. Method *Init* creates the queue and initializes all data members. Method *Empty* reports the state (empty/not empty) of the queue. Method *Eque* adds items to the queue while method *Dque* removes items form the queue. Method *Top* returns the top item of the queue. Listed below are the class attributes, restrictions and pre and post-conditions for the queue class. Method *Empty* does not affect the attributes of the queue (non-attribute effecting method), and it can be invoked at any place in a method sequence once the queue has been initialized. Hence, pre- and post-conditions for method Empty are omitted.

Class Queue

Attributes: 1. Count = number of elements in Queue (q).

Restrictions: 1. Once a queue is created it cannot be recreated in the same instance.
2. Queue is unbounded and there are no other resource limitations.

3. All operations must be performed on a queue that has been initialized.
4. Count cannot be negative.

Pre- and Post Conditions

Method *Init* (q:Queue)

Pre-condition:
1. Queue (q) does not exist

Post-condition:
1. Queue (q) exists
2. Queue (q) is empty

Method *Empty* (q:Queue)

Pre-condition:
1. Queue (q) exist

Post-condition:
1. Return 1 if Queue (q) is empty (count = 0)
2. Returns 0 if Queue (q) is not empty (count > 0)

Method *Eque* (q:Queue, e:element)

Pre-condition:
1. Queue (q) exist

Post-condition:
1. Element e added to the tail of Queue (q)
2. Queue is not empty (count = old count + 1)

Method *Dque* (q:Queue, e:element)

Pre-condition:
1. Queue (q) exists
2. Queue is not empty (count > 0)

Post-condition:
1. Element (e) removed from the front of Queue (q)
2. Count = count – 1
3. Queue (q) exists

Method *Top* (q: Queue, e: element)

Pre-condition:
1. Queue (q) exist
2. Queue (q) is not empty (count > 0)

Post-condition:
1. First element (e) returned
2. Queue (q) exists
3. Queue is not empty (count > 0)

3.2 Method Sequencing Constraints for Class Queue

Method sequencing constraints are derived manually by evaluating the pre- and post-conditions of each method. Several examples are shown below that illustrate how a few of the constraints (a, pT, and pF) are derived. The remaining constraints for this example are listed in [4]. The post-condition of method *Init* and the pre-condition of method *Eque* are as follows:

Method Init (q: Queue)

Post-condition:
1. Queue (q) exist
2. Queue (q) is empty

Method Eque (q: Queue, e: element)

Pre-Condition:
1. Queue (q) exist

Since, the post-condition of method *Init* satisfies the pre-condition of method *Eque*, invoking method *Init* followed by method *Eque* is *always* valid. Thus, the always constraint a[init; → eque] is derived.

To illustrate derivation of possibly true and possibly false constraints, consider the post-condition of method *Dque* and the pre-condition of method *Top*.

Method Dque (q: Queue, e: element)

Post-condition:
1. Element (e) removed from the front of Queue (q)
2. count = count – 1
3. Queue (q) exists

Method Top (q: Queue, e: element)

Pre-condition:
1. Queue (q) exists
2. Queue (q) is not empty (count>0)

The post-condition of method *Dque* implies the pre-condition of method *Top* if and only if the queue is not empty. Hence the possible true constraint: pT[dque;→ top] with the condition (queue (q) is not empty) and the possible false constraint: pF[dque;→ top] with the condition (queue (q) is empty) are derived.

Method sequencing constraints for several of the methods in the queue example are shown below. When illustrating the method sequences, "#" denotes the start of a method sequence. Refer to [4] for a complete listing of all method sequences.

Method Init (q: Queue)

S1. a[#;→ init]   S4. ~[init; → init]
S2. a[init; → eque]   S5. ~[init; → top]
S3. ~[init; → dque]

A queue must be initialized first (S1). Once the queue is created it is always valid to invoke method *Eque* (S2). It is invalid to invoke method *Dque* (S3) or *Top* (S5) immediately after method *Init* (queue is Empty). It is invalid to invoke method *Init* once a queue has previously been initialized (S4).

Method Eque (q: Queue, e: element)

S6. ~[#, → eque]   S9.   a[eque; →eque]
S7. a[eque; → dque]   S10. ~[eque; → init]
S8. a[eque; → top]

It is always valid to invoke methods *Dque* (S7), *Top* (S8) and *Eque* (S9) immediately after method *Eque*. It is invalid to invoke method *Init* once a queue has previously been created (S10) and it is invalid to start a method sequence with *Eque* (S6).

Method Dque (q: Queue, e: element)

S11. ~[#;→ dque]   S15. pF[dque;→ dque]   Queue (q) is empty
S12. a[dque;→ eque]   S16. pT[dque;→ top]   Queue (q) is not empty
S13. ~[dque;→ init]   S17. pF[dque;→ top]   Queue (q) is empty
S14. pT[dque;→ dque]   Queue (q) is not empty

It is always valid to invoke method *Eque* (S12) immediately after method *Dque*. If the queue is not empty, it is always valid to invoke method *Dque* (S14) and *Top* (S16) immediately after invoking method *Dque*. If the queue is empty, invoking methods *Dque* (S15) and *Top* (S17) are invalid. It is invalid to invoke method *Dque* once a queue has previously been initialized (S13) and it is invalid to start a method sequence with *Dque* (S11).

4. Method Sequencing Test Coverage Criteria

This section discusses several test coverage criteria used in generating method sequences. These test coverage criteria (a, a-s, a/pT, a/pT-s, a/pT-s/pF/~) and their definitions are shown in Table 1, and they follow the CSPE test coverage criterion defined in [14]. To demonstrate how method sequences are derived from the test criteria, we use two types of method sequences: 1) valid method sequences and 2) invalid method sequences. A valid method sequence is a sequence of method names such that every two consecutive method names satisfy the "always" or "possibly true" constraint for these two methods. Thus, a valid method sequence specifies a correct sequence of method invocations. An invalid method sequence is like a valid method sequence except that the last two method names satisfy the "never" or "possible false" constraint. Thus, an invalid method sequence specifies an incorrect sequence of method invocations such that any proper prefix of the sequence is a valid method sequence.

4.1 Valid method sequences for class queue

Following we list the always and the always possible true constraints for the queue example.
Always constraints: (S1, S2, S7, S8, S9, S12, S19, S20, S22)
Possibly True constraints: (S14, S16)

Next we show two method sequences one satisfying the (a) criterion and the other satisfying the (a/pT) criterion. For each method sequence, we show the sequence of constraints covered by every two consecutive methods, except that no constraints are given for method Empty.

(a) Criterion
1. #.init.empty.enque.enque.deque.enque.top.top.enque.top.deque
   (S1, S2, S9, S7, S12, S8, S22, S20, S8, S19)

(a/pT) Criterion
1. #.init.empty.enque.enque.deque.enque.top.top.enque.top.deque.deque.top
   (S1, S2, S9, S7, S12, S8, S22, S20, S8, S19, S14, S16)

Below we list method sequences satisfying the (a-s) and (a/pT-s) test criteria respectively. Unlike the (a) and (a/pT) criteria, it is not necessary to cover "always" and "possibly true" constraints with a minimum number of sequences.

(a-s) Criterion
1. #.init.empty.enque.enque.top.deque.enque
   (S1, S2, S9, S8, S19, S12)
2. #.init.empty.enque.deque.enque.enque.top.top.deque
   (S1, S2, S7, S12, S9, S8, S22, S19)
3. #.init.empty.enque.top.enque.deque
   (S1, S2, S8, S20, S7)

(a/pT-s) Criterion
1. #.init.enque.deque.empty.enque.top
   (S1, S2, S7, S12, S8)
2. #.init.empty.enque.enque.enque.deque.deque.enque.empty
   (S1, S2, S9, S9, S7, S14, S12)
3. #.init.enque.enque.top.empty.top.enque.deque.deque.top.deque
   (S1, S2, S9, S8, S22, S20, S7, S14, S16, S19)
4. #.init.empty.enque.enque.top.deque.top
   (S1, S2, S9, S8, S19, S16)

4.2 Invalid method sequences for class queue

The list below contains all "possible false" and "never" constraints for the queue example.
Never constraints: (S3, S4, S6, S10, S11, S13, S18, S21)
Possibly False constraints: (S15, S17)

Method sequences derived from possible false and never constraints are composed of a valid method sequence that is modified to be invalid. Hence, a method sequence is created that covers several valid (always or always/possible True) constraints and one invalid constraint. Suppose we want to create a method sequence that covers the possible false constraint: pF[dque;→dque] Queue (q) is empty. We first start with a valid method sequence (sequence 1 below). To make sequence 1 invalid, three additional dque operations are added to the sequence. Now sequence 2 below satisfies all of the valid constraints in sequence 1 plus the invalid possibly false constraint, S15.
1. #.init.empty.enque.enque.enque.deque.deque.enque.empty-valid
   (S1, S2, S9, S9, S7, S14, S12)
2. #.init.empty.enque.enque.enque.deque.deque.enque.empty.deque.deque.deque-invalid
   (S1, S2, S9, S9, S7, S14, S12, S15)

The (a/pT-s/pF/~) test criteria combines the (a/pT-s), and (pF/~) test criteria, thus a more extensive level of coverage is created. Method sequences that satisfy the (a/pT-s/pF/~) criteria are created by adding an invalid sequence that corresponds to a possible false or never constraint to the end of method sequence derived from the (a/pT-s) criteria. Other method sequences not shown in this paper can be found in [4].

5. Empirical Study

This section presents the results of our empirical study. The objective is to evaluate the effectiveness of the method sequence generation test criteria in detecting software faults. We also consider other issues such as redundancy of method sequencing constraints and variations in the size of method sequence sets.

When testing individual methods of a class, the goal is to examine whether a method returns the correct results and has the desired affect on the called object [8]. Method testing is typically done by treating each method as a function and mapping some input space to some output space, selecting elements of that input space, and examining the outputs for correctness [7]. There is nearly universal agreement that the class is the smallest testable unit and that testing methods in isolations is not effective [2, 3]. In our approach we assume that using constraint-based testing is sufficient for method and intra-class testing.

A valid method sequence is used to cover "always" and "possibly true" constraints, and an invalid method sequences to cover "always" and "possibly true" constraints before the end of the sequences and a "never" or "possibly false" constraint at the end of the sequences. When a valid method sequence S for a class C is used to test an implementation of C, an exception is raised if the execution of C according to S detects an error (due to error checking inside C). When an invalid method sequence S' for C is used to test an implementation of C, an exception is raised if the execution of C according to S' results in one of the following two conditions: 1) this execution detects an error before the execution of the last method of S', and 2) this execution does not detects an error during the execution of the last method of S'. Note that condition 2) implies that the implementation of C has successfully executed an invalid method sequence for C.

In our empirical study, we implemented three C++ programs: 1) bound stack, 2) unbound queue, and a 3) banking example. The mutation tool "Proteum" [5] was used to create mutations of each program. Once the mutations were completed on the C programs the errors were translated back to C++. Method sequences are then derived from the method sequencing criteria for each of the three programs.

5.1 Types of Mutants

To evaluate the effectiveness of different method sequence coverage criteria, four sets of mutants were developed for each example.

Original

The first set of mutants implement the original code in a self checking manner. For example, in the unbound queue, before an item is removed from the queue a check is made to determine if the queue is empty. There are no additional modifications to the source itself.

Post

Post-conditions defined in Larch/C++ [11] and Assertion Definition Language (ADL) [13] were used to implement the second set of mutants. In this set, post-conditions were added to the original self-checking code and rewritten in C++ and inserted into each method. Before any value is returned, post-conditions are checked to verify the global variables and data members have been properly updated before the next method is executed. By evaluating data before it is returned to another method, post-conditions can be used to check methods that return data as well as methods that do not return data. If the method contains mutation errors that affect global variables or data attributes, post-conditions will catch these errors and the program invokes an exception. Post-conditions mutants collect exceptions raised by the original code plus exceptions raised by the post-conditions.

Oracle1

The third set of mutants implement a test oracle. The oracle is used to verify return values from each method. In this particular testing technique, methods that do not return values are not checked. For example, for the stack, the push method does not return a value. Hence, there is no way for the oracle to verify whether the correct value has been pushed onto the stack. In checking these types of errors, we rely on other methods (such as pop), to indicate errors in the push method. Methods that return values back to the test driver program are written to a file. These return values are then compared to an oracle file for verification. If the results do not correspond with the test oracle, an exception is raised and recorded. Test oracle mutants collect exceptions raised by the original code plus exceptions raised by the oracle itself. Unlike the post-condition mutants, the test oracle will catch invalid returned values due to defects in the return statement.

Oracle2

The fourth set of mutants implement post-condition checking and a test oracle. These mutants simply combine the implementations of the two techniques described above. This set of mutants collects exceptions raised by the original code self-checking code, exceptions raised by post-conditions and exceptions raised by the test oracle.

5.2 Mutation Errors

The mutation tool "Proteum" allows mutants to be generated from 71 mutation operators [6]. As previously stated, "Proteum" is a C mutation tool and not a C++ mutation tool. Therefore, the mutation operators were applied to the body and functions of the C programs. These seeded faults were then transformed to the C++ examples. Further explanation of the selected mutant operators are listed in [4,6]. In transforming the mutants back to C++; several mutants were discarded due to compilation errors. We also removed functionally equivalent mutants.

5.3 Test Driver Program

In order to test the methods within a class a test driver program is built for each example that initializes global variables to the appropriate values, invokes methods, executes method sequences and checks output. The test driver program initially reads pre-defined method sequences from a file that corresponds to member functions invocations. Once the object is instantiated and the method invoked, the driver program records any exceptions that are raised.

All four sets of mutants were run on three datasets. Each dataset is composed of method sequences derived from specific test coverage criteria defined in Table 1.

Dataset 1

The first dataset contains method sequences that correspond to relatively small data structures. Implementation of the queue and the stack were limited to five data items and the banking example created and manipulates four accounts. Dataset 1 contains method sequences that were derived to satisfy the following five criteria: (a), (a-s), (a/pT), (a/pT-s) and (a/pT-s/pF/~). In some instances it is impossible to cover just the always constraints. Due to the implementation of the banking example, it is impossible to cover all of the "always" constraints without covering some possible true constraints. In this case, it may be necessary to modify the criteria for deriving (a) and (a-s) method sequences to include coverage of only those possible true constraints that will enable coverage of the always constraints.

Dataset 2

Dataset 2 contains method sequences that correspond to larger data structures. The maximum size of the stack and queue are increased to about twenty. To increase the size of the data structures, each constraint is covered multiple times. Dataset 2 contains method sequences to satisfy (a/pT) and (a/pT-s) criteria. In addition, method sequences in Dataset 2 are modified such that the constraints are repeated at a higher rate than sequences in Dataset 1.

Dataset 3

Dataset 3 is designed to investigate placement of these non-attribute effecting methods for the Queue and the Stack class. Method sequences in Dataset 3 satisfy the same criteria as method sequences in Dataset 1, however non-attribute affecting methods are placed at the end of the sequences. These methods are used simply to report the state of the object and do not affect the attributes of the objects. Dataset 3 is not run on the banking example because in the banking example there are no non-attribute affecting methods.

5.3 Data Analysis and Results

For Dataset 1 we will first look at the effect of valid sequences in detecting faults. If an exception is raised by a mutant from a valid sequence, this mutant is "killed". If no exception is raised, the mutant is considered "live".

Number of Sequences

In comparing a concise set of test sequences to several sequences in all test criteria for Dataset 1, the data in Table 2 indicates a slight increase (2%-7%) in most of the criteria in the number of killed mutants as the number of sequences increases. Hence, in most cases several sequences are slightly better then 1 sequences in detecting faults.

Comparing Criteria

In looking at the differences in coverage criteria for Dataset 1, the results from Table 2 show that as the criterion for creating method sequences changes from (a) to (a/pT), in most cases more (3%-9%) mutants are "killed" for mutants that implemented either post-conditions or a test oracle. In addition, as the criterion for creating method sequences changes from (a-s) to (a/pT-s), between 3–13% more mutants are "killed" for mutants that implemented post-conditions or a test oracle.

Mutants that implement additional checking mechanisms such as a test oracle, post-conditions or both post-conditions and a test oracle "killed" significantly more mutants than the original code alone for all test criteria. Post-conditions found between 68 – 87 % of the errors within the program. If no additional checking is used only 21 – 49 % of the errors are found using valid method sequences. The data indicates that test oracle1 and test oracle2 are the most effective, in that both techniques found 100% of the errors. However, since test oracle1 only implements checking of return values while test oracle2 implements both post-condition checking and checking of return values, we see that test oracle1 is just as effective as test oracle2 without the additional checking of post-conditions.

Redundancy

Dataset 2 addresses the issue of redundancy of sequences and it's effect on detecting faults. In examining redundancy, we compared method sequences in Dataset 1 that satisfy the (a/pT) and the (a/pT-s) criterion with the methods sequences in Dataset 2 that satisfy the same criterion. Previous research [7] has indicated that in general longer sequences may be more effective in detecting faults. The results in Table 2 indicate that in comparing these two datasets , we again see a very minor increase in the number of mutants "killed". It is important to note that for the (a/pT-s) criterion, the test oracle1 and test oracle2 testing technique give us 100% coverage (all mutants are killed) without increasing the redundancy of the constraints. Hence, since full coverage can be achieved without increasing the redundancy of the constraints adding additional redundancy in the coverage of the constraints is not necessary.

Non-Attribute Methods

Dataset 3 addresses the issue of placement of non-attribute affecting methods. The results listed in Table 2 for Dataset 1 and Dataset 3 do not show any significant impact on placing these methods at the end or beginning of the sequence. Although no conclusive results are shown for Dataset 3, it is essential that these (non-attribute affecting) methods be tested. Hence, these methods should be included in the test sequence at least once.

Invalid Method Sequences

To determine the effectiveness of the method sequences, valid and invalid method sequences are executed on invalid programs. Note that both "valid" and "invalid" sequences are valid. Let M be a set of mutants, V a set *valid* sequences, and I a set of *invalid* sequences. Either a valid or an invalid sequence (or both) could kill mutants within set M. When we apply a valid sequence to a mutant, this mutant is killed if an exception occurs. In looking at invalid sequences, assume that the invalid sequences are constructed by extending some valid sequences. When applying an invalid sequence (which is a valid sequence followed by an operation according to a pF or ~ constraint) to a mutant, this mutant is killed if: 1) An exception occurs before the last operation of I or 2) An exception does not occur after the completion of I. Thus, the number of mutants in M killed by the union of V and I =((the number of mutants killed by V)+(the number of mutants killed by I))– (number of mutant killed by both V & I).

The results in Table 3 show that invalid method sequences do increase the capability of detecting faults in the original code mutants. For post-conditions mutants, in most cases invalid method sequences do not increase the capability of detecting faults.

6.0 Conclusions

Our intra-testing approach involves the following three steps: 1) generation of pre- and post-conditions for methods in a class, 2) derivation of method sequencing constraints, and 3) generation of valid and invalid method test sequences. Step 1) requires the use of a formal specification notation. Step 2) was done manually in this paper, but it can be automated by using some logic induction tools. An alternative is to let the designer of a class manually derive method sequencing constraints according to informal specification of methods in the class. Step 3) was done manually in this paper. In [9] an algorithm is shown for test sequence generation using sequencing constraints for concurrent programs. This algorithm can be further modified to automatically generate method test sequences according to method sequencing constraints.

The empirical results show that this technique of method sequence generation is very effective in detecting software faults and that in most cases generating several method sequences that cover the constraints at least once is very effective in fault detection. Testing mechanisms such as adding post-condition checking, a test oracle or a combination of both can significantly increase error detection.

This work supported by a NASA fellowship and in part by NSF grant CCR-9320992

References

[1] A. V. Aho, J. E. Hopcroft, and J. Ullman, *Data Structures and Algorithms*, Addison-Wesley, Reading, MA, 1983.
[2] S. Barbey, M. M. Ammann, A. Strohmeier, "The Problematics of Testing Object-Oriented Software," Software Quality Management II, Building Quality into Software, Commuter Mech. Pub., Southampton, UK 411-426, 1994.
[3] R. V. Binder, "Testing Object-Oriented Software: A Survey," Software Testing, Verification and Reliability, Vol. 6, No 3, Sussex, England, , 125-252, September – December, 1996.
[4] F. J. Daniels, "Producing Dependable Object-Oriented Software Using Testing & Design Patterns," Ph. D. Dissertation, Dept. of Computer Engineering, North Carolina State University, 1998.
[5] M. E. Delamaro, and J. C. Maldanado, "Proteum: A tool for Assessment of Test Adequacy for C Programs," Proceeding of the Conference on Performability in Computing Systems, East Brunswick, New Jersey, 79-95, 1994.
[6] M. E. Delamaro, J. C. Maldanado and A. P. Mathur, "Integration Testing Using Interface Mutation," ISSRE, White Plains, New York, 112-121, 1996.
[7] R. Doong and P. G. Frankl, "The ASTOOT Approach to Testing Object-Oriented Programs," ACM Transactions on Software Engineering and Methodology, Vol. 3, No. 2, 101-130, April 1994.
[8] S. P. Fledler, "Object-Oriented Unit Testing," Hewlett-Packard-Journal, 69-74, 1989.
[9] B. Karacali and K. C. Tai, "Automated Test Sequence Generation Using Sequencing Constraints for Concurrent Programs", to appear in Proc. Inter. Symposium on Software Engineering for Parallel and Dist. Sys, May 1999.
[10] S. Kirani and W. Tsai, "Method Sequence Specification and Verification of Classes," JOOP, 28-38, Oct. 1994.
[11] G.T. Leavens, "Larch/C++ Users Guide: An Interface Specification Language for C++," Iowa State Univ, 1997.
[12] B. Meyer, *Object-Oriented software Construction*, Prentice Hall, Upper Saddle River, New Jersey, 1997.
[13] [Sha94] S. Shanker and R. Hayes, "Specifying and test software components using ADL," Technical Report SMLI TR-94-23, Sun Microsystems Laboratories, Inc. Mountain View, California, April 1994.
[14] K.C. Tai and R. H. Carver, "A Specification-Based Methodology for Testing Concurrent Programs," Proc. 5th European Software Engineering Conference, Lecture Notes in Computer Science, Vol. 989, 1995, 154-172.
[15] R. H. Carver and K. C. Tai, "Use of sequencing constraints for specification-based testing of concurrent programs", IEEE Trans. Software Engineering, Vol. 24, No. 6, June 1998, 471-490.

Table 1: Method sequencing test criteria

Criterion	Definition
Always Coverage (a)	The always coverage criterion requires that all "always" constraints be covered at least once with a minimum number of test sequences.
Always-Several Coverage (a-s)	The always-several coverage criterion requires that all "always" constraints be covered at least once with more than the minimum number of test sequences.
Always/Possibly True Coverage (a/pT)	The always/possibly true coverage criterion requires that all "always" and each "possibly true" constraints is covered at least once with a minimum number of test sequences.
Always/Possibly True-Several Coverage (a/pT-s)	The always/possibly true-several coverage criterion requires that all "always" and each "possibly true" constraints be covered at least once in more than the minimum number of test sequences.
Possibly False/Never Coverage (pF/~)	The possibly false/never coverage criterion requires that all "possibly false" or each "never" constraints be covered once in one test sequence.
Always/Possibly True-Several/ Possibly False/Never Coverage a/pT-s/pF/~)	The always/possibly true-several, possible false/never coverage criterion requires that all "always/possibly true" constraints be covered at least once in more than the minimum number of test sequences. In addition, each "possibly false/never" constraint must be covered in one test sequence.

Table 2: Comparison of test criteria for datasets 1, 2, and 3

			Original		Post		Oracle1		Oracle2	
			killed	live	killed	live	Killed	live	killed	live
Dataset 1	Queue 155 mutants	(a)	34	121	128	27	146	9	152	3
		(a-s)	34	121	133	22	149	6	153	2
		(a/pT)	34	121	136	19	151	4	154	1
		(a/pT-s)	34	121	136	19	155	0	155	0
	Stack 144 mutants	(a)	50	94	110	34	120	24	121	23
		(a-s)	50	94	110	34	124	20	125	19
		(a/pT)	57	87	123	21	133	11	133	11
		(a/pT-s)	57	87	126	18	144	0	144	0
	Bank 124 mutants	(a/pT)	69	55	94	30	124	0	124	0
		(a/pT-s)	69	55	94	30	124	0	124	0
Dataset 2	Queue 155 mutants	(a/pT)	35	120	136	19	151	4	155	0
		(a/pT-s)	36	119	136	19	155	0	155	0
	Stack 144 mutants	(a/pT)	57	87	125	19	135	9	135	9
		(a/pT-s)	57	87	129	15	144	0	144	0
	Bank 124 mutants	(a/pT)	70	54	95	29	124	0	124	0
		(a/pT-s)	70	54	95	29	124	0	124	0
Dataset 3	Queue 155 mutants	(a)	34	121	134	21	140	15	149	6
		(a/pT)	34	121	134	21	146	9	149	6
		(a/pT-s)	34	121	135	20	155	0	155	0
	Stack 144 mutants	(a)	50	94	110	34	126	18	129	15
		(a/pT)	57	87	124	20	135	9	135	9
		(a/pT-s)	57	87	125	19	144	0	144	0

Table 3: Results for valid plus invalid sequences

		Original		Post		Oracle 1		Oracle 2	
		killed	live	killed	live	killed	live	killed	live
Queue 155 mutants	(a/pT-s)	34	121	136	19	155	0	155	0
	(pF/~)	15	140	0	155	0	155	0	155
	Total	49	109	136	19	155	0	155	0
Stack 144 mutants	(a/pT-s)	57	87	126	18	144	0	144	0
	(pF/~)	9	135	0	144	0	144	0	144
	Total	66	78	126	18	144	0	144	0
Bank 124 mutants	(a/pT-s)	69	55	102	22	124	0	124	0
	(pF/~)	47	77	9	115	0	124	0	124
	Total	99	25	102	22	124	0	124	0

A New Metrics Set for Evaluating Testing Efforts for Object-Oriented Programs[*]

K. Periyasamy and X. Liu
Department of Computer Science
University of Manitoba
Winnipeg, Manitoba, Canada R3T 2N2
{kasi, xliu}@cs.umanitoba.ca

Abstract

Software metrics proposed and used for procedural paradigm have been found inadequate for object-oriented software products, mainly because of the distinguishing features of the object-oriented paradigm such as inheritance and polymorphism. Several object-oriented software metrics have been described in the literature. These metrics are goal-driven in the sense that they are targeted towards specific software qualities. In this paper, we propose a new set of metrics for object-oriented programs; this set is targeted towards estimating the testing efforts for these programs. The definitions of these metrics are based on the concepts of object-orientation and hence are independent of the object-oriented programming languages. The new metrics set has been critically compared with three other metrics sets published in the literature.

1: Introduction

Software metrics were primarily used for cost estimation in the 70's, but were later applied for productivity measurement, reliability models and very recently for capability maturity measurement [20]. Software metrics can be used by all people involved in the development processes; depending on who uses the metrics, a different set of definitions is used for describing the same software product. The popularity of the object-oriented approach to software development has created an intensive interest and more challenging problems to metrics development and metrics evaluation. Chidamber and Kemerer defined a metrics suite for object-oriented design [5, 6]. This metrics suite was considered to be a pioneering work in the area of object-oriented software metrics. Basili and others [3] assessed Chidamber and Kemerer's metrics by collecting data on the development of eight medium-sized information management systems based on identical requirements. According to Basili's experiment, Chidamber and Kemerer's metrics suite has been generally found suitable for predicting class fault-proneness during the early phases of the life cycle.

Churcher and Shepperd [7] indicated that it was premature to apply Chidamber and Kemerer's metrics, since there remained uncertainty about the precise definitions of the quantities to be observed and their impact upon subsequent indirect metrics. Graham [11] reported the LCOM metric defined by Chidamber and Kemerer appears to increase with cohesion where it is expected to decrease. Therefore, he gave a new definition for LCOM that decreases as cohesion increases and

---

[*] This work was partially funded by a grant from Natural Sciences and Engineering Research Council of Canada.

gives values that discriminate classes of intuitively different cohesion. Gowda and Winslow [10] reported that Chidamber and Kemerer's metrics basically address the class structures, their attributes and methods, but do not assess the overall system design.

Abreu *et al.* proposed the MOOD (Metrics for Object Oriented Design) metrics set [1, 2]. The goal of Abreu's metrics set was to improve the object-oriented design process to achieve better maintainability. Each metric in MOOD quantifies a distinct feature of object-orientation such as encapsulation, inheritance, polymorphism and message-passing. Kim *et al.*'s metrics [17, 18] are proposed for computing the complexity of an object-oriented program. These metrics are used to examine program complexity from three viewpoints: syntax, inheritance, and interaction.

Since the definition of a metric is based on some specific quality of software, the need for some standard assessment for each metric definition became mandatory. Weyuker proposed a set of properties to serve as a basis for the evaluation of metrics [21], which was one of the first attempts to assess metrics. These properties have been used by several researchers to evaluate their metric definitions, which include the metrics for object-oriented software. Several researchers criticized Weyuker's properties as being inadequate and too abstract. Despite these criticisms, Weyuker's properties are still used to assess new metrics definitions.

We describe a new set of object-oriented metrics in this paper, called *Liu's metrics set*. The goal of Liu's metrics is to estimate the testing efforts required for object-oriented programs. The metric values do not provide the actual number of test cases; rather, they will provide a subjective but quantitative estimation of testing efforts. The definitions of metrics in Liu's metrics set are based on the concepts of object-orientation and hence Liu's metrics set is independent of the object-oriented programming languages. In this paper, we compare Liu'e metrics set with the three metrics sets: Chidamber and Kemerer's metrics suite[5, 6], Kim's metrics set[17, 18] and MOOD metrics set[1, 2]. In addition, we have analytically evaluated Liu's metrics set against Weyuker's properties [21] and against a framework developed by Kim and others [18]. We also applied Liu's metrics set to two fairly large programs. The results of the two analytical evaluations and the results of the empirical evaluation have not been included in this paper due to space limitations; they can be found in [19].

The rest of the paper is organized as follows: Liu's metrics set is introduced in Section 2. In Section 3, we critically compare Liu's metrics set with three other metrics sets found in the literature. The paper concludes in Section 4 with comments on future work in this direction.

2: Liu's Metrics Set

Liu's metrics set is divided into three categories: (i) Metrics based on inheritance hierarchy; (ii) Metrics based on polymorphism; and (iii) Metrics based on interactions among objects. According to Harrold and McGregor [14], these categories differentiate object-oriented programs from procedural programs; at the same time, these categories make testing methods for procedural programs become inadequate for object-oriented programs.

2.1: Metrics Based on Inheritance Hierarchy

Inheritance is a mechanism which implements generalization/specialization relationship among classes in an object-oriented program. The specialization relationship describes how a subclass can be made as a specialization of a superclass by adding more features to, by redefining some of, or by restricting some of, the inherited features of the superclass. Since subclass objects can be substituted for superclass objects due to polymorphism, testing a superclass requires testing of all its subclasses as well. We define the following metrics in this category: metrics based on changing features (IHC); metrics based on adding new features (IHA); and metrics based on deleting features (IHD). While defining the metrics based on inheritance hierarchy, we use the notation "$\langle classname \rangle\_tree$" to indicate the tree/subtree rooted at "$\langle classname \rangle$" in the inheritance hierarchy. We further attach a level number to each node in the inheritance hierarchy. These level numbers are used in the metrics definitions. The root node of the hierarchy has the number zero, with its immediate descendents having level number 1; subsequent levels will have their numbers uniformly increased.

Metrics Based on Changing Features (IHC)   The term "changing feature" refers to an attribute or a method in the superclass whose name is retained in the subclass, but its type (in case of attribute) or definition (in case of methods) changed in the subclass. Generally, object-oriented programming languages do not permit changing a type of an attribute in the subclass. Therefore, we consider only inherited methods in this section. The methods with same name but different signature will be considered as being changed. The metric IHC represents the efforts required to test a superclass due to redefinition of its methods in the subclasses. As the inheritance hierarchy becomes higher and higher, it becomes necessary to test all subclasses for a given superclass. Consequently, the redefinitions of a superclass method increase the testing efforts of the method. The IHC metric is defined as follows:

IHC($\langle classname \rangle\_tree$ at level m)

$$= \text{IHC}(all\_subclasses \text{ at level } (m+1)) +$$
$$\sum_{i=1}^{n} \text{IHC}(\langle class_i \rangle\_tree \text{ at level } (m+1)) \tag{e-1}$$

where n refers to the number of immediate subclasses of $\langle classname \rangle$, and

IHC($all\_subclass$ at level $(m+1)$)

$$= \frac{\begin{array}{c}\text{number of changed methods} \\ \text{in subclasses at level } (m+1)\end{array}}{\begin{array}{c}\text{number of all the methods} \\ \text{in subclasses at level } (m+1)\end{array}} \times (\text{Method Percentage}) \tag{e-2}$$

If there is no subclass for $\langle classname \rangle$, then IHC($\langle classname \rangle\_tree$) = 0. Formally,

$$\text{IHC}(all\_subclasses \text{ at level } (m+1)) = \left(\frac{\sum\limits_{i=1}^{n} \text{MC}}{\sum\limits_{i=1}^{n} \text{AD} + \sum\limits_{i=1}^{n} \text{MD}} \times 100 \right) \% \tag{e-3}$$

where

MI($subclass\_i$) : number of methods in $subclass\_i$, which are inherited but not modified

MC($subclass\_i$) : number of methods in $subclass\_i$, which are inherited and redefined in $subclass\_i$

MA($subclass\_i$) : number of newly introduced attributes in $subclass\_i$

MD($subclass\_i$) : number of all methods in $subclass\_i$; MD = MI + MA + MC

AD($subclass\_i$) : number of all attributes in $subclass\_i$; AD = AI + AA

n : number of immediate subclasses for a given class named $\langle classname \rangle$

MP($all\_subclasses$) : Method Percentage for all subclasses in $\langle classname \rangle\_tree$

$$= \left(\frac{\sum\limits_{i=1}^{n} \text{MD}(subclass\_i)}{\sum\limits_{i=1}^{n} \text{AD}(subclass\_i) + \sum\limits_{i=1}^{n} \text{MD}(subclass\_i)} \times 100 \right) \%$$

Metrics Based on Adding Features (IHA)   The "adding features" refers to a set of attributes and/or methods which are newly defined in the subclasses. The metric IHA indicates the efforts needed to test a superclass due to the increasing of new attributes and methods in the subclasses. The IHA metric is defined below:

$IHA(\langle classname \rangle\_tree$ at level $m)$
$= IHA(all\_subclasses$ at level $(m + 1))$ $+$
$\quad \sum IHA(\langle subclass \rangle\_tree$ at level $(m + 1))$ $\hfill$ (e-4)

where n is the number of immediate subclasses of $\langle classname \rangle$, and

$IHA(all\_subclasses$ at level $(m+1))$

$$= \frac{\text{number of added attributes in subclasses at level } (m+1)}{\text{number of all the attributes in subclasses at level } (m+1)} \times (\text{Attribute Percentage})$$

$$+ \frac{\text{number of added methods in subclasses at level } (m+1)}{\text{number of all the methods in subclasses at level } (m+1)} \times (\text{Method Percentage}) \qquad \text{(e-5)}$$

Formally, $IHA(all\_subclasses$ at level $(m+1)) = $

$$\left(\frac{\sum\limits_{i=1}^{n} AA + \sum\limits_{i=1}^{n} MA}{\sum\limits_{i=1}^{n} AD + \sum\limits_{i=1}^{n} MD} \times 100 \right) \% \qquad \text{(e-6)}$$

where

$AI(subclass\_i)$: number of attributes in $subclass\_i$, which are inherited from $superclass$
$AA(subclass\_i)$: number of newly introduced attributes in $subclass\_i$
$AP(all\_subclasses)$: Attribute Percentage for all subclasses in $\langle classname \rangle\_tree$

$$= \left(\frac{\sum\limits_{i=1}^{n} AD(all\_subclasses)}{\sum\limits_{i=1}^{n} AD(all\_subclasses) + \sum\limits_{i=1}^{n} MD(all\_subclasses)} \times 100 \right) \%$$

Metrics Based on Deleting Features (IHD)   The term "deleted features" refers to those features from the superclass which are deleted or restricted in the subclass. Though many object-oriented programming languages do not provide explicit syntax for deleting an inherited feature, it is still possible for a subclass not to use all of the inherited features. Therefore, we provided this metric just for the sake of completion. The IHD metric is defined as follows:

$IHD(\langle classname \rangle\_tree$ at level $m)$
$= IHD(all\_subclasses$ at level $(m + 1))$
$\quad + \sum IHD(\langle subclass\_i \rangle\_tree$ at level$(m + 1))$ $\hfill$ (e-7)

where

$IHD(all\_subclasses$ at level $(m+1))$

$$= \frac{\text{number of attributes which are deleted or not used in subclasses at level } (m+1)}{\text{number of attributes in subclasses at level } (m+1)} \times (\text{Attribute Percentage})$$

$$+ \frac{\text{number of methods which are deleted or not used in subclasses at level } (m+1)}{\text{total number of methods in subclasses at level } (m+1)} \times (\text{Method Percentage}) \qquad \text{(e-8)}$$

Formally, IHD(*all_subclasses* at level $(m+1)$) $= \left(\dfrac{\displaystyle\sum_{i=1}^{n} \text{ANU} + \sum_{i=1}^{n} \text{MNU}}{\displaystyle\sum_{i=1}^{n} \text{AD} + \sum_{i=1}^{n} \text{MD}} \times 100 \right) \%$ (e-9)

where

ANU(*subclass_i*) : number of attributes inherited by *subclass_i*, but not used
MNU(*subclass_i*) : number of methods inherited by *subclass_i*, but not used

2.1.1: Further Discussions

A close observation of the three equations (e-3), (e-6) and (e-9) reveals that the denominator for all the three equations is the same; i.e., $\displaystyle\sum_{i=1}^{n} \text{AD} + \sum_{i=1}^{n} \text{MD}$. This represents the sum of all attributes and all methods in subclass i. We claim that this denominator will never be zero; if zero, it indicates that the subclass does not have any structure or behavior. The non-zero denominator is very important in computations and will not produce infinite values for the metrics; Kim's metrics set has been criticized for having a possible zero denominator.

We next discuss the implications of some of the values of the three metrics based on the inheritance hierarchy. When a subclass inherits a superclass, the number of attributes and methods it inherits and those it defines decide the value of IHC, IHA and IHD. There are four possible cases in a subclass.

Case 1: AA $\gg$[1] AI, and MA $\gg$ MI+MC

In this case, the subclasses collectively define more attributes and methods than they inherit. IHC will be close to 0, while IHA will be close to 1. This indicates that the subclasses may have quite different structure and/or have quite different behavior as compared to the particular superclass under consideration.

Case 2: AA $\lll$[2] AI, and MA $\lll$ MI+MC

The subclasses in this case inherit more attributes and methods than they additionally define. IHA will be close to 0, and IHC will be close to 1. This indicates that the subclasses share a lot of information where the shared information originates at the superclass under consideration. The inheritance mechanism in this case has been better utilized.

Case 3: AA $\lll$ AI, and MA $\gg$ MI+MC

Most of the attributes for subclasses in this case are coming from their superclasses, while the subclasses define a lot of new methods. IHC will be close to 0. This means the subclasses keep same data identity, but have quite different behaviors. This is a better utilization of behavioral polymorphism.

Case 4: AA $\gg$ AI, and MA $\lll$ MI+MC

This is a situation where the subclasses perform a lot of similar functions with quite different data structures. IHC will be close to 1. It indicates a better utilization of structural polymorphism.

2.2: Metrics Based on Polymorphism

In this section, we define metrics based on behavioral polymorphism in which an operation may have been implemented differently in different classes.

---

[1]The symbol $\gg$ means the value on the left is much larger than the value on the right.
[2]The symbol $\lll$ means the value on the left is much smaller than the value on the right.

Polymorphism Factor Based on Overriding Methods (PFOM)   The metric PFOM represents the efforts needed for testing a superclass when one or more its methods being overridden in sub-classes.

$$\text{PFOM} = \frac{\text{actual number of overridden methods in an inheritance hierarchy}}{\text{maximum possible number of override methods}} \qquad \text{(e-10)}$$

$$\text{PFOM}(\langle classname \rangle\_tree) =$$

$$\frac{\sum_{i=1}^{m} \text{NIV}(subclass\_i) + \sum_{i=1}^{m} \text{NOLO}(subclass\_i)}{m \times [\text{NIV}(superclass) + \text{NOP}(\langle classname \rangle\_tree)]} \qquad \text{(e-11)}$$

where

NIV($subclass\_i$)	:	number of methods in $subclass\_i$, which are the implementations of the same virtual method defined in the *superclass*
NOLO($subclass\_i$)	:	number of overloaded operators in $subclass\_i$
NOP($subclass\_i$)	:	number of system-defined operators which have been overloaded in this $subclass\_i$
m	:	number of all the subclasses of the $\langle classname \rangle\_tree$

Average Changing Rate of Abstract Methods (ACRV)   This metric compares number of statements in an abstract method[3] defined in a *superclass* and those in the overridden versions of the same method in subclasses. It is defined as follows:

$$\text{ACRV}(\langle classname \rangle\_tree) = \frac{\sum_{i=1}^{m} \sum_{j=1}^{k} \text{NSV}(subclass\_i, virtual\_method\_j)}{m * \sum_{j=1}^{k} \text{NSV}(superclass, virtual\_method\_j)} \qquad \text{(e-12)}$$

where

NSV(*class, method*)	:	number of statements in *"method"* defined in *"class"*. It is is zero in the program, we set it to 0.5. The justification for this arrangement is not to leave the denominator be zero. Moreover, a value of 0.5 is reasonably small.
m	:	number of all the subclasses in the *superclass_tree*.
k	:	number of virtual-methods defined in the *superclass*.

When a subclasses chooses to implement an abstract method, the number of statements for this method in the subclass will increase. The numerator in (e-12) will greater than or equal to the denominator. Therefore, the value of ACRV(*superclass_tree*) will be greater than or equal to zero. ACRV being equal to zero indicates that no subclasses implement any of the abstract methods, which is less possible to happen.

2.3: Metric Based on Interactions among Objects

Object interactions are defined by message passing and hence any changes to a class definition will directly affect the interactions of objects of this class with other objects.

Interactions of Objects from Program Viewpoint (IFPV)   This metric examines the interaction from the viewpoint of the whole program. The result indicates the percentage of classes in the

---

[3]An abstract method is the one whose implementation is incomplete; it is similar to a virtual function in C++, a deferred routine in Eiffel or an abstract method in Java.

program which have relation with a particular class C.

$$\text{IFPV}(Class\_C) = \left(\frac{\text{NCP}(Class\_C) + \text{NTC}(Class\_C) + \text{NSUP}(Class\_C)}{\text{NCIP}} \times 100 \right) \%$$

(e-13)

where

NCP	:	number of distinct class pointers used in $Class\_C$
NTC	:	number of template classes used in $Class\_C$, other than itself. Every class pointer will be counted only once, even if it might appear several time.
NSUP	:	number of superclasses of $Class\_C$, other than itself. Every class pointer will be counted only once, even if it might appear several times.
NCIP	:	number of classes in the program.

Interaction of Object from Class Viewpoint (IFCV) This metric examines the interaction of a method with other methods within the same class and/or with other methods defined in other classes. It indirectly represents the strength of dependency between structural and behavioral components of a particular class C with those in other classes with which C has either association or aggregation relationship.

$$\text{IFCV}(Class\_C) = \left(\frac{\text{NDC}(Class\_C) + \text{NPC}(Class\_C) + \text{NRC}(Class\_C)}{\text{AD}(Class\_C) + \text{MD}(Class\_C) + \text{NPAR}(Class\_C)} \times 100 \right) \%$$

(e-14)

where

NDC	:	number of attributes/parameters/methods in $Class\_C$ whose types are other class names
NPC	:	number of attributes/parameters/methods in $Class\_C$ that are pointed to by other classes
NRC	:	number of attributes/parameters/methods in $Class\_C$ that are referenced by other classes
NPAR	:	number of parameters of all the methods in $Class\_C$

3: Comparison of Metric Sets

In this section, we will compare Liu's metrics set with three metrics sets: Chidamber and Kemerer's metrics suite [5, 6], MOOD metrics set [1, 2] and Kim's metrics set [17, 18]. While there are numerous publications on object-oriented software metrics, the three sets of metrics chosen for comparison have somewhat similar features as that of Liu's metrics set. In particular, these three sets of metrics are independent of any object-oriented programming languages. Since it is hard to establish a one-to-one comparison between the metrics, we select only a subset of metrics from the above three sets. A justification for the partial comparison comes from the fact that these three metrics sets as well as Liu's metrics set are all targeted towards different goals. So, we select only those fundamental metric components and their compositions in arriving at the definition of a metric.

3.1: Metrics Based on Inheritance Hierarchy

Chidamber and Kemerer proposed two metrics based on inheritance hierarchy: *Depth of Inheritance Tree* (DIT) and *Number of Children* (NOC). They claimed that DIT and NOC can be used to predict the external characteristics[4] of a design such as design complexity and testing efforts.

---

[4]External characteristics are the characteristics such as design complexity and class reusability, which can only be measured with respect to how the product, process, or resource relates to other entities in its environment [8].

However, this claim is hard to prove. Many researchers criticized that Chidamber and Kemerer's metrics suite is inadequate to evaluate external characteristics of a design [8, 16]. Binkley and Schach [4] conducted experiments to evaluate several object-oriented metrics including Chidamber and Kemerer's. According to their experiments, DIT and NOC had a success rate of only 28% in predicting design complexity. Binkley and Schach also pointed out that DIT and NOC are at a high level of abstraction and are not adequate for evaluating a design.

There are two metrics in MOOD metrics set based on the inheritance hierarchy: *Attribute Inheritance Factor* (AIF), and *Methods Inheritance Factor* (MIF); these two define respectively the ratio of inherited attributes to the total number of attributes in a complete program and the ratio of inherited methods to total number of methods. The authors of MOOD metrics set claim that both AIF and MIF indicate the level of reuse in more detail when compared to those of Chidamber and Kemerer. This is because they are defined on the internal structures of the classes.

Kim's metrics suite proposes only one metric based on inheritance: *Degree of Reuse* (DOR) which defines the ability or potential of reuse of a class. Thus, DOR is computed for each class separately. It is computed based on the interactions of the number of classes and hence is at the same level of abstraction as that of Chidamber and Kemerer.

The metrics IHA, IHC and IHD of Liu's metrics set are based on the inheritance hierarchy. These three metrics are quite comparable to AIF and MIF of MOOD metrics because they are based on the internal structure of a class. Thus, the level of abstraction of Liu's metrics is lower than that of Chidamber and Kemerer's and Kim's metrics sets. While the goal of MOOD metrics set is to evaluate the level of reuse, the goal of Liu's metrics set is to evaluate the testing efforts required to test individual classes. Thus, the focus of the latter is on the individual hierarchies, while the former is targeted towards the entire program. It is quite common that all the classes in a program do not participate in a single inheritance hierarchy or not in any inheritance hierarchy. In this context, we claim that Liu's metrics set is more detailed than MOOD metrics set.

3.2: Metrics Based on Polymorphism

None of the metrics in Chidamber and Kemerer's metrics set and in Kim's metrics set evaluate polymorphism. Therefore, in this section, we compare only MOOD and Liu's metrics sets. MOOD contains only one metric based on polymorphism: *Polymorphism Factor* (PF) which is a measure of inherent polymorphism. PF is computed as the ratio of inherited methods and the maximum number of possible distinct polymorphic situations in a program. This metric can be viewed as an indirect measure of the relative amount of dynamic binding in a program, which is strongly related to polymorphism and inheritance. The authors of the MOOD metrics set claim that an appropriate use of polymorphism in object-oriented project designs should decrease the defect density as well as rework [2]. However, higher value of PF tend to reduce the benefits achieved through this metric. Harrison [12, 13] reported that PF exhibits an unexpected discontinuity when the denominator is zero. Since the denominator includes the number of subclasses of a superclass ($DC(C_i)$), the value of the denominator for a system without any inheritance will be zero, which will give an infinite value for the metric itself.

The metrics PFOM and ACRV defined in Liu's metrics set are related to polymorphism. The metric PFOM is quite comparable to PF of MOOD metrics set. As the goals of MOOD metrics set and Liu's metrics set are different, the focus of metrics PFOM and PF are different, with PFOM focusing on the inheritance hierarchies individually and PF focusing on the entire program. The metric ACRV of Liu's metric indicates the level of polymorphism from within the classes of each individual inheritance hierarchy. It can also give an indication of the efficiency of late binding.

3.3: Metrics Based on Interactions between Objects

Chidamber and Kemerer defined two metrics related to interactions between objects. These are *Coupling between object classes* (CBO) which, for a class C, indicates the number of other classes that are coupled with (interacting with) C; and *Response for a class* (RFC), which indicates the number of occurrences of calls to other classes from C. Binkley and Schach [4] suggested CBO provided only crude estimate of the coupling. There is no distinction made between different types of coupling, such as the number of parameters and how they are passed. On the other hand, RFC does not distinguish between different types of coupling. For example, parameters passed by value or by reference appear identical under this measurement. However, compared to CBO, RFC can give better prediction, because RFC examines every call of all the methods in a class. Binkley and Schach showed that the successful prediction rate of RFC is much higher than that of CBO [4].

The metric *Coupling Factor* (COF) in MOOD metrics set is based on interactions between objects. This metric is defined as the actual number of couplings not caused by inheritance, divided by the maximum possible number of couplings in a program. The coupling factor gathered by COF refers to the whole system.

Kim's metrics set includes three metrics based on interaction between objects: *Degree of coupling of inheritance* (CBI), *Number of classes used in a particular class* (UCL), and *Number of "send" statements of a class* (MPC). CBI for a class C is defined as the product of total complexity of methods (calculated by another metric called *Degree of Internal Method Complexity* IMC)) of C and the number of subclasses of C. UCL concentrates on a class as a whole while MPC focuses on individual methods in a class.

The metrics IFPV and IFCV in Liu's metrics set are based on the interaction among objects. Both IFPV and IFCV is somewhat similar to CBI. However, IFPV and IFCV include more implementation options, such as templates and references, which tend to include more information on interactions between objects. The metrics UCL and MPC denote actual counts to present the interaction complexity, while IFPC and IFCV use a relative measure.

4: Conclusion and Future Work

This paper is a contribution to the quantitative analysis of object-oriented programs. We have introduced a new set of metrics for object-oriented programs, targeted towards evaluating the efforts required for testing object-oriented programs; this new metrics set is called *Liu's metrics set*. As mentioned earlier, Liu's metrics set does not indicate the number of test cases or test data required for a program; rather, it gives an indirect measure of the testing efforts required. The equations for Liu's metrics have been derived with testing efforts as the target.

We have evaluated Liu's metrics set (1) by comparing it with three other metrics sets chosen from the literature, and (2) by analytically evaluating against Weyuker's properties and Kim's framework. Liu's metrics set has also been applied to two large programs. The results of the analytical evaluations and the empirical evaluation are shown in [19]. Currently, we do not have tool support for applying Liu's metrics. The tools which we used to extract the necessary data from object-oriented programs were too specific and were inadequate for applying Liu's metrics. As a result, much work in the empirical evaluation of Liu's metrics as reported in [19] was done manually. It is for this reason that, at this stage, we are unable to provide experimental data to show that the metrics indicate what they are intend to measure. As part of the continuing work in this project, we have planned to develop a tool (i) to extract the necessary data for applying the metrics, and (ii) to graphically display the results.

References

[1] F.B. Abreu, M. Goulao, and R. Esteves. "Toward the Design Quality Evaluation of Object-Oriented Software Systems", *Proceedings of the 5th International Conference on Software Quality, Austin, Texas, USA, pp. 44-57, October 1995.*

[2] F.B. Abreu and W. Melo. "Evaluation the Impact of Object-Oriented Design on Software Quality", *Proceedings of the 3rd International Software Metrics Symposium, Berlin, Germany, pp. 90-99, March 1996.*

[3] V.R. Basili, L. Briand, and W.L. Melo. "A Validation of Object-Oriented Design Metrics as Quality Indicators", *IEEE Transactions on Software Engineering, Vol.22, No.10, pp. 751-761, October 1996.*

[4] A.B. Binkley and S.R. Schach. "A Comparison of Sixteen Quality Metrics for Object-Oriented Design", *Information Processing Letters 58 (1996), pp. 271-275, 1996.*

[5] S.R. Chidamber and C.F. Kemerer. "Towards a Metrics Suite for Object-Oriented Design", *OOPSLA '91, Phoenix, Aeizona, USA, pp. 197-211, 1991.*

[6] S. R. Chidamber and C. F. Kemerer. "A Metrics Suite for Object-Oriented Design", *IEEE Transactions on Software Engineering, Vol.20, No.6, pp. 476-493, June 1994.*

[7] N.I. Churcher and M.J. Shepperd. "Comments on 'A Metrics Suite for Object Oriented Design' ", *IEEE Transactions on Software Engineering, Vol.21, No.3, pp. 263-265, March 1995.*

[8] N. Fenton. "Software Measurement: A Necessary Scientific Basis", *IEEE Transactions on Software Engineering, Vol.20, No.3, pp. 199-206March 1994.*

[9] N.E. Fenton and S.L. Pfleeger. *Software Metrics: A Rigorous and Practical Approach*, International Thomson Computer Press, 1997.

[10] R.G. Gowda and L.E. Winslow. "An Approach for Deriving Object-Oriented Metrics", *Proceedings of the IEEE 1994 National Aerospace and Electronics Conference NACON, Vol.2, pp. 897-904, 1994.*

[11] I. Graham. "Making Progress in Metrics", *Object Magazine, Vol.6, Iss.8, pp. 68-73, October 1996.*

[12] R. Harrison, S. Counsell, and R.Nithi. "An Overview of Object-Oriented Design Metrics", *8th International Workshop on Software Technology and Engineering Practice, 1997.*

[13] R. Harrison, S. Counsell, and R. Nithi. "An Evaluation of the MOOD Set of Object-Oriented Software Metrics", *IEEE Transactions on Software Engineering, Vol.24, No.6, pp. 491-496, June 1998.*

[14] M.J. Harrold, and J.D. McGregor. "Incremental Testing of Object-Oriented Class Structures", *Proceedings of 14th International Conference on Software Engineering, pp. 68-80, May 1992.*

[15] B. Henderson-Sellers. "OO Metrics Programme", *Object Magazine, Vol.5, Iss.6, pp. 72-76,78-79,95, October 1995.*

[16] M. Hitz and B. Montazeri. "Measuring Product Attributes of Object-Oriented Systems", *Proceedings of the 5th European Software Engineering Conference, Barcelona, Spain, pp. 124-136, September 1995.*

[17] E.M. Kim, O.B. Chang, S. Kusumoto, and T. Kikuno. "Analysis of Metrics for Object-Oriented Program Complexity", *Proceedings of COMPSAC'94, pp.201-207, 1994.*

[18] E.M. Kim, S. Kusumoto, T. Kikuno, and O.B. Chang. "Heuristics for Computing Attribute Values of C++ Program Complexity Metrics", *1996 IEEE 20th Annual International Computer Software and Applications Conference, Seoul, Korea, pp. 104-109, August 1996.*

[19] X. Liu, "Object-Oriented Software Metrics", Masters Thesis, Department of Computer Science, University of Manitoba, Winnipeg, Manitoba, Canada, 1999.

[20] K.H. Möller and D.J. Paulish. *Software Metrics.* Chapman & Hall, London UK, 1993.

[21] E.J. Weyuker. "Evaluating Software Complexity Measures", *IEEE Transactions on Software Engineering, Vol.14, No.9, pp. 1357-1365, September 1988.*

Benchmark Metrics for Enterprise Object Request Brokers

M. Vilicich & S. Aslam-Mir[1]

Expersoft Corporation, a Vertel Company

research@expersoft.com

Abstract

The growing interest in using Common Object Request Broker Architecture (CORBA) to distribute application objects over heterogeneous environments has led to an explosive growth in the number of Fortune-500 companies deploying major, mission-critical applications using such client/server (c/s) architectures. Unfortunately, there is little in terms of literature that describes the complexities and issues encountered in scaling these architectures. This is due, in large part, to the relative infancy of CORBA technology when compared to other client/server architectures. This paper attempts to address some of the potential issues involved in large-scale deployments of CORBA technology in highly scaled configurations. The paper makes some empirical assessments of appropriate design-guiding parameters for scalability, and discusses how to arrive at these parameters through a traceable lifecycle process. The paper also provides some guidance on what measures are appropriate to use when estimating an ORB's performance envelope, so as to appropriately extrapolate its behavioral characteristics in fully scaled production deployments.

1. Introduction

Industry and academic efforts toward evolving CORBA into an enterprise-capable technology have steadily increased the quality of available products and current knowledge base, but still leave the customer searching for a means of choosing the right ORB or distributed client/server technology. This paper attempts to address some of the potential issues involved in large-scale deployments of CORBA technology in highly scaled configurations. The paper makes some empirical assessments of appropriate design-guiding parameters for scalability, and discusses how to arrive at these parameters through a traceable lifecycle process. The paper also provides some guidance on what measures are appropriate to use when estimating an ORB's performance envelope, so as to appropriately extrapolate its behavioral characteristics in fully scaled production deployments. Because CORBA is commonly implemented as server-centric, most opportunities to improve performance and scalability present themselves on the server side[1] and this paper will therefore focus on server issues.

Due to the condensed nature of the proceedings publication, please see the complete white paper including charts and figures posted on our website at www.expersoft.com.

1.1. What is CORBA?

For the most part, this paper assumes the reader is familiar with distributed architectures. For those less familiar with ORBs, and CORBA in particular: CORBA stands for Common Object Request Broker Architecture. This architecture is specified and ratified by the Object Management Group (OMG). The OMG is the governing body for the CORBA standard and

---

[1] Mark Vilicich and Shahzad Aslam-Mir (Ph.D.) are VERTEL engineers focussed on the design and architecture of of object request brokers and how this relates to benchmarking and proving their performance envelopes.

includes over 800 member companies internationally. The specification[2] is used by vendors to build ORBs with specific functionality; it is not used as a design document to define an implementation.

1.2. What does the enterprise developer test?

Architects considering the design of distributed systems would do well to avoid the common mistake of relying on the performance tests provided in the ORB vendors' evaluation kits or relying on published results of so-called generic tests. Implementing a pilot study for the target deployment will yield more realistic results. There is no unit-level IDL interface that can convey how the whole ORB works because the ORB must handle so many different data types and combinations/permutations. Unit-level testing results are, therefore, misleading. Customer-based experience proves that a proper pilot study using the ORB in the context of the specific application domain, simulating the captured use-case and hardware configuration, will best serve the end-user.

2. Benchmarking metrics

To discover the primary test cases, it is necessary to begin with the design of the system architecture. An enterprise solution begins in the business domain with a study of the business processes to be automated. The analysis of the business domain in the design process yields both an object model and a set of use-cases. Designers can derive the distribution strategy from the resultant object model and the use-cases indicate common usage patterns with which they can identify required CORBA services. From these, the software architect may draw clues as to how to generate the IDL interfaces that enable the functionality required for object distribution. Principle use-cases help identify the benchmark transactions and the IDL defines the APIs necessary to implement the use-cases in the test applications. Key measures to study with these use-cases include performance, scalability, reliability, interoperabililty, and any project-specific requirements sometimes pre-specified in the form of *Service Level Agreements* (SLAs).

These processes should occur both in a pilot study and in the actual design process. However, the pilot study allows the customer to use this knowledge to evaluate the underlying technologies of the design, including ORB selection, and so best achieve the desired overall performance.

2.1. Test results analysis

Before scaling up a test run to include multiple clients, we need accurate baseline measurements of the invocation times for client requests. Charting invocation time vs. number of invocations determines baseline ORB performance and repeatability. The data provides timings charted for the client's request of a basic data type such as a string versus each individual invocation of the request. The chart illustrates a narrow band of behavior representing consistent results, regardless of the number of invocations. Few outliers appear in this data set.

In contrast to the narrow band of response times in the baseline, the next charted output shows an atypical data set of number of invocations vs. invocation times with 40 clients over a busy LAN. This chart exposes a near-normal distribution with the addition of a "fat tail" at the end (a cluster of data on the right side of the chart). The outlying data points to the right are significant to the overall test results; when combined they provide the tallest column of the data set. This data suggests that other, concurrently running processes, such as network collisions, packet drops, retransmits, or message fragmentation are affecting, and due to the quantity, invalidating the results.

2.2. Enterprise performance

Because the performance of ORBs can vary widely between vendors and products, careful evaluation of ORBs intended to support large-scale installations is essential. In a general sense, an ORB's performance can be used to denote the product's overall capability to meet its requirements and serve its intended purpose. Commonly however, "performance" often means the ORB's perceived processing speed. This perception results from reliance on performance tests to determine an ORB's ability to marshal basic IDL types. This test can often be misleading, because "real" IDL (i.e., production code rather than test code) is more complex in construction.

Performance considerations need to include:

1) The benchmark transactions identified from research of the systems design, or even better, from the pilot study, should identify your primary performance concerns in the form of key fingerprint use cases. These tests should be performed across actual LANs and WANs.
2) Firewalls present significant performance bottlenecks and need attention in the design phase.
3) Stress testing is vital to account for the harsh conditions in which most deployments operate. Be sure to stress the test system with noisy LANs, network hardware failures or drop-outs, poor network configuration, etc.
4) Load testing using standard tools has great value in achieving the maximum scale possible with a minimum of development time. Put these benchmark transactions under heavy server load as well to measure any performance degradation in these conditions.
5) Evaluating the test results needs to ascertain whether the required and agreed upon levels of Quality of Service (QoS) are maintained at the performance levels desired. By QoS here, I mean the allowed number of errors per a certain load, say 100 clients in the system and 2 errors per hour.

2.2.1. Enterprise required ORB features: In general, understanding some of the internal mechanisms of an ORB offers insight into the ORB's performance and the enterprise-level requirements placed on it. Though client-side performance issues exist, testing suggests that "of the client/server pair, it is the server who influences the performance most,"[3] so we emphasize server-side mechanisms here. CORBAplus, the CORBA 2.0-compliant ORB from Expersoft, is used here as an example, but the features discussed are generic at the enterprise level and are generally implemented to varying degrees in the other commercial CORBA ORBs on the market, or should be.

Some commonly experienced issues relating to enterprise ORB performance are: message fragmentation, excessive marshalling overhead, deadlocking, and frozen GUIs. These are addressed by ORBs with a variety of enhancements. For example, buffer tuning addresses the problem of message fragmentation, the co-location optimizer addresses excessive marshalling overhead, and active blocking addresses deadlocking and frozen GUIs.

Buffer tuning allows adaptation of the communication layer to your messaging needs. You can configure the transport buffers to adapt to your most common message size, thus increasing overall performance. The size of these transport buffers does impact the performance of applications because the ORB, in general, is constantly copying application buffers into transport buffers, passing them onto the wire, and copying again on the receiving side. Note: Designing for zero copy buffers inside the ORB is considered optimal for performance considerations, but is not yet offered with many ORBs.

Another performance enhancing feature is the co-location optimizer which refers to how the ORB libraries automatically detect if the requesting and replying objects are located in the same process. No marshalling to the wire or exercising the protocol stack occurs if this is true and access time is equal to one pointer de-reference. To verify that an ORB supports this feature, look for an obvious difference in timing studies of calls to local versus remote objects.

Performance is also enhanced with active blocking which is a mechanism used for handling outstanding synchronous events. A client process with active blocking enabled can seem to handle outstanding events concurrently, even in single-threaded applications. A simple example of this is the starvation condition encountered when handling GUI events in real time. If the application is single-threaded and makes a synchronous call, a concurrent GUI event will freeze thereby disallowing user interaction until the synchronous call completes.

With active blocking the ORB checks all outstanding connections during a synchronous block, and can handle requests on all outstanding connections, including timer events. This is a form of I/O multiplexing where incoming requests will be dispatched as well as the results from outstanding asynchronous calls. This is how active blocking prevents starvation when synchronous invocations are made.

Additionally, some applications to which CORBA has been introduced, specifically in the areas of real-time systems that may require complicated scheduling, are susceptible to specialized forms of undesirable phenomena when subjected to high (enterprise level) loads. This is due to the stringent predictability (and hence schedule-ability) requirements that these systems have.

Two examples of such phenomena are jitter and priority inversion.

- Jitter is defined as the difference between the worst case and best case times observed to process some task (in this case a request).
- Priority inversion is defined as the inappropriate scheduling of prioritized tasks such that higher priority tasks in the ORB may run at lower priorities than the design intended due to inappropriate resource contention among tasks.

The greater the observed jitter, the more difficult it is for an ORB to reliably schedule the processing of requests that may require intensive CPU processing. To solve this problem in hard, real-time CORBA applications, the use of scheduling analysis and prioritized tasks has been proposed [Schmidt]. A popular and successful approach for this has been the use of a specific algorithm known as Rate Monotonic Scheduling, which serves to avoid, or at least minimize, other phenomenon such as priority inversion.

2.2.2 Performance Benchmarking: Performance benchmarking is a vital area of development for the OMG in regards to CORBA, with a Special Interest Group organized to support further development. The SIG has been accepting responses to a Request for Information regarding the status of, and issues regarding, CORBA benchmarking technologies[4]. The resulting benchmarks from the combined responses should prove insightful for both the end-users to determine the appropriate ORB for their needs and guide development by the ORB vendors towards higher performing architectures. Though ORB comparisons and research studies presently do not include all available ORBs at once, the reported testing is often made available in source code and can be a valuable addition to any pilot study or internal evaluation program.

Examples of published tests we have found useful come from Washington and Charles Universities with the FTP sites listed in the References section to obtain source code samples of the tests. These tests primarily measure the message throughput of an ORB under varying conditions and provide a good first benchmark to spec against. Results from these tests comparing multiple ORBs are included below for example purposes. For those interested in reading material regarding CORBA testing or a more detailed description of the tests, highly recommended papers are available from both these universities including those sighted in the bibliography[56][3].

The four ORBs included in Expersoft's internal studies are CORBA 2.0-compliant and were selected for the reasons to be described. With ORB A we are internally researching performance concepts which will evolve into a generally released CORBA ORB product. Currently it outpaces the comparison ORBs and continued testing will further refine the ORB until its release. ORB B is currently a public domain ORB often considered the fastest ORB publicly. ORB C is the fastest of the leading commercially available ORBs on the market today, at least by our testing. ORB D is a university-based research ORB targeting realtime implementations. Assembling data from this grouping of ORBs using well known benchmarks provides both valuable data and credibility for the information gathered.

The next figure in the presentation shows the results of tests that were first performed by the Washington University group of research workers[7]. The tests measure the volume throughput of a CORBA ORB by determining its data transfer rate (measured in kilobytes/sec) for one-way and roundtrip calls to a remote server as a function of the size of message being passed in bytes. The test clearly illustrates that, as the volume being transmitted increases, all ORBs become more efficient per unit data size.

The presentation continues to illustrate a comparison between the aforementioned ORBs using the experimental setups described in the Charles University tests[8]. In these experiments, we passed a variety of primitive CORBA types between client and server in a oneway operation and measured invocation times. The test increases in complexity from left to right by next passing arrays of the same types instead of just one value. Then we pass CORBA sequences of the same primitives instead of arrays, increasing the complexity for the marshalling engine of any ORB. The times to pass the same simple and progressively complex types are measured and presented for the ORBs.

The next figure (see presentation) illustrates the *idl cubit*[9] test, also devised by the Washington University group to measure the request processing speeds of an ORB's request and marshalling engines combined on both the client and server sides simultaneously. This test measures the number of calls an ORB can make per unit time to perform a single CORBA reference invocation. The CORBA reference invocation is defined arbitrarily as an invocation made upon a remote server in which the client sends a numeric value. The server cubes the value and returns it to the client.

The cubit test can be used to identify the latency, jitter, CPU utilization, and priority inversion of the ORB[9].The measurand of interest in this test was determined by the researchers at the time to be the number of calls the client could make per second to the remote server to perform this operation.

2.3. Enterprise Scalability

Scalability is perhaps one of the most scrutinized elements of an ORB[10], and is critical to the maturing of the technology. Enterprise scalability, as defined in this paper, is the ORB's ability to support applications without degrading the overall performance and stability of the server, (i.e., continuing to meet a predefined level of service). A given ORB may exhibit abrupt limits in its ability to function in large configurations, i.e. at some point, begin to exhibit adverse non-linear behavior or may simply fail. Other ORBs may exhibit severely decreased performance as system size increases until they are effectively unacceptable. Testing the ORB in a simulated environment is vital to determining the effective scalability for the desired deployment.

Scalability means many things to many people; One way of quantifying a scalability measure is to chart invocation response time of some key call/invocation vs. number of clients connected to the server for two ORBs under comparison. By most standards, the lower graph in the resulting figure would be considered an example of fairly good scalability and the more desirable ORB due to its relatively flat slope and linear scalability as client load increases. The small slope in this chart represents a small increase in response time for an increase in the number of active clients. Of course, a perfectly flat line would be the ideal and a vertical line would indicate failure.

The figure (see presentation) which shows invocation time vs. number of clients is a simple example of using the quantitative analysis of scalability values to create a scalability graph. The test consisted of a CORBA server on a host platform with remote clients all making invocations on an object in that server. Note that the data points are normalized values consisting of the standardized invocation time over a sample of one thousand method calls run during the test. The times were then reduced by the value from timing studies of CORBA oneway calls, which minimizes the effect of the particular socket-stack implementation in the resulting values. Linear regression applied to the data, as seen here, provides the ability to extrapolate the data to the expected client load if it is beyond the range of the test load. This gives an initial estimate of the scalability of this invocation with this server implementation and environment.

Unfortunately, scalability testing often concludes at this point without actually considering the ORB's scalability limit. Differences in the slope are important, but more difficult to manage is the ORB's efficient use of system and network resources. On the right side of the graph in the figure (see presentation), the plot reaches a "non-linear" transition and appears as a bend in the curve. All ORBs reach this point. The further to the right on the x-axis (i.e., at a greater number of clients) this point appears, the higher the server load and the better for ultimate scalability. This point is often referred to as "hitting the wall." The ORB can go no further; and neither can the small-scale project when it moves to full scale or when it is asked to go beyond initial expectations. This then is the limit of the performance envelope of the ORB configuration for that type and level of load.

2.3.1 Enterprise Required ORB Features: Enterprise-level deployments using ORBs must use network resources efficiently, support fine-grained objects, and use threads effectively in the target applications. Designers of CORBAplus considered shared connections, thread models, and memory management/footprint issues very carefully at the ORB's inception and the resulting implementations are discussed below in greater detail.

The goal of achieving minimal consumption of network resources meant to the designers that any communication protocol based on network broadcasts and/or an ORB that required the normal two connections between any two interacting processes were unsuitable. If one process is a pure client and the other a pure server, then only one connection should be necessary. In CORBAplus, multiple logical CORBA connections are multiplexed across a single transport connection using a shared connections mechanism within the ORB. CORBAplus I/O multiplexing was a unique feature for its time, allowing efficient support of many fine-grained objects.

Within the core architecture of CORBAplus lie multiplexer and demultiplexer conduits, used for handling shared connections efficiently. The multiplexer conduit on the sending side funnels requests across a single transport connection. The conduit on top of the multiplexer conduit hands off the request without regard to which connection the request will travel. On the receiving end, a corresponding demultiplexer reads the request from the single transport connection and passes the request up the conduit stack. Roles are reversed for handling replies.

It is important to analyze a server's memory footprint in the test phase, rather than waiting until production to discover the transient and steady state levels. Scalability ratio tests are plotted with the server private bytes vs. number of clients, showing that the server's private bytes grow as the number of clients increases. After reaching a peak number of clients, the test continues by decreasing the server load and observing the behavior. Here the memory is consumed on increase of server load and not returned when the load decreases; in short, a residual hysteresis effect is evident. Although this can result from the application code/design, it is also possibly the result of poor cleanup by the ORB or inappropriate use of transport protocol under the ORB.

Performance and scalability demands often drive designs toward multithreaded CORBA server implementations. The ORB should be able to both operate in a multithreaded environment and provide optimized message retrieval. One of the most profitable aspects of multithreaded CORBA server implementations is the "availability of a wide variety of options for handling requests."[1]

Several threading models are possible, including one thread-per-object, one thread-per-process, and one thread-per-request. With a thread pool model, a number of worker threads are spawned at startup and then paired with incoming requests. Experience shows that a thread pool model in which threads are assigned per request is the most adaptable. However, in general, an appropriate model should be chosen based on server application requirements. To review the main thread models:

- For one thread-per-object, for example, assume there are two objects and two threads. As requests come in, they are handed only to the thread servicing the requested object. Therefore, one object could receive many requests, resulting in one process-bound thread while the other thread remains idle.
- In a one thread-per-process or -client scenario, each client is responded to by a dedicated thread. Thread startup occurs only on initial connection, decreasing the threading burden for high numbers of requests per client. However, this model does not scale effectively. When inactive clients consume all available threads, or when a high message load exists on a minority of the clients, the server is unable to make new client connections.
- In a thread-pool model, the user defines a pool of threads for the process. Each request is submitted on a separate thread from the pool of available threads. When all threads have been exhausted, subsequent requests are queued until a thread is freed for use. In other words, threads are bound to events and adapt to the load on objects. This design is adaptable because it virtually guarantees optimal use of the allocated threads. It supports more clients and objects than available threads, enabling the server to avoid a scalability wall under load. Add to this the notion of a dynamic thread pool, which spawns more threads if the load passes some set limit to further enhance scalability. Potential drawbacks to this model include a high context-switching burden under high load conditions and requires a siginificant amount of locking.

Knowing the advantages of multithreading, the developer needs to both measure the CORBA server's scalability and identify any anomalies in the server's expected behavior. Though it is noted that threaded servers can perform faster than non-threaded servers on single-CPU machines[1], it is wise to verify the value of a multithreaded design when possible. One figure in the presentation charts invocation time vs. number of clients; the upper line represents the multithreaded server and the lower line, a single-threaded version. Here the single-threaded version of the same server performs much better and suggests further investigation into the thread model used. Other options include hosting the multithreaded server on an SMP machine and re-testing, or verifying by test whether the multithreaded version's performance surpasses the other at higher client loads assuming that scalability requirements extend further.

2.4. Enterprise Reliability

Reliability is at the heart of software quality and addresses the traditional definition of quality (i.e., "Is it buggy?")[11]. Networking software quality/reliability is primarily the responsibility of the ORB vendor, but every user and developer is also concerned with the resultant system's reliability. In regards to this enterprise-level reliability, we may define enterprise reliability as consistent server performance while servicing multiple clients over time. Even with this definition, often ORB "problems with reliability demonstrate themselves only in unusual settings or unusual load patterns"[12] and this area is still difficult to verify in tests.

The work of verifying ORB reliability comes in testing the required features and any unusual settings or load patterns identified during the pilot-study phase. Feature testing involves, for example, whether the object's state is stored and recovered properly. If one of the servers is shut down, is the client's request forwarded to an active server? Can the required service, such as a trader, be replicated? Internal ORB features that play an important role in protecting the server from failure and the client/server connection from momentary network failures include smart connections, server-side governors, and automatic spawning.

The ORB handles network disconnects internally using smart connections. If a momentary disconnect occurs for any reason, smart connections reconnect the client and server and verifies that the object reference is still valid. The power of this feature is in its invisibility to the client and server application code.

Server failures can occur as a result of swamping the server host's resources. When a request comes in, it is read from a transport buffer, memory is allocated from the buffer pool, and a new message is created and queued for processing. As a consequence of this design, the buffer pool may exhaust all available memory in order to handle a high volume of incoming traffic. For example, a single client may send many asynchronous requests without waiting for any of them to complete, or many clients simultaneously send requests to the same server and swamp the buffer pool in the process. Some form of management, such as a governor, is necessary to preclude swamping server host resources. The governor provides an overall high quality and consistent level of service by limiting the amount of memory used to handle incoming requests. This prevents requests on one object within a server from overwhelming a machine.

Automatic Spawning also provides management of server host resources to prevent failure under load. This is accomplished through client access with Basic Object Adapter (BOA) activation (i.e., Automatic Spawning), which starts up server applications on request and shuts them down on completion, thereby managing overall server load and resource consumption. Upon startup of the server object, the BOA daemon returns a reference for the requested server object to the client. Fault tolerance is also enhanced by enabling a restart of the process across a list of registered servers and makes for highly available ORB services.

2.4.1 Enterprise Termination Test: A form of "unusual setting or load pattern" that falls more under the category of a stress test or possibly a "negative test"[13] is the termination test. This test is a recreation of 0900 hours on Monday morning with the dynamic load transients typical for enterprise-level environments. This environment includes a high volume of connects in the form of logon simultaneous with significant network volatility and partial failures distributed across the system simultaneously. To the authors' knowledge, the termination test hasn't been discussed in the context of CORBA ORB testing though the deployment environment eventually realizes the condition. It is the back-breaker for any server, CORBA or basic vanilla, often not investigated sufficiently until just before system test and QA in the enterprise deployment environment.

An ORB's response to this condition requires high efficiency in resource usage and connection management to handle the server's large volume of client connection dropouts. Our experiences show a wide variety of results between various ORB implementations, as well as from platform to platform, suggesting platform issues exist along with ORB issues. The CORBA server used in the termination test should be accessed by remote clients using one-way calls and synchronous or asynchronous connections (if your ORB supports them). Clients should repeatedly connect, forcibly terminate their sessions, and restart. Individual tests should be run for each of the connection modes, and single or multithreaded servers. These tests may run for minutes, days, or weeks depending on the overall configuration and test goals. ORB features such as the governor, and test features such as the rate of client restart, number of clients, and message types should be configured to best represent the target environment or satisfy expectations to obtain meaningful data. Representing the target environment can often be difficult to approximate and with the results being much more valuable on a comparison basis.

2.5. Interoperability

Interoperation between ORBs requires that functionality, performance, and reliability is preserved. CORBA enables interoperation through IIOP (Internet Inter-ORB Protocol) and guarantees every ORB to work with another. This guarantee is backed up both by the membership of the 800+ OMG member companies, which depend on vendor interoperability, and by a recent move from the OMG with the CORBA Brand Program, managed by The Open Group. The Branding Program uses the VSOrb and VSJOrb test suites to passively monitor correct IIOP message generation and actively monitor for proper exceptions generated under error conditions[14]. The Branding Program is currently available for the CORBA 2.1 specification.

Interoperability not only addresses whether the ORB will interoperate with other vendor's ORBs, but also how well it will enable the integration of other technologies and products. The CORBAplus ActiveX Bridge, for example, enables interaction with COM/DCOM objects. Commercial ORBs are beginning to also offer this feature since many installations desire interaction with Microsoft at some level, on the desktop at least.

CORBA also defines language bindings for several programming languages and the user should test a C++ server against both C++ and, perhaps, Java clients if that is a target technology. Since the Java client is essentially written with another ORB inside it, this should be done much like testing interoperation between ORBs.

If the target system needs to cross firewalls or operate across the Web, performance, configuration, and security considerations are primary issues and need to be evaluated with appropriate testing. Often, legacy systems are integrated into a deployment and the developer needs to test for the ORB's ability to pass specialized objects, such as RogueWave Objects, or access wrapped legacy databases.

3. Conclusions

This paper described enterprise CORBA, specifically with regard to the performance, scalability, reliability, and interoperability requirements for such scale of deployment. Design guidelines for testing have been presented and a survey of the literature pertaining to such testing, as performed by eminent researchers in the field has also been presented. The findings of this research will be of interest to both vendors and consumers of CORBA technology today. These are:

- Accurate portrayal of fingerprint use cases of the intended target distributed architecture.
- Extensive testing through pilot studies to identify bottlenecks in the application layers versus the middleware/ORB communication layers.
- Executing stress tests in representative simulated environments.
- Use of effective, industry-wide accepted third party testing tools, e.g. LoadRunner®, Purify®, ClearTest®.
- Seek to provide normalized benchmarks for customer.
- Perform statistical analysis on gathered data and extract empirical guidelines from that analysis to be able to present the customer with a predictable model of the resultant system.
- Verify that the load levels simulated are truly representative. Identify ORB performance envelope relative to these loads.
- Seek to identify and characterize observed anomalies in test data collected from pilot studies. Aim to solve them or inform the customer of their possible adverse affects such as multithreading.

Acknowledgements

We would like to acknowledge the assistance of all the staff of Expersoft Corporation. Special thanks goes to Susan W. Gallagher, Joey Garon, Scott Herscher, Gail Slemon, and Ernest Tomlinson.

Note: Tradmarks referenced in this article are the property of their respective owners.

References

[1] M. Henning and S. Vinoski, "Advanced CORBA programming with C++," Addison Wesley Longman, 1999.

[2] "The Common Object Request Broker: Architecture and Specification", 2.2 edition, 1998, http://www.omg.org/library/documentation.html .

[3] Distributed Systems Research Group, "CORBA Comparison Project", Charles University, Prague, June, 1998.

[4] Object Management Group, "ORBOS Platform Task Force Benchmark RFI", OMG document bench/98-05-02, ftp://ftp.omg.org, 1998

[5] A. Gokhale and D. Schmidt, "Measuring the Performance of Communication Middleware on High-Speed Networks", in Proceedings of SIGCOMM '96, Stanford, CA, Aug. 1996, ACM, pp. 306-317.

[6] A. Gokhale and D. Schmidt, "Measuring and Optimizing CORBA Latency and Scalability Over High-speed Networks", in special issue of IEEE Transaction on Computers, Volume 47, No. 4, April, 1998.

[7] D. Schmidt, Washington University, http://siesta.cs.wustl.edu/~schmidt/ACE_wrappers/TAO/performance-tests/Thruput .

[8] A. Buble, P. Tuma, "THROUGHPUT test – sources", http://www.kav.cas.cz/~buble/corba/comp/test/through/src/, 1998.

[9] D. Schmidt, Washington University, http://siesta.cs.wustl.edu/~schmidt/ACE_wrappers/TAO/performance-tests/Cubit .

[10] P. Carando, "Toward the Development of an Object Request Broker Evaluation Instrument," in OOPSLA-96 Workshop, 1996.

[11] J. Lakos, "Large-Scale C++ Software Design", Addison-Wesley, 1996.

[12] F. Plasil, P. Tuma, A. Buble, "CORBA Benchmarking", Charles University, Prague, Oct. 1998.

[13] I. Jacobson, M. Christerson, P. Jonsson and G. Overgaard, "Object-Oriented Software Engineering – a Use Case Driven Approach", Addison-Wesley, 1992.

[14] "The Open Brand for CORBA Program Data Sheet", The Open Group, Oct. 1998

Analysis Techniques for Testing Polymorphic Relationships *

Roger T. Alexander
Software Productivity Consortium
2214 Rock Hill Road
Herndon, VA 20170-4117 USA
email: alexande@software.org

A. Jefferson Offutt
Information and Software Engineering
George Mason University
Fairfax, VA 22030-4444 USA
email: ofut@ise.gmu.edu

Abstract

As we move from developing procedure-oriented to object-oriented programs, the complexity traditionally found in functions and procedures is moving to the connections among components. More faults occur as components are integrated to form higher level aggregates of behavior and state. Consequently, we need to place more effort on testing the connections among components. Although object-oriented technology provides abstraction mechanisms to build components to integrate, it also adds new compositional relations that can contain faults, which must be found during integration testing. This paper describes new techniques for analyzing and testing the polymorphic relationships that occur in object-oriented software. The application of these techniques can result in an increased ability to find faults and overall higher quality software.

KEYWORDS: Integration, Testing, Components, Inheritance, Polymorphism

1: Introduction

A number of researchers have asserted that some traditional testing techniques are not effective for object-oriented software [7, 6]. The emphasis in an object-oriented language is on defining abstractions (e.g. abstract data types) that model concepts relative to some problem and solution domain [10]. These abstractions appear in the language as user-defined types that have both state and behavior. Although abstract data types can help achieve a higher quality design, how we test software may change. A major factor is that shifting from procedure-oriented software to object-oriented software causes us to shift the complexity in the software from residing primarily in the software units, to the way in which we connect software components. Thus, we are finding that we need less emphasis on unit testing and more on integration testing.

Another factor is due to the inherent complexity in the nature of the relationships found in object-oriented languages [4]. The compositional relationships of inheritance and aggregation, combined with the power of polymorphism, makes it harder to detect faults that result from the integration of components. This is because component integration is different in object-oriented languages [3].

The primary distinction between the types of languages discussed in this paper is in the mechanisms used for abstraction. Procedure-oriented languages use procedures and functions as the primary abstraction mechanism. In contrast, both object-based and object-oriented languages use data abstraction as the primary mechanism. In addition, object-oriented languages use the integration mechanism of *inheritance*. New types created by

---

This work is supported in part by the U.S. National Science Foundation under grant CCR-98-04111.

inheritance are *descendants* of the existing type [9]. Inheritance differs from aggregation in that the encapsulation of the inherited type may not be preserved, that is, the new type can have access to the internal representation of the ancestor types.

When combined with inheritance, polymorphism (which requires dynamic binding) can strongly affect component integration. When a call is made to a polymorphic method, which version is executed depends on the type of the object [10]. Thus inheritance and polymorphism provides new forms of integration that must be dealt with when testing objects, neither of which has a procedure-oriented counterpart.

1.1: Testing object-oriented software

This paper presents results from an ongoing research project that has the goal of improving the quality of object-oriented software. This paper presents initial results towards a solution to the problem of finding errors in the polymorphic relationships among integrated components. The general strategy for this solution is to formalize, via new coverage criteria, routine aspects of testing at the integration level. Formal coverage criteria offer the tester ways to decide what test inputs to use during testing, making it more likely that the tester will find any faults in the program and providing greater assurance that the software is of high quality and reliability. Such criteria also provide stopping rules and repeatability.

Unit and module testing (or just unit testing) is the testing of program units and modules independently from the rest of the software. *Integration testing* refers to testing interfaces between units and modules to assure that they have consistent assumptions and communicate correctly [2]. *System testing* is testing applied to an entire integrated system.

Test requirements are specific things that must be satisfied or covered, for example, reaching statements are the requirements for statement coverage, killing mutants are the requirements for mutation, and executing DU pairs are the requirements in data flow testing. A *testing criterion* is a rule or collection of rules that impose requirements on a set of test cases. Test engineers measure the extent to which a criterion is satisfied in terms of *coverage*, which is the percent of requirements that are satisfied.

2: Definitions and Background

The concepts presented in this paper are largely independent of language. However, the examples, terminology, and many of the specifics by necessity must be related to one or more languages. We choose Java, and try to point out where the rules would change for other languages.

The fundamental building block in object-oriented programming is the *class*, which is the mechanism by which new types are defined. A class encapsulates state information in a collection of variables, referred to as *state variables*, and also has a set of behaviors that are represented by a collection of methods that operate on those state variables. A class defines a type that all of its *objects* share.

There are two types of relationships that can be used to compose class types to form new types. The first of these, *aggregation*, is the traditional notion of one type containing instances of another type as part of the its internal state representation. The second form of compositional relationship is inheritance. Inheritance allows the representation of one type to be defined in terms of the representation of a set of other types. When this occurs, the type being defined is said to inherit the properties of its ancestors (that is, behavior and state). The definition of the ancestors becomes part of the definition of the new descendant type.

2.1: Polymorphism and dynamic binding

Polymorphism permits variable instances to be bound to references of different types according to the structure of the inheritance hierarchy. *Dynamic binding* permits different method implementations to execute depending upon the actual type of an instance that is bound to a particular reference; this actual type is independent of its declared type [10].

2.2: Coupling-based testing

The work in this paper is based on previous work by Jin and Offutt [8]. They presented an approach to integration testing of procedure-oriented software that is based on coupling relationships among procedures.

Coupling was originally proposed to measure design [5, 11], and the original papers presented up to twelve various types of coupling in lists that were ordered in terms of severity. For testing, only three unordered types are needed: *parameter coupling, shared data coupling*, and *external device coupling*. Parameter couplings occur whenever one procedure passes parameters to another. Similarly, shared data couplings occur when two procedures reference the same global variable. Finally, external device couplings occur when two procedures access the same external storage device.

Jin and Offutt's approach requires that programs execute from each definition of a variable in a caller to a call site, and then to the uses of the corresponding formal arguments in the called procedure. The execution path from the definition to the use must be *definition-clear*, that is, the variable must not be redefined along the path. The underlying idea is that to have a high degree of confidence in the resulting software, all of the definitions of variables in one procedure must be correctly used in the called procedures. This approach is called *coupling-based testing* (CBT).

3: Handling Polymorphism and Inheritance

This paper extends the previous work in coupling-based testing by using coupling to detect the faults that result from the polymorphic relationships among components in an object-oriented program. This is done by first extending the CBT coupling path definitions to allow for the additional relationships in object-oriented programs. This requires the definitions for all forms of coupling-defs, coupling-uses, and external references to be modified. Next, a set of techniques and formalisms are defined to test object-oriented coupling relationships. Finally these techniques and formalisms are used to define a set of test adequacy criteria.

3.1: Coupling in the presence of polymorphism

In the following definitions, o is an identifier whose type is a *reference to an instance* of a class. A reference points to a memory location that contains an instance (value) of some type. The reference o can only refer to instances whose actual instantiated types are either the base type of o or a descendant of o's type. The instance referenced by o is indicated by o_r.

Programmers can define new types in procedural languages such as C and Pascal and object-based languages such as Ada 83 and Modula-2. Strongly typed object-oriented languages such as Java, C++, and Ada 95 also allow new types, but programmers can go further by grouping user defined types into *families* of types. All members of a given type family share a common behavior, which allows instances of any member of a type family to be freely substituted for an instance of any other member. Type families are created by utilizing inheritance and polymorphism.

Every type definition (i.e. a class definition) defines a type family. Members of the family include the base type that defines the family, and all types that are descendants of the base type. Figure 1(a) illustrates this with four type families, each defined by one of the classes in the hierarchy.

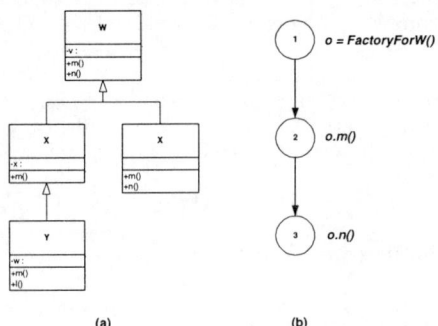

(a)   (b)

Figure 1. (a) Sample Class Diagram (b) Sample Control Flow Fragment

In OO languages, method calls can occur in two circumstances: (1) with respect to some instance, or (2) where there is no instance. Instance methods are called with respect to instance variables, and *class methods* have no instance. Instance methods can make the instance *explicit*, as in $o.m()$, or *implicit*, as in $p()$. For the call $o.m()$, $m()$ executes in **the context of the instance that is bound to the reference** o. For a shorthand convenience, we say that $m()$ executes in the context of o, or o is $m()$'s instance context.

For the call to $p()$, there must be an implicit object reference. That is, p must appear in the program text of a method that was called through an explicit instance (e.g. $o.m()$), and p must be defined in the same class with o. Java and C++ allow the implicit object to be referred to with the keyword "*this*".

An object (instance) o_r is defined (i.e. assigned a value) when one of the variables of the object is defined. An *indirect definition*, or *i-def*, occurs when a method m defines one of o_r's variables. Similarly, an *indirect use* (*i-use*) occurs when m references the value of one of o_r's variables.

Again, consider the class diagram shown in Figure 1a. Assume that W includes a method *FactoryForW()* that returns an instance of W. Figure 1b shows a control flow fragment, with an instance of W bound to o. This is a local definition of the object reference o that results from the call to the method *FactoryForW()*.

When discussing the indirect definitions and uses that can occur at call sites through object references, we must consider not just the syntactic call that is made, but all of the methods that can potentially execute. Because of polymorphism and dynamic binding, this depends on the type of the instance that is bound to the object reference. To analyze this, we introduce the term satisfying set:

Definition 1 *The **satisfying set** of a call to a method m through an object reference o contains all methods that override m, plus m itself.*

Thus, when considering the set of indirect definitions or indirect uses that can occur at a call site, it is first necessary to determine the set of methods that can satisfy the call. For each such method, identify all state variables that are defined and used. The result is the set of *definitions* and *uses* for each satisfying method. Returning again to Figures 1a and

1b, the *i-def* set for the call at node 2 is the following set of ordered pairs:

$$i\_def\ (2, o_r, m)\ =\ \{(W :: m, \{W_r.v\}),\ (X :: m, \{W_r.v, X_r.x\}),$$
$$(Y :: m, \{W_r.v, Y_r.w\}),\ (Z :: m, \{W_r.v\})\} \tag{1}$$

Each pair indicates a satisfying method s for m and the corresponding set of state variables that s defines. In this example, $X::m$ defines state variables v and x contained in classes W and X.

As Table ?? shows, the corresponding *i-use* set for node 2 is the empty set, as none of the satisfying methods for m reference any state variable. However, considering node 3, Table ?? shows that there are two methods that satisfy the call to $o.n()$ that have non-empty *i-use* sets (but their *i-def* sets are empty), which yields the following *i-use* set:

$$i\_use\ (3, o_r, n)\ =\ \{(W :: n, \{W_r.v\}),\ (Z :: m, \{W_r.v\})\} \tag{2}$$

3.2: Differences in coupling paths in OO programs

When polymorphism is used, it is difficult for programmers to keep track of which methods are called, and if not careful, it is easy to allow data flow anomalies and other integration faults to creep into the implementation. From a coupling and integration perspective, the two primary issues are determining what calls can be executed in the presence of inheritance and polymorphism, and what effects the calls have on the corresponding state space.

Alexander has analyzed how method calls are made in object-oriented languages and has identified twelve cases that must be considered when analyzing coupling paths [1]. The twelve cases can be partitioned into three categories. Category I cases are when the call is made in an implicit or explicit instance context. Category II cases are when the call is made in no instance context. Category III cases are when the call is made in no instance context, but there polymorphism may be involved. Category II cases are not effected by inheritance or polymorphism and are handled by the original CBT definitions. Category I and Category III cases require extensions to the definitions and additional analysis techniques. Space does not allow a detailed analysis of each of these cases, they appear in the technical report [1].

4: Object-oriented Coverage Definitions

This section describes extensions to coupling path definitions that are necessary to support object-oriented languages. Section 4.1 provide additional coupling definitions necessary to account for the structural and semantic peculiarities of object-oriented languages. Section 4.2 introduces the definition of a *coupling sequence* and associated concepts for understanding coupling paths with object-oriented programs. Section 4.3 describes coupling paths that result from indirect definitions and uses of state variables through an instance context. Section 4.4 extends the description of instance coupling paths to account for the possible presence of polymorphic method calls. Section 4.5 briefly discusses considerations for coupling-based testing criteria for object-oriented programs.

4.1: Extended coupling definitions

The original CBT definitions must be modified in a number of ways to account for the various calling contexts that occur in object-oriented programs. In the following definitions, m refers to a program unit, including methods that appear in class definitions. V_m is the set of variables that are referenced by m, and N_m the set of nodes in m.

defs (i) is the set of variables that are defined at node i, and *uses (j)* is the set of nodes that are used at node j. A *def_clear_path (m, i, j, v)* returns true if there is a definition-clear path from node i to j with respect to v, where i, $j \in N_m$. *first (p)* is the first node in path p and *last (p)* is the last node. *paths (i, j, m)* is the set of paths that start at node i and that end on node j, where $i, j \in N_m$.

entry (m) is the entry node of method m, and *exit (m)* is the exit node of m. *signature (m, n)* returns true if the signature of method m matches that of n. *overrides (o, m, p)* is true if method m overrides n, where *class (n)* = *class (o)* $\wedge$ *class (m)* $\in$ *family (class (o))* $\wedge$ *signature (m, n)*.

class (m) is the class that contains the definition of m, and *class (o)* is the class that is the declared type of object reference o. *family (c)* is the set of classes that belong to the type family specified by class c. Note that $c \in family\ (c)$. *state_vars (c)* is the set of state variables that directly or indirectly comprise the state space of class c. *instance (t)* is a function that returns an instance of type t.

i_defs (m) is the set of variables in the state space of the class containing m that are indirectly *defined* by a call to m made through some instance context. Formally:

$$i\_defs\ (m) = \{v \in state\_vars\ (class\ (m)) \mid \exists j \in N_m \bullet v \in defs\ (j)\}$$

i_uses (m) is the set of variables in the state space of the class containing m that are indirectly *used* by a call to m made through some instance context. Formally:

$$i\_uses\ (m) = \{v \in state\_vars\ (class\ (m)) \mid \exists j \in N_m \bullet v \in uses\ (j)\}$$

4.2: Coupling sequences

Coupling sequences are pairs of method calls made within the body of a specific method f and are made through a common instance context accessed through an object reference o. Further, there is at least one coupling path between the two methods with respect to some commonly defined and used state variable. An example is illustrated in Figure 2. As shown, method f contains a coupling sequence $s_{j,k}$ that starts at node j with the call to $o.m$ (the *antecedent method*) and extends through paths that end at node k where the sequence ends with the call to $o.r$ (the *consequent method*). The nodes containing the antecedent method and consequent method are referred to as the *antecedent node* and *consequent node*, respectively. Note that there is at least one path between the call sites that is definition clear with respect to o and to those indirect definitions made in the antecedent method that have corresponding indirect uses in the consequent method. Such paths are referred to as *transmission paths*.

A particular coupling sequence $s_{j,k}$ is with respect to a set of state variables that are defined by the antecedent method and subsequently use by the consequent method. This set of variables is referred to as the *coupling set* $\Theta_{s_{j,k}}$ of $s_{j,k}$, and each member of this set is a *coupling variable*. The coupling set for the sequence $s_{j,k}$ shown in Figure 2 is:

$$\Theta_{s_{j,k}} = \{class(o)::v\}$$

That is, $\Theta_{s_{j,k}}$ contains exactly those state variables referenced through o that are defined by the antecedent method and used by the consequent method in the coupling sequence $s_{j,k}$.

A coupling sequence consists of three parts, each consisting of a distinct set of path segments defined with respect to the elements of $\Theta_{s_{j,k}}$. These segments are used to generate the set of coupling paths for $s_{j,k}$. The following sections describe each of these sets in detail.

4.2.1: I-def paths

For a given coupling path in the coupling sequence $s_{j,k}$, there are a set of paths in the antecedent method that begin at nodes that have *last-definitions-before-return* of the

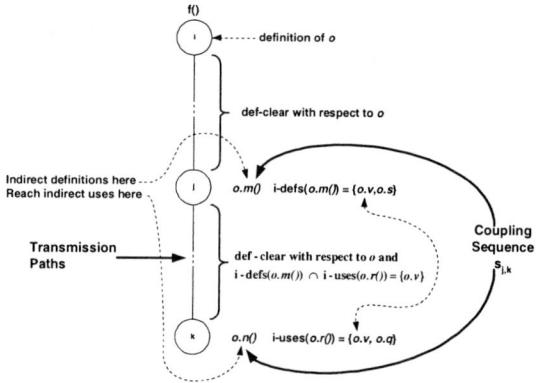

Figure 2. Example Coupling Sequence $s_{j,k}$

variables contained in the coupling set $\Theta_{s_{j,k}}$. For each such node l, the path to $exit(m)$ is definition clear with respect to the corresponding coupling variable defined at l. These paths constitute the *indirect-def path set* (or *i-def-path-set*) of the coupling sequence. Each of these paths is referred to as an *indirect definition path* (or *i-def-path*). Formally:

$$
\begin{aligned}
i\_def\_paths(c, m, V) \;=\; & \{(i, exit(c::m)) \mid i \in N_{c::m} \bullet \\
& (\exists v \;\in\; V \bullet v \in defs(i)) \wedge \\
& v \;\in\; state\_vars(c) \wedge \\
& def\_clear\_path(c::m, i, exit(c::m), v))\}
\end{aligned} \tag{3}
$$

where c is the class, m is either defined or inherited by c, and $V = i\_defs(o, m) \cap i\_uses(o, n)$.

4.2.2: I-use paths

The *indirect-use path set* (or *i-use-path-set*) of the coupling sequence $s_{j,k}$ is the set of paths that are definition clear with respect to the particular coupling variable used at j. That is, the set of paths in the consequent method r that begin at $entry(r)$ and end at a node $j \in N_r$ such that j has a *first-use-in-callee* of a variable in the coupling set $\Theta_{s_{j,k}}$

$$
\begin{aligned}
i\_use\_paths(c, r, V) \;=\; & \{(entry(c::r), j) \mid j \in N_{c::r} \bullet \\
& (\exists v \;\in\; V \bullet v \in uses(j)) \wedge \\
& v \;\in\; state\_vars(c) \wedge \\
& def\_clear\_path(c \;:\; :r, extry(c::r), j, v))\}
\end{aligned}
$$

where c and V are as defined in equation (3), and r is a method that is defined or inherited by c.

4.2.3: Transmission paths

For a given coupling sequence $s_{j,k}$, there is some set of paths T that connect the antecedent node m and the consequent node r, such that each $t \in T$ is definition clear with respect to $i\_def\_path\_set(m) \cap i\_use\_path\_set(r)$. This set of paths is referred to as the *transmission path set* (or *t-path-set*) of $s_{j,k}$, and each t is a transmission path (*t-path*) with respect to a specific coupling variable in $\Theta_{s_{j,k}}$. These paths transmit the value of a coupling variable from the defining method to the using method. Formally:

$$
\begin{aligned}
t\_paths(f, j, k, o, V) \ = \ & \{p \in paths(j, k, f) \mid j, k \in N_f \bullet \\
& def\_clear\_path(f, first(p), last(p), o) \wedge \\
\exists v \ \in \ & V \bullet def\_clear\_path(f, first(p), last(p), v)\}
\end{aligned}
$$

where f is the calling method, j and k are the antecedent and consequent nodes, respectively, o is the object reference that defines the instance context of coupling sequence $s_{j,k}$ appearing in f, and V is as defined in equation (3).

4.3: Instance coupling paths

From a testing perspective, we are interested in all of the indirect definitions that can reach indirect uses with respect to a particular instance context. Thus, we desire to identify all *instance coupling paths* that extend from a node containing a *last-def-before-return* in an antecedent method to a node in a consequent method that contains a *first-use-in-callee* with respect to the coupling variable of interest. We form these instance coupling paths by taking the cross product of the *i-def path set*, *t-path set*, and *i-use path set* for a particular coupling sequence. Formally,

$$
\begin{aligned}
InstanceCouplingPaths(f, j, k, o, m, n) \ = \ & \{(d, t, u) \bullet & (4) \\
d \ \in \ & i\_def\_paths(class(o), m, V) \wedge \\
t \ \in \ & t\_paths(f, j, k, o, V) \wedge \\
u \ \in \ & i\_use\_paths(class(o), m, V)\}
\end{aligned}
$$

where $V = i\_defs(o, m) \cap i\_uses(o, n)$, f is the calling method, $s_1, s_2 \in N_f$, o is the object reference that defines the instance context, and $m, n \in class(o)$.

4.4: Polymorphic coupling paths

The instance coupling paths described in section 4.3 do not take into account the possibility of polymorphic behavior resulting from dynamic variation of types that can be bound to an object reference. With the possibility of polymorphic behavior, a given instance coupling results in one path set for each member of the associated type family. The size of these sets is determined by the number of overridden methods within a given type, either defined directly or inherited from another type. Pragmatically, this has the potential to result in a combinatorial explosion of path sets. The number of path sets is a function of the depth and breadth of the inheritance relations. However, as an optimization to reduce the number of sets, those types that do not have overriding methods will have an empty type set. This is possible since any coupling path that could be executed through the type will necessarily appear in the path sets of other ancestor types that are members of the same type family.

To see an example of polymorphic coupling paths, consider the class hierarchy shown in Figure 3a. This hierarchy forms a type family with respect to class A, the root of the hierarchy. Instances of every class in this family can be used anywhere that an instance of A is required. Because of this, the actual execution path resulting from a given method call can vary depending upon the actual type of the instance context, which results in different indirect coupling paths.

To see this, consider the method control flow fragment shown in Figure 3b that shows method $F::a$ containing call sites at nodes j, k, and l where method calls are made in the context of the instance bound to o. The methods that actually execute for each of these calls, shown in Figure 4, are dependent upon the actual type of the instance that is bound to o through the assignment at node i. Since the declared type of o is A, any instance whose type is a member of the type family defined by A may be bound to o. Thus, instances of any of the classes shown in Figure 3a may used. When o is bound to an instance of A, the method calls at nodes j, k, and l result in the execution of $A::m$, $A::p$, and $A::r$, respectively. When the instance is of type B, the call at node k results in the execution of overriding method p defined in a class. Since B does not override any other method defined by A, the calls at j and l result in the execution of $A::m$ and $A::r$, respectively. Similar reasoning applies when the instance bound to o is an instance of class C or D, but with overriding methods for m and r, respectively.

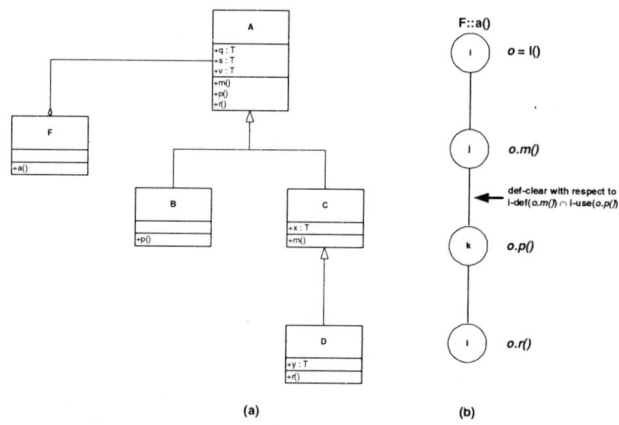

(a)   (b)

Figure 3. (a) Sample Class Diagram (b) Control Flow Fragment for Method $F::a$

To determine the instance coupling paths for a polymorphic call site, it is necessary to consider all of the coupling paths that could possibly result. This is accomplished by considering all of the possible types that the object reference providing the instance context of a call can take on. Determining this is simply a matter of examining the inheritance hierarchy whose root is the declared type of the object reference, and then identifying the set of descendant types D. Sets of instance coupling paths are then computed for each element of D. Formally, using equation (4), the maximal set of instance coupling paths is:

$$PolyCouplingPath\,(f, j, k, o, m, n) = \bigcup_c InstanceCouplingPaths\,(f, j, k, instance(c), m, n)$$

where $c \in family(class(o))$.

Each path set generated from a class c represents those coupling paths that would exist if the dynamic type of the instance bound to the object is an instance of c.

4.5: Coupling criteria

Each coupling path represents a semantic dependency between two methods for a specific instance of a type with respect to a specific state variable. The significance of these paths

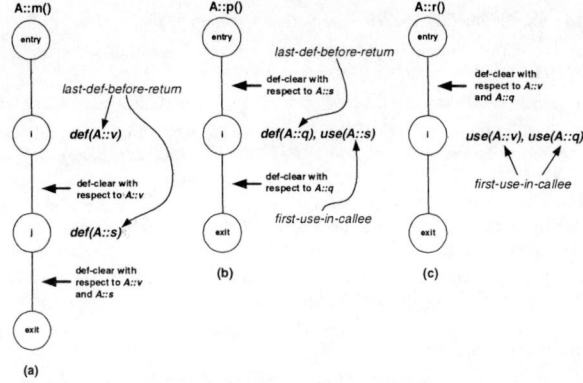

Figure 4. Control Flow Fragments for Methods $A::m$, $A::p$, **and** $A::r$

is that they represent connections among components that define behavior and state and a way for methods to interact. From a testing perspective, we want to identify faults that hide within these connections. The next focus of our research is to take the extended coupling definitions and derive test adequacy criteria that are practical and effective for object-oriented programs. We envision that these criteria will exist in a subsumptive hierarchy similar to the traditional data flow test adequacy criteria, but structured differently to account for the effects of inheritance and polymorphism.

5: Conclusions

This paper has introduced a new integration analysis and testing technique for object-oriented software. This technique is based on previous work for procedure-oriented software called coupling-based testing (CBT). Analysis was presented that showed how object-oriented software differs from procedure-oriented software, and the specific ways in which the CBT technique does not suffice for object-oriented software. This analysis was used to construct new definitions to analyze coupling relationships among OO software components. Specifically, the traditional notion of software coupling has been updated to apply to object-oriented software, handling the relationships of aggregation, inheritance and polymorphism. This allows the introduction of a new integration analysis and testing technique for object-oriented software, object-oriented coupling-based testing (OOCBT). OOCBT can benefit practitioners who are performing integration testing on object-oriented software.

Future plans are to develop algorithms for analyzing the relationships among object-oriented software components, build a proof-of-concept coverage analysis tool for this OOCBT, and to use the tool to empirically evaluate the method.

References

[1] Roger T. Alexander. Testing the polymorphic relationships of object-oriented components. Technical Report ISE-TR-99-02, Department of Information and Software Engineering, George Mason University, February 1999. http://www.ise.gmu.edu/techrep.

[2] Boris Beizer. *Software Testing Techniques*. Van Nostrand Reinhold, New York, New York, 2nd edition, 1990.

114

[3] Edward V. Berard. *Essays on Object-Oriented Software Engineering*, volume 1. Prentice Hall, 1993.

[4] Robert V. Binder. Testing object-oriented software: A survey. *Journal of Software Testing, Verification & Reliability*, 6(3/4):125–252, September/December 1996.

[5] L. L. Constantine and E. Yourdon. *Structured Design*. Prentice-Hall, Englewood Cliffs, NJ, 1979.

[6] Donald G. Firesmith. Testing object-oriented software. In *Eleventh International Conference on Technology of Object-Oriented Languages and Systems (TOOLS USA, '93)*, pages 407–426. Prentice-Hall, Englewood Cliffs, NJ, 1993.

[7] Jane Huffman Hayes. Testing of object-oriented programming systems (OOPS): A fault-based approach. In E. Bertino and S. Urban, editors, *Object-Oriented Methodologies and Systems*, volume LNCS 858. Springer-Verlag, 1994.

[8] Zhenyi Jin and A. Jefferson Offutt. Coupling-based criteria for integration testing. *The Journal of Software Testing, Verification, and Reliability*, 8(3):133–154, September 1998.

[9] Bertrand Meyer. *Introduction to the Theory of Programming Languages*. Prentice Hall International Series In Computer Science. Prentice Hall, 1990.

[10] Bertrand Meyer. *Object-Oriented Software Construction*. Prentice Hall, Englewood Cliffs, New Jersey, 2nd edition, 1997.

[11] A. J. Offutt, M. J. Harrold, and P. Kolte. A software metric system for module coupling. *The Journal of Systems and Software*, 20(3):295–308, March 1993.

Technical Papers

Java 1

When to trust mobile objects: access control in the Jini™ Software System

Charles Crichton, Jim Davies, and Jim Woodcock[†]

Oxford University Computing Laboratory
Parks Road, Oxford, OX1 3QD, UK

Abstract

Future developments in computing, and in consumer electronics, will involve a considerable degree of convergence: applications will work together to locate and provide services. If this convergence is to be implemented successfully, then a shared model for reliable service provision is required.

The recently-released Jini™ Software System (1.0) is an attempt to meet this requirement through object-orientation. Based entirely upon existing Java™ 2 technology, Jini is a set of protocols and programming models for peer-to-peer service provision using downloaded code and remote method invocation.

This paper examines the way in which the Jini Software System will be used. It shows that the existing mechanisms for access control and secure operation provided by Java may prove inadequate in a Jini environment: a Jini-enabled device will be vulnerable to attack from its peers. Similar problems may be encountered in other, related technologies, such as Enterprise Java Beans.

An account of the Jini technology is followed by an exploration of the inadequacies and vulnerabilities; concrete examples are provided to illustrate the possible attacks. The paper ends by showing how the existing specification may be enhanced to produce a secure system without significantly reducing either functionality or flexibility.

1   Introduction

As computing devices become more sophisticated and powerful, we may expect to see a greater degree of convergence: devices and applications will be able to work together to provide a wide variety of services, without any need for manual installation or configuration of hardware and software.

If this convergence is to be implemented successfully, then a shared model for service provision is required. The plug-and-play standard for personal computers is a simple example of such a model: new devices are designed to be detected by a *plug-and-play bios*; the operating system will then locate a suitable driver; applications can then take advantage of the service that the product provides.

The Jini Software System [4] is intended to take this process one step further. Based entirely upon existing Java technology [6], Jini is a set of protocols and models for service provision using downloadable code and remote method invocation. In a Jini system, devices

---

[†]mail: Charles.Crichton@comlab.ox.ac.uk, phone: +44 1865 283508, fax: +44 1865 273839

can provide their own drivers, passing them directly to any applications that wish to use them.

Once a Jini-enabled device has been connected to a network, it can automatically locate and use whatever services are available. For example, a Jini-enabled camera would be able to locate a Jini-enabled printer, download the associated software, and use that software to access the printer, all of this without the need for human intervention.

In the Jini system, the concept of service extends far beyond the notion of a device driver. Indeed, anything that can be implemented in Java can be provided as a service in Jini. All that is required is an interface definition, a collection of classes, and a serialized object. The Jini specification envisages services as varied as transaction management, persistent storage, and remote processing.

Downloading foreign objects and classes is a hazardous activity: the foreign code could corrupt data, export secrets, or prevent other code from operating correctly. Java was designed to cope with downloaded code, and has a fine-grained system of security management, examined thoroughly in [1]. Access to methods is granted on a class-by-class basis, and a call from an untrusted class will result in a security exception.

However, the existing implementation of security management is not enough to guarantee the security of Jini-enabled devices. The procedures for downloading objects and classes require extension and modification. At present, a Jini-enabled device may be forced—quite unnecessarily—to trust in the good intentions of others.

In this paper, we explain why the existing provision for security may prove inadequate. We use a number of simple examples to illustrate the need for a more restrictive approach to downloadable code, and demonstrate how this can be achieved without any significant reduction in either functionality or flexibility.

The paper begins with an introduction to the technology: the Jini system and the relevant features of Java. In Section 3, we demonstrate that the existing security is inadequate, and explain briefly how the various problems could be resolved. In Section 4, we discuss alternative approaches to the construction of secure Jini Systems. The paper ends with a brief summary and a short bibliography.

2   The Jini Software System

We will begin with a brief description of the Java 2 technology employed in the implementation of Jini. We will then outline the core aspects of the Jini system and present a brief example of Jini lookup in practice.

2.1   Java technology

The Jini Software System relies upon four important aspects of Java technology: remote method invocation, serialization and marshalling, jar archives, and security policies.

The first aspect facilitates communication between objects on different machines. The second makes it possible to transfer objects from one machine to another. The third provides a simple mechanism for transporting class files, and the fourth provides a mechanism for restricting the behaviour of downloaded objects.

2.1.1   Remote Method Invocation

Remote Method Invocation (RMI) [5] allows an object to be shared by two or more virtual machines. It provides facilities for the creation of surrogate stub objects on remote machines; these stubs have the same functionality as the original object, but that functionality is implemented through remote methods.

Each stub has the ability to communicate with the original object. A method call on a stub will result in a matching method call on the object: argument data is passed from the stub to the object, which is still on the original machine, and any results are passed back. To facilitate this transfer of information, a *marshalling* facility is provided, based upon *serializable* objects.

2.1.2   Serialization, and marshalling

Any object that implements the Java *Serializable* interface can be serialized: converted into a stream of bits which can be stored locally or passed to a remote machine. Naturally, an object can be deserialized only if its original class, or a suitable substitute, has been loaded into the local machine.

If a serialized object is of an unknown class, then additional class files must be obtained before deserialization can begin. To facilitate this, Java 2 allows a serialized object to be annotated with a reference to a codebase: a collection of code and data available via http. The annotated, serialised object is called a *marshalled object*, and may itself be serialized for storage or transmission. When a marshalled object arrives, any unknown class files in the codebase will be downloaded before the contents are deserialized.

2.1.3   Jar files

The Jar package provides facilities for handling Jar files: zip archives with an optional manifest file. These archives are used to transport class files and data from one machine to another. The manifest file is used to hold meta-information: files listed here may be signed to prevent tampering or falsification.

In addition, the manifest may record that certain packages are to be *sealed*. If a package is recorded as sealed, class files in that package can be loaded only from the current archive. If a class is loaded from one archive when its package is sealed in another, a security exception will be thrown.

2.1.4   Security policies

Any class loaded into a machine can be made the subject of a *security policy*. Whenever an object of that class calls a method that has been identified as security-critical, this policy is consulted. If the class has not been granted permission for such a call, a security exception is thrown.

If a class has been signed, then it is made subject to the security policy associated with the matching certificate. Unsigned classes, or classes for which no certificate is held, are loaded subject to the general security policy of the local machine: this is intended to be quite restrictive.

2.2 Jini technology

A Jini system contains a collection of components that interact to provide services: to each other, or to users of the system. The design philosophy of Jini is entirely service-based, to the extent that the Jini architecture specification [4] refers to the components themselves as *services*.

2.2.1 Service items

Before a client can make use of a service, it must obtain an appropriate *service item*: a marshalled object comprising a serialized object and a codebase. Once deserialized, the object will provide the data or functionality required to use the service; if deserialization requires additional classes, they can be obtained from the codebase via http.

2.2.2 Discovery

A collection of Jini services—a Jini *federation*—is dynamically reconfigurable: services may be added or deleted at any time. New services may announce their presence, and take steps to discover what other services are available. Departing services may be replaced as their clients search for alternatives.

This is achieved through the provision of a special type of service: the *lookup* service. If a new service wishes to announce its availability, it sends out a multicast request. When a lookup service receives such a request, it responds with a unicast message containing a lookup service registrar.

2.2.3 Join

After obtaining whatever class files are required from the lookup service, via http, a new service can deserialize the contents of lookup service item: a local proxy for the *service registrar*. Once deserialization has taken place, the new service is then linked to the lookup service via RMI.

By calling a method on the stub object, the new service can send its own service item to the lookup service. This item will provide the data or functionality required to make use of the new service, together with a matching codebase reference. The new service has then *joined* the lookup service.

2.2.4 Lookup

A lookup service stores and forwards service items belonging to other services. A client looking for a new service will employ the same discovery protocol described above: requesting and deserializing a registrar proxy, and obtaining a link to the lookup service. A client can then use this link to ask about services that have already joined the lookup service.

To make use of a new service, the client requests the corresponding service item from the lookup service. It uses the codebase to obtain whatever additional class files are required, and then deserializes the contents. In most cases, this will produce a stub object for the new service; the client is then linked to this new service via RMI.

2.2.5 Leasing

Once linked to a service via RMI, a client can negotiate for a *lease* upon the service; this will allow access to the service for some period of time. This avoids the possibility of a malicious or faulty client monopolising a service indefinitely, and provides a basis for measuring—and charging for—the use of a service.

The Jini system does not prescribe a particular method of managing a lease, but the default solution is to download a lease stub: a proxy for the actual lease object, which remains on the service. Leases can then be managed, and renewed, through an RMI link.

2.2.6 Event notification

An additional component of the Jini model is *event notification*. Clients may leave stub objects on a service to be used in specific circumstances; when used, these objects will send events to the original client, or to a designated third party.

For example, a client that has failed to locate a particular service may leave an event object on a lookup service. If this lookup service subsequently encounters a service that matches the description in the event object, the client will be notified.

2.3 Example

If a Jini-enabled printer is connected to a network, its first action will be to send out a multicast request for lookup services. If there is a lookup service on the network, it will respond with a lookup service item, comprising a serialized service registrar and a reference to a codebase on the lookup server.

To deserialize the contents of the service item, the printer will need to load additional classes. These are stored in a Jar file on an http server associated with the lookup service. Using the codebase reference in the service item, the printer is able to locate and load the classes required: see Figure 1.

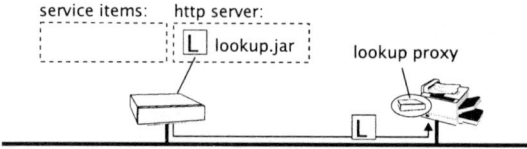

Figure 1. Deserializing a lookup proxy

The printer can use the service registrar proxy to join the lookup service, supplying an appropriate service item via RMI. If a Jini-enabled PDA is then connected, it can discover the lookup service in exactly the same way. Instead of joining, however, it wishes to locate and use a service. Using its new service registrar proxy, the PDA will make a request for a printer service item: see Figure 2.

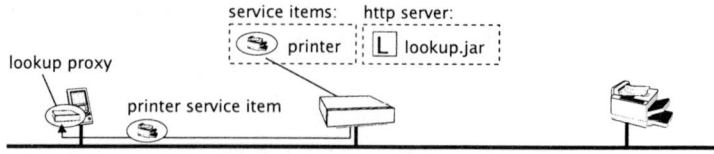

Figure 2. Downloading a printer service item

As the lookup service already has a suitable item, a copy will be passed to the PDA via RMI. The PDA will then deserialize the contents of the item, loading any additional class files from the specified codebase—in this case, a Jar file stored on an http server associated with the printer: see Figure 3.

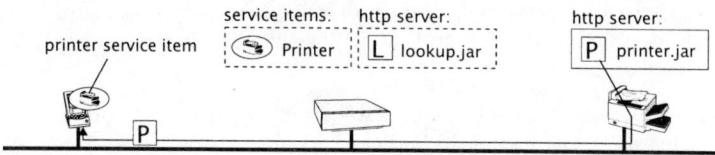

Figure 3. Deserializing the contents

Deserializing the contents of the printer service item will establish an RMI link between the PDA and the printer. The PDA can now negotiate directly to obtain a lease upon the printer service: see Figure 4. The lookup service is no longer required: the PDA can renew the lease by talking directly to the printer.

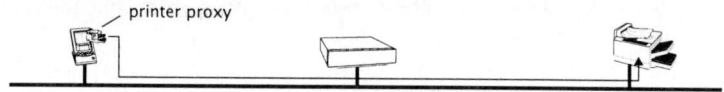

Figure 4. Using the printer service

3   The existing technology is not enough

Any system that admits downloaded code into its run-time environment is vulnerable to attack. The security mechanisms in Java are intended to minimise the possible effects, imposing restrictions upon the access available to downloaded objects and classes. Jini inherits these mechanisms; in this section, we will demonstrate that they are not enough.

In the following, we will use the phrase *trusted code* to refer to signed code for which a certificate exists which will grant certain permissions. *Untrusted code* is unsigned code, or code with a signature that is not recognised. The examples that follow are based upon an internal network, secured behind a firewall that admits only http traffic. Inside the firewall, all devices are initially trustworthy.

3.1   If untrusted code is granted network access

It might seem unlikely that we would intentionally grant network access to untrusted code, but there are ways in which this might occur. Finding that a particular service is not available on the local network, a client might be tempted to look elsewhere. Lookup services can advertise their presence widely, and an external lookup service might be one of the services offered by a lookup service inside the firewall.

To use a lookup service, a client must first obtain its service registrar, and give the deserialized proxy access to the local network. Using an untrusted service registrar is one way of granting network access to a piece of untrusted code; we will now examine the possible consequences.

Problem 1 (Portscan) Untrusted code with local network access can scan local ports. If the code is a registrar proxy, or a stub of a different kind, it can send this information through the firewall. □

Problem 2 (Remote object duplication) Stubs for remote objects are checked against each other using an *equals* methods. Such a check may give a piece of untrusted code a reference to the another remote object; it can then make a serialized copy, and send this copy to an untrusted host.

Remote objects that can be exported in this fashion include service registrars, lease objects, and event listener objects. In each case, the consequences can be disastrous.

- A stolen service registrar can give an untrusted host access to an internal lookup service; the lookup service can then be be used to provide untrusted services; its clients may be misdirected and misinformed.

- A stolen lease stub gives an untrusted host an opportunity to use a protected, internal resource. It may also be able to interfere with any other leases that the client holds: renewing them or cancelling them at will.

- A stolen event listener stub can be used to send a variety of messages to the recipient's event listener. The event mechanism is intended to allow one device to coordinate the actions of a number of others, so a significant degree of manipulation is possible.

□

It is important to note that the *discovery permissions* mechanism provided in Jini is easily bypassed. This is intended to restrict access to lookup services; when an object attempts to contact a particular lookup service, the mechanism checks the associated policy file to see if the service is one of those to which the object has been granted access.

However, a piece of code with network access has no need to use the Jini *lookup discovery* mechanism: it can talk directly to the socket. If it has the IP address of a lookup service, it can contact that service using its own implementation of unicast discovery.

If it does not, then it can bind to the required multicast socket, and broadcast independently of the existing multicast discovery mechanism: there is no limit to the number of multicast sockets that can be bound to a single port. What is more, it can stipulate that the service should reply to another port of its own choosing.

The two problems described above cannot be solved using discovery permissions. The only solution is to ensure that untrusted code has no network access whatsoever.

3.2 If untrusted code is loaded at all

The existing mechanism of security policies, if used properly, can ensure that untrusted code has no direct access to the network. However, there are other ways in which untrusted code can subvert the behaviour of the virtual machine.

Problem 3 (Untrusted service registrar) An untrusted service registrar, denied network access by the access control system, may still be asked to provide services. It may then create an instance of the service being requested, based on trusted code, but with an initial state of its own design.

If the request were for a printer service, for example, then the registrar could create a service item whose codebase points to trusted class file but whose content, when deserialized, turns out to be a stub for an untrusted remote object. This stub could redirect a print job to a host outside the firewall, or subvert the printing service in other ways. □

Problem 4 (Exploiting the RMI class loader) On a Jini-enabled device, the environment of the virtual machine will include an RMI security manager. Once this manager is present, any piece of code can *attempt* to use the RMI class loader by creating a marshalled object and attempting to deserialize it.

This can be done by first creating an array of bytes—in a buffer—that looks just like a serialized, marshalled object, and turning the buffer into a stream. Calling the *readObject* method on the resulting stream will produce a marshalled object of our own design.

We may set the codebase to point to an untrusted host, and encode any data that we wish to send as the class name of the serialized contents. If we call the *get* method of our marshalled object, the RMI class loader will send a request to our untrusted host containing the encoded data.

In this way, a piece of untrusted code may export any information that it has access to. For example, a downloaded stub may serialize and send any stubs that it can reference; the consequences of this are discussed in Problem 2 above. □

Problem 5 (Accessing protected members) A Jini service may need to call another service in order to satisfy its client. If it passes this second service a reference, then it may be giving untrusted code access to its protected members. This is possible whenever the classes associated with the two services are stored in separate Jar files, and the Jar file for the first service is accessible to an untrusted party.

To see how this might occur, consider the example of a database service that calls a graphing service in order to present data to its client. We have only to add our own version of the classes implementing the graphing service to the Jar file for the database service, together with an additional class that claims to be in the same package as the database classes.

If the database service passes the graphing service a reference to an object that it has defined, the additional class can be loaded; it may then access the protected members of that object. Even if the database classes are package-sealed, this will not deter the class loader: the additional class has been stored in the same Jar file. □

All of the problems outlining here can be solved with a simple modification to the class loader mechanism: only those files that have been signed by a trusted party should be loaded; anything else should be ignored. This should apply to *all* files, and not simply those recognised as classes.

3.3   Trusted code, untrusted data

If untrusted code is denied access to the local machine, then all of the problems described above are eliminated. However, it is still possible to affect the behaviour of a client by tampering with the marshalled objects that it downloads.

Problem 6 (Substituting a service item) If an untrusted host has access to a lookup service on the internal network, then it may substitute its own service for one of those offered: it has only to register a new service with the same service ID; the lookup service will then assume that the original service has moved.

The new service item can have the same codebase as the original: every class file downloaded will be properly signed and trusted. However, the contents of the service item may be different; when deserialized, they might produce a stub for a remote object on an untrusted host. The consequences of this have already been described in Problem 3 above.

Note that it is not necessary to *substitute* for an existing service; simply adding a new service will make it available to clients on the internal network. If more than one service matches a request, then a lookup service may provide any of those available: the choice is randomised to provide a degree of load-balancing. □

To solve this problem, we require a mechanism for signing the serialized contents of a marshalled object. It is not necessary, or desirable, to sign the codebase reference. Before such a mechanism can be implemented, the *MarshalledObject* class in the current version of the RMI package must be replaced; it is a final class, and cannot be extended.

4 Secure Jini Systems

Jini is an object-oriented architecture for providing services on dynamically-reconfigurable networks. It exploits the potential of object-orientation to the full, separating the abstract notion of a service from its implementation. The choice of implementation can be delayed until the service is required, and can be revisited at a later date.

Jini-enabled devices can be established with minimal functionality; additional functionality can be added later, automatically, when the need arises. Legacy devices can be Jini-enabled through a proxy; again, object technology is the key. The design of Jini is an excellent model for the network operating system of the future.

However, the security of the Jini system depends upon the security mechanisms provided with Java 2. As we shown above, these prove inadequate when objects are exchanged freely between different virtual machines, and when classes may be obtained from an untrusted source. A secure version of Jini might employ:

- a class loader that loads only those classes that are signed and certified by a trusted party; other data must be discarded;

- a new version of RMI in which the serialized contents of a marshalled object can be signed and certificated.

A secure system for distributing keys and certificates would also be required; this could be provided as a Jini service, with a built-in authentication mechanism. The alternative to this is a system of security policies applied to objects, rather than classes.

Without a suitable set of extensions, the Jini system is not ready for adoption in a supposedly-secure environment. The Jini version of plug-and-play is based around the free exchange of code; without some system of certification, or isolation, a Jini-enabled device will be forced to trust in the good intentions of others.

Sun Microsystems have released a test suite, which can be used to check that a Jini-enabled device will use the various interfaces and components in an appropriate fashion.

An obvious move would be to extend this suite to check that a device has a good sense of its own security: at the very least, it should not grant network access to untrusted code.

5 Conclusion

Jini is an exciting development in distributed, object-oriented computing. Despite inheriting a system of access control and security management from Java, the Jini system is not ready for use in a secure environment: certain extensions are required. The object-oriented nature of Jini means that these extensions would be easy to implement.

In a sense, the existing security fails because it is not object-oriented enough: it works with classes, when it should be working with objects. A class-based approach may be enough for basic Java, but the presence of mobile objects in systems such as Jini and Java Enterprise Beans makes an object-based approach essential.

Acknowledgements

This work was supported by grants from the Defence Evaluation and Research Agency, Malvern, UK. The authors would like to thank Susan Haines, Colin O'Halloran, Tom McCutcheon, and Anthony Smith for their assistance.

References

[1] Gary McGraw and Ed Felton, *Securing Java: Getting down to Business with Mobile Code*, John Wiley & Sons, 1999.

[2] Sun Microsystems, *Jini Lookup Service Specification*, available at http://www.javasoft.com/products/jini/, January 25th 1999.

[3] Sun Microsystems, *Jini Distributed Event Specification*, available at http://www.javasoft.com/products/jini/, January 25th 1999.

[4] Sun Microsystems, *Jini Architecture Specification*, available at http://www.javasoft.com/products/jini/, January 25th 1999.

[5] Sun Microsystems, *Java Remote Method Invocation Specification*, available at http://www.javasoft.com/products/jdk/rmi/, 8th December 1998.

[6] Sun Microsystems, *Java 2 Documentation*, available at http://www.javasoft.com/products/jdk/1.2/, 8th December 1998.

Detecting Evolution Incompatibilities
by Analyzing Java Binaries

Mira Mezini[1], Jens U. Pipka[1,2], Thorsten Dittmar[2], and Wim Boot[2]

[1] Department of Electrical Engineering and Computer Science (FB 12),
University of Siegen, Hölderlinstr. 3, D-57068 Siegen, Germany
Email: {jensuwe, mira}@informatik.uni-siegen.de

[2] Daedalos Consulting GmbH, D-58456 Witten, Germany
Email:{wim.boot, thorsten.dittmar}@daedalos.de

Abstract

Customizing component functionality to application needs generally involves inheritance, known to suffer from the fragile base class problem: changes in a base class may cause preexisting inheritor classes to malfunction, or even become undefined. In this paper, we present a framework for binary detection of such incompatible changes at component (re)integration time. This avoids unexpected erroneous runtime behavior of the integrated components.

1. Introduction

Object-oriented programming is praised for better supporting large-scale engineering of software systems, especially via application framework technology. In order to adapt the semifinished design of a framework for particular application, programmers generally exploit both object composition with forwarding semantics, and inheritance. Inheritance suffers from the *fragile base class problem*. The core of the problem is that current technology only enables the description of usage interfaces; the "contract" between components in an implementation hierarchy is not clearly defined. The implementation of the inheritor component makes assumptions about the implementation of the base component. This might lead to incompatibilities if the implementation structure of the framework changes later, which cannot in general be detected by the compiler.

An example of how changing a base class may affect its subclasses is shown below. It illustrates one of the possible incompatibility types, the so-called *accidentally captured methods* problem [12]. The problem occurs if (a) a new operation is added in the modified base component, and (b) there are inheritors that have already extended the component with an operation which accidentally has the same signature as the operation added in the modified component: the inheritor implementation of the operation may get invoked in new contexts it was not intended to. In our example, the integration of the modified component with the inheritor will result in erroneous instantiation semantics of ExtendedInstanceCounter. This is because ExtendedInstanceCounter::onInstanceCreation() will be invoked twice: (a) in the intended context of ExtendedInstanceCounter(), and (b) accidentally in the context of InstanceCounter() due to the super call within ExtendedInstanceCounter(). This is only one of the possible instances of the fragile base class problem. Descriptions of other instances, such as *unanticipated mutual recursion* or *negation of inheritor specializations* are described in [12, 8, 10]. In [10], the reader can also find instances of the problems that are specific for statically typed languages like Java, which has been ignored by the rest of the literature.

```
// Base:                              Modified Base:
// -----                              --------------
class InstanceCounter {               class InstanceCounter {
    public InstanceCounter() {            public InstanceCounter() {
        instanceCounter += 1; }               onInstanceCreation(); }
    public static int instanceNo() {      protected void onInstanceCreation() {
        return instCounter; }                 instCounter += 1;
    private static int instCounter;           instances.addElement(this); }
}                                         public static int instanceNo() {
                                              return instCounter; }
                                          private static int instCounter;
                                          private static java.util.Vector instances;
                                      }

// Inheritor:
// ----------
class ExtendedInstanceCounter extends InstanceCounter {
  public ExtendedInstanceCounter() { super();
                                     onInstanceCreation(); }
  public void onInstanceCreation() { timestamps.addElement(new Date().getTime()); }
  protected static java.util.Vector timestamps;
}
```

Tackling the fragile base class problem has motivated several works [4, 5, 12, 9, 11, 8]. Most of these works [4, 5, 11, 9] are of a preventive nature: they propagate the design of more disciplined inheritance mechanisms that in certain cases would prevent conflicts from happening. The work presented in this paper is of a more pragmatic nature. It assumes the current state of the art: inheritance implies non-encapsulated components, whose later evolution will very likely be characterized by conflicts with customizations performed prior to the evolution. Consequently, adequate tools are needed to detect evolution incompatibilities and their sources when the modified base component is integrated with existing extensions.

This paper is organized as follows. Section 2 presents the key idea behind the binary analysis approach and a framework for *binary conflict detection* (BCD). Section 3 discusses related work. Section 4 summarizes and discusses areas of future work.

2. A Framework for Binary Conflict Detection (BCD)

Our approach is based on extracting information about the implementation structure – especially about the self-invocation structure – of the involved components before and after the evolution. This information includes superclass relationships, the set of signatures defined in a class, their corresponding method definitions and the set of methods invoked by a method definition via the self-reference. A comparison of the structures before and after the evolution reveals the operations applied to the original base to gain the modified version. The applied operations, in turn, indicate the presence of instances of the fragile base class problem. We extract the needed information by analyzing Java binaries. We advocate binary rather than source code analysis because source code availability is rather unlikely. In addition, source code analysis is difficult for languages with a non trivial block structure, such as Java. It ends up duplicating a good part of the work that is done by the compiler. However, conducting binary analysis implies that component binaries contain enough information about the underlying program and allow inspection of this information. Fortunately, this is the case with Java binaries. This section presents a Java framework that provides binary detection of evolution conflicts for Java components. As shown in Fig. 1, the framework consists of five mostly independent modules.

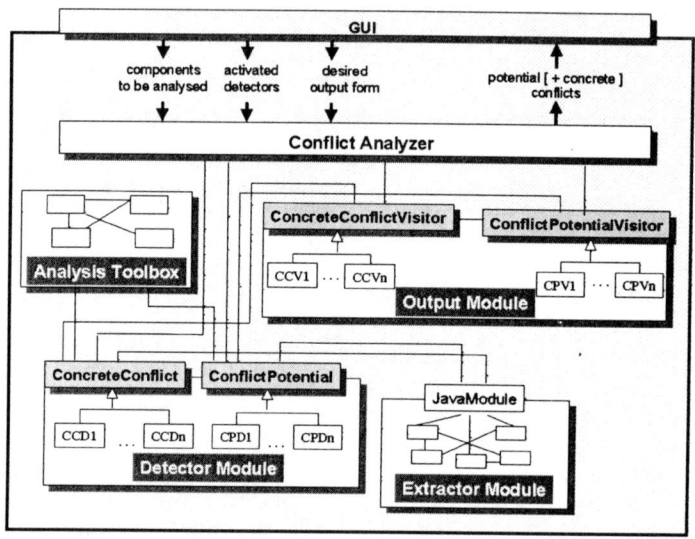

Figure 1. Overview of the Framework Design

2.1. Extractor Module

The responsibility of the *extractor* module is to (a) extract relevant information about the implementation structure of the involved components, Base, ModifiedBase and Inheritor by parsing their corresponding binaries and (b) provide this information in a suitable high-level form to the rest of the framework. This information includes, e.g., the names of the classes in a component, what interfaces are implemented by each class, the methods defined in a class, their self-invocation graph, etc. There are two main elements of the extractor module: (a) a binary parser of Java .class files, and (b) a metalevel infrastructure for representing the extracted information.

The metalevel infrastructure is organized in a similar way as the Java Byte-Code (J-Code). At the top level is the class JavaModule. An instance of JavaModule reifies the relevant information about the implementation of exactly one Java component. It contains a set of ClassDefinitions which in turn contain instances of MethodDefinition, FieldDefinition, etc. The metalevel infrastructure is an extension of the standard Java reflective API (java.lang.reflect). Java's reflective API was not sufficient because it does not provide crucial information needed to detect evolution conflicts, such as information about the protected part of a class's implementation and the self-invocation structure.

The construction of the meta-level infrastructure from Java binaries is realized by a rudimentary decompiler, we have implemented in the class JavaClassParser. Information about a class and the method and field definitions included in it can be extracted directly from Java .class files using the Java virtual machine specification [6]. The information about the self-invocation graph is, on the other hand, not directly available. To extract this information the binary parser simulates the execution of the Java virtual machine: instead of executing the current opcode, the parser evaluates the opcode and eventually corresponding operands, extracting and storing valuable information in respective instances of the metalevel infrastructure.

In order to facilitate accessing the information stored in the JavaModule hierarchy for the rest of the framework, we have applied the *facade pattern* [1]. The class JavaModule plays the role of a facade for the whole metalevel infrastructure, i.e., all relevant access operations are provided at the level of JavaModule.

2.2. Analysis Toolbox

Given the meta-object structures constructed by the extractor module for the Base and ModifiedBase components, the analysis toolbox filters out the difference between them and provides it to the detector module. The toolbox consists of a set of individual tools: a part of the analysis toolbox hierarchy is shown in Fig. 2. The root class AnalysisToolBox, and the individual tools such as MethodDefinitionTools and MethodSignatureTools, are implemented as singleton classes. AnalysisToolBox serves to the rest of the framework as a facade [1]. When requested to analyze the difference between a base and its modification (extractDelta(Base, ModifiedBase)), AnalysisToolBox executes the following loop:

```
public void extractDelta(base, modifiedBase) {
  ClassDefinitionPair[] correspClasses = correspondingClasses(Base, ModifiedBase);
  for (int i = 0; i < correspClasses.length; i++) {
    baseDef = correspClasses[i].base():
    modDef = correspClasses[i].modified();
    String className = correspClasses[i].base().getName();
    ClassDeltas.add(className, ClassTools.analyze(baseDef, modDef));
  } }
```

In response to receiving analyze(base, other), ClassTools invokes extractDelta on each individual tool – its singleton subclasses. All invocations of extractDelta share the same "input parameters", base and other, and store the results in a shared "return value", Delta, a class variable inherited from ClassTools. The overall result of AnalysisToolBox' extractDelta is ClassDeltas – a hash table indexed by classes in the original component; the value associated to a class is a representation of the changes of the class during the modification. For illustration, determining the Base/ModifiedBase delta for the example in Sec. 1 is schematically shown in Fig. 3. The difference between the two versions of InstanceCounter stored in delta consists of (a) the added method onInstanceCreation and (b) the added invocation to onInstanceCreation within the preexisting constructor InstanceCounter().

2.3. Detector Module

There is a pair of detectors for each conflict type: a conflict potential detector (CPD) and a concrete conflict detector (CCD). A CPD examines the Base–ModifiedBase delta constructed by the analysis toolbox, for changes that carry a conflict potential. The abstract class ConflictPotential provides the interface and partial implementation for all conflict potential detectors. Each CPD class implements the abstract detection interface for

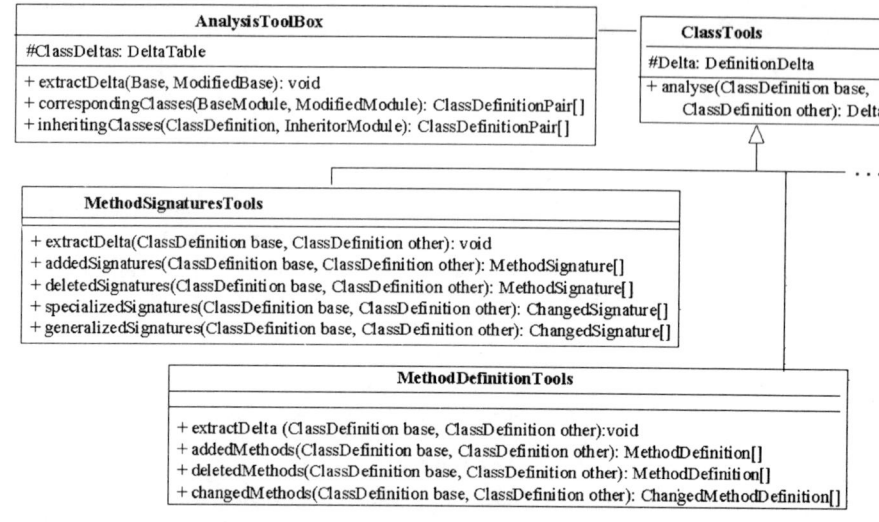

Figure 2. Analysis ToolBox

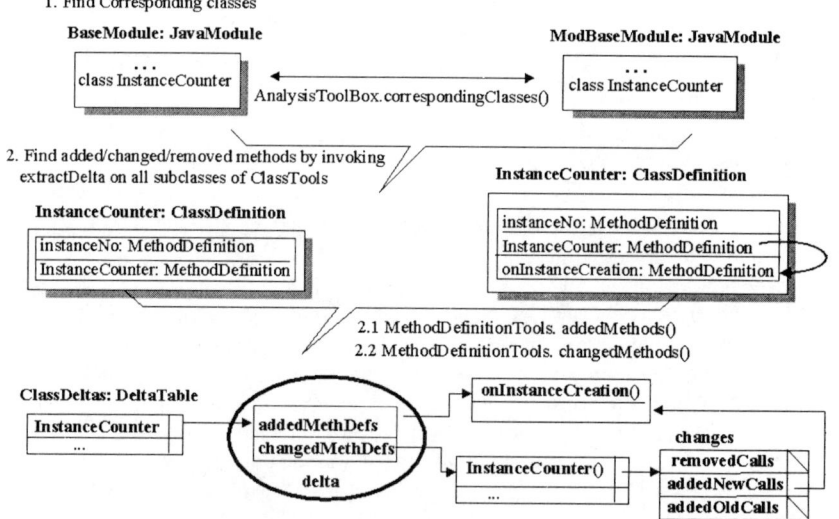

Figure 3. An Example for Delta Extraction

a particular conflict type, specifically interpreting the delta information stored in Analysis-ToolBox. In Fig. 4, the collaboration diagram for the CPD for the accidentally captured method conflict – the conflict illustrated by the example in Sec.1 – is given for illustration. There is a potential for this kind of conflict if (a) there are new operations implemented in the modified module and (b) the implementation of previously existing operations has been changed to invoke the added operation. The overall result of the potential conflict detection is a set of ConflictPotentialData objects.

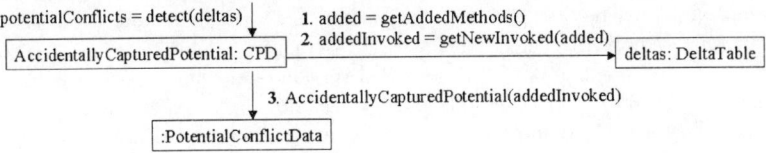

Figure 4. Collaboration Diagram for the Accidentally Captured Methods CPD

Whether changes that carry a conflict potential lead to an actual conflict depends on the implementation of individual inheritors. For this reason, in the second step, the CCD (concrete conflict detector) corresponding to a CPD analyzes InheritorModule with respect to the potential conflicts found by the first step. The BCD framework provides the abstract class ConcreteConflict which lays down the interface for the implementation of any concrete conflict detector. A CCD is initialized with the corresponding conflict potential data and the Inheritor component. Based on this information, it finds out, specifically for the conflict type it detects, whether conflict potentials are actually conflicts in the context of the given inheritor. For storing the result, the framework provides the base class ConcreteConflictData that can be derived to store the conflict information that is specific for an implemented conflict situation. For illustration, the actions taken by the concrete conflict detector for the example conflict from Sec. 1 are shown in Fig. 5.

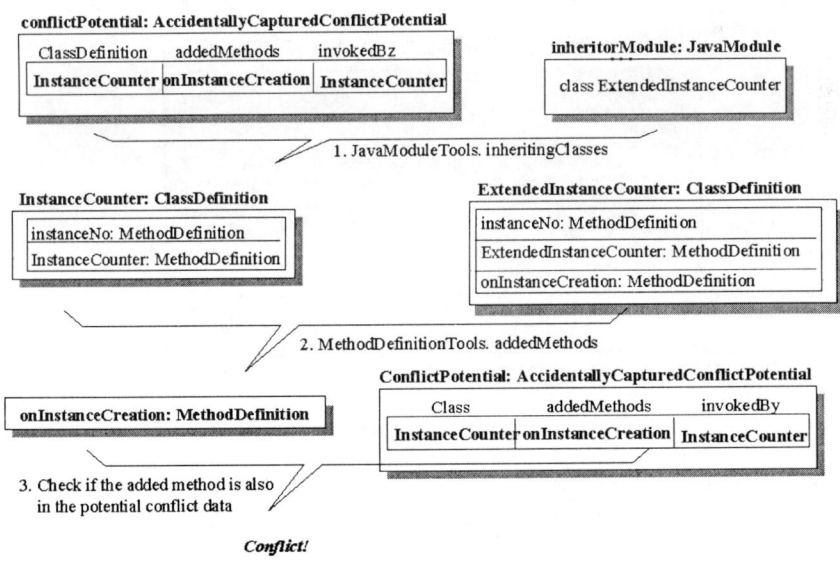

Figure 5. An Example of Concrete Conflict Detection

The output of the detector module is a list of conflict objects, with each conflict object encapsulating the information on a particular conflict produced by the detection process. As far as the immediate use of the framework is concerned, these objects are simply printed out. However, different applications building on top of the framework may have different requirements on the detection process. For instance, a debugging tool attached to the framework could require the detection process to switch into debugging mode as soon as a conflict is detected passing along a decompiled version of the affected class binaries, the methods and the position in the methods where the conflict appears, etc. A binary adaptation tool on the other side would have quite different requirements. Enabling applications to extend the framework with their specific semantics is the responsibility of the *output module*. For this reason the design of this module and its connection to the detection module makes use of the visitor pattern [1].

2.4. The Conflict Analyzer Module

The *conflict analyzer* module is the "controller" of the framework; it coordinates the work of the other modules by determining the control flow among them. In this section, we briefly outline how the framework is used for its primary purpose as a complementary tool to compilers. First, the user chooses the components to be analyzed (Base, ModifiedBase, and Inheritor). In addition, the user can customize the analysis process via a range of choices. First, he/she can choose between potential/concrete conflict detection only, or both at the same time. Second, the user can choose a subset of detectors from those supported by the framework to be activated during the analysis. Third the user can choose/customize the level at which the analysis is performed and the output is produced. The screen snapshot in Fig. 6 shows the default output produced by a potential conflict detection process applied to the example components in Sec. 1.

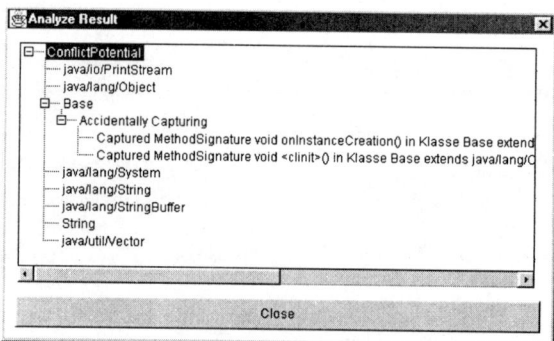

Figure 6. Analysis Process' Output

To give a better understanding of the ConflictAnalyzer module, the main control flow of the analysis process for a potential conflict detection is presented in Fig. 7. After the construction of the corresponding JavaModule metaobjects by the extractor module, the conflict analyzer module passes the control to the analysis toolbox. Given the delta structure constructed by the toolbox, each detector currently registered in the framework and activated by the user is requested to scan the delta structure finding out whether it carries the potential for the corresponding conflict. The result is a set of conflict potential objects, which is printed out.

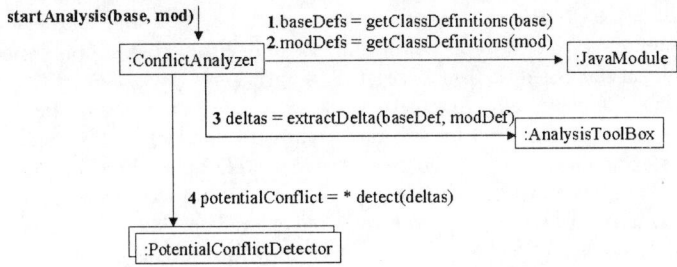

Figure 7. Overview of the Analysis Process

There are two ways of using the framework, depending on whether the potential detection phase of the analysis is performed at developer vs. inheritor site. The first alternative is to perform the analysis for conflict potentials at the developer site prior to delivering the modified component. The deliverables after a component modification are: the modified component plus the serialized data about the detected potential conflicts. The analysis for concrete conflicts is performed at inheritor site. The other alternative is to perform both conflict potential and concrete conflict analysis at the inheritor site.

There are two principal ways to extend the framework: (a) by adding new conflict detectors to extend the set of conflicts that can be detected, and (b) by adding new visitor classes to extend the range of applications that built on top of the framework. This is illustrated in Fig. 1 by filling the boxes for the base classes ConflictPotential, ConcreteConflict, ConflictPotentialVisitor, and ConcreteConflictVisitor with a greyscale. These are the "entry points" for both framework extensions, i.e., the classes that will be subclassed. The implementation of new conflict detectors will make use of the analysis facilities provided by AnalysisToolBox. Furthermore, certain detectors may require the implementation of new analysis facilities and/or data structures for storing the conflicts that are not available in the toolbox. The conflict analyzer module does not hard codes any knowledge about the individual analysis tools and/or conflict detectors present in a certain instantiation of the framework. Instead, it uses reflection to instantiate the appropriate detector/tool classes. As a result, as long as added tools and detectors provide the interface expected by the conflict analyzer module, their integration is transparent to the rest of the framework.

3. Related Work

In [4], Kiczales and Lamping motivate the need for approaches to discipline white-box composition. They named the special interface between a class and its subclasses *specialization interface*. The main question posed in this work was: given the specialization interface of a class, what are the legal modifications a subclass can apply and how should this be declared and imposed? Lamping [5] proposes a type system approach to improve the control over the specialization interfaces. According to this approach, type systems should be extended with indications about the resources of the class that each method utilizes during its execution.

In contrast to [5], Stata and Guttag [11], propose a methodology for specialization interfaces that is specification-oriented instead of type-system oriented. Type systems rarely address semantic issues. For this reason, the approach by Stata and Guttag extends the *object behavioral specifications* proposed by Liskow and Wing [7] to support specialization interface specifications besides client interface specifications.

Minsky et al. [9] have done extensive work on *law-governed regularities in software systems*. They motivate the need for software architectures which provide mechanisms for explicit specification and automatic enforcement of system internal regularities.

BCA [3] is an approach to adapt third party Java components to specific application needs by changing their binaries. Changes to a component are specified as so-called deltas. We have classified this approach as preventive, because only those deltas are allowed that ensure release-to-release compatibility. Similar to the framework proposed in this paper, the BCA approach recognizes the importance of supporting the evolution of reusable components at the binary level.

Related work presented so far is characterized as preventive: the common approach is to discipline inheritance by enforcing customizations to follow certain rules. The imposed rules relax to a certain extent the provider–inheritor coupling, with the expectation that certain conflicts would be avoided. This is in contrast to our *"detect-emergence-before-happening"* approach: let inheritors use the power of inheritance unharnessed and try to shield them from the consequences by detecting conflict situations at composition time (when emerging), i.e., before runtime (when happening). The following two approaches are similar to our work in this respect.

The concept of *reuse contracts* is introduced in [12] as an artifact associated with each class to document the design relevant part of the specialization interface of the class. The reuse contracts and the work presented in this paper share the detective approach. However, there are important differences between them. First, in contrast to reuse contracts, no additional documentation artifacts need to be specified by the developer of the component. Second, reuse contracts use operation names to specify the calling structure of a class. As indicated earlier in the paper this information would be insufficient in languages that support finer-grained structuring as it is the case with the inner classes in Java. Last but not least, reuse contracts do not consider conflicts that are specific for statically typed languages.

In a previous work [8], we proposed to enhance the subclassing semantics of the object-oriented languages to account for detecting and possibly removing evolution conflicts. The proposed composition mechanism was called *smart composition* because it adapted its semantics to the results of the analysis, ensuring that at least the user was informed, or in the best case that the conflicts were removed. This work revealed the limitations of an approach to conflict analysis at the level of source code. This approach is categorized as mixed, because it also supports the declaration/enforcement of certain design properties by the developer of the base component as other preventive approaches do.

4. Summary and Future Work

This paper considered problems with maintaining object-oriented components related to unpredictable effects that this may have on existing inheritor code. We argued that adequate support is needed for detecting incompatible changes in the modified component.

For this reason, we presented a framework for performing this detection process at the binary level during component reintegration. Our approach does not require source code access, so it can be applied to third-party components. The framework is extensible to support new conflict types as needed. Regardless of how many conflict types are supported by the instance of the framework in use, the user can customize the analysis process to his/her specific needs by activating/deactivating detectors on demand.

Performance optimizations as well as extensions of the framework with new detectors will be subject of future work. Furthermore, we plan to conduct case studies on real projects.

References

[1] E. Gamma, R. Helm, R. Johnson, and J. Vlissides. *Design Patterns. Elements of Reusable Object-Oriented Software.* Addison-Wesley, 1994.

[2] Goldberg A. and Robson D. *Smalltalk 80: The Language and its Implementation.* Addison-Wesley, 1983.

[3] Keller R. and Hölzle U. Binary Component Adaptation. In *Proceedings of ECOOP '98*, 1998.

[4] Kiczales G. and Lamping J. Issues in the Design and Documentation of Class Libraries. In *Proceedings of OOPSLA '92*, ACM SIGPLAN Notices, Vol. 27 No. 10, pp. 435–451, 1992.

[5] Lamping J. Typing the Specialization Interface. In *Proceedings of OOPSLA '93*, ACM SIGPLAN Notices, Vol. 28, No. 10, pp. 201–214, 1993.

[6] Lindholm T. and Yelling F. *The Java Virtual Machine Specification.* The Java Series, Addison Wesley, 1997.

[7] Liskow B. and Wing J. A Behavioral Notation of Subtyping. In *Proceedings of OOPSLA '94*, ACM SIGPLAN Notices, Vol. 16, No. 16, 1994.

[8] Mezini M. Maintaining the Consistency of Class Libraries During their Evolution. In *Proceedings of OOPSLA '97*, Sigplan Notices Vol. 29, No. 10, pp.1–22, 1997.

[9] Minsky N. Law-Governed Regularities in Object Systems. In *Theory and Practice of Object Systems (TAPOS)*, Vol. 2, No. 4, John Wiley, 1996.

[10] Pipka J. U. Master Thesis (in German). University of Siegen, 1999.

[11] Stata R. and Guttag J. Modular Reasoning in the Presence of Inheritance. In *Proceedings of OOPSLA '95*, ACM SIGPLAN Notices, Vol. 21 No. 10, pp. 200–214, 1995.

[12] Steyaert P., Lucas C., Mens K., and D'Hondt T. Reuse Contracts: Managing the Evolution of Reusable Assets. In *Proceedings of OOPSLA '96*, ACM SIGPLAN Notices, Vol. 31 No. 10, pp. 268–286, 1996.

[13] Szyperski C. *Component Software. Beyond Object-Oriented Programming.* Addison Wesley, 1997.

Specifying Java Frameworks Using Abstract Programs

Anna Mikhajlova

Turku Centre for Computer Science, Åbo Akademi University
Lemminkäisenkatu 14A, Turku 20520, Finland
e-mail: Anna.Mikhajlova @ abo.fi

Abstract

In this paper we propose a novel approach to specifying, documenting, and reasoning about object-oriented frameworks. The novelty of our approach is in combining standard executable statements of a programming language (we choose Java as an example) with possibly nondeterministic specification constructs. A specification of the intended behavior given in this language can serve as a precise documentation for users of the framework and its extension developers. To illustrate the applicability of our method to specification of object-oriented frameworks, we demonstrate how one can specify the Java Collections Framework which is a part of the standard Java Development Kit 2.0.

1 Introduction

Documenting object-oriented frameworks poses a serious problem - informal descriptions are imprecise and ambiguous, whereas providing code as a part of documentation leads to over-specification, rendering future upgrades impossible. Precise specifications in the form of abstract programs succinctly and unambiguously expressing the functionality of framework classes can solve the problems with framework documentation. The key feature of such abstract programs is that they combine executable statements of a programming language, e.g. method invocations, with possibly nondeterministic specification constructs, which permit abstracting away from implementation details. These specification constructs are not necessarily implementable, as they are intended to serve as high level descriptions of the kind of behavior the framework developers are interested in achieving. Implementations differ from abstract programs only in that they have no specification constructs.

In this paper we present a specification method based on a uniform treatment of specifications and implementations. The method is based on a language *JINSLA - Java INterface Specification LAnguage* - which combines standard executable statements of the Java language with possibly nondeterministic specification statements. The formal basis for the method supporting specification and development of provably correct object-oriented frameworks has been originally described in [9] in application to systems with unified interface and implementation inheritance hierarchies. Here we focus on object-oriented frameworks employing separate interface inheritance and implementation inheritance hierarchies, and illustrate how our method can be used to specify the Java Collections Framework (JCF). We propose to associate with Java interfaces formal descriptions of the behavior that classes implementing these interfaces and their subinterfaces must deliver. Interfaces always have an informal semantics as expressed in their names and in the names and parameter types of their methods, we just make this semantics explicit and express it mathematically. Naturally, such precise specifications can be distributed as part of the framework documentation, contributing to the detailed understanding of its functionality and guiding extension development. Our specifications of JCF are entirely based on informal descriptions of the interface semantics as presented in the documentation [5], and in the process of specifying this semantics we identify a number of ambiguities and inconsistencies in the documentation.

2 Specifying object-oriented frameworks

As a basis for our specification language we choose (a non-concurrent subset of) Java. Before describing the specification constructs of the language, let us make a note about the notation used in this paper. We describe functions using λ-abstraction and write $f\ x$ for the application of function f to argument x. Whenever necessary to clarify the argument in the application of a function, especially in the case when the argument is a tuple of elements, we also use brackets around the argument, writing $f(x)$.

The use of equality and assignment symbols deserves special attention. The Java language uses $=$ to denote assignment and $==$ to denote equality of two values. Being reluctant to redefine the symbol $=$ traditionally used to denote mathematical equality, we will use it to denote equality of two values and $:=$ to denote assignment.

The language JINSLA that we use for specifying and reasoning about Java programs is essentially a combination of specification constructs and standard statements of the Java language. Every construct in JINSLA has a precise mathematical meaning in the refinement calculus [3, 11, 4] as described in [9, 2]. The specification constructs that we use here are *assertion, nondeterministic assignment,* and *nondeterministic choice.* The intuitive meaning of these additional statements is described in Fig. 1 and their formal semantics can be found, e.g. in [4].

The assertion is a statement found in many programming languages, such as, e.g. Eiffel and C++, and, as pointed out by many researchers, e.g. Bertrand Meyer in [8], it is indispensable for the development of correct object-oriented software. Assertions can be used to state contractual obligations between methods of some object and the client program invoking these methods. For example, a method m with input parameter c of a reference type can use a statement assert $c\ != null$ to express that a client invoking m and passing it an object reference $objC$ must assert that $objC\ != null$.

The nondeterministic assignment allows us express "what is being done without saying how it is being done", i.e. abstract away from implementation details, yet specify precisely what functionality should be achieved. For example, if we want to specify a method calculating a square root of x with the precision e, provided that the precision is positive, we

assert p	skips if p holds in a state and aborts otherwise
$[x := x' \mid b]$	assigns to x a value x' satisfying the boolean condition b
choose S_1 or ... or S_n	executes one of the alternatives S_1 through S_n

Figure 1. Specification statements of JINSLA

can use a nondeterministic assignment preceded with the corresponding assertion:

$$\text{assert } e > 0; [x := x' \mid -e < x'^2 - x < e]$$

In fact, the statement $\text{assert } p; [x := x' \mid q]$ corresponds directly to the pre- and postcondition specification (p, q) stating that the postcondition q, which is a predicate over initial and final values of x, will be established whenever the precondition p holds in the initial state.

Related to nondeterministic assignment is the nondeterministic initialization of local variables. A variable x, which is local to a block containing a statement S, can be nondeterministically initialized according to a predicate b, written $\{ type\ x \mid b; S; \}$, where $type$ is the type of x. Initializing x in this way corresponds to declaring it followed by nondeterministically assigning it a new value satisfying the predicate b.

The nondeterministic choice allows us express the nondeterminism in selecting one behavior among several possible behaviors. For example, we can specify a menu offering the choice of opening a new file, opening an existing file, and closing an open file as follows:

$$\text{choose } fm.OpenNew\ () \text{ or } fm.Open\ (f) \text{ or } fm.Close\ (f)$$

where fm is a file manager object with the interface including the corresponding method signatures.

Apart from standard Java language constructs, we use the multiple assignment statement $x_1, \ldots, x_n := e_1, \ldots, e_n$ which stands for a simultaneous assignment of expressions $e_1, \ldots, e_n$ to variables $x_1, \ldots, x_n$ respectively. The multiple assignment allows us to express nondeterminism in the order of the corresponding individual assignments. Assuming that $x_1, \ldots, x_n$ do not occur free in $e_1, \ldots, e_n$, the multiple assignment can always be rewritten as a sequential composition of the corresponding individual assignments in arbitrary order.

There is a natural inter-relation between the executable statements of the Java language and the specification statements of JINSLA. In particular, asserting truth corresponds to skipping, $\text{assert } true\ =\ \text{skip}$, and assigning a functional value in a nondeterministic assignment is the same as assigning this value in an ordinary way, $[x := x' \mid x' = e]\ =\ x := e$.

Apart from the ordinary imperative statements of the Java language and the specification statements that we have described above, our specification language naturally supports object-oriented constructs such as objects, methods and classes, and mechanisms such as subtype polymorphism and dynamic binding. The formal semantics of these constructs and mechanisms is presented in [9, 2]. Using this specification language, we can freely intermix executable statements, such as method invocations, with nondeterministic statements, such as nondeterministic choices, as was demonstrated in our file management menu example above. A specification of object behavior given in JINSLA can be very succinct and precise and benefit from encapsulation and modularity, because it can include method calls to other objects, eliminating the need for approximating the behavior of these methods and building upon other specifications in a modular fashion. No less important, such a specification can be abstract and general enough to permit different implementations: the availability of nondeterministic statements allow us to abstract away from unnecessary implementation details and express the behavior common to several implementations.

Interfaces in Java frameworks can be extended with formal descriptions of the behavior that classes implementing these interfaces and their subinterfaces must deliver. Such formal descriptions in a language which is essentially Java with a few additional constructs should help framework users and extension developers understand the behavior of the corresponding interfaces and their implementations precisely, without being exposed to the bulk of

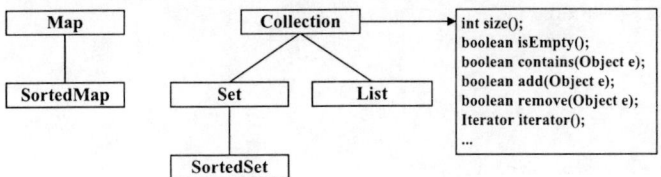

Figure 2. Collection hierarchy

source code, which otherwise can be the only way to achieving this understanding. Let us now illustrate how our method of framework specification can be used to specify the Java Collections Framework.

3 Specifying the Java Collections Framework

As was stated in the documentation of JCF [5], "A collections framework is a unified architecture for representing and manipulating collections." This particular framework contains three parts: interfaces, implementations, and algorithms. In this paper we focus on the interfaces, formalizing their informal descriptions as given in the documentation [5]. The following description of JCF is based on [5].

The interfaces at the core of JCF form a hierarchy as shown in Fig. 2. The root of the hierarchy, the *Collection* interface, represents a group of objects, known as its elements. *Collection* is used to pass collections around and manipulate them when maximum generality is desired. Some *Collection* specializations allow duplicate elements and others do not. Some are ordered and others are not. For example, *Set* is an unordered collection that cannot contain duplicate elements, and *List* is an ordered collection that can contain duplicates.

In the *Collection* interface the method names suggest the intended functionality, for example, the method *size* returns the size of the underlying collection. The interface type *Iterator* returned by the method *iterator* is used to access collection elements and structurally modify the collection. This interface has three methods *hasNext*, *next*, and *remove* which check whether there are more elements in the collection, return the next element, and remove the current element respectively. The description of JCF states that the behavior of an iterator is unspecified if the underlying collection is structurally modified while the iteration is in progress in any way other than by calling the method *remove*.

To specify the behavior of *Collection* methods we must model the underlying data structure the methods operate on. It appears to be rather natural to model this data structure by a bag (multiset) of *Object*[1] elements, as we want the collection to contain polymorphic elements, possibly duplicated or unordered. Furthermore, to specify the history of structural modifications, we will use an integer attribute *modified* which will be increased whenever elements are added to the original collection or removed from it. Accordingly, we specify the data attributes, the constructor, and the basic operations of *Collection* as follows:

---

[1]In Java the standard class *Object* is a superclass of all other classes, and a variable of type *Object* can hold a reference to an object of any other type.

```
public interface Collection {
    bag of Object elems;
    int modified;

    Collection() {
        elems, modified := ⟦⟧, 0;
    }

    int size() {
        return min (#elems, Integer.MAX_VALUE);
    }

    boolean isEmpty() {
        return (#elems = 0);
    }

    boolean contains(Object o) {
        return (o ∈ elems);
    }

    boolean add(Object o) {
        boolean r | r = false;
        if (o ∈ elems) {
            choose {skip; }
            or { elems, modified, r := elems + ⟦o⟧, modified + 1, true; };
        }
        else { elems, modified, r := elems + ⟦o⟧, modified + 1, true; };
        return r;
    }

    boolean remove(Object o) {
        boolean r | r = false;
        if (o ∈ elems) {
            elems, modified := elems \ o, modified + 1;
            r := true;
        }
        return r;
    }

    Iterator iterator() {
        Iterator i := new Iterator(this);
        return i;
    }
```

In this specification highlighted in bold is the original *Collection* interface and the rest is the precise description of the intended behavior. The behavior of the constructor and the methods is specified in terms of operations on bags and integers, with # returning the number of elements in a bag, ∈, +, and \ representing containment of an element in a bag, bag summation, and element removal respectively. The definitions of these operations are given in Table 1. As bags are functions from elements to the number of their occurrences, function application $b\ e$ returns the number of elements e in the bag b. The conditional expression $b\ ?\ e_1 : e_2$ is equal to the expression e_1 if the boolean condition b holds and to e_2 otherwise.

Table 1. Operations on bags

$\#b \ \hat{=}\ \sum e \cdot b\ e$	$b_1 = b_2 \ \hat{=}\ (\forall e \cdot b_1\ e = b_2\ e)$
$e \in b \ \hat{=}\ b\ e > 0$	$b_1 \subset b_2 \ \hat{=}\ b_1 \subseteq b_2 \land \#b_1 < \#b_2$
$b_1 + b_2 \ \hat{=}\ (\lambda e \cdot b_1\ e + b_2\ e)$	$b_1 \setminus b_2 \ \hat{=}\ (\lambda e \cdot \max((b_1\ e - b_2\ e), 0))$
$b \setminus a \ \hat{=}\ (\lambda e \cdot (e = a) ? \max((b\ e - 1), 0) : b\ e)$	$b_1 \subseteq b_2 \ \hat{=}\ (\forall e \cdot b_1\ e \leq b_2\ e)$

Although the specifications of the constructor and the methods intuitively are quite straightforward, a few points are of interest here. First of all, assignment of a bag to a variable of type *bag of Object*, as in the constructor, results in the corresponding variable containing the value which is equal to the value being assigned, in this case $\llbracket\,\rrbracket$, with equality on bags $b1 = b2$ defined by $(\forall e \bullet b1\ e\ =\ b2\ e)$.

The description of method *contains* in [5] states that this method "returns true if and only if this Collection contains at least one element e such that $(o == null\ ?\ e == null\ :\ o.equals\,(e))$". Looking up the description of method *Object.equals*, we see that "for any reference values x and y, this method returns true if and only if x and y refer to the same object ($x == y$ has the value true)". Our specification states that the object reference o, be it a null or a non-null value, is one of the elements in the bag *elems*, which directly corresponds to the above description, still being more succinct and concise.

The description of method *add* states that it ensures that the current *Collection* instance contains the specified element, returning true if *Collection* changed as a result of the call and false if it does not permit duplicates and already contains the specified element. The nondeterministic choice operator choose used in our specification allows us to express these variations in the behavior succinctly and precisely: if the element to be added is already present in the current instance of *Collection*, this element can either be added to *Collection* or the addition of the element can be skipped, with the choice between the options made nondeterministically. When the element is not present, it is necessarily added to *Collection*.

The method *remove* is described as an operation removing an element e such that $(o == null\ ?\ e == null\ :\ o.equals\,(e))$, if *Collection* contains one or more such elements. Further it is stated in [5] that this method "returns true if the Collection contained the specified element (or equivalently, if the Collection changed as a result of the call)". In our specification we stipulate that if o is present in *Collection* at least once, its number of occurrences is decreased by one and the method returns true.

The iterator returned in the identically named method of the interface *Collection* is constructed by calling the constructor *Iterator* and passing it the reference to the current instance of *Collection*. Although *Iterator* is just an interface which cannot be used to produce instances, we provide its formal specification in the same way as for *Collection*, and by giving the specification of *Iterator*'s constructor, we define the precise meaning of its invocation in the method *Iterator* of *Collection*. An implementation of *Iterator* will have to define its own constructor, and an implementation of *Collection* will then return an instance created by this constructor in the method *Iterator*.

Before presenting a formal specification of the interface *Iterator*, let us consider a collaboration between a collection and iterators attached to it. As described in [5], "*Iterator.remove* is the only safe way to modify a collection during iteration; the behavior is unspecified if the underlying collection is modified in any other way while the iteration is in progress." Obviously, this description is rather ambiguous, because it is unclear the behavior of which methods is unspecified, and how modifications are being monitored, and what it means for an iteration to be in progress. To get an intuitive understanding of object interaction in this case, let us consider Fig. 3. Suppose that two iterators i_1 and i_2 are used to iterate over a collection implemented as a list, as shown in Fig. 3(a). Now, if we execute $i_2.next();\,i_1.next();\,i_1.remove()$, the iterator i_2 will be indexing a non-existing list element, as shown in Fig. 3(b). Further invocations of methods on i_2 will produce erroneous results or simply abort. However, the iterator i_1, which has carried out the structural modification of the underlying collection, will continue to work correctly. Accordingly, we have to specify

Figure 3. Simultaneous modification of a collection by different iterators

the conditions under which iterators can be sure that the underlying data structure hasn't been structurally modified. The data attribute *modified* of *Collection* can be used for this purpose. Maintaining in *Iterator* an invariant that its own *modified* data attribute is equal to the one of the underlying *Collection*, helps solve the problem. Furthermore, the description of method *remove* states that this method can be called only once per call to *next*. To reflect this requirement in the specification, we maintain a data attribute *canRemove* and set it to true after resetting the next element and to false after removing the current element. The interface *Iterator* can, therefore, be specified as follows:

```
public interface Iterator {
    Collection col;
    bag of Object current;
    boolean canRemove;
    int modified;
    Object next;
    invariant I            =     col != null ∧
                                 (canRemove ⇒ next ∈ current)
    interclass invariant intI  =  current ⊆ col.elems ∧
                                 modified = col.modified

    Iterator(Collection c) {
        assert c != null;
        col, current, canRemove, modified, next := c, ⟦⟧, false, c.modified, null;
    }

    boolean hasNext() {
        return current ⊂ col.elems;
    }

    Object next() {
        assert current ⊂ col.elems;
        [next := e | e ∈ (col.elems \ current)];
        current, canRemove := current + ⟦next⟧, true;
        return next;
    }

    void remove() {
        assert canRemove;
        col.elems, col.modified := col.elems \ next, col.modified + 1;
        current, canRemove, modified := current \ next, false, modified + 1;
        next := null;
    }
}
```

As elements in a bag cannot be indexed, we use the data attribute *current* to store the elements of the underlying collection that have been returned by the method *next* in the current iteration. The attribute *next* stores the element returned by the last call to the method *next*. The class invariant *I* states that the iterator is always attached to an existing collection (*col* != *null*) and that the next element to be removed is one of the elements currently "indexed" (*canRemove* ⇒ *next* ∈ *current*). This class invariant holds of all *Iterator* instances during their whole life cycle, being established by the constructor and preserved by all the methods. Apart from the class invariant, *Iterator* maintains another invariant *intI* which captures the invariance in the relation between the attributes of *Iterator* and the attributes of *Collection* that it aggregates, stating that the elements returned by the method *next* are always in the underlying collection (*current* $\subseteq$ *col.elems*) and that structural modifications made so far have been made by the current instance of *Iterator* (*modified* = *col.modified*). This invariant is different from the class invariant proper in that it is maintained mutually by *Iterator* and *Collection*. We choose to call this invariant "interclass invariant" to reflect that, on the one hand, it is an invariant established by the constructor and preserved by all the methods of *Iterator*, and, on the other hand, it is the predicate which cannot be assumed to hold of all *Iterator* instances at all times because *Iterator* alone cannot guarantee its preservation between method calls to its methods. In other words, creating an instance of *Iterator* through calling the constructor establishes *intI*, and, although there are no guarantees that *intI* holds at all moments in a life cycle of this instance, if it does then a call to any method of *Iterator* will preserve it. Note that the methods *add* and *remove* of *Collection* break *intI* which suggests potential behavioral problems with structural modification of the underlying collection by different iterators. The interclass invariant of a particular *Iterator* instance will be preserved only if this instance is used by the underlying collection to structurally modify itself through calls to *Iterator* methods. In this respect, the fact that *Collection* has the method *add*, while *Iterator* does not, might indicate the possibility of inadequate framework design.

Bertrand Meyer in [8] discusses the problem of interclass invariants, although in a slightly different setting with two classes maintaining mutual references to each other, and proposes to do run-time monitoring of these invariants, effectively adding them to pre- and postconditions of methods in the classes whose attributes are related through such invariants. We define the semantics of the interclass invariant construct similarly, by adding it as the implicit assert condition in the end of the class constructor and the implicit assume\assert conditions in, respectively, the beginning and the end of every class method. Proving consistency of a class with respect to its class invariant and interclass invariant amounts to verifying that both kinds of invariants are established by the class constructor and preserved by all its methods.

The constructor creates a new *Iterator* instance only under the condition that the collection referred by *c* is some existing object, as expressed in the assertion assert *c* != *null*; otherwise, the constructor aborts. The method *next* returns a next object in the underlying data structure only under the condition that the end of the structure hasn't been reached, as expressed in the assertion assert *current* $\subset$ *col.elems*. Note that the element to be returned by this method is chosen nondeterministically from the elements in the underlying collection that haven't been returned by *next* in the current iteration run. This element is added to the bag of currently iterated elements *current* and the boolean flag *canRemove* is set to true, permitting removal of the next element. In turn, the method *remove* agrees to remove the next element only if *canRemove* holds in a state, encoding the requirement that *remove* can be called only once per call to *next*.

Note that in the specification of *Iterator* we directly modify data attributes of the aggregated collection *col*. Normally, in object-oriented programming such practice is rightfully criticized for breaking encapsulation. In specifications, however, we will permit such direct access and modification because this significantly simplifies specifications, as there is no need to specify the behavior solely in terms of method calls on the aggregated objects. There is no danger of breaking encapsulation because implementations can (and usually will) use completely different attributes for achieving what is required in the specification, and in the implementations direct access to data attributes of another class will be completely eliminated and substituted with method calls preserving encapsulation.

The interface *Collection* also contains methods for converting collections to arrays and methods for performing bulk operations on collections, but we omit their specifications for lack of space. An extended version of this paper [10] contains a complete specification of *Collection* as well as specifications of other core interfaces of the framework.

4 Conclusions and related work

The approach to specification of object-oriented frameworks that we present in this paper is based on using abstract programs which combine executable statements with specification constructs. This uniform treatment of specifications and implementations permits abstracting away from implementation details in a specification, yet being precise about important behavioral issues, such as, e.g. a fixed method invocation order or an iterative execution of a particular statement.

Our approach to specification based on combining executable statements with specification statements has a number of advantages, as compared to the traditional approach based on pre- and postconditions. First of all, as pointed out by Clemens Szyperski in [12], specifications in terms of pre- and postconditions fail to capture subtle interdependencies which arise due to a specific order of method invocations, especially in the presence of *callbacks*, i.e. self-referential method calls that get redirected to subclasses of the class that originated the call. Our specification language includes method calls and, therefore, allows specifying callbacks as well as fixing an invocation of a method or a certain order of method invocations. Richard Helm et al. in [7], recognizing the need to express behavioral dependencies between co-operating objects, also include method calls in abstract specifications of contracts. No less important, as noted by several authors including Szyperski in [12], specifications of object-oriented programs in terms of pre- and postconditions have only semi-formal semantics, which excludes formal (ultimately, computer-assisted) verification. In our specification language every construct has a precise mathematical meaning in the refinement calculus [3, 11, 4] as described in [9, 2]. Finally, pre- and postconditions on operations merely specify *partial correctness*, i.e. state the postcondition for a given precondition under the assumption that the program terminates. Our approach guarantees *total correctness*, i.e. no termination assumption has to be made, and the termination can also be proved if so desired.

Treating specifications and implementations in a uniform logical framework permits formal reasoning about their relationship and properties. Of particular interest is the verification of behavioral conformance between specifications of interfaces and implementations of these interfaces. Verifying behavioral conformance of implementations to their specifications as well as behavioral conformance of subinterface specifications to the corresponding superinterface specifications permits ensuring correctness of the whole system. Our approach to reasoning about object-oriented systems supports this kind of verification as described in [9]. Applying this verification approach to ensuring correctness of JCF is presented in an extended version of this paper [10].

Related work in formal specification of object-oriented systems includes William Cook's specification in [6] of Smalltalk-80 collection class library. Although the library is organized by inheritance, Cook argues that interface inheritance or subtyping is a logical basis for the library organization, supporting this claim by specifying the interfaces and revealing several problems with the current organization of the library. With the Java Collections Framework that we specify here, interface inheritance is separated from the implementation inheritance and, since the former forms the basis for polymorphic object substitutability in client programs, we associate behavioral specifications with interfaces, as does Cook. One of the main differences of our work from that of Cook is that his specifications are given in terms of pre- and postconditions, following Pierre America's approach in [1], while we use a specification language combining specification statements with executable ones. More importantly, America's approach used by Cook is rigorous rather than formal, while in JINSLA every statement has a precise mathematical meaning, and reasoning about our specifications and their relation to executable Java programs can be carried out completely formally, in a unified logical framework.

There are a few issues that we haven't addressed in this project, in particular, the role of exceptions, their relation to assertion statements and their formal semantics are left as a topic for future work. Another direction of developing this work includes extending the specification method described here to handling concurrency.

Acknowledgements

Joakim von Wright, Emil Sekerinski, Ralph Back, and Gary Leavens have provided very useful comments on an earlier version of this paper.

References

[1] P. America. A behavioural approach to subtyping in object-oriented programming languages. Technical Report 443, Philips Research Laboratories, April 1989.

[2] R. Back, A. Mikhajlova, and J. von Wright. Class refinement as semantics of correct subclassing. Technical Report 147, Turku Centre for Computer Science, December 1997.

[3] R. J. R. Back. *Correctness Preserving Program Refinements: Proof Theory and Applications*, volume 131 of *Mathematical Center Tracts*. Mathematical Centre, Amsterdam, 1980.

[4] R. J. R. Back and J. von Wright. *Refinement Calculus: A Systematic Introduction*. Springer-Verlag, April 1998.

[5] J. Bloch. Java collections framework: Collections 1.2. http://java.sun.com/docs/books/tutorial/collections/index.html.

[6] W. R. Cook. Interfaces and Specifications for the Smalltalk-80 Collection Classes. In *Proceedings of OOPSLA'92*, pages 1–15. ACM SIGPLAN Notices, 27(10), October 1992.

[7] R. Helm, I. M. Holland, and D. Gangopadhyay. Contracts: Specifying behavioural compositions in object-oriented systems. In *Proceedings of OOPSLA/ECOOP'90*, ACM SIGPLAN Notices, pages 169–180, Oct. 1990.

[8] B. Meyer. *Object-Oriented Software Construction*. Prentice Hall, New York, N.Y., 1997.

[9] A. Mikhajlova and E. Sekerinski. Class refinement and interface refinement in object-oriented programs. In *Proceedings of 4th International Formal Methods Europe Symposium, FME'97*, LNCS 1313, pages 82–101. Springer, 1997.

[10] A. Mikhajlova and E. Sekerinski. Ensuring correctness of Java frameworks: A formal look at JCF. Technical Report 250, Turku Centre for Computer Science, March 1999.

[11] C. C. Morgan. *Programming from Specifications*. Prentice–Hall, 1990.

[12] C. Szyperski. *Component Software – Beyond Object-Oriented Software*. Addison-Wesley, 1997.

Technical Papers

Frameworks 1

Component Frameworks – A Case Study

Herbert Praehofer, Johannes Sametinger, Alois Stritzinger
Johannes Kepler University, Linz, Austria
hp@cast.uni-linz.ac.at, sametinger@acm.org, stritzinger@swe.uni-linz.ac.at

Abstract

This paper reports on an effort to use both the system theoretic DEVS (discrete event simulation) formalism and the JavaBeans component model as a basis for a component-based discrete event simulation framework. The result of the synergism of DEVS and JavaBeans is a powerful component-based simulation framework together with a set of flexible bean components for building simulation systems.

Component frameworks are dedicated and focused architectures with a set of policies for mechanisms at the component level. In this paper we describe the component framework we have developed for discrete event simulations. Simulation components are based on this framework and can be composed for the creation of various simulation scenarios.

1. Introduction

We have developed a set of JavaBeans components for the creation of discrete event simulations. The goal was to investigate how discrete event simulation applications can profit from an up-to-date component technology. The idea was to create a component framework for discrete event simulation, a set of basic simulation components together with visualization and animation components that can be arranged and connected on a worksheet. The modeling approach is based on the DEVS, a system theoretic formalism for discrete event modeling that provides a theoretic framework for modular, hierarchical modeling [5, 6].

Component frameworks are dedicated and focused architectures with a set of policies for mechanisms at the component level [3]. Component frameworks have similarities with application frameworks. They provide a framework for components rather than objects but are not necessarily used for the creation of entire applications. A component framework for discrete event simulation has to provide mechanisms for simulation control and item flow. Simulation is controlled by events that activate components. In order to be part of the simulation, components have to be registered for events at certain points of time. Additionally, components have to process, provide and receive items, thus allowing items to flow from component to component and being processed by these components. In order to enable item flow, all components have to adhere to a mechanism defined by the framework.

In Section 2 we describe the component-based simulation methodology. The component framework is described in Sections 3. Design considerations of the framework are described in Sections 4. Conclusions are drawn in Section 5.

2. Component-based simulation methodology

A component-based modeling and programming framework for simulation applications has to enable developers to interactively pick components from libraries and place them onto a worksheet. Such components comprise simulation components as well as visualization, animation and statistics components. As a next step, connecting these components has to be accomplished, such that signals and data can be exchanged among them. Additionally, convenient interactive customization of parameters has to be supported. The component system has to be simply executed and used as a simulation application or as a more complex component in other simulation applications.

We envision a component-based simulation methodology which provides component libraries for different purposes, different users, and different applications, see [1, 2]. Components advocate and support a plug and play framework. It should be possible to develop simulation systems with less effort by mainly selecting, extending, customizing, and connecting components. It should be less effort for developers to realize specific components or specific simulation systems and environments. The component provider is faced with the challenge of designing components in a way so that they can be reused in a wide range of applications.

3. Component framework

Components for discrete event simulation need to have a common basis for basic simulation principles, e.g., a common simulation time and a common mechanism for event scheduling. Additionally, they need to have a common understanding of how items are constituted and how item flow is realized. These aspects have to be defined in the component framework. Any components being based on this framework may be combined for construction of simulation scenarios. The component framework for discrete event simulations consists of the simulation kernel and a set of interfaces for component coupling. They will be described subsequently.

3.1. Simulation kernel

The simulation kernel provides the simulation infrastructure and implementation concepts for the simulation components. The kernel is specific for different types of simulations, e.g., there is an infrastructure for discrete event simulation, for continuous simulation and for combined simulation.

For discrete event simulation, the kernel includes support for
- event scheduling and event handling,
- models, model containers and hierarchies of models,
- state variables and property change mechanism, and
- utility services for data collection and analysis.

In order to participate in a simulation scenario, a component has to register itself to the simulation kernel, see Fig. 1. Additionally, it can register itself for activation at a certain point of time. A simulation scenario is built by composing simulation components that have to communicate with the simulation kernel, as well as components for visualization, animation and statistics. Components that are not directly involved in the simulation, e.g., visualization components, do not have to be aware of the simulation kernel. Therefore, arbitrary components may be included for animation, for visualization, and for statistical evaluations.

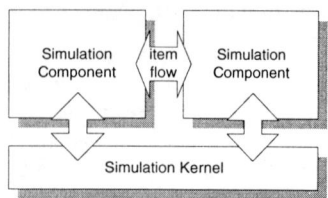

Figure 1. Simulation kernel

The simulation kernel drives the simulation by processing events that have been registered by components. The effect of an event depends on the component that is activated thereupon. For example, a component may generate or process items. The simulation kernel does not have any influence on what events trigger. Additionally, the kernel does not care about items. Components have to take measures to handle items and their flow through the system, i.e., to receive items from other components and to provide items to other components. In order to enable item flow, all components have to adhere to the same mechanism, which is also defined in the framework, and described in the next section.

In order to enable communication between the simulation kernel and components, two interfaces have been designed, interface DEVS and interface Resource, see Fig. 2. DEVS defines the interface to the simulation kernel, whereas Resource defines a minimal interface to components. The simulation kernel defines a routine to register components. This is necessary to control a simulation run and, for example, allows the kernel to reset all components before a new simulation run is started. The simulation kernel defines another routine to register events, i.e., components are registered to be triggered at a certain simulation time. These events are triggered by calling the routine trigger when the specific simulation time has arrived.

3.2. Simulation components

For discrete process simulation we have identified the following principal types of elements:
- *resource components*, which are active or passive and may be occupied by items,
- *items*, which flow through a system of resource components, and
- *glue components*, which control item flow among resource components.

A simulation system, therefore, is viewed as consisting of several resource components, where items are placed and processed, and a coupling structure which realizes the flow of the items from one resource component to the next. Glue components decide which items can flow from which resource components to the next based on requirements of items and space availability of resource components. This is a general, abstract view which fits to all types of discrete event simulation. Systems differ in what type of resource components are used, the types of items used, the glue structure, and in particular, who is in control and how is the control of the item flow. The components were designed according to those principal types.

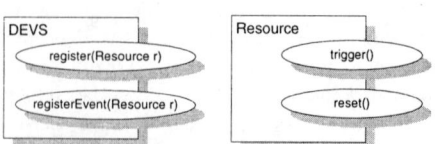

Figure 2. Interfaces DEVS and Resource

3.3. Resource components

Resource components form the key elements from which simulation systems are built. They are specific for the application domain, i.e., there is a library of resource components for different types of simulation, e.g., discrete event simulation (as discussed here). Resource components are crucial for the success of the component-based simulation framework. It is the challenge to foresee a wide range of applications in the domain and provide a set of easy-to-use and easy-to-extend components.

Resource components of discrete event simulations include what we call generators, sinks, processors, queues, places, and delays. Generators make new items available after some production time. Processors can process one single item at a time. Upon receipt of an item they get occupied and immediately start processing. After some processing time, they signal that an item is available and wait that it is accessed by another component. Delay components are never occupied and can always receive items. They delay items for some time and then make them available for access again. Place components can take one item. They signal that they need an item when there is no one on the place. When they receive an item they signal that they are occupied and that they have an item available for access. Other components behave in analogous way.

A resource component can be active, i.e., it can do some processing on an item, or it can be passive, i.e., it can only passively store items. In any case, their elementary functions are to receive items, hold them, and provide them to other components. While a passive storage component will only store received items and provide them for access, an active component will process received items, which will take some time, and afterwards want to get rid of them. Also components may have space available, i.e., they may need or be able to take further items.

Two interface definitions are crucial to the realization of item flow. These are the *Receiver* interface for components which may receive items and the *Provider* interface for components which may provide items. Receivers may be occupied and not be able to receive further items. Providers signal the availability of items and provide access to them. The interfaces for providers and receivers define methods to provide/receive an item and to inspect/test an item. They also signal an event when they have/need an item. Additionally, they signal an event whenever they actually provide/receive an item, see Fig. 3. For example, a generator, i.e., a component generating items, only implements the provider interface and makes new items available. More complex components are built by either coupling together components in a hierarchical way or by implementing them in Java using elementary simulation functions. By implementing the provider/receiver interfaces, they can be used in bigger coupled models according the same coupling concepts.

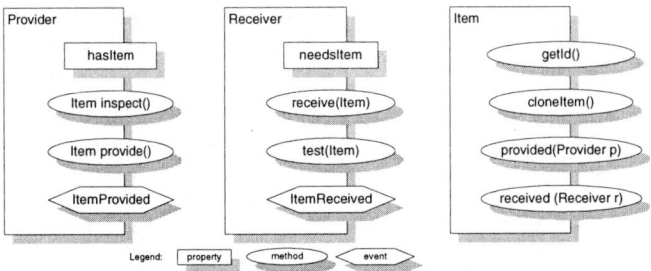

Figure 3. Provider, Receiver and Item interfaces

3.4. Items

Items are also described by an interface. They have a unique ID and provide several methods that may be called when events occur, e.g., when the item has been received or provided, i.e., when it has been moved on from a resource component, see Fig. 3. Components can implement the provider/receiver interfaces in different ways. They can also implement the item interface and, thus, be used as flowing items. Therefore, components are not of a particular type but rather they play the role of a particular type. They may also play various roles of different types. For example, a transportation component may on the one hand serve as a container, i.e., be a resource for some items (a resource component), but on the other hand it may flow as an item through the transportation system itself.

3.5. Glue components

The provider and receiver interfaces are not coupled directly, but rather additional glue components are used. The general idea of glue components is that they listen to property changes (hasItem and needsItem) of resource components and react to those by distributing items between providers and receivers based on an individual control scheme.

We use the event and bound property change concepts to realize event coupling and communication in discrete event models. Models which rely on states of other models are registered as listeners of the other model's state property and are, thus, informed whenever a change in state happens. For example, a processor needing a particular item registers itself as a listener of the needsItem property of the appropriate item provider. Everything flowing through the system is regarded as being an item, e.g., tools needed to process other items (work pieces). As soon as an item gets available, the processor is informed and can access the item. Control and coupling can be arbitrarily complex, ranging from simplest linear forwarder to a transportation system built up by a complex coupled model by itself. Fig. 4 shows a glue component coupling one provider and two receivers. Thick arrows from the glue component to the resource components designate method calls, thin arrows from resource components to the glue component designate the flow of events.

Examples of prefabricated glue components are what we call *forwarder, receiverDecisionPoint* and *providerDecisionPoint*. A forwarder realizes a direct flow of items from a provider to the next receiver. It listens to the hasItem property of the provider and the needsItem property of the receiver and, when both are true, takes the item from the provider and hands it over to the receiver. No control decision is needed here. An extension to the forwarder is the receiverDecisionPoint. It is used to couple a single provider with a set of receivers. The selection of the receiver of the next available item is based on a control strategy, i.e., a component selecting from a set of receivers. Components realizing different control strategies can be envisioned, for example, selecting at random, based on given percentages, the receiver waiting longest, etc. In the same way a providerDecisionPoint couples a set of providers with a receiver. With the mentioned glue components coupled systems can be built which are typical for *flow shop* models.

A different coupling scheme should be used when modeling a robotized manufacturing cell. Here the item flow and control scheme is much more complex. A robot has direct access to the places in a cell and the control has to take the whole cell state into account. Nevertheless, we use the same components and coupling principals. The cell controller listens to the hasItem and needsItem properties of cell components and generates transport commands to the robot. The robot then realizes item flow by accessing items from the specified provider and by placing them on the specified receiver.

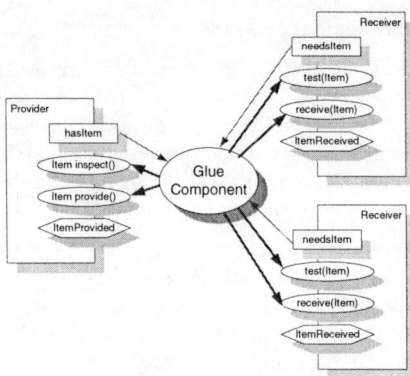

Figure 4. Glue component

3.6. Framework architecture

Fig. 5 depicts how the JavaBeans component model, the simulation component framework, simulation components and regular JavaBeans components interrelate. JavaBeans builds the foundation enabling any JavaBeans components to be included in simulation scenarios. The simulation kernel is built on top of the JavaBeans component model and contains the central event mechanism. All simulation components have to be built on top of the simulation kernel. In addition, they have to adhere to the framework's interfaces in order to exchange items. Item distribution is separated from item processing by providing resource components and glue components, thus providing more flexibility in building simulation scenarios.

4. Design considerations

We have implemented the component framework in Java and the components as JavaBeans [4]. JavaBeans provides an attractive platform-independent component model, making our components platform-independent and allowing us to easily integrate components for visualization, for animation, and for statistical evaluations from other sources. JavaBeans offers simple mechanisms for component coupling, i.e., events and the property change mechanism. The Java interface concept corresponds to the roles of components. A component playing a particular role has to implement the corresponding interface.

In this section we describe design considerations of the component framework. There were two central design decisions. First, in the simulation kernel we had to decide issues based on the event mechanism. Second, item flow among components can be realized in many different ways. Picking a suitable solution is interesting and offers insights in the way components can be connected.

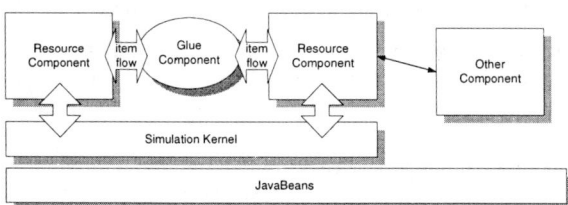

Figure 5. Simulation component framework

4.1. Event handling in the simulation kernel

The simulation kernel needs to control simulation time and has to trigger events based on event registrations of resource components. The simulation kernel is based on the JavaBeans component model. The Beans specification does not define the semantics of invocation order and synchronization of multiple event handlers listening to the same event. A default implementation is given for synchronous event handling (class PropertyChange-Support). However, this mechanism is not appropriate for simulation events.

In a simulation scenario it is typical that a resource component signals, for instance, the availability of a new item. The first listener being notified about such an event reacts by requesting the item and processing it. Other registered listeners get informed about the event when actions of the first listener have already taken place. For example, a component intended to trace item flow will get notified about the event too late because through the actions of another component the information provided by the event is outdated.

It is quite typical that event handlers react upon notification and modify the state of the event source, e.g., receiving and processing an item. In this situation problems arise, because conceptually parallel event handling is simply serialized such that each component performs event handling actions before the next component is notified about the event. The solution for this problem is the use of asynchronous event handling. Events must not be processed immediately, but have to be collected in a global event queue. When a component triggers an event, event objects for all registered listeners are queued, then event handling takes place in a first-in-first-out order whereby new events may be appended to the queue. As a consequence, events have to know their listeners, such that they can be delivered when being taken out of the queue.

Synchronous events can only be used for components that do not have any influence on the state of resource components. For example, whenever an item is received by a component, this should be visualized by corresponding components immediately, even when the item is put forward. Asynchronous events are important when several listeners are registered with the same provider. The first listener receiving the event would get the item before the second one has a chance of even getting the information that there is an item available, i.e., the second listener would get the information when the item is not available any longer. Summarizing, we use synchronous events for animation and visualization components and asynchronous events for glue components.

4.2. Item flow

Item flow among components is of utmost importance for efficient simulation applications. Any component that is intended to be used within a simulation has to adhere to the component framework in order to participate in the item flow, i.e., in order to be coupled with other components and to provide and receive items. Subsequently, we will describe different solutions and discuss their advantages and drawbacks.

4.2.1. Property changes: Property changes are simple and can be used for the connection of any JavaBeans component. Thus, it is possible to integrate visualization components with simulation components, even though visualization components are not based on the simulation component framework. The concept of bound properties is based on events. Whenever the property of a component is modified, an event is triggered in order to notify listeners. This mechanism can be used to inform an item receiver that an item provider has an item available, see Fig. 6a.

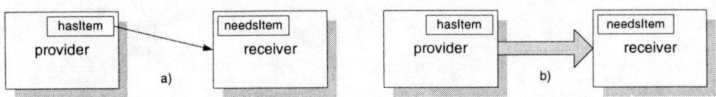

Figure 6. Component coupling a) with bound properties b) with interfaces

In the example of Fig. 6a an event is sent to the receiver component whenever the boolean property hasItem of the provider component is modified. This connection can simply be established by the following Java code, which is usually generated by a building tool:

```
provider.addPropertyChangeListener("hasItem",receiver);
```

The receiver can check the value of the hasItem property of the provider and, if available, receive the item. However, it turns out that communication between components becomes clumsy and unnecessarily complex, because after the property change has occurred, the provider and the receiver have to identify themselves and to negotiate about item flow. This is necessary because several receivers can be registered at the same provider. They all get notified when an item is available, but only one receiver may actually receive the item.

The concept of property changes is not powerful enough to realize sophisticated component coupling, but for simple data exchange among components it is a possible solution. The main disadvantage of this type of item flow is that the simple mechanism of bound properties is burdened with complex communication and because it is not possible to control item flow. For example, it is not feasible to move items to receivers based on a specific strategy. Another disadvantage of using bound properties is the fact that there is no static type check, i.e., it can only be detected at runtime whether components are listening to the properties they are interested in.

4.2.2. Abstract interfaces: For intensive cooperation abstract interfaces are a useful means to define operations. Such interfaces make cooperation more efficient, but all cooperating components have to implement the specific interfaces, see Fig. 6b. In the example of Fig. 6b the provider knows the identity of the receiver and can use various operations defined in the receiver's interface in order to move an item forward. Such a connection can again be established by a simple Java statement:

```
provider.setItemReceiver(receiver);
```

Using interfaces provides flexibility, but there is still a major drawback. First, components have to know each other. Second, the provider (or the receiver) has to make decisions on where items should be delivered. Thus, the provider not only has to know all the receivers, it also has to have additional information in order to implement a distribution strategy, e.g., to randomly or linearly distribute items. This means, that the same resource component has to be available in different forms, implementing different distribution strategies. Additionally, all resource components should provide all distribution strategies, leading to a vast number of similar components.

4.2.3. Adapters: A more flexible form of cooperation can be reached by using adapters that listen to bound properties and communicate via interfaces. Fig. 7a demonstrates the use of an anonymous adapter. Such a connection can be established with an anonymous Java class, i.e., it is necessary to manually write Java source code:

```
PropertyChangeListener adapter = new PropertyChangeListener {
    void propertyChange (PropertyChangeEvent e) {
        if (provider.hasItem() && receiver.needsItem())  receiver.receive(provider.provide())
    }
};
provider.addPropertyChangeListener("hasItem",adapter);
receiver.addPropertyChangeListener("needsItem",adapter);
```

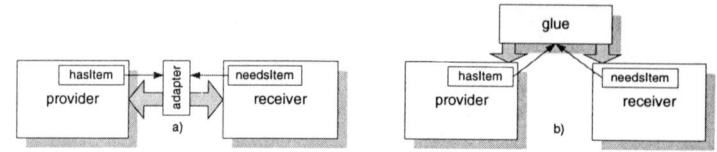

Figure 7. Component coupling a) with anonymous adapter b) with glue component

Adapters provide additional flexibility over the previous solutions, but coupling is rather cumbersome having to implement distribution strategies into anonymous classes. From this point the next step seems obvious, i.e., using components rather than anonymous adapters.

4.2.4. Glue components: Glue components implement various distribution strategies and can simply be placed among arbitrary provider and receiver components, see Fig. 7b. The source code to establish the necessary connections is as follows:

```
provider.addPropertyChangeListener("hasItem", glue);
receiver.addPropertyChangeListener("needsItem", glue);
glue.addProvider(provider);
glue.addReceiver(receiver);
```

Like adapters, glue components register with their provider and receiver components in order to get informed about item availability and item requests. Resource components know nothing about coupling and only send events and property change notifications. (Listeners have to be administered of course.)

4.2.5. Design rationale: Component systems in general and simulation systems in particular may grow to huge systems consisting of thousands of components. It becomes extremely hard if not impossible to understand and maintain such systems, especially when there are arbitrary dependencies among the components. Restricting the dependencies to be only in one direction leads to a layered architecture that is easier to comprehend and maintain. We have paid attention to the fact that communication among components is clearly defined and only one way as much as practical. For example, resource components communicate with their environment only via broadcasting events. Glue components listen to these events and call specific methods of the resources in order to realize item flow, i.e., they have specific knowledge about all the resource components involved in item flow.

It is sometimes impossible to completely restrict communication to one direction. In such cases we use events as dedicated communication vehicles; the number of events has been kept to a minimum with their semantics easy to comprehend and globaly known. In other words, we use a layered architecture, i.e., components know nothing about components of layers above them. Whenever it is necessary to communicate signals or data to higher layers, we define appropriate events and listener types. Event sources broadcast events and only know that there may be registered listeners.

The same communication mechanism is used for specialized visualization components that listen to events of resources and may also access specific data of the resources for better visualization. Naturally, resource components are unaware of any visualization mechanisms. Hence, this model-view component architecture is practical not only for a separation of models and views, but also for the realization of layered architectures.

5. Conclusion

We have described a component framework for discrete event simulation that is based on the JavaBeans component model. We regard the framework as being typical for component based software engineering in that it provides an infrastructure that is necessary in a specific domain. Effective coupling of components will only be successful on top of component models that enable simple composition of arbitrary components as well as on top of specific component frameworks that enable more complex and more effective composition of domain-specific components.

So far we have implemented a basic set of resource and glue components as well as some domain specific items. New components can be implemented by extending existing ones. We have also defined abstract classes that contain basic functionality needed for the implementation of resource components like registering with the simulation kernel. We are confident that discrete event simulation applications highly profit from component technology in terms of reusability and flexibilty.

We have used the components developed so far for the simulation of simple scenarios only. Due to the good experiences we have made, we have decided to make the system more mature in order to additionally serve as a simulation framework for real world applications. We also plan to extend the framework to allow continuous and combined simulation. The main objective is not only to extend the functionality of the framework and the components, but to gain additional insight into problems and solutions of component based software construction.

Many questions remain unanswered and need more work to be done in the future. For example: Are the design principles of our framework typical for the domain or may they be applied to other domains as well? Are there general mechanisms used in our framework or in frameworks of other domains, that may be included into the component model for better coupling of arbitrary components?

6. References

[1] H. Praehofer , A. Stritzinger, and J. Sametinger, "Using JavaBeans to teach Simulation and using Simulation to teach JavaBeans", ESM98, 12th European Simulation Multiconference, Manchester, UK, June 16-19, 1998.

[2] H. Praehofer, J. Sametinger, A. Stritzinger: "Discrete Event Simulation using the JavBeans Component Model", WEBSIM99; 1999 International Conference On Web-Based Modelling & Simulation, San Francisco, California, January 17-20 1999.

[3] C. Szyperski, Component Software: Beyond Object-Oriented Programming, Addison-Wesley, 1998.

[4] Sun Microsystems: JavaBeans, http://java.sun.com/beans/.

[5] B.P. Zeigler, Multifacetted Modelling and Discrete Event Simulation. Academic Press, 1984.

[6] B.P. Zeigler, Object Oriented Simulation with Modular, Hierarchical Models. Academic Press, 1990.

Answerer: A Design Pattern for Dynamical Conditional Execution

Mari OMORI, Nobuyuki IKEDA, Jun-ichi YAMAMOTO
Toshiba Corporation, System Integration Technology Center
3-22, Katamachi, Fuchu-shi, Tokyo, 183-8512 Japan
E-mail: mari@sitc.toshiba.co.jp

Abstract

In this paper, we propose a new design pattern named Answerer whose purpose is to eliminate the effort of recompiling a program due to changes of run-time environments. Most programs have to behave differently to accommodate with various run-time environments. As usual, the behaviors of such programs have to be specified in conditional blocks. When the run-time environment of a program changes, these blocks need to be modified and recompiled.

The Answerer pattern applies the reflection architectural pattern to take care of conditional execution. The reflection architectural pattern provides a mechanism for changing structure and behavior dynamically. Based on this idea, the Answerer pattern provides:

(1) a model of conditional execution and specification rules,

(2) a mechanism to structure a model dynamically from information acquired at run-time,

(3) a mechanism to create and execute a conditional operation from a model created from (2).

We developed the Answerer pattern with following two steps. Firstly, we found that it is necessary for structural items of (1) to implement the following information in order to implement the Answerer design pattern based on the above model and mechanisms:

(a) an information about environmental factors that should be observed

(b) an information about behavior that should be executed according to the factors

Secondly, we created the Answerer design pattern that implements (2) and (3).

In this paper, we explain how we applied and implemented the Answerer pattern with an example of Java applet of DVD authoring tool.

1. Introduction

A software system depends on its run-time environment such as operating systems, web browsers and other software systems. Some software systems are expected to run on a variety of run-time environments for many years. For example, an applet has to run on some kinds of web browsers. Each web browser has its particular characteristics, and they have been upgraded frequently. Then, the applet has to adapt itself to some released browsers and to browsers that will be updated or newly released in the future, too[1].

Nowadays, run-time environment for software systems changes rapidly with advance in hardware and software technologies. Thus, if software is adaptable for many environments, it needs less maintenance cost. Especially if software is adaptable for a new environment without source code modification, its maintenance becomes easier. However, development of such software is difficult because (1) there can be many complicated conditions to adjust the system to run-time environment, and (2) future environments cannot be expected during the system development.

We propose a design pattern *Answerer* which makes software adaptable for a variety of run-time environments dynamically. Software design patterns[2][3] are the core abstractions from successful recurring problem solutions in software design. Because they define neither the context nor the proposed solution, we can reuse someone's idea repeatedly.

The *Answerer* pattern is a specialized *Factory Method* pattern[2] in adaptability to a various run-time environments. A software system developed using the *Answerer* pattern contains a module to select an appropriate object for the current run-time environment. The relation between the run-time environments and the system's behavior is represented in two types of tables separately from its source code, which makes the system adjusted to multiple environments without source code modification. The tabular representation also enhances the readability of the condition and solves the difficulty (1) explained above. Regarding the difficulty (2), the *Answerer* pattern can cope with unexpected future changes by modifying the tables.

The *Answerer* pattern applies the *Reflection* architectural pattern[4] to take care of conditional execution. The *Reflection* architectural pattern provides a mechanism for changing structure and behavior of software systems dynamically to a program.

The rest of this paper is organized in the following way. Firstly, we show our motivation and analyze the problem by using an example. Secondly, we show our approach to solve them. Thirdly, we propose the *Answerer* design pattern in which our approach is implemented. Fourthly, we give an example of the application of the *Answerer* pattern. The fifth is a discussion and the last part is a conclusion.

2. Background

In this chapter, we show a problem and a sample to deal with.

2.1. Problem

Some software systems run on various run-time environments. Such software has to detect the current run-time environment and adjust its behavior to the environment dynamically.

One way to develop such software is to implement run-time condition directly in its source code. This implementation style may increase the maintenance cost of the software. As run-time environment is changing rapidly, some software will have to modify its behavior on a certain environment, or run on a new environment.

If software can cope with the change in environment without source code modification, its maintenance cost will decrease. However, designing software for the future change is not easy because (1) there can be many complicated conditions to adjust the system to run-time environment, and (2) future environments cannot be expected during the system development. We will illustrate this situation in the next section.

2.2. Sample case

Consider a Java applet for authoring a DVD data as an example. The applet is executed under three kinds of web browsers: Internet Explorer (IE), HotJava and Netscape Navigator (NN). The applet has to get some security privileges to execute some operations on each run-time environment because:

(1) The applet has to access dynamic-linkage files that stored in local file system to access and manipulate a DVD media

(2) In general, applets are prohibited from loading such executable programs in local file system.

(3) Therefore, applets had to acquire an appropriate security privilege to load these programs.

Problem is that the methods to acquire an appropriate privilege differ in each web browser. You write source code with a conditional executive operation to detect what browser is used and prepare an implementation for each web browser. Then, you release that applet. It works well. In the future, you may want to deal with next three demands without modifying the source code of the original applet:

1) A new web browser "WebStar" will be released. You want to modify the conditional executive operation like that; if the applet is running on a "WebStar", the module for "WebStar" is selected by the conditional executive operation to execute the operation for acquiring the security privilege.

2) Originally, there are no special modules only for NN. If the applet is running on NN, a default module is selected to acquire a security privilege. Then, you have to prepare a special module for NN. Therefore, you will make a module for NN. You want to make the conditional executive operation updated.

3) Originally, the conditional execution depends on only one factor, that is, the kind of web browser. Then, it becomes to depend on the version of NN, too. Therefore, you want to add a new operation that checks the web browser's version to the original conditional operation.

3. Approach

Our problem is that the program has to behave differently to accommodate with various run-time environments. Our approach to solve the problem is preparing the following model and mechanisms to adapt the program to the run-time environment dynamically by facilitating the selection of appropriate procedure from the conditional part of the program:

(1) a model of conditional execution and data format to represent the model,
(2) a mechanism to structure a model dynamically from information acquired at run-time,
(3) a mechanism to create conditional operations from the model structured by (2) and to execute them.

Firstly, we found that it is necessary for structural items of (1) to implement the following two types of information in order to implement our approach:

(a) an information about environmental factors that should be observed. It describes the number and contents of conditional execution. See Section 4.1 *factor-map*.
(b) an information about behavior that should be executed according to the factors. It describes rules adapted to execute conditional execution. See Section 4.1 *label-map*.

Secondly, we created a new design pattern *Answerer* that implements (2) and (3),
In the following chapter, we explain how we applied and implemented this policy as the *Answerer* pattern.

4. Solution : the *Answerer* pattern

In this chapter, we propose the *Answerer* design pattern that makes software adaptable for a variety of run-time environments dynamically. In the *Answerer* pattern, conditional execution is composed of switch-clauses and information about the structures that will be acquired from outside of the program when it is executed.

In Section 4.1, we define terms used in this paper. In Section 4.2, we define a *goal* with these terms and decompose it into three *subgoals*. In Section 4.3, we show a class structure to implement our approach.

4.1. Definitions of terms

In this section, we define some terms (a term is defined in the form 'term_name: explanation') to represent a conditional execution. We define terms in next two steps. Firstly, we define terms about structural items of a conditional execution.

choosing: A conditional execution. Figure 1 shows an example of a *choosing*. A *choosing* can be represented by tree structure as illustrated in Figure 2.

factor: An item that a *choosing* refers to select an answer (e.g., the vendor-name of a web browser) (see Figure 2). In Figure 1, *factors* are *S1*, *S2* and *S3*.

label: A candidate for a value of a *factor*. In Figure 1, *labels* are the values of the constant expressions in the case-labels (i.e., *1a*, *1b*, *2a*, etc.).

chosenValue: An answer that is chosen by a *choosing* (see Figure 2). In Figure 1, a *chosenValue* is one of *A*, *B*, ... *H*.

```
choosing1
  switch(S1){
    case 1a : chosenValue = A; break;
    case 1b : {
      switch(S2){
        case 2a : chosenValue = B; break;
        case 2b : chosenValue = C; break;
        default : chosenValue = D; break;
      }
    }
    case 1c : {
      switch(S3){
        case 3a : chosenValue = E; break;
        case 3b : chosenValue = F; break;
        default : chosenValue = G; break;
      }
    }
    default : chosenValue = D;
  }
choosing
```

Figure 1. *Choosing*

Next, we describe operations executed by a conditional execution using maps. A map associates keys with values. A map cannot contain duplicate keys; each key can be associated with at most one value. We can create two maps shown in Figure 3 from a *choosing* shown in Figure 2. The definitions of these maps are as follows:

factor-map: A map that associates a *choosing* with a set of *factors* (see Figure 3). A value of this map describes the number and the contents of *factors* used by the *choosing*.

label-map: A map that associates sets of possible *labels* of *factors* with *chosenValues* (see Figure 3).

In a *label-map*, a character '-' means that the *factor* corresponding to the character '-' is irrelevant to this *choosing*. Similarly, a character '*' means a "default" *label*.

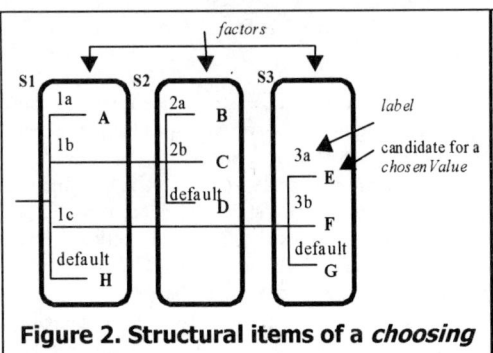

Figure 2. Structural items of a *choosing*

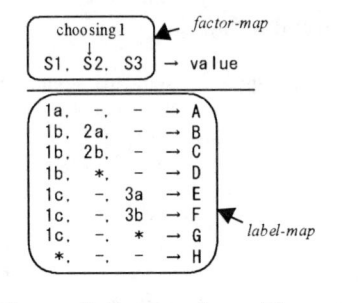

Figure 3. Expression with maps

Enhancing an Event-Based OO Framework for Distributed Programming

Bilhanan Silverajan, Jarmo Harju

Dept. of Information Technology, Tampere University of Technology,
P.O. Box 553, FIN-33101 Tampere, Finland
Tel: +358-3-365 3906 Fax: +358-3-365 3808
email: {bilhanan \ harju}@cs.tut.fi

Abstract

This paper discusses an asynchronous event-based object-oriented framework, OVOPS, employing the usage of design patterns to incorporate and interwork with a CORBA enabled environment. Distributed programming is constantly evolving into a very realistic technology which enhances systems integration through interoperability, adaptability and flexibility. However such advantages, coupled with performance, can only be gained by the proper analysis and design of the systems or frameworks in question. A critical examination would reveal that such a framework can be made realistically possible through the usage of object-oriented methods combined with the elegance of design patterns and the advances made in CORBA technology. The described environment will ensure consistent creation of protocols and other such similar services through reusable object-oriented components communicating over a heterogeneous network while addressing certain shortcomings, such as ensuring asynchronous communication remaining guaranteed and providing native event and message based features without resorting to CORBA-based messaging and event services. It also attempts to shield the developer from network specific issues by providing a more generic but very consistent technique to interface to the underlying services. Two areas in which such a framework can be employed are described within the Intelligent Networks realm to illustrate the available methods and practices.

1. Introduction

Currently protocol standards contain both the specification of abstract service interfaces and the specification of the protocol itself. Yet, the communications software products resulting from the multi-layer specifications are large and complex, and modularity achieved by applying traditional methods of structured programming in the layered protocol architecture has been considered insufficient. To ease the deployment of object oriented methods in protocol engineering, object oriented frameworks for implementing protocol software have been developed. One such framework which has been successfully designed is OVOPS, which serves as a middleware operating asynchronously using event and message based mechanisms. Advances in distributed programming, especially CORBA, having become undeniably significant and ubiquitous, have forced designers to rethink about having a consistent and easy-to-use open framework which can be used in a distributed environment and communicate in a compliant manner. In this paper, such a framework was successfully designed by modifying the OVOPS development environment. Such interworking between legacy systems

0-7695-0278-4/99 $10.00 © 1999 IEEE

and CORBA clients and servers can be done in several ways. The core CORBA specifications, for example, discuss the usage of the Dynamic Invocation Interface and the Dynamic Skeleton Interface mechanisms to implement gateways capable of interoperating with foreign object systems [1]. In order to better support asynchronous communication for CORBA compliant frameworks which need event and message based features, CORBA services such as the Event Service [2] have been defined and other services such as the Messaging and Notification Services are being actively studied by the relevant OMG working groups. This is primarily due to the fact that the core CORBA specifications do not guarantee support for asynchronous or one-way messaging. Interworking can be done in other ways too, such as building specialized Object Adapters and using the Internet Inter-ORB Protocol.

In this paper, an alternative and innovative approach of interworking with CORBA systems has been studied to those proposed by OMG, by using and adapting design pattern techniques. It shows how design patterns can be used to overcome the same issues without suffering any loss in functionality nor needing any overheads of using CORBA-based messaging or event services. At the same time it still supports rapid development and lower learning curves for both novice and adept users of the OVOPS framework to reap the advantage of load-sharing over multiple machines. Although this paper explores the interworking with CORBA systems, it also shows how, by using these design patterns, the interworking of OVOPS with other kinds of distributed object models can quickly and easily be incorporated, without being tied to one particular type of distributed technology such as CORBA.

2. OVOPS – A protocol implementation framework

In protocol engineering, work usually begins at the formal language definition level. Proceeding this, the protocol engineer often has to employ compilers and development and runtime environments. OVOPS provides such an environment suited to interfacing the various applications and protocols whilst itself not being a FDT.

The Object Virtual OPerations system (OVOPS) [5] supports the design, implementation and prototyping of protocols and distributed applications by providing an object oriented framework with class libraries and tools, that are often needed in the development of communications software. OVOPS has also been successfully employed to develop medium to complex protocols widely used in telecommunications, as well as asynchronous communications in client-server architectures. Figure 1 illustrates the OVOPS general model.

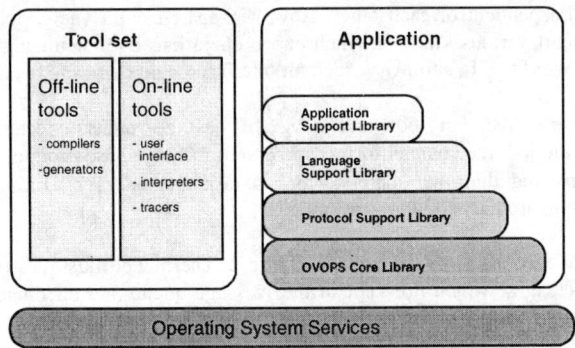

Figure 1. The OVOPS general model

The basic services and tools as provided by OVOPS libraries encompass the following features:

- scheduling of OVOPS tasks either with the default or user implemented scheduler
- asynchronous message passing between tasks through the usage of port classes
- I/O handler, interfaces to devices and other operating system services
- graphical and textual protocol tracers for message tracing and debugging
- hierarchical symbol interface to support user interactions in a symbolic form
- efficient, flexible and controllable memory management
- timers, frames and other useful classes.

A protocol support class library eases the programming of routine issues related to the creation of protocol implementations. Of specific interest in understanding the design and implementation of protocols are the PTask, StateMachine, IFace and PortMux classes. These classes play an active role in helping automate many routine tasks a programmer would face in the event of implementing a protocol.

At the topmost level OVOPS provides support for the development of applications via the component library containing protocol modules that can be used by applications. OVOPS does not provide a kernel-like environment. An entire OVOPS application, which typically incorporates various OVOPS task entities, a scheduler and an I/O Handler, is run as a single user-level process. This has the advantage of having a significant performance gain when tasks are scheduled within a single operating system process [6]. Simple distribution is achieved in OVOPS chiefly using socket based communication techniques. Therefore OVOPS by itself does not manage concurrency and scheduling issues among the several processes which may comprise a distributed application. Instead, the underlying operating system assumes the responsibility of handling the scheduling and concurrency methods amongst these processes.

2.1 Tasks, ports, channels and messages

The OVOPS methodology reduces any protocol to be built into a set of interacting tasks, channels and messages. Tasks communicate via messages sent asynchronously. Each task has ports which form the endpoint of a channel. Each message received by a task usually depicts an event. The direct implication of this model is that all channels are dedicated bi-directional port pairs, with each port thus being able to connect to only one other port. This way, tasks in OVOPS remain independent of each other. However, apart from asynchronous operations, a task can also support various kinds of synchronous operations by announcing these as public operations via its interface. In summary, such an interface could therefore be said to consist of 2 parts:

- The task's sending/receiving port and the set of messages understood by the task which could be sent through the channel for asynchronous, message based communication.
- The operations and their parameters which a task announces by means of its public interface for synchronous communication.

An abstract model of a task is depicted in Figure 2. The model illustrates the principles of how ports and messages, which are kept in the message queue, are encompassed within an OVOPS task. The model also brings attention to the existence of finite state machines implicitly existing within each event driven task. During execution, the task would remove messages from the message queue to investigate the type of event reported, and depending on its current state, perform a series of actions. The implementation of the finite state machine is left to the user or to the tools and supporting libraries provided by the OVOPS Protocol Support Library.

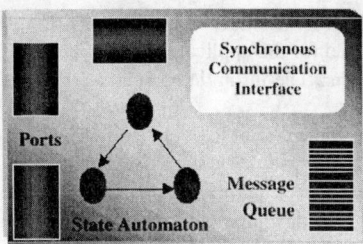

Figure 2. Task abstraction

As the system is not pre-emptive, only one task is executed at any one time. The executing task, upon completion must relinquish control to other tasks inside the process waiting for the end of execution of the running task. A scheduler handles decisions regarding allowable execution time for these tasks.

2.2 Scheduling and I/O handling subsystems in OVOPS

Scheduling within an OVOPS application can be achieved either through the scheduler provided by the OVOPS system or by using a user written scheduler. Upon creation, the task calls the inform operation of the scheduler for notifying that a new task has been created and should be scheduled. Accordingly the scheduler becomes responsible for the provision of execution turns to those tasks until the load of the executing task reaches zero. When there are no requests from the OVOPS tasks for execution turns, the scheduler would pass the execution turn to the I/O Handler and eventually blocks on the I/O Handler waiting for external events.

The I/O Handling in OVOPS can be regarded as a subsystem in its own right and provides the functionality needed to interface to external systems. The I/O Handler is an operating system specialized class which controls all device instances. These instances provide a way to model real life devices so that they present a gateway for the OVOPS system to inter-communicate with external events.

Essentially, the management by the I/O Handler of its devices in OVOPS is very similar to that between the scheduler and tasks. The *inform* and *forget* functions of the I/O Handler are invoked whenever a device is created or destroyed. By registering with each device, the I/O Handler is able to monitor for the occurrence of external events upon obtaining execution turns from the scheduler by checking the status of each device and performing the appropriate callback function specified by each device. If no such event has occurred, the I/O Handler would block. In UNIX terms, each device basically monitors one file descriptor, and the I/O Handler uses the *select()* UNIX system call to block on events on these file descriptors. Upon the arrival of an event on any of the devices, the I/O Handler would request an execution turn from the scheduler and subsequently invoke a callback function on the waiting device to process the event. This principle of operation closely corresponds to the Reactor Pattern [7] as presented by Schmidt.

2.3 OVOPS applications implementation methodology

In the main routine, such as the *main.C* file of an OVOPS application, prior to the invocation of the scheduler's *run()* function, activities pertaining to instantiations, initializations and interconnections of the various classes must be defined. These could be:

- Initialization of the OVOPS Memory Manager (OMM).Various types of memory managers could be employed for the application.
- Instantiation of the scheduler. The instantiated scheduler could either be OVOPS supplied or user implemented.
- Instantiation of the I/O Handler. Usually only one I/O Handler is ever needed, and the initialization of the I/O Handler would lie in registering it with the scheduler.
- Instantiations and the interconnecting/binding relationships among the various tasks
- Optionally, various debugging development time utilities and tracers if needed
- Any other application-specific instantiations, checks and operations, such as the usage of timers and devices.

Once these are accomplished, the scheduler's *run()* function is invoked in an infinite *while* loop which is broken either when the process has ended (during runtime) or when the *Exit* command is issued in the TPT (during development time).

3. Extending OVOPS towards CORBA object integration

For a pure CORBA based system, the general order of activities in the main routine are similar. The following sequence is loosely adopted for the server implementations:
- Initialization of the ORB
- Initialization of the OA (Object Adapter)
- Instantiation of the object implementations the server is prepared to offer.
- Other service specific operations

For an OVOPS application which also wishes to serve as a CORBA server, integration cannot be achieved by simply combining the sequence described above with that of the preceding section, as there are two event loop operations; the first with the OVOPS scheduler's *run()* function called within the *while* loop, and the second with the OA's *impl_is_ready()* function.

The solution is to be able to create and manage ORB-related event device class instances within OVOPS which will then work together with the I/O Handler, so that in the case of any CORBA events occurring, the scheduler can pass execution turns to the ORB for event processing. This implies that the ORB implementation should be able to provide a callback functionality which will inform the OVOPS system whenever any I/O operations occur. Orbix is one of a several ORBs which provides exactly this functionality in the ORB's *registerIOCallBack()* function call [8]. This function call, could, for example, trigger a notification to the I/O Handler that there are CORBA specific events waiting to be handled, and a subsequent request from the I/O Handler to the scheduler for an execution turn to process the awaiting events using the OA's *processEvents()* operation.

The addition of two new classes in the OVOPS core make possible the design methodology discussed. Two abstract base classes, ORBDevice and CORBAGateKeeper have been designed; ORBDevice is a base class from which concrete ORB classes which represent vendor-specific ORBs can be derived. CORBAGateKeeper handles the creation and destruction of the various individual connection specific ORBDevice-based instances by managing them in a list. This is necessary in order to comply with the design philosophy of the I/O Handler: each device instance should only handle exactly one file descriptor.

The employment of the Singleton Pattern [9] guarantees that only one instance of the CORBAGateKeeper exists in any one application which is globally accessible, while the usage of the Factory Method Pattern [9] allows the definition of an interface for creating the

ORBDevice object, but enables the deferment of class instantiation to subclasses. This allows the usage of multiple ORB implementations with OVOPS as long as they are able to support the basic mechanism described in the preceding paragraphs. Figure 3 illustrates these operations.

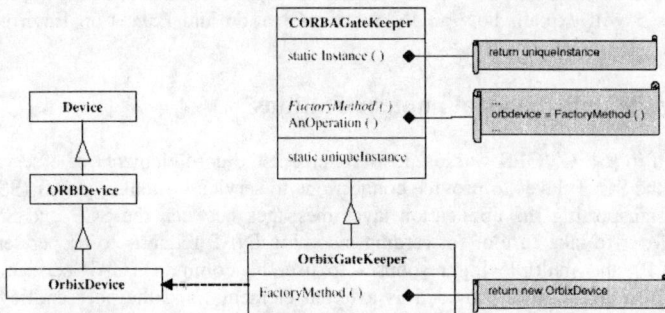

Figure 3. Class derivations for interworking with Orbix

Figure 4 depicts a Message Sequence Chart showing the order of events which could easily occur that enable an OVOPS application to pass scheduled execution turns to the ORB via some intervention by the I/O Handler.

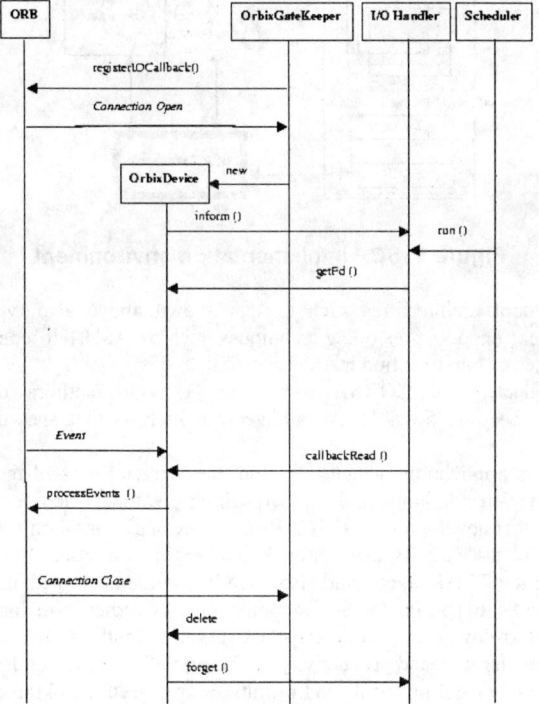

Figure 4. Message Sequence Chart

The integration of CORBA technology in this manner opens several plausible opportunities to apply such distribution to application areas traditionally employing OVOPS to build either protocol implementations or client-server applications, as well as other areas which would benefit from such an alliance. The next two sections describe such scenarios within the domain of Intelligent Networks. Section 4 will discusses a CORBA enhanced protocol implementation, while Section 5 will explain how an IN Service Creation and Execution Environment was implemented.

4. Building possible protocol implementations

As reported in [5], OVOPS was used to implement the core elements of a service control point (SCP): the SCCP layer to provide connections to service switching points (SSP), TCAP protocol for transporting the application layer messages between the SCP and SSP and an INAP multiplexer to take care of forwarding incoming INAP requests to proper service logic programs (SLP) and multiplexing responses to use the common TCAP service. The SSP simulator and the SLPs were provided as external elements, and the peer entities of INAP, TCAP and SCCP protocols at the SSP simulator were provided by a non-OVOPS based commercial software. For simplicity, TCP/IP sockets were used to connect the SCP process and the SSP simulator below the SCCP layer, instead of the SS7 message transfer protocols (MTP 1 - 3), as conceptually depicted in Figure 5.

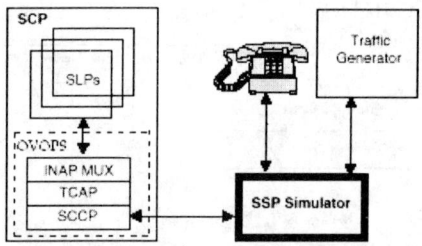

Figure 5. SCP implementation environment

Traditional protocol architectures such as that shown above also typically depend on platform independent encoding/decoding techniques such as ASN.1 to communicate reliably over the socket based communication methods present.

With the introduction of CORBA technology, a wide plethora of implementation architectures could become possible. An architecture such as that shown in Figure 6 was achieved easily.

The model covers applications which may find the characteristics of the ORB such as its reliability, security, marshalling and unmarshalling features rich enough to directly communicate at higher level protocols. TCAP, as an example, uses only the connectionless feature of SCCP, identifying its peer through its Destination Point Code and Subsystem Number. Therefore the TCAP layer could also directly communicate with its peer by using the ORB using object calls, bypassing the SCCP completely, if overheads such as ASN.1 encoding and the construction of lower layer connectionless service primitives are not needed. This will obviously lead to greater ease and productivity on the part of the protocol designer as he or she would now be able to model protocols and primitives as objects invoking operations directly on each other, passing data as parameters to the appropriate operations instead of as PDUs.

This is one approach which is currently being studied by the OMG CORBA/IN Interworking committee [10].

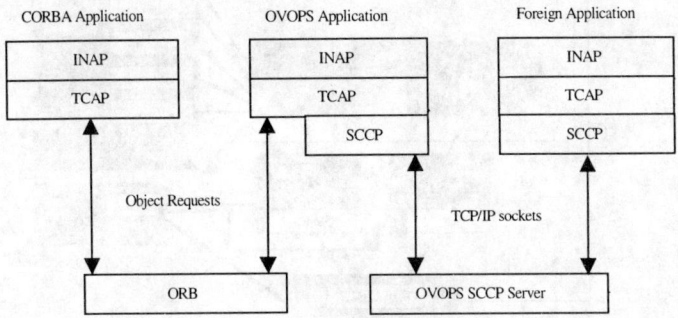

Figure 6. Possible protocol implementations

5. Building an Intelligent Network Service Creation Environment

Directly harnessing these CORBA-enhanced protocols, a Service Creation Environment (SCE) to create and model real-life services within the Intelligent Network area could be built. A Service Control platform provides a service logic execution environment (SLEE) within which service logic processing programs (SLPs) run to provide pertinent service processing.

An SLP is a service application program invoked by the SLEE and is used to realize service processing under the control of the SLEE. The simultaneous invocation and execution of multiple SLPs are also managed by the SLEE. When an SLP is selected and invoked, it is referred to as a service logic processing program instance (SLPI). In contrast to an SLP, a corresponding SLPI is a dynamic entity that actively controls the flow of service execution.

This flow of service execution is broken down into a sequence of service independent building blocks (SIBs) which are standard reusable networkwide components, each encompassing a complete monolithic activity, that can be chained together in a variety of combinations to define a service.

Figure 7 illustrates the SLEE which also acts as a Service Creation Environment. The CoreINAP Driver provides an implementation of the ETSI Core Intelligent Network Application Protocol (INAP) which is a Remote Operations Service Element (ROSE) user protocol [11]. It connects to the underlying Signalling Stack Number 7 to communicate with other Service Points in the network and is responsible for converting ASN.1 messages to IDL datatypes and vice-versa.

This model supports the synchronous as well as the asynchronous models of communication. All protocol specific transmission is guaranteed to be reliable, as synchronous calls are used for CORBA object requests (which are subsequently translated into OVOPS-specific messages) and OVOPS provides reliable delivery with via event-based mechanism. Thus, no additional CORBA service for messaging or event-handling is needed.

The CoreINAP Driver, Naming Service, and Database Driver all provide object implementations for interfaces specified in IDL. These components of the architecture are supplied by a third party vendor for the HP-UX 10.20 platform while the service specific SLPFactories, their associated call instance handling tasks as well as the SIB Inventory had been developed and execute on the Solaris 2.5 platform.

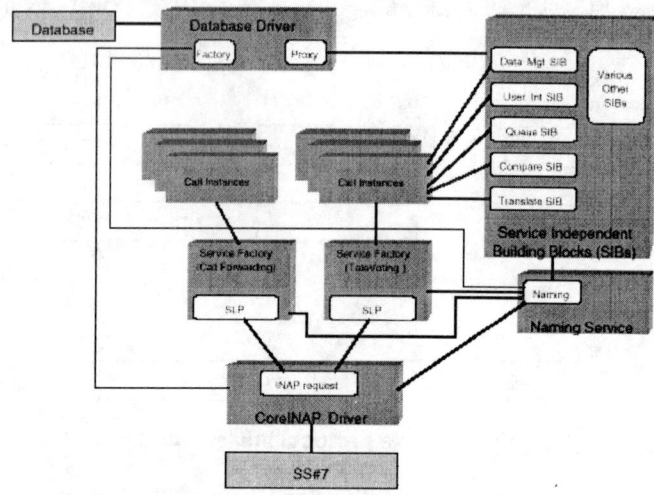

Figure 7. Service Creation Environment

The SLPFactories, derived from OVOPS tasks attempt to isolate the network specific information flow from the service specific information flow. This will essentially mean that the services created would become independent of the underlying protocol which is used to communicate with the other service entities across the network, providing the advantage of being able to run the service over multiple protocols. Also the architecture harnesses the multiplexing and multiple connection handling facilities that OVOPS provides in the manner in which the OVOPS tasks representing individual call instances (SLPIs) are managed. The resulting concrete factories are usually enforced with the Singleton pattern, since every application typically needs only one instance of a concrete Service Factory per service [12].

The SIB Inventory provides a sub-set of fully implemented SIBs which can be easily used as building blocks for a service. The instantiation of the SIBs should be as minimal as possible to avoid a proliferation of an extremely large number of SIB instances and thus the SIBs have been designed following the principles of design similar to the Flyweight Pattern [9].

A major deviation from the standard Flyweight Pattern arises from the usage of CORBA technology. The Flyweight Factory is no longer necessary as it can be replaced by the ORB working in the shared activation mode. Flyweights however, cannot assume the context in which they are operating. All such data must therefore be managed by the SLPI.

Each SLPI is an event-driven task which possesses state information and depending on the current state and the type of Information Flow (IF) it receives from its concrete service factory, it launches a predetermined chain of SIBs to perform the necessary series of actions. The SLPI thus forms the "glue" which holds all the necessary data and parameters needed by the SIBs, since the SIBs themselves are independent blocks which have no notion of service.

The State Pattern [9] when modified, together with the Singleton pattern, provide an easy behavioural technique for managing this complexity by introducing a set of abstract classes which represent and store the state*input combinations of the SLPI and the temporal data specific to each combination.

6. Conclusions

The ability of OVOPS applications to interoperate as CORBA server implementations is a significant step in enhancing the nature of distribution in OVOPS. Better still, such integration had been achieved by extending the behaviour at the core level. Although the integration of OVOPS with CORBA had been successfully achieved in a rather elegant manner, still open questions remain over certain key issues. The most pressing issue is that seamless integration can possibly only occur through a modified scheduling algorithm. This reduces the burden on the I/O Handler freeing it to handle other kinds of events but retains a certain level of performance and reliability, provided a suitably decent scheduling algorithm is used.

The design methodologies presented in this work, including the usage of the design patterns and their modifications thereof, were also used to achieve the maximum portability possible for independence from underlying operating systems. Much of the techniques presented could have used alternatives such as synchronous multithreading mechanisms. However, threads often have high performance overheads and require a deep knowledge of synchronization patterns and principles in order to manage access to shared resources. Threading may also not be available on all platforms.

Design patterns are also constantly growing given the vast pool of emerging experiences and the rapid acceptance of object-oriented methodologies. The work described in this paper verifies that the usage of technologies such as CORBA as well as design patterns combined with the usability and power of OVOPS holds great promise.

7. References

[1]   OMG: The Common Object Request Broker: Architecture and Specification. CORBA V2.2, February 1998.
[2]   OMG : CORBAservices, Common Object Services Specification, December 1998
[3]   OMG : Messaging Service Document orbos/98-03-12
[4]   OMG : Notification Service Document telecom/98-01-01
[5]   J. Harju, B. Silverajan, I. Toivanen: OVOPS – Experiences in Telecommunications Protocols with an OO Based Implementation Framework Proc. ECOOP '97 Workshop on Object Oriented Technology for Telecommunications Services Engineering, Jyvaskyla , Finland June 9 - 13, 1997.
[6]   J.Harju, B. Silverajan: OVOPS – An Object Oriented Implementation Framework For Communication Protocols. Proc. IEEE MICC '97, Kuala Lumpur, Malaysia, November 10 –13, pp S22B.3.1-S22B.3.6
[7]   D. C. Schmidt: Reactor: An Object Behavioural Pattern for Concurrent Event Demultiplexing and Event Handler Dispatching. Pattern Languages of Program Design (J.O. Coplien and D. C. Schmidt, eds.), Reading, MA: Addison-Wesley, 1995.
[8]   IONA Technologies : Orbix 2.2 Reference Guide, March 1997
[9]   E. Gamma, R. Helm, R. Johnson, J. Vlissides: Design Patterns, Elements of Reusable Object-Oriented Software. Addison-Wesley 1995.
[10]   OMG: IN/CORBA Interworking, document telecom/98-06-03
[11]   ETSI: Recommendations ETS 300 374-1, Intelligent Network Capability Set 1 (CS1) Core Intelligent Network Application Protocol (INAP) Part 1: Protocol Specification, ETSI 1994.
[12]   B. Silverajan: A CORBA-Enhanced Implementation Environment for Distributed IN Service Creation, MSc Thesis, 1998.

Technical Papers

Methods 1

Use Case Pitfalls:
Top 10 Problems from Real Projects Using Use Cases

Susan Lilly
SRA International, Inc.
4300 Fair Lakes Ct.
Fairfax, VA 22033
susan_lilly@sra.com
703-227-5103

Abstract

One of the beauties of use cases is their accessible, informal format. Use cases are easy to write, and the graphical notation is trivial. Because of their simplicity, use cases are not intimidating, even for teams that have little experience with formal requirements specification and management. However, the simplicity can be deceptive; writing good use cases takes some skill and practice. Many groups writing use cases for the first time run into similar kinds of problems. This paper presents the author's "Top Ten" list of use case pitfalls and problems, based on observations from a number of real projects. The paper outlines the symptoms of the problems, and recommends pragmatic cures for each. Examples are provided to illustrate the problems and their solutions.

Introduction

Over the past few years, we have seen a number of projects make their first attempts at developing use cases. These projects have used use cases in a number of ways: as the entire system requirements specification, as part of the system requirements, as an analysis technique to elicit user requirements that were subsequently specified in other forms (e.g., traditional "shalls"), and as software subsystem-level requirements. The project teams that developed the use cases have included developers and/or analysts; in some cases the project teams have included customers or end users as well.

Although the project teams had little trouble getting started with use cases, many of them encountered similar problems in applying them on a larger scale. These problems include undefined or inconsistent system boundary, use case model complexity, use case specification length and granularity, and use cases that are hard to understand or never complete. These have been grouped and summarized here as a *"Top Ten"* list of use case pitfalls and problems, which may be encountered by inexperienced practitioners.

A sample problem is used to provide simple examples throughout this paper. *The Baseball Ticket Order System* is a computer system that is to be deployed to simplify customer sales for baseball games. Customers may view the season schedule and reserve tickets at kiosks placed in convenient locations, such as malls. Alternately, customers may call an 800 number and a phone clerk will reserve tickets for them. The customer may pay by credit card, or may pay at the time the tickets are picked up at the stadium on the day of the game.

The Top Ten List

Problem #1: The system boundary is undefined or inconsistent.

Symptom: The use cases are described at inconsistent system scope -- some use cases at business scope, others at system or even subsystem scope.

One element of the use case model is a labeled box that indicates the system boundary; the actors go outside of this box, and the use cases go inside. Before we determine the actors and use cases, we must be explicit about what we mean by "system." Is it a computer system? An application? A component or subsystem? Or is it a whole business enterprise? Use cases might be used to describe any of these "system" boundaries, but should only focus on one at a time. The actors and use cases appropriate at one system boundary are likely to be incorrect for a different system boundary. A common problem is the mix of both scopes in the same use case model, or even within a single use case specification.

Example: A *Kiosk Customer* uses the computer system to order tickets. Alternately, a *Phone Customer* may call the ticket business, and a *Phone Clerk* (an employee of the ticket business) may use the computer system to order tickets. Who are the actors? Figure 1 illustrates a mixed-up system boundary: The modelers have tried to show both the users of the business and the users of the system in the same use case model.

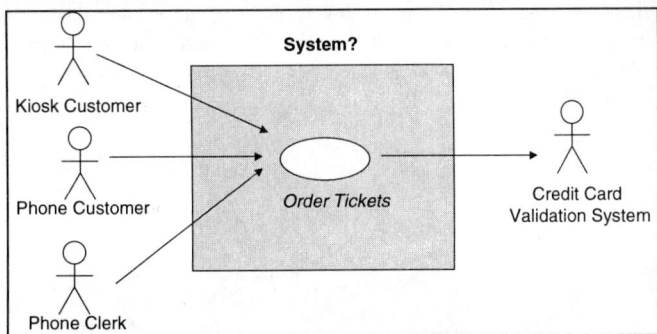

Figure 1: Use Case with Mixed-Up Scope

Cure: Be explicit about the scope, and label the system boundary accordingly. Say: "Yes, the business model is very interesting, but right now we are defining our use cases at the computer system scope" -- and then stick to it. *Example:* In Figure 2, the system boundary represents a computer system, and *Kiosk Customer* and *Phone Clerk* are actors who use the **Order Tickets** use case.

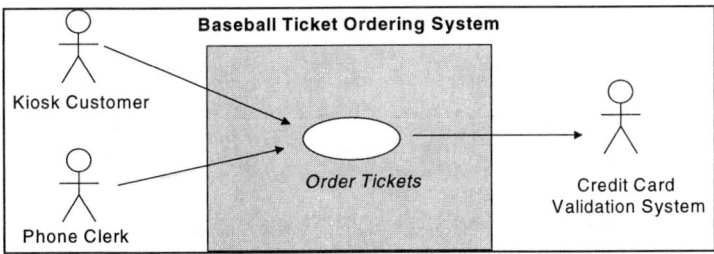

Figure 2: Use Case at Computer System Scope

In Figure 3, the system boundary represents a whole business enterprise. The actor, *Phone Customer*, is a user of the ticket business, but is not a user of the computer system. Both of these are appropriate ways to model; the choice between them depends on whether we are trying to define the requirements of a computer system (use Figure 2), or using use cases in business process modeling or reengineering (use Figure 3).

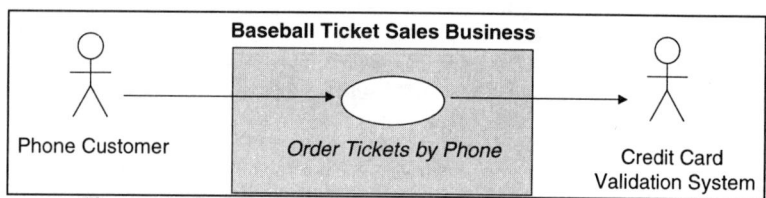

Figure 2: Use Case at Business Enterprise Scope

Symptom: Looking at the use case model, it's not really clear what's inside and what's outside the system. This problem often comes up when the use cases are modeled using a visual modeling/CASE tool (including the leading one on the market) that doesn't show the system boundary on the use case model.

Cure: Draw the system boundary (at least in your head). If the modeling tool does not draw a system boundary, place the use cases inside and the actors outside an imaginary box. *Example:* Figure 4 shows the same use case model, formatted in different ways. The model on the left has mixed up the actors and use cases; the one on the right has placed the use cases in the middle ("inside") with the actors on the "outside."

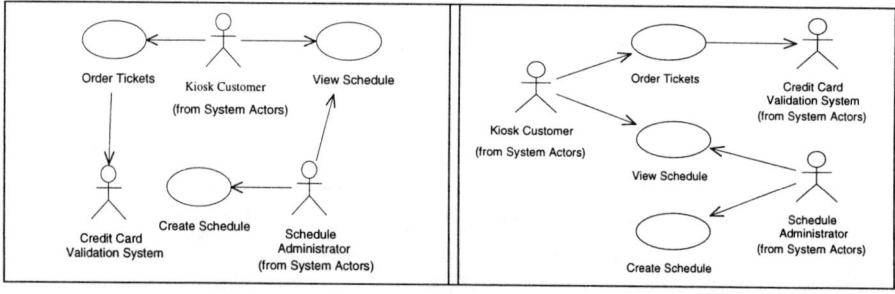

Figure 3: Use Case Model Formatting (bad and better)

Problem #2: The use cases are written from the system's (not the actors') point of view.

Symptom: The use case names describe what the system does, rather than the goal the actor wants to accomplish.

Cure: Name the use cases from the perspective of the Actor's goals. *Example:* **Process Ticket Order** and **Display Schedule** are things the system does (bad use case names). **Order Tickets** and **View Schedule** are goals of the system's users (good use case names).

Symptom: The steps in the use case specification describe internal functionality, rather than interactions across the system boundary.

Cure: Focus on what the system needs to do to satisfy the actor's goal, not how it will accomplish it.

Symptom: The use case model looks like a data/process flow diagram.

Cure: Watch out when the use case model includes use cases that are not directly associated with an actor, but are associated with *<<uses>>* or *<<extends>>* relationships. Sometimes this is an appropriate way to model the use cases. But many neophyte use case modelers (especially those who are programmers, or who have a process modeling background) misuse these associations, functionally decomposing the problem, rather than focusing on the interactions between actors and the system. Take a look at the specifications of used or extension use cases, to ensure that the steps in them describe interactions between the actor (of the base use case) and the system. If the steps are entirely focused on internal processing, the used and extended use cases are probably being used as a mechanism for functional decomposition. (If so, they don't belong in the use case model.)

Problem #3: The actor names are inconsistent.

Symptom: Different actor names are used to describe the same role. This is amazingly easy to do, since different sources of requirements often use variant names for the same thing -- and similar names for quite different things. When a problem is large, there are often multiple teams working on use case models for different parts of the problem, and the same (logical) actor may appear with variant names from model to model. *Example:* The role of the person who manages the online baseball schedule is called "Schedule Administrator" in one model, "Schedule Manager" in another, and "Scheduler" in a third.

Cure: Get agreement early in the project about the use of actor names (and other terms). Establish a *glossary* early in the project and use it to define the actors. The glossary should specify the actor name, its meaning, and any aliases that this name is known by. Include the glossary as an appendix to the use case document.

Problem #4: Too many use cases.

Symptom: The use case model has a very large number of use cases.

Cure: Make sure that the granularity of the use cases is appropriate. Use cases should reflect "results of value" to the system's users -- the attainment of real user *goals*.

- Combine use cases that describe trivial or incidental behavior that are actually fragments of the real use cases. Use cases are sometimes chopped into fragments when there is an attempt to associate user interface screens to use cases in a 1-to-1 relationship.
- Remove use cases that describe purely "internal" system processing ("internal" with respect to whatever system boundary is being used).

Example: In Figure 5, the Happy *Kiosk Customer* actor is associated with a use case called **Order Tickets** -- the customer's real goal in walking up to the kiosk in the mall. The Sad *Kiosk Customer* actor is associated with three different use cases. They all describe interactions between the *Kiosk Customer* and the system, but they represent incidental steps in the attainment of the actor's real goal (to order tickets). How did the "real" use case get split into three sub-goal use cases? The modelers were attempting to make a separate use case for each user interface element.

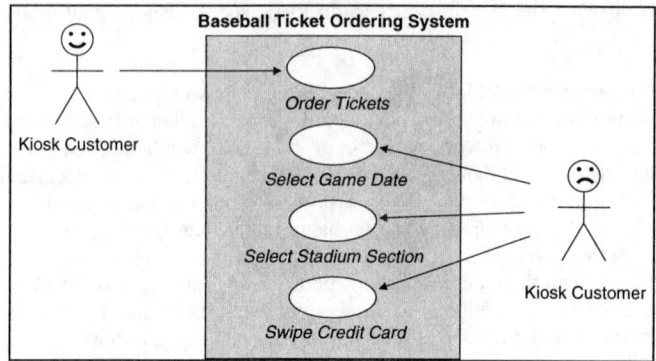

Figure 4: Real Use Cases vs. Incidental Actions

If the granularity of the use cases is right, but the system is simply very large, partition the set of use cases. Break the use case model into use case *packages*, each of which contains a cohesive set of use cases and a limited set of actors. *Example:* Figure 6 shows a use case model that has a large number of use cases. Figure 7 illustrates the same set of use cases, partitioned into 5 packages. Each package should contain a "cohesive" subset of the use cases, grouped around one or more actors who share common goals.

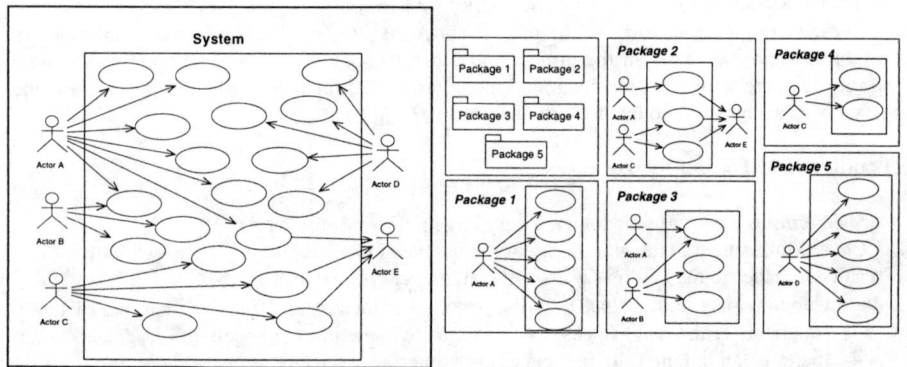

Figure 5: Model Needs Partitioning   **Figure 6: Model with Packages**

Problem # 5: The actor-to-use case relationships resemble a spider's web.

Symptoms: (a) There are too many relationships between actors and use cases. (b) An actor interacts with every use case. (c) A use case interacts with every actor.

Cure: The actors may be defined too broadly. Examine actors to determine whether there are more explicit actor roles, each of which would participate in a more limited set of use cases. *Example: Employee* is very general, and is associated with a large number of use cases.

Phone Clerk and *Schedule Administrator* are more specific; each of these is associated with a smaller, more role-oriented set of use cases.

There may be cases where recognition of a more general class of actors helps to simplify a model. This often occurs where two or more actors are associated with the same set of use cases, because of some commonality in their roles. The resulting use case model has a spider's web of crossed lines between actors and use cases, as shown in Figure 8.

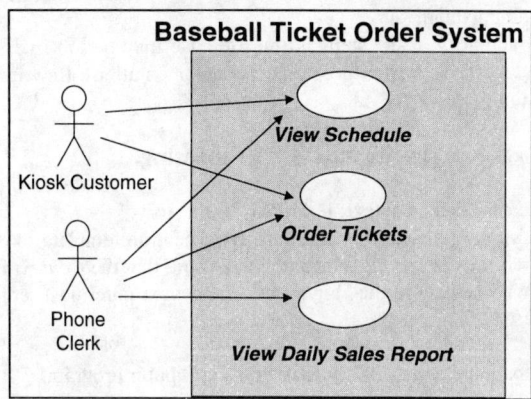

Figure 7: Actors with Overlapping Roles

The use case modeling notation provides a mechanism, **actor generalization**, for explicitly recognizing the commonality of actor roles. Figure 9 shows how the use case model can be redrawn with actor generalization to simplify the relationships between actors and use cases. This model says that *a Kiosk Customer* is a kind of *Ticketer* and that a *Phone Clerk* is a kind of a *Ticketer*. Any *Ticketer* may view a schedule or order tickets. A *Phone Clerk* (but not a *Kiosk Customer*) may additionally view a sales report.

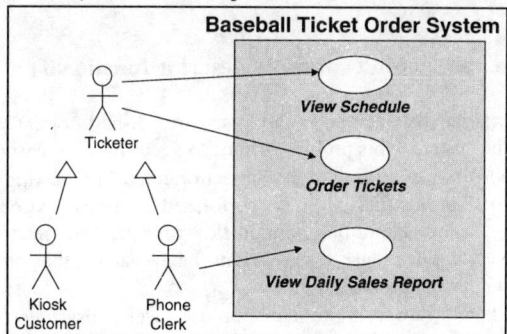

Figure 8: Use Case Model with Actor Generalization

Note that it would not have been correct to simply model *Phone Clerk* as a specialization of *Kiosk Customer*, in place of *Ticketer*. While the actor-to-use case relationships would be correct, the actor-to-actor relationship is semantically unsound: A *Phone Clerk* is **not** a kind of *Kiosk Customer*. (I saw that example in a recent use case book, which modeled a *Sales Rep* actor as a subclass of a *Customer* actor, in order to inherit the overlapping use case relationships.)

Problem #6: The use case specifications are too long.

Symptom: A use case specification goes on for pages.

Cure: The granularity of the use case may be too coarse. *Example:* **Use Schedule** (a use case that includes everything any user might want to do with a schedule) is too broad. More narrowly defined, specific use cases (such as **View Schedule** and **Create Schedule**) tend to be shorter and easier to understand.

Alternately, the granularity of the steps in the use case may be too fine. The steps may be too detailed or include purely internal processing (implementation). Rewrite them to focus on the essential interaction.

Problem #7: The use case specifications are confusing.

Symptom: The use case lacks context; it doesn't "tell a story."

Cure: Include a *Context* field in your use case specification template to describe the set of circumstances in which the use case is relevant. Make sure that the *Context* field puts each use case in perspective, with respect to the "big picture" (the next outermost scope). Don't just use it to summarize the use case.

Symptom: The steps in the normal flow look like a computer program.

Cure: Rewrite the steps to focus on a set of essential interactions between an actor and the system, resulting in the accomplishment of the actor's goal.

- Break out conditional behavior ("If...") into separately described alternate flows, leaving the normal flow shorter and easier to understand.
- Use case steps are not particularly effective for describing non-trivial algorithms, with lots of branching and looping. Use other, more effective techniques to describe complex algorithms (e.g., decision table, decision tree, or pseudocode).
- Make sure that the steps don't specify implementation. Focus on the external interactions. Consider expressing some of the behavior as "rules," rather than algorithms.

Problem #8: The use case doesn't correctly describe functional entitlement.

Symptom: The associations between actors and use cases doesn't correctly or fully describe who can do what with the system. This problem seems to occur for two reasons:

- The use case modelers were trying to be "object oriented," by making fat use cases that include all possible actions that might be performed on a business object. (I call these "CRUD use cases," since they often contain flows for creating, reading, updating, and deleting the object.) These use cases often have names that include the words "maintain," "manage," or "process."
- The use case modelers were trying to match up use cases to user interface screen. Faced with a view screen, that could also be edited (by a user with the right authority), they combined viewing and updating into a single use case that relates to the single screen design.

Example: Figure 10 shows a use case **Process Game Schedule**, that describes everything that any actor might want to do with a game schedule. Its specification has a "normal flow" for viewing the schedule, and alternate flows for updating the schedule. The *Kiosk Customer* actor may use the normal flow, but cannot use the alternate flow. Only the *Schedule Administrator* is functionally entitled to perform the schedule update.

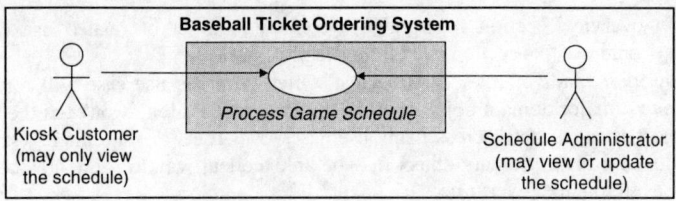

Figure 9: Confusing Functional Entitlement

Cure: Make sure that each actor associated with a use case is completely entitled to perform it. If an actor is only functionally entitled to part of the use case, the use case should be split. *Example:* The **Process Game Schedule** use case should be split into two: **View Game Schedule** and **Update Game Schedule**, as shown in Figure 11. Now it is clear, at a glance, that the *Kiosk Customer* may view, but not update, a schedule.

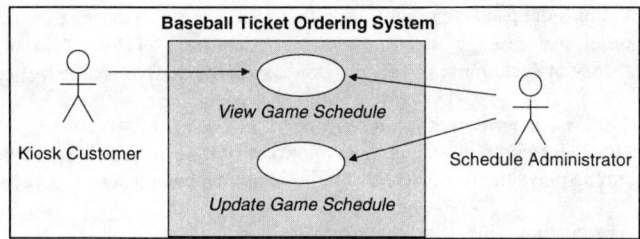

Figure 10: Use Cases with Correct Functional Entitlement

Problem #9: The customer doesn't understand the use cases.

Symptom: The customer doesn't know anything at all about use cases, but has been given a use case-based requirements document for review or approval. (Of course it's best when customers/end users have been included in the use case development. However, the person who reviews or approves the requirements may not have been involved in developing the use cases.)

Cure: Teach them just enough to understand.

–   Put a short (1-2 page) explanation of use cases in the use case document, as a preface or appendix. The explanation should include a key to reading the model and specifications, and a simple example.
–   Lead a short training session when use case document is distributed for review.
–   Think long and hard about using *<<uses>>* and *<<extends>>* relationships in the use case model. They are a modeling convenience, but are not at all intuitive to the inexperienced reviewer.

Symptom: The use cases don't tell a story.
Cure: Add information to tell the story:
–   Include a *Context* section in the use case template.

- Add an overview section that provides context to a set of related use cases (e.g., a package), and use this section to "tell the story."
- Include other kinds of models as needed. Often, a single use case will result in a state change to a major domain object, but the use case model alone won't tell the story of how the object changes state across many use cases over time. A state model (state transition diagram) of a major domain object may be an excellent way to show how several related use cases fit together over time.

Symptom: The use case organization doesn't match the way the customer thinks of the problem.

Cure: Determine what strategy for organizing the use cases makes the most sense to the customer. Listen to how the customer describes the business.

- How to partition the use cases into packages: Break out the use cases by major roles/actors, or by major events in the customer's business. *Example:* The customer talks a lot about "Spring Setup" -- when they put the new game schedule, stadium section definitions, and ticket prices into the system. Even if that's not the way the system developers think about the system, that's the package organization that makes sense to the customer.
- How to order use cases within a package: Order the use cases "chronologically," to describe a story of system use over time. Don't order the use cases alphabetically!

Symptom: Use case is written in "computerese."

Cure: Watch out for computer slang that is not part of the customer's vocabulary. *Example:* Say "The system displays the result screen," rather than "The result screen is invoked."

Symptom: The customer just hates the use cases.

Cure: Deliver what the customer wants. This doesn't mean that use cases can't be used as a requirements elicitation technique, if use cases are really the right technique for the job. But they might not be a primary delivered work product. *Example:* One customer has its own requirements document template, and it's not use-case based. But the system is highly operational in nature, and we feel that use cases are the best approach for eliciting and modeling the requirements. We perform the use-case based analysis, and then write the requirements in the format that the customer wants, based on what we learned in that analysis. The use cases might be included in an appendix to the requirements document, or they might not be a deliverable at all.

Problem #10. The use cases are never finished.

Symptom: Use cases have to change every time the user interface changes.

Cure: *Loosely couple* the user interface details and use case interactions. The user interface design is likely to change, and you don't want your system requirements to be dependent on design. (The dependency goes the other way -- the user interface design must satisfy the use case requirements.) A little coupling is okay -- "low fidelity" pictures of the user interface can aid understanding of the use case. But don't overly tie the fundamental interactions to the UI mechanisms (which are more likely to change). In the flows, focus on the essentials of what the actor does (e.g., "selects a game," "submits a request") rather than how the interaction is done (e.g., "double-click on the Submit button").

Specify use case "triggering" events as preconditions (e.g., "user has selected a game, and requested to order tickets"), rather than screen navigation details. Keep the screen navigation information in a (separate) user interface design document, not in the use case model.

Symptom: The use cases require change every time the design changes.

Cure: The easy answer is "Don't put design in your use cases." That's generally good advice when the use cases are at a computer system scope. The use cases should record what the system must do, not the design/implementation details. Make sure that your use case steps are not unnecessarily low level; that is, they should completely specify what they system must do, but no more than that. Put design information discovered during analysis into a separate Design Guidance document.

When use cases are defined at a subsystem scope, changes in system-level design (e.g., how functionality is partitioned between subsystems) can affect the subsystem requirements. Until the system design is stable (and explicitly documented), the subsystem requirements, including the use cases, will not stabilize.

Symptom: There are so many possible alternate cases!

Cure: Watch out for "analysis paralysis." There is a point at which the requirements are adequately specified, and further analysis and specification does not add quality. Cover the "80%" cases; do your best on the rest within the allocated budget of time and money.

Symptom: The requirements are just unknown.

Cure: Use cases have a simple, informal, and accessible format. This may lead to the deceptive conclusion that developing use cases is easy. However, the simplicity of the format does not mean that the requirements analysis process is any less critical or any easier. *Use cases are a mechanism for defining and documenting operational requirements, not magic.*

Conclusions

The pitfalls and problems described in this paper are not an indictment of use cases, but rather problems in the *application* of use cases by inexperienced practitioners. In our experience, most use case development teams include inexperienced members. Use cases may be a new technique to the organization, and are being used by the development team for the first time. Even when the analysts or system developers have experience with use cases, other team members may not. The ideal use case team includes customers, end users, and/or domain experts. In most cases, these team members will have no prior experience with use cases. The simplicity of the use case modeling notation and natural-language specifications make use cases extremely accessible to such team members. They may fully participate in the use case modeling and specification, but are likely to encounter the pitfalls described in this paper.

One suggestion for teams in which some or all of the members are new to use cases is perform periodic informal "in-progress" reviews of the use case models and specifications, in order to catch problems early in the development, and to educate the team members. Of course, a formal review or inspection of a finished use case document is also appropriate. The reviews can be made more effective by the use of a checklist to help identify these common problems. An example of such a checklist is available by email on request from the author.

Use Case Modeling Guidelines

Donald G. Firesmith

Lante Corporation

Don_Firesmith@Lante.com

1. Abstract

Use case modeling has become the most popular de facto standard technique for performing software requirements analysis and specification. However, use case modeling has its well-known problems, and different requirements engineers typically perform use case modeling differently. This paper provides a hierarchically organized set of detailed guidelines for use case modeling.

2. Introduction

Over the last decade, use cases have become the most popular de facto standard technique for software requirements analysis and specification within the object community. However, use case modeling has numerous well-known problems [1] [2] [3] [4]. It is inherently more functional than object-oriented, leading to a significant chasm and paradigm shift between requirements engineering and OO modeling. Putting the use case approach into practice also often illuminates problems that are not addressed in books and most articles on use cases, and different requirements engineers typically perform use case modeling differently.

This paper provides a hierarchically organized set of detailed guidelines for use case modeling. I have collected these guidelines from numerous real projects during the last six years and recently refined them using lessons learned while creating the software requirements specification for a large, embedded, distributed real-time system (the control software for an automated digital tape library).

3. Definitions

The following terms clarify use case modeling and the following guidelines:

- An **external [object or class]** (a.k.a., actor) is any relevant object or class that is external to the *application* (whether system or software) and interfaces (either directly or indirectly) with it. Externals can be stereotyped as [human] actors, data repositories, hardware externals, and software externals. For example, a digital thermostat *system* may have only a single external: its user. However, the *software* controlling the digital thermostat may have the following externals, many of which are internal to the system: actual temperature display, actual temperature sensor, desired temperature display, decrement actual temperature button, decrement desired temperature button, increment actual temperature button, increment desired temperature button, on/off button, status display, and user.

- A **use case** is a functional abstraction that captures a general way that an external interacts with a business or application to achieve some goal. A use case is primarily defined in terms of interactions between the business or application and its associated externals. Note that a use case is neither an operation of an external nor a business or application operation (function). Rather, a use case is typically that part of an external's operation that involves the business or application. For example, a simple digital thermostat may have the following use cases: "Change the state of the digital thermostat", "Change the desired temperature of the room", and "Control the actual temperature of the room".

- – An **essential use case** is a pure requirements-level use case that does not contain any unnecessary design constraints (e.g., GUI design details).

- A **use case path** (a.k.a., course) is a contiguous set of referential relationships traversed by the interactions of the use case. Because a single use case will typically have an indefinitely large number of paths that traverse it due to branching and looping, only a minimal basis set of paths is typically identified and analyzed. Each path is stereotyped as either a **normal path** (i.e., it achieves the underlying goal of the use case) or an **exceptional path** (i.e., it does not). For example, the normal paths through the "Change the desired temperature of the room" use case may be "Decrement the desired temperature" and "Increment the desired temperature". The exceptional paths of the "Control the actual temperature of the room" use case may include "Handle temperature sensor failure".

- A **usage scenario** is a single set of contiguous interactions that traverses a use case path. Whereas a use case is very general and a use case path is more specific, a usage scenario is totally specific. The large collection of usage scenarios that traverse the same path form an equivalence class with regard to software testing. For example, the following uniquely identifies a usage scenario: Increment the desired temperature when the digital thermostat is in the on state, the current desired temperature is 68°F, and the actual temperature is 69°F.

- A **use case diagram** is a kind of context diagram that documents blackbox use cases, externals, and the important relationships between them.

- A **sequence diagram** (a.k.a., timing diagram) is a kind of interaction diagram that documents the dynamic behavior of objects in terms of a sequence of interactions between them.

  - – A **blackbox sequence diagram** is one that treats the application as a blackbox interacting with externals. Interactions on blackbox sequence diagrams are typically specified using narrative English rather than as programming language messages between internal software objects.

4. Use Case Modeling Guidelines

The following guidelines for performing use case driven requirements analysis and specification, use case driven scheduling, and use case driven testing have been proven by experience to be cost-effective. They fall into the following categories:

- General Guidelines
- Modeling Languages and Tools
- Modeling Externals
- Modeling Use Cases
- Modeling Use Case Paths

4.1 General Guidelines

- **Training.** Provide initial classroom training for all relevant personnel (requirements engineers, marketing, domain experts, customers, developers, and testers) who will either develop, inspect, or read the use case section of the requirements specification. Provide ongoing on-the-job training for all members of the requirements team including analysts, domain experts, and testers. *Rationale*: Use case modeling is still relatively new to most people. Requirements analysts who are new to use case modeling tend to produce many defects in the use case model and resulting requirements specification. Developers, who are used to traditional requirements specifications, also often have difficulty interpreting and understanding use case-oriented specifications, especially items intended for others (e.g., the use case categorization that is used by independent testers to prioritize testing).

- **Operational requirements only**. Use a use case model to analyze and specify the operational (a.k.a., functional) requirements of an application. Do not use case modeling for specifying quality requirements (e.g., extensibility, operational availability, portability, reliability, and reusability). *Rationale*: Use cases provide a powerful, industry-standard technique for analyzing and specifying operational requirements in a user-centered manner. However, quality requirements cannot be reasonably stated in terms of interactions.

- **Avoid use case driven design**. Do not drive the architecture or design from the structure of the use cases. Instead, use domain experts and object modeling to identify the key business abstractions. Use externals and the information passed with the interactions of the use cases to identify additional classes of objects. *Rationale*: Use cases are functional abstractions that are often functionally decomposed. Thus, use case driven design often results in a functional decomposition design based on god-like controller objects violating the encapsulation of dumb data objects.

- **Design verification**. Verify the object-oriented design against the use case model by tracing paths through the design. *Rationale*: The design must implement the requirements captured in the use case model.

- **Requirements validation**. Use the technique of use case driven testing to validate the implemented application against the use case model. *Rationale*: Functional test cases can be chosen to exercise use case paths because they capture the operational requirements

- **Use an iterative, incremental, parallel development cycle**. Iterate the use case model during the course of development. Develop the use case model in a series of increments associated with the builds. Develop the use case model in parallel with design, development, and testing. *Rationale*: The requirements are never known completely and correctly at the start of requirements elicitation, analysis, and specification. Domain experts and users are much better at identifying what is wrong or incomplete with a partial model than specifying it perfectly up front. The use case model of any nontrivial application is too large to develop efficiently in a single phase. Incremental development allows the associated application to be incrementally developed and tested. It also allows for course corrections that insure that the delivered application is not obsolete as soon as it is released. This guideline results in higher productivity and user (e.g., designer, tester) satisfaction. Design, coding, and testing against the use case model will identify defects and holes, resulting in a higher quality.

- **Schedule later builds by use cases and paths**. Although the initial builds should provide a foundation of core classes that capture an object-oriented architectural framework, later builds and releases should be scheduled in terms of use cases and paths in the use case model. *Rationale*: Schedules based on use cases and use case paths provide incremental value to the users (actors) and provide testable increments to the independent test team. However, scheduling all builds on use cases without an overriding architectural vision tends to produce a functional design that requires significantly more iteration than is necessary.

4.2 Modeling Languages and Tools

- **Standard modeling language**. Use a single industry standard modeling language to document the use case model. Start with UML, but extend it with the latest approved version of the OPEN Modeling Language (OML). *Rationale*: A standard modeling language promotes communication among developers. It also promotes increased productivity and model quality. This extension of the Unified Modeling Language (UML) is easier to learn, more expressive and intuitive than vanilla UML. It also better supports different kinds of externals, relationships between use cases, and logic.

- **CASE tools**. Use an upperCASE tool that supports all necessary aspects of the chosen modeling language to electronically capture the results of use case modeling. But do not let the choice of tool drive the choice of modeling language. *Rationale*: This guideline ensures that the tool actually does what is intended.

4.3 Modeling Externals

- **Clearly differentiate the boundary of the use case model**. Decide whether one is modeling a business, a *system* application, or a *software* application. Be consistent. Label the boundary on relevant diagrams. *Rationale*: Unless you clearly distinguish what you are modeling, it will be difficult to determine what the externals are. Because a system may contain software, hardware, paperware (documentation), and wetware (personnel), an external to a software application may be internal to the larger system.

- **Externals should be cohesive**. Externals should have a cohesive set of goals and responsibilities. Every external should not involve every use case. Use inheritance to factor out common external characteristics. *Rationale*: This guideline makes externals and their resulting use cases easier to understand.

- **Properly name the externals**. Provide a unique, meaningful name to each external. The name should be consistent with, and implied by, the associated definition and responsibilities. Watch out for unintended synonyms due to parallel development. *Rationale*: Remember that the name of a human actor need not be a job title, because the same person may play multiple roles when interacting with the application. *Bad Example*: Button pusher. (What the user of a digital thermostat does, not who the actor is.) *Better Example*: User

- **Define the externals**. Provide a clear, concise, glossary definition of each external that is consistent with the name of the external and its responsibilities. Rationale: Because externals need not be job titles, they may be new concepts, even to domain experts. Because domain experts and requirements analysts often have different undocumented definitions for the same terms, formally defining the externals helps avoid confusion. *Bad Example*: The user is the person who presses the buttons on the digital thermostat. *Good Example*: The user is the actor who uses the digital thermostat to control the temperature of a room.

- **Specify external responsibilities**. Specify the responsibilities of each external. Where appropriate, include responsibilities for doing, knowing, and enforcing business rules. Specify responsibilities rather than specific tasks or operations that implement the responsibilities. *Rationale*: An external is largely defined in terms of its responsibilities. An external should have a cohesive set of responsibilities. *Bad Example*: The following "responsibilities" of the user of a digital thermostat are at too low of a level of detail:
  - Turn on the digital thermostat.

- Turn off the digital thermostat
- Decrement the desired temperature of the room.
- Increment the desired temperature of the room.

Good Example: The following responsibilities are above the level of abstraction of an operation:

- Change the state of the digital thermostat.
- Change the desired temperature of the room.
- Observe the display.

- **Document external state behavior**. Document the state machines of any externals. *Rationale*: This guideline clarifies use case path preconditions and postconditions.

- **Specify actors rather than people or job descriptions**. *Rationale*: Remember that human actors are roles, not persons or job titles. A single person may play multiple roles when interacting with an application.

- **Do not specify requirements on externals.** *Rationale*: The use case model specifies requirements on the blackbox business or application rather than the externals with which it interacts.
  Bad Example: The user shall control the temperature of the digital thermostat.
  Good Example: The digital thermostat shall permit the user to set the desired temperature of the digital thermostat to any temperature between the minimum and maximum desired temperatures.

- **Document required actor expertise**. Specify the required expertise and training for all human actors. Different users of an application require different levels of training and expertise. *Rationale*: By specifying the required levels, training plans can be developed.
  Example: An average six year old should be able to successfully use the digital thermostat with minimal (i.e., 5 minutes of) training.

- **Organize by externals**. Organize the use case model into packages, first by external stereotype (e.g., actor, hardware, software) and then by specific external (e.g., customer, user). Within a package, use a standard sort order, either chronologically or alphabetically. Those subordinate use cases that are not primarily associated with any one external should be grouped into a package associated with the application. *Rationale*: This guideline provides a natural organization to the use case model that is both easy to use and user-centric.

- **Specify interfaces to externals**. Specify any required interfaces to externals, especially to existing hardware devices and software applications. *Rationale*: This guideline ensures that the designers have adequate requirements to implement the interface across which the interactions flow.

- **Document all relevant externals**. Document both externals that directly interface with the application as well as externals that indirectly interface via other externals *Rationale*: The object model often includes classes corresponding to both indirect externals and direct externals. Direct externals (e.g., keyboard, console) are sometimes less important than the indirect human actors that use them.

- **Summarize the context**. Use one or more context diagrams to summarize the static environment of the application in terms of its externals and the relationships between it and its externals. Also, document all significant relationships between externals on the context diagram. Provide narrative English description of the context diagram that clarifies anything that is not totally obvious. Also, summarize the workflow between externals. *Rationale*: Context diagrams help one understand the context of an application. Relationships between externals often make the resulting context more understandable, especially inheritance relationships or associations when the order of use cases depends on interactions between externals. This guideline makes it easier for domain experts and others less familiar with this diagram to understand it. The overall goals of the business or application are implemented by workflows that often involve multiple externals and use cases.

- **Externals should be cohesive**. Externals should have a cohesive set of goals and responsibilities. Every external should not involve every use case. Use inheritance to factor out common external characteristics. *Rationale*: This guideline makes externals and their resulting use cases easier to understand.

- **Identify external stereotypes**. Differentiate the different stereotypes of externals with intuitive icons. *Rationale*: This guideline makes context diagrams and use case diagrams easier to understand and avoids confusion (e.g., when the UML stick figure is used for hardware and software externals as well as human actors).

4.4 Modeling Use Cases

- **Use cases should be functionally cohesive**. Each use case should fulfil all related business or application responsibilities involved in the primary external's goal. Do not base use cases on GUI screens. *Rationale*: This guideline makes use cases easier to understand.

- **Properly name the use cases**. Name each use case with a unique meaningful active verb phrase. Name the use cases from the external's viewpoint rather than the system viewpoint. Optionally, include the name of the primary external that benefits from the use case. *Rationale:* Verb phrases are best because use cases are functional abstractions. This guideline increases understandability.
  Bad Examples:
  - Turn on the digital thermostat. (This is really a use case path)
  - Desired temperature is changed. (This is not an active verb phrase and is from the wrong viewpoint.)
  - Temperature Control. (This is not a verb phrase and is from the wrong viewpoint.)
  Good Examples:
  - Change the state of the digital thermostat.
  - The user changes the desired temperature of the room. (Optional external)

- **Specify use case requirements**. Provide a uniquely identified, textual requirement for each use case that captures its functional abstraction and external's goal. *Rationale*: This guideline provides an overview of the use case. A textual requirement is also the information expected by domain experts who are used to textual requirements specifications.
  Bad Examples:
  - The user changes the desired temperature of the room. (This is not a requirement, but rather an observation.)
  - The user shall change the desired temperature of the room. (This constrains the user. It is not a requirement on the digital thermostat).
  Good Examples:
  - The digital software shall permit the user to change the desired temperature of the room. (Written as a requirement - "shall" - on the digital thermostat.)

- **Create use case diagrams**. Create a top-level use case diagram for each primary external that summarizes the behavioral context of the application in terms of the primary external's use cases, any related externals, and the relationships between them. Optionally create a lower-level use case diagram for each use case that has numerous relationships to other use cases. Identify the primary external associated with each use case on the use case diagram. Provide narrative English descriptions of the use case diagrams that clarify anything that is not totally obvious in the diagram. Also, document the boundaries of the blackbox application on each use case diagram, and label the scope of each diagram. *Rationale*: Applications often have too many externals and use cases to document on a single top-level use case diagram. By limiting the scope of the diagram, the diagram becomes simpler, more focused, and therefore easier to understand. The diagrams also become easier to maintain because the impact of changes is more localized.

- **Provide a business justification**. Document the business justification for each use case. Ensure that the business justification actually justifies the use case and is more than merely a restatement of the use case requirement. *Rationale*: This guideline ensures that the use case specifies a real requirement.

- **Use essential use cases**. Avoid unnecessarily specifying design decisions in use cases by using essential (i.e., analysis level) use cases. Use preconditions rather than screen navigation details. *Rationale*: By including design information in use case models, the distinction between requirements and design is blurred. Design-level use cases must be updated each time the design changes.
  Bad Example:
  − The user chooses an account type from a pull-down menu bar on the GUI.
  Good Example:
  − The user requests an account type from the application.

4.5 Modeling Use Case Paths

- **Properly name the use case paths**. Name each use case path with a unique, meaningful phrase that captures the essence of the path. The name should be consistent with, and implied by, the associated requirement, preconditions, interactions, and postconditions. *Rationale*: This guideline improves communication by improving understandability.
  Bad Example:
  − Control the actual temperature of the room fails. (May fail multiple ways.)
  Good Example:
  − Handle temperature sensor failure.

- **Specify use case path requirements**. Provide a uniquely identified, textual requirement for each use case path that captures its functional abstraction, preconditions, and postconditions. *Rationale*: This guideline makes the use case path easier to understand and promotes the testability of the resulting implementation.
  Bad Examples:
  − The user successfully increments the desired temperature of the room. (Not written as a requirement.)
  − The user shall be able to increment the desired temperature. (Vague − temperature of what. Written as a requirement on the user, not the digital thermostat.)
  Good Example:
  − The digital thermostat shall allow the user to increment the desired temperature of the room.

- **Capture exceptional paths and interactions**. Specify the exceptional basis paths as well as the normal paths through a use case. Also document exceptional interactions as well as normal interactions, but avoid analysis paralysis due to trying to cover too many, extremely unlikely exceptional paths. *Rationale*: Too often, requirements only specify how an application must function under normal circumstances, but not how it should function during abnormal circumstances. Requirements are therefore incomplete if only normal paths are specified. Exception handling software can often make up to 80% of business-critical or safety-critical software needing high operational availability and reliability. Unless exceptional paths are specified, there is little likelihood that they will be implemented or implemented correctly, and exceptional interactions must be documented if exceptional paths are to be completely documented. This guideline is critical if the resulting application is to be robust or have high operational availability.
  Example path:
  - Handle temperature sensor failure.
  Example interaction:
  - The digital thermostat software shall display the string "ERR" on the actual temperature display when the temperature sensor fails.

- **Document relevant assertions**. For each use case path, document both the preconditions and postconditions. *Rationale*: Without preconditions, there is no way to determine what is required to successfully execute the path. Without postconditions, there is no guarantee that the execution was correct, even if the visible interactions were correct. Postconditions can be used to specify otherwise hidden internal constraints. This greatly helps with the specification of the associated test cases.
  Examples:
  - Preconditions of the "Increment desired temperature" normal path of the "Change the desired temperature" use case include:
    - The digital thermostat is in the on state.
    - The desired temperature is below the maximum.
  - Postconditions of the "Increment desired temperature" normal path of the "Change the desired temperature" use case are requirements and include:
    - The digital thermostat shall be in the on state.
    - The new desired temperature shall be one degree larger than the old desired temperature.

- **Document the interactions**. Completely document each interaction between the application and externals including the client and server of the interaction, the interaction itself, and any information that flows with the interaction. Optionally document interactions between the externals if it helps one understand the purpose of the interactions. Ensure that each interaction is actually an interaction and not really a precondition, postcondition, or traditional textual functional requirement or hidden calculation. *Rationale*: It is important to know which is the client and which is the server in order to determine who provides the resulting service. In addition, only the interactions initiated by the application represent requirements. The specification is incomplete if it does not specify what information is passed with the interaction, and this information helps to identify classes in the corresponding object model. The interactions are confusing and hard to understand if preconditions, postconditions, and traditional textual functional requirements are incorrectly labeled as interactions.
  Bad Examples:

- The user presses the on/off button. (Not part of the increment desired temperature path. Use a precondition instead.)
- The digital thermostat shall increment its desired temperature. (Actually, a postcondition on internal data that technically is not visible at the interface.)
- The desired temperature display displays the new desired temperature. (Actually a postcondition.)
- The digital thermostat software shall display the desired temperature. (Not specified as an interaction. What is the external?)

Good Examples:

- The user presses the increment desired temperature button.
- The increment temperature button interrupts the digital thermostat software with the string "increment desired temperature".
- Within .1 second of the user pressing the increment desired temperature button, the digital thermostat software shall request the desired temperature display to display the desired temperature of the room as a 1 to 3 digit integer followed by either "°F" or "°C".

- **Factor out common interactions**. Use subordinate use case paths and the "invokes" relationship to factor out common cohesive sets of interactions. However, watch out for excessive functional decomposition of the use cases. *Rationale*: This guideline simplifies the interactions and improves maintainability by eliminating unnecessary redundancy.

- **Document the logic**. Where appropriate, document the logic of the use case (e.g., branching, looping, critical regions) using pseudocode in the interactions and using logic boxes on sequence diagrams. However, branching can be ignored if interactions and sequence diagrams are documented one per path. *Rationale*: This clarifies the actual behavior of the interactions.

- **Categorize the paths**. Categorize each use case path with its stability (how likely is it to change), frequency (how often does it execute), criticality (how important to the user is it), probability of defects (how likely are the developers to implement it correctly), and resulting risk. Use values of high, medium, and low. Calculate risk as a function of stability, frequency, criticality, and probability of defects. *Rationale*: The implementation of unstable paths may be postponed until the paths solidify, or else implementation may be moved forward in the schedule so that early prototyping may stabilize them. Reliability may be improved if limited test resources are allocated to paths that are executed frequently. Testers can emphasize the paths, the correct execution of which is critical to the user. Testing resources should also be allocated to those paths most likely to contain defects due to complexity or uncertainty (e.g., exceptional paths). This guideline allows one to identify the risk associated with each path in order to prioritize the scheduling of the development and testing of each path.

- **Create sequence diagrams**. Use blackbox sequence diagrams to document complex paths containing numerous interactions or complex logic. *Rationale*: Complex interactions are easier for most readers to understand if they are documented graphically.

- **Some interactions are requirements**. Formally specify those interactions that are initiated by the application as requirements using the standard terminology of requirements (e.g., the use of the term "shall"). Uniquely identify each such requirement including each item in the list of information passed with the interaction. *Rationale:* Any interaction initiated by the application is visible behavior and therefore required.

Bad Examples:
- The user shall press the increment desired temperature button. (This improperly constrains an external.)
- The digital thermostat displays the new desired temperature to the user. (Not written as a requirement.)

Good Example:
- The digital thermostat shall display the new desired temperature to the user.

- **Postconditions are requirements**. Document each postcondition as a requirement using the standard format for requirements (e.g., the use of the term "shall"). Uniquely identify each postcondition. *Rationale:* A postcondition of the application is a required outcome of a use case path.

  Bad Example of postconditions of the "Decrement desired temperature" normal path of the "Change the desired temperature" use case include:
  - The desired temperature shall be decremented. (Merely repeats the use case name.)
  - The new desired temperature is one degree less than the old desired temperature. (Not written as a requirement.)

  Good Examples of postconditions of the same path:
  - The digital thermostat shall be in the on state.
  - The new desired temperature shall be one degree less than the old desired temperature.

- **Specifying complex internal algorithms**. If a new value is the result of a complex calculation that occurs internally to the blackbox application, use a postcondition to explicitly specify the complex algorithm to be used to calculate the new value. *Rationale*: Because the interactions only specify visible interactions between the application and its externals, they are not appropriate for specifying the complex algorithms sometimes needed to calculate a post-execution value.

  Example:
  - The new account balance equals the function foo() of its original value.

- **Standardize interaction formats**. Use a standard format to document interactions. For example, interactions may be stereotyped as requests, responses, and event notifications. *Rationale*: This guideline greatly increases understandability and maintainability by avoiding insignificant differences that may confuse the reader.

  Example formats:
  - External 'A' sends a 'B' request to 'the application,' which includes the following information: X, Y, and Z.
  - 'The application' shall send an 'A' response to external 'B', which includes the following information: X, Y, and Z.
  - 'The application' shall send an 'A' event notification to external 'B', which includes the following information: X, Y, and Z.

5. References

[1] Donald G. Firesmith, "Use Cases: The Pros and Cons," in *Wisdom of the Gurus: A Vision for Object Technology*, Charles F. Bowman, ed., SIGS Books Inc., New York, New York, 1996, pp. 171-180.

[2] Alistair Cockburn, "Structuring Use Cases with Goals," *Journal of Object-Oriented Programming*, SIGS Publications, Sep-Oct 1997 and Nov-Dec 1997.

[3] Tim Korson, "The Misuse of Use Cases," *Object Magazine*, 8(3), SIGS Publications, 1998, pp. 18-20.

[4] Susan Lilly, "Use Case Pitfalls: Top 10 Problems from Real Projects, in the *Proceedings of TOOLS USA '99*.

Cooperative Software Development: Concepts, Model and Tools

Josef Altmann, Gustav Pomberger
C. Doppler Laboratory for Software Engineering
Johannes Kepler University Linz
Altenberger Str. 69, A-4040 Linz, Austria
{altmann, pomberger}@swe.uni-linz.ac.at

Abstract

The development of large software systems demands intensive cooperation among multiple project team members with different responsibilities. The development process is often distributed across time and space and takes place within and between specialized workgroups. This necessitates finding appropriate answers to questions related to division of labor, to communication, and to coordination and cooperation in the planning, development and maintenance of software systems.

Development environments that explicitly support group work are an important prerequisite for the production of high-quality software systems. Most of the software development environments in use today support primarily technical aspects and have shortcomings in the area of organizational support. This paper describes a model for cooperative work processes in software projects and a corresponding development environment that provides balanced support for both organizational and technical aspects of software development.

The work toward the conception of the model and the implementation of the development environment have been completed, and the evaluation of the proposed approach has begun. Experience to date with using the developed environment confirms the assumption that the cooperative, cluster-oriented development improves both productivity and quality. The presented approach excels primarily in its easily understandable model, the intuitive usability of the tools and the comprehensible presentation of process- and product-related information.

1. Introduction

The prerequisites for the economical and professional production of high-quality software products extend beyond technical aspects and encompass in particular the process of distribution of development tasks and activities within a project team, the establishment of communication and coordination relationships, and the support of creative problem-solving processes.

Due to the spatial and temporal distribution of a large software project, collaboration between project team members is often asynchronous. Regular synchronization and the ability of developers to record momentary states and events are essential for efficient collaboration. Important aspects of supporting cooperative software development include the following:

- spontaneous collaboration
- direct and indirect communication
- building of group consciousness

- knowledge about details and particulars of the project and its current state
- the reuse of experience-based knowledge

Such aspects influence the economy of the development process and the quality of the target product.

A survey of current research approaches and the development environments used today reveals that group-supportive aspects are underrepresented or often fail to meet the requirements for efficient support of communication and coordination [1]. Although some tools do support group work in software projects (electronic mail, workflow managemnt systems, group editors, synchronous debugging tools, etc.), these are generally not integral components of a development environment or they support only selected activities.

Process-centered software engineering (see, e.g., [2]) or approaches from computer aided software engineering (see, e.g., [3]) strive to formally describe complex processes of software development in order to enable their (partial) automation. The prerequisite is a precise description of the software development process. However, the development process normally evades adequately precise a priori description due to continuous dynamic change; therefore the formalized process model approach seldom achieves success in practice. Furthermore, the application of strictly formal process models and ensuing automated control instruments fails to reap the potential of creative processes that can be decisive for product quality.

Beginning with a problem-oriented view of software projects that enables enumerating the significant characteristics of distributed, cooperative software development, this paper derives universal design principles for a work environment to support cooperative, distributed software projects. The identified design principles serve as the basis for the development of a model for cooperative work processes, which forms the starting point for the analysis, structuring, management and synchronization of divided-labor software development tasks. Next the paper provides an overview of a group-supportive work environment for cooperative software development; this enables the practical implementation of the developed model for cooperative work processes in software projects. The summary contains a short report on our experience with the use of the developed process model and the supportive development environment as well as a preview of planned research activities.

2. The role of cooperation in software development processes

Starting with a general view of the cooperation aspects of distributed teamwork, this section introduces the terms communication, coordination and cooperation. Next, the general characteristics of software development processes and finally the specific characteristics that distinguish distributed, cooperative software development processes are discussed with regard to the special needs of communication and cooperation.

2.1. Cooperation aspects of distributed teamwork

Cooperation processes such as software development in a team demand coordination processes in order to coordinate the cooperative activities of the individual team member with one another. Coordination processes in turn demand communication processes, such as the exchange of information across the various development activities. Based on [4], we use the terms communication, coordination and cooperation as follows:

Communication encompasses the process of transfer and exchange of information that takes place between communication partners. If the exchange of information serves to coordinate activities among team members, then this type of communication serves as the basis for the coordination of processes.

Coordination is based on suitable communication processes and encompasses all activities that are necessary for coordinating divided-labor tasks in the realm of a work process. While those involved in coordination processes pursue different goals, in the realm of cooperation multiple persons work together in a planned and coordinated way toward a common goal.

Cooperation is the manner of coordination that is necessary for agreeing on common goals and for the coordinated achievement of common work results among the participants.

Discussions of the concept of cooperation show that the organization, coordination and control of divided-labor tasks occurs on the basis of communication and coordination processes. Depending on the degree of freedom of the involved team members, we distinguish different forms of cooperation. We identify the following forms of cooperation on the basis of the influence and organizational possibilities of the participants:

- Team cooperation is characterized by the influence on the part of the other cooperation partner on the activities to be carried out. There is freedom in the establishment of internal organizational structures and process flows. The cooperative work occurs on the basis of agreed-upon goals and negotiated rules of cooperation. The cooperation partners are equals.
- Structured cooperation is enforced by formal mechanisms. Collaboration occurs primarily on the basis of objective and technical elements of the service generation process. Standardized workflows and formalized processes lead to external coordination and restriction of the alternatives for action. Cooperation routes are largely prescribed along with rigid spatial and temporal assignment of workplaces and work tasks. The cooperation partners occupy different hierarchical positions and are normally not equals.

The effects of structured cooperation on the software production process have been designated by Pasch [5] as software bureaucracy. A distinguishing characteristic of this bureaucracy is the formal embedding of the individual developer in a rigid organizational structure. Activities are coordinated and controlled by an external position (e.g., process modeller, workflow management system). The process of negotiating interests and resolving conflicts is largely suppressed.

Team cooperation supports unstructured, unplanable task completion and self-organization in a cooperative work context. Conflict serves as the starting point for a continuous process of coordination that can be guided and controlled by the participants. Team cooperation supports individual action and creativity and accommodates the current work context. In contrast to structured cooperation, computer-aided tools of the teamlike category are characterized by a supportive view. This view enables the participants to build mutual understanding of the cooperative work. The automation of a work process is not in the foreground.

The above discussions have shown different perspectives of cooperative work. The following subsections discuss first the important characteristics of software development processes and then the characteristics of distributed, cooperative software development processes.

2.2. Characteristics of software development processes

The software development process is significantly influenced by the underlying process model. A process model abstractly describes the general sequence of the development process along with its subtasks, their dependencies, and the targeted results as well as the quality assurance measures that are used. The superordinate work steps are called phases. In the realm of software engineering, various phase models have been developed and compared. One of the main problems in the application of phase models is the distinction of the individual phases from one another and the consideration of the mutual effects between the phases. This paper does not describe the various phase models, but refers instead to the literature [3], [6], [7].

However, we do consider Meyer's cluster model [7] because on the one hand it refers to the object-oriented software technology in practice today and on the other hand by subdividing a project among various development teams it seeks to help avoid the main problems in the use of process models. As with most process models, Meyer's distinguishes among various project activities such as analysis, design, implementation and maintenance. In contrast to traditional phase models (e.g., waterfall model) sequential activities are not considered to be independent, isolated steps but as subsequent system extensions. Figure 1 depicts this development process according to Meyer, which reflects the essence of object-oriented development.

The software development process is not primarily characterized by phase-orientation and the resulting sequence of intermediate products, but by the development of components. The development team is responsible for all phases, and the strict phase distinction is relaxed; that is, the borders between the phases often disappear. This type of organization of the development process demands intensive communication and coordination within and between the development teams of the individual project clusters, because, to achieve flexibility and to exploit creative potential, neither the phase results within the cluster nor the cluster results are completely and formally specified in advance.

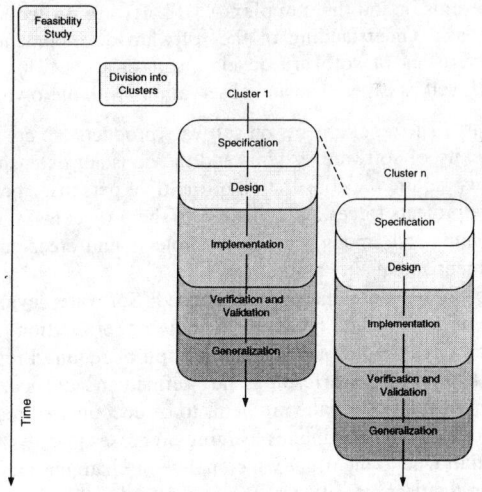

Figure 1. Meyer's cluster model [7]

Meyer's model differs significantly from conventional phase models in that a decomposition into subprojects takes place after the establishment of a rough architecture for the overall system. The resulting clusters represent subsystems (components) that are implemented by small development teams. Figure 1 shows the cluster model strives for a sequentialization of the development process, although not for the overall system. On completion of the decomposition of the overall project, for each cluster a mini-lifecycle is defined. The subprojects can run simultaneously or staggered over time. Various project goals are achieved at different deadlines. At the end of each subproject comes a generalization phase in order to identify reusable software components and then make them available across cluster and project boundaries. This results in a parallel or overlapping development process that demands intensive communication and coordination of the involved development teams.

Floyd and Züllighoven [8] distinguish between product- and process-related development activities in software production.

- Product-related activities encompass requirements definition and system development. In the foreground is the software product with the corresponding development results, consisting of prototypes, programs and documents. The production process can be structured on the basis of predefined phases with predefined intermediate results.
- Process-oriented activities serve the purpose of coordination and cooperation in the development process and encompass product management, quality assurance and project coordination. In a running project, reference lines are introduced for the purpose of assuring intermediate results. Reference lines define project states that the developer and user have agreed upon for synchronization of their cooperative work processes.

One problem is that software development is often viewed from only one of the two perspectives. The product-oriented view focuses on the divided-labor software product with its specific document types and system versions. By contrast, the process-oriented view encompasses the divided-labor development process, which is reflected in various documents. Thus an integration of the two views is appropriate to master the problems in and the complexity of software projects.

Based on this basic understanding of the software development process, below we outline the characteristics of software development projects. This outline is based on literature studies as well as experience and observations with our own software projects.

- Rising complexity: The requirements on software products are continuously rising. The growing complexity of software systems and the constant extension and adaptation to new requirements require the cooperation of multiple persons. The size and complexity of most software projects forces a distribution of the project tasks. Collaboration occurs in specialized teams and among various subprojects and areas such as programming, project management and quality assurance.
- Processes that cannot be formalized or automated: Software development differs from the production of most other products in that the proportion of required creative activities is significantly higher than the proportion of required reproductive activities. In creative work processes the result is not defined in advance. The multiplicity of software development tasks and the problems to be encountered require a high measure of flexibility, creativity and continuous learning processes [9].
- High risk potential: Due to the usually incomplete or changing requirements and due to the difficulties in the decomposition of the project tasks, the planning and execution of a software development project is accompanied by uncertainties and risks [10]. The number of collaborating subprojects or project groups whose development activities have mutual influence cannot be determined at the start of the project.
- High communication requirements: In contrast to other production processes (e.g., for hardware systems), due to the characteristics listed above, especially informal information exchange among the project team members is of particular importance. In contrast to formal communication, which is specified by a process model its defined

results, Bischofberger et al. [11] indicate the necessity and importance of informal communication during the project. The distributed shared decision making and the coordination in the team usually require spontaneous and flexible exchange of information between software developers.

- High documentation requirements: In addition to product documentation, the documentation process also requires process documentation in order to assure the comprehensibility of development decisions. The high degree of freedom and the low measure of available proven theoretical concepts does not always make design or implementation decisions readily comprehensible. Making use of knowledge about technical and administrative decisions, difficulties and their causes and corrections, conversations held between software developers, and modification and error statistics is an important prerequisite in order to support collaboration among the developers.

In an empirical study of 29 software projects in 19 firms, Hesse and Frese [12] determined that the effort for coordination processes, e.g., to exchange information, consumes ca. 40% of the overall development effort. The greater the dependency of development activities of various project team members, the more intensively they must cooperate with one another, inform one another, and keep each other up to date.

2.2. Characteristics of distributed, cooperative software development processes

The considerations of the general characteristics of the software development process in the previous section make it clear that software systems of a certain complexity cannot be realized in monolithic form, but must be decomposed into subsystem. The associated task-related spatial and temporal distribution of a cooperative software development process has the following characteristics:

- Task-related distribution: The rising complexity of software systems requires task-related decomposition of a project into subprojects as well as specialization within a development organization extending beyond project boundaries. In accordance with their capabilities, staff member and teams are assigned to specific subprocesses in software development. This demands a suitable coordination strategy.
- Temporal distribution: Depending on the scope of the project, subprojects are handled sequentially or in parallel. Various subprojects can be handled simultaneously. Various project goals are achieved at different times and so require synchronization or coordination of the work processes.
- Spatial distribution: Beyond the task-related and temporal distribution of development activities, there is also a distribution of project activities to different teams that, for organizational and/or economic reasons, can be spatially distributed. Spatial distribution requires providing a suitable communication infrastructure to cover the communication, coordination and cooperation requirements.

Based on the general concept of cooperation and the corresponding characteristics of distributed software development processes, we define the term cooperative software development as follows:

Cooperative software development encompasses covering the communication and coordination requirements within a software development process that are necessary for the planning, execution and coordination of all task-related, spatially and temporally distributed activities. Accordingly, cooperative software development encompasses all process- and product-related activities on the part of all participants whose common goal is the production of a software product.

Distributed, cooperative software development requires not only organizational support but also adequate tool support. In the area of computer-supported cooperative work, recent years have seen the development of various tools to support cooperative work. These systems generally fail to offer adequate support for the cooperative software development because they usually lack sufficient conceptual and technical integration of process and product views and insufficiently support the flexible, informal exchange of information.

3. Design principles for tool support

On the foundation of characteristics of distributed, cooperative software development processes introduced in Section 2, this section derives the design principles for the support of group work in software projects. The identified design principles form the basis for the development of a model for cooperative work processes in software development projects, and the model forms the basis for the implementation of a development environment to support cooperative software development processes. These design principles are the following:

- Transparency: The term transparency can be considered in the context of software engineering or in the application domain; here we limit the scope to the application domain. Applied to the support of cooperative software development, this means that the software developer is informed about the location of archives for artifacts, the distribution of development activities, and the competition situation with respect to other cooperating project team members. The project team members should have a comprehensible picture of limitations of resources and their spatial, temporal and task-related distribution. The coordination processes and the effects of access to artifacts should be clearly recognizable.

- Individual and group-oriented views of the current work process: Due to the task distribution, the project team members need an individual view of the current development process in order to achieve an overview of their responsibilities for certain activities. In addition, a group-oriented view is necessary for the cooperating software developer in order to be able to evaluate the activities in the overall context and to synchronize or coordinate the work processes in the team.

- Shared work space: The purpose of a shared work space is to provide and consistently manage process- and product-related artifacts. In addition, the team members must have an available cooperation environment in which to organize, structure and carry out their work. The organization of the work space includes the identification of the associated team members, the working materials and the tools that can be used for collaboration. The introduction of roles and their associated privileges and duties enables differentiation among team members of a work space and regulates access to artifacts.

- Promoting group consciousness: Building group consciousness requires making the structure of the development process clear to all software developers. This requires a notification service that automatically informs the project team members about completed and running activities and enables an overview of the activities of the cooperation partner in a software project. Dourish and Bellotti [13] call such consciousness about individual and group activities awareness.

- Negotiability of a conflict resolution: Conflict situations (e.g., competitive access to artifacts) should not be regulated completely by formal and automatable workflow descriptions. On the contrary, the cooperative support environment should be conceived such that control over the cooperative work process is left completely with the cooperating software developers and the responsible use of freedom of action is permitted [8]. The nature of the cooperation in a given development process can vary according to priorities and conditions. Cooperation models and conventions describe and regulate collaboration within a software development team.

- Availability of predefined workflows: The workflow sequence of selected development activities in cooperative work processes should be made available in the form of schedules, directions and process patterns that describe the workflow of a task (e.g., code inspection). This is intended to support the cooperating persons in their mutual coordination and execution of work steps and in the determination of responsibilities. In the sense of Suchman [15], such coordination schedules should not be viewed as algorithmic, executable rules and regulations. Coordination schedules or predefined workflows should represent an outline and orientation for the divided-labor execution of a task – without a closed workflow in the formal sense and without the need for strictly following such a workflow.

- Explicit and implicit exchange of information: Explicit exchange of information among software developers occurs by sending messages, project reports, comments, etc.; the cooperation medium can be electronic mail or electronic bulletin boards. Implicit exchange of information needs to take place when changes occurred in the artifacts of a shared work space. Such changes should be propagated automatically by tools and made visible in the shared work environment. An event or signal mechanism notifies affected project team members of changes in shared artifacts; this notification could be in the form of a message or via appropriate representation in the user interface of the affected team members' development environment.

- Transparency of the process history: A process history evolves during the development process; this history should be appropriately documented and made available for later access by the project team members. This documentation should contain information about the activities carried out, problems encountered, dependencies on other activities, alternative solutions, knowledge gained, etc. This improves overall understanding and assures efficient problem solutions through reuse of the project team members' knowledge from experience.

- Status and context information: The status information about a project that team members require can be either organization-related or project-specific in nature. Organization-related information includes the composition of the work groups and their responsibilities. Project-specific information concerns the status of activities, causes for modifications and instructions for the programming of extensions. A cooperative support environment should provide such status and context information to facilitate the project team members' orientation in the current work context.

From these design principles, the following section derives a model for cooperative software development processes. The proposed model forms the basis for the implementation of a corresponding cooperation environment.

4. A model for cooperative software development processes

The goal of the model is to describe development activities along with the associated project team members and the relationships among the workflows. Figure 2 depicts the components that are most important for understanding the overall model (in OMT notation).

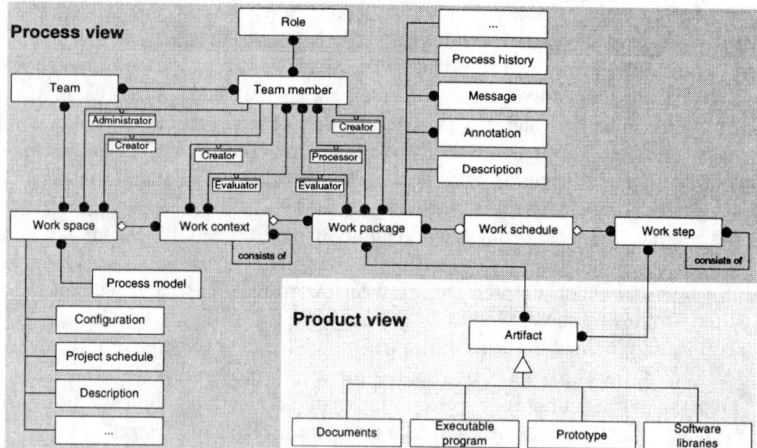

Figure 2: Model of cooperative software development processes

The model comprises two logically connected areas:

- **Process view:** The components for mapping the process view, which belong to the core of the model, form the basis for coordination and cooperation during the software development process. The process-related model describes the tasks of the development activities and their relationships. This also includes assigning the process participants to the individual tasks and ensuring that the development process is recorded.
- **Product view:** The product view includes the results of a software project. The development results consist of documents, executable programs, prototypes and software libraries.

The following subsections introduce the components of the model and explain the important terms in this context.

4.1. Process view

The core of the model is the process model. The process-related structuring of a software development project occurs via decomposition of an overall task into multiple smaller subprojects and subtasks. A subtask is represented in the model by a work package and consists of one or more work steps. A work context describes a subproject and manages a group of logically associated work packages. Multiple work contexts together form a shared work space that combines all development activities of a certain subproject. The shared work space serves the team members as an entry point into a software development project and forms the basis for the coordination and cooperation of the development activities. Depending on their roles, the individual team members can access the process- and product-related information and inform themselves about the status of the development process. The activities that are carried out with individual artifacts are visible to certain participants, depending on the configuration of a work space, and are recorded in a process history.

After the basic concept for the decomposition of a software development project has been defined, selected components of the model are discussed to enhance understanding.

- **Process model:** A process model in the sense of the proposed model defines the basic structure of a development process, which consists of prefabricated work contexts, work packages and work steps. As a rule the process model is not re-invented for each new project. Generic process models for various types of software projects are stored in a process model catalog and are available as starting points for launching new development projects.
- **Work step:** A work step represents an activity within a work package. A work step is represented by its designation, a description, the process status, and a link to the next work step. The description contains work instructions for carrying out the work step. Template documents can be provided as input documents. A work step can be refined via other work steps. This creates a hierarchical structure of work steps that represents a work schedule for processing a work package.
- **Work schedule:** A work schedule consists of work steps. In this model the work schedule serves as instructions for activities or as a hierarchical guide to support the processing of a work package. Work schedules are not process regulations that completely control the activities of the project team members. Depending on the respective project conventions, which are established at the start of a development project, deviations from the prescribed work schedule can be justified by project team members and documented in the respective work steps. Proven work schedules (best practice) for various development activities (e.g., error correction, integration test) are collected in a catalog and made available for the creation of other work packages.
- **Work package:** A work package describes a goal-oriented processing order that forms a logical unit and is executed by a project team member. The creator of a work package can be the one to handle the work package or can delegate it to a member of the project team. A project team member can handle the assigned work package, reject it, or after coordination with the creator delegate it to another team member. The coordination of the work process as well as the assignment of access privileges for parts of a work package are the responsibility of the creator. An evaluator is responsible for checking and receiving the results of a work package. The creator bears the responsibility for the achieved results and coordinates the handling of corrective suggestions between the evaluator and the processing team member. A work package description contains specifications concerning the creator, the processor, the evaluator, the role(s) that the processor must assume in order to be allowed to handle the work package, the types of tasks, the priority, the completion status, the date of creation, the planned and actual date of completion, the modification dates and the evaluation date. The documentation of work progress, the achieved results, and the results of the evaluation process are appended electronically to the work package description by the respective project team members. Every work package contains a process history that consists of a list of executed work events. The work package is the most important medium to support collaboration among the project team members. The exchange of work packages constitutes the divided-labor software production process. Additionally, annotations and package-related messages support informal cooperation in a development team and the documentation of development decisions.
- **Work context:** In a work context, logically related work packages are managed; the work context serves as a hierarchical structuring medium for a work space. A work context in turn can be refined by means of additional work contexts. The creator of a work context coordinates the sequence and execution of the work packages and bears the responsibility for the results of the work context. The evaluator of a work context checks the overall result of a work context, which comprises the component results of

the individual work packages. The creator of a work context delegates the corrections suggested by the evaluators to those responsible for the respective work packages and monitors the timely and correct execution of the revisions. Work contexts divide a shared work space into various areas of interest. This promotes orientation in cooperative development processes, since coordination and cooperation are no longer restricted to individual work packages, but occur in a larger context, the work context.

- **Work space:** A work space encompasses multiple development activities that are necessary to achieve the common goal of one or more project groups. A work space is structured hierarchically into various work contexts and work packages. The description of a work space contains all information necessary for planning and executing a project. The most important artifacts are the project order and the description of the project organization. The structure of a work space, consisting of work contexts and work packages, is continuously complemented and updated by the project team members. In certain intervals the project leader checks the work space structure and adapts it to the current process. A prescriptive description of the development process is not supported by the proposed work space, since this would not correspond to the low a priori specification and high complexity of software development processes.

4.2. Product view

The product view relates to the software product to be developed. The software product comprises programs, libraries of reusable software components, prototypes, and development documents. The product view is represented abstractly by an artifact that can occur in multiple instances with various forms.

Artifact: An artifact represents a work object in the software development process. Both the executable program system itself and all documents of the development process are artifacts.

This section has presented the base model proposed for modeling (i.e., structuring and describing) a software development process. In the foreground are the concretization of the responsibilities of the individual project team members, the mutual coordination of the work processes, and the description of work scenarios.

5. A work environment for cooperative software development

This section introduces a work environment for cooperative software development that enables practical application of the model for cooperative work processes in software projects described in Section 4. The work environment supports spatially and temporally distributed project team members in the context of typical software development activities.

The work environment Cooperation Assistant was developed as an experimental platform at the C. Doppler Laboratory for Software Engineering at Johannes Kepler University of Linz [15]. The concepts implemented in Cooperation Assistant to support distributed, cooperative software development strive to harmonically unify the product- and process-related views. The environment is based on the approach of shared work spaces. A task to be cooperatively handled is represented in the work space as a work package.

Introducing all the tools of this extensive work environment and discussing implementation details would exceed the scope of this paper. Hence we present the Cooperation Assistant only as an overview on the basis of an application scenario. For reasons of compatibility with other integrated software development tools and due to the wide usage of the language, C++ was chosen as the implementation language. As implementation platform we chose the framework ObjectWire [16], which was developed at the C. Doppler Laboratory and particularly supports the implementation of distributed, object-oriented software architectures.

Figure 3 shows an overview of the selected tools of the cooperation environment from the viewpoint of a project team member. The Cooperation Assistant provides tools for structuring, monitoring and processing cooperative work processes. Due to space considerations, we restrict our description to the tools Agenda ①, Work Context Manager ② and Work Package Editor ③.

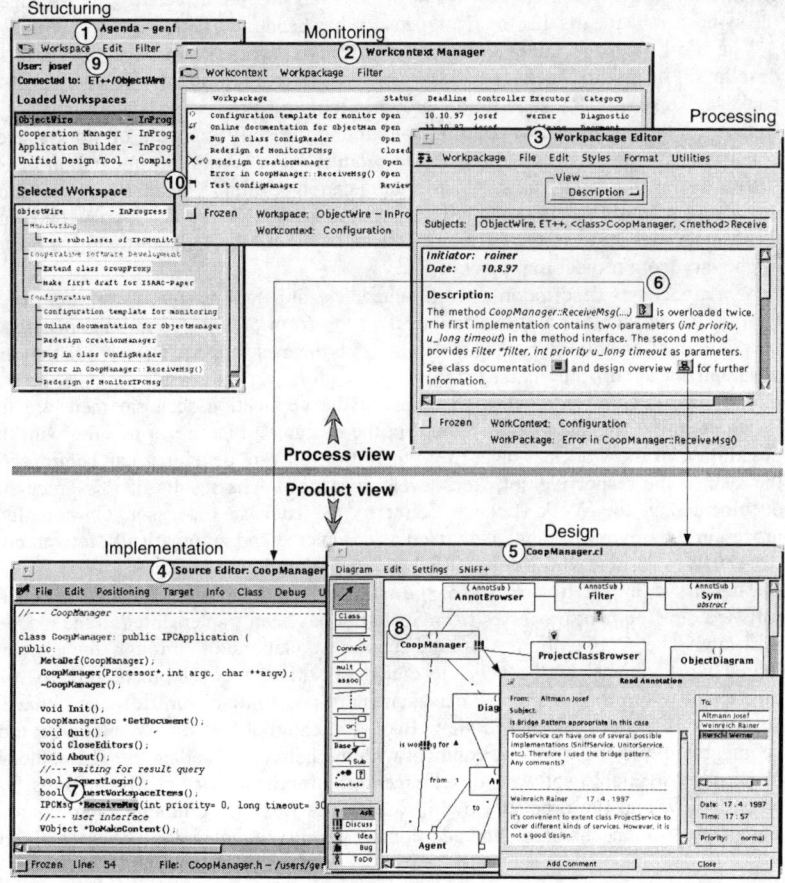

Figure 3. Application scenario

Figure 3 shows the project structure of the development project ObjectWire (in progress), which is depicted in the Agenda ①. The presented structure of the software development project gives project team member josef ⑨ an overview of the logical associations of the individual development activities of the project group. The overall project in this application scenario consists of the subprojects Monitoring, Configuration, and Cooperative Software Development, as established by the project leader at the start of the project.

Monitoring the sequence and work progress of the development activities of a subproject occurs in the Work Context Manager ②. Figure 3 shows a Work Context Manager that represents all current and completed work packages of the work context Configuration. On a state transition of a work package, the event service of the cooperative work environment creates an event object. For example, a state transition in the creation, sending, rejection or acceptance of a work package. The reporting service informs the project team members about the events that occur. The events are depicted graphically in the Work Context Manager ② alongside the affected work packages; e.g., the symbol at ⑩ means that the work package has been modified.

The Work Package Editor ③ supports collective processing of development tasks. The description of a work package reflects both the description and the processing of a work package. The Work Package Editor provides tools for processing a work package and to support communication and coordination among the staff members of work spaces. The connection of the process view with the product view occurs via integration of existing software development tools. In the application example, TakeFive's programming environment SNiFF ④ [17] and a design tool developed at the C. Doppler Laboratory ⑤ were integrated into the Cooperation Assistant. The tools available for the product view might vary from project to project.

Work package descriptions, work schedules, annotations and comments are put in relation to one another and to documents in the form of links. The links inserted in the description of the work package complement the task specification with the software development documents that are necessary for processing the work package; activating a link ⑥ invokes the external application. In the application scenario there are links to locations in the implementation ⑦ and in the design ⑧ that are in relation with the task description of the work package. From there the software developer can begin processing the task in the respective software development tool. The results of this processing are documented in the Work Package Editor by the package processor. On completion of processing, the work package is marked as completed and automatically forwarded to the respective evaluator, who was specified with the Work Package Editor.

The above application scenario shows that the model for cooperative, distributed software development processes from Section 4 has been implemented in the Cooperation Assistant. The Cooperation Assistant supports collaboration through the exchange of shared work objects and covers the complete software development process. General functionality for process-oriented management of cooperative workflows was linked to the artifacts with a product-oriented view. Likewise, external software development tools can be integrated into the work environment with the help of tool adapters. The authors know of no other available software development environment that equally supports both the process view and the product view; also provides flexible communication, coordination and cooperation mechanisms; and additionally permits the integration of external tools.

6. Summary and perspectives

The proposed model for cooperative software development and the development environment Cooperation Assistant based on this model serve as a contribution toward correcting the shortcomings of software development environments; in addition, they provide an experimental environment that permits empirically-based support or rejection of the thesis that the cooperative, cluster-oriented development approach is superior to the rigid phase-oriented development approach with respect to exploitation of productivity and improvement in quality potential, especially for spatially and temporally distributed project organization.

The work toward the conception of the model and the implementation of the development environment have been completed, and the evaluation of the proposed approach has begun. Experience to date with using the Cooperation Assistant confirms the assumption that the cooperative, cluster-oriented development improves both productivity and quality. The presented approach excels primarily in its easily understandable model, the intuitive usability of the tools and the comprehensible presentation of process- and product-related information.

The evaluation research activities have not been completed yet, and the presently available analysis data do not suffice for empirical evaluation and conclusion with respect to support or rejection of the above thesis. Evaluation will continue to take some time, since only the results of a correspondingly large number of extensive, complex software projects can provide the basis for such evaluation.

Open issues that are the subject of continuing research and development work include the integration of network techniques for the control and monitoring of tasks and deadlines, the integration (acquisition and use) of metrics for process optimization, and the conception and availability of tools for user-controlled analysis, filtering and sorting of product- and process-related information.

7. References

[1]   J. Altmann, "Cooperative Software Development: Computer-Supported Coordination and Cooperation", PhD-Thesis, Trauner, Linz, 1999.

[2]   P.K. Garg and M. Jazayeri, "Process-Centered Software Engineering Environments: A Grand Tour", Technical Report TUV-1841-95-02, Distributed Systems Group, Technical University of Vienna, 1995.

[3]   I. Sommerville, "Software Engineering", 5th Ed., Addison-Wesley, Harlow, 1996.

[4]   K. Bauknecht, T. Mühlherr, C. Sauter, and S. Teufel, "Computerunterstützung für die Gruppenarbeit", Addison-Wesley, Bonn, 1995.

[5]   J. Pasch, "Software-Entwicklung im Team", Springer, New York, 1994.

[6]   B. W. Boehm, "A Spiral Model of Software Development and Enhancement", in: IEEE Computer, Vol. 21, No. 5, 1988, pp. 61-72.

[7]   B. Meyer, "Object-Oriented Software Construction", Prentice Hall, London, 1997.

[8]   C. Floyd and H. Züllighoven, "Softwaretechnik", in: P. Rechenberg and G. Pomberger (eds.), "Informatik Handbuch", Hanser, Vienna, 1997, pp. 641-665.

[9]   C. Floyd, "Theory and Practice of Software Development", Proceedings of the Sixth International Conference on Theory and Practice of Software Development, Springer, New York, 1995, pp. 25-41.

[10] B. Curtis, M. I. Kellner, and J Over, "Process Modelling", Communications of the ACM, Vol. 35, No. 9, 1992, pp. 75-90.

[11] W. R. Bischofberger, T. Kofler, K.-U. Mätzel, and B. Schäffer, "Computer Supported Cooperative Software Engineering with Beyond-Sniff", Proceedings of Software Engineering Envrionments, IEEE, 1995, pp. 135-143.

[12] W. Hesse and M. Frese, "Zur Arbeitssitutation in der Software-Entwicklung", in: Informatik Forschung und Entwicklung, Vol. 9, No. 3, Springer, 1994, pp. 179-191.

[13] P. Dourish and P. Bellotti, "Awareness and Coordination in Shared Workspaces", Proceedings of the Conference on Computer-Supported Cooperative Work, ACM Press, New York, 1992, pp. 107-114.

[14] L. Suchman, "Plans and Situated Actions", Cambridge University Press, 1987.

[15] J. Altmann and R. Weinreich, "An Environment for Cooperative Software Development: Realization and Implications", Proceedings of the Thirty-First Annual Hawaii International Conference on System Sciences, Collaboration Systems and Technology, IEEE, Los Alamitos, 1998, pp. 27-37.

[16] R. Weinreich and J. Altmann, "An Object-Oriented Infrastructure for a Cooperative Software Development Environment", Proceedings of the Fifth International Symposium on Applied Corporate Computing, ITESM, Monterrey Mexico, 1997, pp. 45-53.

[17] SNiFF: TakeFive Home Page. http://www.takefive.com.

Technical Papers

Frameworks 2

View Programming for Decentralized Development of OO Programs

Hafedh Mili, Joumana Dargham, Ali Mili*, Omar Cherkaoui, and Robert Godin
Département d'Informatique
Université du Québec à Montréal
Case Postale 8888, Station Centre-Ville
Montréal, Québec H3C 3P8, Canada
*Institute for Software Research
1000 Technology Drive, Suite 1000
Fairmont, WV 26554, USA
{Hafedh.Mili@,dargham@larc.info,Omar.Cherkaoui@}uqam.ca
amili@cs.wvu.edu

Abstract

*There has been a lot of interest recently in the problem of building object-oriented applications by somehow combining other application fragments that provide their own overlapping definitions or expectations of the same domain objects. We propose an approach based on the split objects model of prototype languages whereby an application object is represented by a varying set of instances-- called views-- that implement different parts of its domain behavior but that delegate its core functionalities to a **core instance**: an object's response to a message depends on the views currently attached to its core instance. Our approach is not purely prototype-based in the sense that core instances and views are members of classes. Further, we recognize that the behavior inherent in views (classes) is often an adaptation of a generic behavior to the domain object at hand, and define **viewpoints** as parameterized class-like algebraic structures to embody such a generic behavior. In this paper, we first describe view programming from the perspective of the developer. Next, we sketch a semi-formal model of view programming, and describe the steps needed to implement it in a class-based statically typed language, for instance, C++. Third, we look at the challenges and opportunities provided by view programming to support safe, robust, and efficient distributed applications.*

1. Introduction

As object-oriented systems scale-up from desktop applications to enterprise-wide information systems, developers are faced with the problem of supporting a myriad of functional areas within the same object model. While the objects manipulated may refer to the same real-world objects, each functional area may have its own data requirements, nomenclature, and classification. Traditionally, this problem has been handled in information modelling by modelling the data required by the functional areas separately, normalizing them, integrating them into a unique *complete* model, and re-deriving the *partial* views needed by the functional areas from that model (see e.g. [10]). Notwithstanding the difficulties inherent in programming and manipulating objects through separate data views, this process works best in the context of a centralized and pre-planned development activity. In practice, centralized and pre-planned development are neither practical, nor always possible, and may not even be desirable.

The concept of views in OOP was first introduced by Shilling and Sweeny [9] as a *filter* of a global interface of the class, but the views are not separable or separately reusable. Harrison and Ossher proposed *subject-oriented programming* as a way to build integrated "multiple view" applications by composing application fragments, called *subjects*, which represent compilable and possibly executable functional slices [4]. In principle, independently developed programs/subjects can be composed a-posteriori, making it possible to decentralize ownership and development of OO applications. In practice, the code of subjects must adhere to specific programming guidelines to make subjects composable [7]. Further, subjects cannot be composed dynamically.

In our approach, an application object consists of a core object, to which we can add and remove functional slices, or *views,* reflecting the changing roles of the object during its lifetime. The set of views "attached" to an object determine the messages to which it can respond, and the way it responds to them. We introduce the concept of **viewpoint** as a generic template that is mapped to domain objects to yield views. *Viewpoints* abstract functional behavior in a domain-independent way, and are developed independently of the classes to which they apply. This supports the decentralized development of integrated OO applications, and removes many of the visibility and ownership dependencies that create development bottlenecks and that reduce the reusability of the resulting applications. Further, to the extent that views embody different functional areas, there is every expectation that the underlying data reside, and/or be owned, in different sites, and the aggregation inherent in view programming appears to provide a reasonable boundary with regard to data distribution. Such a naive scheme would probably be inefficient because of the high traffic between the core object and views, and we show various optimizations that can help reduce the overhead.

In the next section, we present view programming scenarios, and introduce some of the basic structural and behavioral mechanisms. A formal model of viewpoints, views, and *viewable objects* is introduced in section 3. In particular, we discuss a number of issues related to typing, and briefly describe a tool set aimed at supporting view programming in C++. We discuss distribution issues in section 4, and conclude in section 5 by highlighting directions for future research.

2. Programming with views

2.1 Basics

Typically, we assume that each object of the application domain supports a set of core functionalities that are made available, directly or indirectly, to all the users of the object, and a set of interfaces that are specific to particular uses, and which may be added or removed during run-time. The interfaces may correspond to different types of users with similar functional interests or to different users with *different* functional interests. We would like client programs to be able to access several functional areas or *views* simultaneously, provided that the views are not mutually exclusive. We would also like to have a consistent and unencumbered protocol to address objects that support several views simultaneously. Existing approaches to view programming do not support the run-time addition and removal of functional views; all of the views that a user (programmer) might wish to address are «declared»/attached at compile time.

Figure 1 shows an aggregation/delegation-based implementation of this idea. The core object (a **Truck**) includes several state variables (_id, make, etc.), and supports several operations. The view objects, which point to the core object, may add state (e.g. OTruck adds 'schedule', which is a list of reservations on the truck), behavior (e.g. FTruck adds the method 'getAmortizationRate()), or simply redirect existing behavior (all three redirect calls to 'getSerialNumber()')). In this case, upon invoking the operation getSerialNumber() on any view, the request is forwarded to the core object (a **Truck**), and *the operation getSerialNumber() is executed in the context of the core* *object.* The same is true for references to the shared state variables (not shown here). Practically,

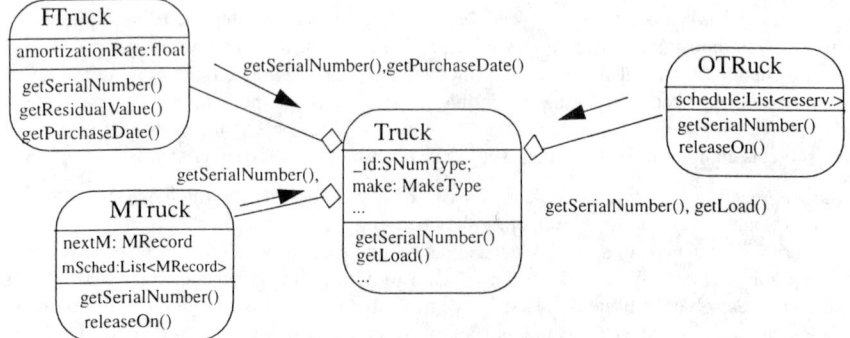

Figure 1. A model of objects with views.

there will be a single copy of such variables, stored in the core object, and read/write requests will be forwarded to the core object. Our approach to sharing state variables is consistent with delegation, but our approach to behavior sharing (methods) is different from the typical delegation or prototype-based approaches where the operation in the object being delegated to is executed in the context of the *delegator* [5]. In our case, we have a purely *forwarding mechanism*.

2.3 Lifecycle behavior

We look at three aspects of an object's manipulation: 1) object creation, 2) view attachment and removal, and 3) behavior invocation on objects. We will distinguish between two kinds of situations, (i) the case where we use a single view on an object, and (ii) the case where several views are used simultaneously. This distinction is important because we want single-view programming to "reduce" to regular programming, with no overhead for the developer. We illustrate our approach using an example in C++ to identify the issues that will have to be addressed in the context of a statically typed language such as C++.

We consider a merchandising organization that manages a fleet of trucks. The finance department views trucks as assets which are amortizable over a certain period of time. The operations department, which operates merchandise deliveries, views trucks as allocatable time-exclusive resources. It also views them as machinery that requires parts, scheduled maintenance, and incidental repairs. Let **Truck** be the interface of the core object (see Figure 2). We will refer the financial, operations, and maintenance views as **FTruck**, **OTruck**, and **MTruck**, with the C++-like interfaces (see Figure 2 for **FTruck**). These interfaces show one way of implementing behavior forwarding, whereby each view points to the core object (data member _truck in classes FTruck, OTruck, and MTruck). Similarly, the core objects refers to the active views through a collection instance variable called _views.

2.3.1 Object creation

The lifetime of an application object is bounded by that of its core instance; the lifetimes of the views are included within those bounds. For the case of single view programming, the developer need only see the definition of the view class, and should be able to create instances of the application object through the view. The following excerpts illustrate what we mean:

```
(0)    #include <ftruck.h>
(1)    FTruck* anFtruck = new FTruck(123);
```

The line (0) includes the file that contains the definition of the view class (**FTruck**). In line (2), we "bring about" the application object with serial number 123, and that supports the functionalities of **FTruck**. The idea here is that, behind the scenes, if an instance of **Truck** with Id 123 existed already, either in persistent storage, over the network, or in main memory, then 'anFtruck' is attached to it, and is used to access it functionalities; if no such instance of **Truck** existed, then one is created. This behavior can be obtained if we make sure that all view classes have a one argument constructor that calls some sort of a "core object broker".

For the case of multiple views, developers are aware of both the core object class and of the view classes, and they have to instantiate the core object *explicitly*, and 'construct' view instances for that core instance. This is illustrated in the following code excerpts:

```
(0)    #include <truck.h>
(1)    #include <ftruck.h>
(2)    #include <otruck.h>
(3)    #include <mtruck.h>
(4)    Truck* myTruck = new Truck(id);
(5)    FTruck* myFTruck = new FTruck(myTruck);
```

class Truck:... {
 public:
     ...
     SNumType getSerialNumber();
     MakeType getMake();
     Year getModelYear();
     Date getPurchaseDate();
     float getLoad();
     static Truck* getTruck-
             WithSNum(SNumType anId);
 protected:
     void setSerialNumber(SNumType);
     void setMake(MakeType);
     ...
 private:
     SNumType _id;
     List<View> _views;
     static Dict<IdType,Truck> _knownTrucks;
 ...
 }
 // The core class
	class FTruck {
	 public:
	     FTruck(IdType anId);
	     ...
	     SNumType getSerialNumber();
	     Date getPurchaseDate();
	     float getResidualValue();
	     static float getAmortPeriod();
	     static float getAmortRate();
	     float getActPurchVal();
	 protected:
	     void setActPurchVal(float);
	 private:
	     Truck* _truck;
	     float _actPurchaseValue;
	     float _purchaseValue;
	     ....
	 }
	 // The financial view

Figure 2. The core class and financial view of a truck.

In this case, we include the core class as well as the view classes. Line (5) shows a way of attaching a view to a core instance using the one argument constructor. View attachment and detachment is discussed below.

2.3.2 View attachment and removal

For the case of single view programming, view creation and attachment is indistinguishable from "object creation" since the same operation does both. With several views, view creation is a separate operation. Our intent is to make the behavior embodied in a view available to the core object as long as the view is attached, but also to be able to switch that behavior on and off during the lifetime of the object. Because views may maintain independent state variables, we distinguish between view creation and attachment, on one hand, and view activation on the other, and between view desactivation, on one hand, and view detachment and removal on the other. For instance, we would like the state of views to survive the desactivation (or non-availability) of a view to a particular program or program run. The distinction between view creation and view activation is the same as that between creating a data object, and bringing up into main memory. The same thing for view desactivation and removal: desactivation is like persisting the sate of the view, and removing it from main memory, whereas view removal removes it from the database. This analogy will become more relevant when we deal with distribution issues across ORBs.

Within a given application, we might have several requests to create a view of a particular object; a single view should be created, independently of the number of requests to create such a view, where the first request creates the view, and the subsequent ones return the existing view.

2.3.3 Behavior invocation

With single view programming, developers see only the interface of the view class, and all the behavior in that interface is available. Behind the scenes, some of the methods that are "callable" from the view are actually delegated to the core object. For example, "getSerialNumber()" is available in the **FTruck** interface, but its implementation forwards to **Truck::**getSerialNumber(). When we have several views, messages are sent primarily to the core object. If one of the views that are currently attached supports the requested behavior, the request is satisfied. Otherwise, the request is denied. In a reflective language such as Smalltalk, this behavior can be accomplished by modifying the dispatching mechanism [6]. In a typed and (mostly) statically bound language such as C++, this behavior can be obtained by performing the appropriate compile-time code transformations. Consider the following program excerpts.

```
        #include <truck.h>
        #include <ftruck.h>
        #include <otruck.h>
        #include <mtruck.h>
(1)     Truck* myTruck = new Truck(132);
(2)     FTruck* myFTruck = new FTruck(myTruck);
(3)     OTruck* myOTruck = new MTRuck(myTruck);
(4)     Date t0 = myTruck->getDateNextMaintenance();
(5)     myTruck->releaseOn(t3);
```

In line (4) the programmer invoked a behavior that is available in the MTruck view on the instance of Truck, without referring explicitly to the view instance. The underlying mechanism is a pre-processor that replaces line (4) with the following line:

```
(4')    Date t0 = myTruck->getView('MTruck')->getDateNextMaintenance();
```

because it knows that 'getDateNextMaintenance()' is available in the view class **MTruck** [6], but it does *not* know for sure that *at the time* that the call is made, an **MTruck** view is *attached* and *active*[1], and we cannot sort this out at compilation time.

Assume now that the method 'releaseOn(Date)' (see line (5)) is supported by the operations view (**OTruck**) and the maintenance view (**MTruck**). We adopted the approach advocated by Harrison & Ossher [4] which consists of *composing* the various method implementations. Our approach relies on a *universal composition view* which is automatically generated to contain default implementations for the all the multiply defined methods:

```
class __Truck_CompositionView {
public: ...
        void releaseOn(Date t)   {
                _truck->getView('OTruck')->releaseOn(t);
                _truck->getView('MTruck')->releaseOn(t);}
                ...
```

Developers can edit it to conform it to their intent (see e.g. [7]); the actual mechanics of composition views are slightly more complex [6].

By using a code rewriting approach, we strove towards making view programming as natural and transparent as possible. There are, however, some implicit assumptions that developers usually make when dealing with a class hierarchy, that would be violated because of delegation [6]. In terms of visibility and access properties, it is useful to think of the relationship between a view and a class as the private subclass relationship in C++[2] where one has to think explicitly of what to export through the subclass relationship. The distinction between the core class hierarchy (**Truck**) and the view class hierarchy (**FTruck**)-- which is transparent to the single view user-- manifests itself when we want to extend the view class **FTruck**: that extension should not break the forwarding mechanism. This leads to a number of more or less easily enforceable guidelines, which compelled us to forbid view extension, but use *viewpoint specialization* to the same effect [6].

2.4 Viewpoints: «horizontal reuse» of functional slices

We recognize that the functionality provided by a view such as the financial view above may be useful for other kinds of objects/assets and propose to define some sort of a template of a functional view that is parameterized by the elements of the *required interface* of the core object. This template, called *viewpoint*, can then be instantiated for different types of assets, be they trucks or buildings or machines or computers. For example, the _serialNumber attribute is seen as a special case of a general inventory ID, and may be replaced by other domain object specific identifiers. Using *viewpoints*, views may be seen as the mapping between a view and a domain object. The use of viewpoints provides an additional reuse dimension, one for the *developers* of views.

3. Implementing viewpoints and views in C++

3.1 A framework for viewpoints and views

A viewpoint is a parameterized type VP[*TH*], where *TH* is a *theory* describing the type of the domain object to which VP may be mapped. We illustrate the syntax through an example:

---

1.   The actual code substitution is more fault tolerant and allows for a graceful degradation in case no such view is *currently* attached.
2.   Intuitively, A is a *private* subclass of B, if the knowledge of the subclass relationship is private to A's methods, i.e. only A's methods can refer to (non-private) data and function members of B

> **VIEWPOINT** FinancialAsset
> **REQUIRES** *CapitalAssetTheory* [*AgeType* -> **Year**,
> *PurchaseValueType* -> *CurrencyType*]
> **EXTENDS**
> void *setPurchaseDate*(**Date** d)   **after**
> {setAmortizationPeriod(**Year**(Date::today() - d)); }
> **PROVIDES**
> **variables**
> **Year** _amortizationPeriod;
> *CurrencyType* _residualValue;
> **operations**
> *CurrencyType*   getResidualValue () {return residualValue;}
> void setAmortizationPeriod(**Year** y){_amortizationPeriod = y;}
> ...
> **END VIEWPOINT**

Figure 3. A viewpoint definition.

The requirements on the (type of) objects to which the viewpoint may be applied are described in the **requires** clause. In this example, we specify such a requirement in terms of a previously defined theory, *CapitalAssetTheory*, whose *sort* or type parameter *AgeType* was bound to the type **Year**, and whose sort *PurchaseValueType* was replaced by the sort *CurrencyType*. The **extends** clause allows us to specify blocs of code that are to be executed by the generated view before (**before**) or after (**after**) the specified core object methods (which must be part of the **requires** interface), in much the same way method wrappers work in CLOS. Other syntactic flavors for the specification of viewpoints have been provided, including the in-line specification of new theories, or in-line extensions of existing ones [6].

A view *V* is generated by instantiating a viewpoint *VP*[*Th*] for a type *T* that satisfies the theory parameter *Th* for a given correspondence Σ, i.e. $T =>_\Sigma Th$, and we write $V = Vp [Th ->_\Sigma T]$. The one-to-one correspondence Σ maps names of *sorts*, *variables*, and *operations* of the *theory* to the corresponding constructs in the type (e.g. class interface). In C++, we may write:

$$V = T \text{ as } VP [s_1 ->\Sigma(s_1),..., v_1 ->\Sigma(v_1),..., op_1 ->\Sigma(op_1),...];$$

where the "clauses" '$x -> \Sigma(x)$' represent the various substitutions to replace the component constructs of the theory (e.g. sorts or variables) by the corresponding constructs in the type *T*. The reader will notice that the code for the **extends** and **provides** methods of the viewpoint is aggregation-unaware. hence, in addition to the aforementioned substitutions, view generation will transform references to **required** (or **extended**) variables and methods to delegated references[1]. For example, if *f* is a method that is part of the **provides** clause, and if *f* calls the **require**'d method "getPurchaseDate()", then its code:

> void *f*(...){...
> Date d = getPurchaseDate();
> ...}

will be transformed into:

---

1. This choice is motivated by our desire to repackage existing code where several views are implicitly merged with the core object functionality, into viewpoints (see [6] and section 4.1). Also, we want our model of viewpoints to be independent of the implementation mechanism-- in this case, aggregation.

```
        void f(...) {...
                Date d = _truck->getPurchaseDate();
                ...}
```

where _truck is a variable of type **Truck*** that is automatically added to the view[1]. References to **require**'d variables are handled the same way [6]. In both cases, we have to make sure that the required variables and methods are somehow accessible to the generated view class[2]. We won't expand further on view generation; the reader is referred to [6] for a more complete catalog of transformations and outstanding problems.

3.2 Typing issues

With view programming, there are various hierarchical (symmetric, transitive) relationships between the various constructs with different implications on reuse, behavioral substitutability, and the like. We examined three kinds of relationships:

1. The specialization/subsumption of viewpoints, as a way of incrementally specifying and reusing viewpoints,
2. Subtyping, and more generally, behavioral substitutability of views derived from hierarchically related viewpoints, or from views derived from the same viewpoint, but for hierarchically related core classes, and
3. Dynamic subtyping, and more generally, behavioral substitutability of hierarchically related core objects, to which we attach views, possibly generated from hierarchically related viewpoints.

For the purposes of this paper, we will be content to highlight the major issues raised by our framework:

- The multiple specialization of viewpoints raises the issue of combining *before* and *after* methods (our solution: using defaults, that can be overridden),
- Identifying conditions under which the application of two hierarchically related viewpoints to a class yields two hierarchically related (from a typing perspective) view classes,
- Supporting *pure*[3] dynamic typing in a statically typed language in a way that strikes the right balance between flexibility and safety, or at the very least, graceful degradation.

There is a host of other issues discussed in [6].

Implementation-wise, we are interested in statically typed languages to be able to perform relatively type-safe code transformations; we chose C++ because it is widely used. Our approach consists of adding non-ambiguous syntactic constructs to the C++ language to define views and viewpoints, and putting programs that use these constructs through a bunch of pre-processors that ultimately, generate standard C++ code. Our tools are being developed with flex and yacc (bison),

---

1. In reality, there are two possible code transformations, the one shown above, and one to _truck->get-CompositionView()->getPurchaseDate(...) so that the view code gets to use whichever version of get-PurchaseDate(...) is available to the truck at the time of the invocation, including one (or several) view versions. In effect, using getCompositionView(...) is like opting for dynamic binding. Most approaches to delegation use the latter interpretation. We choose to also support the former mode in case views correspond to different access rights/privileges.
2. In C++, they have to be public members of the core class, or else, the view must be a friend of the core class [6]
3. This is not just of matter of picking the right implementation for a signature that was known at compile time, in principle, we don't even know which signatures an object will support at run-time because of the dynamic attachment and removal of views.

and we keep discovering unsuspected joys of dealing with C++ semantics.

4. View programming and distribution

4.1 Issues

View programming supports the decentralized development of applications that span a variety of functional domains because viewpoints and viewpoint hierarchies can be developed independently from core classes, and the generation of views for a particular class does not require owning the definition of the class. In this section, we are more interested in the distributed implementation of an object with several views. Figure 4 shows a possible distribution scenario involving the same object of Figure 1. we make the distinction between two kinds of "distribution". First, we have the case where a given site sees (and "believes") a single view, or a subset of views, and is not aware of the existence of the other views. Second, we have the case where a site knows of all the views, but hosts only one, or a subset thereof. The two situations raise different sets of issues. We assume in this example that site 3 is not aware of the existence of a core object behind the view, or of OTruck and MTruck, and the behavior of these should not be available to it, except indirectly as a

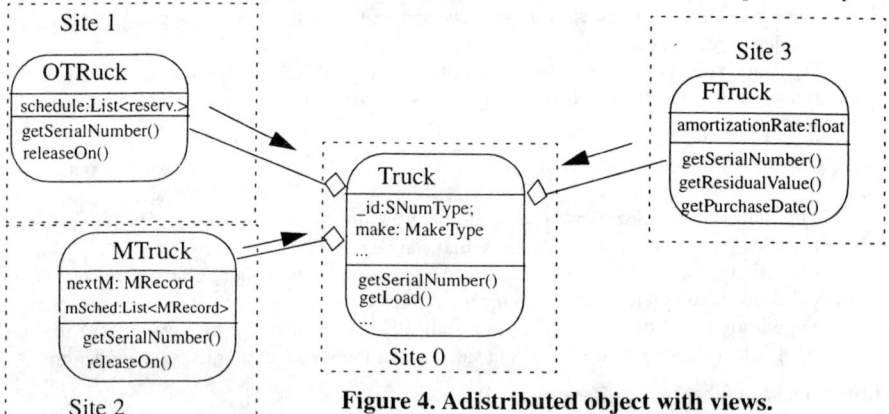

Figure 4. Adistributed object with views.

side effect of methods called on the core object (e.g. through the *before* and *after* methods). For the case of sites 1 and 2, they know about OTruck and MTRuck, but don't know about FTruck, and any behavior invoked on the core object should only invoke the methods that are explicitly provided by OTruck and MTruck (or as side effects of such behaviors).

4.2 A model of distribution

We address our model of view programming from the perspective of a CORBA/RMI-like model where a single state-holding copy of an object is available over the network whereas different proxies/stubs route requests to that object through ORBs. Figure 5 illustrates such a model. We assume for simplicity that a single ORB manages requests on behalf of all sites. The issues to consider in this model are:

1.   where to put the distribution boundaries, and which objects to replicate, if any, and
2.   re-evaluating the code transformations implemented to support message forwarding in light of the performance factors of a distributed implementation.

Having a single system-wide copy of any object and stubbing all the objects that are not local to a given site, may have severe performance problems. Consider the code excerpts shown earlier. Assume that the core class **Truck**, and the view classes **OTruck** and **MTruck** reside on sites 0, 1, and 2, respectively, and that we are writing an application on site 1, that uses both views[1]. We assume that the invocation of the constructor of the Truck stub will do the right thing, i.e. either locate a live object with identifier 'id', and return a reference to it, or invoke the lifecycle service to create or reanimate such an object from site 0.

```
                  #include <truck.h>
                  #include <otruck.h>
                  #include <mtruck.h>
(1)        Truck* myTruck = new Truck(id);                              // remote
(2)        OTruck* myOTruck = new OTruck(myTruck);                      // local &
remote
(3)        MTruck* myMTruck = new MTRuck(myTruck);                      // remote
(4)        Date t0 = myTruck->getDateNextMaintenance();                // remote
(5)        myTruck->releaseOn(t3);                                     // remote &
local
```

Line (2) involves both local and remote access: the creation of the view is local but the connection to the core object is remote. Line (3) involves two remote accesses, one to create (or reactivate, or return reference to an existing) OTruck view, from site 1 to site 2, which passes the ORB reference of the core object to the view in site 2, and from site 2 to site 0, to connect the remote view to the remote core object. Line (4), when transformed, becomes:

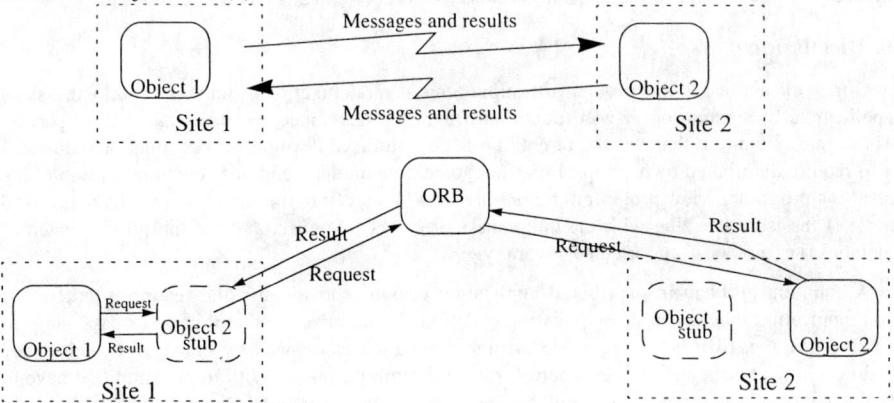

Figure 5. A CORBA-like distribution model.

(4')   Date t0 = myTruck->getView('MTruck')->getDateNextMaintenance();

Under this transformation, we need a first remote access to get an ORB reference to the **MTruck** instance (through the "getView('MTruck')" call), and then a remote method invocation of 'get-DateNextMaintenance' on that instance. It is clear in this case that the remote call to "getView(...)" is somewhat redundant since instruction (3) has already fetched a reference to that object. A more efficient transformation would yield:

(4")   Date t0 = myMTruck->getDateNextMaintenance();

---

1. We assume that the client versions of **Truck** and **MTruck** are also called *Truck* and *MTruck*.

Generally speaking, the view pre-processor can generate variables that will contain references for the views, which will be initialized on the first call, and used thereafter.

Because the method "releaseOn(...)" is provided by two views, line (5) is replaced by:

(5')   myTruck->getCompositionView()->releaseOn(t3);

Here again, the code pre-processor could save an ORB reference to the composition view in a local variable to save one remote call. Using the default implementation, i.e.:

```
void __Truck_CompositionView::releaseOn(Date t){
        _truck->getView('OTruck')->releaseOn(t);
        _truck->getView('MTruck')->releaseOn(t);}
```

Using the normal processing mode, the execution of "__Truck_CompositionView::release-On(...)" will invoke the following remote calls:
1.   One remote call to invoke __Truck_CompositionView::releaseOn(...) from site 1 to site 0,
2.   One remote call to invoke OTruck::releaseOn(...) from site 0 *back to* site 1, and
3.   One remote call to invoke MTruck::releaseOn(...) from site 0 to site 2.

Because the composition view holds no state, having duplicates carries no overhead, and thus, we can duplicate it in all the sites. This will obviate the need for the first remote call. By explicitly storing pointers to the attached views (rather than going through the core object), the call to OTruck::releaseOn(...) becomes local, and that to MTruck::releaseOn(...) still requires a single remote call. We have thus saved two remote invocations out of three, notwithstanding any remote invocations one of the two methods might make to the core object's methods.

6. Discussion

Our work addresses the problem of supporting several functional domains within the same application, by composing at will functional fragments developed by independent third parties. Those same situations that require, or could use, decentralized development of functional domains also require distributed ownership of the functional domain data, and distributed execution of the resulting programs. View programming seems like a perfect fit to the extent that we have resolved most of the issues dealing with the uniqueness of object reference, and the multiple dispatch of methods (i.e. methods supported by several views).

A common problem in distributed application design is to identify the recurrent patterns of communication inherent in the application code to help optimize the distribution of data and processing (see e.g. [8]). In our case, we assume that data are "owned" by the sites in which they reside, and cannot be moved elsewhere for optimization purposes. With duplication, we have to find a trade-off between performing all computations at the place where data resides (i.e. no duplication), or, duplicating everything everywhere, and incurring heavy network traffic to propagate changes between duplicates. The way in which views slice an object *may be used in this case to optimize duplication*: within a given site, we only duplicate the slice of the core object that we need—the view mechanism is then used to coordinate the various slices. We have started exploring these issues whereby *view-induced slice* of an object is the—conservatively computed (see e.g. [3])—transitive closure of the **required** interface of the corresponding viewpoint, through the call relationship. Concept formation methods are used [2] to find objects' optimal slices. We continue to work on this an other issues, both from a theoretical and a practical (implementation) point of view.

Acknowledgments: We thank William Harrison and Harold Ossher whose work subject-oriented pro-

gramming and subject-composition helped us identify (and sometimes solve) some of the issues discussed in this paper. This work was sponsored by Nortel, DEC, IBM, CAE Electronics, Teleglobe, and Machina Sapiens, within the context of the SYNERGIE industry-university initiative (Quebec), by NSERC (Canada), and by YAGO Technologies.

References

[1]   Saniya Ben Hassen, Irina Athanasiu, and Henri E. Bal, "A Flexible Operation Execution Model for Shared Distributed Objects," *ACM SIGPLAN Notices*, vol. 31, no. 10, OOPSLA'96 Proceedings, San Jose CA, October 1996, pp. 30-50.

[2]   Robert Godin, Hafedh Mili, Guy Mineau, Rokia Missaoui, Amina Arfi, and Thuy-Tien Chau, "Design of Class Hierarchies Based on Concept (Galois) Lattices," *Theory and Practice of Object Systems,* vol 4, No 2, pp. 117-134, 1998.

[3]   David Grove, Greg De Fouw, Jeffrey Dean, and Craig Chambers, "Call Graph Construction in Object-Oriented Languages," *ACM SIGPLAN Notices*, vol 32, no 10, OOPSLA'97 Proceedings, Atlanta, GA, October, 1997, pp. 108-109.

[4]   William Harrison and Harold Ossher, "Subject-oriented programming: a critique of pure objects," in *Proceedings of OOPSLA'93*, Washington D.C., Sept. 26-Oct 1, 1993, pp. 411-428.

[5]   Jacques Malenfant, "On The Semantic Diversity of Delegation-Based Languages," *Proceedings of OOPSLA'95*, Austin, TX, pp. 215-230.

[6]   Hafedh Mili and Joumana Dargham, *View Programming in C++: A co-reference based approach*, rapport technique, département d'informatique, Décembre 1997.

[7]   Harold Ossher, Matthew Kaplan, William Harrison, Alex Katz, and Vincent Kruskal, "Subject-oriented composition rules," in *Proceedings of OOPSLA'95*, Austin, TX, Oct. 15-19, 1995, pp. 235-250.

[8]   Sandeep Purao, Hemant Jain, and Derek Nazareth, "Effective Distribution of Object-Oriented Applications," *Communications of the ACM*, vol. 41, no. 8, August 1998, pp. 100-108.

[9]   John Shilling and Peter Sweeny, "Three Steps to Views," *Proceedings of OOPSLA'89*, New Orleans, LA, pp. 353-361, 1989.

[10]   Jeffrey D. Ullman, *Principles of Database Systems*, C S Press, 2nd ed., 1982.

[11]   Michael Van Hilst and David Notkin, "Using Role Components to Implement Collaboration-Based Designs," in *Proceedings of OOPSLA'96*, San-Jose, CA, 6-10 October, 1996, pp. 359-369.

Object Lessons Learned from an Intelligent Agents Framework for Telephony-Based Applications

Demetrios Yannakopoulos
IBM Global Services
dy@digital.net

Michael Ferretti
IBM Global Services
ferretti@digital.net

Mark Schultz
IBM Global Services
ootech@ibm.net

Abstract

Contact Center-related activities, at the business level, are common regardless of parent organizations or industries. The implementation of such activities is unlikely to change throughout the lifetime of the Contact Center and, therefore, it could be the basis ("framework") upon which customized solutions can be built. Specifying such framework is mainly a business rather than a technical problem. Programmers create "what" a system does while business analysts determine "when" the system takes certain actions. Factors influencing the framework architecture are the requirements for small, mobile, intelligent components, the ability for run-time modifications, and a reasonable foreknowledge of the technology that will minimize risks. In this paper, we present a distributed, object-oriented, telephony framework based on Intelligent Agents and coupled with a rules engine. The goals are reuse, platform independence, support for a distributed environment, system scalability, and adherence to standards. The framework's core is an inference engine that accepts external stimuli and, based on business rules, determines the resulting actions. This engine is an intelligent agent, that can be attached to any object for which intelligence is needed and thus, it is able to create an integrated, customizable solution. We discuss our architectural decisions, limitations, design choices, and experiences in development, customization, and operation of the framework. Tools and procedures used during implementation of specific solutions are also reported.

1. Introduction

The primary aim of software consulting-services organizations is to develop successful systems for customers. From a commercial standpoint, a system's success is measured by whether its implementation, deployment, user training, and, ultimately, its potential reuse have met their respective acceptance levels. *Contact Center*[1] businesses need applications that effectively assist their service representatives or, in more advanced cases, their customers in determining the most appropriate resolution to a given task or request. Regardless of the center's line of products or business, every contact center's practices and policies are essentially homogenous across industries. In addition, center-specific activities and strategies are logically complex but well known. Since these processes are enduring, (at the generic as well as the center-specific level,) they can be used as an ideal

---

[1] The phrase, "contact center" epitomizes, more eloquently, the combination of all transactions that can occur from the integration of a traditional call center with e-commerce channels over the Internet.

common foundation for a reusable contact-center application. For more than four years, our team members, have been involved with contact centers and have had the opportunity to observe, record, and apply simple principles of reusability in implementing the center's enduring activities. From these engagements, a framework, *Customer Service Series (CSS)*, has evolved. As a customer solution, the CSS model consists of the following four elements.

1. **Inference Environment.** The framework utilizes a rules-based module capable of evaluating events and determining an appropriate course of action. Unique in the proposed solution is the fact that the Inference Environment can be attached to any module/object for which intelligence is needed. This allows for flexibility, decentralization, low cost, and small size of the modules. Roughly speaking, a rule is a pair of an *event* and an *action*, created by a *business analyst*, and registered with a Rules Manager module. When a particular event occurs, a specific action is triggered.

2. **Telecommunications modules.** There are the modules that essentially form a contact center. Specific telephony and web-enabled packages are included, but a customer may elect a different selection.

3. **Organizational and project management aspects.** CSS, as a product of a large organization, has the advantage of using well-established supporting environments (e.g. repositories, communications procedures, etc.) as well as methodologies that define the software engineering approach for an engagement.

4. **Core Team.** A small team of experts (in both organizational and technical areas) maintains and improves the framework. They also assist customers in site-specific implementation and deployment issues. By rotating the team members between the core team and various engagements, the framework is always "in touch" with its intended problem domain. Members of the organization are exposed to both the framework and the customers' needs, and reusability of skills is achieved by mentoring.

The framework allows any software packages to interface with the Inference Environment and therefore the ensuing system is able to take advantage of the Intelligent Agents (IA) technology at the business level.

2. Background

2.1 Today's Contact Centers

Contact Centers today face a challenge; in almost every aspect of life, the consumer is presented with automation that integrates many of the every-day functions under one casing. The center's policies, procedures, heuristic shortcuts, and traditional routines from the simplest to the most complex transaction should be unambiguous, effortless to apply or follow, not redundant, simple to modify, easy to train employees on, and uncomplicated to create. Those who know a specific business (business analysts) and those who are called to automate it (developers) are usually two different groups. There is a growing need for a powerful and easily customizable tool that would allow the business analyst to capture the center's policies and procedures and to instruct a system as to whether a certain action should be taken. "When" something is supposed to happen cannot be controlled by a central location (centralized computing) anymore. This goes beyond hardware/network considerations. Therefore, software has not only to be small but also to possess considerable intelligence in any level. In other words, small, mobile, intelligent components that allow for run-time modifications and expansions are preferable.

2.2 Frameworks

Productivity increase, project cost reduction, and time-to-market consideration are some of the factors that dictate some degree of "automation" (*reuse*) in a software project. A good approach is for reuse to be achieved during construction time. Modules that are "similar and yet not the same" are constructed, and result in run-time executables that are able to meet the needs of specific problem domains. Reusability has three important construction-time properties.

 i. **Generality.** In how many contexts or situations can a reusable entity be utilized?

 ii. **Adaptability.** How much work is required for a reusable entity before it can be used within another context?

 iii. **Usability.** Is the resulting software product useful and efficient during run time?

The need to utilize entities that (a) are the *same as* some already built and used modules, and (b) have the ability to be adopted by other entities during construction, has led us to the *framework technology*. ([2]) A framework is not a specific (physical) entity. It is generic in the sense that it contains variables that allow it to create, with the proper adaptation, an infinite amount of specific entities. Inside a framework, there are program instructions and variables, and framework instructions and variables. As expected, during run-time, program instructions act on program variables that manipulate data. Framework instructions, on the other hand, manipulate frameworks **at construction time** by acting on framework variables. Consequently, frameworks can adapt, and be adapted by, other frameworks. Framework instructions implement the concept "*same as, except.*" Usually, the instructions enable a framework to select any of the properties it needs from its surrounding environment, and then overwrite, add, modify or manipulate them by a knowledgeable designer.

2.3 Business Rules

Each enterprise has a structure that represents policies, controls, and constraints that define its operations. These are the enterprise's *business rules* ([8], [17]). They are classified into one of the following three categories. ([8], Pg. 261.)

 i. **Functional.** Generally, these rules are more global in scope than any other type of rules. They control and describe the enterprise's strategic imperatives. Mainly structured as axioms, they usually answer the various "whats" and "whys" about the enterprise. (E.g. "A credit card and its associated PIN are shipped to a card holder separately.")

 ii. **Structural.** They describe the enterprise's elements, entities, and the relationships amongst them. Mainly expressed as declarative statements, these rules are the policies that the enterprise's elements should conform to, as their responsibilities change. (E.g. "Profit = Revenue – Expenses".)

 iii. **Behavioral**. They control the flow of the enterprise's process. Mainly structured as either procedures or state changes, they usually answer the various "when" questions about the enterprise's business. For this reason, behavioral rules have *preconditions* and *postconditions*. (E.g. "Most valued customer is a customer who has placed 100 or more orders within a year or less").

Conceptually, business rules are a shorthand language capable of specifying unambiguously and without redundancies the business knowledge.

2.4 Intelligent Agents

According to Wooldridge and Jennings ([25], pg. 2), an Intelligent Agent is a hardware or (more usually) software-based computer system that enjoys the following properties:

i. **Autonomy.** Agents operate without the direct intervention of humans or others, and have some kind of control over their actions and internal state.

ii. **Social ability.** Agents interact with other agents or humans via some kind of agent-communication language.

iii. **Reactivity.** Agents perceive their environment and respond timely to changes that occur in it.

iv. **"Pro-activeness."** Agents do not simply act in response to their environment; they are able to exhibit goal-directed behavior by taking the initiative.

Meeting these properties with various degrees of completeness classifies the complexity of the IA's design.

3. Architecture

The CSS framework is designed to support telephony packages from different vendors. These packages are expected to support telephony features such as *connect, disconnect, call transfer*, etc. A contact center's computer and telephony systems are integrated as part of the CSS-based application (*Computer Telephony Integration* or CTI). Thus, CTI integrates voice and data into a *soft-phone* exchange between customers and agents of a contact center. While the customer is physically talking to the agent, the customer's data are shown on the agent's screen. As the transaction progresses, all related data is saved to a call history database.

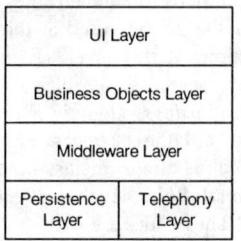

Figure 1. Logical Architecture

The logical layer architecture of the framework is presented in Figure 1. The first layer, *UI layer*, is used to communicate data to the system's "user." Users of a CSS-based system are not only human beings (in which case the UI is a GUI) but also any other software system tailored to communicate with the components of the framework. Following this layer, the *Business Objects Layer* represents the changeable logic that governs the business. The *Middleware Layer* is used to link packaged data between front-end components and supporting data stores and telephony. Finally, the last two layers incorporate any type of storage medium whose lifecycle is beyond a Contact Center's transaction (*Persistence Layer*), and all necessary modules that allow a customer to communicate with the system's user (*Telephony Layer*).

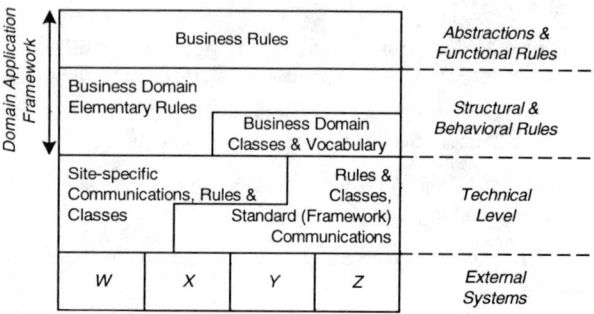

Figure 2. Rules Architecture

Figure 2 is a general implementation architecture, which makes the main distinctions among components in the rules subsystem. The primary distinctions are pertinent to the role that the code plays and not upon the scenarios in which it participates or the classes involved. It reflects a standard layered architecture, where usage relationships are only downward. Lower levels of the architecture represent code with decreasing probability of change over time; the frequency of change is expected to increase at higher layers. The following descriptions detail the components of the subsystem. At the *Technical Level*, rules and classes support the direct connection to the external systems. This level has been identified during Design as an implementation-oriented layer, in addition to the categories discussed in section 2.3. It consists of a collection of technical components, which implement primitive rules via which data will be communicated. Primitive rules are likely to provide a general interface to particular external entities (e.g. a message window) which can be made more specific (and more comprehensible) at a higher level. Also at this level, there are class definitions for the entities used at this level. Rules here are written for events that only apply to actions at this level. (E.g. temporarily switching to a "hot" backup server when the main server is disabled.) At the next level, *Structural and Behavioral Rules*, there are the *Business Domain Elementary Rules* which are intuitively meaningful rules, oriented toward the business domain. Here, there is also a set of *Business Domain Classes*, which is almost a class library. Finally, the Business Rules, at the *Abstractions and Functional Rules* level, are generic or application-specific rules describing the actual business. These rules are written based on the vocabulary available in the layer(s) below. The two topmost levels, *Domain Application Framework*, are distinguished from a class library in that they also implement the object interactions common to the application's domain. Two things are accomplished here: (a) implementation of the invariant object interactions for the domain, and, (b) provision of a "vocabulary" that will permit the business analyst to compose the remaining behavior of the system.

In the CSS framework, the rules affect primarily the decisions and actions that the system's agents undertake in the process of satisfying a customer's request. An Agent (Figure 3) is the person or system that receives, controls, and processes an

Interaction or set of Interactions. An Interaction (not shown here) may be a transaction during which the contact center serves a customer, or simply an internal call between operators of the center. PersonalInfo is the Agent's profile and contains the Agent's demographics and various settings (e.g. login to a telephone switch, passwords, telephone numbers, etc.). Workspace is the Agent's working area. It may be a GUI front end. All steps of processes related to a fulfillment of an Interaction are performed within a Workspace in the contact center. It contains the following entities:

1. An InferenceEnvironment package, which is a set of classes that intelligently assist the Agent in analyzing incoming events and reaching appropriate decisions on actions that should be taken.

2. ExternalSystem abstract package, which is the chosen product(s) that handles telecommunications issues.

3. Zero or more WorkFolders, which are organizational classifications of the various Interactions an Agent is charged to handle. During installation of the framework, WorkFolder entities (workflow items) are defined in a manner that makes sense to the specific contact center's policies and practices.

4. A WorkQueue that contains the various workflow items that an Agent is currently working on.

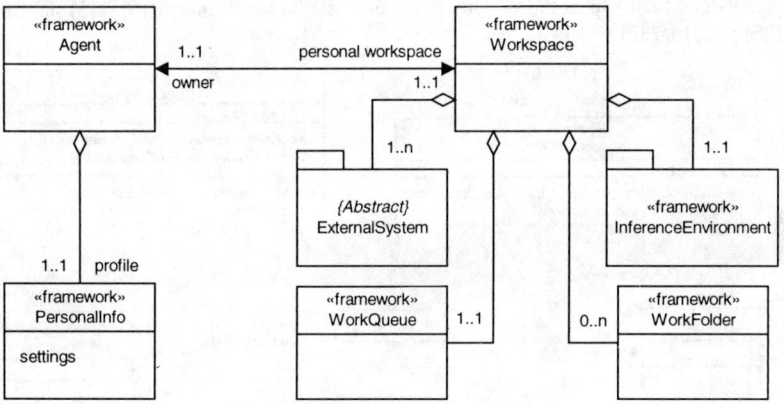

Figure 3. Agent and Workspace classes

The InferenceEnvironment (Figure 4) contains BusinessRules that govern an Agent's actions and the AI engine (RulesManager) which analyzes incoming events and decides how to act according to the BusinessRules. BusinessRules are rule scripts dictated by the business Process (not shown here) that governs each site in which the InferenceEnvironment is installed. This may be an individual Agent's workstation or an Organization's centralized command and control point (e.g. a server). After the InferenceEnvironment reaches an "intelligent" decision depending on the external events and its internal rules it may instruct the ExternalSystem associated with it or another Agent on the appropriate actions that need to be taken.

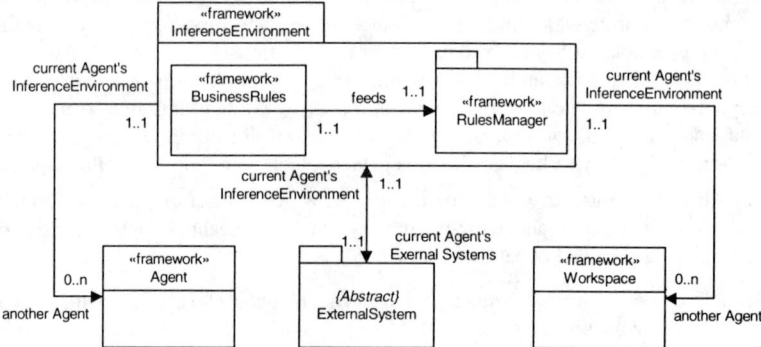

Figure 4. InferenceEnvironment class

4. Design

4.1 Intelligent Agents

During the prior four years, the authors have been researching the area of Intelligent Agents and their use in the various fields of business applications ([6], [15] pg. 261-275, [25] pg. 219-232).

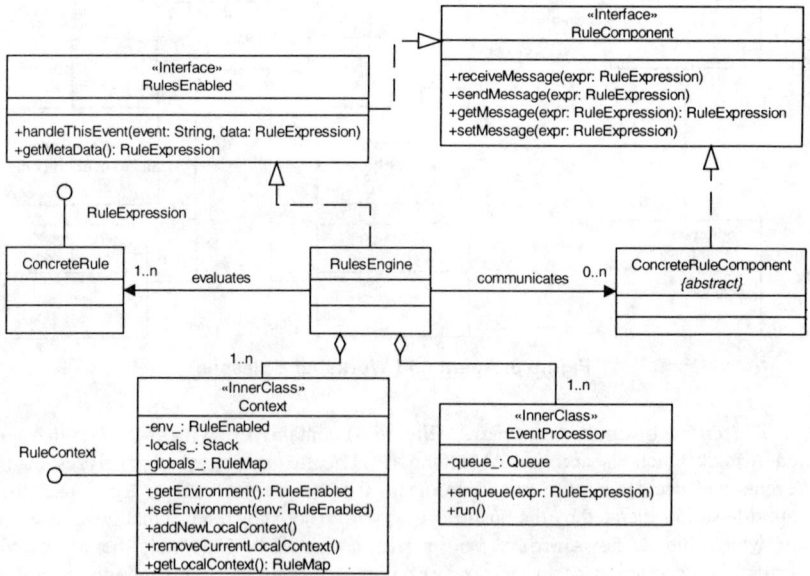

Figure 5. Design of an Intelligent Agent

Any component that needs the benefit of a rules-based environment should implement the RuleComponent interface (Figure 5). The RulesEnabled interface allows any class to encapsulate business rules and their behavior. The RulesEngine is an example of such class. Since different classes are allowed to encapsulate different business rules, we avoid the need for a monolithic rules-based engine. The domain classes can include local or remote (CORBA, RMI) classes. The `ConcreteRuleComponent` can be the front-end of any software package needed for the implementation of a contact center. Telephony, workflow, and persistence packages are of this type. These instances register with a `MessageDispatcher` (not shown here) instance to receive messages of a specified type. The `RuleContext` interface allows rules to interact with the `RulesEnabled` component within which they are running, and to maintain and access a local context. The `Context` provides an environment in which the rules run. A `Context` is created for each rule event and is passed to rules during evaluation. The `Context` includes nested local contexts (for instances of expressions created by the rules) and the `RulesEnabled` component within which the rules are running. The `EventProcessor` runs on its own thread and evaluates rules on a thread per rule-event. `RuleExpressions` are rules-language elements and the language used to communicate with rule components. Their types include attribute containers, primitive semantics (*For*, *If-Then-Else*, etc.), and various rules-language extensions. Domain objects can also implement the `RuleExpression` interface to allow them to be created and used from the rules script.

The strategy used to evaluate the rules (Figure 6) is currently a fixed interface that runs in the `Context` provided by the rules engine. The *sponsor-selector* design pattern ([14]) allows selection of the appropriate evaluation strategy and rules-based environment. The `RuleRepository` provides storage for the events and metadata associated with rules. The metadata associated with rules is the definition of scripted entities. Instances of scripted entities can be instantiated from the metadata. Environment attributes are attributes of the environment in which rules are running. A `RuleMap` is a named collection of attributes that describe an entity in the business domain or commands used to communicate with `RuleComponents`. The `Queue` contains all `items` that have been selected by the `RulesEngine`. Each `item` executes in a separate thread.

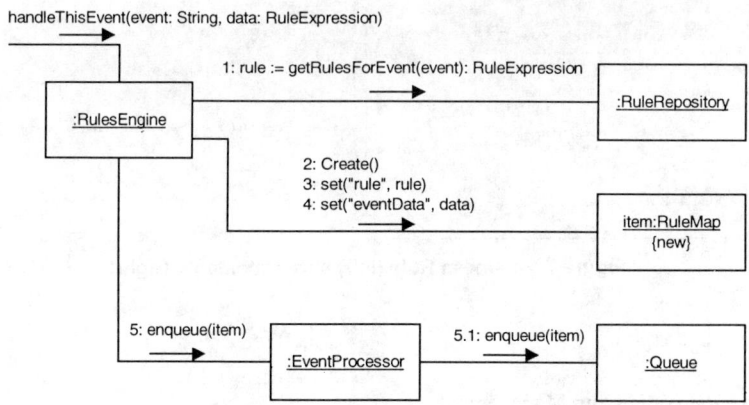

Figure 6. Using rules to evaluate events

4.2 Rules

In the CSS framework, all rules are described in an English-like language. Every system "entity" (node, workstation, package, user account, etc.) which needs specific sets of policies and procedures (i.e. rules), is linked to scripts that contain descriptions of those rules. The framework uses a compiler that creates the run-time rules structure from ASCII text files that contain the rules scripts. The compiler consists of two segments, the *Rule Maker,* and the *Rules Compiler* that can be either part of a local or a distributed process. The Rule Maker gets a reference to a Rules Compiler from a distributed service (*Rules Compiler Gateway*), reads and preprocesses a script. Individual lines are then sent to the Rules Compiler. The Rules Compiler reads rule scripts and builds a structure that contains rules, statements, and the metamodel (attribute descriptions for rule entities). A *Grammar* is responsible for creating and completing *Expression Builders* (*interpreter,* and *builder* patterns, [9]). A Context class encapsulates the particular aspects of an individual compilation session, including configuration options, results, and builder and parameter stacks (internal parameters created as a result of a recursive resolution process).

The rules-language's keywords are themselves objects and they can be renamed or have their semantics changed very easily. Two simple examples of rules are shown in Figure 7. At the left, there is a Business rule, from a sales organization, describing the addition of a purchased item into a customer's order form. The customer information is first retrieved from the persistence area then the item's price is calculated and the updated order is displayed on the screen. Four Statements are presented at the right. A CSS Statement is always called by a rule, while a CSS Rule is triggered by an external event. Most of the rules in the Technical Level (section 3) are therefore Statements. The Statements shown implement the ideas expressed in the Rule. In this example, note that the first Statement transfers control to a Java program that calculates some values based on a standard formula. Since the formula will never change, there is no need for expressing it using the rules language. The fourth Statement transfers control to GUI program. Also note the effort made for the rules-language to resemble natural English by expressing the OO notion of "*Object.attribute*" as "*Object's.attribute.*"

```
Rule for "add <item> to <order> for customer with <id>"

// retrieve data
Customer is a customer from datastore with id
if (is item available == false) then
    // show warning, availability date, etc.
end

if (Customer's.type == "GOLD") then
    item's.price = Discount item's.price by GoldDiscount
end
if (Customer's.type == "PLATINUM") then
    Offer volume discount for item
end

Add item to order
Show OrderView for Customer

End
```

```
Statement for "Discount <price> by <percentage>"
    return on the Calculator perform "Discount" \
                                  with price, percentage
    // Calculator is a java class
End

Statement for "Is <item> available"
    //...
End

Statement for "Offer Volume discount for <item>"
    // ...
End

Statement for "Show Orders for <customer>"
    On the ViewController perform "show orders for customer" \
                                  with customer
End
```

Figure 7. Business Rule (left) and Statements (right)

5. Process

5.1 Organization and Management

The team has evaluated various interpretations of the "time boxes" management technique ([2], [13]) and has created its own version. In an effort to combine essential progress with contained risk, short periods (*time boxes*) with fixed, not-to-be-altered deadlines are set, within which certain less-than-perfect results are expected. Since deadlines are fixed, only tasks may be modified to mitigate risk. Each time box is treated as a complete project, and since each project has various phases, time boxes may overlap in time. This approach not only encourages the most critical results to be produced first but also makes all parties concerned painfully aware of any scheduling disharmonies as soon as they emerge. Some of the advantages of this technique are the following. Early feedback is provided to the team. Requirements do not change for each time box (due to the short duration of each time box). Results are shown early for both the customer (since each time box is its own project) and the developers (since the most critical issues are addressed first).

A central repository containing a work-products database, guidelines, schedules, "issues/problems" databases, discussion forums, the organization's development methodology and its examples, templates and assets, QA packages, as well as various notification programs is used for supporting the CSS engagements. All CSS-related personnel have access to the repository and thus not only many of the reusability issues are resolved, but continuing education and mentoring is also served.

5.2 Work Products and Deliverables

Work products (tangible artifacts produced during the project, [10]) are models, reports, diagrams, plans, code and other documents which are direct "stepping stones" to final deliverables. Not all work products are deliverables but all deliverables consist of work products or parts of work products. In CSS, there exist work products and relationships among them for all domains of an engagement, from management to software development.

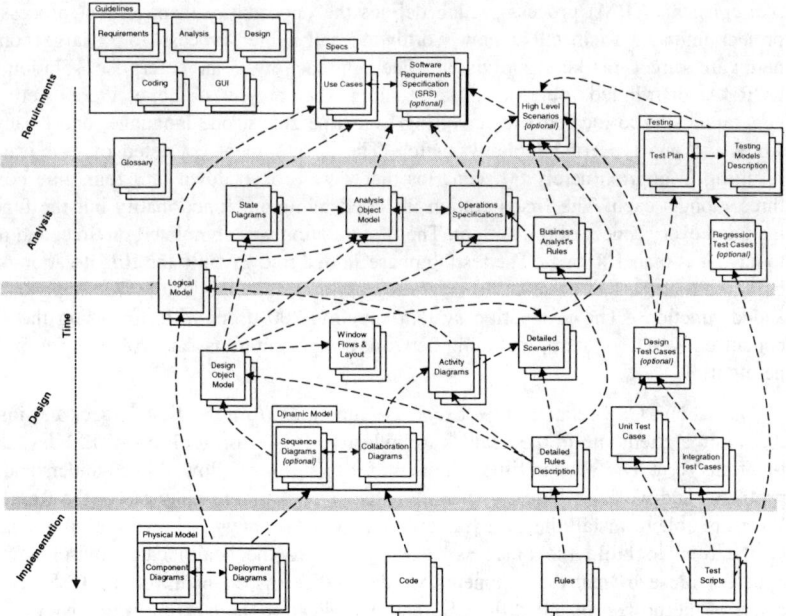

Figure 8. Software work products dependency diagram

In Figure 8, the work-products dependency diagram for the software development effort are shown. The three-block stack is a UML stereotype representing a work product. Similar dependency diagrams exist for other engagement domains. The closer a work product is to the top of the diagram the earlier it is completed during the project's life cycle. Arrows indicate primary dependency. Secondary dependencies are not shown here for the sake of clarity. Double arrows denote a strong interdependency indicating an almost synchronous development of the related work products. Optional work products may be omitted depending on time and/or specific application considerations. The development of work products on top of a project-phase separator (horizontal solid bar) spans more than one phase. Wherever possible, the UML terminology for OO artifacts and their contents was followed. A brief explanation of the non-UML work products follows. *Operations Specification* is a Fusion/OMT work product that characterizes the effects of each system operation in terms of the state-change it causes and the output events it sends. Each Operation Specification uses *Preconditions* and *Postconditions* to describe each system operation. The *Business Analyst's Rules* work product is the Business Rules' counterpart to the Analysis Object Model. It baselines the business areas for which rules should be written and describes them in an abstract way. *Window Flows & Layout* are GUI specifications. *Detailed Rules Description* is the Business Rules' counterpart to the UML's Dynamic Model. Finally, the *Glossary* describes all terms, names, and entities used throughout Software Development.

6. Projects

Currently, three projects are using the CSS model. The first project can be described as the project that created the CSS framework and refined IBM's *Customer Relations Management* (CRM) process, which defines the opportunity management process. This project intended to install a new worldwide call center process for a large computer hardware direct marketing division. The approach was an enterprise solution using CORBA distributed objects. After scaling the project's scope there were three geographically co-located sites covering four time zones, one language, one legacy data store, and one type of telephony switch. The development consisted of four use cases resulting in approximately 60 scenarios that were broken down into four time boxes of three months each. The first iteration included minimum functionality but the functions included every aspect of the system. The first iteration was completed on time, and proved to have less than 100 bugs. The testing phase started midway into the first iteration of each build, so that the test team could create regression test scripts or update scripts based on added functions. The production system supports 700 users with 450 using the system concurrently. The system, including network design, supports data volumes for 500 calls per hour.

The second CSS-related project took the functions from the first project and installed them into a client site in the health-care industry. This effort took about 120 days and all functions were available on time. The work for this project allowed us to understand reuse problems and work on industry-specific extensions that were planned for the framework. We were able to install the base framework in about 45 days and then took the remainder of the time to build the business layer specific to the health care environment. The apparent reuse of many components validated them as elements of the CSS. The first phase of the project installed the CSS-based application, connecting it to legacy systems, and allowing five agents to use the system in a production environment.

The third project was for a large US airline. The client wanted to install both the Inference Environment (in order to gain the IA benefits,) and the telephony modules.

While the framework was built to use many types of Middleware, this project was defined to use CORBAservices. The overall project required the installation of the two components in a lab area. There, advanced functions could be prototyped and verification of ideas on new ways to automate airline functions from customer reservations to crew scheduling and aircraft maintenance may be achieved. For this project, the base framework was extended to create large grain components that plugged into existing services. The project was scheduled for 120 days and installed the two components and a Web collaboration ability as one of the first prototype functions.

7. Lessons Learned

7.1 Components and Tools

A) Common to all contact centers are the requirements for platform independence, telephony response-times less than three seconds, and a thorough but simple user training process, all of which are met by CSS. Currently, there is no good methodology for creating business rules for an enterprise. In our opinion, rules-based packages are not popular for this reason. While businesses have documented their processes very elaborately, they have not defined the business rules in an exhaustive and effective manner.

B) Although the rules' "Technical Level" has been helpful, the core team is considering eliminating it. Because of Java's flexibility, we feel that this level could be substituted by Java classes. We have also found that it is hard to find analysts knowledgeable enough that are willing to create rules at this low level. At this level, there are only a few policies or procedures that are standard across the various external systems or even common to all contact centers.

C) During development of the CSS framework, reuse focused on creating *technical* components (e.g. GUI, rules manager, and communications module) and neglected the creation of *functional* (business) components (e.g. Telephony component). This omission was addressed during consecutive refinements of the framework.

D) CSS supports Java Telephony API (JTAPI) standards that give flexibility and portability. Using JTAPI increases the number of PBX switches that CSS-based applications can accommodate. (Otherwise, customized code supporting vendors' proprietary telephony packages for their supported PBX switches would have to be written.)

E) One of the key issues affecting persistence and legacy systems integration is the obvious incompatibility of the underlying models, namely, object orientation vs. procedural approaches. We have concluded that the issue has to be decisively and unambiguously resolved at early stages.

F) Validating components as part of the framework can happen only during consecutive projects. Initially we felt that GUI elements could not be reused and therefore they should not belong in the framework. However, during the second project we discovered that certain design elements as well as several implementation abstractions are reusable and therefore they belong in the CSS framework.

G) CSS has been created with reuse in mind. There are various levels of reuse, ranging from simple code reuse to reuse at Global or Industry level. We feel that with the CSS we have accomplished reuse at the *Enterprise* level ([4], pg. 34-48). Table 1 below, demonstrates the percentage of entities reused in each of the major phases of the projects

234

described in section 6. Since each project is related to a different Industry, the table also underlines the extension of reuse across vertical industries accomplished by CSS. Note that during Project 1, which created the framework initially, the only elements that could be reused were Analysis and Design patterns.

Table 1. CSS reuse per project

	Requirements	Analysis	Design	Implementation	Testing
Project 1	0%	10%	15%	0%	0%
Project 2	60%	80%	50%	60%	60%
Project 3	80%	80%	60%	60%	60%

H) There are no COTS security packages for generic client/server models. Consequently, we wrote our own security modules with the intention to evaluate and adopt any future security packages for distributed Java applications as they become available.

I) Software development is solidly guided by the Object Oriented methodology. Specifically, for both framework and applications we chose UML with several additions from the Fusion Method. Finally, the operating systems used are Windows NT 4.0 workstation and OS/2 for the client, and AIX for the server. The software packages include IONA's Orbix, CallFlow (IBM's telephony-oriented package), Swing V1.03 GUI class library, and Sun JDK V1.1.7. The network protocols include SNA APPC (LU6.2), LU2 (FEPI), and TCP/IP.

7.2 Organization and Management

A) Our first realization is that regardless of the technology involved the process is of paramount importance. The key to having a successful organization is to have a well-defined process that both managerial and technical personnel can utilize. A work-products repository is beneficial in establishing and using the process.

B) Reuse is not the same as development in more than one way. It requires a different mindset. Elements of a software development cannot be named "reusable" until they can be employed in a second environment. Unfortunately, "politics," old management culture, and uneducated customers may inhibit its proper exploitation.

C) Dealing with both the application and the underlying framework is arduous. Therefore, senior developers who are exposed to the design issues of the framework should carry out application performance tuning.

D) Time boxing is an instrumental and highly successful technique. However, it should be understood by all parties involved, and be applied with strict discipline. Otherwise, it may lose its effectiveness.

E) We found that requirements did not identify business rules independently of the underlying business process. Educating customers on the importance of well-defined business rules is tedious. In many occasions the customer was under the false impression that the CSS core team should discover and define the customer's business rules.

F) Unfortunately, not many software consulting-services organizations have a customer-centric development philosophy. Within our own organization, we found people whose attitude, designs, and views are focused on their own processes and development practices. Flexibility to embrace new customer needs and technology is not achieved easily.

7.3 People

A) In CSS, multiple, hard interviews resulted in highly motivated, knowledgeable, experienced, and capable team members. Hierarchy within the team is dynamically formed depending on the tasks involved, rather that being statically fixed according to individual job titles. Rotation of members and a mentoring program has effectively allowed for "human reusability." Dealing with multiple customer-sites renders telecommuting essential. However, communication protocols, project management issues, and problem-solving procedures should be defined early on.

B) People assigned to the CSS-based application development lacked solid engineering and coding skills, exhibited inadequate knowledge of OO, and overall had no experience with managing large software projects.

C) The software development techniques, methodology and methods, as well as enterprise-level practice, that CSS represents, require a higher level of commitment by the customer. At first, not only the scheduling (time boxes), but also the notion of frameworks and reuse may be unfamiliar to the customer. The customer not only should be introduced to a framework and its benefits, but should also be aware of the fact that the framework, **without any customer-specific development**, could be used at other similar environments as well.

7.4 Future and Related Work

A) Researching the best representation of the business rules took place concurrently with, but independently of, the definition of the Object Constraint Language (OCL), which has become a part of the UML standard ([22]). Despite our efforts to make the rules look like English, their syntax is remarkably similar to OCL. Since we are committed on using standards whenever possible, we are investigating ways of transitioning to OCL.

B) Currently a business analyst creates and modifies rules by handling ASCII files. Since this is inefficient and error-prone, a GUI rules-builder capable of graphically assisting business analysts in creating sound rules, and most importantly allowing them to effortlessly validate and verify their correctness holds the highest priority in our future plans.

C) The use of IAs has allowed CSS to contain several specialized, small, and efficient Inference Environments with limited domains that, temporarily at least, have lowered the need for implementing reasoning (AI) algorithms. However, in the future, we plan to investigate several rules algorithms whose efficiency is asymptotically independent of the number of rules. (The *Rete* or the *Treat* processing algorithms for instance.)

D) As CORBA 3 becomes commercially available, we plan to extend CSS to allow a better interface to the CORBAfacilities. We also plan to redesign certain Middleware modules in order to take advantage on the reuse offered by the Java Beans API technology.

E) Finally, several companies have applications similar to CSS. Neuron Data, Inc. (http://www.elements.com), Chordiant Software, Inc. (http://www.chordiant.com), and iLOG Inc. (http://www.ilog.com) offer very good rules-based applications. However, we claim, that CSS presents not only a reusable framework, but also a development and deployment process along with a core team of experts.

8. Conclusions

We have described the architecture, design, people skills, and project management issues of a rules-based framework for telephony-oriented applications. Using Intelligent Agents, the framework allows contact centers to automate procedures based on English-like scripts that describe business rules. We have explained the value of the framework in coordinating telephony, data, and process in contact centers. We have discussed the lessons learned during the implementation of the framework and the framework's deployment at three contact centers. The framework is feasible and, presently, unique. Our approach is attractive because it addresses issues specific to CRM, while offering robust and scalable solutions which can be implemented in a timely fashion.

9. References

[1]   L. Bass, et al. "Software Architecture in Practice." Addison-Wesley 1998.

[2]   P. Bassett. "Framing Software Reuse. Lessons from the Real World." Prentice Hall 1997.

[3]   G. Booch, et al. "The Unified Modeling Language User Guide." Addison-Wesley 1998.

[4]   W. Brown et al. "AntiPatterns: Refactoring Software, Architectures, and Projects in Crisis." John Wiley & Sons 1998.

[5]   F. Buschmann et al. "Pattern Oriented Software Architecture." Wiley & Sons, 1996.

[6]   F. Farhoodi, I. Graham. "A Practical Approach to Designing and Building Intelligent Software Agents." PAAM 1996.

[7]   M. Fowler. "Analysis Patterns: Reusable Object Models." Addison-Wesley 1996.

[8]   T. Gale, J. Eldred "Getting Results with the Object Oriented Enterprise Model." SIGS Books, 1996.

[9]   E. Gamma et al. "Design Patterns, Elements of Reusable Object Oriented Software." Addison-Wesley, 1995.

[10] IBM's Object-Oriented Technology Center. "Developing Object-Oriented Software." Prentice Hall 1997.

[11] M. Knapik, J. Johnson. "Developing Intelligent Agents for Distributed Systems." McGraw-Hill 1998.

[12] R. Malan, et al. "Object-Oriented Development at Work: Fusion in the Real World." Prentice-Hall, 1995.

[13] J. Martin, J. Odell. "Object Oriented Methods: Pragmatic Considerations." Prentice Hall, 1996.

[14] R. Martin, et al. "Pattern Languages of Program Design 3." Addison-Wesley 1998.

[15] J. Muller, et al. "Lecture Notes in AI: Intelligent Agents III." Springer-Verlag 1997.

[16] D. Peppers, M. Rogers. "Enterprise One to One." Currency/Doubleday, 1997.

[17] R. Ross. "The Business Rule Book: Classifying, Defining, and Modeling Rules," Database Research Group, Inc. 1997.

[18] J. Rumbaugh. "OMT Insights." SIGS Books, 1996.

[19] J. Rumbaugh, et al. "The Unified Modeling Language Reference Manual." Addison-Wesley 1998.

[20] I. Sommerville, P. Sawyer. "Requirements Engineering." Wiley & Sons, 1997.

[21] C. Szyperski. "Component Software: Beyond Object-Oriented Programming," Addison-Wesley 1997.

[22] J. Warmer, A. Kleppe. "The Object Constraint Language: Precise Modeling with UML" Addison-Wesley 1999.

[23] B. Webster. "Pitfalls of Object-Oriented Development." M&T Books, 1995.

[24] E. Wegschieder. "Next Generation Business Application Development Environment." White paper, ObjectQuest.

[25] M. Wooldridge, N. Jennings. "Lecture Notes in AI: Intelligent Agents." Springer-Verlag 1995.

Tool Support for Testing and Documenting Framework-based Software

Wolfgang Strunk
Micrologica AG
Bahnhofstraße 24
22941 Bargteheide, Germany
ws@micrologica.de

Carola Lilienthal
University of Hamburg
Department of Computer Science,
Software Engineering Group
Vogt-Kölln-Str. 30,
22527 Hamburg, Germany
lilienth@informatik.uni-hamburg.de

Abstract

Complex object-oriented applications are these days built on the basis of frameworks. While it is clear that a framework and the applications built using the framework conform to some design, we experienced a mismatch between the "idealized" software architecture presented in the documentation and the architectural structures actually existing in the source code. This mismatch belongs either to the failures of the developer in implementing the proposed architecture or to the lack of tool support. By providing tool support for dynamic diagrams, applications can be animated for debug and optimization purposes and actual design documentation can be extracted from the implemented model. Framework inspection using a true object-oriented approach enables the software engineer to access the source-level using an object-oriented map of the observed application instead of switching to a procedural way of working.

1. Introduction

To benefit from a framework programmers need to understand the design details embodied in the framework, and become familiar with the classes therein. As Booch states, "the most profoundly elegant framework will never be reused unless the cost of understanding it and then using its abstractions is lower than the programmer's perceived cost of writing them from scratch." [3]

Frameworks contain a particular model of an application domain. They are composed of concrete and partially implemented abstract classes that represent this model. A framework calls client functions, controls the flow of execution, defines object interaction, provides default behavior and customization by subclassing. This process of understanding how the components of a framework are to be used individually and in combination, is heavily dependent on the enclosed documentation. "Since frameworks are reusable design, not just code, they are more abstract than most software, which makes documenting them difficult" [10]. Unfortunately documentation on the dynamic interaction and communication between objects is often lacking, because it can't be generated out of the source code but has to be drawn manually.

Our motivation for building tool support for dynamic diagrams stems from our efforts in designing frameworks and teaching framework use and development. While it is clear that a framework and the applications built using the framework conform to some design, we experienced a mismatch between the "idealized" software architecture presented in the documentation and the architectural structures actually existing in the source code. This mismatch belongs either to the failures of the developer in implementing the proposed architecture or to the lack of tool support. Even if case-tools are used for drawing design documents, very often only the static structure is documented due to the amount of work needed for building sequence diagrams or state charts.

We decided to design and implement a toolset which enables the framework developer as well as the user of a framework to generate documentation of the system dynamics from the running program. Our approach is to build a toolset that analyzes the behavior of object-oriented programs at runtime and enables visualization by different diagram techniques. The diagrams present the interaction amongst objects on different levels of abstraction and provide a good basis for framework documentation.

2. Framework design documentation

Teaching frameworks and applying framework technology in industrial projects provides us with specific knowledge about documentation. A framework used extensively tends to be used in ways never conceived by its designers. This unexpected use normally leads to alteration and development in the framework components. Intimate knowledge of a framework's inner workings is indispensable in building extensions. The most demanding aspect here is understanding the dynamic interaction between the various framework components.

To build components which fit in the flow of control enclosed in the framework a heightened understanding of the framework is necessary. To fully understand these framework processes the programmer has to use and understand an example application as well as the provided pattern language. A cookbook full of recipes is a common starting point for building the first applications based on a framework. Recipes consist of step by step instructions and are often combined with an example. The recipes usually comprise the following instructions:

- which classes are to be inherited
- which methods to overwrite
- where methods from superclasses can be called
- where to send which events that initiate framework processes

Typically the enthusiasm in using frameworks wanes however when the lack of documentation becomes obvious: How could the framework be used to bring life to the new application? What occurs when filling predefined abstract sequences with concrete operations? The problem of understanding the dynamics has to be mainly solved without the aid of written documentation. Debugging the code is still the primary, mostly unsatisfactory source of information. The programmers request specific techniques for visualizing the dynamic interaction between objects. The need to create and preserve individual views of the framework parts at work is also felt.

Therefore we maintain that the following conclusions can be applied to all framework contexts:

- Development of frameworks is only possible when a detailed understanding of the dynamic interaction between framework components takes place.
- An example is a good starting point for learning how to use a framework. Dynamic behavior of the framework can be more readily understood by observing the interaction between an example and a framework rather than merely inspecting the source code.
- Programmers becoming familiar with a framework should be spared the task of debugging the code. The dynamic behavior should be visualized on higher levels of abstraction. Visual debugging should ideally start on the design and the pattern level .

- Understanding the dynamic behavior should be supported by various views of the framework at runtime. Programmers should be enabled individual views of parts of the framework.

3. Dynamic documentation using VOOP

Documenting the dynamic behavior of program components is still a field of research. We were able to use and extend several techniques from this area and apply them to dynamic documentation for frameworks [13]. The set of diagram techniques that we found to be useful consists of:

- **Construction diagrams** show the objects responsible for the creation of another object, the objects created and when this occurs. The construction diagrams allow a software developer to observe which objects are created by which framework class.
- **Interaction diagrams** visualize objects and how they interact dynamically by calling each other. The basic notation of interaction diagrams was presented by Jacobson [8] and these have also been used for pattern documentation in [4]. The syntactical extensions to interaction diagrams proposed in [13] are now part of the standard defined in the UML.
- **Message diagrams** show the actual state of the example application. The state is expressed by a stack of methods called on objects. The topmost message is the method just being executed.
- **Reference diagrams** graphically display which objects refer to which other objects. Reference diagrams assist the programmer in inspecting how application classes combine with framework classes on a use-relation level.

These diagrams portray different aspects of dynamic interaction between framework and application components. Most of the diagrams can be drawn manually by the use of case tools but are rarely drawn in real projects.

Our toolset VOOP (visualizing object-oriented program architecture[1]) though generates diagrams of the system dynamics from the running program. We will explain VOOP's features by showing and explaining some screen dumps of it's user interface. At the moment interaction and construction diagrams are depicted by separate monitors. We have shown the generation of construction diagrams in [13] and we present an interaction diagram in fig. 1 of this article. The only precondition to apply VOOP to an executable program is to compile the executable with debugging information enabled. If you build applications for the Microsoft Windows platform you can tell the compiler to generate the debug information in a separate file and simply remove this file when delivering your application

Information can be extracted from the dynamic diagrams by pointing and clicking on any object icon or method call label to display a popup menu. The following additional information is available:

Data	Show the state of the object in a data browser.
Messages	The list of member functions available in a particular object can be viewed by selecting this option.
Source	Show the class source for the selected object.
Definition	Display the class definition for the selected object.
Where Created	Navigate to the point in the source where the object was created.

---

[1] Many tools already display the static architecture of programs with class diagrams. Therefore our main focus for VOOP is to visualize dynamic behavior. Class diagrams can easily be added to VOOP's toolset.

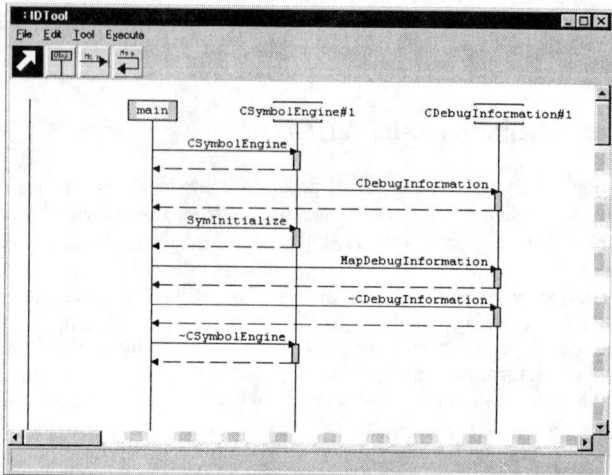

Figure 1: VOOP Screen Dump portraying a generated interaction diagram

Classes and Objects[2] can be removed from the display (fig. 2). This has the benefit of enabling only the objects that are of particular interest to be viewed. The objects can then be added to the display again if they still exist in the application. This technique also has the advantage of reducing the overall drawing time for the display.

After starting VOOP the user selects the application he likes to inspect. As in a traditional debugger the program is loaded into memory. The difference is that you can deal with object-oriented abstractions of the application from now on. Fig. 1 presents a snapshot of one of VOOP's tools: the ID Tool (InteractionDiagramm Tool). The ID Tool is displaying an interaction diagram of VOOP itself as the running application. The snapshot is restricted to two application objects. All method calls shown in fig. 1 are recorded automatically. The observed application can be started and stopped like in a traditional debugger. The main difference is that breakpoints are set implicitly dependant on the classes and objects selected.

To make automatically generated diagrams useful for documentation purposes, it is important that the ID Tool works as an interaction diagram editor too. The user can eliminate

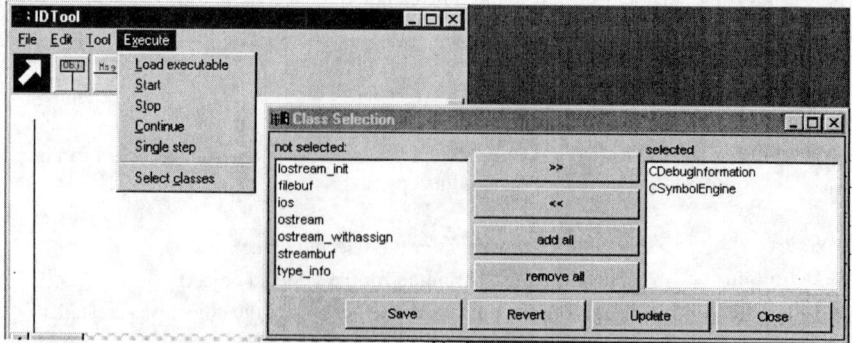

Figure 2: Selecting classes and controlling the executable

[2]If VOOP would be rebuilt for Java programs packages would be another possible item to exclude from the display.

method calls or objects he is not interested in. He can also change the layout of methods and objects or even add new objects and method calls.

4. Tool animation of diagrams

The implementation phase of an application is normally supported by tools that tend to neglect the object-oriented structure of applications and frameworks. The debugger or profiler for example restrict themselves to the path of control flow. A tool that supports framework use and understanding should allow a software developer to think in the terms dealt withduring design. The design of object-oriented applications is described in class terms, in object terms and, on a higher level of abstraction, in design patterns. The following sections will describe fundamental design decisions for both the debugger and the visualization tools in detail.

4.1. Architectural overview

VOOP is a debugging and visualization toolset which is focused completely on developers building object-oriented applications. The design of VOOP is independent of the programming language but the current implementation only supports C++ as the implementation language of the observed application.

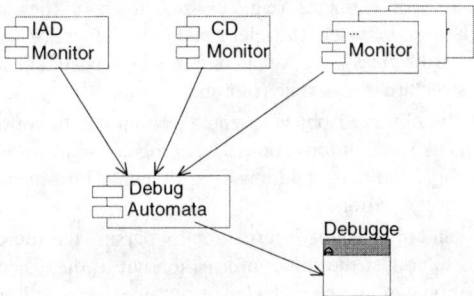

Figure 3: VOOP component architecture

Although we only implemented two different visualization tools, the design is more general and provides a basis for implementing several other tools. The heart of the toolset is an *debug automata* which is starting and controlling the target program (which we will call *debuggee*). The debugger is responsible for starting the application (debuggee) to be observed. For every class the user is interested in, a breakpoint is set to the constructing methods of that class.

Inside the automata a *conceptual model* of the debuggee is built. The breakpoints set on the constructors of each observed class enable the debug automata to collect information about any created object of the selected class. Even if the class of the object has no constructor defined, or if the constructor is in-line, object creation is recorded. With this information creation and message diagrams can be constructed. To provide interaction diagrams and reference diagrams breakpoints have to be attached to each method, available at the object's interface.

Several visualization tools are built on top of the debug automata. These tools are primarily monitoring changes in the conceptual model and manipulating the set of observed program entities. Each monitor provides its own specific view of the debuggee. These views can be graphical or textual representations of a set of regarded program entities.

The debug automata also works as a monitor coordinator. Every change in the debuggee is notified and reproduced in the model. The monitor applications register for changes in the conceptual model. When a change occurs events are sent from the monitor coordinator to the different monitors. By using the monitor coordinator approach we gain several advantages for monitor development:

- Monitors can be developed independently of one another and of the monitor control itself. Monitors can be individually loaded and attached to the program to be monitored at run time.
- Monitors can be written to observe very specific program behavior. Instead of placing specializations in the debug automata, monitors can build their own abstractions on top of the meta model.
- Specialization of the monitors simplifies the task of presenting information.
- New tools can easily be added to the toolset. Adding a new tool does not require recompiling or even relinking the debug automata or any of the other visualization tools.

4.2. Collecting information

The first step in supporting the analysis and evaluation of a software architecture is to extract a concrete model, a representation of the implemented system. Such a representation contains a collection of elements (e.g., classes, method, files, variables, objects) and a collection of relations between the elements (e.g., "function calls method," "class has method ", "object is of class A"). A concrete model may reflect several views of a system, such as its static structure or dynamic (runtime) nature.

The model of the observed object-oriented system has to consist of static and dynamic information. Typical static information describing an object-oriented application are the class descriptions and the class relationships, dynamic information for example describes method calls or object creation.

In general we can collect static information by parsing the source code of an application. Another option is to collect the static information out of the executable or even at runtime. Dynamic information can just be collected at runtime, because it is only partly contained in the source code. There are two possibilities to collect the information portraying the dynamic behavior of example and framework classes: *source code instrumentation* ([2], [17]) and *object code inspection* ([14], [20]).

We decided to use object code inspection for several reasons:
- No recompiling is necessary. Frameworks are often not available in source code.
- The selection of the observed components can be changed during inspection. Source code instrumentation requires to select the observed parts in advance.
- The full functionality of a debugger can be integrated. Source code instrumentation implies the extension of the observed application to allow direct communication between the visualization tool and the application.

We took into account that object code inspection slows down the application's execution, due to process switching and inappropriate debugger interface. Information about the observed program is collected on two levels: first the static information about classes and functions is collected by object code inspection. Afterwards information about objects and the use relationships is collected by inspecting the running system. As our current implementation focuses on applications built with C++, we rely on the program compiled with debug information. From the collected data a conceptual model comparable to the one described in [18] is built. The collected information serves as a base for generating all kinds of diagrams.

Technically the static information about the software system is extracted from the object code of the system by reading the debug information. The prerequisite for doing so is that the system is compiled with debug options. We implemented the parser for reading debug information both for the STABS debug format used in Unix based systems and the Win32 debug format. The object code contains class names, names of base classes, the attributes of a class as well as the methods that a class provides.

4.3. Conceptual modeling of the debuggee

Every visualization tool in the VOOP toolset provides a different view to the same amount of information: a view to a model of the inspected application. We explicitly build this model of the inspected application when we examine it's debug information. We call this model conceptual model because it is a model of the object-oriented model inherent to the observed application. The conceptual model is changing constantly and reflecting the actual state of the debuggee.

The conceptual model is itself modeled in an object-oriented manner: an object is created for each class used in the application, for each method and each created object. We decided not to model method calls explicitly. To our understanding method calls are conceptually only an event without a permanent state and thus they can not be modeled as objects with state information.

Even though we do not model method calls as elements of the conceptual model, the monitors need to be notified when a method is called. The method calls therefore initiate an event to be sent to every monitor which is interested in this method. In addition the conceptual model offers mechanisms for selecting and searching individual meta elements or sets of meta elements. By using the conceptual model we are able to reduce interprocess communication between the debuggee and the VOOP toolset to a minimum as all selections, searches and every navigation can be done on the conceptual model.

Each object in the application is modeled by a corresponding meta-object in our conceptual model. The meta-object contains information about every object holding a reference to the modeled object. The meta-object knows in which context the original object is created.

Classes are modeled by tClass objects in the conceptual model. The most important properties of tClass are the methods "GetBaseClasses" and "getMethods". These two methods provide the means for navigating in the conceptual model. In addition "GetMethods" enables us to select the constructor of a class and to set breakpoints to the constructors. Thereby the conceptual model is informed about every object creation and can create a corresponding meta-object.

The class "tFunction" is the meta element which mirrors a method in the debuggee. It contains the method's name and signature. A tFunction object knows whether a method is a member function, a constructor or a destructor. As C++ generates constructing and destructing methods during compile time if they are not specified by the programmer, it is important to distinguish between generated and programmer defined constructors and destructors.

4.4. Controlling the debuggee

The debuggee is controlled via the debug automata as shown in figure 4. As stated in the previous chapter, most of the control can be done on a method basis.

The debug automata sets breakpoints in the debuggee. The breakpoints are set in correspondence to the selections done by the monitors. The following events are recorded in the debug automata:

- construction of objects
- destruction of objects
- method calls
- returns from method calls.

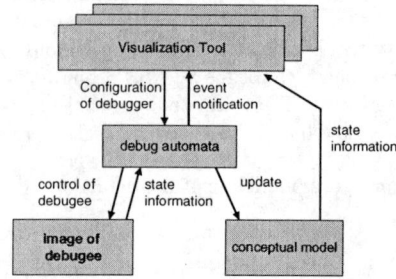

Figure 4: Event and control flow

The conceptual model is reacting to changes in the debuggee. These changes get propagated to the conceptual model when a breakpoint on one of the above mentioned four events is reached. If the debuggee is stopped due to a breakpoint, every monitor interested in the event is notified and the corresponding diagrams can be updated. Traditional debuggers were not designed to debug object-oriented systems. The STABS format is interpreted by the debugger, but not the complete information is available at the debugger's interface.

4.5. Benefits from applying VOOP

Framework inspection using a true object-oriented approach has several advantages to normal debugging. It becomes possible to access the source-level using an object-oriented map of the observed application and there is no longer a need to switch to a procedural way of working. The dynamic diagrams provide point and click access to the framework details, allowing navigation to data and source code. The switch between the object model used for design and procedural source-level access is done by selecting graphical components of the diagrams. For example, by selecting an object, a breakpoint can be set to stop every time this object gets active. If execution stops on this breakpoint, the member functions can be listed and again stop points on entry/exit or on a specific line in the source code can be set.

The consistency between conceptual object-oriented design and the portrayed views of a framework leads to quicker framework understanding. Applications can be develop more efficiently, because the developer can interact with and navigate to the source-level in an intuitive object-oriented manner.

5. Related work

Other work in the field of describing dynamics of object-oriented systems can be classified in different directions:
- The information about the observed system is either gained by modifying the source code or by expecting only the normal debug information.
- There are approaches that build a protocol of a program execution which can be investigated afterwards and others that allow the observation of a program at run time.
- Tools for describing dynamics are built for reverse engineering of existing applications or for debugging purposes.

5.1. Runtime visualization vs. recording

Approaches that build protocol of the program execution in a first step record every procedure call, object creation and object deletion and assignment. In a second step a statistical analysis and even an animated view of the recorded execution is possible.

Every information is available at the beginning of the animation. Thereby every forthcoming change is known in advance and the layout of the presented information is more simple. Every situation can be replayed several times with different viewpoints or different levels of details in the presentation [11], [2].

Runtime observation on the other hand provides the possibility to use and inspect an application at the same time. The use of the application is mirrored immediately in the dynamic diagrams [17]. In combination with object code inspection runtime observation enables to vary the set of observed components [14], [20].

In [20] one feature of the tool Look! is described that will influence our future work: Look! provides a dynamic filter mechanism. In contrast to select the sections of the application that should be visualized, as we do in our tool, Look! provides a C++ like language for defining a filter description.

5.2. Tools for reverse engineering

In the development lifecycle of large software systems the need to reverse engineer applications. Reasons may be maintenance problems or a degraded structure after a long time of development. Programmers use execution monitoring tools to help them gain insight about a program when they cannot obtain sufficient understanding by studying the program text or the design documents.

Some of the work in program monitoring tools stems from this need to support reverse engineering of existing applications. At University of California, San Diego, the StarTool program analysis tool is developed ([1], [5] [12], [6]). The tools support restructuring of existing applications by refactoring similar code into methods or abstract base classes.

In [19] the focus is on the evolution of legacy systems. They try to capture the architectural rational of existing systems automatically to find those parts, that can be used in the software systems. Murphy and others defined a technique they call reflexion models ([15], [16]). Their motivation is to help developers in understanding the source code of large complex systems. They provide automatic generation of call graphs between modules which developers usually sketch by hand.

5.3. Graphical debuggers

Unfortunately most programming languages are not developed with monitoring capabilities in mind, and facilities generally are integrated into the programming environment as an afterthought instead.

Using a traditional debugger, the user needs to have a good idea about where to look for the problem, because the runtime information in a debugger is procedure oriented while his design is object oriented. By providing tool support for dynamic diagrams, applications can be animated for debug and optimization purposes [14], [17]. Newer approaches for graphical debugging are [7] and [9]. The approach of Jeffery and others shows a lot of similarity to our approach in that they also built a toolset as a base for different monitors instead of building only one tool.

6. Conclusions and outlook

We introduced a toolset for portraying the dynamic behavior of object-oriented systems. The diagrams and the tool have already proven effective in teaching as well as in several industrial projects. Our approach is still weak in presenting the static information of the debuggee. We will have to link our tool to software development environments or case tools thereby enabling integrated software development. In the use of interaction diagrams it became clear that our tool could not only be employed to document frameworks, but used in both error detection and optimization. We could envisage that our tool even be used in comparing design documents with the actual program at work. We believe by using automatically generated diagrams that can manually be changed and refined, each developer can sketch his own understanding of the software he is investigating on.

7. Bibliography

[1]   D.C. Atkinson and W.G. Griswold: The Design of Whole-Program Analysis Tools. In: Proceedings of the 18th International Conference on Software Engineering (ICSE-18), March 25-29, 1996, Berlin, Germany.

[2]   G. Cheng, N.A.B. Gray: *A Program Visualisation Tool*, TOOLS '92, pp. 365-369, 1992

[3]   G. Booch: *Designing an Application Framework*, Dr. Dobb's Journal 19, No. 2. p. 24, February 1994.

[4]   E. Gamma, R. Helm, R. Johnson, J. Vlissides: *Design Patterns, Elements of Reusable Object-Oriented Software*, Addison-Wesley Publishing Company, Reading, Massachusetts 1995

[5]   W. G. Griswold, M. I. Chen, R. W. Bowdidge, Jenny L. Cabaniss, Van B. Nguyen, J. D. Morgenthaler: *Tool Support for Planning the Restructuring of Data Abstractions in Large Systems*. UCSD CSE Technical Report CS97-559, October 1997.

[6]   J. J. Hayes: *A Method for Adapting a Program Analysis Tool to Multiple Source Languages*. Masters Thesis, Technical Report CS98-600, Department of Computer Science and Engineering, University of California, San Diego, September 1998.

[7]   D. R. Hanson and J. L. Korn : *A Simple and Extensible Graphical Debugger*. In: Proceedings of the USENIX 1997 Annual Technical Conference, Anaheim, CA, Jan. 1997, pp. 183-174.

[8]   I. Jacobson, M. Christerson, P. Jonsson, G. Övergaard: Object-Oriented Software Engineering - A Use Case Driven Approach, Addison-Wesley, 1992

[9]   C. Jeffery, W. Zhou, K. Templer and M. Brazell: *A Lightweight Architecture for Program Execution Monitoring*. To appear in ACM SIGPLAN Workshop on Program Analysis for Software Tools and Engineering Montreal, Canada, 14 June 1998.

[10] R.E. Johnson: Documenting frameworks using patterns, OOPSLA '92, Conference Proceedings, pp.63-76, 1992.

[11] M.F. Kleyn and P.C. Gingrich: *GraphTrace - Understanding Object-Oriented Systems Using Concurrently Animated Views,* OOPSLA '88, Conference Proceedings, 1988

[12] W. F. Korman: *Elbereth: Tool Support for Refactoring Java Programs*. Master Thesis, UNIVERSITY OF CALIFORNIA, SAN DIEGO, 1998

[13] C. Lilienthal and W. Strunk: *Documenting Frameworks by visualizing dynamics*, Proceedings of TOOLS' 96, 1996

[14] S. Mukherjea, J.T. Stasko: *Toward Visual Debugging: Integrating Algorithm Animation Capabilities within a Source-Level Debugger*, ACM Transactions on Computer-Human Interaction, Vol. 1, No. 3, pp.215-244, Sept. 1994

[15] G. C. Murphy and D. Notkin: *Lightweight Lexical Source Model Extraction*. ACM Transactions on Software Engineering and Methodology, Vol. 5, No. 3, July 1996, Pages 262–292.

[16] G. C. Murphy and D. Notkin: *Reengineering with Reflexion Models: A Case Study*. Computer 30, 8, 1997, pp.29-36.

[17] W. de Pauw, R. Helm, D. Kimelman, J. Vlissides: *Visualizing the Behavior of Object-Oriented Systems*, OOPSLA '93, Conference Proceedings, pp. 326-337, 1993.

[18] W. de Pauw, D. Kimelman, J. Vlissides: *Modeling Object-Oriented Program Execution*, ECOOP '94, pp. 163-182, 1994.

[19] H. Richter, P. Schuchhard, and G.D. Abowd: *Automated capture and retrieval of architectural rationale*. College of Computing, Georgia Institute of Technology, Atlanta, Technical Report 98-37, 1998

[20] A. West: *Animating C++ Programs. Dynamic C++ Animation,* White Paper, Objective Software Technology Ltd., 1993

Technical Papers

Methods 2

Contracts: From Analysis to C++ Implementation

Reinhold Plösch, Josef Pichler
C. Doppler Laboratory for Software Engineering
Johannes Kepler University Linz
Altenbergerstr. 69, A-4040 Linz, Austria
[ploesch, pichler]@swe.uni-linz.ac.at

Abstract

Standard C++ does not provide mechanisms for working with assertions in the spirit of design by contract (DBC) as proposed by Meyer. We earlier developed a set of techniques and tools facilitating the prototyping of object-oriented architectures based on the idea of design by contract. As it is crucial for us to support evolutionary prototyping, we need to provide mechanisms to automatically transform the classes and assertions specified in our prototyping environment to C++. Therefore we developed a system that automatically transforms classes and assertions of our prototyping system to C++. As a side effect our environment provides general mechanisms for realizing design by contract for the programming language C++.

1. Motivation

Prototyping is a development approach to overcome the shortcomings of traditional software life cycle approaches by developing executable prototypes for experimental purposes.

A number of available experience reports ([6], [5], [3], [17]), illustrate the impact of prototyping on software construction and on the overall development process. Bäumer et al. [1] summarize the experience gained in the application of prototyping in industrial projects. Although they draw very positive conclusions, the emphasis of analysis in this and the other experience reports cited above is on user interface prototyping.

Currently established object-oriented development approaches consider prototyping to be an important methodology but deal with it in a superficial way. Booch [2], Rumbaugh [16] and Jacobson [7] mention prototyping but do not give precise advice on how to use it in the context of object-oriented development.

It is widely accepted in the research community [19] that a prototype is a working model of a system. The essential difference between a prototype and a model produced with object-oriented methods like OMT [16] is expressed by the word *working*: a prototype is always a usable model implemented on a computer. It is also commonly accepted that the end users have to be involved in the validation of the prototype; i.e., user participation is of vital importance.

The main factor determining successful prototyping is choosing appropriate methods/techniques with appropriate tool support. A number of experience reports clearly indicate that prototyping could only be applied successfully in cases where appropriate tool support was available.

Earlier we developed a set of techniques and tools that facilitate the prototyping of object-oriented architectures by employing the ideas of design by contract (DBC) as described by Meyer in [11] and [12]. In principle, assertions are elements of formal specifications and

0-7695-0278-4/99 $10.00 © 1999 IEEE

express correctness conditions for classes and methods. Assertions are part of the implementation and are checked at run time. The prototyping environment we developed is based on the object-oriented programming language Python [10] (we give some details in section 2) and consists of a run-time environment and a number of high-level graphical browsers and editors (see [14] and [15] for more details).

Although the provided tool support facilitates the construction of prototypes and their evolution and thus has positive effects for analysis and early design, we need to have the possibility to (semi)automatically transform the prototype to a target platform for system implementation, in our case C++. First, this requirement is pragmatic, as we favor reusable prototypes (in contrast to throwaway prototypes) in order to reduce development costs and development time. Second, and more important, we do not want to lose the formal specifications derived through analysis and expressed by means of assertions; these partial specifications are of vital importance for the overall software development process, as they facilitate the derivation of test cases and contribute to general quality attributes like maintainability and correctness.

Beyond the issue of prototype transformation, this article also shows how to provide DBC (design by contract) support for the programming language C++. There are a number of technical problems to overcome; we want to solve them in an elegant manner in order to keep the C++ code readable and maintainable. As we will see, this implementation approach for DBC for C++ can also be used in the implementation phase of C++ projects — independently of our prototyping approach and our prototyping tools.

In section 2 we briefly describe our DBC model for Python/C++. Section 3 illustrates the architecture chosen for transforming assertions from our prototyping environment to a C++ production environment. In section 4 we discuss a number of technical problems related to the transformation process, and in section 5 we draw our conclusions on the usefulness of this approach for a prototyping-oriented software development approach.

2. Assertions in Python

Our DBC model for Python supports the specification of class invariants, preconditions, postconditions and check instructions. The semantics of our model corresponds to the support available in Eiffel [12], which is the only commercial object-oriented language with full support for invariants, preconditions and postconditions. An invariant is a correctness condition imposed on a class, i.e., a condition that must not be violated by any method of a class. A precondition is associated with a particular method and imposes a correctness condition on the client of the method; i.e., the client must ensure that the precondition is fulfilled; otherwise the method is not executed. A postcondition is also associated with a particular method, but it imposes a correctness condition on the implementation of the method; a violation of a postcondition indicates an error in the implementation of the method. A check instruction ensures the correctness at a specific point in the implementation of a method.

Loop invariants (as provided by Eiffel) are currently not considered in our DBC model for Python, as they are a lower-level kind of specification compared to invariants, preconditions, postconditions and check instructions. In this context, our emphasis is not on correct software but on providing mechanisms to combine formal approaches with object-oriented technology. For this purpose we do not consider loop invariants.

This section only briefly describes our model. To fully understand the idea of DBC, we refer to [12], [13], and our previously published work on this subject [14], [15].

Preconditions and postconditions are specified in the documentation section of a method (see method *SetProperties* in Figure 1). There may be an arbitrary number of *require* and *ensure* clauses, i.e., preconditions and postconditions, for one method. The preconditions of overridden methods are automatically *or*-ed with the original preconditions, and the postconditions of the overridden methods are automatically *and*-ed with the original postconditions according to the underlying theory.

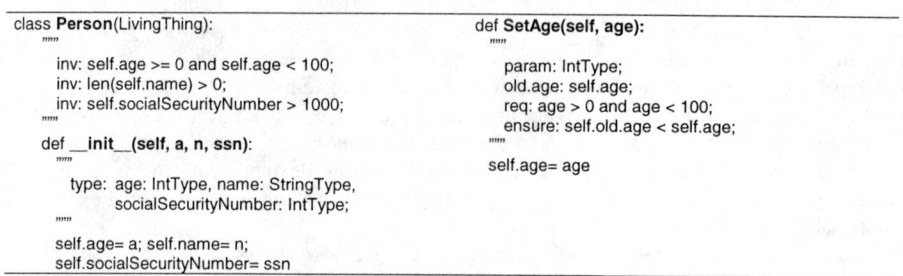

Figure 1. Assertions in Python

Old expressions (see method *SetAge* in Figure 1) may be specified and allow to access the value of instance variables or parameters at method entry in the postcondition of a method. The right side of the *old* expression may consist not only of elementary data types but also of arbitrary class types. In the latter case, a deep copy of the object is created at method entry. *Param* expressions allow the specification of types for method parameters; such type specifications are treated as preconditions and that are checked accordingly at run time. This is an important feature, as the underlying programming language Python is not statically typed.

Invariants are specified in the documentation section of a class. The class invariants are checked according to the theory. Comparable to the *param* precondition, *type* clauses may be specified in the constructor method (see method *__init__* in Figure 1) of a class to specify types for instance variables. *Type* expressions are treated as invariants and are checked accordingly at run time, i.e., before and after execution of any method.

The infrastructure tools provide support for parsing and run time checking. In our context only the parsing activities are of interest. The symbol information extracted by the parser can be stored persistently in symbol files. These symbol files, whose structure is well defined by means of a grammar, contain all necessary information, i.e., assertion information and information about classes, methods, inheritance relationships and file location. The prototyping tools, which we cannot describe in detail in this article, rely on this symbol information.

3. Architecture for Assertion Support in C++

We developed a transformation tool that relies, as do the prototyping tools, on the symbol information provided by the parsing tool. In this paper we emphasize C++ code generation. Additionally, a configuration tool is supported that allows parameterization of the configuration process, e.g., renaming of classes and methods, exclusion of assertions.

Before we describe the general structure of the generated C++ code, let us state a number of requirements that were taken into account in the design and prototypical implementation of the tool support.

- *Support for iterative development:* The tool for transforming our Python assertions to C++ must take our iterative software development approach into account. It must therefore be possible to step back into analysis, to change the analysis model (i.e., our prototype) and to regenerate the C++ code without any loss. This is the most important requirement.
- *Standardization:* The generated C++ code must be compilable with a standard C++ compiler; i.e., it is not feasible to extend or change the syntax and semantics of standard C++.
- *Readability:* The generated C++ code must be readable; in particular, this means that the code for assertion checking must be clearly separated from the implementation of a method or class.
- *Theory compliance:* The semantics of the Python assertion model and thus the semantics as defined by Eiffel must be preserved.
- *Configurability:* The configuration process must be configurable; in particular, it must be possible to selectively disable the generation of individual assertions in the C++ code.
- *Efficiency:* For efficiency reasons it must be possible to selectively activate and deactivate assertion checking on a class level. No run-time penalties may be associated with deactivated assertion checking.

Beyond Eiffel, a number of interesting approaches have been proposed for integrating behavioral specification into statically typed programming languages. In our opinion the most important approaches are:

- **Larch/C++:** Larch [9] allows the specification of the behavior of a C++ program. The underlying mathematical model is closely related to concepts of Z [18]. Due to the underlying programming language and due to the underlying formal semantics, this approach is interesting for ensuring correctness of C++ implementations. Nevertheless it does not fit our approach, as it is not compliant with the design by contract theory, which is of vital importance for us.
- **Annotated C++ (A++):** A++ is an annotation formalism and a proposed C++ programming tool supporting object-oriented annotation for C++. The features contained in A++ were inspired by Eiffel and other specification systems and are not compliant with the design-by-contract theory. Furthermore, A++ changes the standard C++ programming language.
- **iContract:** The iContract system [8] implements DBC for the programming language Java. The basic ideas are similar to our approach; nevertheless, the implementation of DBC for Java differs significantly, as C++ imposes design choices different from those of Java. Furthermore, iContract is not integrated with a prototyping environment.

In our system, a C++ class is generated for every Python class. The necessary information (class name, superclass, method signatures) can be extracted from the symbol files mentioned above. Instance variables and types of parameters can only be generated correctly if the appropriate *param* expressions and *type* expressions are available. For each generated class, a parallel check class is generated. This generated check class comprises instance variables and methods for assertion checking. Each class inherits from its superclass (provided it has one) and from the generated check class; thus multiple inheritance is used. Figure 2 shows the principle structure of the generated C++ classes. The name of the check class is equivalent with the name of the core class extended by the string "*__dbc*". The class "*Root__dbc*" is the

252

root class for all check classes and defines the common protocol for all check classes. The code generation tool allows subsequent regeneration of the code without loss of any C++ implementations made in the meantime.

The generated assertion check code is called via the *Require* and *Return* macros as depicted in Figure 3. The code generation tool automatically inserts both macros. The *Require* macro calls the *Person__dbc::Require_SetAge* method and passes the parameters to this check method. As Figure 4 shows, the method *Person__dbc::Require_SetAge(int &a)* automatically calls the *Invariant()* method of this check class. This ensures that the invariant checks take place with each method invocation that conforms to the underlying theory. Since a method may be exited from various points in the implementation of a method, it is not sufficient to place the code for calling the postcondition check method at the end of a method. To overcome this problem, we introduce a *Return* macro. The code generator replaces every *return* statement with our *Return* macro and inserts the *Return* macro at the end of a method in case no *return* statement can be found.

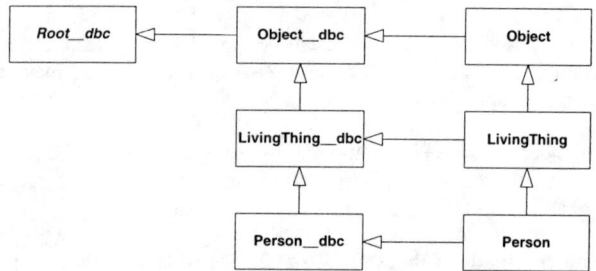

Figure 2. Structure of generated code

The assertion code for invariants, i.e., the corresponding boolean expression derived from the Python assertion, is generated into a method *Invariant()* of the check class. The generated code ensures that the *Invariant()* method of all superclasses is called. Figure 4 shows an example of the generated code. We discuss the generated code, i.e., the transformed Python assertions and the problems associated with this task, in more detail in section 4.

```
void Person::SetAge(int a)
{
    Require(Person, SetAge, (a));
    age= a;
    Return;
}
```

```
bool Person__dbc::Require_SetAge(int &a) {
    if (stack.Top().Switch()) {
        InitRequire();
        stack.Top().AddParam(a);
        this->Invariant();
        stack.Top().Switch(false);
    }
    return LivingThing__dbc::Require_SetAge, (a)
        || Check("self.age > 0", self->age > 0); }

bool Person__dbc::Ensure_SetAge(MCI &I) {...}

bool Person__dbc::Invariant() {
    return Check( ... ) &&
    LivingThing__dbc::Invariant(); }
```

Figure 3. Calling assertion check code   **Figure 4. Generated check classes**

For all preconditions of one method, one check method is generated (in Figure 4 it is method *Person__dbc::Require_SetAge(int a)*). Figure 4 shows a typical example of the generated code. The details are described in section 4. For all postconditions of one method, one check method is generated too (in Figure 4 it is method *Person__dbc::Ensure_SetAge(MCI &i)*).

To ensure that the check method for postconditions can access the parameters of the method, references to the parameters are stored in a vector by the *Require_SetAge(int &a)* method (see the call of method *AddParam()* in the *Require_SetAge(int &a)* method. Besides other information, the info object passed to *Ensure_SetAge(MCI &i)* as parameter includes this vector.

4. Implementation Details for Assertion Support in C++

This section describes a number of implementation details necessary to understand the problems and our solutions in conjunction with assertions in C++.

4.1. Supporting Preconditions and Postconditions

The call of the check method for the preconditions can be resolved by the *Require* macro since the method name and the parameters are passed to the macro. The call of the ensure-check method cannot be resolved directly by the *Return* macro because neither the method name nor the parameters are passed to the macro. Therefore, at the time of method entry, a pointer to the *Person__dbc::Ensure_SetAge()* method is initialized (*pEnsure*) by the *Require* macro. This pointer is generated as a local variable of the checked method. The corresponding ensure-check method can be called via this pointer. The definition and initialization of the pointer to the *Person__dbc::Ensure_SetAge()* method of the above example, done by the Require macro, looks like this:

```
bool (Person__dbc::*pEnsure)(MCI &i) = &Person__dbc::Ensure_SetAge;
```

The initialization statement requires the class name and the method name, which are both passed as parameters to the *Require* macro. Since the name of the method pointer as well as the parameter of all ensure-check methods are the same for all ensure methods, the corresponding method call in the *Return* macro can be resolved without macro parameters to *(this->*pEnsure)(info)*. The parameter *info* (of type *MCI*) contains the vector with the references to the parameters of the *Person::SetAge(int a)* method and thus provides access to them.

For every checked method, the *Require* macro pushes an *MCI* object onto the stack; this object is initialized with the class name and method name. The instance variables are added to this info object in the *InitRequire()* method, a generated method of the check class. The parameters of the checked method are added in the *Require_SetAge(int &a)* method. Instance variables of the class and parameters of the check method are stored in the *MCI* object in two ways: one vector contains references to the instance variables and parameters of the method to provide access to these variables for the check methods for postconditions; a second vector contains copies of the instance variables of the class as well as of the parameters of the checked method. This enables access to the variables in the check method for postconditions with the values at method entry. Since a method may invoke other methods which again are checked for preconditions and postconditions, the *MCI* objects must be organized in a stack hierarchy similar to the activation records of methods. The *MCI* object is pushed onto the stack before the check method is invoked for the preconditions. After the return of the check method for the postcondition, the *MCI* object is popped from the stack. The check method always accesses the top entry on the stack.

4.2. Handling Parameters

Parameters of methods and instance variables of a class can be of arbitrary types. To hold variables of different types in one vector, every variable is wrapped by a wrapper object that holds a reference to the proper variable. With the wrapper classes defined in Figure 5, a vector of type *vector<Wrapper*>* is able to manage variables of different types.

```
class Wrapper {};

template<class T>
class Var : public Wrapper {
public:
  Var(T &v) { value = v; }
  T &var() { return value; }
protected:
  T value; };
```

```
template<class T>
class PtrVar : public Var<T*> {
public:
  PtrVar(T *v) { value = new T(*v); } };

template<class T>
class Ref : public Wrapper {
public:
  Ref(T &r): reference(r) { }
  T &ref() { return reference; }
private:
  T &reference; };
```

Figure 5. Wrapper classes for parameters

- The wrapper *Var* holds a copy of the variable (copy is caused by the assignment in the constructor), which is accessible via the *var()* method of the wrapper.
- For pointer types, the wrapper *PtrVar* initializes the value with a copy of the object. The statement *value = new T(*v)* in the constructor of *PtrVar* creates a copy of the object by calling the copy constructor of the class *T*.
- The wrapper *Ref* holds a reference to the variable that was passed to the constructor. The *ref()* method provides access to the variable held by the wrapper.

The instance variables and parameters can be accessed by a check method via these wrappers. In our above example, the *SetAge(int i)* method has one parameter of type *int*. The corresponding wrapper objects stored in the MCI object are therefore *Ref<int>(a)* and *Var<int>(a)*, respectively. Assuming that the wrapper objects are stored at position 0 in the vectors *vars* and *olds*, access to the variable and to the copy of the variable is handled by the following expressions:

```
int a = dynamic_cast<Ref<int>*> (info.vars.at(0));
int copyA = dynamic_cast<Var<int>*>(info.olds.at(0))
```

The index of the particular instance variable or parameter in the vectors *vars* and *olds* corresponds to the declaration order of the instance variables of a class and the parameters of a method, where instance variables are located before the parameters.

4.3. Invocation Sequence Order

For our discussion of the check method invocation sequence of overridden methods, Figure 6 shows the generated methods of method *Base::Set()* overridden by method *Derived::Set()* in a simplified notation. The method invocation *anObject->Set(...)* on the object *anObject* of type *Derived* leads to the following sequence of check method calls: First, the method *Derived__dbc::Require_Set()* is called (performed by the *Require* macro). Before the preconditions are checked, the invariants have to be proved by calling the *Derived__dbc::Invariant()* method (*switch* was set true in the *Require* macro), which in turn calls *Base_dbc::Invariant()*. Therefore all invariants along the inheritance line to the root class are checked.

Base	Precondition and postcondition	Invariant

Base::Set (...) {
Require (...);
Return;
}
	Base__dbc::Require_Set (...){
	if (switch) this->Invariant();
	switch = false; }
	
	Base_dbc::Ensure_Set (...){
	if (switch) this->Invariant();
	switch = false; }
		Base__dbc::Invariant(){
		...
		}

Derived	**Precondition and postcondition**	**Invariant**

Derived::Set (...) {
Require (...);
Return;
}
	Derived__dbc::Require_Set(...){
	if (switch) this->Invariant();
	switch = false;
	Base__dbc:: Require_Set(...); }
	Derived__dbc::Ensure_Set(...){
	if (switch) this->Invariant();
	switch = false;
	Base__dbc::Ensure_Set(...); }
		Derived__dbc::Invariant(){
		Base__dbc::Invariant();
		}

Figure 6. Check methods for overridden methods

After all invariants have been proofed, *switch* is set to false. Since the *Derived::Set()* method overrides *Base::Set()*, the preconditions of the overridden method have to be proved too (call of *Base__dbc::Require_Set()*). At this time no more invariant checks are necessary because all invariants have been proved already. Therefore *switch* is used to determine the caller of the check method. If the caller was one of the macros *Require* or *Return*, the invariants of the class have to be proved; if the caller was a check method, the invariants of the class need not be proved.

4.4. Recursive Invocations of Check Methods

The invocation of a method of a class in the invariant expression of the same class would lead to an infinite recursive method call. Consider the invariant expression *age() > 0* of a class Person, where *age()* is a method of the same class. The invocation of the *age()* method on an object of the class *Person* forces a check of the invariants. The expression of the invariant calls the *age()* method again, which in turn forces a check of the invariants of class *Person*. Since the use of method calls in invariant expressions is possible, the generated check code has to determine such recursive method calls at run time and prevent an infinite loop. A simple approach to overcome this problem is to lock the method that checks the invariants. Before a invariant check method is entered, a lock is set by simply initializing a boolean switch to true. After execution of the invariant checks, the method is unlocked by setting the switch to false. The switch introduced to avoid multiple invariant checks on overridden methods can be used for this task. The switch must be unique for every checked method and thus is included in the MCI object.

4.5. Handling Run-Time Errors

In case an assertion is violated at run time, corresponding information is stored in a log file. The log file entry describes the class and method, records where the assertion violation occurred, and also indicates which assertion caused the violation. We consider this approach to be sufficient: as demonstrated by the application of our C++ model in the implementation phase, where it suffices to know that an exception occurred that contradicts the developed domain model. From a technical perspective it would be possible to integrate the handling of assertion violations by means of the exception handling mechanism provided by the programming language C++.

4.6. Controlling the Code Generation Process

There are several reasons why it is desirable to control the assertion generation process, i.e., to selectively enable or disable assertion checking for certain classes or methods:

- Usually the specification changes throughout the software production process. These changes may also affect the assertions. Thus it is convenient to disable assertion checking for affected classes as long as the analysis model and thus the assertions are being altered. This change process may take some time, as an impact analysis must be carried out and possible stakeholders must be informed about the changes.
- It is convenient to disable assertion checking for performance reasons for classes that are yet implemented and that are thoroughly tested.
- In case of major redesigns, it is convenient to disable assertion checking during the redesign process, as assertions might be violated as the classes being redesigned are not stable yet.

Due to the use of macros and multiple inheritance, it is easy for us to selectively enable or disable assertion checking on a class or method basis. In addition, it would be desirable to see at a glance for which classes or methods assertion checking is currently disabled. This allows specific investigation about the reasons for disabling certain assertions and thus contributes to the overall quality of the software process. A tool with a graphical user interface providing this overview is currently under construction.

5. Conclusions

In the introduction to section 3 we stated a number of requirements on the code generation tool. Here we report the extent to which these requirements have been met.

- *Support for iterative development:* This requirement has been fulfilled, as the transformation from an analysis model to the implementation can be done incrementally.
- *Standardization:* This requirement is fulfilled, as no language or compiler extensions are used in our approach.
- *Readability:* Due to the use of macros, a high degree of readability has been attained. The code of the application programmer is only changed by inserting the *Require* and *Return* macro. The complicated code for implementing the assertion checking mechanism is separated by means of distinct check classes, which are integrated with the ordinary code by means of multiple inheritance. The major drawback of our current prototypical implementation is that the application programmer has no direct association between a method (class) and its assertions. From a technical perspective it would be very easy to generate C++ comments for every method and class. These comments would contain the assertions in readable form (comparable with the approach we used for our Python implementation; see Figure 1); this would enhance readability.
- *Theory compliance:* This requirement is fulfilled, as the semantics of the Python assertion model and thus the semantics as defined by Eiffel are preserved.

- *Configurability:* This requirement is fulfilled, as the technical solution used, i.e., macros and multiple inheritance, facilitates selective enabling and disabling of assertion checking on a method or class basis.
- *Efficiency:* This requirement is fulfilled, as the macro approach used allows selective activation and deactivation of assertion checking on a class or even method level without run-time or memory penalties. This is not our merit, of course, but is facilitated by the C++ language.

From a prototyping perspective, the transformation mechanisms described in this paper are suitable for migrating a prototype to a C++-based implementation system without sacrificing the valuable assertion information derived during analysis and captured in the working models — in our case implemented using Python and using our Python-based prototyping environment.

Furthermore, the model described here is fairly independent of our prototyping approach. From a technical perspective, the C++ code generation mechanism relies only on the symbol files provided. Thus it would be very easy to change the input source for the code generation process (provided that the underlying semantics of DBC is not altered) and still to use the code generation mechanisms described in this paper.

Bibliography

[1] Bäumer D., Bischofberger W. R., Lichter H., Züllighoven H.: "User Interface Prototyping - Concepts, Tools, and Experience", Proceedings of the 18th International Conference on Software Engineering (ICSE), Berlin, Germany, March 1996, pp 532-541

[2] Booch G.: Object-oriented Analysis and Design with Applications, The Benjamin Cummings Publishing Company, 1994

[3] Carey J. M., Currey J. D.: "The Prototyping Conundrum", Datamation, June 1, 1989, pp 29-33

[4] Cline M.P. and Lea D.: "The Behavior of C++ Classes", Proceedings of the Symposium On Object-Oriented Programming Emphasizing Practical, Applications 1990, pp 81-91

[5] Goma H.: "Prototypes – Keep Them or Throw Them Away", in: Lipp M. E. (ed.): Prototyping – State of the Art Report, Pergamon Infotech Ltd, Maidenhead, 1986, pp 41-54

[6] Gordon S., Bieman J.: Rapid Prototyping and Software Quality: Lessons from Industry, Technical Report CS-91-113, Department of Computer Science, Colorado State University, 1991

[7] Jacobson I.: Object-Oriented Software Engineering – A Use Case Driven Approach, Addison-Wesley, 1993

[8] Kramer R.: "iContract-The Java Design by Contract Tool", Proceedings of TOOLS USA '98 conference, 1998

[9] Leavans G. T.: An Overview of Larch/C++: Behavioral Specifications for C++ Modules, TR 96-01d, February 1996, revised March, April 1996, January, July 1997, Department of Computer Science, Iowa State University, 1997

[10] Lutz M.: Programming Python, O'Reilly & Associates, Sebastopol, 1996

[11] Meyer B.: "Building Bug-Free O-O Software: An Introduction to Design by Contract", Object Currents, SIGS Publication, Vol. 1, No. 3, March 1996

[12] Meyer B.: Eiffel - The Language, Prentice Hall, Object-Oriented Series, Hemel Hempstead, 1992

[13] Meyer B.: Object-Oriented Software Construction, 2nd Edition, Prentice Hall Inc., 1997

[14] Ploesch R.: "Design by Contract for Python", Proceedings of joint APSEC'97, ICSC'97 conference, Hong Kong, IEEE Computer Society, Press, 1997, pp 213-219

[15] Ploesch R.: "Tool Support for Design by Contract", Proceedings of TOOLS USA 98 conference, Santa Barabara, USA, IEEE Computer Society Press, pp 282-294, 1998

[16] Rumbaugh J.: Object-Oriented Modeling and Design, Prentice Hall, 1991

[17] Sobol M. G., Kagan A.: "Which Systems Analysts are more Likely to Prototype?", Journal of Information System Management, Summer 1989, pp 36-43

[18] Spivey J. M.: The Z Notation: A Reference Manual, International Series in Computer Science, Prentice-Hall, New York, 1992

[19] Vonk R.: Prototyping, The effective use of CASE Technology, Prentice Hall Inc, 1990

A Comparison of Defensive Development and Design by Contract™

Donald G. Firesmith

FiresmithD@AOL.com

Abstract

This paper briefly defines and discusses assertions and their uses before summarizing Design by Contract and Defensive Development. This provides a foundation for the following comparison of their similarities as well as their respective strengths and weaknesses. The paper concludes by arguing that Defensive Development is superior to Design by Contract, largely because of how they differ in assigning the responsibility for checking and ensuring preconditions.

1. Introduction

Assertions are a class-level, quality assurance technique used to address the following important problems:

- **Abstraction.** Because each class and type (e.g., Java interface) should model a single abstraction, it should capture the essential characteristics of the concept being modeled while ignoring the inconsequential or diversionary details. Although each class should also be given an English definition of the concept it models, the resulting informal narrative text can be vague and ambiguous. Even if its responsibilities for doing, knowing, and enforcing are also documented, they are still captured in narrative English text. How can one unambiguously document the abstraction of a class or type?

- **Correctness.** How do you know that a class or type is correct? How should this correctness be enforced? A relatively formal, yet practical, technique is needed to ensure that a class or type correctly captures its abstraction.

- **Encapsulation.** Encapsulation is the combination of localization and information hiding.

  - **Localization.** How should the specification (the 'what' and 'why') and implementation (the 'how') of a class be localized? Unless the specification is localized with the implementation, it becomes increasingly unlikely that they will remain consistent as the design and software are iterated and maintained. However, the specification should clearly be separated from the resulting implementation. Otherwise, it becomes hard to know whether the software meets its requirements (i.e., the implementation fulfills the specification). How does one localize defect detection and handling software with the associated operational software that contains the defects without mixing the two and thereby cluttering up the software?

  - **Information hiding.** Information hiding makes it harder and less efficient to determine from outside an object whether or not the abstraction of the object has been violated. The object should not have to export read and write accessors just for testing purposes because this decreases encapsulation and thus increases coupling. Such accessors may also be misused as a trapdoor for purposes other than testing.

- **Inheritance**. How can one ensure that inheritance is used properly to capture the "a kind of" specialization relationship between a child and its parent(s)? How can one avoid the loss of polymorphic substitutability? How can one ensure that test software is inherited as well as operational software?

- **Exception handling**. When should exception handling be used? How can developers avoid misusing it as a glorified "goto" (or rather "come from")?

- **Defensive development**. It is important that an object protect its abstraction from violation no matter what messages are sent to it, what exceptions are raised to it, or in what order these interactions occur. Moreover, if the abstraction of an object is violated, it is important that this violation be immediately recognized so that appropriate action can be taken. This action could be to notify the developer during testing so that debugging can occur or to ensure the robustness of the delivered objects.

- **Robustness**. More and more applications are mission or safety critical. It is insufficient if the application only works under normal conditions. Applications must also continue to function appropriately, even with bad input or the failure of controlled hardware. Such applications often have severe requirements concerning reliability and operational availability. Such systems must be fault tolerant and therefore self-testing and self-correcting. How should such software be built in order to meet required levels of robustness, reliability, operational availability, and fault-tolerance?

- **Testing**. How can testability be maintained when encapsulation inherently makes classes less observable and controllable (and therefore less testable)? What design for testability techniques for classes provide the most testability? How can objects be made self-testing so that the defect that caused the failure is identified when it happens so that debugging can be performed? Information hiding also emphasizes blackbox testing that does not depend on knowledge of the hidden implementation of the class. What should be the basis for class-level blackbox testing?

- **Reuse**. How can we be know that a class is suitable for reuse without spending an inordinate amount of time researching its implementation? How do we know that it will perform as advertised when reused in a new environment?

2. Assertions

An **assertion** is a rule in the form of a condition that must be true at certain times during the execution of the software. An assertion is a Boolean expression that constrains certain properties of the software. When properly used, assertions form an essential part of the formal specification of a class or type, documenting the required behavior of its instances.

Typical examples of assertions include:

- The value of an attribute or parameter must be of a certain type (strong typing) or fall within a certain range.

- The multiplicity of a certain association must fall within a given range (e.g., a certain link must not be void).

- A certain formula describes the value that must be returned by an operation.

- An operation must raise a certain kind of exception (strong typing) under certain circumstances.

- The valid states of an object are defined in terms of certain values of certain attributes.

When properly used, assertions provide the following key benefits:

- Assertions capture business rules and the responsibilities for enforcing them.

- Assertions simplify operational code by separating it from rule checking and rule violation handling code.

- Assertions increase understandability by capturing the designer's intent and formally specifying the protocol of the class or type.

- Assertions more formally specify the abstraction than do narrative English comments.

- Assertions increase quality and reliability. By specifying the assertions of a class, developers take a major step towards ensuring that the class actually meets its specification.

- Assertions monitored at runtime form a basis for:
  - Systematic class-level testing and debugging.
  - Ensuring robustness.

Assertions come in the following major kinds:

- **Protocol assertions**. These assertions are visible to senders and document the protocol of the associated class or type:
  - **Invariants** – define the valid states of an object that exist before and after the correct execution of its visible[1] operations[2].
  - **Preconditions** – define the conditions that must be true before a specific operation can execute correctly.
  - **Postconditions** – define the conditions guaranteed to result from the correct execution of a specific operation.

- **Implementation assertions**. These assertions are hidden from senders and constrain the implementation of the class or type:
  - **Ad hoc assertions** – define a condition that must be true at an arbitrary point in some operation.

Because of encapsulation, protocol assertions should not involve private properties of the object; instead, they should be specified in terms of its logical properties (i.e., externally meaningful concepts). The ability to use precisely defined queries to capture logical properties provides great power to assertions because the implementation of these queries can be arbitrarily complex (e.g., quantifiers such as "there exists" and "for all"). However, information hiding suggests that such queries should be used primarily for assertion checking because arbitrary use by senders of the object increases coupling. The Law of

---

[1] A visible operation is visible to some external class. Different implementation languages recognize multiple kinds of visibility. For example, "visible" in Java means one of the following: public, protected, and package; hidden thus means private.

[2] Whereas preconditions and postconditions can be used with non-object-oriented models and software (e.g., use cases), invariants only make sense when applied to objects.

Demeter[3] also suggests that assertions should not include the logical properties of logical properties.

Thus, assertions can be Boolean expressions involving the following:
- Logical properties of the object.
- Message parameters.
- Logical properties of message parameters.
- Exceptions handled.
- Logical properties of exceptions handled.

3. Design by Contract™

Design by Contract is the collaboration-level specification and design approach developed by Bertrand Meyer, the creator of the Eiffel programming language. Thus, Design by Contract is directly supported in the Eiffel language and a fundamental part of the Eiffel mindset. Design by Contract views each interaction between two objects as if it were a legal contract between a customer and a service provider. Each such contract documents the respective obligations and benefits of each party; whereby the obligations of one party result in benefits for the other party. By analogy, the interaction between the operation sending the message (the customer) and the associated operation implementing the message (the service supplier) can be viewed as a contract between them specified in terms of assertions. For example, consider the pop operation of a bounded stack. The associated contract's obligations and benefits are documented in the following table:

BoundedStack.pop()	Obligations	Benefits
Customer (message sender)	Satisfy following preconditions: • Stack not empty.	Obtain from postconditions: • Top item is returned. • Stack is properly updated.
Supplier (receiver operation)	Satisfy following postconditions: • Stack is not full. • New size equals old size minus 1.	Obtain from preconditions: • Can assume that the stack is not empty; no need to check.

The metaphor of contracting can be extended to subcontracting. A superclass uses *inheritance* to subcontract out some of its obligations to its subclasses. A sender uses *delegation* to subcontract out some of its obligations to its receivers.

Design by contract is based on the following principles and assumptions:

- A run-time violation of an assertion is caused by a fault (defect, bug) in the software.

- The customer (sender object) is responsible for establishing the precondition. Therefore:

    - A violation of a precondition implies a defect in the customer's code.

---

[3] The Law of Demeter (a.k.a., the "Don't talk to strangers" pattern) minimizes coupling and enforces encapsulation by restricting who should receive messages from an object. An object should only send messages to itself, its properties (i.e., attributes, parts, entries, members, and objects that it is directly linked to), the parameters of messages sent to it, and any exceptions that are raised to it.

- Thus, every logical property appearing in the precondition of an operation must be visible to every customer of the operation so that the customers can verify/ensure the precondition.

- If the customer does not establish the precondition of the supplier, then the supplier can do anything it wants because the result of calling the supplier operation is undefined. The following are direct quotes from Bertrand Meyer, the inventor of Design by Contract:

  - "If the client's part of the contract is not fulfilled, that is to say if the call does not satisfy the precondition, then the class is not bound by the postcondition. In this case, the routine may do what it pleases: return any value; loop indefinitely without returning a value; or even crash the execution in some wild way." [2]

  - "The definition of class correctness leaves the routines of the class free to do as they please for any class that violates the precondition or the invariant [2]

- In concurrent software in which a customer cannot guarantee the precondition of the supplier because of race conditions, the precondition becomes a wait condition rather than a correctness condition. The supplier waits until the precondition holds before executing the requested operation.

- The supplier (receiver object) is responsible for establishing the postconditions and invariants. Therefore, a violation of a postcondition or invariant implies a defect in the supplier itself.

4. Defensive Development

Defensive Development [2] is a class-level specification, design, and implementation approach designed to defend an abstraction from misuse or bugs. Unlike Design by Contract, it places all responsibilities for ensuring the abstraction of a class on the class itself. It is interested in both correctness and robustness. It is based on the following important principles:

- Each class and type captures a single abstraction. As such, it is correct and complete to the extent that it properly captures all essential aspects of the concept it models while ignoring all unimportant or diversionary details.

- Because you cannot defend an abstraction that is not specified, assertions and their associated exceptions are used to formally specify the behavior of the abstraction. Because assertions and exceptions capture a critical part of the abstraction, they must therefore be localized with the abstraction they specify.

- Objects must be instantiated in a valid state (i.e., ensure its invariants). Otherwise, it is already too late to defend them because their abstractions were already violated on creation.

- To the extent practical, an object should defend itself by not allowing its abstraction to be violated (e.g., respond inappropriately, be put in an invalid state) regardless of:

  - What messages it receives.
  - What exceptions it handles.
  - In what order the interactions occur (i.e., its state).

- If an object's abstraction is violated, the object should recognized that fact and react appropriately:

  - Reestablish its valid state.

  - Use *appropriate* exceptions to warn its senders that it cannot respond appropriately.

- Senders are *not* responsible for establishing the preconditions of receivers; they often cannot be responsible if multiple objects are sending messages to the same receiver. Neither is it the responsibility of the receiver to establish its own preconditions. Instead, the checking of all assertions is the responsibility of the receiver class that specifies them, whereas the handling of assertion violations resides in both the receiver (reestablish invariants and throw exception) and sender (handle failure).

- Because concurrency may lead to race conditions between multiple senders attempting to use the same receiver, visible operations of concurrent classes must be synchronized (i.e., critical regions guaranteed to run to completion without interruption) if correctness is to be guaranteed.

5. Comparison of Defensive Development and Design by Contract

Defensive Development and Design by Contract have a great deal in common:

- They are both based on the use of assertions.

- They use the same kinds of assertions.

- They both consider the receiver responsible for ensuring invariants and postconditions.

- They both allow the raising of exceptions upon assertion violations.

- They both therefore derive many of the same benefits from assertions.

Because of how it assigns responsibility for ensuring preconditions and emphasizes exception handling, Defensive Programming is superior to Design by Contract for the following reasons:

- **Defensive Development improves reliability.** Reliability is the combination of correctness and robustness. Design by Contract is only concerned with correctness, whereas Defensive Development is also concerned with robustness. Although it may be OK in the legal world for one party to abandon a contract if the other party violates the contract, such behavior is neither acceptable nor practical for software. It is critical that software continues to function, even if one party violates the contract. Whereas Design by Contract would allow the receiver operation to do anything on violation of its preconditions, Defensive Development mandates that an appropriate exception be thrown, thereby allowing the sender to take appropriate actions. Defensive Development also supports robustness by providing more guidance on exception handling. Defensive Development therefore produces software that is more reliable and robust than software produced by Design by Contract.

- **Defensive Development decreases message coupling.** The two different techniques result in different numbers of messages being sent between objects:

  - Design by Contract usually forces the sender to first send a query message to the receiver object to determine if each precondition of a desired operation is true before sending the associated message. The counter argument that the sender need not send queries in order to guarantee the precondition does not usually hold in either practice or examples provided by proponents of Design by Contract.

- With Defensive Development, however, the sender assumes that the preconditions hold when sending messages. Thus, there is no need to send query messages to check the precondition, and only in those rare occasions in which a precondition is violated is an exception raised and handled.

- By requiring fewer messages, Defensive Development causes less message coupling between classes than does Design by Contract.

- The sequence diagrams in Figures 1 and 2 use stacks to illustrate how Defensive Development and Design by Contract differ with regard to interactions.

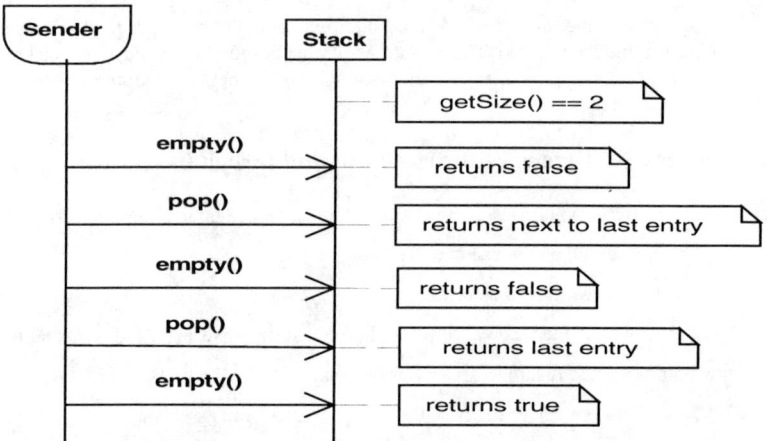

Figure 1. Interactions using Design by Contract

- **Defensive Development better supports encapsulation.** Defensive Development supports encapsulation better than Design by Contract:

  - With Design by Contract, the sender must ensure the receiver's preconditions. Thus, either the sender must send query messages concerning every logical property in the preconditions or the receiver must export the associated physical properties. Either the query operations must be public (instead of protected) or else (and worse) the associated physical properties must be public. Neither case maximizes encapsulation.

  - With Defensive Development, the receiver is responsible for ensuring its own preconditions. Therefore, many of the logical properties can be hidden if they only are used in the preconditions.

- **Defensive Development improves localization and cohesion.** Design by Contract violates the guideline "Never do for an object what an object can do for itself." Instead of having the supplier responsible for its own preconditions, the associated precondition checking code is scattered across all of the senders of the associated message. Defensive Development better localizes precondition checks with the operations having the preconditions, thereby improving the cohesion of the class.

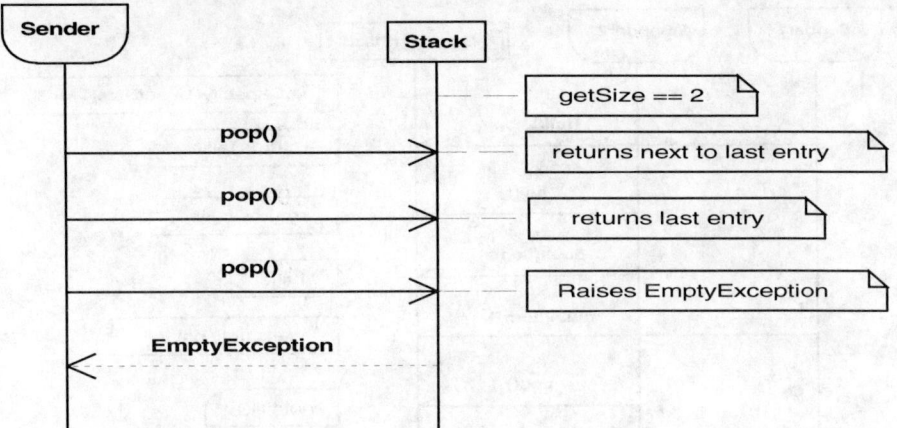

Figure 2: Interactions using Defensive Development

- **Defensive Development eliminates concurrency bugs.** More and more classes must exist in a concurrent environment. Design by Contract and Defensive Development greatly differ in how they handle concurrency:

  - Design by Contract would have the sender check or establish the precondition of the receiver. However, even if one sender were to establish the preconditions or determine that they were true, a second sender could send another message that causes a precondition violation before the first sender could send its intended message. Such race condition defects cause intermittent failures and are therefore very difficult to test for and debug. For this reason, Design by Contract only uses preconditions to ensure the correctness of sequential software; it uses preconditions to signify wait conditions for concurrent software.

  - Because the receiver of the message is responsible for monitoring its own preconditions and responding correctly, Defensive Development does not need to change the meaning or uses of preconditions when dealing with concurrent software.

  - The sequence diagrams in Figures 3 and 4 use bounded-stacks to illustrate how the behavior resulting from Defensive Development and Design by Contract differ greatly with regard to concurrency. Note that parallel lines signify that the senders and the bounded stack are concurrent (i.e., execute in *parallel* on their own threads). The shield on the bounded stack further indicates that it is thread safe. Note that Design by Contract requires the use of asynchronous messages, whereas Defensive Programming allows synchronous messages.

- **Defensive Development decreases complexity.** Design by Contract simplifies the supplier code (by not having it check the preconditions) at the cost of increasing the complexity of the code of each customer and increasing the number of interactions between the customer(s) and the supplier. Because a single supplier often has multiple customers that must each redundantly check the preconditions, Design by Contract results in a net increase in overall complexity.

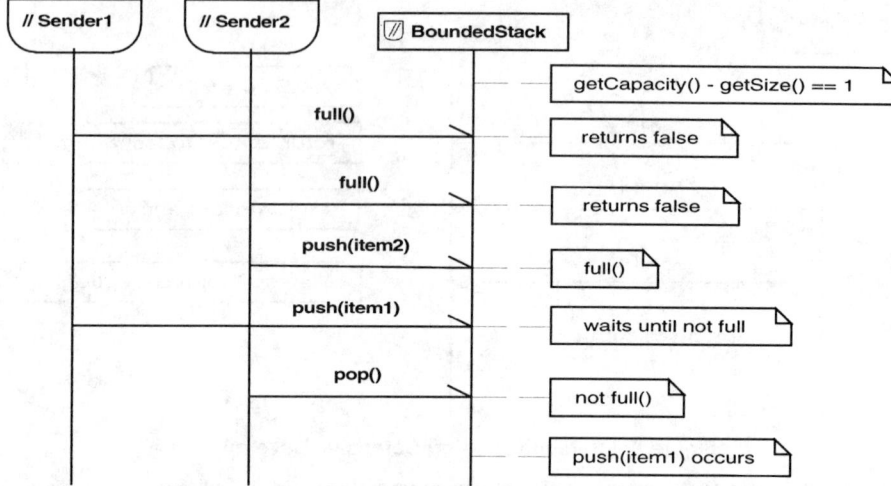

Figure 3: Concurrency using Design by Contract

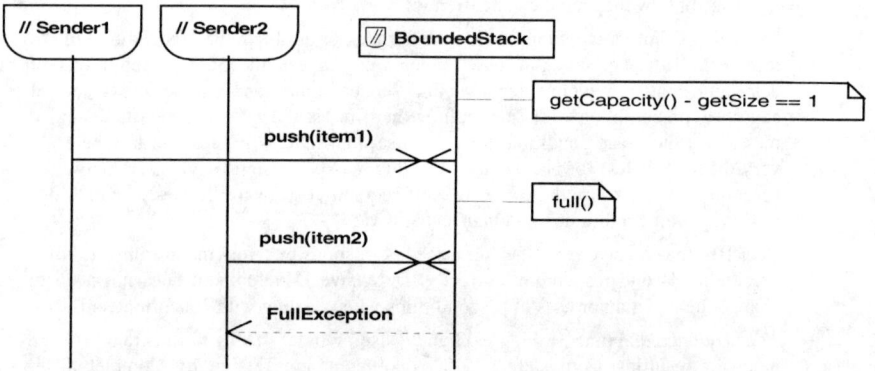

Figure 4: Concurrency using Defensive Development

- **Defensive Development eliminates redundant code by reusing precondition-checking code.** Whereas Defensive Development checks preconditions only once (at the beginning of the called operation), Design by Contract redundantly includes precondition checking code in each sender. Thus, Design by Contract increases overall code size and the costs of the associated maintenance. If the preconditions change, each sender must be found and modified in an identical manner; something that would be unnecessary if the receiver was responsible for enforcing its own preconditions.

- **Defensive Development increases maintainability.** It increases maintainability by decreasing complexity, eliminating redundant client code, and better separating normal from abnormal code.

- **Defensive Development increases performance.** Because assertions should only rarely be violated, exception raising and handling code will only rarely execute. By not requiring (typically unnecessary) query messages between classes to check preconditions, Defensive Development significantly increases the performance of the resulting code. This is especially true when the instances of the classes belong to different processes on different processors.

- **Design by Contract is based on false assumptions**. Design by Contract is partially based on the following false assumptions:

  - Only one customer per supplier.

  - The violation of a precondition is a symptom of a defect in the sender. Such a violation could be the result of bad user input, or merely the fact that multiple concurrent senders are interacting via the same receivers (i.e., a race condition occurs).

  - The violation of a postcondition is a symptom of a defect in the receiver. This is an over simplification because such a violation could be the result of a failure of either a collaborator of the receiver or a hardware device that is controlled by the receiver. Thus, violations of postconditions may signify the robustness of the receiver rather than a defect.

- **Defensive Development increases consistency**. Defensive Development provides a single consistent way of handling all assertions (the receiver is responsible), sequential and concurrent classes treat preconditions the same way, and most commercial-off-the-shelf (COTS) class libraries are based on defensive programming (at least logically). Design by Contract does not.

- **Defensive Development provides greater separation of concerns**. Defensive Development physically separates normal processing code, code to detect assertion violations, and code to handle assertion violations (exceptions). However, Design by Contract commingles precondition violation detection code and normal processing code in the sender and does not emphasize the use of exception handling code.

- **Defensive Development produces specifications that are more complete**. By specifying the specific exception to be raised by each violated assertion, Defensive Development provides more complete specifications that does Design by Contract, which tends to emphasize assertions over their associated exceptions.

6. Conclusion

The proper use of assertions solves many important problems with the specification, design, implementation, and verification of classes and types. Whereas Design by Contract has greatly advanced software engineering and is the de facto industry standard approach for the use of assertions, Defensive Development (when properly based on assertions) provides all of the advantages of Design by Contract but also avoids many of Design by Contract's limitations, especially those associated with how to handle preconditions. This paper therefore argues that Design by Contract should be superseded by Defensive Development.

7. References

[1] Bertrand Meyer, *Object-Oriented Software Construction, Second Edition*, Prentice Hall, Englewood Cliffs, New Jersey, 1997.

[2] Donald G. Firesmith, "Pattern Language for Testing Object-Oriented Software," *Object Magazine, Vol. 5, No. 8*, SIGS Publications Inc., New York, New York, January 1996, pp. 32-38.

Interaction Schemata: Compiling Interactions to Code

Neeraj Sangal[*], Edward Farrell[*], Karl Lieberherr[†], David Lorenz[†]
[*]*Tendril Software, Inc, Westford, MA 01886-4133*
[†]*Northeastern University, Boston, MA 02115-9959*

Abstract

Programming object interactions is at the heart of object-oriented programming. To improve reusability of the interactions, it is important to program object interactions generically. We present two tools that facilitate programming of object interactions. StructureBuilder, a commercial tool, achieves genericity with respect to data structure implementations for collections, following ideas from generic programming, but focussing only on the four most important actions add, delete, iterate and find that are used to translate UML interaction diagrams into code. The focus of StructureBuilder is to generate efficient code from interaction schemata that are an improved form of interaction diagrams. DJ, a new research prototype intended for fast prototyping, achieves genericity with respect to the UML class diagram by dynamic creation of collections based on traversal specifications.

1 Introduction

The Unified Modeling Language (UML [BRJ96]) defines 9 kinds of diagrams, listed in Figure 1, to help in the construction, analysis and comprehension of object-oriented programs. Of those diagrams, this paper focuses on one important kind: *object-interaction diagrams*. Class diagrams give the *static* view of how classes relate to each other. Object-interaction diagrams give the *dynamic* view of how a program organizes the interaction of instances of these classes to perform specific functions. Design tools (like *Rational Rose* [S98], *StructureBuilder* [SB], etc.) make it possible to generate code from class diagrams; and visualization tools make it possible to construct object-interaction diagrams by tracing the execution of the program (e.g., *Program Explorer* [LN95]).

Performing the translations in the opposite direction is possible albeit more complex. For class diagrams it is not that hard. By parsing the class code, or using reflection capabilities, a class diagram can be produced by means of reverse engineering (e.g., the on-going work at MIT on generating object models from Java [J99]). Indeed, with Java and other object-oriented languages, it has become possible to map class diagrams to code and vice versa. For object-interaction diagrams, however, there is a key difficulty. There is not enough information in the interaction diagram to do the job. One can try to overcome this difficulty and construct code by abstracting over *execution patterns* [DLWV98] in object-interaction diagrams. But this would require a working program to begin with. In this paper, we show an incremental direct technique for moving from an interaction diagram to code.

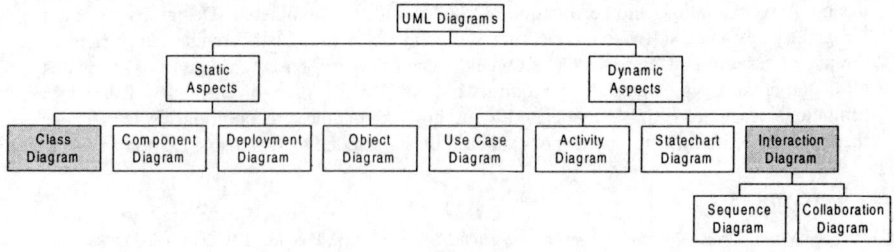

Figure 1

1.1 Motivation

Diagrammatic notations must be very precise to express the design accurately and yet imprecise enough to permit different implementations. Interaction diagrams are no exception. What makes interaction diagrams useful is that they contain enough information to embody the essential aspects of the object interaction but not too much to become identical to code. The challenge addressed in this work is in specifying interaction diagrams in sufficient detail so that code can be generated, while maintaining the essential simplicity, which is necessary for human communication.

The technique presented in this paper lets you start from an object-interaction diagram and generate actual Java code from it. In working towards this goal, we use the following guidelines:

- The generated code captures just the sequence diagram. The user is expected (and enjoys the freedom) to add additional code which embodies the application logic not captured within the sequence diagram.

- We made a simple generalization of messages. Instead of thinking of messages as just method calls, we treated them as code fragments. This allows us to treat iterations and conditionals as messages. It also allows us to capture common data structure manipulations in actions, that we call: *add*, *delete*, *iterate* and *find*. By parameterizing these actions with properties we found that we were able to capture most of the common usage patterns. These actions embody and convey what they do at a high level, and fit very well into the sequence diagram paradigm. On the other hand, the properties associated with these actions contain enough detail to generate the code. We call descriptions comprising of such actions: *interaction schemata*.

What is so striking about this approach is that an interaction schema conveys an overview of the function in a manner that is easy to understand. The details of the data structure are abstracted away from the user. The properties of each of these actions on the other hand contain the details of what it takes to implement the interaction schema. You can experiment with different class diagrams and different data structures. Interaction diagrams facilitate communication between software developers. Most software development will be done in teams and these teams are going to change over time. Using class and interaction diagrams that are guaranteed to be current is an excellent way to communicate what the program does.

In the rest of this paper, we identify the missing information required to convert an interaction diagram to code. We explain why it is so difficult to generate code from a sequence diagram, and list what we believe the programmer does *inside his head* when converting an interaction diagram into code. We demonstrate two approaches implemented in two tools. The first tool generates large parts of your program for you. Furthermore the parts that are generated relate to object interaction and tend to be more tedious and error prone. This approach can eliminate many errors in these parts. Therefore, it opens up the possibility of writing highly reliable programs. The process of incremental development is critical to good software development. The second tool uses the Java Generic Library and a traverse action in combination with a domain specific language for object traversal.

2 A Library System Example

Consider a *library system* whose design is given by the class diagram in Figure 2 using the UML notation. The edges represent associations. The **Library** class is associated with the **Book** and **User** classes, which in turn are associated with the **Copy** class. An edge marked with * indicates zero-to-many relationships, but the implementer is free to choose which collection type to use to realize the association. The roles *books* and *users* (the labels on the arrows from **Library** to **Book** and **User**) suggest that a **Library** instance contains multiple **Book** instances and multiple **User** instances. The arrow directions indicate the direction of the references. However, one can imagine an implementation in which, e.g., the **Book** or the **User** instances point to the **Library** instance, or an implementation in which external objects model the associations.

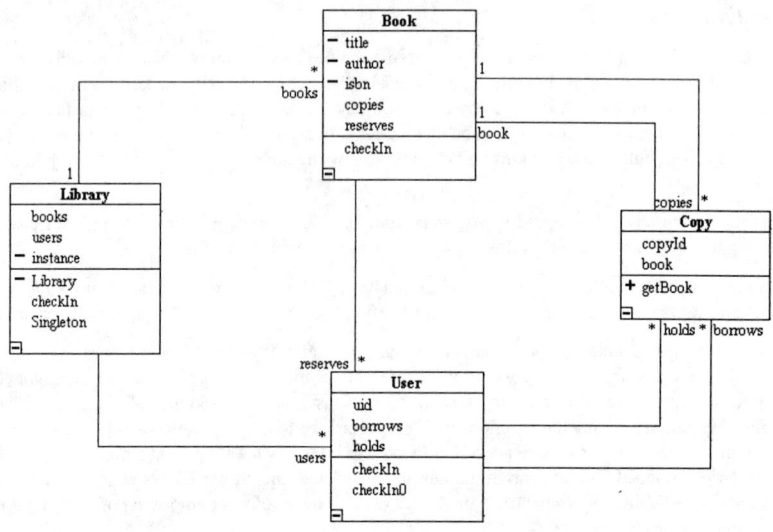

Figure 2

For the purpose of this illustration, nevertheless, all of the associations are assumed to be implemented as in memory structures. Since the library may have multiple copies of a book, each book contains multiple **Copy** instances. Each **User** instance contains multiple instances of **Copy,** one for each (copy of a) book that is checked out by that user (the *borrows* role). Each **User** also holds a collection of copies: the ones that are ready to be picked up (the *holds* role). Each **Copy** instance references a single **Book** instance. The zero-to-many relationships are implemented using the basic Java collections: Vector and Hashtable. Note that the thrust of this paper would be unaffected whether different collection types were used or whether a persistence mechanism such as a database is employed.

2.1   Returning a Book

Consider now a sequence diagram for the library system. For clarity, we shall concentrate only on sequence diagrams, but the technique described is applicable also to collaboration diagrams and other kinds of object-interaction diagrams. Sequence diagrams illustrate how objects of these classes are used for specific functions. Note that it is not necessary to specify a class diagram prior to creating a sequence diagram. However, as you iterate over the design, you will begin filling in the class diagram as you continue to refine your sequence diagram.

The sequence diagram in Figure 3 shows the details of checking in (i.e., returning) a book by a user. First we find a user with the specified **uid**. Then we remove the copy from the user's list of borrowed books. Next we access the book of the removed copy, and remove the first user from the reservation queue. Finally, we add the removed copy to the **holds** list of the reserver and notify him.

Note that a number of data structure operations are hidden behind several of the messages. For instance, the message **find** will operate on the data member **library.users.** It will iterate through the collection looking for the appropriate user.

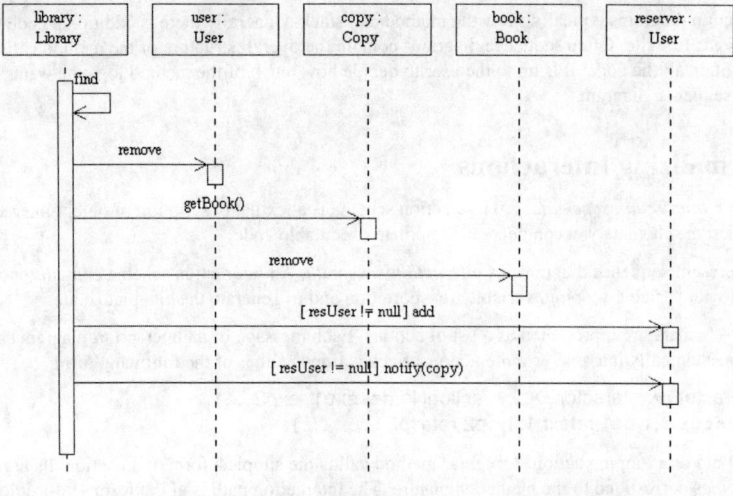

Figure 3

2.2 Going from Interaction Diagram to Code

First, we must figure out *from where* the objects come, and locate the origin of the objects **library**, **book**, **user**, **copy** and **reserver**. Looking at the diagram, we can deduce that **library** is the object which the method is called on and corresponds to the *this* object in the method. On the other hand, it is not immediately clear how **user**, **book** and **copy** objects were accessed. The creator of the interaction diagram knows that **user** is an object which is discovered by **find**, **book** is the object returned by **getBook**, and that **copy** is the object which is returned by *remove*. But we don't.

Second, we must figure out how objects are *transported*. It isn't clear from the sequence diagram how these objects are passed around between different methods. This is a tedious task for the programmer.

However, the problem is even harder than just being an issue of a programmer not being diligent in maintaining interaction diagrams. Interaction diagrams support the notion of *iteration* and *conditionals*; therefore, objects of an interaction diagram are subject to the same *scoping* and *visibility* rules that programmers encounter in programming languages. Indeed, it is easy to construct interaction diagrams, which violate these rules and therefore cannot be used to generate correct code.

Iterations and conditionals limit the visibility of new objects within their scope. This is true when writing code and remains true within interaction diagrams. Any access to such objects outside the scope is illegal. Since sequence diagrams describe collaboration of multiple objects that may be of different types, the code for implementing a collaboration spans multiple classes. Therefore, method parameters and return variables enable those variables to be visible within the appropriate method.

Third, we must fill in the missing details. There are many details that may be missing from sequence diagrams:

- The iteration specified in an interaction diagram does not contain enough information. Frequently, iterations are over a collection of objects. Interaction diagrams generally do not specify what that object is. Often iterations are subject to conditions, e.g., iterate over all elements in a collection that meets certain constraints.

- The method calls need to have parameters and return types. Conditionals need boolean expressions.

- Interaction diagrams typically show the method call stack. Generally there is additional code that a user needs to write. Often sequence diagrams contain the overall structure of the method calls but do not contain all the code. It is up to the user to decide how much of the method logic he wants to show in the sequence diagram.

3 Formalizing Interactions

We introduce *interaction schemata*. An interaction schema is a textual description of object-interaction. From interaction schemata you can generate complete executable code.

Now we represent sequence diagrams as *interaction schemata*. An interaction schema contains enough details to deal with variable scoping, variable transportation and to generate the complete code.

Interaction schemata are represented as a list of actions. Each message of an interaction-diagram can be translated mechanically into one or more actions. Each action is either of the following form:

[interactor → interactor → ...] . actionName (exp1, exp2, ...)
    return (type1 retexp1, type2 retexp2, ...) {...}

or a conditional or a looping action. A regular method call is the simplest form of an action. Its arguments and return types correspond to the method signature. The interaction path is of the form [interactor$_1$ → interactor$_2$ → ...] where interactor$_1$ is an object in the interaction diagram and interactor$_2$ is an instance variable of interactor$_1$, and so on. Note that some actions such as conditional and looping actions can contain other actions. The scope of each returned variable is limited to being inside the innermost enclosing conditional or iterative action.

For example, if we have a sequence diagram of the form:

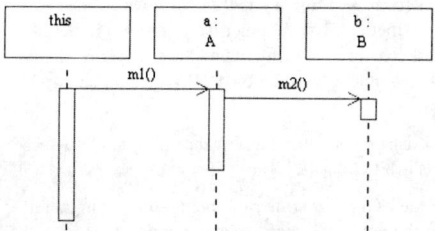

it would be represented in terms of actions as:

```
a.m1() {
        b.m2()
}
```

A conditional message of the form:

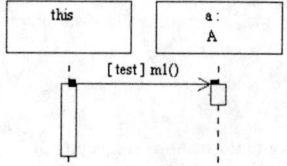

would be represented in terms of actions as:

```
if (test) {
        a.m1();
}
```

As we alluded to earlier we have defined additional actions which allow us to capture certain common data structure manipulations. These actions are *iterate, find, add,* and *remove*. These actions are defined on collection types and the generated code is appropriate for the type of collection.

Now let us look at the action description of the **checkIn** method:

```
Library.checkIn(UID uid, Copy copyId)
```

It takes as inputs a **uid** and a **copyId**. The **uid** identifies the borrower and the **copyId** identifies the copy of the book being returned.

The following sequence of actions describes the program. Each of the actions takes as input a set of expressions, which are the properties associated with them, and which serve to parameterize the generated code. Properties for many of these actions are shown after the interaction schema. We have added comments to each of the actions to assist the reader in understanding the interaction schema.

```
Library.checkIn(UID uid, Copy copyId)
{
    // Find the user with the specified uid
    [library→users→uid].find(uid'current == uid)
        return (User users'current as theUser)

    // Remove the copy with the specified copyid
    [theUser→borrows→copyId].remove(copyId'current == copyId)
        return (Copy borrows'current as theCopy)

    // Call method on copy
    [theCopy].getBook()
        return (Book book as theBook)

    // Find the first user who is on the reserve collection
    [theBook→reserves].remove(reserves'index == 0)
        return (User reserves'current as theReserver)

    // Conditional action
    if (theReserver != null) {
        // Add this copy to the reservers hold list
        [theReserver→holds].add(theCopy)

        // Call method on reserver
        [theReserver].notify(theCopy);
    }
}
```

3.1 Object Transportation

In order to translate the schema into code, the issue of object transportation must be resolved. For example, the action

```
[theUser→borrows→copyId].remove(copyId'current == copyId)
    return (Copy borrows'current as theCopy)
```

leads to the generation of the method *checkIn* in the classes **Library, User,** and **Copy** (Figures 4a, 4b, and 4c show the generated code.) The value **copyId** needs to be passed into the methods *checkIn* from the main method *checkIn* in **Library**. This is an example of an *external* transportation across actions, i.e., between methods which where generated from different actions. Transportation can also occur *internally*. Internal transportation refers to the passing of an object to several generated methods within a single action.

There are many delicate issues involved in object transportation. The object name may change. Multiple objects may need to be returned through a single method requiring the use of wrappers (if the language does not support multiple return values.) Conditionals within actions can lead to unexpected transportation.

There are two approaches to translating to code. StructureBuilder, a Java design tool, takes a code generation approach, in which code is generated for each instance of each action, and method signatures are updated to perform object transportation. DJ [DJ99], a research project at Northeastern University, takes a generic approach, in which traversal specifications are adapted to be used with predefined generic algorithms in the Java Generic Library [JGL], and reflection is used to customize the traversals at runtime. DJ also provides important traverse actions (traverse, gather, fetch, etc.) to support the Visitor Design pattern [GOF] without the problem of structure hardening.

3.2 StructureBuilder: A Code Generation Approach

When code is generated there are a number of issues to consider:

- The actions themselves can embody method calls because not all of the objects that they act upon are accessible in the method specified. In a interaction diagram, the programmer would explicitly specify the method necessary. Structure-Builder, on the other hand will automatically generate a method call if necessary.

- When methods are generated, it is necessary for objects to be

Figure 4a: Method Generated in class Book

```
/** @SBGen Generated Method (2), created by Li-
brary.checkIn(UID, Copy) (Library.2,-5)   */
User checkIn()
{
  // SBgen: Action Remove User from reserves (5)
  User resUser = null;
  int size = reserves.size();
  if (size > 0) {
    resUser = reserves.elementAt(0);
    reserves.removeElementAt(0);
  }

  // SBgen: End Remove
  // SBgen: Return resUser
  return resUser;
}
```

Figure 4b: Method Generated in class Library

```
/**
 * @param uid
 * @param copyId
 * @SBGen Generated Method (2)
 */
void checkIn(UID uid, Copy copyId)
{
  // SBgen: Action Find User in users (2)
  User user = null;
  Object tmpKey;
  Enumeration i = users.keys();
    while(i.hasMoreElements()) {
      tmpKey = i.nextElement();
      user = (User)users.get(tmpKey);
      if (user.uid==uid)
        break;
    }

  // SBgen: End Find
  // SBgen: Call generated method on User (-3)
  Copy copy = user.checkIn(copyId);

  // SBgen: Action Execute method on Copy (4)
  Book book = copy.getBook();

  // SBgen: Call generated method on Book (-5)
  User resUser = book.checkIn();

  // SBgen: Action If (6)
  if (resUser != null) {
    // SBgen: Call generated method on User (-7)
    resUser.checkIn0(copy);

    // SBgen: Action Execute method on User (8)
    resUser.notify(copy);
  }
  // SBgen: End If (6)
}
```

transported correctly to the generated methods. It is also necessary for generated objects to be transported back. StructureBuilder will generate methods with the correct signature and return type.

Notice, however, that this is simply an implementation issue. Normally the programmer sets up his method signatures so that scoping issues are dealt with appropriately. Indeed, we could bypass the whole issue of object transportation by leaving it up to the programmer to specify the method signature completely.

3.3 DJ: A Generic Approach

The DJ tool [DJ99] provides an alternative technique to implement actions by making them more generic. The first observation of DJ is to note that actions like *add*, *find*, *delete* etc. also appear in Generic Programming (GP) as generic algorithms or as methods of container interfaces [MS94, JGL]. Therefore DJ attempts to reuse those generic algorithms. The second observation of DJ is that traversal-visitor style programming is a frequently recurring pattern and therefore DJ offers a traverse action that simplifies traversal visitor style programming.

Figure 4c: Methods Generated in class User

```
/** @SBGen Generated Method (2), created by Li-
brary.checkIn(UID, Copy) (Library.2,-3)   */
Copy checkIn(Copy copyId)
{
    // SBgen: Action Remove Copy from borrows (3)
    Copy copy = null;
    int i, size = borrows.size();
    for (i=size-1; i>=0; i--) {
        Copy tmpVar = (Copy)borrows.elementAt(i);
        if (tmpVar.getId() == copyId) {
            copy = tmpVar;
            borrows.removeElementAt(i);

            // SBgen: Begin actions (3)
            // SBgen: End actions (3)
            break;
        }
    // SBgen: End Remove
    // SBgen: Return copy
    return copy;
}

/** @SBGen Generated Method (3), created by Li-
brary.checkIn(UID, Copy) (Library.2,-7)   */
void checkIn0(Copy copy)
{
    // SBgen: Action Add Copy to holds (7)
    holds.addElement(copy);

    // SBgen: End Add
}
```

```
class ClassGraph {Object traverse(Object o, TravSpec s, Visitor v);}
```

ClassGraph-objects are constructed from the Java programs (either in compiled or source form). TravSpec-objects (traversal specifications [L96]) encapsulate a domain-specific language for navigation through object structures and visitor-objects define what needs to be done on top of the traversal. The third observation of DJ is that traversal specifications are an ideal ingredient for Generic Programming lifting the level of genericity by an order of magnitude.

Generic Programming (GP) is about expressing algorithms with minimal assumptions about data abstractions, and vice versa, thus making them as interoperable as possible. A second goal of GP is to lift a concrete algorithm to as a general level as possible without losing efficiency. In GP, the algorithms are parameterized by iterators and data structures are connected to the algorithms using iterators as connectors. In Demeter [L96], algorithms are parameterized by traversal specifications and data structures are connected to the algorithms using traversal specifications as connectors. A good way to integrate GP and Demeter is to view traversal specifications as "superiterators" and to have a conversion function that translates a traversal into an iterator that gives access to collection methods (e.g., *find*, *select*, *findIf*) of some generic library such as the Java Generic Library. The goal is to reuse the useful work done in GP and not to reinvent many of the operations already provided by GP. Given a class graph *classGraph*, a traversal specification *sg* and an object *og*, we can create a container *TGC(classGraph,sg,og)* which can be used as argument for many generic algorithms such as *forEach*, *lexicographicalCompare*, *mismatch*, *accumulate*, *count*, *countIf*, *reject*, *select*, *adjacentFind*, *detect*, *every*, *find*, *findIf*, *some*, etc. The generic algorithms operate directly on *og* without creating a new collection object duplicating the information in *og*.

276

```
                        Figure 5: The checkIn method in DJ
void checkIn(UID uid, Copy copyId)
{
    // [library→users→uid].find(uid'current == uid)
    //    return (User users'current as user)
    Container LibraryToUserContainer = new TraversalGraph(
        Main.classGraph,
        new TravSpec("From Library to User").container(this));
    User user = Finding.findIf(
        LibraryToUserContainer, new FieldEquals("uid",uid));

    if (user == null)
        return;
    // [user→borrows→copyId].remove(copyId'current == copyId)
    //    return (Copy borrows'current as copy)
    Container UserToCopyContainer = new TraversalGraph(
        Main.classGraph,
        new TravSpec("From User through borrows to Copy").container(user));
    Copy copy = Finding.findIf(
        UserToCopyContainer, new FieldEquals("copyId",copyId));

    if (copy == null)
        return;
    Removing.remove(UserToCopyContainer,copy);
    // [copy→book→reserves].remove(reserves'index == 0)
    //    return (User reservers'current as reserver)
    Container CopyToUser = new TraversalGraph (…) ;

    Container UserToCopyHoldsCont = new TraversalGraph(
        Main.classGraph,
        new TravSpec("From User through holds to Copy").container(user));
    User reserver =
        (User)CopyToUser.remove(CopyToUser.elements());
    if (reserver != null) {
        //[reserver→holds].add(copy)
        UserToCopyHoldsCont.add(copy);

        //[reserver].notify(copy);
        reserver.notify(copy);
    }
}
```

In Figure 5, we demonstrate the DJ approach by rewriting the interaction schema for **checkIn** in DJ. Method **checkIn** is for class Library. We annotate the Java code with the interaction schema to show the correspondence between the two. FieldEquals extends UnaryPredicate from JGL.

The fourth and final observation of DJ is that sequence diagrams can be automatically generated from DJ code to facilitate the understanding of the code at various levels of details. In our current implementation, DJ does no generation or pre-processing of user code.

4 Related Work and Conclusions

This paper describes a new technique for object-oriented programming, which can lead to the production of much higher quality software, and to significantly quicker development. This technique uses *interaction schemata* and has been implemented in StructureBuilder, a development tool for Java Programming, from Tendril Software [SB]. DJ [DJ99] provides additional genericity and ease of maintenance but a slower implementation based on Java Reflection.

The origins of this technique are in a decade long research program at Northeastern University on Adaptive Programming called the Demeter Project [L96]. Like Demeter, StructureBuilder internally views the programming process in terms of navigating through the object model. This view of thinking of objects as a network and providing for their transportation is of what a large part of the programming task consists. Even though programmers don't always conceptualize their task in these terms, this is an essential aspect of virtually all programming. Indeed, object oriented programming is an attempt to organize this network of objects and to provide programmers with rules on how they might access the network.

Generic actions address two important problems in software development. First, tangling of object collaboration code. We have shown how object collaborations can be more easily expressed using generic actions. Each generic action describes a multi-object collaboration in a succinct way. A generic action cross-cuts the class structure and it is easy to read because all relevant information is part of the generic action and not spread out across several classes and tangled with lots of other code [HL95, K+97]. Second, maintaining UML interaction diagrams is tedious during evolution of the class structure. Generic actions are structure-shy and fairly robust under changing class structures.

Acknowledgements

We thank Josh Marshall and Doug Orleans for designing and implementing DJ and their feedback.

References

[BRJ96] Grady Booch, James Rumbaugh, and Ivan Jacobson. The Unified Modeling Language for Object-Oriented Development, July 1996.

[DLWV98] Wim De Pauw, David Lorenz, Mark Wegman, and John Vlissides. Execution Patterns in Object-Oriented Visualization. In *Proceedings of The Fourth Conference on Object-Oriented Technologies and Systems*, pages 219-234, Santa Fe, New Mexico, April 27-30, 1998. USENIX.

[GOF] Erich Gamma and Richard Helm and Ralph Johnson and John Vlissides, Design Patterns: Elements of Reusable Object-Oriented Software, Addison-Wesley, 1995

[HL95] Walter L. Hürsch and Cristina Videira Lopes. Separation of Concerns, College of Computer Science, Northeastern University, 1995, February, NU-CCS-95-03, Boston, MA

[J99] Daniel Jackson and Allison Waingold, Lightweight Extraction of Object Models from Bytecode, International Conference on Software Engineering, 1999, May, Los Angeles, CA, http://sdg.lcs.mit.edu/womble/

[JGL] Object Space, Inc., Java Generic Library, 1997, http://www.objectspace.com/developers/jgl/

[K+97] Gregor Kiczales, John Lamping, Anurag Mendhekar, Chris Maeda, Cristina Lopes, Jean-Marc Loingtier, and John Irwin. Aspect-Oriented Programming, ECOOP'97, 220-242, Springer Verlag, 1997.

[L96] Karl J. Lieberherr, Adaptive Object-Oriented Software: The Demeter Method, PWS Boston, 1996.

[LN95] D. B. Lange and Y. Nakamura. Interactive visualization of design patterns can help in framework understanding. In OOPSLA'95, pages 342-357, Austin, Texas. ACM SIGPLAN Notices 30(10) Oct. 1995.

[DJ99] Joshua Marshall, Doug Orleans, and Karl Lieberherr. DJ Home Page, Northeastern University, May, 1999. http://www.ccs.neu.edu/research/demeter/DJ/

[MS94] D. R. Musser and A. A. Stepanov, Algorithm-Oriented Generic Libraries, Software--Practice and Experience, 1994, July, 24(7)

[S98] Robon Schumacher. Products Hands-On Reviews: Rational Rose 98. DBMS Magazine 11(10), September 1998.

[SB] StructureBuilder 3.1 Tutorial. http://www.tendril.com/

Technical Papers

Teaching

Recording User Actions in a Smalltalk Programming Environment

Malcolm Macgregor, Pete Thomas, Mark Woodman
Computing Department, The Open University, Walton Hall, Milton Keynes,
England MK7 6AA
{m.d.macgregor, p.g.thomas, m.woodman}@open.ac.uk

Abstract

AESOP (An Electronic Student Observatory Project) is a system for recording, replaying and analysing user actions in LearningWorks, a Smalltalk programming environment. The project aims (i) to inform educators how best to effect object technology transfer by improving their teaching, (ii) to provide an apparatus for identifying problems neophytes experience while learning to program and (iii) to provide empirical evidence for improving the design of the programming environment. Initially AESOP is being targeted on a large-scale distance learning course enrolling 5,000 mature students per year. This paper describes the project and gives a flavour of the research questions of how neophytes learn programming concepts, in particular object concepts as exemplified by Smalltalk. The implementation of a selection of tools is described and sample data is also explained. Current project status is reviewed and many issues are raised concerning what sort of data to collect.

1   Introduction

A strategy for unobtrusive, mass observation of students learning software development has been developed for the course *M206 Computing: An Object-oriented Approach* [1] offered by the Open University (OU). The teaching of programming on M206 uses the OU LearningWorks Smalltalk environment [2] with its in-built HTML browser, simulations, and programming tools. It is an instantiation of the LearningWorks framework [3] produced in collaboration with Adele Goldberg. M206 students rely mainly on the course materials, with supplementary help from a tutor by phone and email. The AESOP project aims to improve teaching by gaining a better understanding of how beginners learn software.

OU LearningWorks consists of LearningBooks that provide microworlds and programming tools. AESOP's first task is to record the user's navigation through the LearningBooks, and their use of microworlds and software tools. Events deemed significant for observing how neophytes learn are recorded in a format amenable to replaying and analysis. This paper describes the pedagogic use of LearningWorks and how LearningBooks interact with the tools. Some early results are sketched, and problems with designing for instrumentation are raised.

2   Learning aims and objectives

After studying Smalltalk programming students should be able to: skilfully use the software involved; write correct code; show initiative in developing solutions to set problems; develop limited Smalltalk applications including graphical user interfaces (GUIs). The account of software systems is object-oriented and, to avoid learning misconceptions [6], very Smalltalk-oriented. The pedagogy [7] is highly practical, and painstaking, in its adherence to object-oriented concepts [8]. Within a few weeks students are expected to understand the notions of objects, behaviour, messages, methods, instance variables, state, classes, subclassing, polymorphism and inheritance, and how to use them in practical programming contexts.

0-7695-0278-4/99 $10.00 © 1999 IEEE

Smalltalk-80 was an important choice for the course: it was judged suitable for distance learning [9] and ideal for customising for learning-by-doing [10]. With multimedia fully deployed, we had the opportunity to innovate in the evaluation of the course [11]. The malleable nature of the LearningWorks Smalltalk environment has facilitated the development of the set of instrumenting classes and support tools that comprise AESOP.

3   Use of LearningWorks

OU LearningWorks is described in detail elsewhere [1, 2]. Here we describe the parts of the programming environment necessary to provide context for subsequent explanations. The environment offers a set of "LearningBooks", i.e. software modules of objects and classes that use a book metaphor. Each LearningBook is organised into sections, each section into pages. Each page is a Smalltalk application [12] which can be a Web-style HTML page, a programming tool, or a microworld. A page may be "detached" from its book. The first section always contains an HTML-browser page of practical exercises. Subsequent sections contain microworlds and programming tools.

One microworld – using instances of classes Frog, Toad and HoverFrog – is a touchstone for *all* object concepts. It is introduced in a simple version (Figure 1), to illustrate concepts like messages, state, behaviour, inheritance and polymorphism. As the student progresses, it evolves to a full-blown version (Figure 2) which integrates with all the programming tools. This microworld shows a view of amphibians whose behaviour and state are affected by messages from action and menu buttons. Thus in Figure 1, the instance of Frog called frog5 can be moved right by clicking the button labelled right. Code evaluation is first provided in an input field (Figure 1) and later in a more flexible workspace page (Figure 2).

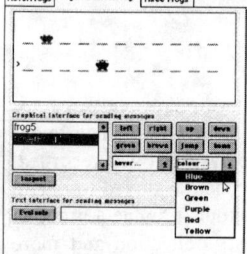
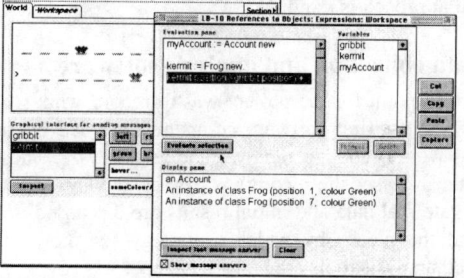

Figure 1: Amphibian world   **Figure 2: Amphibian world with Workspace in foreground**

Using increasingly sophisticated browsers [2] (Figure 3, 4) students learn how to define new messages, and the visual effect of any new behaviour can be immediately displayed.

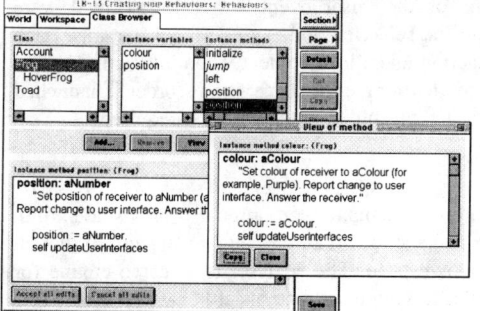
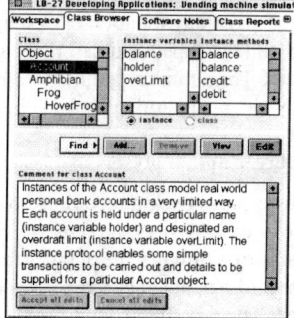

Figure 3: Simplest browser on four classes   **Figure 4: Full browser on all classes**

Text in each book contains Practicals, and Discussions (comments on the Practicals). A book is opened from a *launcher*, a metaphorical bookshelf (Figure 5), which shows the LearningBooks. Typically, a student works through the table of contents (Figure 6).

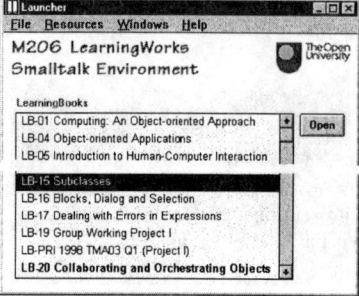

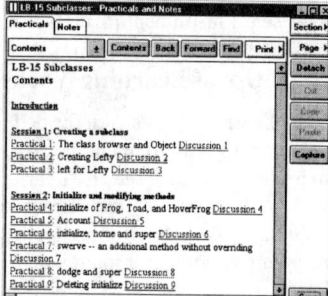

Figure 5: Launcher (bookshelf of LearningBooks)   Figure 6: Typical work structure

The identification of appropriate questions about how students learn object concepts is a significant research task. Some appropriate questions are:

(i)   Were this practical and its discussion adequate?
(ii) Did students attempt the practical and read the discussion?
(iii) Did they take too much time?
(iv) Do they realise when they have gone wrong? Do they recover?

Once appropriate questions have been prioritised, the required data and instrumentation have to be determined. Since the questions are likely to change as the project progresses, an incremental approach is required.

4 Data collection and analysis software

The starting point for the project was to record what students do during practical sessions. This identified the first software component needed by the project, a *recorder*. Two other components were needed: a *replayer* and an *analyser*. The former replays what was recorded, and the latter analyses the recordings in various ways. All three have been deployed to obtain and investigate real data and initial results are discussed in [5]. These tools provide a proof of concept and the means by which a strategy for more extensive data collection and more sophisticated analysis tools are being designed.

4.1 Recorder

This writes a file of text representations of the "user events" that we decided were important, e.g. page turns, button clicks, hyperlink selection and expression evaluations. Each user event is time stamped and describes an action taken by a student when interacting with a LearningBook. To minimise perturbation of the learning experience, the recorder is launched automatically when a LearningBook is opened (i.e. no student intervention is required).

4.2 Replayer and analyser

The replayer plays back a recording so that an investigator can observe what a student did. The replay can be as fast as the replayer can manage, or it can be "single stepped" so that an observer can move through the steps at their own pace. The analyser is a search engine for examining recordings. It enables the investigator to search for patterns of behaviour across sets of recordings. The recordings hold time information, so queries like, "how long did it take to do this task", can be asked. A wide variety of possible analyses have been identified, and several implemented, including:

Time Tool: attempts to distinguish the time that a student spends doing various activities. It identifies long pauses and flags them or filters them out.

Significant Event Trace Tool: This tool outputs a trace of significant event(s) with their time. A typical significant event is the evaluation of an expression in a workspace. This tool is particularly useful for determining what work a student does using his own initiative.

Patterns Tool: This tool enables the investigator to experiment, looking for patterns. It assumes that the investigator has identified a short *sequence* of events (not necessarily adjacent) that represent some meaningful learning or difficulty on the part of the student. The tool finds each occurrence of the sequence (if any exists). For example, students may be instructed to perform a sequence of activities such as reading a particular practical page, performing some evaluations, and then reading a specific discussion page. The tool identifies whether or not such a pattern was followed within a given recording.

5   Sample recording

In the current second pilot, around 80 students volunteered to use the recorder software. Students e-mail their recordings of LearningBook use to the AESOP team via their tutors. So far, the recordings have been used to prove and refine the recorder. Also, the recordings have highlighted errors in the basic teaching materials, and a wide variety of learning styles and misconceptions in students. For example, students can become confused by the simple syntax of keyword messages (those requiring arguments) and can be forgetful of class protocol. Clearly the course team were correct to devise and implement progressive disclosure [2], but the initial findings suggest the need for further automated assistance.

LearningBook 9, Practical 5 asks students to evaluate the syntactically incorrect expression series highlighted in Figure 7. (A period is missing after the first expression.) Note, the practicals page is left in the LearningBook, the amphibian world and workspace are detached.

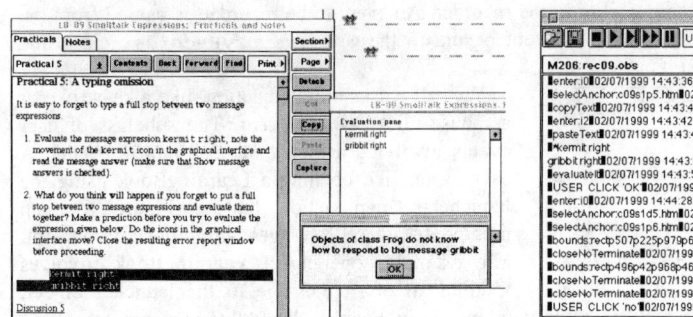

Figure 7 LearningBook 09, Practical 5   Figure 8 Replaying Practical 5

Figure 8 shows the replay tool with a recording of events a student has caused (numbers in parentheses are annotations for this commentary). The ■ symbol occurs in pairs that delimit the textual representation of events. Each closing ■ is followed by a time stamp. Line (1) indicates the student has copied the highlighted text in the practical (Figure 7). (2) shows that the workspace window has been made active. (3) records the pasting of the two lines. The * on line (4) shows that a student has entered the text. (4) and (5) indicate the selection which has been evaluated while (6) records the click of an 'evaluate selection' button.

The exercise deliberately asks students to execute incorrect code. The missing period results in `kermit right gribbit left` being evaluated, in which `gribbit` is determined to be a message to the result of `kermit right`. Thus, the evaluation causes an exception dialogue box to appear (Figure 7); this is dismissed by clicking on **OK** (7). (8) shows that the student has re-entered the window containing Practical 5. From here, it might be hoped the student would deduce that a period should be inserted after `kermit right`. Unfortunately, it appears this is not the case as line (9) shows that three seconds later the student proceeds via a hyperlink anchor (**c09s1d5**) to Discussion 5. An instructor might think the student would read this discussion, learn of their error, and attempt a correct evaluation. But no, within four seconds, shown in line (10), this student moved onto the next practical. This recording shows a typical study pattern for this particular student–a type of pattern that the analysis tools can locate.

6   Implementation architecture

Because our research project should minimise interference with student learning, we separated the AESOP classes from those of M206's LearningWorks environment [2]. We use a LearningWorks facility for loading classes on start-up: if anything goes wrong, it is trivial for a student to circumvent the loading of these classes. The loaded AESOP classes make all course-standard LearningBooks record their use. The following are the main classes:

`ObservatoryRecorder` – contains the functionality for recording user events.

`ObservatoryReplayer` – contains the functionality for replaying recorded user events, and an application to control the replaying

`ObservatoryAnalyser` – the core class for launching analyses.

Due to lack of space, we describe samples of recording instrumentation only.

6.1   Recording events in LearningWorks and VisualWorks

To produce recordings we instrument appropriate methods in the framework classes, especially the classes that implement LearningBooks, microworlds, and tools. Such classes are part of the Smalltalk environment. Instrumentation is minimised in framework classes by delegating recording responsibility to the recorder. An event to be recorded is passed from the (instrumented) object in which the event occurs to the `ObservatoryRecorder` class that initiates the recording (Figure 9).

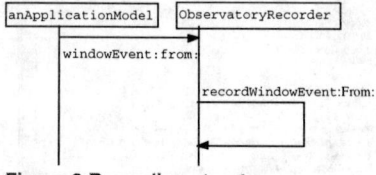

Figure 9 Recording structure

We call a user-initiated action, like a keystroke or a mouse click, a *user event*. The subclass of user events involving a mouse we call *mouse events*. A user event, like opening a LearningBook using the launchers **Open** action button (Figure 5), can precipitate several messages within the environment. For example, opening a LearningBook involves sending an `open` message to the launcher object, followed by messages which open the window, set its bounds, display its contents, tab to the first section in the LearningBook, and so on.

For each user event we do not record the myriad of messages it generates, we simply record one message that is isomorphic to the user event. We call this a *user message*. This message, on replaying, should generate the same behaviour in the LearningWorks environment as the original user event. Also, on analysis, the message (with its time stamp) should give us the information we need about the original user event.

VisualWorks provides a class, `ApplicationModel`, whose subclass instances manage an application's user interface and components. Goldberg *et al.*'s LearningWorks programming framework [3] provides a subclass, `LwinSystem`, as a model of a LearningBook. OU

LearningWorks specialises this as OULwinSystem. Hence, when an M206 LearningBook is opened a user interface is seen whose application model is an instance of OULwinSystem. One of the components of this application model is the window that contains it and, in turn, the window's main component is the application model.

A user moving a window is a user event that must be recorded. The Smalltalk system translates this user event into a Smalltalk event. In the following, when we speak of "an event" we can mean a user event, a Smalltalk event, an event recorded in a text file as a message, or an event (identical to the user event) that happens on replay. The meaning should be clear from the context. However, variable anEvent refers exclusively to a Smalltalk event object. The Smalltalk system forwards anEvent to the object representing the current window. The current window object relays anEvent to its application model by sending the message windowEvent: anEvent from: anApplicationWindow to the application model. To record a window event requires altering the method windowEvent:from: in the application model by adding one expression:

    ObservatoryRecorder recordWindowEvent:anEvent from:anApplicationWindow

The method recordWindowEvent:from: in ObservatoryRecorder can deal with different Smalltalk events. For instance, if a user moves or re-sizes a window, this causes a #bounds event to be generated (see recording in Figure 8), and the recording probe for dealing with #bounds events is:

    (key anEvent = #bounds)
        ifTrue: [self recordBounds: anEvent from:anApplicationWindow]...

The recordBounds:from: message results in a textual representation of an event being stored in a text file. For example, bounds:rectp507p225p979p644 window:i2 (Figure 8). p507p225p979p644 are the co-ordinates of the window's bounding rectangle and i2 is a reference used by the replayer object, indicating which window has been given new bounds. This is sufficient information for the replayer to play back this particular event.

Besides window events, there are also user interface events, such as a user clicking on the **Open** button of the LearningWorks launcher application (Figure 5) – the user event that causes a LearningBook to open – that must be recorded. Every ApplicationModel class has a postBuildWith: method, which is activated when the application model is opened in a window. It makes sense to send the recording message from the postBuildWith: method, because every subclass of ApplicationModel is sent a postBuildWith: message when it opens. As mentioned previously, OULwinSystem is the application model class that describes a LearningBook. So OULwinSystem's postBuildWith: method contains the line:

    ObservatoryRecorder recordBookOpening:self

This records a line like openUserVersion:false. There may be two versions of a book: an "original" and a "user" version that includes student changes. The occurrence of false in the above line tells us that the original version of the LearningBook was opened.

6.2   Dealing with spurious user messages

When opening a LearningBook an "openUserVersion:" message is recorded. But, unless measures are taken, a "bounds:" message is also recorded because bounds are set when a window opens. We cannot disallow the recording of bounds messages altogether because they can be user messages (e.g., representing "window drags"). To avoid recording a spurious user message, we need a way to distinguish between it and a true user message (even though both might be the same string of characters). One way would be to use a flag IsUserEvent (a class variable in the class ObservatoryRecorder) which becomes true when an input device is used and false when the user message has been recorded. Unfortunately this user event flag cannot be used, as we shall now show.

First, consider a situation where the `IsUserEvent` flag would work. When an "open LearningBook" event occurs in a window, the operating system passes it to the Smalltalk environment. The Smalltalk environment can be instrumented to set `IsUserEvent` to true on receiving such an event. As stated previously, an `openUserInterface:` user message records the fact of a book opening. `ObservatoryRecorder` could set `IsUserEvent` to false after the `openUserInterface:` message has been recorded. This would stop further recording until another mouse manipulation occurred.

Now consider a situation where the `IsUserEvent` flag would not work. When a window is dragged, you would think that `IsUserEvent` could be set to true, and a "bounds" message could be recorded, after which `IsUserEvent` could be set to false. But, on investigation, we found that mouse events occurring in the title bar of the window are not propagated into the Smalltalk environment as Smalltalk events. When the window is dragged "window damage" and "window move" events are passed directly into the Smalltalk environment from the operating system and appear, and act, in the Smalltalk environment exactly like Smalltalk events produced without user intervention. So, there is no way to set `IsUserEvent` to true, and so no way to record such an event as a user message.

To circumvent this "no user message" problem, we could record every Smalltalk event that happens due to a user event. For instance, a window drag cannot be flagged by the mouse event that causes it, but it is flagged by the Smalltalk events, which follow as side effects of the mouse event. The problem is that there may be so many of these events that replaying and analysis become onerous. Depending on operating system settings, the window may refresh continually meaning that there can be dozens of messages recorded for every drag event.

So we are left with not recording any "bounds" events if we use the user event flag mechanism, or too many if we just let all such events be recorded. To get round this, and other similar problems, we have to make special case provision. For instance, the recorder has been programmed to reduce all sequences of "bounds" messages to the final "bounds" message. This means we lose some user events–e.g. sequences of window movements. But, for our present interests, such details are not important.

6.3 Sample recording instrumentation

Here we sketch the instrumentation that resulted in lines (4) to (9) of the example described earlier (Figure 8). After the student selected and evaluated `kermit right gribbit right` the message `evaluateIt` was sent to the Workspace. Its method has been instrumented by two expressions (where the expression `source selection` returns the selected code):

```
ObservatoryRecorder record:'*', source selection.
ObservatoryRecorder record:'evaluate it'.
```

The exception `Dialog` object has been instrumented to record that the **OK** button has been clicked, thus:

```
ObservatoryRecorder record:'User CLICK ''OK'''
```

The `enter:i0` event occurs when the user clicks on the window containing the practicals. The recording is performed by the expression:

```
ObservatoryRecorder recordWindowEvent:anEvent from: anApplicationWindow
```

`ObservatoryRecorder` determines that anEvent is an "enter window" user event, and records the required user message.

The HTML viewer class `OUHTML` has been instrumented to record which hyperlink anchor is clicked by adding the following expression to the method `changedReference`,

```
ObservatoryRecorder record:'selectAnchor:', aPath
```

From these examples it can be seen that the code is specific to the methods being instrumented. It would be interesting to seek ways of refactoring the code to make it more general and easier to maintain [15]. Also, it can be seen that the recording software cuts across groups of functional components, so it becomes "tangled" up with the original software. This introduces numerous opportunities for programming error, makes version control difficult, and leads to code that is difficult to understand and evolve. It would be useful to express the recording aspect in the Smalltalk environment in a separate and natural form. This recording aspect could then be automatically combined with the objects requiring use of it using automatic tools. Such an approach is in-line with the exciting new research area of Aspect-Oriented Programming (AOP) [16], and we hope to use the fruits of this research to enhance our instrumentation.

6.4   Dialogue boxes

Dialogue boxes are a problem because they are implemented to expect input from a user, not from the replayer. In VisualWorks dialogue boxes are modal and therefore should not appear on replaying to avoid usurping the replayer's control. Because of the variety of dialogue boxes, and the variety of ways in which responses from them are handled, the present system does not deal with them automatically. Instead, the user of the replayer must check which dialogue button was clicked by the user by looking at the replayer's status box, and then click on the dialogue box in the same way. The automatic handling of dialogue box manipulations will be a useful addition to the next version of the system.

7   Future work: preparing for mass observation

Before the AESOP system can be deployed on a large scale, further tools are needed, and analysis of the pilot results is needed to clarify research questions and further instrumentation.

7.1   Proposed tools

Comparison Tool: The aim is to build a tool to compare what a student does with what they have been asked to do. This is difficult because there is ample scope for students to do additional work or simply experiment. Some instructions are not specific enough for a simple search to work. As a first step, we intend to search a recording for hyperlink usage and hence determine which pages have been visited. Given the normal collection of introduction, practical and discussion hyperlinks in each LearningBook, it will be easy to list all those pages visited and compare them with the pages provided by the LearningBook.

The idea of comparing an actual recording with an "ideal" recording is being actively pursued. In the ideal recording we are flagging methods and code evaluations that require students to use their initiative.

Concept Tracking Tool: Somewhat ambitious, this tool is to have built into it lists of the significant concepts being taught, and will then examine student LearningBooks to record the frequency of errors associated with the concepts. Discovering whether the errors decrease over time will be important. The evaluations in workspaces and methods created are likely to be the significant sources of such data.

7.2   Further research questions

Achieving a State: The outcome of particular practical exercises is often determined by the achievement of some state. Recording the changes to the "values" of variables (i.e. object references) which describe the state of a LearningBook should enable us to determine when it was in a state that the student had been asked to achieve. This will provide a mechanism for comparing what the student is asked to do with what the student actually does. In many cases, we believe that the sequence in which actions occur does not matter.

Given that an event causes a change of overall state, our recordings already reflect changes. Indeed, when a recording is replayed, the LearningWorks environment changes state but we do not (currently) have automatic access to the variables which describe that state. By saving, as part of a recording, the values of selected variables (which still have to be determined) will enable an analysis tool to search for specific states. The recorded state would be the set of values of all selected variables, but we might only be looking for a pattern that is characterised by a subset of those variables.

Longitudinal Data: We wish to examine data from a succession of LearningBooks to see how a given concept is used as time progresses. If, for example, a concept is introduced in one LearningBook, it should be possible to see that concept being used in later LearningBooks. If that concept is used incorrectly we should observe errors – and perhaps be able to deduce that the error was made because a concept was not picked up at an earlier stage.

If we see patterns of behaviour that are common to many students, it will be possible to say something useful: probably that the teaching of that concept is flawed and must be changed. Whilst this may be useful information to the course team it is not answering the central question of how students learn. It could be much more informative to examine what the student does immediately after being confronted by an error message. At present the only way to detect student's understanding of concepts is to look at practicals where they have had to think out answers for themselves, rather than just following a "monkey-see monkey-do" process. We are actively considering whether to include more structured self-tests in the LearningBooks.

Completeness of Answers: LearningBooks assume that students will read the accompanying printed texts but the recordings do not show what the student does or how long the student spends doing it. It may be the case that students continually refer to the accompanying texts in order to clarify concepts whilst tackling the practical. It may be worthwhile, therefore, supplying electronic copies of printed texts so that, when performing the practical, the student can refer to the computer-based text. We could then record when a student accesses particular information and begin to address the issue of whether a substantial gap between recorded events represents time when the student is interacting with other materials or taking a break.

Note Taking: A dilemma the project faces is the degree to which we can perturb students study. If we could encourage students to write down more about what they are doing and learning, say using the Notes pages, we might have additional useful data to access automatically, for example, answers to self-tests. We are investigating the use of audio recordings for this purpose.

8   Conclusion

The aim of the electronic student observatory project is to study the way students learn software concepts, particularly those of object technology and Smalltalk. The subjects of the study are taking the large-scale distance learning course M206, *Computing: An Object-oriented Approach*, from the Open University. Current work is focusing on the identification of research questions about learning and the refinement of instrumentation and analysis software. A significant constraint is that the collection of data should be unobtrusive, for both ethical and data quality reasons.

The project depends on the automatic recording, replay and analysis of data collected from neophyte student-programmers while they use the OU LearningWorks programming environment. The project concentrates on electronically based, largely quantitative studies that can be supplemented by other evaluations [11]. The AESOP approach allows investigators to re-construct the processes students use when programming for the investigation of concept acquisition and change, the analysis of factors affecting performance, the identification of points of difficulty or misconception, and so on.

Here we have given a flavour of the questions we are trying to specify and answer concerning how neophytes learn object concepts. We have described the implementation of a selection of the AESOP tools and explained sample data. There remain many technical problems to overcome but we believe we have identified the main ones and are confident that we have a robust recorder and useful replayer, and some basic analysis tools.

Early results, validated by conventional course assessment, suggest that general use of LearningWorks in the early part of the course is as intended, though several problems were identified in teaching and in our tools. During 1999 we are concentrating on determining whether we have identified appropriate questions and have instrumentation in place for the more complex concepts taught. When deployed to the mass of M206 students, the observatory will provide a rare, if not unique, view of student learning.

Acknowledgements
We would like to thank Marian Petre of the Open University, who largely initiated the project and our colleagues on the M206 course team. We also thank Mike Martin of the University of Denver for his contributions whilst on sabbatical at the Open University.

References
1. Woodman, M. Griffiths, R., Macgregor, M., Holland, S., and Robinson, H., "Separable UI Architectures in Teaching Object Technology", TOOLS USA 1999 (this conference).
2. Woodman, M. Griffiths, R., Macgregor, M., Holland, S., and Robinson, H., "Exploiting Smalltalk Modules In A Customisable Programming Environment", *Proceedings of ICSE 21, International Conference on Software Engineering*, Los Angeles, May 1999.
3. Goldberg, A., Abell, S., and Leibs, D. (1997) "The LearningWorks Delivery and Development Framework", *Communications of the ACM*, 40(10): 78–81.
4. Goldberg, A., and Robson, D. (1983) *Smalltalk-80: The Language and its Implementation*. Addison-Wesley Reading, MA.
5. Thomas, P.G., Martin, M., and Macgregor, M. (1998) *"AESOP - An Electronic Student Observatory Project"* Frontiers in Education 98, Phoenix, USA, November 1998.
6. Holland, S., Griffiths, R., and Woodman, M. (1997) "Avoiding Object Misconceptions", *Proceedings of the 28th SIGCSE Technical Symposium on Computer Science Education*, San Jose, February 1997.
7. Woodman, M. and Holland, S. "From Software User To Software Author: An Initial Pedagogy For Introductory Object-Oriented Computing", *Proceedings SIGCSE/SIGCUE '96*, Barcelona, Spain, June 1996.
8. Cook, S. (1994) "Analysis, Design, programming: What's the Difference", in A.J. O'Callaghan and M. Leigh (eds.) *Object Technology Transfer*, Alfred Waller, Henley-on-Thames.
9. Woodman, M. and Griffiths, R. (1996) "Programming Language Choice for Distance Computing", in M. Woodman (ed.), *Programming Language Choice,* International Thomson Computer Press, London.
10. Goldberg, A. and Ross, J. (1981) Is the Smalltalk-80 System for Children? *Byte*, **6**, No. 8, August 1981.
11. Woodman, M. and Taylor, J. (1999) "Evaluating A Redefinition Of Computing", submitted to *Journal of Computers in Mathematics and Science Teaching*
12. Sumner, T. and Taylor, J. (1998) "New Media, New Practices: Experiences in Open Learning Course Design". *Proceedings CHI '98*, pp. 432–439, Los Angeles.
13. Howard, T. (1995) *The Smalltalk Developer's Guide to VisualWorks*, SIGS Books, New York.
14. Cook, S. and Daniels, J., (1994) *Designing Object Systems*, Prentice Hall International, Hemel Hempstead.
15. Roberts D., Brant J., Johnson, R.E. (1997) "A Refactoring Tool for Smalltalk", *Theory and Practice of Object Systems*, 3(4): 253–263.
16. Lopes, V.L. and Kiczales, G. "Recent Developments in AspectJ", *Proceedings of the European Conference on Object-Oriented Programming (ECOOP)*, Twente, Netherlands, June 1998.

Separable UI Architectures in Teaching Object Technology

Rob Griffiths, Mark Woodman, Simon Holland, Malcolm Macgregor, Hugh Robinson
Computing Department, The Open University, Walton Hall,
Milton Keynes, England MK7 6AA
tel: +44 1908 274066
email: r.w.griffiths, m.woodman, s.holland, m.d.macgregor, h.m.robinson@open.ac.uk

Abstract

This paper concerns the critical role of separable user interface design in teaching object-oriented systems. M206 "Computing: An Object-oriented Approach" is a large-scale university-level introduction to software development designed from scratch for distance learning, using an objects-first approach with Smalltalk. The course is degree-level, counting as one sixth of a degree, and is being offered in the UK, Western Europe and Singapore. To address the needs of industry we have developed a radical syllabus that adheres to the principle of designing complex systems by separating view and model, and have developed a programming and learning environment to support these ideas. In the paper we examine how separable user interface architectures have guided our teaching of object technology and the design of powerful microworlds that are both usable and extendible by neophytes. The course and relevant teaching with software is outlined and the technical design and pedagogic use of the microworlds and GUI builder tool are described.

1 Introduction

The Open University (OU) is the UK's largest university and its courses are offered almost exclusively in the distance mode. Since it was established in 1969 more than two million people from the UK, Europe and world-wide have studied with the OU. After four years of development, the OU has launched its flagship course *Computing: An Object-oriented Approach* (M206). For those in our degree programme the course is worth one sixth of a degree and introduces computing to thousands of people per year and radically recasts it for others. Currently M206 is enrolling over 5,000 students per year in the UK and an additional 600 are taking the course at the Singapore Institute of Management. In late 1999, the course will become available in the USA.

The course is not just about object-oriented programming, it also includes analysis and design, loosely centred around the CRC approach of Wirfs-Brock *et al.* [1] but with a flavour of the more formal treatment of associations given by Cook and Daniels [2], and Human–Computer Interaction, especially the separation of domain model and user interface classes which we make central to our pedagogy. Syllabus and multimedia details are on the Web (at http://www-cs.open.ac.uk/~m206/). The main course objectives are that, after successfully studying the course, students should, inter alia:

❑ have obtained practical, generally applicable skills in using software, e.g. programming, telecommunications and multimedia software;

❑ have sufficient knowledge of the object-oriented paradigm to analyse software artefacts and problems in terms of it, to sketch the design of systems, and to make design choices, and to complete or extend an application;

❑ be capable of developing small applications composed of separable user interfaces and domain models.

After much debate [3] we decided on an "objects-first" approach to computing and to adopt a pure object-oriented language for the course, thereby avoiding the confusion and misconceptions that can arise when teaching a hybrid language. This was especially important as the course is designed for the distance learning mode where individual practical help is not immediately at hand. The programming language which best suited our purpose was Smalltalk-80 [4, 5]. For us its primary benefits were that the language is based on just a few concepts and, importantly, its programming environments have the following properties:

❑ they are simple embodiments of object technology;
❑ they lend themselves to tailoring;
❑ all aspects of the system can be explored interactively and reflectively;
❑ they are suitable environments in which to produce student-alterable microworlds.

The curriculum is designed for students planning to major in computing, and also to be fully comprehensible to students planning to major in other subjects. This particular requirement, posed a number of problems. In order to address these problems, we developed a new programming environment that integrates the following elements: a purpose-designed variant of the MVC graphical user interface architecture, a specially designed GUI builder, a set of custom-built programming tools, and a series of educational microworlds. Our programming environment is designed to progressively reveal its more powerful and complex features as the course unfolds. It initially appears to be extremely simple, but by the end of the course it is comparable in power to an industrial-strength programming environment, which enables our students to develop non-trivial applications with fully separable graphical user interfaces. Moreover, the introductory microworlds are designed with similar properties of progressive disclosure: unlike many other simulations, the microworlds progressively allow students to control, modify (e.g. add new behaviour or state), and extend them (e.g. by subclassing).

2 Rationale for Learningworks

The requirement that the course be accessible to non computer science majors led us to the conclusion that the available professional Smalltalk environments were too complicated for real beginners. We needed an environment that would make the experience of beginning students as worry-free as possible. For example:

❑ Some form of simple switching between applications or text windows to attend to the difficulties of window navigation for people with little sophistication in this area.
❑ A range of parameterised browsers to avoid the paralysis felt by many people when confronted by a dauntingly large class library, and who mistakenly think they need to understand it all before proceeding.
❑ Simple and helpful evaluation and inspection facilities that would improve upon the ways in which Smalltalk environments provide transcript and workspace windows.

We concluded that we would have to develop our own environment. However, shortly after embarking on our own development we established a collaboration with the Smalltalk pioneer Adele Goldberg and her colleagues on an object-oriented framework for learning environments called LearningWorks [6]. LearningWorks allows a Smalltalk environment to be used as a vehicle for interactive courseware and programmers to specialise it to produce their own customised system. As far as learners are concerned LearningWorks offers a set of "LearningBooks", which are software modules that are presented to the user as a book metaphor: a LearningBook is organised into sections, and sections into pages, each page being an arbitrary application. And, like in a loose-leaf binder, a page may be "detached" from its book and left on the desktop, allowing the user to continue to view a page from one section, having moved to another. LearningWorks, also provides a class and method scoping mechanism for LearningBooks called the "vision".

This framework proved ideal for our pedagogy, as we were able to write our own microworlds and programming tools as pages for LearningBooks, furthermore the vision mechanism enabled our browsers to progressively reveal more of the class library as the student worked through the LearningBooks. So initially we can present our students with LearningBooks that appear to be extremely simple programming environments, where very few classes are made visible, and within these very little visible implementation code. By the end of the course however we can present LearningBooks which are comparable in power to industrial-strength programming environments[7].

We now review our use of two microworlds which are designed to fit the separate user interface architecture strategy: they adhere to it and by doing so enable students to explore them simply and effectively.

3   Microworlds as Filtered Views

Smalltalk is inextricably linked with simulation [8] therefore we were culturally well disposed to introduce simulations into our interactive learning environment in the form of microworlds. One in particular was used as a touchstone for reasoning about object concepts – an amphibian microworld that models the behaviour of instances of classes Frog and Toad and of a subclass of Frog, HoverFrog. The simulation has been devised to expose all object concepts, starting with the simplest: initially the simulation shows objects of the classes Frog and Toad which have identical state attributes – position and colour – and identical message protocols, such as green, brown, home, right and left, which respectively set the receiving object's colour to green, and brown, and change its position to the "home" position and move left and right. Students select any of the objects in the microworld from a regular scrolling list and use the GUI widgets to send the corresponding messages. This simple user interface not only allows message sending to be visualised, it allows apparently advanced notions such as polymorphism to be demonstrated. For example, when a frog is selected and the **home** button is clicked (resulting in the message home being sent) the receiving frog moves to the leftmost position; but, if a toad is selected, and so receives the message home, it moves to the *rightmost* position – the "home" position for toads.

Right from the beginning of the course we introduce our students to the notion of domain models and separable user interfaces. An innovation of LearningWorks we used heavily to sustain this idea is the provision of *page-local* and *section-local* variables, implemented in page and section dictionaries respectively. In practice the latter are the most useful. For example, any objects of any class created in a Workspace page and assigned to section-local variables are accessible by all pages in that same section. Therefore, to facilitate the visualisation of separable user interfaces, assignment, object creation and disposal, our amphibian microworld was built not as an arbitrary application, but, in effect, as a *filtered* graphical view of the section variable dictionary. This graphical view of the section dictionary is filtered in the sense that it only displays objects of certain classes of initial interest (e.g. frogs, toads, hoverfrogs). The result of this design decision is that simply creating an object of the relevant class in the Workspace page and assigning it to a section variable will cause its graphical representation to appear in the microworld automatically.

Figure 1 shows a LearningBook which is open at the Amphibian World page. Overlaid, next to it is a Workspace page that has been detached from the same section of the book, i.e. placed on the desktop. The scrollable list to the top, right of the workspace is a list of local variables: gribbit, kermit and myAccount. The variable myAccount is currently referencing an `Account` object and therefore the amphibian world will not display it; however, the microworld is displaying the `Frog` objects referenced by `kermit` and `gribbit`. This demonstrates that a separable interface can, and should, determine which elements of the domain model to display, i.e. those it is concerned with. So a workspace shows all variables, but an amphibian world shows only representations of amphibians. Students can send messages to these amphibian objects either by clicking buttons on the amphibian World page, or by textually sending messages to amphibian objects using Smalltalk in the Workspace page. In either case the effect of any state-changing messages, such as `right`, `left` or `colour:`, will be reflected in the amphibian world.

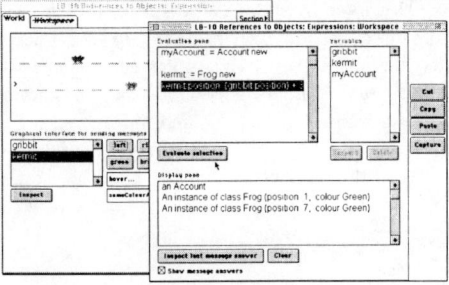

Figure1.

This combination of microworld and Workspace provides a powerful visual aid in the teaching of reference semantics and assignment and in particular helps our students avoid a number of misconceptions [9] such as:

❑ only one variable can reference to a given object at a given time;

❑ once a variable references a given object, it will always reference that object;

❑ a variable that refers to an object uniquely specifies it for all time;

❑ if you have two different variables, they must refer to two different objects.

For example if a student evaluates the assignment expression `gribbit := kermit`, the `Frog` object previously referenced by `gribbit` will have no remaining references to it, and the automatic garbage collection of that object will be graphically dramatised in the immediate disappearance from the microworld of its graphical representation. The fact that `gribbit` and `kermit` now reference the same object can also be graphically demonstrated as state changing messages to the sole remaining frog object can be sent via `kermit` or `gribbit`. Students quickly become proficient in this style of microworld manipulation and programming and our account of how user interfaces are implemented and separated from domain models is a crucial part of our pedagogy. Furthermore, due to the separable interface discipline, all of the relevant model code can be inspected, modified and understood by students without them being distracted by the interface code. Eventually they are able to construct new kinds of objects from the ground up and – provided they are subclassed from a displayable object and no new state added – the objects, their state and their behaviours will all automatically be displayed in the microworlds, without students having to pay any attention to explicit graphical interface programming.

As the course progresses students are introduced to other microworlds, for example a microworld simulating an air traffic control system. Figure 2 shows two pages: an air traffic control microworld (detached from the book) and a Workspace, where issues of design and safety-critical software development are explored. The microworld is a separable interface that graphically represents the three queues of plane objects that comprise the domain model. Again, the separation between interface and domain model allows us to easily introduce several interfaces without interfering with the model – in this case it is the

Workspace which again acts as another interface to the domain model. This teaches students (by example rather than preaching) that the same user interface can be used with several different domain models. In our teaching we discuss the necessary behaviour for these queues and discussion leads students to suppose that a subset of the OrderedCollection protocol would provide the necessary behaviour. Hence initially the queues are instantiated as OrderedCollection objects. The queues are referenced by section local instance variables so students can send messages to them from the user interface or from the Workspace. When these queues are manipulated from the microworld, planes can be landed safely as the GUI only sends the agreed subset of the OrderedCollection protocol to the queues. However from the Workspace students are free to send any of the messages from the OrderedCollection protocol to the queues, sometimes with dramatic results. For example sending at:put: messages to a queue will cause planes to be lost from the system. Once they realise how easily the queue abstraction can be broken we can teach them various strategies for designing and implementing a bespoke Queue class. Once they have implemented this new class they can trivially instantiate the queues in the microworld as objects of this new class.

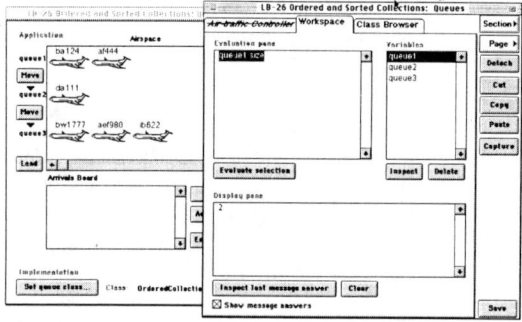

Figure 2.

4 Simplifying MVC

For the notion of separable user interface architectures to mean anything to novices, they have to be able make concrete the abstract by eventually implementing their own user interfaces using a GUI builder, and to write all of the domain model and user interface code necessary to make these interfaces work. The most general goal of this part of our pedagogy was that students should understand, in detail, the advantages of allowing user interface and domain model development to be pursued independently. Specifically, our students should be able to:

❑ create their own user interfaces, and connect them to domain models, thus creating applications.

❑ understand and use the broadcast dependency mechanism and the messages involved;

❑ alter existing user interfaces built with a GUI builder;

❑ give a model multiple user interfaces simultaneously;

❑ reconnect a user interface to different domain models (i.e. to a different instance, or, to an instance of a different class where appropriate).

One of the earliest and most developed architectures in Smalltalk is Model/View/Controller (MVC) [10]. MVC is an approach to application development that divides the application into the information of interest (model), the visual representation of that information (view), and the handling of user input (controller).

In order to allow various kinds of flexibility, the VisualWorks instantiation of MVC introduces a kind of "impedance matcher" or buffer class whose instances stand between the model and the various widgets. This class is called ApplicationModel. In effect, application models absorb the messiness of practical linking between model and user interface widgets, and translate model-accessing messages from the widgets into the domain-specific protocol of the model in question. The cost of this approach is that a lot of knowledge about both domain model and user interface needs to be built into the application model by the programmer. Indeed, the application model may end up mirroring and hence duplicating much of the domain model. This architecture works very well for professional programmers. It allows tremendous flexibility in the fine detail of how widgets can be used, and it keeps user interface logic out of domain code. However, even for experienced programmers, using the MVC mechanism [11] can be very daunting. For any given application there are multiple models, views and controllers. For example, the "model" for even a small application will consist of the application model, and possibly multiple models from the domain model. The user interface will consist of many views (the graphical representation of widgets). Each widget will be a dependent of some different aspect of the application model rather than the whole user interface simply being a dependent of some domain object. Therefore, for the beginner, this complexity tends to obscure the essential simplicity of the separable user interface idea.

In a degree course aimed principally at first-time computing students, the complexity of the MVC architecture behind the VisualWorks GUI builder poses a problem that is not mitigated by the friendly and simplifying front end of LearningWorks, even with our principle of progressive disclosure [7]. We did not want students merely to learn to use a GUI builder. We wanted them to understand and to work with separable user interfaces, to understand the architecture that makes them possible. To this end we devised a simplified version of MVC which we term MUI, Model–User Interface. MUI, is an architecture that allows beginners to easily create GUI applications by binding domain objects (models) to instances of user interface classes that they create using a simple GUI building tool.

Before we introduce the MUI architecture to our students, they are taught about the broadcast dependency mechanism from which the *Observer* pattern is abstracted [12, 13]. Using this mechanism one object (the observer) is made a dependent of another object (the observed). They learn that to notify an observer object of any state changes the observed must include self changed message expressions in its state-changing methods. The model's only responsibility is to notify its dependents when its state changes. In that way the model need not take any account of what its dependents are, or indeed whether it has any. The responsibility is on any user interface components to respond appropriately to such notifications, and, where appropriate, to query the model about its current state so that they can update themselves suitably.

Our design goal for MUI was that an arbitrary model could be bound to an arbitrary user interface via this broadcast dependency mechanism. In other words, we wanted an architecture in which a user interface class could be made a direct dependent of a model rather than the individual widgets being dependent on value models in an application model as is the case with the VisualWorks instantiation of MVC. Furthermore, as long as the model provided the protocol expected by the widgets in the user interface it should simply work without any further "glue" code being written by the user. In fact, the only user interface related code that appears in the model is the self changed expression mentioned above so that the user interface can be alerted via the broadcast dependency mechanism that the state of the model has changed.

5 Building Simple GUIs

The OpenGUI tool appears as a page in a LearningBook (see Figure 3). It looks like a fairly standard (if very simple) tool for laying out interface widgets and giving them property values. OpenGUI supports the following widgets: label, divider, group box, action button, check box, radio button, slider, text editor, input field and list box. We considered various ways of implementing menu buttons and other more complex widgets, but inevitably interface code ends up in the model and so they were rejected.

The amphibian microworld displays graphical representations of Frog objects. Their protocol includes the messages position and position:, which are used to get and set the position instance variable representing a frog's position attribute. With this information students can construct an alternative user interface to control instances of the Frog class.

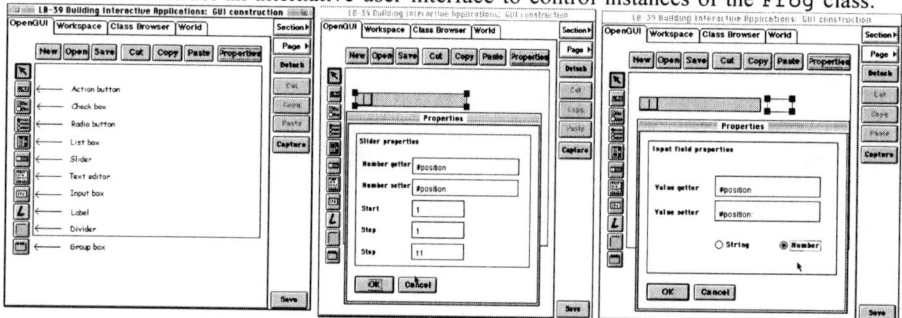

Figure 3.   Figure 4.   Figure 5.

In the OpenGUI page the student selects the slider drawing tool and draws the slider to the required size on the canvas. With the drawn slider still selected the user clicks on the **Properties** button to open a dialogue box which will allow the properties of the slider to be set. (See Figure 4.) As sliders can only work with numerical information the user is asked to supply the names of messages that will get and set a numerical instance variable in the prospective model (in this case a frog). Note that in the VisualWorks GUI builder the user would be asked to supply the name of a value model in the application model, rather than a message from the domain model's protocol. Other values requested are highest and lowest values that the slider can set in the model using the set message, and the size of the increments the slider can make. To complement the slider an input box can be added to the canvas as in Figure 5. Note again that the user supplies get and set messages from the model's protocol rather than the name of a value model in the application model. As we mentioned earlier some of our widgets are much simpler than the equivalent VisualWorks widgets. As you can see in Figure 5 the OpenGUI input field supports only two types – number and string. Also input fields are always editable. To make another property "editable" would be trivial to implement but this was resisted in the cause of simplicity.

We have incorporated extensive error checking into both OpenGUI and the MUI mechanism. When saving the properties of a widget, OpenGUI ensures:

❑ that none of the fields in the properties dialogue box are blank;
❑ that any getter is a legal unary selector;
❑ that any setter is a legal single keyword selector.

Before saving the user interface as a class, OpenGUI checks that:

❑ the user interface is complete and consistent and the user is warned if they are using the same selector in more than one way in the same user interface;
❑ the class is either a new class or an existing student-authored user interface class.

Figure 6.

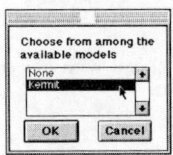

Figure 7.

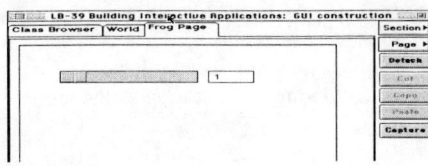

Figure 8.

The user interface class is then saved as a subclass of `OUGUIAbstractInterface`, itself a subclass of `ApplicationModel` in VisualWorks. Such a user interface class consists of a single class method, `windowSpec`, which specifies how the user interface is to be drawn. When an instance of the user interface class is opened, methods in the superclass `OUGUIAbstractInterface` (which hides the detail of implementation) dynamically create all the value models needed to support the MVC architecture that underpins MUI.

Attaching an instance of this new interface to a suitable model is achieved through the LearningBook's **Page** menu button. Selecting the **Add...** option opens up scrollable list of available user interface classes (Figure 6). After selecting the desired user interface class the neophyte programmer is then prompted to select an appropriate model from the section dictionary (Figure 7). This simple reference to a suitable model must have previously been established in the workspace in the same section. An instance of the user interface is then created and inserted as the current page in the LearningBook (Figure 8).

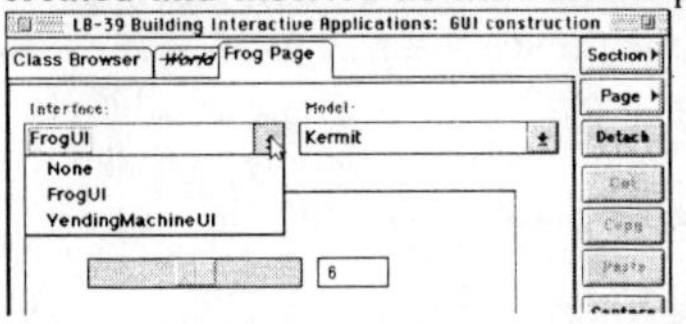

Figure 9. 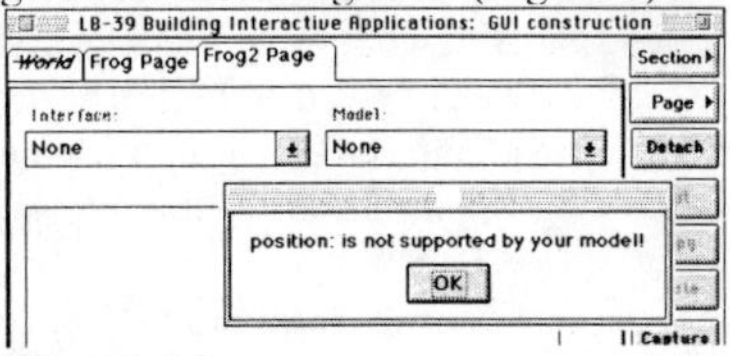   Figure 10.

Exceptions and errors involving user interface classes and models in VisualWorks are next to impossible for the neophyte programmer to debug or reason about because of the huge number of complex classes involved. With the MUI architecture, students do not need to see MUI-specific classes or VisualWorks runtime GUI code to understand any errors associated with binding an instance of a user interface class with a model – problems are caught and reported in terms of objects and code created directly by the student. Indeed, to guarantee that a contract between a user interface and a model can be properly established, before a user interface is inserted as the current page in a LearningBook, the MUI behaviour inherited by the particular user interface first carries out extensive checks on the model's protocol and if the right methods are not present in the model, or if they return a message reply of the wrong type, details are reported and a test page is inserted into the LearningBook (see Figure 9). From this page the user can select other pairs of local variables and interface classes. In Figure 10, the user has attempted to bind an instance of the `FrogUI` class to a model which is of class `Account` rather than of class `Frog` – `Account` objects do not understand the message `position:`.

Similarly, once a user interface is opened, MUI detects the following errors:
- ❑ that the get or set methods it needs to use are no longer understood by the model (i.e. the user has deleted the method since the interface was opened);
- ❑ the return value of a getter or the argument of a setter does not match the appropriate type (because the user has edited the method since the user interface was opened);
- ❑ that a method in the model causes an exception.

These errors are reported to the user and again a test page is substituted for the current user interface page. Finally, if the method called by a widget results in an infinite loop and the user presses break, they are told which method was probably in the infinite loop and a safe recovery is made.

A model from the section dictionary can be associated with any number of user interfaces pages within the same section as the model.

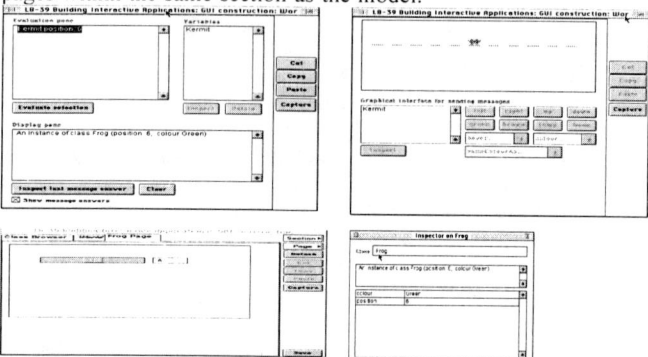

Figure 11.

By detaching a Workspace and an amphibian world from the same section of the LearningBook, and placing them side by side with the new user interface page, students can view the effect of sending state-changing messages to the model from a Workspace, the state changes will of course be reflected in both user interfaces. Similarly, changing the state of the model from either user interface will be reflected in the other user interface and can be confirmed by inspecting the model from the Workspace. Thus reinforcing the notion of separable user interfaces. See Figure 11.

At any time the user can choose **Test mode** from the **Page** menu button to associate a new model (from the section dictionary) with the page's user interface (see Figure 9). This new model need not be of the same class as the previous model, the only proviso is that it understands the required protocol and that the appropriate setter methods include the `self changed` message expression.

There are some significant restrictions in the current implementation of OpenGUI. For instance, the requirement that a local variable be used to link a user interface to a model means that a collection of models cannot be linked to collection of user interface instances. And, of course OpenGUI is much simpler than a commercial GUI builder, in that it supports fewer widgets, and it assumes that a user interface can only deal with one model at a time. However, it is conceptually straightforward and simple for beginners to use. In effect, we have traded off some loss of flexibility with a tool that allows the unconfident to experiment concretely with all of the key concepts of separable interface architectures.

6   Conclusion

Industrial-strength pure-object programming environments can be intimidating to the complete beginner, particularly in a distance education context or in other situations where individual practical help is not immediately always at hand. We have described how we have addressed this problem by designing, implementing, and delivering to students a programming environment that adheres to two major principles. First, it provides progressive disclosure in a carefully tailored way. This allows, for example, given classes and methods to be hidden initially, and unsafe message expressions to be carefully filtered in the early stages, but with the system ultimately unfolding to a fully permissive industrial strength environment. Second, it adheres to the principle of separable user interfaces, which addresses another systemic problem relating to graphical simulations.

Graphical simulations are a good vehicle for promoting the approach outlined above. However, there have historically been practical problems in allowing beginning students to explore, modify, and create from scratch their own graphical simulations in Smalltalk. The standard separable interface architecture known as MVC is too complicated for beginning students to understand in their early stages of learning. One historical response to this problem has been to forfeit the principle of keeping the user interface separate from the model, and to allow user interface code to mix with the model code. In exchange for short term simplicity, this approach introduces longer term problems such as loss of modularity, loss of flexibility, unnecessary coupling and bad design and coding habits. Another possible approach is to provide students with a GUI builder, but to pass over in silence how this is linked to the model, and to leave the nature of the connection between the visible parts of the simulation and the underlying model perceived as essentially magical. We have described in detail our solution to this impasse. Namely, we have designed, implemented, and delivered to students a highly error-protected, dynamic and simplified variant of MVC called MUI that illustrates all of the key principles of separable user interfaces, yet is simple enough for beginning students to understand in great detail. This allows students to explore and modify existing simulations and their user interfaces, and to create their own graphical simulations, applying complete modularity to user interface and model.

More generally, we have deployed a wide range of technologies to support learners grappling with fundamental concepts of object technology in a way that is appropriate to the distance mode. We have devised a simple, consistent pedagogy and constructed a programming and learning environment to match the pedagogy, using LearningBooks to package work, systems and tools. We have shown how, using LearningWorks, novices can progress from using and extending systems through "game play" microworlds, to designing and implementing their own applications with separable user interfaces.

References

[1] Wirfs-Brock, R., Wilkerson, B. and Wiener, L. *Designing Object-oriented Software*, Prentice Hall, Englewood Cliffs, NJ, 1990.

[2] Cook, S. and Daniels, J., *Designing Object Systems*, Prentice Hall Int., Hemel Hempstead, 1994.

[3] Woodman, M., Holland S. and Price, B., Pervasiveness of a Programming Paradigm: Questions Concerning an Object-oriented Approach, *Proceedings CS Education*, Dublin, 1994.

[4] Goldberg, A. and Robson, D. *Smalltalk-80: The Language and its Implementation*. Addison-Wesley Reading, MA, 1983.

[5] Woodman, M. and Griffiths, R., Programming Language Choice for Distance Computing, in M. Woodman (ed.), *Programming Language Choice*, Int. Thomson Computer Press, London, 1996.

[6] Goldberg, A., Abell, S., and Leibs, D., The LearningWorks Delivery and Development Framework, *Communications of the ACM*, 40(10), 78–81, 1997.

[7] Woodman, M., Griffiths, R., Macgregor, M., Holland, S., and Robinson, H., Exploiting Smalltalk Modules In A Customizable Programming Environment, *Proceedings of ICSE 21*, International Conference on Software Engineering, Los Angeles, May 1999.

[8] Goldberg, A. and Ross, J., Is the Smalltalk-80 System for Children?, *Byte*, 6(8), August 1981.

[9] Holland S., Griffiths R., Woodman M., Avoiding Object Misconceptions, *Proceedings SIGCSE 97*, San Jose, February 1997

[10] Krasner G. E. and Pope S. T., A Cookbook for using the Model View Controller User Interface Paradigm in *Smalltalk 80 Journal of Object-oriented Programming*, Vol 1, #3 pages 26–49, 1988.

[11] Howard, T., *The Smalltalk Developer's Guide to VisualWorks*, SIGS Books, New York, 1995.

[12] Gamma E., Helm R., Johnson R. and Vliffides J. *Design Patterns: Elements of re-usable Object-oriented Software*, Addison Wesley, 1994.

[13] Alpert S. R., *The Design Patterns Smalltalk Companion*, 1998, Addison Wesley, 1998.

Visualizing O-O Testing in Virtual Communities - Distributed Teaching and Learning

Sita Ramakrishnan

School of CSSE, Monash University, Australia

sitar@csse.monash.edu.au

Abstract

The Internet has been recognised not only as a tool for communication in the 21st century but also as an environment for enabling changes in the paradigm of teaching and learning. This paper describes our research effort on the design and delivery of quality educational material on object-oriented (O-O) testing in an Internet environment. O-O software testing has the advantage of being easily visualizable in terms of state changes and data-flows. We have attempted to show the inner workings of the complex processes involved in O-O testing. The O-O testing case studies considered contain visual images, animation, and interactive lessons, to assist active participation by learners to result in better understanding and knowledge retention. The distributed teaching and learning approach discussed in this paper employs appropriate UML diagrams, makes the diagrams test ready by including details of constraints as part of state/event transitions, and provides interactive lessons for learning O-O software testing. Furthermore, this paper describes a development process in visualization and interactivity to achieve improved learning outcomes of O-O software testing in an Internet based environment - (see http://www.sd.monash.edu.au/ sitar/se_educ_proj).

1: Introduction

Traditionally, students of undergraduate courses in software engineering have been taught techniques to design and develop relatively small programs, with only minor emphasis on software testing and maintenance. However, testing is an important activity both at the development and maintenance phases of software development. Industry data show that around 60% of software costs go into the maintenance phase of the software life cycle. As an extreme example, the explosion of the first Ariane-5 rocket 30 seconds after lift off in June 1996 was found to be due to hidden assumptions in software elements having been reused from a previous rocket in Ariane-5 without a clear understanding of the testing required [9, 7]. It is important that software engineering students learn systematic testing of software systems.

O-O technology encourages modular and incremental development of large systems. At Monash University, we teach O-O software development for building complex systems, in which testing is an integral part. However, a lack of adequate teaching tools support has made it difficult for students to master the complexity of software testing. O-O software testing has the advantage of being easily visualizable in terms of state changes and data-flows. By making use of this advantage, we have attempted to show the inner workings of the complex processes involved in O-O testing. The O-O testing case studies considered contain visual images, animation, and interactive lessons, with a belief that active participation by the learners result in better understanding and knowledge retention. This paper describes the extensions to our previous work [19] on an Internet environment for learning O-O testing processes. The aim of this work is to enhance the state of the art in learning O-O testing by visualizing O-O testing and interactive courseware in virtual communities.

2: Testing O-O Software

Software testing procedure includes the development of many test cases, each of which is intended to test a particular element of the application. Test results are analysed to check the correctness of the software. The tester checks the outcome of each test case in the test suite by executing a feature (method) and comparing the actual results obtained with expected results. Unit testing is used to check the correctness of the algorithms implemented in the class and the conformance of return values to expected results. Integration testing deals with how well single units work together.

2.1: Testing techniques

The basic goal of achieving high productivity in testing is to create a minimum number of test cases to uncover the maximum number of defects for a given amount of effort. We can produce test cases by concentrating on all the individual substates for small systems. This will, however, result in a significant increase in the number of test cases for larger systems. So, often we try to reduce the number of test cases by identifying tests that are more likely to reveal errors, and working out the errors that may be revealed by the selected tests[1]. Test case selection usually involves defining the purpose of the test and creating tests to satisfy each test purpose. Test purposes are derived manually such as from use-case descriptions or from checklists of common programming mistakes [12]. Test selection techniques require categorising tests as either structural tests, functional tests or integration tests [14, 13], and recognising the level of testing supported by a given technique.

2.1.1: Functional Test Cases

Functional test cases, also known as black box test cases, are constructed based on the specification of a component. The specification of a class includes a class invariant and specification with pre and postconditions for each method. A method is executed to verify conformance to its assertions. More test cases are used to check invariants. We can produce adequate coverage by building test cases based on analyses of the public interface of classes with precondition, postcondition for the methods, and class invariant. We illustrate black-box testing in case study 1, and visualize test paths for a simple Account object, using UML state diagram and design by contract notions.

2.1.2: Structural Test Cases

Structural test cases, also known as white box test cases, are constructed by identifying individual paths through the method. This allows us to capture errors/bugs that were not detected in functional testing. In section 4, we discuss the testing process for a VCR system case study, where each of the components (VCR, remote control and TV monitor) in a JavaBean application has to undergo structural code-based testing.

2.1.3: Integration Test Cases

Integration test cases deal with interactions between methods within a class (intra-class testing), and interactions between methods in different classes (inter-class testing). It focuses on checking methods, which may cause errors due to interactions. Test cases are produced by checking values of attributes used or set by these methods, or parameters passed between these methods. During integration tests, care needs to be taken with inheritance, polymorphism, and dynamic binding, which affect the dynamic run-time type of an object in object-oriented languages. We have employed event flow testing technique (described in section 4) in deriving system level test cases for the VCR case study.

2.2: O-O Testing method with UML and Design by Contract

In O-O systems, although we test the individual features (methods) within a class, we are more interested in class testing, which combines some aspects of unit testing and integration testing.

Unified Modeling Language (UML) modelling diagrams are used in the testing process. Unit tests use class diagrams and state diagrams; integration tests use collaboration diagrams, state diagrams and component diagrams; and the system tests implement use case diagrams to validate that the system behaves according to the definitions in these diagrams [8].

Verification and validation are two approaches employed to check for conformance between the specification and an implementation. Validation determines if software is correct; verification determines if software is built correctly. A correct implementation is complete (sufficient) and consistent. However, it is important that one makes certain that a specification completely describes the properties of a system that it is supposed to cover. Consistency and completeness properties are complementary [15]. For any query expression, one must be able to derive only one value: at least one (sufficient completeness), but no more than one value(consistency). Verification at 100 % may not be possible for the 3 C's - completeness (data complete, no junk such as method not found messages), consistency and conformance, as different % are applicable for different things.

2.3: Design by Contract

Design by contract (and subcontracts), developed by Bertrand Meyer [15], is a well regarded paradigm for building quality O-O systems in the Eiffel world. In Eiffel language, we are able to specify the constraints of the methods in a class in terms of pre and postconditions, and the assertions that must be met by all methods of the class in terms of invariants. Design by subcontract extends this notion for subclasses by weakening the preconditions and strengthening the postconditions for overridden methods. This design by contract is shown in a tabular format (see fig. 4), and forms the basis for our extension of UML diagrams to make them test ready. We use the preconditions, postconditions, and invariants as part of the state diagrams in our case studies, and the constraint values dictate the paths taken during a state transition.

3: Distributed Teaching and Learning Communities

3.1: Motivation

"Object-oriented Programming Systems" and "Systems Quality, Verification and Validation" are third year level single semester undergraduate subjects at Monash University. Students are required to learn to develop software systems using an O-O approach in these two units with an emphasis on testing. Our conventional approach can only teach software testing as static observational models on paper or on electronic medium. We believe that an interactive multimedia system for teaching software testing based on Internet programming will be an effective teaching vehicle.

The results of the ongoing software engineering experiments conducted by the author [18] that measure students' understanding, correlated well against other assessment components for the subject [17]. But, it also highlighted the benefits of developing software testing as part of our ongoing experiment to teach a deeper understanding of how testing really works.

The current work fits well within the ongoing software engineering measurement experimental framework. It provides an additional alternative self-paced teaching environment for software testing. Students are required to complete these self-study teaching modules of varied complexity before attempting major assignments. Students develop O-O software systems by following a methodology that involves deriving software designs from software models satisfying certain conditions. These requirements (conditions or rules) are included in the implementation using an O-O language and become part of the test data definition. Although this link in software design, coding and testing is covered during lectures, it does not explicitly cover the difficult area of visualizing the complex processes involved in developing software systems. Students are likely to benefit by interacting and visualizing the paths followed during testing. The system is expected to improve the quality of test plans, test cases and the O-O test strategy employed by the students.

3.2: Expected benefits of our approach

Learning outcomes: Students are expected to undertake this task of software testing systematically by visualizing execution paths and state changes in the tested program. Also, students are expected to produce better test data (for their assessable components) that takes the possible states of the objects and their interaction during system execution by simulated and animated examples using UML's state diagrams augmented with constraints.

Student-centered Learning: The project shifts the learning process from the traditional teacher-centered approach to student-centered approach. It is argued [5] that the traditional educational process is similar to the practice of the waterfall model of analysis, design, implementation and evaluation by the software engineering community. The shift from the waterfall to a rapid prototyping approach in software system development is due to an emphasis on customer involvement in the decision-making process. Similarly, the change from a traditional teaching paradigm to a distributed learning and teaching in virtual communities is aimed to engage the student in active participation as part of the learning process. Since software testing is a complex process, the learning pace of students may not be uniform and therefore this shift to resource-based learning in the students' labs in the University should help the students. A significant number of students have home computers with connections to the Internet. By providing the system on the Internet, students have the flexibility of learning at their own place. Thus we provide both time and space flexibility in the learning process. Computer based animation and visualization are powerful and motivationally attractive education techniques, which can simplify the presentation of the conceptual frameworks and schematic overviews [10], thereby enhancing learning. It is vital for students to internalize the notion of testing so that they can produce systems, which are reliable, and of good quality.

4: O-O Testing on the Internet

Our current work entitled, "LIGHT VIEWS", for learning the process of O-O testing is an interactive hypermedia courseware geared towards a distributed learning community model for visualizing O-O software testing process through web-based software. The Internet technology has been used as an enabler for creating pedagogically sound material, such as active participatory learning in collaborative environments. The courseware has adopted the good principles of instructional design and human computer interaction. A short textual description of the problem is provided interspersed with passive learning material containing UML diagrams. These diagrams can be stepped through in a system directed fashion. We also provide active participatory learning material with UML diagrams by enabling the learner to control the interactivity. Links to O-O theory, and glossary terms of relevance to O-O testing in general and to those case studies in particular are also part of the courseware.

4.1: UML, Constraints and Visualization of O-O Testing Processes

We use UML diagrams and build O-O models as part of our software development process. Apart from the UML diagrams for analysis and design, we use the dynamic UML models such as state machines for visualizing the test paths of a system. We include design by contract by specifying the constraints that must be satisfied for an object to transition from one state to another. This enables us to build a constrained interaction with state machines, which facilitates guided experiential learning. By varying the constraints, students are able to move through various paths of the state machines. They are able to direct and control the interactions. This helps them to immerse in the activity by asking, "what if the parameter value is such and such - how does it affect the constraint and its impact on the state transition" and learn about test selection and test coverage. They can do this activity at their own pace; experiment with various parameter values to see the paths taken, represented as Java applets (visualized state machines). When the parameter values satisfy the constraints (preconditions, postconditions & invariants), they are visually shown as ticks. Crosses are used to indicate constraint violation (Refer figs. 2 - 3).

4.2: Java applets and interactive visualization of O-O Testing processes

The use of Java applets for passive and active illustration of dynamic O-O models suits our requirement to make the courseware accessible on a platform independent basis. We have used DreamWeaver, a visual authoring tool for creating and managing web pages. We have implemented some animations using Java. However, we have also used the tool, Flash, to draw and animate a number of these diagrams, and Macromedia's scripting language, Lingo, for producing interactive illustrations of the test paths. Since our learning environment is an interactive, web based environment, we convert these diagrams to Java applets for ease of distribution.

For a web based distant learning to work, the designer must take care of the content, web instructional design, interactivity, and take the students' feedback and assessment of the effectiveness of the material into account. This evaluation may necessitate redesign and reimplementation. Since we wanted to experiment with a number of test strategies, and take the students' feedback to evolve the solution, we have chosen to use these authoring tools to develop an Internet solution.

4.3: Case Studies

We have included four case studies in the courseware, geared to learn about the various test strategies employed in testing O-O software systems. We focus on various aspects of O-O testing: black-box testing of a simple account object, systems testing and white-box testing in a VCR system, event based testing and applets, and network/distributed testing. In this paper, we have discussed the first two case studies in detail.

4.3.1: Case Study 1

This case study has been used to illustrate black-box testing by firstly making the learners to walk through the various states of a simple account object with a state transition diagram (see fig. 1). We have specified the Account object with five states: *open, overdrawn, frozen, inactive* and *closed*. The conditional transition from a state to the next state is expressed with the associated precondition, postcondition and invariant. For e.g., the precondition, balance = 0, must be satisfied for this account object to transition to *closed* from *open* state.

From the state model, they can proceed with the test case design by developing a transition tree. They can click through to see a transition tree being built. The initial state is the root node of the tree. So, the root node for Account class is the initial state of Account - open. For each transition from the root state, a branch is created to a node that represents the next state. This is repeated for each state unless the next state is the final state or the next state appears in the ancestor node [2]. The next phase of test design is to get the test sequences from the transition tree. Each branch of the tree becomes a test case (Chow's algorithm [3]). Covering this tree will discover bugs that may be missed by just testing each method, transition, or state once. Finally, they can work interactively on the state diagram by keying in parameter values, which control the paths taken (see figs 2 - 3).

From figure 2, they can work out that the deposit operation is allowed to proceed as precondition is satisfied. Figure 3 shows that withdrawing $1500 is disallowed when the current balance is zero as it violates the class invariant which has been set at -$1000 for minimum balance. These visual cues are used to reinforce their understanding of how to use assertions in building functional test cases.

The test sequence is created by traversing the state transition graph. The test sequence should start from the initial state, go through all the possible transitions, and return back to the initial state, in a depth-first fashion [3]. The parameters or arguments of the operations (if applicable) are relevant in this context. The test plan is produced by identifying the method arguments & their values, and the expected state and possible exceptions for each transition. The actual test run involves setting the object under test (OUT) to the initial state, applying the test sequence, and checking the final state.

4.3.2: Evaluation

Students of Class 98 were required to study Case Study 1 as part of their learning and assessment. They were required to complete the on-line questionnaire in the case study to provide feedback about their thoughts on the effectiveness of the material and provide suggestions for improvements. Quizzes were used to provide instant feedback and collect evaluation data on their understanding of the material covered. The system logged the student id, number of attempts per quiz, and the result. Analysis of the data has revealed that students who understood the material by either getting it correct the first time, or having mastered it after a number of attempts, have produced better annotated state charts with constraints and followed it through with better test cases and test strategies for their assignments. We can claim from the results that we found that for this case study, our students found the UML state diagrams annotated with these easy to understand visual cues to be beneficial and effective in improving their understanding of test selection, test coverage, and inner workings of a of simple UML dynamic models. We are continuing our evaluation efforts on all the four case studies to validate our claims.

4.4: Case Study 2

This case study has been used to illustrate testing for a JavaBeans application by visualizing the interaction of a remote control navigator object with a VCR object and a TV monitor. The focus here is on test case selection based on event flows (see figs 5 - 6).

OO Testing Process in simulating functionalities of a VCR: An OO software system development is described which is meant to simulate the functionality of a VCR. The system is used to verify the high level design of the control program to be installed in the microcomputer unit of a new model VCR. We focus on the behaviours required by the VCR user to derive the scenarios, and use UML diagrams to describe our OO testing process. The VCR offers a number of functionalities such as timer recording, audio dubbing, and tape dubbing that can be treated as separate use cases. We rank timer recording as of the highest priority, and so, explore it as the first use case.

A discussion of test selection techniques follows in the next subsection: system level testing for scenario 1, and unit level and integration level testing for scenario 2. Integration tests use collaborative diagrams and sequence diagrams to validate the interactions between objects.

Selecting Test cases for a VCR system: System testing is about using meaningful functional test cases to check the working of the system. We derive meaningful test cases by using testing techniques that focus on related events that occur in the system level model[11] of the VCR system. Here, in event flow testing, we focus on the effect of system level events on subsequent events. On the other hand, in data flow testing at the unit testing level, we select test cases that cover the definitions and uses of variables in a program.

Using the event flow approach, test cases can be generated automatically with the program model represented in the nested state diagrams. However, we may need manual intervention in some cases where paths that are not feasible are generated automatically. This happens when a transition depends on the occurrence of other transitions.

Our VCR system model acts as a kind of simulation of the modelled operations of the VCR. This model includes the states that the system can be in, the events that cause the state changes, and the event sequences that can occur (fig.5). Such a model state chart at this abstraction level shows just event sequencing. However, the specification model state charts would show how these events are generated by software. The specification model also allows objects of a subtype substitute for objects of a supertype, enabling software to be assembled from components.

We consider system testing of the VCR system with the event semantics of the specification model and leave the state charts with message semantics of the design/implementation models for other forms of testing. The VCR system has a number of interacting objects such as the VCR, TV Monitor and a Remote Control (Navigator).

In scenario 1 for setting timer details, the VCR system is required to simulate the remote control operations by setting the timer operations of the VCR. It uses the TV Monitor as the user interface medium while setting the timer details.

In scenario 2, we require the remote control object to control the VCR operations such as play, fast forward (ff), vol+ and others, and display the video pictures on the monitor. We also require the monitor surface for visualizing the state diagram that shows the interaction between VCR & Monitor objects.

Here, we describe how we select system level test cases from the specification model's state chart diagrams for the timer recording scenario 1. We work out first which events are related. Using the event flow testing technique, we focus on the effect of system level events on subsequent events. This technique is used to select test cases to cover sequences of events that occur from a particular system level event to a related event.

We begin to represent the high level behaviour of the system by specifying how the Monitor and VCR timer objects react to system level events under the control of the remote control object. How does the VCR timer recording system (operation) react to events such as Monitor.On and Monitor.Off? How does it interact with the timer operation of the VCR with events such as VCRTimer.On and VCRTimer.Off.

We specify that the remote control (navigator) is working and sending stimuli to the other objects for their interactions to system events. That is, navigator event is on. Monitor.On and Monitor.Off events are related under the control of the navigator. We also want to consider the VCR timer here and include its events, VCRTimer.On and VCRTimer.Off, as the timer recording function visualized on the monitor is the essence of this scenario 1.

We select tests by identifying the sequence of transitions between these events that we need to cover.

1.Navigator.Off, Navigator.On - this sequence is about turning the remote control on.

2.Navigator.On, Monitor.On, Monitor.Off - this test sequence is about turning the monitor on to start the timer recording process, and switching the monitor off before starting the timer operation.

3.Navigator.On, Monitor.On, VCRTimer.On, Monitor.Off - this test sequence is about turning the monitor on with the remote control, starting the timer recording process, and switching the monitor off before finishing the setting of the timer operation.

4.Navigator.On, Monitor.On, VCRTimer.On, VCRTimer.Off, Monitor.Off - this test sequence is about turning the monitor on, starting the setting of VCR timer recording on, turning it off after setting the recording details, and switching off the monitor.

We have thus created a number of test cases that cover the system requirements as specified by the system modeller. The test team would select test cases from these models by walking through events in the diagram, which illustrate how the VCR system should work. With the event flow technique of test case sequences as shown above, we can automate the test selection process from the model (fig. 5).

We now proceed to expand the nested state, SetVCRTimer. We have a nested state with a superstate, SetVCRTimer, and substates, setDate, and setTime, which can be decomposed further. Setting the VCR timer recording function involves setting the date and time, and any errors during this process is displayed on the monitor. The transition, VCRTimerOff is at the setVCRTimer superstate level indicating that the timer recording can be stopped at any time, and is controlled by the remote control (fig. 6).

This means that the test sequences must always include VCRTimerOff like so:

1. Navigator.On, Monitor.On, VCRTimer.Off, Monitor.Off
2. Navigator.On, Monitor.On, Date Set, VCRTimer.Off, Monitor.Off
3. Navigator.On, Monitor.On, Date Invalid, VCRTimer.Off, Monitor.Off
4. Navigator.On, Monitor.On, Date Set, Time Set, VCRTimer.Off, Monitor.Off
5. Navigator.On, Monitor.On, Date Set, Time Invalid, VCRTimer.Off, Monitor.Off

We have included Monitor.Off in all sequences as the monitor is turned off after the VCR-TimerOff event is executed. We complete the test sequence generation by decomposing abstract states, SetVCRTimer and Error. We must expand the transitions into and out of the state. The transition out of the abstract state is VCRTimerOff and MonitorOff. The transition from the decomposed setVCRTimer to Error must be covered. We have 3 transitions - Date Set, (set Start Time, set End Time) from setting time, and 3 events - setting date, startTime and endTime.

We must also include the transition to error by including the transition pairs (invalid Date, VCRTimer.Off), (invalid EndTime, VCRTimer.Off), (overlapped time, VCRTimer.Off) and (Too many Programmes, VCRTimer.Off) in our test sequence.

4.5: Discussion

Our system is unique in its combination of multimedia, Internet, and student-centered approach in the learning of software testing. Projects that use Internet based multimedia for computer mediated education have been reported in the literature such as the Brown University's Exploratory Research program [20], European Consortium's Conceptual Learning of Sciences through experimentation with simulation environments [4], and Instructional Technology Programs at University of California, Berkeley [16]. However we are not aware of any package for teaching software testing.

Proprietary tools like Statemate, Quid and Protob are used in research establishments; these however are not developed for educational purposes, but are visual O-O software modelling tools and do not focus on testing. Research tools such as ASTOOT [6] on O-O testing do exist. The major difference between our system and systems like ASTOOT is that our intention is to develop a system to learn OO-testing, where testing itself is only one component. The more important aspects are visualization and interactivity with the system under test, instructional material on preparing test plans, and provisions for evaluation and feedback.

5: Conclusion

We are designing an Internet environment to visualize the inner workings of the complex processes involved in O-O testing. Our objective is for students to learn the basic goal of achieving high productivity in testing by being able to create a minimum number of test cases to uncover the maximum number of errors for a given amount of effort. To achieve this objective, we have used four case studies to explore the various test selection techniques. We have discussed the specification based black-box testing - at the unit level in case study 1 for an Account object, and at the system level in case study 2 for a JavaBean application. For unit level black-box testing, we have shown how to use the UML state diagram augmented with design by contract notions as part of the transition, to verify the behaviour of an object with few test cases. For system testing, we have shown how to derive meaningful test cases by using testing techniques that focus on related events that occur in the system level model of the VCR system.

In 1998, the author's final year undergraduate students studying a subject entitled "Object-Oriented Programming Systems" have learned about OO testing using the case study on Accounts as the web-based interactive teaching resource, in addition to standard classroom lectures. They have taken part in formative evaluations of the material and completed on-line quizzes to check their understanding. These students have received this material very positively. This approach presents a new road to self-paced learning by enabling learners in distributed locations to follow the new ROAD - Read the on-line material, Observe the static and animated O-O diagrams (Passive learning), Absorb, and Do (Active learning). The interactivity features allow the learner to direct the test paths taken by the system. We are also currently working on using this design experience in interactivity to develop a framework in Java for learning O-O testing strategies and processes.

Acknowledgements: The author gratefully acknowledges the funding support for this work by the Australian National CUTSD98 grants, and also the support by the School of CSSE. She also acknowledges the work done by D Browne, T-L Nguyen, T Kanzaki, H McCarthy and D Thompson. Thanks are extended to Prof John McGregor, Clemson University and to Monash academics for offering constructive feedback, and thanks also to author's class of 98, and McGregor's class of 99.

References

[1] A. Bader, A. S. M. Sajeev, and S. Ramakrishnan. Testing Concurrency and Communication in Distributed Systems. In *International Conference on High Performance Computing, IEEE Computer Society, Chennai*, Dec. 1998.

[2] R. Binder. State-based testing. *Object Magazine*, pages 75–78, Jul-Aug 1995.

[3] T. S. Chow. Testing Software Design modeled by finite-state machines. *IEEE Transactions on Software Engineering,*, 4:3:178–187, May 1978.

[4] CoLoS. Conceptual Learning of Sciences (CoLoS),. *On-line at <http://hpwww.ec-lyon.fr/colosHp/>*, June 1997.

[5] B. Cox. *Evolving a Distributed Learning Community, The Online Classroom in K12, Eds. Z Berge and M Colins, On-line at <http://www.virtualschool.edu.cox/OnlineClassroom.html/>*. Hampton Press, 1998.

[6] R. K. Doong and P. G. Frankl. The ASTOOT Approach to Testing Object-Oriented Programs. *ACM Transactions on Software Engineering and Methodology*, 3:2:101–130, 1994.

[7] ESA. ESA Launchers. *European Space Agency and Space Transport Systems, On-line at < http://www.esrin.esa.it/htdocs/esa/progs/launch.html>*, May 1997.

[8] M. Fowler. *UML Distilled*. Addison-Wesley, 1997.

[9] J. M. Jezequel. Engineering Telecom Systems with Eiffel. *Tutorial held in conjunction with TOOLS Pacific 96*, 1996.

[10] S. Kent. Constraint Diagrams: Visualising Invariants in OO Modelling. In *OOPSLA97, ACM Press*, 1997.

[11] W. B. Liu and P. Dasiewicz. Selecting system test cases for object-oriented programs using event flow. In *Canadian Conference on Electrical and Computer Engineering (CCECE'97)*, 1997.

[12] B. Marick. *The Craft of Software Testing: Subsystem Testing Including Object-based and Object-Oriented Testing*. Prentice-Hall, 1995.

[13] J. McGregor. *A Practical Guide to Testing Object-Oriented Software (Draft)*. to be published by Addison-Wesley, 1999.

[14] J. D. McGregor and T. Korson. Integrating Object-Oriented Testing and Development Processes. *Communications of the ACM*, 37:9:59–77, Sept. 1994.

[15] B. Meyer. *Object-Oriented Software Construction, 2nd Ed.* Prentice-Hall, 1997.

[16] B. Pray. Instructional Technology Program. *University of California, Berkeley, On-line at <http://www.itp.berkeley.edu/>*, April 1998.

[17] S. Ramakrishnan. An Experimental Approach to Object-Oriented Software Process and Product Measures. In *TOOLS Pacific 95, Prentice-Hall*, pages 91–97, November 1995.

[18] S. Ramakrishnan, T. Menzies, M. Hasslinger, P. Bok, H. McCarthy, B. Devakadadcham, and D. Moulder. On Building an Effective Measurement System for OO Software Process, Product and Resource Tracking. In *TOOLS Pacific 96*, pages 239–247, November 1996.

[19] S. Ramakrishnan and A. S. M. Sajeev. An Internet Environment for Learning Software Testing Processes. In *International Conference on Software Engineering and Applications*, pages 33–40, Dec. 1997.

[20] A. van Dam and J. Hughes. Exploratory - seeing, interacting, learning. *Brown University Graphics Group, On-line at <http://www.cs.brown.edu/exploratory/home.html>*, April 1998.

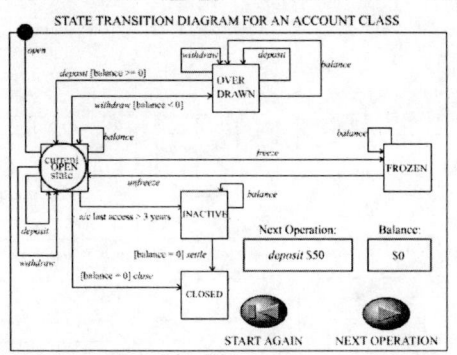

Figure 1. System Directed Interaction

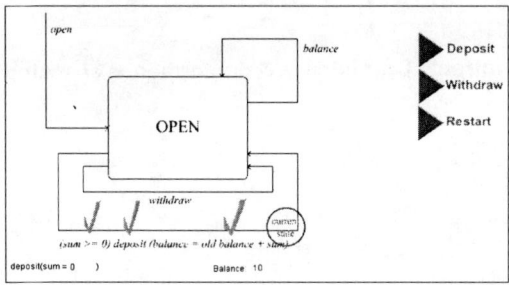

Figure 2. Student directing the interaction - depositing $10 - precondition satisfied, balance now = $10

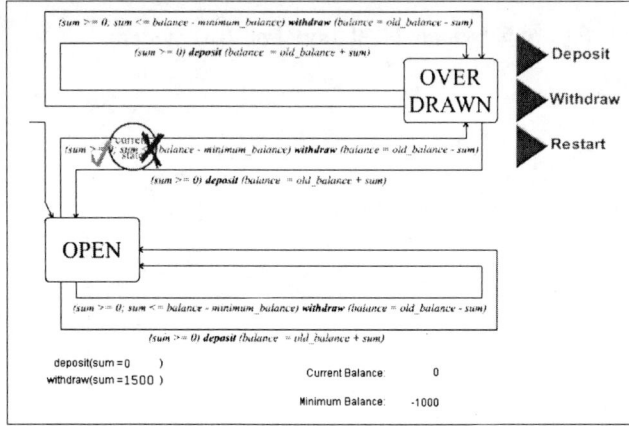

Figure 3. Withdraw violating constraint - see parameter value of withdraw & invariant value of minimum balance

SuperClass S / SubClass s	Precondition P	Postcondition Q	Invariant I
precondition p	P \ true(t) false(f); p t: ✓ E_s; f: ✓ ✓	Q \ true(t) false(f); p t: ✓ E_s; f: ✓ ✓	I \ true(t) false(f); p t: ✓ ✓; f: E_s ✓
post-condition q	P \ true(t) false(f); q t: ✓ ✓; f: E_s ✓	Q \ true(t) false(f); q t: ✓ ✓; f: E_s ✓	I \ true(t) false(f); q t: ✓ ✓; f: E_s ✓
invariant i	I \ true(t) false(f); i t: ✓ ✓; f: E_s ✓	Q \ true(t) false(f); i t: ✓ ✓; f: E_s ✓	I \ true(t) false(f); i t: ✓ ✓; f: E_s ✓

Figure 4. Design by contract - Correctness & conformance checking with assertions

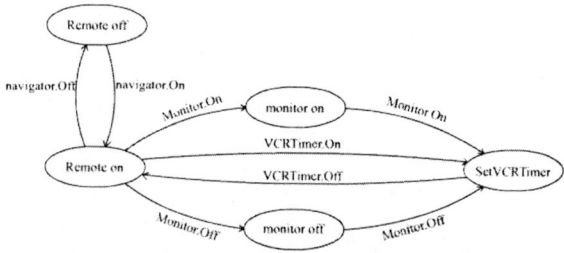

Figure 5. System level model of VCR system

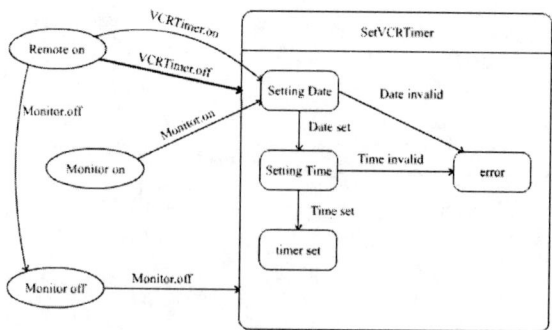

Figure 6. Nested State Diagram - SetVCRTimer

Technical Papers

Java 2

Storing Java Objects in any Database

Raimund K. Ege
High Performance Database Research Center *
School of Computer Science, Florida International University
University Park, Miami, FL 33199
ege@cs.fiu.edu

Abstract

Typical Java applications involve access to a database system. Database systems store data according to their type system, even object-oriented databases generally have their own storage structures. It is therefore necessary to convert Java objects as they are stored in a database, and to re-convert them when they are read. Ideally, this should be done behind the scenes by a support package. Our paper presents an approach that automates the conversion process without involving pre- or post-processing of Java code: we use a reflection mechanism, where Java code is inspected at run-time and changed to include the convert and re-convert effort. The result is a flexible and transparent Java database access.

1. Introduction

Accessing a database system from the Java programming language is a common occurrence. For typical database systems, i.e. those based on relational technology, there are several packages available that enable Java to store and retrieve data. For object-oriented database systems it is desirable to allow Java to store and retrieve its objects directly, i.e. in a seamless manner. Several approaches to the integration of a Java program's object model with an object-oriented database have been proposed and demonstrated. Some advocate a strong and strict integration, some allow loose coupling. Either approach has advantages and disadvantages.

In this paper we will describe an API based on a novel approach that allows Java objects to be maintained by an object-oriented database system. Our approach employs a reflection mechanism that allows for an application program to explore itself and the database schema: it is neither strict nor excessively loose. We use reflection, i.e. self inspection and change of a running program, to map Java classes to database classes and to enable persistence. Reflection allows a program to inspect itself and to affect its own execution. In an object-oriented program that means that at run-time the class of an object is accessible, in our case, the classes of the Java application program as well as the classes of the database API.

And unlike other approaches that add persistence capabilities to Java our approach does not change the Java language nor does it require changes to the Java Virtual machine. The result is a very flexible and efficient style of Java database access.

This research was supported in part by NASA (under grants NAGW-4080, NAG5-5095, NAS5-97222, and NAG5-6830), NSF (CDA-9711582, IRI-9409661, HRD-9707076, and ANI-9876409), ARO (DAAH04-96-1-0049 and DAAH04-96-1-0278), AFRL (F30602-98-C-0037), BMDO (F49620-98-1-0130 and DAAH04-0024) DoI (CA-5280-4-9044), and State of Florida.

This paper is organized as follows: Section 2 explores the issue of adding persistence to Java objects; Section 3 discusses other efforts that are related to our approach; Section 4 illustrates our reflection-based approach of adding persistence to Java objects and Java classes; Section 5 elaborates and gives examples of common classes, and gives an example of a program; Section 6 briefly outlines the implementation approach and reports on the status of our prototype [Ege et al., 1998a] which is based on SemODB, a semantic object-oriented database system [Rishe, 1992]. Finally, the paper concludes with our future plans.

2. Java Persistence

Both object-oriented programming languages and object-oriented database systems have been in use for some time. And from the early days there was the desire to combine both in a true object-oriented fashion. The programming language uses objects in its model of computation; the database stores objects: therefore, an application programmer interface (API) necessarily should be constructed around objects. Objects occur in two places: (1) the objects stored and retrieved from and to the database, and (2) service objects, that enable the typical database management capabilities, such as transactions etc.

It is classes that describe objects: the schema of the database is just a set of classes; an OO program is also just a set of classes. Several approaches to their integration have emerged: from a loose integration, exemplified by the GemStone OODB for Smalltalk, to the ODMG[Catell et al., 1997] C++ binding, which represents an integration compromise, to tight integration that is proposed for storing Java objects. In a tight integration, Java program objects can be made *persistent*, which causes them to be implicitly stored and managed by an OO database.

The issues involved in allowing Java objects to be persistent are (1) the selection/marking of classes that have persistent instances; (2) the creation of persistent objects; (3) the retrieval of objects from the database; (4) navigation from object to object; (5) updating objects; and also (6) some basic database housekeeping capabilities.

2.1. Persistence-Capable Classes

In order for an object to become persistent, its class needs to be enabled. A Java class has to be made persistence-capable, i.e. we allow that some of its instances reside in the object-oriented database. There are 2 ways to achieve it: *explicitly*, that is to require that the programmer mark persistence-capable classes; or via some *implicit* automatic or derived fashion.

Explicit marking can be done in several ways, e.g. by defining a class as a subclass of a database superclass. Any class in Java is already a subclass of Java class `Object`: the same concept applies now to such a database root superclass. We can now say that any persistent object handled by our Java API is an instance of that class. This class handles the basic correlation between the physical database object and its local Java counter part.

Another approach is more implicit: *any* object can be made persistent, in effect, all Java classes are therefore persistence-capable. The advantage of this approach is that even Java system classes, AWT classes, utility classes, etc. can have persistent instances. This concept is called *orthogonal* persistence. The programmer, of course, need not be aware of this.

The second issue of persistence in Java is how to make individual objects persistent. The desire is to stay minimally intrusive. The first option is to add a variation of a new operation to Java (e.g. pnew); or, to provide a mechanism to tell the database about those objects that are to be persistent; or, as a variation of that, enable a ODMG C++-style set_object_name() operation that declares root objects.

The third issue is how to retrieve objects from the database: 3 sub-options again: (1) allow some general query capability similar to a single SQL project, e.g. "select instance of class whose attribute has value"; (2) extend the Java programming language with a new looping construct that allows to scan instances of a class; or (3) retrieve specific objects that have been given a root name in ODMG C++ style: lookup_object("root name"). As Java objects are moved into the database, member fields that contain references to other Java objects need to be converted. A Java reference is only valid during a single run of a program. Therefore, they need to be converted into more general object identifiers that are valid, i.e. unique, in the context of the entire database. As objects are retrieved from the database these object identifiers will have to be reconverted into valid Java references. Once a persistent object has been retrieved from the database, other objects are reached by following its relationships, i.e. via object identifiers. Objects are automatically fetched as needed from the database. This concept is called *persistence by reachability*.

Updating objects is totally transparent to the programmer. The programmer invokes member functions and goes about the programming business as usual. Member functions can update member fields of persistent objects: that in effect is an update of a database object. The programmer does not have to insert any code to explicitly affect the update to the database. Of course, the final success of an update is dependent on the final success of the transaction.

2.2. Implementation Issues

The above mentioned issues present various degrees of complexity: how to resolve how to make a Java class subclass of the database root class; how to enable objects to be named; how to retrieve objects by name; how to enable traversal of persistent objects; and finally how to enable object update.

ODMG suggests 3 potential ways to address these "how-to" issues in Java: via a preprocessor to Java compilation; via a postprocessor of Java byte codes; or via a change to the Java Virtual machine.

In the preprocessor version, one would parse Java code to add the necessary snippets to enable persistence capability, e.g. make a class a subclass of a database root class. This approach would also allow to insert the necessary checks and additional code to enable the fetch, traversal and update of persistent objects.

In the postprocessor version, one would read and modify Java byte codes for the classes that are to be effected. Since Java byte codes are well defined and documented – tools exist to process them – this version has the same capabilities as the first version, but might even be easier to implement.

To change the Java virtual machine is not a complete solution: it needs to be made aware of objects that are persistent. One could add new byte codes: this approach is used in the PJama approach. However, in our opinion this runs against the spirit of Java: such a modified Java program will not run *everywhere*.

In summary, approaches one and two are doable, however, as a consequence they alter the Java compilation approach: a programmer needs to use a special version of the Java compiler.

Our approach attempts to stay away from changing the compilation approach and from changing the Java virtual machine. Instead we use Java's reflection capabilities, where we generate the necessary changes to the Java program automatically as it runs. The result is limited intrusion into the programmer's model and into the compilation model.

3. Related Work

Many different approaches have been suggested to enable database access from a Java program. Prominent, for example, is the Java Database Connectivity package (JDBC) [Hamilton and Catell, 1996]. Of course, it allows Java to access relational database system[1]. JDBC access can be bridged into ODBC access, or – as is becoming very common – direct drivers are provided by the database management system. Several extensions to this JDBC approach have been suggested: one is JRB (Java Relational Binding) which allows to manage database entities (transactions, queries, etc.) and to store and retrieve Java objects. JRB has been used as further basis for a Java Universal Binding (JUB) which hides the relational aspects of the underlying database system [Xhumari et al., 1997].

Several commercial vendors of ODBMS have provided Java bindings that follow the ODMG recommendation: ObjectStore[PSE, 1998] and GemStone/J[Gem, 1998] are 2 examples.

The most integrated approach is PJama[Atkinson et al., 1996]: here Java truly becomes persistent with minimal intrusion into the programming model, however, at the expense of requiring a non-standard Java compiler and significant changes to the Java Virtual Machine.

4. Reflection

Our approach to enable Java programs to store their objects in an object-oriented database is based on reflection. The term *reflection* means that a computer program is able to observe and/or change itself while it is running. A programming language becomes *reflective* if it enables its programs with reflection, i.e. it enables that the program code is changed by the program at run time [Stemple et al., 1993].

An object-oriented program is described via a set of classes. OO programming languages such as Smalltalk and Java represent these classes as objects and make them available at run-time. Smalltalk has a rich set of meta-classes that enable reflective programming. Java, on the other hand, does not directly support full reflection: its `java.lang.reflect` package allows a program to inspect the class of objects, its member fields and functions, etc., but it does not allow that they are changed. In order to achieve full reflection, access to the Java byte code is necessary. Once a Java class is available in byte code, it can be changed and the class reloaded using the standard Java class loader. Recreation of Java byte codes and dynamic loading can be done at run-time. While not elegant, this avenue in effect enables full run-time reflection for the Java programming language.

In the database context it is quite common to represent and store the schema with the rest of the data in the database and also to make it available to application pro-

---

[1] more precisely, it allows access to database that allow ODBC-style access, and of course, the common commercial OODBMSs have such interfaces.

grams[2]. Our prototype implementation uses SemODB (semantic object-oriented database system)[Rishe, 1992]. Its metaschema contains classes for the database, transactions, file storage, as well as classes "Category" and "Relation" that govern what is stored in the database. "Category" has instances for the classes whose objects populate the database. "Relation" captures the superclass/subclass relationships among classes and class associations. In the semantic object-oriented database approach, attributes are also captured as associations to basic primitive database types.

The Java meta schema on the other hand is quite simple: it contains classes `Class`, `Field` and `Method`. We also need to use the class `ClassLoader` since that enables the dynamic reload of classes at run time.

In addition to the meta classes, the Java program will contain application specific classes, and the database schema will contain content specific classes.

Our API now allows the 2 sets of classes to be reconciled automatically. As the programmers declares objects to become persistent, we inspect – via reflection – the details of the class, then check whether a corresponding class exists in the database, and then – again via run-time reflection – create a proxy class that serves as a bridge to enable Java objects to move into the database, and for database objects to move into the Java execution world. In this fashion, all Java classes mentioned in a program are made persistence capable, including the Java support classes from the standard JDK packages.

Some special cases need to be considered: (1) Java primitive types, e.g. `int`, `char` etc. are mapped directly into equivalent database primitive atomic types; (2) a Java class might not have a corresponding category in the database: we then create the category automatically based on the data members declared for the Java class.

In addition, we enable a caching mechanism, where the proxy classes are also stored with their byte codes in the database, which significantly improves the performance of those Java programs which use common classes. [Ege et al., 1998b]

5. Database Programming with Reflection

For further illustration lets consider a sample Java class (see Figure 1) which is defined without any database access in mind. This class is then used in Java programs that access the database:

5.1. To make an object persist

In order for a Java program to make arbitrary object persistent it will have to make that intention known. Our reflection package provides a helper class `DBAccess` which defines the member function `makePersist()`. This code example illustrates the use:

```
DBAccess db = new DBAccess("demo");
Person p = new Person();
db.makePersist(p, "first");
```

The member function inspects the class of its parameter in the Java program and in the database. If a corresponding database category is not found, a new category is created in the database based on the member fields of the Java class. In any case, a new instance of

---

[2]This is a form of reflection, full reflection would enable dynamic schema evolution.

```
import java.io.*;

class Person {
   String name;
   int age;
   Person [] children;
   void add(Person c) {
      Person [] list;
      if (children != null) {
         list = new Person [children.length + 1];
         for (int i=0; i<children.length; i++)
            list[i] = children[i];
      } else
         list = new Person[1];
      list[list.length-1] = c;
      children = list;
   }
   void print() {
      System.out.println(name + "(" + age + "):");
      if (children != null)
        for (int i=0; i<children.length; i++)
          children[i].print();
   }
}
```

Figure 1. Java Class Person

the category is created in the database. We now create a proxy class which will serve as an intermediary between Java objects and database objects. We add a new member field to the Java class to allow it to be associated with the proxy class. The Java class is further modified to become a subclass of the database root class, unless it is already a subclass of a class other than Object. In this case, its superclass will be modified to become of the database root class. The code of all member functions of the Java class is inspected to check for member field access: where it occurs checks are inserted to ensure related objects are fetched from the database as needed. Of course, if the Java class is already prepared in this way, then makePersist() will not repeat this setup task.

The second parameter to the makePersist() member function is used as root label for the object.

5.2. To retrieve an object

In order to retrieve an object from the database, we provide the member function fetch() in class DBAccess. This code example illustrates the use:

```
p = (Person) db.fetch("first");
```

It allows to find an arbitrary object in database that had been named previously via the makePersist() member function. It gets the database object, inspects its category, searches for the equivalent Java class. If the class is not found, then an exception is raised. It prepares an instance of that class by setting its member fields and converting database object identifiers into Java references. Like before, a proxy class is generated and associ-

```
import java.util.*;

public class DBwrite {
    public static void main(String[] args) {
        DBAccess db = new DBAccess("demo");
        Transaction tx = new Transaction(db);
        tx.begin();

        Person p = new Person();
        db.makePersist(p, "first");

        p.name = "John Doe";
        p.age = 31;
        Person c = new Person();
        c.name = "little guy";
        c.age = 1;
        p.add(c);

        tx.commit();
        db.close();
    }
}
```

Figure 2. Writing Java Objects

ated with the Java class of the retrieved instance. The Java class is also made persistence capable as above.

5.3. To navigate from object to object

Since object creation and retrieval inserted presence checks whenever member functions access member fields, objects can be fetched from the database as needed. Whenever an object is further retrieved it may be possible that it is an instance of a class that has not been encountered yet. We then create the necessary proxy class and modify its Java class as discussed above.

5.4. To update persistent objects

Before a transaction is committed we need to ensure that all persistent objects are stable, i.e. that all its dependents have been recognized and their classes been made persistence capable. The member function `stabilize()` serves this purpose. It is called whenever the programmer commits a transaction.

Figure 2 illustrates a Java program that writes objects into the database. Two Person objects are created, "little guy" as a child of "John Doe". Only "John Doe" is explicitly made persistent, "little guy" becomes persistent implicitly when he is added as a child. Once the transaction is committed, both objects are stored in the database.

Figure 3 illustrates a Java program that reads objects from the database, makes some changes, and then commits the transaction: "John Doe", the person object labeled "first" is explicitly fetched from the database; his child person object is implicitly directly accessible.

```
import java.util.*;

class DBread {
   public static void main(String args[]) {
      DBAccess db = new DBAccess("demo");
      Transaction tx = new Transaction(db);
      tx.begin();

      Person p = (Person) db.fetch("first");

      p.print();

      Person c = new Person();
      c.age = 0;
      c.name = "baby";
      p.add(c);

      tx.commit();
      db.close();
   }
}
```

Figure 3. Updating Java Objects

A new person object "baby" is created and added to "John Doe's" children array. All 3 objects are updated to the database upon the transaction commit.

In summary, the Java programmer will encounter limited intrusion when writing persistent programs. Figure 4 shows the UML class diagram for class DBAccess.

6. Implementation

The architecture of our prototype implementation [Ege et al., 1998a]. has the following components:

1. a Java front-end as described in Sections 4 and 5 of this paper;
2. a substrate, or facilitator, that enables our reflection-based persistence approach;
3. a communications protocol called Icecube, which enables objects to travel in a network of distributed clients and servers;
4. data base servers: either directly implemented database core engines, or proxy servers that interact with other database systems.

Components 2 and 3 are provided in form of a Java package. The package contains the classes DBAccess as well as the meta classes for the semantic object-oriented database system.

Another important element of the architecture is the Icecube communications link: Icecube enables a set of command that allow a Java application program to access the services of the server database system. Java persistent object access is translated into Icecube commands. The commands travel on the socket link to the database server. The database server receives the command through its engine interface (EI). This EI is implemented as

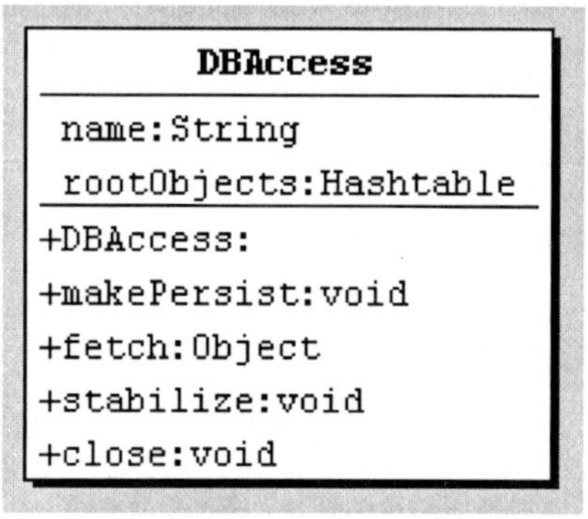

```
┌─────────────────────────────────┐
│            DBAccess             │
├─────────────────────────────────┤
│  name:String                    │
│  rootObjects:Hashtable          │
├─────────────────────────────────┤
│  +DBAccess:                     │
│  +makePersist:void              │
│  +fetch:Object                  │
│  +stabilize:void                │
│  +close:void                    │
└─────────────────────────────────┘
```

Figure 4. Database Access Class

a set of switch statements that make the function calls associated with the method invocation information (Action Code) of an incoming message. The database engine delivers its results through its EI. The EI packages the results into a message and sends it out through the socket.

Our architecture allows for multiple servers to connect to an Java API via our IceCube communications link. 2 servers are envisioned: both are based on the semantic binary database model [Rishe, 1992]: the first is implemented using Java; the second is represented with its C++ API, which maps itself into 2 available servers, one written again in C++, the other simulated on top of a relational database server.

7. Conclusion

In this paper we presented a flexible application programmer interface that allows Java objects to be stored in an object-oriented database system. Our approach uses a reflection mechanism, that inspects and changes a running Java program. Our approach requires limited intrusion into a normal Java program. Especially, it is not necessary to pre-process Java code or post-process Java byte codes. A standard Java compiler can be used. The code is able to run on any standard Java virtual machine.

Our future plans call for an investigation of using the reflection approach for other aspects of object-oriented database systems, such as schema evolution, query optimization, and load balancing.

References

[Atkinson et al., 1996] Atkinson, M., Daynes, L., Jordan, M., Printezis, T., and Spence, S. (1996). An orthogonally persistent java. *ACM SIGMOD Record*, 25(4):68–75.

[Catell et al., 1997] Catell, R., Barry, D., Bartels, D., Berler, M., Eastman, J., Gamerman, S., Jordan, D., Springer, A., Strickland, H., and Wade, D., editors (1997). *The Object Database Standard: ODMG 2.0*. Morgan Kaufmann.

[Ege et al., 1998a] Ege, R. K., Battikhi, Y., Pardo, P., Uppal, J., and Rishe, N. (1998a). A modular java api for object-oriented databases. *Proceedings of IEEE COMPSAC 98*.

[Ege et al., 1998b] Ege, R. K., Liu, J., and Lebedev, V. (1998b). *Using Java to add "Stored Procedures" to Databases*. FIU-HPDRC Technical Report.

[Gem, 1998] Gem (1998). *GemStone/J Programming Guide*. GemStone Systems, Inc., www.gemstone.com.

[Hamilton and Catell, 1996] Hamilton, G. and Catell, R. (1996). *JDBC: A Java SQL API*. Sun Microsystems, Inc., http://java.sun.com.

[PSE, 1998] PSE (1998). *ObjectStore PSE and PSE Pro for Java User Guide*. Object Design, Inc., http://www.odi.com/.

[Rishe, 1992] Rishe, N. (1992). *Database Design: The Semantic Modeling Approach*. Mc-Graw Hill.

[Stemple et al., 1993] Stemple, D., Morrison, R., Kirby, G., and Connor, R. (1993). Integrating reflection, strong typing and static checking. In *Proceedings of the 16th Australian Computer Science Conference*, pages 83–92, Brisbane, Australia.

[Xhumari et al., 1997] Xhumari, F., dos Santos, C. S., and Skubiszewski, M. (1997). Java universal binding: Storing java objects in relational and object-oriented database. In *Proceedings of The Second International Workshop on Persistence and Java(tm) (PJW2)*, Halfmoon Bay, CA.

Using Java to add "Stored Procedures" to Databases

Raimund K. Ege, Naphtali Rishe, Jingyu Liu, Vladimir Lebedev
High Performance Database Research Center *
School of Computer Science, Florida International University
University Park, Miami, FL 33199
ege@cs.fiu.edu

Abstract

The paper describes our approach to adding "stored procedure" capability to a semantic database system using Java byte-codes and Java's ability to dynamically load and execute Java code. Several steps were necessary: first we added a Java application programmer interface to the database system; then we created a database schema to hold Java executable code; then we constructed a Java class loader to allow code to be loaded from the database; then we enabled the creation of Java objects and executed the Java code for them. Our approach is not specific to our semantic database system, rather it can serve as a recipe for adding "stored procedures" to any database system.

1. Introduction

While database systems are meant to store data, increasingly demands arise to allow data manipulation within the database context. The database system typically enables such manipulation by storing procedures [Urman, 1996, Ranking, 1997], i.e. fragments of code, that can execute with data from the database.

Object-oriented database systems [Kim and Lochovsky, 1989, Atkinson et al., 1989] – by their very definition – already deal with procedurality. While an object stored in a database represents data, it is also an instance of a class, which may define applicable methods. These methods – if made available to the database system – can be executed with data, i.e. the objects, from the database, giving the database management system procedural capabilities.

In this paper we describe our approach to add "stored procedures" capability to a database system. Our specific database system uses the semantic modeling approach [Rishe, 1992] which extends the relational database model with user definable types, explicit relations, and inheritance. The semantic database model is close to an object-oriented model, however, it lacks the capability to capture methods.

In order to add procedure capability we considered 2 approaches: (1) to define our own programming language, or (2) use an existing one. Obviously, for choice (1) we would have to specify our own language, provide grammar, parser, compiler, run-time

This research was supported in part by NASA (under grants NAGW-4080, NAG5-5095, NAS5-97222, and NAG5-6830), NSF (CDA-9711582, IRI-9409661, HRD-9707076, and ANI-9876409), ARO (DAAH04-96-1-0049 and DAAH04-96-1-0278), AFRL (F30602-98-C-0037), BMDO (F49620-98-1-0130 and DAAH04-0024) DoI (CA-5280-4-9044), and State of Florida.

environment in order to make it viable. The existence of the Java programming language [Gosling et al., 1996, Jaworksi, 1996] made our choice (2) easy since several of its features greatly simplify our endeavor:

1. Java code is compiled and stored on a per-class basis. One Java class yields one Java compiled-code file (byte-code file).

2. Java code can be loaded dynamically. It does not have to be linked, neither statically nor dynamically at compile time.

3. Java supports reflective programming, i.e. a running Java program can modify itself while running. For example, a Java program can load a class, inquire about its methods, create instances of the new class, and invoke those methods for these instances, all in the same program.

4. Java is platform independent, so operating system dependencies are not present.

5. Java can easily interact with the C++ programming language, which is very important since our database management system is written entirely in C++ and has a C++ interface.

In the following sections we will first outline the basic elements of the semantic data model used in this database system: we will illustrate its C++ application programmer interface (API). Then we discuss the implementation of our Java to C++ bridge, which gives us a Java API to the database system. Next we illustrate a database schema to store Java code and give an example of how to store and retrieve it. And finally we show how to execute Java stored procedures with database data.

The paper concludes with some performance results and our vision of how to further enhance the database system.

2. The Semantic Binary Database System

The target of our research effort, the semantic binary database system [Rishe, 1992], models data in a semantic fashion, but employs a highly efficient binary storage model [Rishe, 1996].

The semantic model allows the definition of categories, relations and database types. Database types exist for the most commonly found types such as numbers (arbitrary varying precision and magnitude), strings, large binary objects etc.. A category is a specification of a class of abstract objects in a database. Each category may have relations with other categories or database types. A relation from a category to a database type is called an attribute. A relation from a category to a category is called an abstract relation. Categories can have sub-categories, which models inheritance.

The storage model consists solely of binary facts, each of which describe an aspect of an abstract object in the database, as well as inverses of these facts constructed in a way guaranteeing optimality of the so-called "basic queries". Examples of such binary facts are:

- an abstract object is an instance of a certain category;
- an abstract object has an attribute with a certain value;
- an abstract object has an abstract relation to a certain category;

More details on this storage model can be found in [Rishe, 1996].

```
#include <iostream.h>
#include <sdb3.h>
main() {
  TDataBase* DB = OpenDataBase("Demo");
  DB->Transaction_Begin();
  // create class with attributes
  Category *cat = NewCategory(DB, "Person");
  NewRelation(DB, "name",  "Person", "String");
  NewRelation(DB, "birthYear","Person", "integer");
  // make instances
  Var p1 = DB->NewAbstract("Person");
  p1.Assign("Person::name","John Doe");
  p1.Assign("Person::birthYear",1958);
  Var p2 = DB->NewAbstract("Person");
  p2.Assign("Person::name","Sue Miller");
  p2.Assign("Person::birthYear",1965);
  // simple query
  SetQuery list = cat->GetObjects();
  Var person;
  while (list.GetVarInc(person)) {
    cout << pChar(person.Query("Person::name").GetVar()) << ", ";
    cout << pChar(person.Query("Person::birthYear").GetVar()) << endl;
  }
  DB->Transaction_End();
  CloseDataBase(DB);
}
```

Figure 1. C++ API Example

The primary application programming interface (API) to this database system is for the C++ programming language[SDB, 1995]. Figure 1 shows a simple C++ example: after opening a "Demo" database and starting a new transaction, we create a category Person, with attributes "name" of type String, "birthYear" of type integer. Then we create 2 instances of category Person and relate them to attribute values. A simple query retrieves the 2 instances from the database and prints their attribute values. The program ends with committing the transaction and closing the database.

The current C++ interface has no capability to define and attach methods to a category. In this example, a method to calculate the age of a person based on the birth year would be useful. In the following sections we will show how Java can be used to make this happen.

3. A Java to C++ bridge

The first step necessary was to create a Java application programmer interface to the semantic binary database. Our approach provides that by mimicking the C++ API with Java using the Java Native Interface [JNI, 1997] capability. We implemented a Java package that contains the same classes and functions as can be found in the C++ API. The Java classes define "native methods" which are implemented in C++ and call the respective C++ API functions.

For example, the C++ API has a function to create a new category: NewCategory(). The Java API defines a class Proc with static methods, one of them is newCategory().

Figure 2 shows a portion of the Java class [1]. Other methods that were also used in the C++ example (Figure 1), such as OpenDataBase() and NewRelation() now appear as methods of class Proc.

```
package JavaSDBAPIBridge;
  public final class Proc extends DataBaseObject {  ...
    public native static TDataBase createDataBase( String databasename );
    public native static TDataBase openDataBase( String databasename );
    public native static void closeDataBase( TDataBase db );
    public native static Category newCategory( TDataBase db, String name );
    public native static Relation newRelation( TDataBase db,
                                        String relation,
                                        String CategoryFrom,
                                        String CategoryTo );
  ... }
```

Figure 2. Java API Proc Class

Figure 3 shows a portion of the Java class Category, which mirrors the C++ Category class. For example, the method GetObjects() (see Figure 1) now becomes a native method of Java class Category. In order to complete the Java package we provide native C++ code that is dynamically loaded whenever the Java class executes. For each native Java method we have a C++ function which simply calls the respective C++ API function. For example, Java native method Category.getObjects() is linked to the C++ function

```
Java_JavaSDBAPIBridge_Category_getObjects__
```

which in turn calls the Category::GetObjects() function in the C++ API. The standard Java developer's kit (JDK) provides helper utilities, such as the javah command, to facilitate the native method interface. The name conventions and further detail can be found in [JNI, 1997]. Since C++ is not platform independent we provide compiled versions for

```
package JavaSDBAPIBridge;
public class Category extends DataBaseObject {  ...
  public native String getName( );
  public native Category[] getSupercategories( );
  public native Category[] getSubcategories( );
  public native Relation[] getRelations( );
  public native boolean hasRelation( Relation relation );
  public native boolean hasSupercategory( Category category );
  public native SetQuery getObjects( );
  ... }
```

Figure 3. Java API Class Category

both environments on which the semantic binary database system is available: Sun Solaris and Windows NT.

With the Java API, we can now rewrite our earlier C++ example. Figure 4 shows the resulting Java code. The Java code quite closely resembles the C++ code of Figure 1: we

---

[1]DataBaseObject is a common superclass to serveral classes in the Java API. It contains operations and attributes that are common to all of its subclasses. SetQuery is a class to capture query results.

```
import JavaSDBAPIBridge.*;
import lang.io.*;.*;
public class Main {
  public static void main( String[] args ) {
    TDataBase DB = Proc.openDataBase("Demo");
    DB.transactionBegin( );
    // create class with attributes
    Category cat = Proc.newCategory( DB, "Person" );
    Proc.newRelation(DB, "name", "Person", "String" );
    Proc.newRelation(DB, "birthYear", "Person", "integer" );
    // make instances
    Var p1 = DB.newAbstract("Person");
    p1.assign("Person::name","John Doe");
    p1.assign("Person::birthYear",1958);
    Var p2 = DB.newAbstract("Person");
    p2.assign("Person::name","Sue Miller");
    p2.assign("Person::birthYear",1965);
    // simple query
    SetQuery list = cat.getObjects();
    Var person;
    while (list.getVarInc(person)) {
      System.out.println(Proc.pChar(person.query("Person::name").getVar())
        + ", " + proc.toLong(person.query("Person::birthYear").getVar()));
    }
    DB.transactionEnd( );
    Proc.closeDataBase(DB);
} }
```

Figure 4. Java API Example Program

open the database, start a transaction, create a class, make instances, issue a simple query, and then commit the transaction and close the database.

The Java program accesses the semantic database as easily as C++.

4. The Java Class Repository

Java source code resides in files that have the extension ".java". While a source code file may contain more than one Java class, once it is compiled it will result in exactly one file with extension ".class" for each compiled Java class. Java ".class" files actually contain Java byte codes, which are executed in the context of a Java virtual machine [Lindholm and Yellin, 1996]. Java virtual machine implementations are available for most modern computing platforms and also are contained within typical Internet browsers. This is the key to Java's platform independence.

Figure 5 shows a simple Java class for our Person category example. It declares two attributes "name" and "birtYear", a constructor, and a simple method for age calculation. This class is quite similar to the Person category of Figures 1 and 4. When compiled, its code resides in file "Person.class".

To store Java code in the database all we need to handle is Java ".class" files. We create a simple category "JavaClassRepository" with attributes "name" and "data". The "data" attribute is of type "binary" which allows to store an arbitrary-long chunk of data.

```
public class Person {
    String name;
    int birthYear;
    public Person(String n, int b) {
        name = n; birthYear = b;
    }
    public int getAge(int when) { return when - birthYear; }
}
```

Figure 5. Java Person Class

```
public static void Store( String[] args ) {
    TDataBase DB = Proc.openDataBase("Demo");
    DB.transactionBegin( );
    // create classes with attributes
    Category cat = Proc.newCategory( DB, "JavaClassRepository" );
    Proc.newRelation(DB, "name", "JavaClassRepository", "string" );
    Proc.newRelation(DB, "data", "JavaClassRepository", "binary" );
    // code to load Person.class into buffer
    File theFile = new File("Person.class");
    DataInputStream fileStream =
        new DataInputStream(new FileInputStream(theFile));
    // allocate a buffer and read the data into it
    byte[] buffer = new byte[theFile.length];
    fileStream.readFully(buffer);
    // make instance
    Var c = DB.newAbstract("JavaClassRepository");
    c.assign("JavaClassRepository::name","Person");
    c.assign("JavaClassRepository::data", buffer);
    DB.transactionEnd( );
    Proc.closeDataBase(DB);
}
```

Figure 6. Storing Class Code

Figure 6 shows the Java program [2] which creates the schema and loads the Person class into the database: it first opens the "Demo" database, starts a new transaction, then makes a new category JavaClassRepository with two relations to attributes "name" and "data". Then it opens and reads the "Person.class" file into a buffer, and finally creates a database object and assigns its name and data. Figure 7 shows how to retrieve a Java class from the database: the code is quite similar to the code in Figure 4. After opening the database, creatin a transaction, we read all classes in the database, then commit and cloase the database.

5. Execution of Java Code

And finally we want to execute Java code. Assuming that the database contains Java class code and also instances for the same class, we need to do the following steps:

1. read Java ".class" code from the database;

---

[2]for clarity, we have ommitted the Java housekeeping and exception handling code.

```
public static void Show( String[] args ) {
  TDataBase DB = Proc.openDataBase("Demo");
  DB.transactionBegin( );
  // find category, read instances
  Category cat = DB.findCategory("JavaClassRepository");
  Relation rel = DB.findRelation("JavaClassRepository::name");
  // show the list of all java classes in the database
  SetQuery list = cat.getObjects();
  Var aClass;
  while(list.getVarInc(aClass) {
    System.out.println(Proc.pChar(aClass.query(rel).getVar()));
  }
  DB.transactionEnd( );
  Proc.closeDataBase(DB);
}
```

Figure 7. Reading Class Code

2. dynamically create a Java class from ".class" code;

3. find instances of a corresponding category in the database;

4. create instance of Java class with data from the database;

5. execute a method.

In order to dynamically create a class in Java we need to create a special class loader. The Java code for a DBClassLoader is shown in Figure 8. It is defined as a subclass of Java class ClassLoader which is part of the Java standard distribution. The critical method is loadClass which first tries to find the class in a local cache – to prevent multiple definitions –, checks whether the requested class is a system class, and then finally calls defineClass which creates a new Java class based on the btye-codes passed in a buffer parameter. The next step is to resolve the class, i.e. to make sure that all other Java names used within the new class are also loaded and present.

With this DBClassLoader class we can now show an example that illustrates these steps. The Java code in Figures 9 and 10 first opens that database and starts a new transaction; it then finds the JavaClassRepository category with its attribute relations; it then reads the Java byte-codes from the database, creates an instance of the DBClassLoader class, and loads the byte-codes using the loadClass method; it then finds the constructor and the getAge method using Java's reflective programming capabilities. Figure 10 then continues with the code find and read Person data from the database, and finally creates Java Person objects and executes the getAge() method.

In the example we loaded only a single isolated class from the database. The Person class only references builtin data types "String" and "int". More complicated classes, of course, will be related to other classes: those classes can either be also fetched from the database or resolved from the local execution environment subject to the normal Java "CLASSPATH" search rules.

The performance of executing "stored procedures" was quite acceptable, posing little overhead in addition to the regular database access times. However, even that can easily be improved. For example, to execute the method "getAge()" we had to construct a Java Person object. As easily we can define a static method "calculateAge()" as shown in Figure 11 and call it instead of "getAge()". Since we do not have the overhead of creating a Java

```
import java.io.*;
import java.util.*;
public class DBClassLoader extends ClassLoader {
  private byte buf[] = null;
  private Hashtable sdbClassCache = new Hashtable();
  public DBClassLoader(byte inBuf[]) {
    buf = inBuf;
  }
  public synchronized Class loadClass(String name, boolean resolve)
        throws Class NotFoundException {
    try {
      // try to find the class in cache
      Class aClass = (Class)sdbClassCache.get(name);
      if (aClass == null) {
        try {
          // check if it's a system class
          aClass = findSystemClass(name);
        } catch (Exception e) {
          System.out.println(" System class: " + name + " not found");
        }
      }
      if (aClass == null) {
        aClass = defineClass(name, buf, 0, buf.length);
        sdbClassCache.put(name, aClass);
      }
      if (resolve) resolveClass(aClass);
      return aClass;
    } catch (Exception e) {
      System.out.println("DBClassLoader.loadClass: " + e.getMessage());
      throw new ClassNotFoundException(e.getMessage());
    }
  }
}
```

Figure 8. Database Class Loader

Person Object, the performance is significantly improved.

We measured the performance by loading 20000 objects from the database: with method invocation per **Person** object the program ran for 11.4 seconds; with static method invocation without creating Java **Person** objects it ran for 10.5 seconds. Without any method invocation, just reading 20000 objects using the Java API, the program ran for 10.1 seconds.

6. Conclusion

Our approach to adding "stored procedure" capability to the semantic binary database system uses the advanced features of the Java programming language. We make it possible to store and retrieve Java code from the database and then immediately execute it with acceptable performance. Our next research step is to use this facility to allow the definition of virtual categories. Virtual categories have attributes that are computed as needed by a query.

The approach described in this paper is actually a recipe that can easily be adopted and applied to other database system that need the capability to execute stored procedures.

```
import JavaSDBAPIBridge.*;
import java.io.*;
import java.lang.reflect.*;
import PersonClassLoader;
public class Execute {
 public static void main( String[] args ) {
    TDataBase DB = Proc.openDataBase("Demo");
    DB.transactionBegin( );
    // find Repository category and it's relations
    Category cat = DB.findCategory("JavaClassRepository");
    Relation className = DB.findRelation("JavaClassRepository::name");
    Relation classData = DB.findRelation("JavaClassRepository::data");
    // retrieve Java class 'Person' from category JavaClass_Repository,
    SetQuery query = Proc.rangeQuery(className, new Var("Person"));
    query.goFirst();
    Var dataClass = new Var(query); // assuming it's not null
    Var aData = dataClass.operatorDot(classData);
    // get the length of java class data
    int expectedBytes = (int)Proc.dbfilelength(aData);
    byte buffer[] = new byte[(int)expectedBytes];
    int readBytes = Proc.dbread(buffer, (short)expectedBytes, aData);
    Proc.dbclose(aData);
    // init class loader
    DBClassLoader classLoader = new DBClassLoader(buffer);
    // load the 'Person' class from the memory buffer
    Class personClass = classLoader.loadClass("Person", true);
    // init 'Person' constructor
    Class[] paramList = { Class.forName("java.lang.String"),
                          Class.forName("java.lang.Integer") };
    Constructor personConstructor = personClass.getConstructor(paramList);
    // init 'getAge' method
    Class[] whenList = {Class.forName("java.lang.Integer")};
    Method ageMethod = personClass.getMethod("getAge", whenList);
```

Figure 9. Executing Java Class Code

References

[Atkinson et al., 1989] Atkinson, M., Bancilhon, F., DeWitt, D., Dittrich, K., Maier, D., and Zdonik, S. (1989). The object-oriented database system manifesto. In *Proceedings of the First Conference on Deductive and Object-Oriented Databases*, Kyoto, Japan.

[Gosling et al., 1996] Gosling, J., Joy, B., and Steele, G. (1996). *The Java Language Specification*. Addison Wesley.

[Jaworksi, 1996] Jaworksi, J. (1996). *Java Developer's Guide*. Sams Net, Indiana.

[JNI, 1997] JNI (1997). *Java Native Interface Specification*. JavaSoft, A Sun Microsystems, Inc. Business, http://www.javasoft.com/products /jdk/1.1/docs/guide/jni/ spec/jniTOC.doc.html.

[Kim and Lochovsky, 1989] Kim, W. and Lochovsky, F. H., editors (1989). *Object-Oriented Concepts, Databases and Applications*. ACM Press, Reading, Mass.

[Lindholm and Yellin, 1996] Lindholm, T. and Yellin, F. (1996). *The Java Virtual Machine Specification*. Addison Wesley.

```
   // Find category, relations which represent class 'Person' in database
   Category cPerson = DB.findCategory("Person");
   Relation rPersonName = DB.findRelation("Person::name");
   Relation rPersonBYear = DB.findRelation("Person::byear");
   // Retrieve all instances of class 'Person' from database
   SetQuery list = cPerson.getObjects();
   Var aClass;
   while (list.getVarInc(aClass)) {
      // retrieve data for each person object
      String name = Proc.pChar(aClass.query(rPersonName).getVar());
      int byear = Proc.toLong(aClass.query(rPersonBYear).getVar());
      Object[] paramList = {new String(name), new Integer(byear)};
      // create an instance and invoke method
      Object obj = personConstructor.newInstance(paramList);
      System.out.println(name+" is "+ageMethod.invoke(obj, 1998)+ " old");
   }
   DB.transactionEnd( );
   Proc.closeDataBase(DB);
}
}
```

Figure 10. Executing Java Class Code (continued)

```
public class Person {
   String name;
   int birthYear;
   public Person(String n, int b) {
      name = n;
      birthYear = b;
   }
   public static int calculateAge(int when, int birthYear) [
      return when - birthYear;
   }
}
```

Figure 11. Java Person Class

[Ranking, 1997] Ranking, R. (1997). *Sybase SQL Server 11 Unleashed.* Sams Publishing.

[Rishe, 1992] Rishe, N. (1992). *Database Design: The Semantic Modeling Approach.* Mc-Graw Hill.

[Rishe, 1996] Rishe, N. (1996). A file structure for semantic databases. *Information Systems,* 16(4):375–385.

[SDB, 1995] SDB (1995). *Semantic Binary Database C++ Interface Version 3.* High Performance Database Research Center, School of Computer Science, Florida International University.

[Urman, 1996] Urman, S. (1996). *Oracle PL/SQL programming.* Oracle Press, Osborne McGraw-Hill.

A Concurrent Object-based Model
and its Use for Coordinating Java Components

S. Majoul, C. Percebois, J.-P. Bodeveix

IRIT, Université Paul Sabatier, 118 route de Narbonne

31062 Toulouse Cedex 4 - France

e-mail: {majoul,perceboi,bodeveix}@irit.fr

Abstract

We present a canonic model expressing the behavior of a system of communicating objects through multiset rewriting. Then, we discuss the integration of the so-defined model into the Java language. The choices and the restrictions made to implement the model as well as the architecture of the system are presented. Finally, we propose to use the prototype that we carried out as a coordination tool for communicating Java components. We focus on applications built around InfoBus, a standard package providing an event-based protocol for dynamic data-sharing between components. We show how our model can be used to coordinate Java events flowing on a software bus.

1: Introduction

The need of coordinating distributed activities has involved the design of coordination models. Some languages introduce the concept of shared dataspace as main tool for coordination. They offer a set of basic associative operations on a unique shared database called tuple space. Linda [9], one of the first advocates of this programming style, defines mainly an interface between a high level language and a database. Several models such as PoliS [5] improve on Linda by introducing multiple shared dataspaces and a more precise interaction protocol relying on the chemical metaphore [2].

On the other hand, the increased popularity of object-oriented programming has lead to the emergence of Linda-like object models such as [10] and [11] where tuples are first class objects. Another family of models relies on a rule-based mechanism integrating both concurrency and object aspects. We can put forward the Maude language [13] which uses a rewriting logic and the COOLL language [4] that relies on a fragment of linear logic. However, the handling of some object aspects in Maude are purely syntactic, notably regarding inheritance. Furthermore, the approach adopted in COOLL is constrained by the underlying logic, which obscures the expression of some features, for example process joining.

Our proposal, presented in section 2, consists in a general framework incorporating multiple data spaces management and parallelism. It relies on an algebraic representation of an object database whose transformations are expressed by rewriting rules. Unlike Maude, inheritance is implicit and is made possible by introducing a partial-order relation on rule heads that reduces the non-determinism by selecting the most specific rules. In section 3, an implementation of the model in the Java language is studied. Then, we propose in section 4 to coordinate Java events on a software bus. Finally, we conclude in section 5 and discuss some directions for future work.

0-7695-0278-4/99 $10.00 © 1999 IEEE

2: The calculus model

2.1: Objects

An object is seen as a multiset of valued attributes called the object *context* or the object *state*. The domain of an attribute is a term of the Herbrand universe. The attributes are separated by the operator ⋄ supposed associative, commutative and with neutral element $\epsilon_\diamond$. A special field called `self` is introduced to designate an object. For example a point p of coordinates 1 and 4 is represented as follows: $\text{self}(p) \diamond \text{x}(1) \diamond \text{y}(4)$.

An object database is represented by a sequence of ground terms denoting the objects which are connected by the associative-commutative operator # having $\epsilon_\#$ as neutral element. In the following, we consider the operator ⋄ as having a higher precedence than #. A database containing, for example, three points $p_1(1,2)$, $p_2(4,6)$ and $p_3(5,3)$ is coded by the term:

$$\text{self}(p_1) \diamond \text{x}(1) \diamond \text{y}(2) \ \# \ \text{self}(p_2) \diamond \text{x}(4) \diamond \text{y}(6) \ \# \ \text{self}(p_3) \diamond \text{x}(5) \diamond \text{y}(3)$$

2.2: Rewriting rules

Object evolution is specified by rewriting rules modulo the associativity and the commutativity of the operators ⋄ and # [3]. These rules apply to terms representing an object database and code state transitions of the database. An execution is a succession of rule applications deducing an irreducible term from the initial one. The syntax of a rewriting rule is the following:

$$\underbrace{s_1^1 \diamond \ldots \diamond s_1^{n_1} \ \# \ \ldots \ \# \ s_p^1 \diamond \ldots \diamond s_p^{n_p}}_{l} \longrightarrow \underbrace{t_1^1 \diamond \ldots \diamond t_1^{n_1'} \ \# \ \ldots \ \# \ t_q^1 \diamond \ldots \diamond t_q^{n_q'}}_{r}$$

where the s_i^j and the t_i^j are first order terms. The rule $l \to r$ applies to a term t if there exists a subterm u of t, a term u' equivalent to u (modulo the associativity and the commutativity of the operators ⋄ and #), and a substitution σ such that $u' = l\sigma$. So, the application of the rule rewrites the term t into $t[r\sigma/u]$ where u is the term matched by l, called pattern, and the term $t \backslash u$ is called the remaining context. Note that rewriting must be atomic in order to ensure the coherence of the object database. Furthermore, the model is essentially non-deterministic.

2.3: Rule classification

In order to reduce the non-determinism inherent in the model, we introduce a partial-order relation on rule heads which restricts the selection to the most specific ones. A rule r_1 is more specific than a rule r_2 if and only if terms reducible by r_1 are also reducible by r_2. Among the most specific rules applicable to a term, one is selected non-deterministically and is applied to the term. We have presented in [12] a formal definition of rule specificity as well as a classification algorithm.

2.4: Message sending

This model supports message sending naturally since a rule may directly insert a term into the context of another object. For reasons of convenience, we define the operator $o : m$ similar to asynchronous method invocation in object-oriented languages by:

$$\text{self}(o) \diamond x \ \# \ o : m \diamond y \longrightarrow \text{self}(o) \diamond x \diamond m \ \# \ y$$

Note that two messages sent to a same object are not necessarily handled in order of arrival.

2.5: Example

We consider the dining philosophers problem as presented in [4]. The following rule specifies the behavior of a hungry philosopher p in the presence of two free forks f_1 and f_2:

$$\text{self}(p) \diamond \text{hungry} \# \text{self}(f_1) \diamond \text{free} \# \text{self}(f_2) \diamond \text{free} \rightarrow \text{self}(p) \diamond \text{eat}(f_1, f_2) \# \text{self}(f_1) \# \text{self}(f_2)$$

When the rule applies, the context of each matched object is consumed an a new one is produced where the philosopher is eating and the forks are no longer free. After eating, the philosopher puts the forks down and thinks. This behavior is expressed by the following rule:

$$\text{self}(p) \diamond \text{eat}(f_1, f_2) \longrightarrow \text{self}(p) \diamond \text{think} \diamond f_1 : \text{free} \diamond f_2 : \text{free}$$

that consumes the message $eat(f_1, f_2)$ from the context of the philosopher p and produces the message *think*. The forks f_1 and f_2 become free by sending the message *free* to each of them.

3: Use of the model for coordinating Java objects

Many researches have been made to coordinate message sending among objects. Most of them introduce a meta-level interception mechanism between senders and receivers. One approach consists in matching messages one by one and redistributing them to the receiver when some condition is fulfilled [1]. However, in this proposal, reaction to a set of messages must be implemented in terms of reaction to a single message. Another approach, suggested by Frolund and Agha in [8], introduces the notion of activator that specifies the firing of an action when a set of messages is present. In the following sections, we show how our model can be used as a multi-object coordination tool based on the second approach.

Our model can be implemented in at least two ways: either as a real programming language or as a tool that can be integrated into an existing programming language. We adopt the second approach because most of the existing programming languages do not provide mecanisms dealing with multi-object coordination. Furthermore, it is easier for a programmer to use tools than to learn a new programming language. The increasing development of concurrent and distributed applications in the Java language has motivated us to implement our model in this language.

3.1: Integration into the Java language

The Java platform contains a large collection of ready-made software components (Java API) grouped into libraries or packages. The prototype that we carried out is provided as a Java package so that programmers can use it like any Java library. Nevertheless, the integration of the model into the Java language was not direct because the former is designed while disregarding any programming language. Hence, some restrictions and choices have to be made in order to comply with the object-oriented principles on which the Java language relies.

3.1.1: Problems raised by the integration

In the proposed model, a left hand of a rule mentions the attributes and messages that should be present in an object context. Exhibiting the state of an object in such a way violates the encapsulation principle of object-oriented programming. Furthermore, the model allows to express the mutation of an object through the production/consumption mechanism, which is incompatible with strong typing in Java. Hence, expressing object mutation in terms of change of membership class might be expensive.

3.1.2: Adopted solutions

The JavaBeans library, defining a software component model for Java, proposes an elegant solution to access private properties of a bean in order to be customized. A bean property can be either a simple data field or a computed value. It can be accessed through *setter* and *getter* methods whose names follow specific rules called *design patterns*. For example, the setter and getter methods of a property foo are respectively:

```
public void setFoo(PropertyType value);
public PropertyType getFoo();
```

We adopt this solution to avoid the violation of the encapsulation principle. So, a rewriting rule may have access to an object property by invoking the corresponding getter method. The property may be updated either through its setter method or through any other method of the object.

We remedy the problem of object mutation by forbidding the production and consumption of object attributes. However, to benefit from the expressiveness of the production/consumption mechanism on which the model relies, we introduce another data type called *message* different from an object method. Messages are atoms which can be added to and removed from the context of an object matched by a rewriting rule. Such messages are only managed by the rules and are not accessible by the Java code of an application. Hence, objects handled by a rule contain a static set of attributes accessible through method invocation and a dynamic multiset of messages.

A left hand of a rule enumerates the set of attributes and the multiset of messages that must be present in the context of the matched objects. As for the right hand, it contains any Java code. The application of a rule removes all the matched messages of the current objects and executes the Java code given in the right side.

3.2: Architecture

The model is implemented as a Java package called jrules that can be used in a Java application. The RuleManager interface, implemented by the RuleGateway class, specifies the methods allowing a Java programmer to use an already-compiled rule base.

```
public interface RuleManager
{   public void register (Object ob, boolean persist);  //registration of an object
    public void unregister (Object ob);
    public void activate (RuleBase rb, int mode);       //activation of the rule engine
    public void desactivate ();
}//end RuleManager
```

An instance of the RuleGateway class defines a gateway to a rule base. It contains at least a rule base, two object bases, one for persistent objects and the other for non-persistent objects and a rule engine undertaking pattern-matching, rule selection and rule application.

3.3: Rewriting Java objects

Rules are grouped into a named rule base. Messages exchanged between objects are declared globally by specifying their signature. Each rule is named and consists in a declaration part, a pattern part and an action part. The action part contains Java code extented with the operators : (message sending), NEW (creation of non-persistent objects) and NEWP (creation of persistent objects). For example, the behavior of a hungry philosopher, specified in §2.5, is defined by the rule:

```
rulebase Dinner
{ message free();
  rule tryToEat
    { var Philosopher p; Fork f1, f2;
          self(p), hungry(b) & {: b == true :}
      #   self(f1), free()
      #   self(f2), free()
      => {: p.eat(f1,f2); f1:free(); f2:free(); p.think() :}
    }
}
```

This rule involves three objects: a philosopher and two forks specified by three occurrences of the keyword `self`. A philosopher is matched by the variable `p` if the value `b` of its field `hungry` is `true`. The two forks are matched by the variables `f1` and `f2` if their respective message boxes contain the message `free`. When the rule applies, a message `free` is retrieved from the message box of each fork and the method `eat` is invoked on `p`. When the philosopher ends its meal, he releases the forks by sending a message `free` to each fork and starts thinking.

3.4: Implementation

The prototype that we carried out comprises two parts. One part deals with rule compilation and code generation. The other one implements pattern-matching, rule selection and rule application.

3.4.1: Rule compilation

The compilation of a rule file generates new classes: for the rule set, for each rule and for each message declaration. Then, the newly generated classes are compiled via the Java compiler.

The `jrules` package contains the `Message`, `RuleBase` and `Rule` classes which constitute the super-classes for the generated ones. The patterns defined in a rule base are compiled into a Rete net [7] allowing to perform associative-commutative pattern matching. The `Rule` class has two abstract methods `verify` and `execute`. In the sub-classes of `Rule`, the first method contains the generated code for the conditions of the current rule while the second one contains the generated code for the action part of the rule.

The Rete net generated at compile time contains four kinds of nodes. A token flowing on the net maintains a reference to an object to be matched and the current rule's free variables called environment. The left side of a rule dealing with n patterns (objects) is compiled into a net with n `EntryNodes` checking the type of the matched object, n sequences of `AlphaNodes`, each starting with an `EntryNode`, $n-1$ `BetaNodes` and an `ExitNode` storing successful tokens. A `BetaNode` joins the `AlphaNodes` ending two sequences. An `AlphaNode`, associated to an object's field or message, tries to unify the environment carried by the token with the field or the message arguments and checks the eventual conditions by invoking `verify` method on the corresponding rule.

3.4.2: Rule activation

Rule activation is ensured by a `RuleEngine` object that encapsulates a control thread. Its task consists in performing pattern matching, selecting a rule from the obtained conflict set and applying the selected rule.

Pattern-matching is achieved by an implementation of a variant of the Rete algorithm [7] that undertakes backtrack with consumption. A token enters the net through an `EntryNode` and tries to reach an `ExitNode`. While the token is progressing on the net, the free variables that it carries are instanciated gradually. In this implementation, each token on the net encapsulates a control thread hence allowing to perform pattern matching concurrently. Granularity of the matching system is managed by a controller object which can be customized according to the machine on which the system runs.

Pattern-matching terminates when all the control threads encapsulated by the tokens terminate. The set of pairs composed by a rule and its corresponding successful tokens, which are stored in the rule's ExitNode, forms the conflict set. In the current version of the prototype, the classification algorithm given in [12] is not implemented yet. Priority is awarded to rules according to their declaration order. Among the set of successful tokens obtained from the most specific rule's ExitNode, one token is non-deterministically selected. Then, this rule is applied by invoking its execute method with the instanciated environment in parameter. Finally, non-persistent objects that are matched by the applied rule are removed from the non-persistent object base.

4: Application

We focus on applications using a software bus as a communication support and requiring multi-object coordination. For this purpose, we use InfoBus[1] [6], a public specification of dynamic data-sharing technology which enables Java developpers to equip their components to communicate with other components in a structured way. Components in an InfoBus application can be classified in three types: *data producers*, *data consumers* and *data controllers*. An individual component can act at once as a producer, a consumer and also a controller. Data flows between components in named objects known as *data items*. Data controllers are specialized components that mediate the *rendezvous* between producers and consumers.

4.1: The InfoBus protocol for data exchange

InfoBus components use an event-based mechanism to announce data availability and request data among other components on the bus. Data exchange is made by name, thereby, components connected to a bus may exchange data without knowing about each other.

A data producer listens for requests and announces data availability or revocation by firing an event of type InfoBusItemAvailableEvent or InfoBusItemRevokedEvent. A consumer listens for availability and revocation events, and requests data by firing an InfoBusItemRequestedEvent. The role of a data controller is to play traffic cop on the bus. It participates in the distribution of events to consumers and producers. The default data controller performs one-to-all communication.

A data consumer (respectively producer) has to implement the interface InfoBusDataConsumer (respectively InfoBusDataProducer) provided by the infobus package. The InfoBusDataConsumer interface specifies two methods:

```
public void dataItemAvailable (InfoBusItemAvailableEvent event);
public void dataItemRevoked (InfoBusItemRevokedEvent event);
```

These methods are called by an InfoBus instance on which data exchange occurs in order to notify the consumer about the availability of some data in the first case, and the revocation of an announced data in the second one. The interface implemented by a producer supplies a method:

```
public void dataItemRequested (InfoBusItemRequestedEvent event);
```

which is also called by the bus in order to inform the producers about a request for a data.

---

[1] InfoBus is jointly designed by Lotus Development Corporation and Sun Microsystems' JavaSoft Division.

An InfoBus participant defines its reaction to a received event by implementing the method(s) specified by the appropriate interface(s). Note that all these methods define the reaction to a single event. The infobus package provides classes and methods defining operations allowing to get information about an event such as its source, the name of the announced data and the data.

4.2: Event coordination

Some applications involve object reactions whose logical cause is a set of events rather than a single event. Nevertheless, the infobus package provides classes and interfaces allowing to implement the reactions of an InfoBus participant caused by the reception of exactly one event. So, programmers must implement reaction to a set of events in terms of reaction to a single event. In order to defer a reaction until a number of events have been received, components must maintain a number of temporary variables which reflect the events received so far. Hence, programmers are forced to intermix two orthogonal design concerns: when to react and how to react [8].

The coordination of an event set received by an InfoBus participant (producer/consumer) can be expressed via a set of rewriting rules. The InfoBus participant has to implement the RuleManager interface supplied by the jrules package using the implementation provided by the RuleGateway class. Its reaction to an event reception consists in registering the event as a non-persistent object so that it can be handled by the rules once. Similarily, the redistribution of events received by a data controller to InfoBus participants can be expressed by a set of rewriting rules.

4.2.1: Example: the dining philosophers problem

We can imagine the following scenarios for the dining philosophers problem. In this example, we are interested in the coordination aspect rather than the resource management aspect.

The arrival A restaurant waiter manages a set of tables. When a group of philosophers arrives, the waiter announces the arrival to all the tables of the restaurant. In response, each table informs the waiter about its state: FREE or BUSY. The waiter waits for the replies and accepts the group if at least one table is free.

In this scenario, the waiter acts both as a producer and a consumer while the table acts as a producer. The waiter is notified by the arrival of a philosopher group through the call performArrival. This method is defined in the class Waiter below. The bus fires on behalf of the waiter an InfoBusItemAvailableEvent carrying the name ARRIVAL when the waiter invokes the method fireItemAvailable on the current bus. This method, provided by the InfoBus class has three arguments: the first one is the name to be announced, the second one is an optionnal description of the data and the last one is the event's source. A reference to the current bus is obtained through the getter method getInfoBus of the interface InfoBusMember supplied by the infobus package.

```
public class Waiter implements InfoBusDataProducer, InfoBusDataConsumer, RuleManager,...
{  private RuleGateway gateway;  private Group group; ...
   public void performArrival (Group g)
   { group = g; getInfoBus().fireItemAvailable("ARRIVAL",null,this);
   }
   public void dataItemAvailable (InfoBusDataItemAvailableEvent e)
   { gateway.register(e,false);
   }
   public Group getGroup () //the getter method of the property group
   { return group;         //invoked during pattern-matching
   }
}
```

When a table receives an event announcing the availability of a data named ARRIVAL, the bus fires on behalf of the table an InfoBusItemAvailableEvent, carrying the name FREE or BUSY according to the table state stored in the attribute isFree. This reaction is defined by the method dataItemAvailable of the class Table below.

```
public class Table implements InfoBusDataProducer,...
{ private boolean isFree; ...
    public void dataItemAvailable (InfoBusDataItemAvailableEvent e)
    { if (e.getDataItemName().equals("ARRIVAL"))
        if (isFree) getInfoBus().fireItemAvailable("FREE",null,this);
        else getInfoBus().fireItemAvailable("BUSY",null,this);
    }
}
```

The reception of all the replies by the waiter can be coordinated according to the rules below. We suppose that the restaurant contains only two tables. The reaction of the waiter to an InfoBus event consists merely in registering the event to a RuleGateway instance referenced by the attribute gateway of the class Waiter.

The Acceptance rule applies when at least one event announces the availability of a free table. In this case, the announced table is returned by the method requestDataItem provided by the InfobusItemAvailableEvent class. The table becomes occupied by the philosophers (method setGroup) which sit down round it (method sitDownRound). If all the received events carry the name BUSY, the Refusal rule applies and the philosopher group is refused by invoking the method noPlaceLeft supposed defined in the class Group.

```
rule Acceptance
  { var InfoBusItemAvailableEvent e1,e2; String n1,n2; Waiter w; Group g;
      self(w), group (g)
  # self(e1), dataItemName(n1) & {: n1.equals("FREE") :}
  # self(e2), dataItemName(n2) & {: n2.equals("FREE") || n2.equals("BUSY") :}
  => {: Table t = (Table) e1.requestDataItem(w,null);
          t.setGroup(g); g.sitDownRound(t);
      :}
  }//end Acceptance

rule Refusal
  { var InfoBusItemAvailableEvent e1,e2; String n1,n2; Waiter w; Group g;
      self(w), group(g)
  # self(e1), dataItemName(n1) & {: n1.equals("BUSY") :}
  # self(e2), dataItemName(n2) & {: n2.equals("BUSY") :}
  => {: g.noPlaceLeft(); :}
  }//end Refusal
```

Figure 1 shows the interaction between the actors participating in this scenario during the negotiation phase. Zigzag arrows depict event firing while the others represent method invocation. The numbers on the arrows indicate the order in which the methods are invoked.

Around the table Around the table, the actors are the forks on the table, the philosophers and the table itself. A fork acts as a producer that announces its availability when it becomes free. A philosopher acts both as a producer notifying that he is hungry and as a consumer that picks up forks. Finally, the table acts both as a data controller that mediates the rendezvous between a hungry philosopher and two free forks, and as a data producer that provides the forks to the

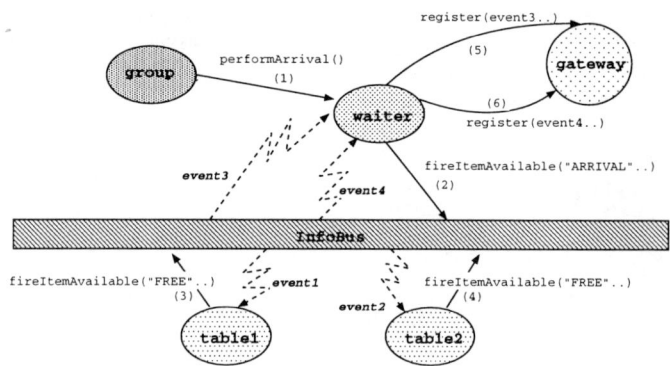

Figure 1. The arrival

philosopher. The Rendezvous rule, given below, fires when three events meet: one announces the availability of a hungry philosopher and the others announce the availability of two free forks.

```
rule Rendezvous
{ var InfoBusItemAvailableEvent e1,e2,e; String n,n1,n2; Table t;
    self(t)
 #  self(e),  dataItemName(n) & {: n.equals("HUNGRY") :}
 #  self(e1), dataItemName(n1) & {: n1.equals("FORK") :}
 #  self(e2), dataItemName(n2) & {: n2.equals("FORK") :}
=> {: TwoForks tf = new TwoForks((Fork) e1.requestDataItem(t,null),
                                 (Fork) e2.requestDataItem(t,null));
      Philosopher p = (Philosopher) e.getSourceAsProducer();
      t.reserveTwoForksFor(tf,p);
      t.getInfoBus().fireItemAvailable("TWO_FORKS",null,t,p);
   :}
}//end Rendezvous
```

When the Rendezvous rule applies, an object tf of type TwoForks is created. It contains the fork announced by the event e1 and the one announced by the event e2. The table reserves these forks to the hungry philosopher p which is the source of the event e. The method getSourceAsProducer, defined in the InfoBusItemAvailableEvent class, returns the source of the current event. The method reserveTwoForksFor, supposed defined in the Table class, associates two forks tf to a philosopher p so that they can be returned to the philosopher when he requests them. Finally, the table requests the bus to directly notify the philosopher p about the availability of two forks. The last parameter of fireItemAvailable represents the consumer that receives the notification event.

```
public class Philosopher implements InfoBusDataProducer, InfoBusDataConsumer,...
{ ...
   public void dataItemAvailable (InfoBusDataItemAvailableEvent e)
   { if (e.getDataItemName().equals("TWO_FORKS"))
      { TwoForks tf = (TwoForks) e.requestDataItem(this,null);
        eat(tf);  releaseForks(tf);  think();  leaveTheRestaurant();
      }
   }
}
```

On the reception of an available event carrying the name TWO_FORKS, the philosopher gets the two forks reserved by the table, eats, releases the forks, thinks and leaves the restaurant. When a fork becomes free, an InfoBusItemAvailableEvent carrying the name FORK is fired on behalf of the fork.

5: Conclusion

We have presented a calculus model for a system of communicating objects. This model relies on a term algebra provided with the associative-commutative operators ⋄ and # used respectively as attribute and object separators. The evolution of an object of the database is specified by a set of rewriting rules. The non-determinism inherent in this kind of model is reduced by introducing a partial-order relation on rule heads restricting the selection to the most specific rules.

The increasing development of concurrent and distributed applications in the Java programming language has motivated us to implement our model in this language. The integration of the model into Java has raised some problems since the model was initially designed while disregarding any programming language. These problems are overcame by making some choices and restrictions. Finally, we have presented the InfoBus protocol for data exchange which relies on an event-based mechanism. We showed how our model can be used to coordinate events on a software bus.

There are at least three directions for future work. One would be to implement the rule classification algorithm based on the partial-order relation over patterns. The second one would be to structure rule bases. Finally, it remains to experiment our prototype with distributed applications.

References

[1] M. Aksit, K. Wakita, J. Bosch, L. Bergmans, and A. Yonezawa. Abstracting Object Interactions Using Composition Filters. In R. Guerraoui, O. Nierstrasz, and M. Riveill, editors, *in object-based distributed processing*, LNCS, pages 152–184. Springer-Verlag, 1993.

[2] G. Berry and G. Boudol. The Chemical Abstract Machine. In *Seventeenth Annual ACM Symposium on Principles of Programming Languages*, pages 81–94, San Francisco, CA., January 1990.

[3] J.-P. Bodeveix, C. Percebois, and S. Majoul. An Object-Oriented Coordination Model based on Multiset Rewriting. In *9th International Conference on Parallel and Distributed Computing Systems*, PDCS'96, Dijon, September 1996.

[4] S. Castellani and P. Ciancarini. Exploring the Coordination Space with LO. Technical Report 94-6, UBLCS, University of Bologna, Laboratory for Computer Science, April 1994.

[5] P. Ciancarini and M. Gaspari. Parallel Symbolic Computing with the Shared Dataspace Coordination Model. Technical Report 94-17, UBLCS, University of Bologna, Laboratory for Computer Science, July 1994.

[6] M. Colan. InfoBus 1.1.1 Specification. http://java.sun.com/beans/infobus/, September 1998.

[7] C. Forgy. Rete: A Fast Algorithm for the Many Patterns Many Objects Match Problem. *Artificial Intelligence*, 19(1), September 1982.

[8] S. Frolund and G. Agha. Abstracting Interactions Based on Message Sets. In P. Ciancarini, O. Nierstrasz, and A. Yonezawa, editors, *in Object-Based Models and Languages for Concurrent Systems*, LNCS. Springer-Verlag, 1995.

[9] D. Gelernter. Generative Communication in Linda. *ACM Transactions on Programming Languages and Systems*, 7(1):80–112, 1985.

[10] Keld K. Jensen. *Toward a Multiple Tuple Space Model*. PhD thesis, Aalborg University, Dept. of Mathematics and Computer Science, Inst. for Electronic Systems, 1994.

[11] T. Kielmann. Designing a Coordination Model for Open Systems. In O. Nierstrasz, editor, *Coordination Languages and Models*, LNCS, pages 267–284. Springer-Verlag, 1996.

[12] S. Majoul, C. Percebois, and J.-P. Bodeveix. Reasoning about Negative Conditions in a Concurrent Rewriting System. In *2nd France-Japan Workshop on Object-Based Parallel and Distributed Computation*, Toulouse, October 1997.

[13] J. Meseguer. A Logical Theory of Concurrent Objects and Its Realization in the Maude Language. In G. Agha, P. Wegner, and A. Yonezawa, editors, *Research Directions in Concurrent Object-Oriented Programming*. MIT Press, 1993.

Technical Papers

Tools

Managing the Software Development by Using the Recursive Multi-Threaded (RMT) Tool

Arturo I Concepcion
Department of Computer Science
California State University,
San Bernardino
5500 University Parkway
San Bernardino, CA 92407
concep@csci.csusb.edu

Sunny Lin
Administrative Computing Services
California State University,
San Bernardino
5500 University Parkway
San Bernardino, CA 92407
slin@csusb.edu

Scott J. Simon
Environmental Systems Research Institute
380 New York Street
Redlands, CA 92373
ssimon@esri.com

Abstract:

A number of software life-cycles for object-oriented software development (Fountain Model, Recursive/Parallel Model, McGregor and Sykes Model, and Chaos Model Life-Cycle) exist today. However, these life-cycles have little or no support for estimating and monitoring progress during the development of the software. The ability to measure progress during the development is significant because it allows both the managers and the developers to determine whether a project is on schedule or not. Identifying that a project is behind schedule allows managers and developers to notify appropriate individuals of any scheduling and/or budgetary impacts at an early stage during the development and to determine appropriate course of action. This paper presents the Recursive Multi-Threaded (RMT) software life-cycle which supports the monitoring of progress during development, addresses the specific needs of the developing object-oriented software, and attempts to resolve deficiencies found in many existing software life-cycles. What makes RMT unique from existing software life-cycles is its use of a "thread" for partitioning and organizing software development activities. Threads support iteration and recursion, which are critical concepts for the development of the software. To implement the concepts of the RMT software life-cycle model, we develop the RMT Tool, which is Java-based. The Tool was used in an actual software development project in our software engineering course to test its functionalities.

1. Introduction and Motivation

One area of software engineering aimed at improving how software is developed, is the definition of a repeatable, systematic process that can be applied to the construction of software, called a software life-cycle. A repeatable process helps eliminate many of the uncertainties common to software development. In order to create a repeatable process, a software life-cycle defines a set of activities, what tasks are performed during each activity, the order that the activities occur, the preconditions that must be met before beginning an activity, and the postconditions that must be met before an activity is complete.

Some common activities included in life-cycles are analysis, design, coding, and testing. These activities, and the life cycle itself, are intended to make the development effort more efficient, so it is equally important that the process does not impede the work of the developers.

Aside from the need for better software development processes because of system failures, there is a need for developing an object-oriented life-cycle that facilitates the monitoring of progress during development. Existing life-cycles (Waterfall [12], Spiral [3], Win-Win Spiral [2], Recursive/Parallel [1], Fountain [7], Chaos Model/Life-Cycle [11], McGregor and Sykes [10], Visual Modeling Technique [6], and Methodology for Object-oriented Software Engineering of System [8]) have little or no support for monitoring progress and/or the structure of existing life-cycles makes progress monitoring difficult. The ability to measure progress during development is significant because it allows managers and developers to determine whether a project is on schedule or not. When a project overruns some planned schedule, the ability to monitor progress during development can help identify that the project is behind schedule earlier during development, rather than at the final delivery date, allowing managers/developers to take appropriate actions to accommodate the situation.

Another motivation is that there is a demand for object-oriented life-cycles because traditional life-cycles are ill-suited for object-oriented technology. While the history of object-oriented programming and object-oriented techniques date back to the 1960's, it was not until the 1980's that object-oriented technology began to be widely used within the software engineering community. The object model focuses on entities (objects), their attributes, and their behavior rather than placing the emphasis on functions. Due to this significant difference, and others, between procedural and object-oriented methods, many traditional life-cycles simply do not address the requirements specific to the development of object-oriented software. Some specific requirements that some traditional life-cycles do not support are iteration or the overlap of development activities, which are common for object-oriented projects.

Estimating progress can be difficult. Without some technique for estimating progress, estimates are simply best guesses based upon the opinions of the developers. Personal opinions will vary between individuals and the accuracy of the estimate depends upon their education, experience, skill, and luck. Even though estimating progress is not explicitly supported by the mentioned life-cycles, additional methods could be used. However, the organization of the development process in each of these life-cycles makes estimating progress fundamentally difficult (but not necessarily impossible) for one of two reasons. The first reason is that some life-cycles are too flexible by allowing development to proceed almost randomly between activities making it difficult to determine the current state and progress of development. The fountain model, chaos life-cycle, and McGregor and Sykes are examples of this flexibility. The other difficulty imposed by some life-cycles, such as VMT and MOSES, on estimating progress is that the smallest unit of management is an iteration, which makes estimating progress difficult (and potentially inaccurate).

2. The Recursive Multi-Threaded (RMT) Software Life-Cycle

Many of the underlying concepts and techniques of RMT are also found in existing life-cycles (e.g., the spiral model [3] and the recursive/parallel model [1]), but the presentation and implementation of those concepts differentiate RMT from these life-cycles. Even though techniques used by RMT, such as iteration and recursion, have also been proposed in existing life-cycles, what differentiates RMT from existing life-cycles is the use of a development "thread" as a conceptual unit to organize development activities and to monitor progress. RMT is a milestone-based, iterative life-cycle that supports incremental and parallel development. It uses a divide-and-conquer technique to system implementation, and supports multiple levels of information abstraction. The use of threads to organize development helps provide a form of control to the complex nature of object-oriented software development (often interpreted as chaotic). There are a number of essential concepts that define the RMT process. Specifically, they are threads, iteration, and recursion. The following sections describe each of these concepts in detail.

2.1 Threads

An RMT thread consists of a set of activities, or phases, that have well-defined goals, inputs, and outputs. These activities are not unique to RMT but are present in many other software life-cycles. An RMT thread is composed of requirement analysis, planning, analysis, design, implementation, testing, and quality assurance phases, see Figure 1. These activities are generally performed in a sequential order, although there may be overlap between some phases. Unlike traditional, sequential life-cycle models, certain thread phases may begin prior to the completion of the preceding phase. The most common overlap of phases occurs in the analysis, design, implementation, testing, and quality assurance phases.

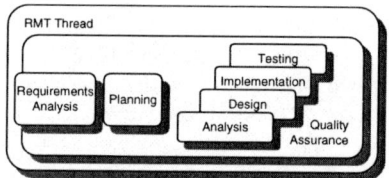

Figure 1. RMT Thread Activities/Phases

Each thread has a team of individuals (one or more) who perform activities to implement software components to satisfy the requirements for that thread. Within a thread team, there is one individual, the thread manager, who is responsible for the software component(s) built by the thread. Developers may work on many different threads and thread managers may manage more than one thread.

2.2 Iterative/Evolutionary Development

When given a set of requirements for a software component (whether they are for an entire system or for a single class), the development of the component should be partitioned into a number of incremental releases, distributing the requirements among the incremental releases. The requirements should be prioritized according to an effectiveness/cost ratio and scheduled so that the highest ranked requirements are included in the earliest releases. It is possible that the planned iterations may change during the course of development. Planned iterations may be removed because system requirements may be deleted or new iterations may be added due to new requirements or the modification of existing requirements. In addition, if technical problems occur, such as design or implementation flaws, new iterations may be required to resolve the flaws.

These incremental releases do not need to be given to the end user or other team members, but may simply be used as an internal development milestone. In fact, an incremental release may not even satisfy any of the given requirements. Early project increments may simply implement a basic system architecture or framework that the remainder of the software system will be built on. Thread iterations may also be used as a way to explore and further define vague or incomplete requirements, evaluate potential risks, or to prove/disprove crucial design decisions. When given vague requirements or the design for a critical component, a thread iteration may simply implement a prototype to clarify requirements or as a proof-of-concept for a design specification. This prototype can be included as a thread iteration during the planning phase for the thread. Figure 2 shows an N thread iteration of a software project or component.

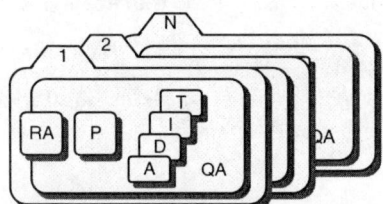

Figure 2. RMT Thread with N-Iterations

2.3 Recursion

Each RMT thread begins with a given set of requirements for a software component that the thread must implement. These requirements may be in varying levels of abstraction, ranging from very high-level (for an entire system) to very specific (for a single class). As previously mentioned, these requirements may be prioritized and implemented in various thread iterations. Within a single thread iteration, the implementation phase begins when enough design information has been defined from analysis and design phases to specify what needs to be implemented (the preconditions of the implementation phase are specified later). If the design information is the specification for a small-grained component (a class or group of classes) then the implementation phase results in the actual coding of the component. If, however, the design is for a higher-level component, then the current design must be further detailed to identify and define all of the classes required to implement the higher-level component(s). To make this process of specialization more manageable, the design of each higher-level component is decomposed into smaller cohesive groups and new, more specialized, threads are spawned to satisfy each of these groups of requirements (i.e., divide-and-conquer). Each of these child threads follow the same rules as its parent thread; they may iterate many times and they may have a number of child threads themselves. The implementation phase of a given thread is completed when all iterations of all its child threads have been completed or it has been terminated prematurely because of some failure. Figure 3 shows a thread spawning a child thread through the implementation phase of the parent thread.

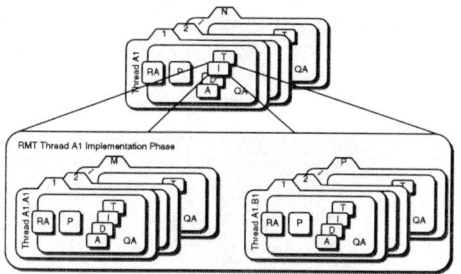

Figure 3. RMT Thread with Recursion

Because threads may create other threads, there may be any number of threads that are being "executed" at any given time, each of which may be in a different phase. In addition, all development initiates from a single thread, the root, which represents the entire system. All other threads are spawned, either directly or indirectly, from the root thread.

2.4 Benefits of Threads

The purpose of using threads as abstractions of the development process is to provide control and management for a complex process. As a result of using threads as a form of control, they provide a mechanism for monitoring progress during development, allow parallel development, and support multiple levels of abstraction. The following sections discuss these benefits in detail.

2.4.1 Monitoring Progress: RMT supports the task of monitoring progress during development by providing a mechanism that makes the process of evaluating and interpreting progress estimates easier for developers. Progress estimation begins at the smallest unit of abstraction in RMT, a class. The implementation of a class is performed within the conceptual unit of a thread, which is partitioned into a number of iterations. Before the implementation of the class actually begins, each iteration is assigned a percentage of overall effort required to implement the class (the sum of the percentages for all iterations is 100%). Progress is measured by summing up the assigned percentages of iterations that have been completed, plus the assigned percentage of the current (incomplete) iteration multiplied by its estimated progress. For example, consider the implementation of a class that is partitioned into three iterations with percentages of 40%, 35%, and 25% of the overall implementation effort, respectively, given to each iteration. If the first iteration is completed and the second iteration is 50% completed, the overall implementation is 57.5% complete $((40\% * 1.0) + (35\% * 0.5) + (25\% * 0.0) = 57.5\%)$.

The progress of an implementation phase is simply the sum of the weighted progress estimates of each of its child threads. For example, if the implementation phase of a thread has two child threads, A and B, where A constitutes 75% of the implementation effort and B constitutes 25% of the implementation effort, weights of 0.75 and 0.25 will be assigned to each of the child threads, respectively. If thread A is 25% complete and thread B is 75% complete, the overall progress of the parent threads implementation phase is 37.5% $((0.75 * 0.25) + (0.25 * 0.75) = 0.375)$

While this still requires the developers to estimate the percentage of overall effort that each iteration and child thread represent, it does provide some systematic method for estimating progress of complex components and an entire system.

2.4.2 Multiple Abstraction Levels: When applying RMT to a particular project, all of the threads are organized in a hierarchy. Each level in the thread hierarchy represents a different level of abstraction. High-level threads address general overall system requirements while low-level threads address the requirements for individual classes. Each thread abstraction level is usually managed and implemented by different developers because each abstraction level requires a different skill set and expertise. While there can be any number of abstraction levels in a particular project, there are three broad classifications: project-level, subsystem-level, and class-level.

Threads in the project-level category address the high-level (broad) system requirements. The highest level thread is the root thread, which represents the entire system being developed. All other threads are spawned from the root thread. Brooks feels that the project architect is responsible for partitioning the overall system into subsystems. [4] Each of these subsystems will have its own architect, which may or may not be the project architect. Class-level threads represent the threads that deal with the lowest level of detail (the most specific), which is the actual implementation of a class. Software engineers and programmers are responsible for class-level threads. Subsystem-level threads represent the intermediate threads between the project-level and class-level threads, which deal with subsystems and modules. Project designers are generally responsible for subsystem-level threads, although the project architect may be involved for higher-level subsystem threads and software engineers may be involved for lower-level subsystem threads, depending upon the availability of resources. Figure 4 shows the multiple level abstractions levels of RMT.

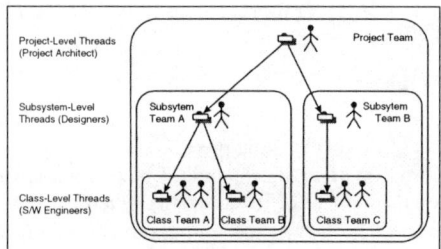

Figure 4. Levels of Thread Abstractions and Thread Managers

3. The Recursive Multi-Threaded (RMT) Tool

The Recursive Multi-Threaded (RMT) Tool is an implementation of the concepts of the Recursive Multi-Threaded software life-cycle model, which supports the object-oriented approach of software development to monitor and predict the progress of software during its development. Table 1 shows the functionalities of the RMT Tool.

Function	Objectives
Project Manager	Creates new project by the project leader and allows personnel to browse the project and artifacts within their security clearance.
Progress Manager	Provides an input function, which allows users to enter new progress or modify the current information of iterations and weights.

Single Project Progress Report	Produces progress reports depending on the user security clearance; the progress report is either in bar chart or text format.
Multiple Projects Progress Report	Produces a graph and determines the critical path for a group of projects.
Project Prediction	Predicts when the project will be delivered; it includes how many days are remaining for completing the project and a calendar day of completion.
Personnel Management	Contains information for all projects and personnel included with the project; the database is maintained by project leader; programmers are added to a project by the project leader or team-leaders; all other personnel can change their personal password for security reason.

Table 1. Functions of RMT Tool

To illustrate the functionalities of the RMT Tool, we applied the Tool to an actual software project called Algorithma [5]. The Algorithma (algorithm animation) Project is a software package that visualizes the effect of algorithm steps to the data structures that it operates. It is an end user product designed to allow students of computer science to explore various algorithms and data structures. Algorithma is being developed as an on-going software project for the undergraduate software engineering course in the Department of Computer Science, California State University, San Bernardino.

3.1 Single Project Progress Reporting

The introduction frame is shown in Figure 5 which shows all four main features: creation of new projects, browsing existing projects, accessing personnel information, and managing of multiple projects. For the creation of new projects, the user is able to enter the name of the project, the number of iterations the development team will take to finish the project, an estimate of how long the entire project will take, and the weight or percentage of each iteration for the entire project (the sum of these weight must be 100%).

Figure 5. Main Menu of RMT Tool.

For browsing an existing project, the user will see an organization tree as shown in Figure 5. On the top-left corner of the screen, the project is given A98 as the project ID. Here we see the entire project is being implemented using two iterations. The root thread has two spawned child threads, the left thread labeled as A981 and the right thread labeled as A982. The root is the thread of the entire project, whose color is partially filled up, meaning that this thread is not yet finished. The two child threads are shown with the left thread whose color is completely filled up, meaning A981 is completed, and the right thread, A982, is not yet completed. Each child thread, labeled by the Team Leader's name, is assigned to different programming teams, as shown in Figure 6. The Team Leaders are shown as leaf nodes of the tree. When the user clicks on the Team Leader's node, a similar tree graph will show the number of threads used for implementing the task assigned to the team and the programmers assigned to implement each thread. When the user clicks on the programmer's node, the thread or threads (depending on the number of iterations) for the programmer is shown.

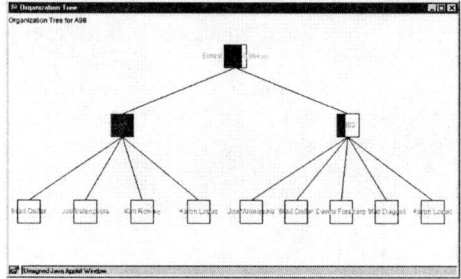

Figure 6. Organization Tree.

The thread A982 of Figure 6 is shown in detail in Figure 7. As can be seen from Figure 7, the implementation phase is partially done and testing has not yet started. If the user clicks on any filled block, the corresponding document will be shown in a new window. For example, when the Requirement Analysis block is clicked, the Software Requirement Specification is displayed and if the user clicks on the Planning block, the Software Quality Assurance Plan will be shown.

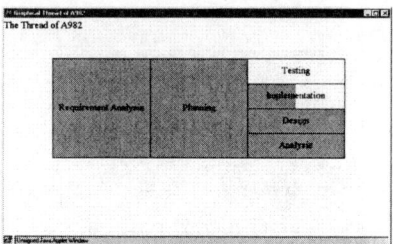

Figure 7. An RMT Thread.

From corresponding thread for a Project Leader, Team Leaders, and Programmers, a bottom-up computation (beginning from the Programmers) is done to compute both the current progress of the project and also the predicted completion date. The result is displayed in a frame. As shown in Figure 8, progress is 82.3% completed and predicted completion date is September 11, 1999. To estimate the completion date, a table of average percentages of time spent on the development phases for 132 Hewlett-Packard projects [14] is used to estimate the remaining time left to finish the project.

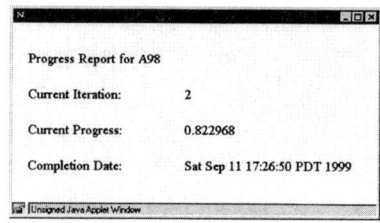

Figure 8. Progress Report and Estimated Completion Date.

3.2 Multiple Project Progress Reporting

Figure 9 shows a multiple project software development consisting of 6 individual software projects. In addition, there are two special nodes called start and end nodes to represent dummy projects with no time duration. Each node, except the special nodes, has filled up colors representing the progress of that particular project. If the node's color is partially filled up, that project is still in progress. To predict the completion date of the entire multiple project software development, the Critical Path Method (CPM) is used. All the edges emanating from a node is given the weight corresponding to either of the following:

- The length of time it took to finish that node (if the project was completed), or

- The computed length of time the node will finish (if the project is currently in progress), or

- The estimated length of time the project will finish as entered by the Project Leader when this project was created (if the project has not started yet).

The end node will contain the computed completion date of the entire multiple-project while the start node will contain the start date of the multiple project.

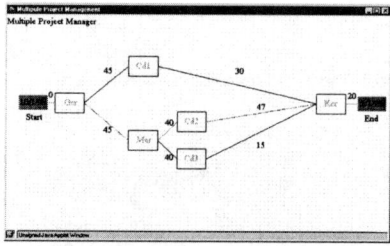

Figure 9. Multiple Project Critical Path Analysis

In Figure 9, the start node shows October1, 1998 when the entire multiple project has begun. All nodes, except start and end node, are labeled by the project ID. The weight on each edge indicates the duration in days of each project. Applying CPM, the critical path consists of 4 projects: Ger, Mer, Cd2 and Ker. The length of this path is 152 days. Using the length of the critical path, the computed completion date is March 1,1999 as shown in the end node.

4. Conclusions and Future Directions

RMT is most useful for medium- to large-scale projects rather than small-scale projects. This is because for small-scale projects the benefits of using RMT are outweighed by the overhead required to manage the threads. A weakness of RMT is the potential for an exponential explosion of threads and thread iterations by misusing recursion and iteration. To help guard against this problem, guidelines should be established by an organization to help prevent this from happening and to identify, at an early stage, when the problem does occur so that it can be corrected before the problem becomes unmanageable.

While thread iterations and recursion can be applied to any project, RMT (and iterative life-cycles in general) is most appropriate for projects where the system requirements are vague or frequently changing. RMT can still be used effectively for the other project types, but the iteration and recursion techniques can be used as internal development styles rather than a means to accommodate changing requirements and/or schedules.

The following additional features are envisioned for the RMT Tool: support for a complete tracing of software artifacts, an object-oriented complexity design analyzer, integration of a design pattern library, and incorporation of SEI Personal Software Process [9] at the Programmer's level checklist.

References

[1] Edward V. Berard, *Essays on Object-Oriented Software Engineering Volume 1,* Prentice Hall, 1993.

[2] Barry W. Boehm, "Using the Win Win Spiral Model: A Case Study," IEEE Computer July 98, pp. 33-44.

[3] Barry W. Boehm, "A Spiral Model of Software Development and Enhancement," IEEE Computer, May 1988, pp. 61-72.

[4] Frederick P. Brooks, Jr., *The Mythical Man-Month: Essays on Software Engineering, Anniversary Edition,* Addison Wesley, 1995.

[5] Arturo I. Concepcion, et. al., "Algorithma 98: An Algorithm Animation Project," Proceedings of the ACM SIGCSE' 99 Technical Symposium, 24-28 Mar 99, pp. 301-305.

[6] F.W. Fang, A. C. So, and R. J. Krindler. "Ther Visual modeling Technique: An Introduction and Overview," JOOP, Jul-Aug 1996, pp. 48-73.

[7] Brian Henderson-Sellers and Julian M. Edwards, "The Object-Oriented Systems Life Cycle, Communications of the ACM," September 1990 Vol. 33, No. 9.

[8] Brian Henderson-Sellers and J.M. Edwards, *Book Two of Object-Oriented Knowledge: The Working Object,* Prentice Hall, 1994.

[9] Watts S. Humphrey, *A Discipline for Software Engineering,* Addison Wesley, 1996

[10] John D. McGregor, David A. Sykes, *Object-Oriented Software Development: Engineering Software for Reuse,* Van Nostrand Reinhold, 1992.

[11] L. B. S. Raccoon, "The Chaos Model and the Chaos Life Cycle," Software Engineering Notes, January 1995, Vol. 20, No. 1.

[12] W. W. Royce, "Managing the Development of Large Software Systems: Concepts and Techniques," 1970 WESCON Technical Papers, Western Electronic Show and Convention, Los Angeles, August 1970, pp. A/1-1-A/1-9.

[13] James Rumbaugh, Michael Blaha, William Premerlani, Frederick Eddy, *Object-Oriented Modeling and Design,* Prentice Hall, 1991.

[14] Stephen R. Schach, *Classical and Object-Oriented Software Engineering,* 3rd ed., Irwin, 1996.

Entity-Relationship
Software Development Environment

Pornsiri Muenchaisri
Dept. of Computer Engineering
Chulalongkorn University
Bangkok 10330 Thailand
muenchp@cp.eng.chula.ac.th

Toshimi Minoura
Dept. of Computer Science
Oregon State University
Corvallis, OR 97331
minoura@cs.orst.edu

Abstract

We designed and implemented a prototype software development environment based on software component composition. *Our software development environment, the* Entity-Relationship Software Development Environment *(ERSDE), uses* extended entity-relationship diagrams *(EERDs) as templates of executable programs. An EERD represents the component types and the relationship types among them within an application domain. The graphical editor of the ERSDE uses an EERD as a menu in constructing application software. An EERD used as a menu can enforce legitimate patterns of relationships among software components, in addition to providing an intuitive view of available components and possible relationships among them. Furthermore, as the ERSDE uses* structural active objects *as the components of a program, we can obtain an executable program if those components are instantiated and interconnected as dictated by an EERD. Two experiments conducted confirmed the effectiveness of our approach.*

1 Introduction

Composing application software from components, as other industrial products are produced, has been an aim of many researchers [3, 4, 5, 7, 9, 11]. By using well-tested software components, we can reduce the development time and enhance the quality of application software. However, none of the current software-component composition methods use *patterns of relationships* among components in constructing applications effectively. They emphasize only how components should communicate with each other. Furthermore, although some code for class definitions can be generated from a diagram, the generated code is not executable.

For example, *Universal Connector (Unicon)* [10], allows relations among components to be specified by *connectors*. The Unicon system, however, is not an object-based system, and it supports only pre-defined components. *Vista* is a prototype environment for visual software composition [6]. A Vista application is specified in terms of component behaviors, component presentations, and a composition model. A Vista composition model is expressed only in a textual notation. The graphical editors of Structural Active-Object Systems (SAOSs) [5] allow applications to be developed by component composition, but they do not show possible relationships among components as menus. Furthermore, a separate SAOS graphical editor is needed for each application domain. A

SAOS graphical editor for simple queuing systems and a SAOS graphical editor for tank systems, for example, are different.

In our approach, we integrate an object modeling technique, a (visual) software component composition, entity-relationship diagrams, and active objects into a software development environment. This approach enables application software in different domains to be composed by pick and place.

Although a class diagram of the Object Modeling Technique (OMT) [8] allows us to specify possible patterns of relationships among instances of classes, such patterns are not explicitly enforced when an application is created. We consider that relationship patterns should be included in the template from which applications are constructed. Then this template will provide an intuitive view of the patterns of relationships in the application domain. When this template is graphically represented and is used as a menu of a graphical editor, its user can easily comprehend the application domain and construct an application.

We designed and implemented a prototype software development environment called the *Entity-Relationship Software Development Environment* (ERSDE), which follows our software component composition methodology for creating executable software automatically. The environment uses an *extended entity-relationship diagram* (EERD) (*domain-specific schema*) as a menu for a graphical editor as well as as a template of executable programs. A programmer can see in an EERD the available entity types and the patterns of the relationships (possible connections) among them. She can compose an application software by instantiating entities from the entity types in the EERD and then by connecting them following the patterns of relationships specified in the EERD. Since entities are implemented as *active-objects*, the application is executable as soon as entities are instantiated and interconnected.

We conducted two experiments in order to evaluate our approach. In the first experiment, EERDs and OMT class diagrams were compared in terms of their effectiveness as design documents. We also asked the subjects their preference between the EERDs and OMT class diagrams. In the second experiment, we compared the ERSDE application editor and the menu-based SAOS graphical editors in terms of the correctness of applications composed and the times required to compose them. We then asked the subjects their preference between the ERSDE application editor and SAOS graphical editors as a software development environment.

We restricted ourselves to object composition instead of functional (or relational), procedural, or process composition, The environment is not meant to be a general purpose software development environment. The basic building blocks of each application are objects. In other words, the focus of this research is to find a software development methodology that allows concurrent applications to be constructed by component composition. By restricting our approach to visual composition of concurrent systems, we could create realistic applications by visual composition. Furthermore, we could create executable programs interactively as active components were provided as editor components.

In Section 2, we provide an overview of our approach by using a simple example. Section 3 presents the architecture of the ERSDE. Section 4 concludes this paper and addresses some future research topics.

2 Overview of the ER Approach for Software Composition

In this section we give an overview of our approach with a simple example. Fig. 1 shows a tank system consisting of tanks, valves, and pumps. A tank contains some kind of liquid, a pump makes liquid flow, and a valve controls the amount of liquid that flows through it. The liquid flows from left to right from tanks to other tanks through valves and pumps.

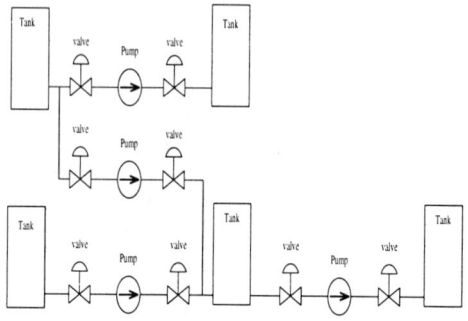

Figure 1. A tank system.

Fig. 2 is a conventional *entity-relationship (ER) diagram* for tank systems consisting of tanks, valves, and pumps. The input end of a pump can be connected to the output end of a valve, and the output end of a pump to the input end of a valve. The input end of a tank can be connected to the output ends of many valves, and the output end of a tank to the input ends of many valves.

A simple way to enhance understandability of an ER diagram is to replace the rectangular representation of entity types by their iconic representations. An iconic entity type looks like a real entity. For example, a picture of a valve can be used to represent an entity type `Valve`. Intuitiveness of a domain-specific schema is enhanced with iconic entity types. Fig. 3 shows an *entity-relationship diagram* of the tank system represented in this way. In this diagram, relationship types are represented by arrows.

However, the representation as shown in Fig. 3 has the following problem. The arrow between the output end of the valve type and the input end of the pump type and the arrow between the output end of the pump type and the input end of the valve type may mislead us to believe that there is a circular connection between a valve and a pump. Similarly, it looks like there is a circular connection between a tank and a valve. This problem will make the diagram confusing or at least unattractive.

To solve the problem described above, we introduce *proxy entity types*. A proxy entity type, which are drawn with dashed lines, is equivalent to the original entity type, and all the connections made to it have the same effect as they were made to the original one. Fig. 4 shows the EERD for tank systems with a proxy of the valve type and a proxy of the tank type. In this way, we can eliminate circular connections which may not exist at the entity level.

3   Architecture of Entity-Relationship Software Development Environment (ERSDE)

In this section we present the architecture of Entity-Relationship Software Development Environment (ERSDE). As shown in Fig. 5, the ERSDE consists of three major parts: the *entity-type editor*, the *schema editor*, and the *application editor*. The major feature of the ERSDE is that it can be used to develop executable application software in different application domains by component composition.

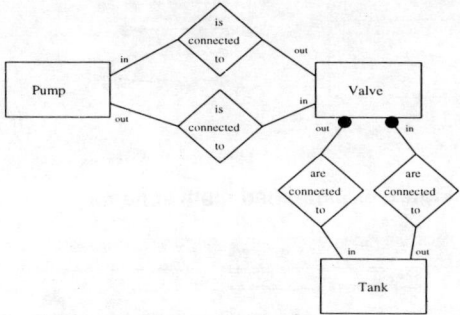

Figure 2. A conventional entity-relationship diagram for tank systems.

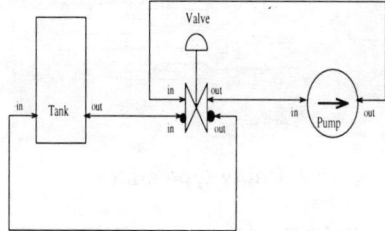

Figure 3. Entity-relationship diagram with iconic entity types.

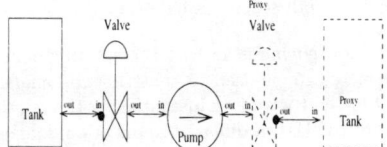

Figure 4. Extended entity-relationship diagram with proxy entity types.

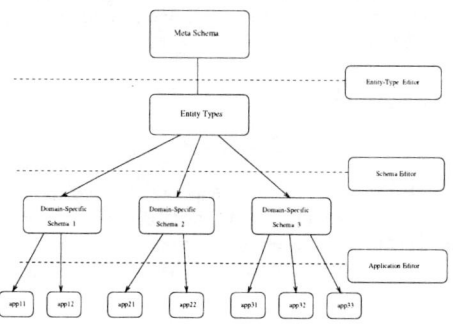

Figure 5. Structure of the ERSDE software development environment.

358

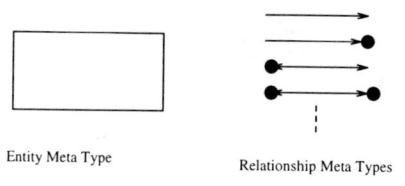

Entity Meta Type   Relationship Meta Types

Figure 6. Simplified meta schema.

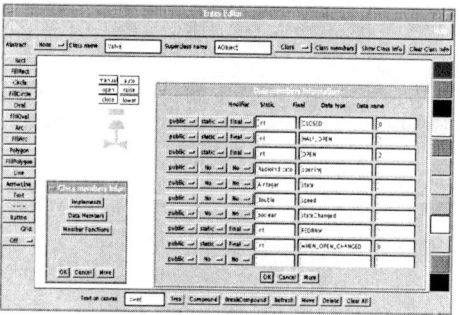

Figure 7. Entity-type editor.

The meta schema, which conceptually consists of the *entity metatype* and the *relationship metatypes* as shown in Fig. 6, is a template for creating *domain-specific schemas*. The entity editor created iconic entity types by instantiating the entity metatype. The relationship metatypes indicate the *cardinality ratios* (*one-to-one, one-to-many, many-to-one, many-to-many*) and the *directions of access*. Additional notations used by the meta schema are described in subsection 3.2.

A domain-specific (application-specific) schema is an EERD consisting of entity types and relationship types among them. The schema editor is used to construct a domain-specific schema by the entity types created by the entity-type editor and by instantiating the relationship metatypes. One schema editor can create and modify EERDs in different application domains.

We can construct applications (instance diagrams) in each application domain with the application editor. This application editor uses the EERD in each application domain as its menu. The application editor allows applications to be composed in different application domains by switching the EERD used as the menu. In the next three sections, we describe more details of the three major parts of the ERSDE.

3.1 Entity-Type Editor

The entity-type editor, as shown in Fig. 7, is used to create entity types to be used in EERDs. The entity metatype provides the rules to be used in creating entity types. Although the generic notation for an entity type is a rectangle, it can be replaced by an iconic representation in a domain-specific schema. The entity-type editor also supports entity subclassing, where an entity type inherits characteristics of its supertype.

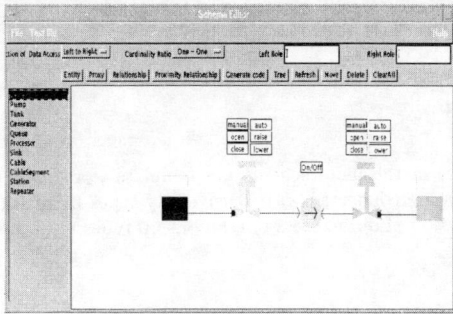

Figure 8. Schema editor.

3.2 Schema Editor

We use the schema editor to build domain-specific schemas. A domain-specific schema displays the entity types and the relationship types used by the application in that domain. The schema editor, as shown in Fig. 8, is a (general) domain-independent graphical editor for creating and manipulating graphical representations of entity types and relationship types in domain-specific schemas.

The meta schema is a template for creating domain-specific schemas. We adopt some conventional notations and propose some new ones for the meta schema. The meta schema as shown in Fig. 9 provides notations for the *entity composition*, *relationship types*, and *proxy entity-types*. The first two notations are extensively used in many object-oriented design methods including OMT [8], Booch [1], and Fusion [2]. However, in our approach, the arrows representing relationship types indicate the directions of data access. A visibility graph of the Fusion method uses an arrow to indicate the direction of data access as we do. However, only one way of data referencing is allowed [2]. The concepts of proxy entity types and relationship representation by proximity, which we describe later, are new.

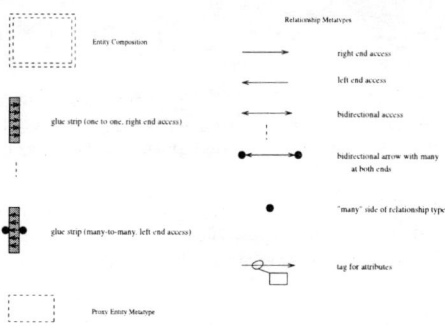

Figure 9. Meta schema.

3.2.1 Composite Entities

Entity composition is a mechanism to allow hierarchical composition of an entity from its component entities. A *composite entity* is an entity created by entity composition. A *composite entity type* is represented by a rectangle with double dashed outlines. Such a rectangle encloses the entity types of its members.

3.2.2 Relationship Types

The relationship metatypes in the meta schema are templates for creating relationship types in EERDs, where entity types are connected with other entity types by relationship types. We allow cardinality ratios and direction of data access of relationship types to be specified.

Cardinality ratios

A relationship metatype is a *unidirectional* or *bidirectional* arrow with small filled-circles at its ends. A small filled-circle (•) means "many". The tag attached to a relationship type represents the attributes of the relationship type. The semantic direction of a relationship is normally from left to right or from top to bottom. In this paper, we refer to the source of a relationship as its left-side entity, and the destination as its right-side entity. There are four possible combinations of these small filled-circles.

Direction of Data Access

The direction of an arrow indicates that of data access. The access direction of data may be different from the semantic direction. There are three possible cases for the direction of an arrow.

1. *Right-end access* (E1 $\longrightarrow$ E2): If an arrow head is at the right end of the arrow, an instance of E1 can access an instance of E2, but the instance of E2 cannot access the instance of E1.
2. *Left-end access* (E1 $\longleftarrow$ E2): If an arrow head is at the left end of the arrow, an instance of E2 can access an instance of E1, but the instance of E1 cannot access the instance of E2.
3. *Bidirectional access* (E1 $\longleftrightarrow$ E2): If arrow heads are at both the right and left ends, an instance of E1 can access an instance of E2, and the instance of E2 can access the instance of E1.

3.2.3 Proxy Entity-Types

We now explain the reasons why proxy entity-types are introduced. The proxy entity types are designed to make an EERD easy to understand. Proxy entity types are equivalent to their original entity types. The following problems are examples that proxy entity types can solve.

1. (Multiple Sheet Problem) When a system is large, multiple sheets are needed to show all the required entity types and relationship types. Then there should be a way to refer to entity types in other sheets. From one sheet we can refer to an entity type given on another sheet with a proxy entity type.
2. (Circular Connection Problem) This problem occurs when some entities are connected to other entities of the same type. In this case, a chain of relationship types originates from and ends at the same entity type.
3. (Multiple Component Problem) This problem occurs when a composite entity type includes multiple occurrences of one entity type as its components. Fig. 10 shows an EERD for an entity type Car which is a composite type consisting of four occurrences of the entity type Wheel and one occurrence of the entity type Body. The fact that a car has four wheels is not intuitively represented. The EERD given in Fig. 11, on the other hand, shows the composite entity type Car by using proxy entity types.

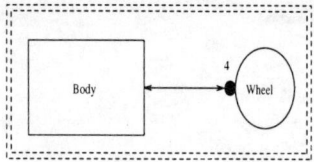

Figure 10. A car as a composite entity type.

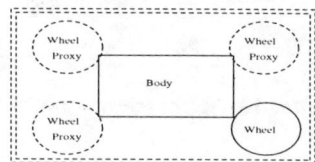

Figure 11. A car as a composite entity type with proxies.

Although the generic notation for a proxy entity metatype is a dashed rectangle, it can be replaced by an iconic representation in a domain-specific schema.

3.2.4   Creating a Domain-Specific Schema or EERD

There are four major steps in constructing a domain-specific schema. First, we use the schema editor to create entity types. Second, we connect entity types to other entity types by relationship types. Third, once an EERD is completed, the schema editor generates skeleton code for the entity types and the pointer structures to access related entities according to the direction of data access specified in the domain-specific schema. Fourth, a programmer is responsible for providing behaviors for each entity type.

We use some new ideas in domain-specific schemas: iconic representations of entity types, proxy entity types, and *relationship representation by proximity*. We can relate entity types to other entity types by placing them closely. This mechanism for creating relationship types is called relationship representation by proximity. Although relationship types shown by this mechanism are semantically not different from those represented by arrows, composite (assembly) entity types shown in this way look more like real entities. We use a *grey glue strip* to represent a relationship type by proximity. The cardinal ratio of a relationship type can be indicated with a small filled-circle within an entity type on the "many" side. An EERD for cars using this notation among its component types is shown in Fig. 12. A `Car` has one `Driver` and multiple `Passenger`s.

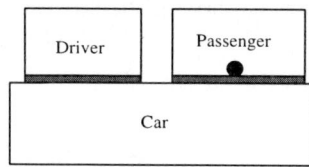

Figure 12. An EERD for a car, a driver, and passengers.

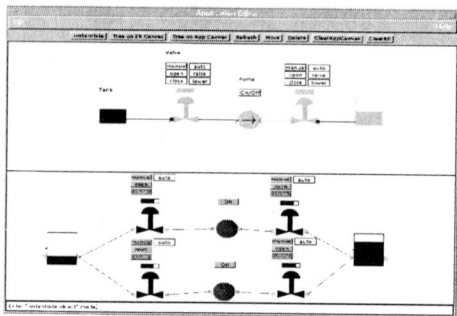

Figure 13. Application editor.

3.3 Application Editor

We can use the application editor to construct applications. In composing an application, a domain-specific schema (EERD) is used as the menu of the application editor to instantiate entity types and connect them in compliance with the connectivity styles specified in the EERD. When used as a menu of a graphical editor, an EERD is more effective than a conventional editor menu since it can show not only entity types but also possible relationships between entities.

The application editor, which is shown in Fig. 13, is a general graphical editor used to create, and move instances of entity types and connections among them. If each entity is an active object, the application can be executed once the entities are connected. The application editor allows us to construct applications in different layouts, and to move, delete, and edit components interactively.

4 Conclusions

We presented a software development environment for composing application software from components. This software development environment, called the *Entity-Relationship Software Development Environment* (ERSDE), uses extended entity-relationship diagrams (EERDs) as templates for application software. Its three major facilities are the *entity editor*, the *schema editor*, and the *application editor*.

We implemented prototypes of the entity editor, the schema editor, and the application editor. With the entity editor and the schema editor, we created the EERDs for queuing systems, tank systems, and local-area network systems. With the application editor and with these EERDs, we successfully created applications for a queuing system, a tank system, and a local-area-network system.

In order to evaluate the effectiveness of the ERSDE, we conducted two experiments and obtained the following results.

1. The proportion of the subjects who composed local area network system applications correctly with the EERD for this application domain was larger than the proportion of the students who did so with the OMT class diagram in the same application domain.
2. Using an EERD and using an OMT class diagram did not make any difference in creating tank system applications.

3. The subjects preferred EERDs to OMT class diagrams as templates for constructing applications.

4. The graphical editor used, i.e., a menu-based SAOS graphical editor or the ERSDE graphical editor, did not affect the correctness of the programs constructed.

5. The subjects took significantly longer to compose applications with a menu-based SAOS editor than with the ERSDE editor.

6. All the subjects preferred the ERSDE editor to the SAOS editors in composing queuing system and local-area-network system applications.

We demonstrated that we can construct an executable application program from its components by connecting them as indicated by the extended entity-relationship diagram in that application domain.

The current system supports only centralized applications. The scope of the ERSDE should be extended to include distributed applications. An EERD can be used to show possible configurations of distributed applications. In the current system, legal connections among entities are restricted by relationship types. To allow more complicated rules for configurations, we need to support patterns each of which contains more than two entity types and one relationship type.

References

[1] Grady Booch. *"Object-Oriented Analysis and Design with applications, 2nd edition"*, Chap. 1, pages 3–26. Benjamin-Cummings, 1994.

[2] Derek Coleman, Patrick Arnold, Stephanie Bodoff, Chris Dollin, Helena Gilchrist, Fiona Hayes, and Paul Jeremaes. *"Object-Oriented Development: The FUSION Method"*, Chaps. 1-4, 8, 9, pages 1–230. Prentice-Hall, 1994.

[3] Brad J. Cox. *"Object Oriented Programming - An Evolutionary Approach"*. Addison-Wesley, 1986.

[4] Ivar Jacobson, Magnus Christerson, Patrik Johnson, and Gunnar Overgaard. *"Object-Oriented Software Engineering: A Use Case Driven Approach"*, Chap. 11, page 291. Addison-Wesley, 1992.

[5] Toshimi Minoura, Shirish S. Pargaonkar, and Kurt Rehfuss. Structural Active Object Systems for Simulation. In *Proceedings of OOPSLA '93*, pages 338–355, ACM, October 1993.

[6] Oscar Nierstrasz and Dennis Tsichritzis. *Object-Oriented Software Composition*. Prentice Hall, 1992.

[7] Oscar Nierstrasz, Dennis Tsichritzis, Vicki de Mey, and Marc Stadelmann. Objects + Scripts = Applications. In *Proceedings of Esprit 1991 Conference*, pages 534–552, 1991.

[8] James Rumbaugh, Michael Blaha, William Premerlani, Frederick Eddy, and William Lorensen. *"Object-Oriented Modeling and Design"*, Chaps. 1-12, pages 1–277. Prentice-Hall, 1991.

[9] Bran Selic, Garth Gullekson, and Paul T. Ward. *"Real-Time Object-Oriented Modeling"*. John Wiley and Sons, 1994.

[10] Mary Shaw. Architecture Issues in Software Reuse: It's Not Just Functionality, It's the Packaging. In *Symposium on Software Reusability*, page 3. ACM SIGSOFT, April 1995.

[11] Mary Shaw, Robert DeLine, Daniel V. Klien, Theodore L. Ross, David M. Young, and Gregory Zelesnik. Abstractions of Software Architecture and Tools to Support Them. *IEEE Transactions on Software Engineering 21*, 4, pages 14–335, April 1995.

MysterX: A Scheme Toolkit for Building Interactive Applications with COM

Paul A. Steckler*
Department of Computer Science
Rice University, MS 132
6100 S. Main St.
Houston, TX 77005-1892
steck@cs.rice.edu

Abstract

MysterX is an object-oriented Scheme toolkit for building applications from off-the-shelf COM components. While the COM support in languages such as Haskell and Mercury requires the use of an interface compiler to generate stub code, MysterX uses the reflective capabilities of OLE Automation to make value-marshalling decisions at run-time. MysterX hosts COM components in windows that display Dynamic HTML, without requiring a separate browser. Scheme code can manipulate HTML elements and their style properties in such windows to create interesting visual effects. Event handlers written in Scheme can be associated with HTML elements and COM objects. By integrating these diverse technologies, MysterX can be used to write complete GUI applications.

1: Introduction

MysterX is an object-oriented Scheme toolkit for building interactive applications with components that adhere to the Component Object Model (COM). COM allows applications to be built from off-the-shelf components. Components and their host programs can be written in any language; a component and its host program may be written in different languages. Most often, COM components are contained in applications built with Microsoft's Visual Basic or with various implementations of C++. Another way of using COM components is to "script" them in Web pages containing code in either JavaScript or VBScript, a browser-hosted version of Visual Basic. Unfortunately, these usual approaches of handling COM components rely on languages that make the task somewhat cumbersome. To overcome this problem, several research groups have developed COM support for languages with clean syntax, structure, and semantics. MysterX, Rice's effort at adding COM support for Scheme, uses Scheme to particular advantage.

By combining other technologies with COM, MysterX is able to use COM components in dynamic, interactive applications. A COM component instance is an object with state; most components have some visual representation. Displayable COM objects are ordinarily hosted in a container, such as a Web browser. In MysterX, COM components are hosted in a window containing Dynamic HTML, though no Web browser is run directly. Therefore,

---

*The author was partially supported by NSF grant CDA-9713032 for this work.

applications created with MysterX can use any HTML elements, such as bitmaps, buttons, drop-down lists, frames, and tables, as well as text. In MysterX programs, Scheme code handles Dynamic HTML events, and can be used to modify HTML elements, in the same way that code written in a client-side Web scripting language, such as JavaScript, performs these tasks in a browser. MysterX extends the capabilities of Dynamic HTML, a Web-based technology, to conventional applications. MysterX thus adds more to Scheme than just COM support — it adds the ability to build full-featured GUI programs.

The remainder of the paper is organized as follows. In Section 2, we describe the document abstraction provided by MysterX; in Section 3, we show how the HTML elements in a document can be modified; in Section 4, we explain how MysterX programs use the reflective capabilities of OLE Automation to get descriptions of methods and properties, and how methods and properties are used; in Section 5, we explain how events are generated in applications, and how they can be handled by Scheme code; Section 6 describes the technical details of the MysterX implementation; we present conclusions in Section 7.

2: MysterX documents

MzScheme, Rice's Scheme interpreter, supports classes for object-oriented programming [Fla98]. Each MysterX window contains a *document*, which is an instance of the Scheme class `mx-document%`. A MysterX document roughly corresponds to the notion of document in the Document Object Model, which is the official basis for Dynamic HTML [Con99]. A MysterX program may create arbitrarily many documents. HTML elements and COM objects in distinct documents may communicate with one another via Scheme glue code.

To create an instance of `mx-document%`, the syntax is:

(make-object mx-document% *label width height x y style*)

where each of the arguments is optional. The *style* argument is a list of options for the resulting window, such as its border and menu. An `mx-document%` instance is a first-class Scheme value. A new instance of a document appears as an empty window.

There are just a few public methods of `mx-document%`. Those that deal with COM objects are:

- **objects**: returns a list of the COM objects, including ActiveX controls, contained in the document. Each object has the Scheme type `<com-object>`, which encapsulates the COM IDispatch interface.

- **insert-object** *coclass*: places an instance of the COM class *coclass* at the beginning of the document.

- **append-object** *coclass*: like **insert-object**, but places the instance at the end of the document.

Note that the *coclass* argument of **insert-object** and **append-object** is a string naming the coclass. Such a string is not guaranteed to uniquely name a COM class, but probably will on a given user's machine. COM classes are uniquely named by a CLSID, a 128-bit descriptor, but these are inconvenient to use. If there is any concern about ambiguity, a MysterX programmer can use a CLSID directly in HTML.

The HTML-related public methods of `mx-document%` are:

Figure 1. A MysterX document.

- `insert-html` *s*: inserts its string argument *s* as HTML at the beginning of the document.
- `append-html` *s*: like `insert-html`, but places the HTML in *s* at the end of the document.
- `replace-html` *s*: replaces all the HTML in the document by the HTML in *s*.
- `find-element` *tag* *id*: returns the HTML element with the given HTML tag and "id" attribute, as an instance of the Scheme class `mx-element%`.

In order for `find-element` to work as indicated, programmers must be sure to include the "id" attribute in the start tag of HTML elements that they wish to manipulate from Scheme.

Here is an example of how these methods are used. The following Scheme code creates a document, inserts a pushbutton, and binds a variable to the pushbutton:

```
(define document (make-object mx-document% "Test program"))
(send document insert-html "<BUTTON id=\"my-button\">Push me!</BUTTON>")
(define button (send document find-element "BUTTON" "my-button"))
```

The resulting window is shown in Figure 1.

HTML elements generate *events*, which can be handled from Scheme. HTML events are instances of the Scheme class `mx-event%`, which we describe in Section 5. The `mx-document%` methods relating to events are

- `register-event-handler` *elt* *fn*: registers an event handler *fn* for the HTML element *elt*. The handler *fn* is a Scheme procedure of one argument, which will be an event.
- `unregister-event-handler` *elt*: removes any existing event handler for the HTML element *elt*.
- `handle-events`: spawns a Scheme thread for handling events for the elements in the document.
- `stop-handling-events`: kills any existing event handler thread for the elements in the document.

We provide more details of event-handling, including event-handling for COM objects, in Section 5.

Figure 2. Changing the style of an HTML element.

3: Modifying HTML elements

Most HTML elements have a *style* attribute, which indicates visual properties such as width, height, background color, font size, and so forth. The style attribute can be supplied in the start tag for an element, or style properties can be assigned to HTML tags in special STYLE blocks. There are complex rules for the inheritance of styles by elements from other elements. For a given element, its style attribute may be derived from several sources. The "Cascading Style Sheet" specification, part of the Document Object Model, indicates how styles flow from element to element [Con99].

MysterX applications can modify the style attribute properties of HTML elements. There are more than eighty such properties. With a few exceptions, the mx-element% class provides a pair of "get" and "set" methods for each style attribute property. As an example, suppose we wanted to create a page with a header whose background color changes when the mouse position changes. Assuming document is a variable bound to a MysterX document, we could write:

```
(send document insert-html
        (string-append "<H1 id=\"my-header\""
                       "style=\"color: white background-color: blue\">"
                       "Header the Charles</H1>"
                       "<p>"))

(let ([elt (send document find-element "H1" "my-header")])
  (send document register-event-handler elt
          (lambda (event)
            (cond
              [(send event mouseover?)
               (send elt set-background-color! "red")
               (send document append-html "red!")]
              [(send event mouseout?)
               (send elt set-background-color! "blue")
               (send document append-html "blue!")]))))

(send document handle-events)
```

The <H1> header background color is initially blue, but the color changes as the mouse is

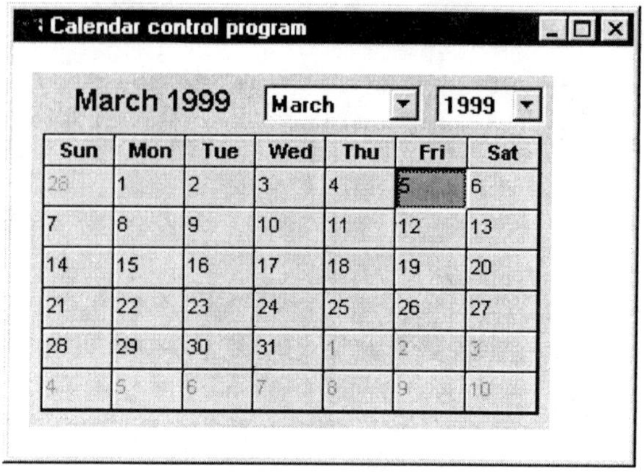

Figure 3. Calendar control, a COM object.

moved over or off the text. With each color change, the name of the new color is appended to the document. Figure 2 shows a document after several such changes.

MysterX also provides a "raw" interface to style properties via the method `set-css-text!`. Programmers can use HTML syntax for those properties. In the program fragment above, to set the background color to red, we could have written

```
(send elt set-css-text! "color:red")
```

An advantage of the raw interface is that many properties can be set at once:

```
(send elt set-css-text! "color:red font:sans-serif font-size:24pt" )
```

Besides allowing the modification of style properties of HTML elements, MysterX allows HTML to be modified by insertion of new elements and by the replacement of existing elements. The `insert-html` and `append-html` methods for `mx-document%`, mentioned earlier, allow placement of new HTML only at the beginning and end of the entire document; the same-named methods for `mx-element%` allow placement of new HTML before and after individual elements. Likewise, the `replace-html` method for `mx-document%` replaces the entire contents of the document; the same method for `mx-element%` replaces just the element.

4: Methods, properties, and COM reflection in Scheme

COM objects, including ActiveX controls, can be inserted into MysterX documents using the `insert-object` and `append-object` methods of `mx-document%`. Alternatively, given a COM class name, the Scheme procedure `coclass->html` returns an HTML string which can be used to load a COM object. For example,

```
(define calendar (send document insert-object "Calendar Control 8.0"))
```

binds `calendar` to an instance of the COM class "Calendar Control 8.0", which appears as in Figure 3. Once we have a reference to a ⟨com-object⟩ value, we can invoke its methods and use its properties. But how do we know what those methods and properties are, and how to use them?

MysterX has the procedure com-help, which takes a ⟨com-object⟩ argument and an optional topic name. This procedure starts either the WinHelp system or the HTML Help system, as appropriate, with the documentation for the COM class that generated the object. Such documentation is often useful in determining how the methods and properties of an object are meant to be used. WinHelp and HTML Help files for COM components are usually pitched to Visual Basic programmers, so the language syntax in these files may be unenlightening to Scheme programmers.

Fortunately, most COM objects that support OLE Automation offer a reflective capability through the ITypeInfo interface. With this interface, a programmer can query an object to determine the names of its methods and properties. For example:

```
> (com-methods calendar)
("AboutBox" "Today" "Refresh" "PreviousYear" "PreviousWeek"
 "PreviousMonth" "PreviousDay" "NextYear" "NextWeek" "NextMonth"
 "NextDay")
```

Similarly, we can obtain calendar's readable properties with

```
> (com-get-properties calendar)
("Year" "ValueIsNull" "_Value" "Value" "TitleFontColor"
 "TitleFont" "ShowVerticalGrid" "ShowTitle"
 "ShowHorizontalGrid" "ShowDays" "ShowDateSelectors"
 "MonthLength" "Month" "GridLinesColor" "GridFontColor"
 "GridFont" "GridCellEffect" "FirstDay" "DayLength"
 "DayFontColor" "DayFont" "Day" "BackColor")
```

Likewise, the procedure com-set-properties returns a list of writable properties for its ⟨com-object⟩ argument.

To use a method or property correctly, we need to know its type. The ITypeInfo interface can also provide such information for most OLE Automation objects. MysterX primitives access the information provided by ITypeInfo. For example, we have

```
> (com-method-type calendar "PreviousWeek")
(-> void)
```

meaning the method takes no arguments, and the return value is the special MzScheme #<void> value. This function type is meaningful to Scheme programmers, and is the translation of the type provided by COM. It turns out that the types of all the calendar methods above are the same — hence all these methods are used for their side effects.

The Calendar Control properties have slightly more interesting types:

```
> (get-property-type calendar "Day")
(-> short-int)
```

Therefore, this property is called with no arguments, and returns a 2-byte integer. The type short-int is not a native Scheme type, of course. In return position, distinguishing this type from the ordinary Scheme integer type is usually unimportant, but in argument position, that distinction is critical: passing a Scheme bignum is a type violation. MysterX detects such type violations when methods or properties are invoked.

Curiously, we have:

```
> (get-property-type calendar "Value")
(-> mx-any)
```

This type indicates that the return value might have any type producible by a COM object. The `mx-any` type is a translation of the COM type `VARIANT`. When it appears in argument position, `mx-any` means we can pass a method or property *any* Scheme value that has a meaningful COM equivalent, and the COM object will try to use that value.

With types in hand, we can experiment with COM methods and properties. Method invocation uses the procedure `com-invoke`, which takes a COM object, the name of a method, and any arguments. Property reading and writing use the procedures `com-get-property` and `com-set-property!`, respectively. For the readable properties mentioned above, we have

```
(com-get-property calendar "Day")
```

which returns an integer, and

```
(com-get-property calendar "Value")
```

returns a value of type ⟨com-date⟩, which is the Scheme version of the COM type `DATE`.

When invoking methods and using properties, Scheme argument values are checked to make sure they are compatible with the COM type given by the `ITypeInfo` interface. If so, the values are marshalled to COM equivalents. Return values are not checked, since we can rely on the safety properties offered by the COM object. OLE Automation return values always come packaged as a VARIANT type, even if the advertised return type is more specific. MysterX unmarshals these values to an appropriate Scheme type.

We wish to highlight the difference between our approach to COM and that used by COM research projects for other languages. The Haskell community has described their work with COM in a series of papers [FLMJ98, JML98, MLH99]. Haskell uses the type descriptions in a COM interface description language (IDL) file, and uses a compiler to generate stub code for gluing with C++. Pucella has built an IDL-to-Standard ML compiler, which can be used to support COM [Puc98]. Similarly, Mercury, a mixed logic and functional language, also compiles IDL specifications to generate bindings for CORBA [JDS99].

These implementations gain the benefit of strong typing in the languages involved, at the cost of a preprocessing step. In contrast, we avoid a preprocessing step, and take advantage of the reflective capabilities of OLE Automation objects. This approach takes the dynamic typing and interactivity of Scheme as its strength. We do lose the ability to use those relatively few COM classes that do not support `IDispatch`, the Automation interface. We also incur a small performance penalty in checking the types of arguments for each COM method invocation, though such a penalty is usual in Scheme. It is possible to add support for non-Automation classes by adding a preprocessing step, though we have not yet felt compelled to do so.

5: Events in MysterX

Events can be generated either by HTML elements or by COM objects. The mechanisms for handling events from these two sources are distinct.

As we have seen, the `mx-document%` class has methods for registering event handlers associated with HTML elements. HTML events are instances of the Scheme class `mx-event%`.

An `mx-event%` instance encapsulates the COM interface `IHTMLEventObj`. An event handler can identify the kind of event that occurred by using predicate methods such as `keypress?`, `keydown?`, and `mousedown?`. The `mx-event%` class also has methods that describe the event in various ways. For instance, the `mousebutton` method returns an integer indicating which mouse button was pressed.

Since MysterX uses the rendering engine underlying Internet Explorer 4, events are propagated as in that browser. Since events bubble up the tree of HTML elements, MysterX listens for events only at the root, the `<BODY>` of the HTML page, not at individual elements. Since events carry tag and attribute information, the MysterX event dispatcher can readily determine which element generated a particular event.

While there is a fixed set of HTML events, COM objects can generate both "standard" events, defined by the ActiveX controls specification, or "custom" events, defined by a particular COM class [Den97]. MysterX uses COM reflection to obtain the events supported by a COM object, and the types required for each event's handler. For the calendar control we saw in the last section, we have

```
> (com-events calendar)
("NewYear" "NewMonth" "AfterUpdate" "BeforeUpdate" "KeyUp"
 "KeyPress" "KeyDown" "DblClick" "Click")
```

and

```
> (com-event-type calendar "Click")
(-> void)
```

We can install a handler for the `Click` event with

```
(com-register-event-handler calendar "Click"
                            (lambda () (printf "Got a click!")))
```

6: Implementation

MysterX relies on two key technologies in its implementation. The first is the functionality offered by the Microsoft Active Template Library (ATL) to load COM objects into a window; the other is MzScheme's extension feature. The implementation consists of three dynamic libraries (.DLL's), MysPage, MysSink, and MysterX, and a small Scheme library.

The MysPage .DLL implements a Dynamic HTML COM class, which encapsulates an HTML page. A instance of this COM class is created for each MysterX document. ATL provides the functionality to host the Dynamic HTML COM object in a window. The underlying HMTL page for the COM object is blank, except for a `<BODY>` containing event handler declarations such as

```
onmousedown='window.external.AtAnyEvent()'
```

and so on for each event we wish to trap. These handler declarations are not visible when the HTML page is rendered. `AtAnyEvent()` is a compiled C++ procedure that is called for each event in the document. The DHTML class has an associated event queue, which is also implemented as a COM class.

The MysSink .DLL implements a COM event sink object that dispatches COM events to registered Scheme handlers.

The MysterX .DLL contains compiled C++ code which implements various primitives callable from Scheme. We use MzScheme's `load-extension` facility to load the .DLL, extending the current environment with bindings for the MysterX primitives. Each new document creates a new window with its own Windows message-handling loop. That loop needs to run in a Win32 thread separate from the MzScheme read-eval-print (REPL) loop, so the latter does not get blocked. As mentioned, `<com-object>` values encapsulate `IDispatch` interface pointers; such values are available from the MzScheme REPL. Unfortunately, COM interface pointers are valid only in their creating thread. To obtain interface pointers that are valid in the REPL, we use the inter-thread interface marshalling features of Distributed COM (DCOM). In fact, we only need to use these features explicitly when obtaining interfaces for the DHTML object and its associated event queue object. At that point, we create proxy versions of those objects, which we can deal with directly in the REPL thread. Thereafter, whenever we obtain a new COM interface, DCOM automatically and invisibly creates a proxy.

We briefly mention an abandoned implementation strategy, which relied on DCOM even more heavily. In that version, a Dynamic HTML COM object was hosted in the Internet Explorer 4 browser, instead of windows directly associated with MzScheme. Therefore, COM objects resided in a separate *process*, and we used DCOM to handle all interprocess communication. Ultimately, we rejected the use of the browser as too cumbersome for users, and the DCOM implementation as too complex.

7: Conclusions

We have built an object-oriented toolkit for GUI applications in Scheme. Our older GUI toolkit for MzScheme, MrEd [FF98], is full-featured, but MysterX can do things that MrEd cannot. MysterX's use of OLE Automation fits in well with interpretive nature of Scheme. A MysterX programmer can try out the methods and properties of an ActiveX control from the MzScheme REPL prompt. By wrapping documents, HTML elements, and events in OO classes, MysterX provides a convenient programming model, much like the one successfully used in MrEd. In fact, the two toolkits can be combined, if desired, to get the capabilities of both.

When we began work on MysterX, we primarily sought the ability to use ActiveX controls and other COM objects. We have achieved that, though not quite in the way we had envisioned. In particular, we did not contemplate using Dynamic HTML for hosting COM objects. Once we went down that path, it became clear that having DHTML available in applications was useful. It is apparent that DHTML is valuable not only for Web pages, but also for many conventional applications.

Let us mention some advanced features offered by MysterX via Dynamic HTML that are not easy to emulate in MrEd. One such feature is the ability to embed Java applets by using the `APPLET` tag, providing another source of software components. Another useful MysterX feature is the ability to use visual filters. Filters transform the appearance of HTML elements. For example, there are filters for grayscaling, flipping an image horizontally and vertically, and blurring. Figure 4 shows a button that has been flipped horizontally. There is much functionality in the Internet Explorer 4 rendering engine that MysterX can use for its own ends.

We would like to test MysterX with a wider variety of COM components, and build

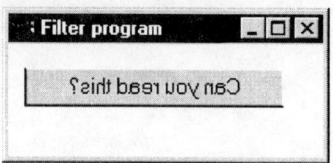

Figure 4. Applying a visual filter to an HTML element.

some large applications. Possible future enhancements include support for non-Automation components and tighter integration into the MrEd framework.

Acknowledgements

The author thanks John Stone and members of Rice PLT for useful comments on this paper. Jim Bullard bravely tested various iterations of MysterX. Microsoft supplied software and documentation.

References

[Con99]   World Wide Web Consortium. Document Object Model (DOM) Level 2 Specification. http://www.w3.org/TR/WD-DOM-Level-2, Mar. 1999.

[Den97]   Adam Denning. *ActiveX Controls Inside Out*. Microsoft Press, 2d. edition, 1997.

[FF98]   Matthew Flatt and Robert B. Findler. PLT MrEd: Graphical toolbox manual. Part of PLT software distribution, July 1998. Version 53.

[Fla98]   Matthew Flatt. PLT MzScheme: Language Manual. Part of PLT software distribution, July 1998. Version 53.

[FLMJ98]   Sigbjorn Finne, Daan Leijen, Erik Meijer, and Simon Peyton Jones. *H/Direct*: A binary foreign language interface for Haskell. In *International Conference on Functional Programming (ICFP'98)*, pages 153–162, New York, 1998. ACM.

[JDS99]   David Jeffery, Tyson Dowd, and Zoltan Somogyi. MCORBA: A CORBA binding for Mercury. In Goyal Gupta, editor, *Practical Aspects of Declarative Languages (PADL'99)*, number 1551 in Lecture Notes in Computer Science, pages 211–227, Berlin, 1999. Springer-Verlag.

[JML98]   Simon Peyton Jones, Erik Meijer, and Daan Leijen. Scripting COM components in Haskell. In *Proc. Fifth International Conference of Software Reuse*, page unknown, 1998.

[MLH99]   Erik Meijer, Daan Leijen, and James Hook. Client-side web scripting with HaskellScript. In Goyal Gupta, editor, *Practical Aspects of Declarative Languages (PADL'99)*, number 1551 in Lecture Notes in Computer Science, pages 196–210, Berlin, 1999. Springer-Verlag.

[Puc98]   Riccardo Pucella. An overview of the ML-IDL compiler (Technical Note #1). http://cm.bell-labs.com/who/riccardo/notes/overview-ml-idl, Nov. 1998.

Technical Papers

Theory

Communication as a Means to Differentiate Objects, Components and Agents

Dwight Deugo, Franz Oppacher, Bruce Ashfield, Michael Weiss
School of Computer Science, Carleton University
1125 Colonel By Drive, Ottawa, Ontario, Canada, K1S 5B6
deugo@scs.carleton.ca, oppacher@scs.carleton.ca, ashfield@computer.org,
michael_weiss@Mitel.COM

Abstract

Choosing the right abstractions is important for managing the complexity of your system. Three important abstractions used today are object, component and agent. Many similarities exist between these abstractions, but to make proper use of each, one should have a good understanding of their differences. Too often, we hear people discussing their agent-based systems when they have simply used the object abstraction. In this conceptual paper, we use communication as a means to differentiate the three abstractions. We describe communications patterns for each abstraction using an abbreviated pattern format, identifying the contexts, forces and solutions to different problems that present themselves for each abstraction. Our objective is to help developers identify the abstractions they are working with so they can make better use of them.

1. Introduction

When you create compound elements, name them, and manipulate them as units, you are forming abstractions. Abstraction helps you separate the details of how an element is implemented from how it is used. This separation makes it easier to replace one element for another since abstraction users are depended only on the abstraction's interface, not on its implementation. Moreover, by hiding the details of the implementation, abstraction users do not have to deal with the complexity associated with the implementation, making their development tasks easier.

You can layer abstractions on top of one another, where any abstraction may use only the services of the abstractions in the layer immediately below, and so on. For example, you can develop interval arithmetic out of the ability to add and subtract rational numbers. You can add and subtract rational numbers by being able to create them and by having access to their numerators and denominators. Finally, you can represent the numerator and denominator with a pair structure and with operations to get at the head and tail of the pair.

The division between an abstraction layer is called an abstraction barrier. One main advantage to using abstraction barriers is that each layer is easier to maintain and modify. Since the layer above depends only on the interface of the layer below, the lower layer can be replaced with new elements or implementations without having to inform the higher layer. You can defeat this advantage by bypassing abstraction barriers in your software, permitting one layer to use abstractions beyond the layer below. This jump results in a tight coupling between the implementations of the software layers, making your software more brittle.

0-7695-0278-4/99 $10.00 © 1999 IEEE

To avoid jumping abstraction barriers, it is important for you to understand your abstractions. Abstractions can take many forms, including procedural, data and language [1]. More recently, object, component and agent have become increasingly important forms of abstractions. Do you know the differences between procedural, data and language abstractions? Most do. Do you know the differences between object, component, and agent abstractions? Most don't, and this is a problem. You cannot use an abstraction properly unless you know what it is.

Bradshaw noted that some consider procedure, object and agent abstractions as identical:

> One person's "intelligent agent" is another person's "smart object'; and today's "smart object" is tomorrow's dumb program [2].

Others have expressed the view that some algorithms can be expressed better using objects rather than with procedures [10]. While others have gone further, stating that it may be easier for developers to represent their programs in terms of agents rather than with objects [5].

We view all of these abstractions as being important and relevant, but for different contexts. Unfortunately, we find that there is much confusion between the object, component and agent abstractions. Given that you must understand an abstraction, before you can use it properly and successfully, we find that it is very important to clarify the distinction between the three. This a highly relevant task today because many developers are making claims about building object, component or agent-based systems without knowing what this implies or which abstractions they are actually using. For example, many are building agent-based systems out of objects [11]. Is this situation possible, or have they mixed abstractions?

We agree that there are many similarities between the object, component and agent abstractions. Some researchers have already tried to differentiate objects from agents [9, 12]. However, we have not found anyone that has attempted to provide a comparison of all three. We do not provide an exhaustive comparison here, but have found that we can use communication as one means to differentiate the three.

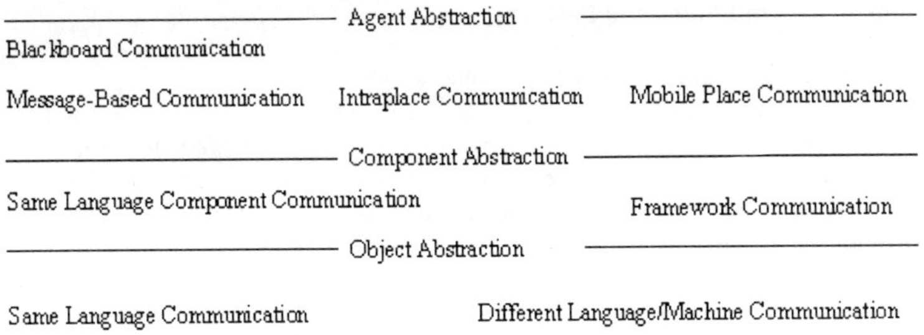

———————————————— Agent Abstraction ————————————————

Blackboard Communication

Message-Based Communication Intraplace Communication Mobile Place Communication

———————————————— Component Abstraction ————————————————

Same Language Component Communication

        Framework Communication

———————————————— Object Abstraction ————————————————

Same Language Communication   Different Language/Machine Communication

Figure 1. Abstraction Barriers and Patterns

In this conceptual paper, we describe each abstraction's main communication patterns. The patterns identify the contexts, forces and solutions to different problems that present themselves for each abstraction. One may be familiar with some of the communication patterns described here. However, the main contribution of the paper is to associate each pattern with a specific abstraction, as shown in Figure 1. The consequence of providing these patterns is that developers will have something to compare their abstractions against, enabling them to determine which one they are using, and, thereby, enabling them to make better use of the abstraction.

For brevity and simplicity, we have used an abbreviated pattern notation. What follows are sections that begin with brief introductions to objects, components and agents and then continue with the main communication patterns of each abstraction. The final section provides a summary and our final thoughts.

2. Object Communication Patterns

In order to discuss patterns of object communication, we begin with a working definition of an object. We agree with the usual definition that an object is an entity that exists, is able to save state (information) and is able to offer a number of operations (behavior) to either examine or change the state [8]. In addition, a common class defines the structure and behavior of similar objects [3]. We also agree that instance variables and methods implement an object's state and behavior [4]. Implicit with this definition is that object-oriented applications are implemented using languages like C++, Smalltalk or Java. Consequently, applications are composed of language specific objects with development teams in control of their implementation.

This object-oriented approach to application development with specific focus on language results in two patterns of communication between objects. In short, either you leave it up to the language to manage the communication between objects or you develop your own add-hoc technique. The point we are trying to make is that once you use an object-oriented approach, rather than a component-based approach or agent-based approach, you form an expectation as to how your objects communicate because of the early commitment to a language.

In the following sections, we describe two communication patterns applicable once you make this choice.

2.1. Same Language Communication Pattern

Problem. How does an object communicate with another object?

Context. You have developed objects for an application and implemented them in the same language. One or more of the objects needs to collaborate with another or to delegate responsibility for a task. You and your development team are in close proximity and can agree on what information must be passed between objects and on its format.

Forces:

- Objects need to collaborate quickly with one another.
- Collaboration and delegation between objects is needed often.
- The implementation language supports the ability for objects to send messages to one another.
- The receiving object must always respond to a message. The response may be null, but this too is considered a valid response.
- A sending object is always willing to wait for a response to its message.

- Custom messaging protocols and frameworks take time to develop and can impact performance.
- The mapping between messages and methods to execute can be determined a priori.

Solution. Use the built-in facilities of the implementation language for communication. The quickest and most efficient means for objects to communicate is by having them send one another predefined messages resulting in the execution of corresponding methods implemented by the receiving object. Let the language facilities work out the details of ensuring the delivery of messages and the returning of their results.

2.2. Different Language/Machine Communication Pattern

Problem. How does an object communicate with another object in a different application on the same machine, on another machine, or written in a different language?

Context. You have developed objects for different applications and implemented them using either the same language or different combinations of object-oriented languages. One or more objects in different applications needs to collaborate with another or needs to delegate responsibility for a task to it. You and your development team are in close proximity and can agree on what information must be passed between objects and on its format.

Forces:

- Objects need to collaborate quickly with one another.
- Collaboration and delegation between objects is needed often.
- The implementation languages do not support the ability for objects to send messages between objects across languages, applications or machines.
- The receiving object may need to respond to a message, but not always.
- The sending does not need to wait for a response to a message.
- Sophisticated messaging protocols and frameworks take time to develop and can impact performance.

Solution. The sending object writes its message to a blackboard that the receiving object looks at periodically. After noticing and processing the message, if necessary, the receiving object writes its response back to the blackboard for the original sending object to read. You can consider shared memory, a file, or even a socket as physical examples of a blackboard.

3. Component Communication Patterns

In order to discuss component communication patterns, we begin with a working definition of a component. We agree with the definition formulated at the 1996 European Conference on Object-Oriented Programming [13]:

> 'A software component is a unit of composition with contractually specified interfaces and explicit context dependencies. A software component can be deployed independently and is subject to composition by their parties.'

The belief is that a component is one abstraction level above an object. For example, we naturally think about methods when we think of object behaviors, since methods are the embodiment of the behaviors. However, this is a result of an early focus of language and implementation. Components change our focus from behaviors to interfaces, contracts, semantics and composition. When working with components, you should not care about how they conduct their operations or their implementation. Rather you should focus on what they can do for your application. In other words, components are the true notion of black box. Therefore, when your application communicates with a component, the language you are using and the one used to implement the component do not matter. Moreover, where objects are dependent on their execution environments and this dependency is yours to manage, components are meant to be independently deployable. This means that components must specify their own needs and any environment can use them provided those needs are met.

In summary, components manage their needs and hide their implementation details, including the implementation language. If you don't know which language was used to implement a component, how do you communicate with it? In the next sections, we describe two communication patterns applicable once you make the choice to work with components, not objects.

3.1. Same Language Component Communication Pattern

Problem. How does a component or an object communicate with other components when they are implemented in the same language?

Context. You decided to use the component abstraction for your building your application. You have either developed your components from scratch or have purchased them from a third party, but in both cases, they are implemented in the same language as other objects in your application. The result is that your application is composed of objects and components implemented in the same language.

Forces:

- Components need to collaborate quickly with one another and with other objects.
- Objects need to collaborate with components.
- Collaboration and delegation between objects and components is needed often.
- The receiving component must always respond to a message. The response may be null, but this too is considered a valid response.
- A sending component is always willing to wait for a response to its message.
- Custom messaging protocols and frameworks take time to develop and can impact performance.
- The mapping between messages and the methods to execute can be determined a priori.

Solution. Since your components are implemented in the same language as your objects, you can apply the same solution as in the Same Language Communication Pattern and for the same reasons. An example of this type of interaction is Java objects interacting with Java Beans.

3.2. Framework Communication Pattern

Problem. How does a component or an object communicate with other components when it is not implemented in the same language, not physically located on the same machine or not in the same application?

Context. You decided to use the component abstraction for your building your application. You have developed or purchased components implemented using a different language from the one used to develop your application's components. Your application's components may need to message to components contained in another application. The result is that your application is composed of objects and components implemented in different languages, and possible on different machines and in different applications.

Forces:

- Components need to collaborate quickly with one another and with other objects.
- Objects need to collaborate with components
- Collaboration and delegation between objects and components is needed often.
- The implementation language supports the ability for objects to send messages to one another.
- The receiving component must always respond to a message. The response may be null, but this too is considered a valid response.
- A sending component is always willing to wait for a response to its message.
- There is no way for you to determine a component's implementation language.
- The mapping between messages and the methods to execute can be determined a priori.

Solution. Since your application is composed of objects and components implemented in different languages, or you are not sure of a component's implementation language, you cannot rely on the communication services provided by a specific language. Therefore, your application will need to work with a framework that can 'install' the components and then use its communication services to communicate with the components. Examples of this type of framework include The Object Management Group's (OMG) Common Object Request Broker Architecture (CORBA) and Microsoft's Component Object Model (COM).

4. Agent Communication Patterns

In order to discuss agent communication patterns, we begin with a working definition of an agent. It is difficult to define an agent since many different definitions exist. For example, Franklin and Graesser [7] describe ten different agent definitions. However, we agree that their definition is best at providing an overall view of an agent:

> *"An autonomous agent is a system situated within and a part of an environment that senses that environment and acts on it, over time, in pursuit of its own agenda and so as to affect what it senses in the future."*

Our belief is that an agent is a level of abstraction above a component. Like a component, an agent is situated in an environment and is capable of autonomous action in this environment. However, unlike an object or component, which have no control over the execution of their methods, agents have precisely this type of control [9]. If an object or component sends a message to another object or component, the receiver has no control over whether the corresponding method executes; the method always executes. This control is provided by the underlying language or framework, not the object or component. With agents, we view communication as a request by one agent to another. Whether the receiving agent performs any action upon receiving the request, is entirely under its control, not with the underlying language or framework.

Another important aspect of agency, is mobility. In the past, we have built distributed systems from objects and components that, once distributed, stay in one place. The only difficulty in having the distributed entities communicate with one another is in finding their locations. Though, once located, you can apply the Different Language/Machine Communication Pattern or the Framework Communication Pattern to provide for their communication. Mobile agents offer another powerful technique for developing distributed applications at a higher-level of abstraction [14]. However, mobility presents a number of new problems for agent communications. For example, it is difficult to message to an agent that never stays in one place long enough to receive its messages.

The agent abstraction creates new demands on communication. The agents rather than the language or framework are in control of receiving messages, and due to their mobility, agent messages will need to locate the agents before being transported in a secure manner. In the following sections, we describe a few patterns that address these problems.

4.1. Message-Based Communication Pattern

Problem. What mechanism should agents use to communicate when security, portability and addressing are primary concerns?

Context. You are developing a multi-agent system in which communication is required. The communication and exchange of data must be encoded, controlled and managed. Regardless of the decisions made later in the design process, message based communication will change very little.

Forces:

- Agent communication (knowledge sharing) must be encapsulated as it cannot be part of a language.
- Messaging must be secure because it may occur across the network.
- Messaging must be portable across platforms, agents and execution engines.
- A single type of message must be understood by all types of agents (i.e. a standard way of communicating)
- Messages must be of minimal size to reduce network load.
- Different vendors will want to define different message formats; therefore, additional work may be required for interworking

Solution. Define a message class independently of how it is to be used and the information that it may contain. This class hides the platform and agent type (e.g., BDI or Reactive) dependent nature of the information sent between agents. Message objects can be grouped into protocols, or sequences, but always remain the basic building block of agent communication.

Next, develop a messaging layer that sits above the agents as part of the execution environment and which performs all access and manipulation of the messages through well-defined API methods. This messaging layer is responsible for providing the security and portability of the information encoded in the message. Use a suitable encoding for communication, such as KQML [6], embedded into the API of the message objects to allow effective collaboration and communication. Additionally, the communication (messaging) layer should employ established technologies such as Corba or RMI to take care of the low-level details of sending messages.

The platform and agent independent nature of the message allows security and portability to be encapsulated. For example, message objects can calculate check sums and verification codes automatically.

Creating a dedicated messaging layer allows agents of different vendors to be interworked, since information can be converted upon receipt to a format that the target agent can understand. This solution allows the agents that make up a system to concentrate on other issues, remain simple and still take advantage of complex messaging features.

4.2. Intraplace Communication Pattern

Problem. How does an agent communicate with other agents located in the same execution engine (machine)?

Context. You are developing a multi-agent system and agent collaboration is required. To complete tasks, agents must communicate with other agents physically located in the same agent execution engine.

Forces:

- Other agents may not know an agent's location or if it exists before communication occurs.
- Agents may not be of the same type; therefore, issues such as capabilities determination are required
- Security is a concern, i.e., Can other agents be trusted. What are their intentions?
- Agents cannot move from engine to engine.
- Agents have limited knowledge of other agents outside of their execution engine.
- Agent communication must be controlled to keep the system in a consistent state (i.e., lost messages need to be managed)
- Agent complexity must be kept to a minimum to avoid creating a high maintenance overhead.

Solution. Use an agent "supervisor" to provide the means for agents to locate and communicate with others. Upon its creation, force an agent to register with a supervising agent (layer). Upon its destruction, force an agent to deregister. When an agent initially registers with the supervisor, have it communicate information such as its goals, intentions and capabilities. This allows the supervisor to match agent queries (clients) with providers (servers).

The centralization of communication in the supervisor allows security, reliability and agent location to be transparently provided for agents. Agents never directly communicate but instead construct messages and pass them to their targets via the supervisor. Although this design can cause a message bottleneck, it increases message flexibility and security. Additionally, the supervisor can implement advanced features such as flow control or caching of messages and queries. Another benefit is that individual agents remain relatively simple and do not have to implement methods to locate and communicate with other agents.

4.3. Mobile Place Communication Pattern

Problem. How do mobile agents communicate and collaborate with other mobile agents?

Context. You are developing a multi-agent system where agents must collaborate with others located in the current execution engine or on other remote engine. Agents are free to move about the network and are not constrained to remain at a single execution engine. Agents may actively move about the network seeking collaborators or wait until collaborators are found and move to their location.

Forces:

- Agents are free to move throughout the network and are aware of the network topology. However, the more they move, the greater the demands placed on the execution engines for transport.
- Not all agents have the same capacities or "type".
- An agent's location and capabilities must be accessible by other agents in the community.
- Network load should be reduced through local processing whenever possible.
- Agents must be portable between execution engines.
- An agent can be assigned a unique identity and home location that do not change during or after it moves.

Solution. Similar to the Intraplace Communication Pattern, upon an agent's creation, force it to register with a supervising agent at its 'home' location. Upon its destruction, force it to deregister. When an agent moves, it informs its home, supervising agent where it will be located. It also informs the remote, supervising agent that it has arrived at a location. Anytime a home, supervising agent is asked to deliver a message to an agent, it forwards the message to the remote, supervising agent where it believes the agent is currently located. The remote, supervising agent finally delivers the message. However, if the agent has moved again and the remote, supervising agent does not know where to forward the message, it informs the home, supervising agent of the situation. The home, supervising agent can send the message again once the agent identifies its new location.

4.4. Blackboard Communication Pattern

Problem. How can agents communicate with others without having to know their locations?

Context. You are developing a multi-agent system in which agents need to share information not knowing the exact location of each other.

Forces:

- Agents cannot directly message between one another. This may be because of performance concerns, or because agents move so frequently that a supervising agent is not practical.
- Communication between specific agents is required.
- Communication may also need to be multi-cast.
- An agent can be assigned a unique identity
- A single consistent messaging interface is required because add-hoc ones do not scale well.

Solution. Create a new system object called a Blackboard. The blackboard is a centralized place where agents can post and retrieve messages in a particular execution engine.

The blackboard handles all communication in a transaction-based manner. This means that agents can post messages or events for other agents and the blackboard ensures their consistency and validity through a transaction model. This model includes support for things such as commit events, retracting messages and sequences of actions. Any agent can poll the blackboard to see if they have any messages.

Agents can post messages directed to specific agents by including the identifier of the target agent in the message, or they can post higher-level, more abstract messages, such as goals, for all agents to read. Permit goals to be seen by the entire agent community and let any agent with the proper capabilities and intentions to post a response.

The blackboard is a passive system object and consequently consumes very few system resources. The flexibility, performance and consistent messaging interface it provides are difficult to match using directed messages. The blackboard can also provide functionality such as persistent messages and the ability to transfer messages to other blackboard, all without any additional agent complexity.

You can extend the blackboard concept with a facilitator agent. Agents register with the facilitator and the blackboard. The blackboard provided the passive services and the facilitator takes an active role by notifying any registered agents if a message was posted for them.

5. Summary

Our goal was to help the reader understand the differences between the object, component, and agent abstractions. To achieve this, we used communication as a means to differentiate them. In short, if you use entities written in the same language and rely on the language for communication support, you are using the object abstraction, even when those entities are on different machines. If you use entities implemented in different languages, but still rely on a sender, a receiver and language support for messaging, you are using the component abstraction. Even with this abstraction, there is a one-to-one mapping between a message and a corresponding method or procedure. For example, when one entity sends a message, a corresponding method or procedure is executed in the receiver. If messages are first class objects with their processing involving the following steps, you are using the agent abstraction.

- locating the appropriate receiving entity(s),
- delivering the message,
- entities reacting with the appropriate behavior determined after the message is received

We based our choice of patterns and pattern format partly due to space limitations and on the fact that we did not intend our patters to be the complete set. This is especially true of the agent abstraction, as we are in the process of documenting an additional ten communication patterns. We attempted to choose those patterns that were important for distinguishing one abstraction from another. We believe the abbreviated pattern format provides enough of the details to help the reader understand the difference between the abstractions.

Are there other dimensions to compare the object, component and agent abstractions? The answer is obviously yes. However, when someone says they are developing an agent-based system in the future, we hope you will now understand what it means, at least from a communication perspective.

6. References

[1] Abelson, H., Sussman, G.J., and Sussman, J., "Structure and Interpretation of Computer Programs", McGraw Hill, 1996.

[2] Bradshaw, J.M., "An Introduction to Software Agents", In J.M. Bradshaw (ed.) Software Agents, AAAI Press/MIT Press, 3-49, 1997.

[3] Booch, G., "Object Oriented Design with Applications", Benjamin/Cummings, 1991.

[4] Campione, M., and Walrath, K., "The Java Tutorial", Second Edition, Addison-Wesley, 1998.

[5] Dennett, D.C., "he Intentional Stance", MIT Press, 1987.

[6] Finin, T., Labrou, Y., Mayfield, J., "KQML as an Agent Communication Language", In J.M. Bradshaw (ed.) Software Agents, AAAI Press/MIT Press, 291-316, 1997.

[7] Franklin, S., and Graesser, A., "Is It an Agent, or Just a Program?: A Taxonomy for Autonomous Agents, In J.P. Müller, M. J. Wooldridge and N. R. Jennings (eds.) Intelligent Agents III Agent Theories, Architectures, and Languages – ECAI 96 Workshop, Springer-Verlag, Heidelberg, 21-35,1997.

[8] Jacobson, I., "Object-Oriented Software Engineering", Addison-Wesley, 1992.

[9] Jennings, N.R., and Wooldridge, M., "Applications of Intelligent Agents", In N. Jennings and M.J. Wooldridge (eds.) Agent Technology: Foundations, Applications, and Markets, Springer-Verlag, Heidelberg, 3-28, 1997.

[10] Kaehler, T., Patterson, D., "A Small Taste of Smalltalk", BYTE, August, 145-159, 1986.

[11] Lange, D.B, and Oshima, M., "Programming and Deploying Java Mobile Agents with Aglets", Addison Wesley, 1998.

[12] Shoham Y., "Agent-Oriented Programming", Journal of Artificial Intelligence, 60(1), 51-92, 1993.

[13] Szyperski, C. and Pfister C., Workshop on Component-Oriented Programming, Summary, In M. Mühlhäuser (ed.) Special Issues on Object-Oriented Programming – ECOOP 96 Workshop Reader, Springer-Verlag, Heidelberg, 1997.

[14] Vogler, H, Moschgath, M., Kunkelmann, T, "Enhancing Mobile Agetns with Electronic Capabilities", In M. Jlusch and G. Weiß (eds.) Cooperative Information Agents II: Learning, Mobility, and Electronic Commerce for Infromation Discovery on the Internet – Second International Woekshop, CIA '98, Springer-Verlag, Heidelberg, 148-159, 1998

Bounding Component Behavior via Protocols

Frantisek Plasil[1,2], Stanislav Visnovsky[1], Miloslav Besta[1,2]

[1]*Charles University, Prague*
Department of Software Engineering
{plasil, visnovsky, besta}@nenya.ms.mff.cuni.cz
http://nenya.ms.mff.cuni.cz

[2]*Academy of Sciences of the Czech Rep.*
Institute of Computer Science
{plasil, besta}@uivt.cas.cz
http://www.uivt.cas.cz

Abstract

In this paper, we enhance the SOFA Component Description Language with a semantic description of a component's functionality. There are two key requirements this description aims to address: first, it should ensure correct composition of the nested architectural abstractions (for design purposes); second, it should be easy-to-read so that an average user can identify a component with the correct semantics for the purposes of component trading. The semantic description in SOFA expresses the behavior of the component in terms of behavior protocols using a notation similar to regular expressions which is easy to read and comprehend. The behavior protocols are used on three levels: interface, frame, and architecture. The key achievements of this paper include the definition of the protocol conformance relation. Using this relation, the designer can in most cases statically verify that the frame protocol adheres to the requirements of the interface protocols, and that the architecture protocol adheres to the requirements of the frame and interface protocols.

1. Introduction

It is widely accepted that in the very near future, the majority of software applications will be composed from reusable, potentially off-the-shelf software components. One of the cornerstones of successful component trading and usage is the possibility to describe their functionality in terms of both internal and external communication taking place through the component interfaces. Such a description should be sufficiently precise in order to allow for automatic checking of correctness of component composition and use, but easy to comprehend for application programmers and simple to write for component designers. From this perspective, one of the current concerns with components is that the usual signature-based interface definitions do not describe the component communication precisely enough. The need for such a definition is reflected in efforts of the object-oriented programming community, e.g., in [2, 10, 14, 15].

1.1. Objects and protocols

An object interface definition can be considered as a service definition. As stated in [9], the sequences of requests that an object is capable of servicing constitute the object's *protocol*, a specification of which should be an integral part of the object's interface definition(s). A typical way [2, 4, 9, 10, 17, 14] to express the object's protocol is to model it as a finite state machine. There are three basic approaches to specify such a machine: (1) directly as a state transition system, e.g. [9,

14, 17], (2) via a parser accepting the valid request sequences, e.g. [4], (3) as a regular-like expression generating the valid request sequences, e.g. [2, 12]. The protocols originate in path expressions [3] which specify synchronization of procedures executed in parallel. Procol [2] might serve as an example of an object language in which protocols are used to describe both the access synchronization and the availability of an object's service.

In all these synchronization schemes, checking the compliance of calls to an object with its protocol was expected to be done at run-time. As emphasized in [10], rather than simply raising exceptions when protocols are violated, it would be desirable to statically validate clients' conformance with protocols and to determine automatically if a protocol can be formally viewed as a "subtype" of another one. In a similar vein, a subtyping relationship on regular types is defined in [9] which allows to statically determine whether a protocol can be replaced by another one.

1.2. Components and protocols

Recently, the component-oriented program design has drawn a lot of attention, mainly because components provide a higher level of design abstractions than objects. Usually, a component can be viewed as a black-box entity which provides and/or requires a set of services (accessed through interfaces). Components can be composed together by binding required to provided services, forming a framework resp. a higher-level component.

With respect to describing component communication, the approaches based on applying the idea of object protocols to components include [1] and [17]. In [1], the protocol is expressed via a set of recursive CSP-based equations. The protocol idea outlined in [17] is based on cooperating pairs of typed interfaces (collaborations). A collaboration description includes the protocol described as a set of sequencing constraints based on a transition system.

1.3. Challenges, the goal of the paper

None of the approaches mentioned in Section 1.2 are based on describing protocol in a form similar to regular expressions which is very easy to read. Moreover, none of these approaches address a step-by-step development of a component's protocol during the design process of the component. Thus, the goal of this paper is to address these two issues: protocol readability and support for step-by-step protocol refinement.

To reflect the goal, the paper is organized as follows. In Section 2, we provide an overview of the SOFA component model which will serve as a proof-of-the-concept base. Section 3 introduces behavior protocols and the underlying model of communication. The key contribution of the paper is provided in Section 4, which shows how behavior protocols can be associated with the SOFA architecture description language (CDL), and in Section 5, where the protocol conformance relation is defined. Moreover, these sections outline seamless fitting of the idea of step-by-step protocol refinement into the SOFA component model, where refinement-based component design is supported by providing both black-box view and grey-box view on a component as a part of the component's type definition. Section 6 is devoted to evaluation and open issues. Related work is discussed in Section 7. Section 8 concludes the paper by summarizing key achievements.

2. SOFA Components

2.1. Component model

The SOFA (Software Appliances) project [11] targets the issue of composing applications from components which can be deployed over a network. In the SOFA component model, an application is viewed as a hierarchy of nested software components. Analogous with the classical concept of an object being an instance of a class, we introduce a *software component* (*component* for short) as an instance of a *component template* (*template* for short). In principle, "template" can be interpreted as "component type".

A template is a pair <template frame, template architecture>. The *template frame* (*frame* for short) of a template T defines the set of individual interfaces any component which is an instance of T will possess. Basically, the frame of T reflects a black-box view of T. Interfaces are defined in the SOFA CDL language. In a template frame, similarly to many other architecture description languages (ADLs), an interface (type) can be instantiated as a *provides-interface* or a *requires-interface*.

The *template architecture* (*architecture* for short) describes the structure of a concrete version of the corresponding template frame implementation by instantiating direct subcomponents (those on the adjacent level of component nesting) and by specifying the necessary component interconnections via interface ties. There are three kinds of interface ties: (1) binding of a requires-interface to a provides-interface, (2) delegating from a provides-interface to a nested component's provides-interface, (3) subsuming of a subcomponent's requires-interface to a requires-interface. Basically, the architecture of T reflects a grey-box view on T. The architecture can be specified as *primitive* which means that there are no subcomponents and the template frame implementation will be given in an underlying implementation language, out of the scope of the architecture specification. When an architecture is not primitive, the nested components are viewed on the level of their frames.

2.2. CDL specification language

The specification of a SOFA component is written in the SOFA component definition language (CDL), which is based on CORBA IDL. The complete syntax of CDL is given in [7]. Here, we just demonstrate CDL on a simple example.

Let us imagine we need to create a component which will serve as a very simple database server (Figure 1). Such a component should provide the *Insert, Delete*, and *Query* operations for inserting and removing records from the database, and querying the contents of the database. The database server will access the underlying database via the *IDatabaseAccess* interface type and will use the *ILogging* interface to log invocations of the provided operations. For this purpose, CDL includes the interface construct which specifies the interface type as a set of method signatures. Our interfaces can be specified as follows:

```
interface IDBServer {
    void Insert(in string key, in string data);
    void Delete(in string key);
    void Query(in string query, out string data);
};

interface ILogging {
    void LogEvent(in string event);
    void ClearLog();
};
```

```
interface IDatabaseAccess {
    void Open();
    void Insert(in string key, in string data);
    void Delete(in string key);
    void Query(in string query, out string data);
    void Close();
};
```

The frame specification contains declarations of provides-interfaces and/or requires-interfaces. Thus, the *Database* frame, representing the intended simple database server, is specified by the following frame construct:

390

```
frame Database {
    provides:
        IDBServer dbSrv;
    requires:
        IDatabaseAccess dbAcc;
        ILogging dbLog;
};

architecture Database version v2 {
    inst TransactionManager Transm;
    inst DatabaseBody Local;
    bind Local:tr to Transm:trans;
    subsume Local:lg to dbLog;
    subsume Local:da to dbAcc;
    delegate dbSrv to Local:d;
};
```

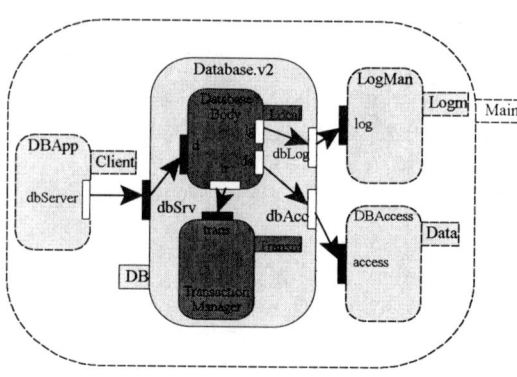

Figure 1. Database architecture

Several versions of the *Database* architecture can be specified. A possibility is to declare a version as *primitive*, i.e., with no nested components. As an alternative, the *Database* architecture version *v2* illustrates how the subcomponents are instantiated and how their ties are specified (distinguishing bind, subsume, and delegate ties). Notice that the subcomponents are specified only at the abstraction level of their frames. As this approach clearly separates the levels of providing architectural details, it allows, e.g., for easy replacement of a subcomponent by its new version.

3. Behavior protocols

3.1. Model of communication

In this section, we describe the essence of the communication model described in detail in [13]. In this model, an agent is a computational entity handling sequences of events. As to handling events, agents can emit events, absorb events, and perform internal events. In general, we say that an agent *exhibits* some *actions*. Agents communicate via peer-to-peer connections. In principle, an agent can communicate with a finite number of agents, and two agents can communicate by means of a finite number of connections. Moreover, we assume that an agent cannot handle more than one event at a time, there is no connection delay, and an agent can emit an event only if its counterpart is prepared to accept it. We pretend that emitting and absorbing a particular event is done as one atomic action.

By *activity* of an agent A on a set of connections CS we understand the sequence of actions A exhibits on CS. By convention, this sequence is represented by the *trace of* A *on* CS. In general, a trace is a sequence of *action tokens*, each of them representing exactly one action. In an action token, the *event name* is followed by the symbol ↑ resp. ↓ which distinguishes *request* resp. *response*. To express whether an event is emitted, absorbed, resp. is internal, we prefix the event name by the *!*, *?* resp. τ symbol. There is a local event namespace associated with every connection. In order to distinguish among actions exhibited on different connections of the same agent, each event name can be qualified by a connection name. In an application, a single global namespace of connection names also exists.

An agent can be *primitive* or *composed*. A composed agent P is constructed by a *composition* of two agents A and B. The connections of P are the union of the connections of A and B. The connections through which A and B communicate with each other (*external* connections from A's and B's points of view) become *internal connections* of P; events on the internal connections of P are referred to as *internal events* of P (analogous with internal actions τ in [8]). Let C be a connection of A. By definition, P shares C with A. The events on C are handled by both P and A jointly (in the sense that the event handling done by A is also considered to be done by P). If C is external both in A and P, the contribution to the corresponding traces of A and P is the same. (Similarly in the case of C being internal in both A and P). However, if C is external in A but internal in P, the handled events are prefixed by τ in the trace of P and by ? or ! in the trace of A.

On a set of connections CS, the set of all possible activities of the agent A is the *behavior* of A on CS. By convention, the behavior of A on CS is represented as a set of traces — the *language of A on* CS (denoted by $L_{A,CS}$). The *event restriction* of a language L on a set of event names N is a function $\varphi_N: L \to L'$, such that $\varphi_N(\alpha_0 x_1 \alpha_1 x_2 \alpha_2 ... x_n \alpha_n) = x_1 x_2 ... x_n$, where $\alpha_0 x_1 \alpha_1 x_2 \alpha_2 ... x_n \alpha_n \in L$, $x_i \in E_N$, $\alpha_i \in (E_L \setminus E_N)^*$, E_N is the set of all possible action tokens the event names of which are in N, and E_L is the set of all action tokens in L. In other words, the restriction is a function which from every trace of the language L omits all action tokens whose event names are not in N. The resulting set of words constitutes the language L'. Furthermore, the restriction of language $L_{A,CS}$ on a subset C of the connection set CS is the language $L_{A,CS}/C = \varphi_{CE}(L_{A,CS})$, where CE is the set of all action tokens, event names of which are qualified by the identification of a connection from C.

The key issue is to find a formal notation able to specify the typically infinite language $L_{A,CS}$ in a finite way. Such a notation should be simple enough to be easily included in an ADL language. The approach we choose is to take advantage of the fact that some of the languages can be expressed by behavior protocols (Section 3.2). At the same time, a language L which cannot be precisely defined by a behavior protocol can usually be approximated by a "closely relative" language L' reflecting well the abstraction level difference between an ADL specification and an implementation in a programming language.

3.2. Behavior protocols

A *behavior protocol* (*protocol* for short) is a regular-like expression, which (syntactically) generates traces. The basic element of a behavior protocol is an action token or NULL (for empty protocol). A protocol can use the following operators and abbreviations, where α, β denote protocols and m denotes an event name.

Operators		Abbreviations	
$\alpha^\wedge$	reentrancy; equivalent to $\alpha \mid \alpha \mid ... \mid \alpha$	$?m\{\alpha\}$	nested incoming call; stands for $?m\uparrow$; α ; $!m\downarrow$
α^*	repetition; equivalent to α ; α ; $...$; α		
$\alpha \mid \beta$	and-parallel; an arbitrary interleaving of traces generated by α and β	$?m$	simple incoming call; stands for $?m\downarrow$; $!m\uparrow$
$\alpha \parallel \beta$	or-parallel; stands for $\alpha + \beta + \alpha \mid \beta$		
α ; β	sequencing; concatenation of traces generated by α and β	$!m$	simple outgoing call; stands for $!m\uparrow$; $?m\downarrow$
$\alpha + \beta$	alternative; either α or β		
$\alpha \sqcap \beta$	composition; similar to $\alpha \mid \beta$ except for when m is absorbed in a trace generated by α and emitted in a trace of β then the simultaneous participation is expressed as internal event		

Intuitively, a behavior protocol can serve for expressing action ordering. For example, if we want to express that an agent emits a request *u* first, then it absorbs any number of requests *x*, *y*, or *z*, and finally a response *v* is emitted, we can describe this behavior by means of a protocol in the form $!u\uparrow$; $(?x\uparrow + ?y\uparrow + ?z\uparrow)^*$; $!v\uparrow$.

4. Associating behavior protocols and SOFA components

4.1. Agents: components at run time

Modeling of SOFA components via agents is straightforward: Every component can be associated with an agent (one-to-one relationship) such that it models the component behavior. Given a component C, we call the agent associated with C the *agent of* C, or simply the C *agent*. In any component C being an instance of T=<F, A>, if A is primitive, the C agent is primitive. Otherwise, the C agent is the composition of the agents of all subcomponents of C (recursively).

Distinguishing the two kinds of interfaces (provides and requires) can be reflected as employing connections with a "provides" and a "requires" end in the sense that the emitting and absorbing of events follows this pattern: A method call m(...) issued by the component C on a requires-interface is modeled as the event pair ...!CON.m↑...?CON. m↓... in a trace of the C agent and ...?CON.m↑... !CON.m↓... in the corresponding trace of the C' agent (CON identifies the connection). A call of a one-way method ow(...) is modeled as an event !ow↑ in a trace of the C agent and

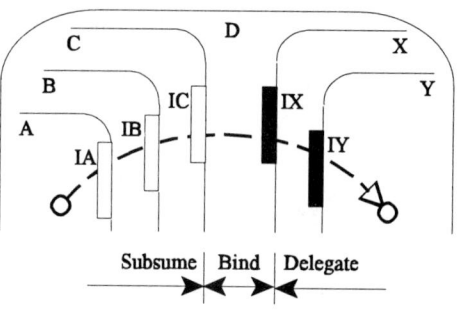

Figure 2. Binding of components

?ow↑ in the corresponding trace of the C' agent. In principle, the set of method names in the interface types involved comprises the event namespaces.

A component C which is an instance of T=<F, A> is basically specified by a set of frame instances involved in the description of A (recursively). To follow the basic philosophy of nesting in CDL specifications, a connection is specified on an incremental description basis. This incremental approach is embodied by tying pairs of interfaces as presented in Section 2. Thus, a connection specification can be seen as a chain of subsume, bind, and delegate clauses spanning across the corresponding hierarchy of architecture specifications, e.g., as depicted on Figure 2. Here, A, B, C, D, X, Y are the component names, IA, IB, IC, IX, IY are the names of the interface instances tied together. Thus, with respect to the composition of agents, the agents of A, B, and C share the "requires" end of the connection and the agents of X, Y share the "provides" end. The connection is internal to the D agent. Technically, the connection is uniquely identified by its *full-chain identification*, taking the form: $D.C.B.A{:}IA{-}D.C.B{:}IB{-}D.C{:}IC \rightarrow D.X{:}IX{-}D.X.Y{:}IY$.

4.2. Bounding behavior of components

As emphasized in Section 3.1, an agent's behavior can be approximated by a behavior protocol. Thus, we could employ the behavior protocols to approximate component behavior. The key issue is to define the exact meaning of the "approximation" of the SOFA component behavior. Our answer to this question is based on the idea that a component's behavior on its provides-interfaces can be "richer" than what is specified by a protocol, while the behavior on its requires-interfaces has to be "narrower" than what is specified by a protocol. Such an approximation is referred to as "bounding" the behavior of a component; formally:

Let C be a component and P_C resp. R_C the sets of all C's provides-interfaces resp. requires-interfaces (recursively including the interfaces of C's subcomponents). We say that the behavior represented as language L_C of the component C on a set of its interfaces SI is *bounded* by a protocol BP if both of the following inclusions hold:

$$(1)\ L(BP)/(P_C \cap SI) \subseteq L_C/(P_C \cap SI) \qquad (2)\ L(BP)/(R_C \cap SI) \supseteq L_C/(R_C \cap SI)$$

Needless to say, a key issue of employing the behavior protocol idea in the component design is to find meaningful sets SI and natural units for which protocols can be easily formed. Obviously, the CDL interface, frame, and architecture concepts are such natural units. We therefore introduce the interface, frame, and architecture protocols in Sections 4.3 – 4.5.

The CDL constructs, however, are inherently generic — at the CDL specification level, the protocols can only contain a generic identification of potential connections. Consequently, the protocols in CDL are specified in a generic form. In particular, the generic connection names are derived from the interface instance identifications as declared in the corresponding CDL frame and architecture constructs.

Because of the step-by-step refinement nature of the component design, the knowledge of the connection identification is also obtained on a step-by-step basis, reflecting the nesting of architectures. Each level of a template T's nesting into another template contributes incrementally to the knowledge of a part of the complete-chain identification of the connections which are involved in T. This implies a step-by-step modification of every protocol P associated with T; we call these intermediate forms of P *semi-instances* of P. After the outmost component is instantiated, each protocol in the component contains a complete-chain identification of the connections; the semi-instance of P becomes an instance of P. It should be emphasized that only an instance of a protocol can bound the behavior of a component. Anyway, bounding the behavior is a run-time issue.

4.3. Interface protocol

To capture the behavior of a service specified by a particular interface type, we enhance the interface type specification by an *interface protocol*. In principle, in an interface protocol associated with a provides (resp. requires) interface, a method invocation is to be prefixed by ? resp. !. In CDL, the interface protocol is written in its generic form, i.e., no ? and ! prefixes are used; the prefixes are automatically added when the corresponding interface type is instantiated.

To illustrate the use of interface protocols, let us consider a protocol for the *IDatabaseAccess* interface from Section 2.2. The intended use of this interface is to call the method *Open* first, then do a modification of the database by invocations of *Insert*, *Delete* and *Query*, and finally to finish the work with the database by invoking *Close*. The corresponding protocol is *Open ; (Insert + Delete + Query)* ; *Close*. If the *Insert*, *Delete*, and *Query* methods were to be designed to handle requests in parallel, we could specify this intention by *Open ; (Insert || Delete || Query)* ; *Close*. This indicates that parallel execution of the *Insert*, *Delete*, and *Query* methods is possible, but any two invocations of *Insert* must be done sequentially (the same holds for *Delete* and *Query*). To specify that a completely parallel invocation of these methods is allowed, the reentrancy (^) operator is to be used instead of the repetition (*), yielding *Open ; (Insert || Delete || Query)^ ; Close*.

4.4. Frame protocol

To allow the specification of a "black-box behavior" of a component, we enhance the frame specification by including a *frame protocol*. Here, the protocol specifies the acceptable order of method invocations on the provides-interfaces and the expected reactions on the requires-interfaces of the frame. Thus, a name of an action is qualified by the name of the interface instance the invoked method belongs to, and is prefixed by ? or !. Method calls can be specified as nested. This semantics can be expressed by curly brackets (Section 3.2).

For illustration, we present the frame protocols of *Database* and *DatabaseBody*:

```
// Database frame protocol                    frame DatabaseBody {
                                                 provides: IDBServer d;
!dbAcc.Open ;                                    requires: IDatabaseAccess da;
(   ?dbSrv.Insert { ( !dbAcc.Insert ;                       ILogging lg;
        !dbLog.LogEvent )* } +                             ITransaction tr;
    ?dbSrvDelete { ( !dbAcc.Delete ;             protocol:
        !dbLog.LogEvent )* } +                     !da.Open ;
    ?dbSrvQuery { !dbAcc.Query* }                  (   ?d.Insert {! tr.Begin ; !da.Insert ;
)* ;                                                       !lg.LogEvent ; ( !tr.Commit + !tr.Abort ) } +
!dbAcc.Close                                           ?d.Delete {! tr.Begin ; !da.Delete ;
                                                           !lg.LogEvent ; (!tr.Commit + !tr.Abort ) } +
                                                       ?d.Query { !da.Query }
                                                   )* ;
                                                   !da.Close
```

In the *Database* frame protocol, the fact that each modification of the database should be logged is reflected by specifying nested calls in the following way: inside every *dbSrv.Insert* invocation, any number of *dbAcc.Insert* calls can be executed, and after each of these calls is finished, the modification is logged by invoking *dbLog.LogEvent*. Similarly, as a part of every *dbSrv.Delete* invocation, deleting is logged by invoking *dbLog.LogEvent*. The specification of the *DatabaseBody* frame illustrates the CDL syntax of employing frame protocol in a frame specification.

4.5. Architecture protocol

For a template T=<F, A>, an architecture protocol specifies a "grey-box" behavior of T's instances. In principle, the architecture protocol is based upon the frames of the direct subcomponents specified in A. The protocol describes the dependencies among the interfaces of F and the outmost interfaces of all subcomponents in A. In CDL, the architecture protocol is not specified directly. Our approach is to generate it, e.g., in a CDL compiler, by combining the semi-instances of the internal frame protocols using the composition operator ($\sqcap$). This eliminates the need for what would, in fact, be a manual rewriting and mechanical modification of protocols when creating the semi-instances. However, this approach does not capture special properties of the architecture, e.g., simple dependencies among internal subcomponents.

To illustrate what a generated architecture protocol looks like, let us consider the *Database* architecture version *v2* which contains two subcomponents: *Transm* (instance of *TransactionManager*) and *Local* (instance of *DatabaseBody*). When the frame protocols are modified into the corresponding semi-instances and the composition operator is applied, we obtain the following architecture protocol of *Database*:

```
(   ?<Local:tr → Transm:trans>.Begin ;
    ( ?<Local:tr→ Transm:trans>.Commit + ?<Local:tr → Transm:trans>.Abort )
)*
⊓
!<Local:da-dbAcc>.Open ;
(   ?<dbSrv-Local:d>.Insert {
        !<Local:tr → Transm:trans>.Begin ; !<Local:da-dbAcc>.Insert ; !<Local:lg-dbLog>.LogEvent ;
        ( !<Local:tr → Transm:trans>.Commit + !<Local:tr → Transm:trans>.Abort )
    } +
    ?<dbSrv-Local:d>.Delete {
        !<Local:tr → Transm:trans>.Begin ; !<Local:da-dbAcc>.Delete ; <Local:lg-dbLog>.LogEvent ;
        ( !<Local:tr → Transm:trans>.Commit + !<Local:tr → Transm:trans>.Abort )
    } +
    ?<dbSrv-Local:d>.Query { !<Local:da-dbAcc>.Query }
)* ;
!<Local:da-dbAcc>.Close
```

5. Protocol conformance

5.1. Definition of protocol conformance

The generic protocols specified in a template T=<F, A> constitute an obligation on the part of all potential implementations of T. The protocols of the components tied together within the template have to correspond to each other, i.e., intuitively, the architecture protocol of A should follow the design intentions embodied in the frame protocol of F and the interface protocols of the interfaces in F and A should comply with the way these interfaces are employed in the protocols of F and A. The definition of protocol conformance reflects this intuition:

Definition: Let T=<F, A> be a template with frame protocol P_F and architecture protocol P_A, and I_1, I_2 be two interfaces with interface protocols P_{I_1} and P_{I_2}. We say that *interface protocol* P_{I_1} *conforms to interface protocol* P_{I_2} *iff* $L(P_{I_1}) \subseteq L(P_{I_2})$. We say the *frame protocol of* F *conforms to the interface protocols of interfaces of* F iff, for every provides-interface P in F with an interface protocol P_P, $L(P_P') \subseteq L(P_F)/\{P\}$ holds, and for every requires-interface R in F with an interface protocol P_R, $L(P_F)/\{R\} \subseteq L(P_R')$ holds, where P_P' (resp. P_R') denotes the semi-instance of P_P (resp. P_R) with respect to F. We say that *architecture protocol* P_A *conforms to frame protocol* P_F iff $L(P_F')/S_{SET} \subseteq L(P_A)/S_{SET}$ and $L(P_A)/R_{SET} \subseteq L(P_F')/R_{SET}$, where S_{SET} is the set of all F's provides-interfaces and R_{SET} is the set of all F's requires-interfaces and P_F' denotes the semi-instance of P_F with respect to A.

Claim: Let T=<F, A> be a template with frame protocol P_F and architecture protocol P_A, $\{S_i\}$ the set of all F's provides-interfaces, and $\{R_j\}$ the set of all F's requires-interfaces. If Ps_i is the interface protocol of S_i and P_{R_j} is the interface protocol of R_j, then $L(Ps_i') \subseteq L(P_F')/\{S_i\} \subseteq L(P_A)/\{S_i\}$ for all provides-interfaces S_i in F and $L(P_{R_j}') \supseteq L(P_F')/\{R_j\} \supseteq L(P_A)/\{R_j\}$ for all requires-interfaces R_j in F, where Ps_i' resp. P_{R_j}' denotes the semi-instance of Ps_i resp. P_{R_j} with respect to A and P_F' denotes the semi-instance of P_F with respect to A.

The definition of protocol conformance ensures that, having a component C as an instance of template T=<F, A>, the architecture, frame, and interface protocols form a hierarchy. The architecture protocol restricted to the frame's interfaces has to conform to the frame protocol and the frame protocol restricted to any frame's interface has to conform to the interface protocol of that interface.

As an example, consider the conformance of the architecture protocol *Database* version *v2* to the corresponding frame protocol. Following the definition above, we have to identify the restrictions and then verify the inclusions. For the requires-interfaces (*dbLog* and *dbAcc*), the restrictions for the frame protocol and for the architecture protocol are shown below. As we can see, the architecture protocol of its requires-interfaces is narrower than the frame protocol. Similarly, the same verification has to be done for the provides-interfaces. For illustration, the restriction here is done on protocols instead of the generated languages. This is not always possible, however, in the cases when we are able to automatize inclusion checking, restriction on languages can be done in an automatized way (Section 5.2).

```
//Database frame protocol restriction

!dbAcc.Open ;
( ( !dbAcc.Insert ; !dbLog.LogEvent )* +
  ( !dbAcc.Delete ; !dbLog.LogEvent )* +
    !dbAcc.Query*
)* ;
```

```
//Database architecture protocol restriction

!dbAcc.Open ;
( ( !dbAcc.Insert ; !dbLog.LogEvent ) +
  ( !dbAcc.Delete ; !dbLog.LogEvent ) +
    !dbAcc.Query*
)* ;
```

5.2. Checking of protocol conformance

The most important problem of design-time protocol conformance checking is the complexity of languages generated by behavior protocols (BPLs). The sequence, repetition, and alternative operators define regular languages. Based on the definition of the | and ⊓ operators, each use of these operators in a protocol can be replaced by a finite expression containing only +, ;, and *. Therefore, the languages generated by behavior protocols with no use of the ^ operator are regular and verification of their inclusion as well as a construction of the language restriction based on intersection can be done in an algorithmic way [6]. But the ^ operator damages regularity of BPLs. Even worse, BPLs are not context-free in general case. It can be easily shown that (a;b;c)^ violates the pumping lemma for context-free languages. The identification of the subclass of behavior protocols for which the inclusion verification is possible, e.g., protocols where the reentrant subprotocols are equivalent, is a hot topic in our current research. Also, we are evaluating the justification of employment of the ^ operator.

At run-time, on the contrary, it is always possible to check if the behavior of a given component is bounded by a behavior protocol (no restrictions in terms of ^ as actual number of reentrant "entries" into the protocol is known) The run-time checking is typically based on intercepting the method calls by a "protocol guard". It can also be used for run-time checking of protocol conformance, but this approach is not very useful as the run-time checks cannot prove the conformance, they can only identify any non-conformance encountered.

6. Evaluation and open issues

The main advantage of the behavior protocols is their intuitively easy-to-comprehend notation for description of communication. Behavior protocols are not designed to be used as a full programming language. For example, they cannot specify any specific number of repetitions, reentrant entries, etc. They only approximate real traces. Balancing the expressive power and the simplicity of protocols, we believe that the argument of an elegant and easy-to-read notation can outweigh some loss in expressiveness and justify application of behavior protocols in ADLs.

Interface protocols are guidelines for using interfaces. They help to distinguish among different types of services which have the same interface signatures. Moreover, they provide information for component trading and enhance opportunities for checking of component design correctness. The idea of frames with frame protocols helps system designers to build a system from components without detailed knowledge of the components' internals. The frame protocol publishes information about communication among interfaces implemented by a component and thus gives advice to implementors about the component implementation. The frame protocols also provide means for reasoning about suitability of components for a specific purpose. Finally, the notion of architecture protocol improves the description of component behavior by revealing behavior at the next level of component nesting. Architecture protocols are not specified explicitly in CDL, but they are rather created by a tool which combines the frame protocols of nested components by means of ⊓.

The fact that the interface, frame, and architecture protocols form a hierarchy implies the possibility of checking compatibility of protocols at different levels of abstraction. To formalize the requirements of such a compatibility, we introduce the protocol conformance relation. There is a tool which can statically decide (in most cases) whether two protocols at different levels of abstraction comply. This allows for reasoning about template design and supports process of design refinement which we consider to be the key contribution of this paper.

The list of open issues includes: (1) Although the tool for checking protocol conformance has been implemented, some problems with the reentrant operator persist. The issue is to better define the conditions under which the reentrant operator can be used in order to preserve the possibility of checking the protocol conformance in an algorithmic way. (2) We consider to use guards for constraining method invocations in protocols. Guards could help to better understand a component's semantics, but it is not clear if the guard predicates should rely on the component methods for their evaluation, or if some abstract properties representing the internal state of the component should be defined. (3) We do not consider the issue of protocol inheritance. At present, we face the challenge to enhance the sound enrichment technique [12] to reflect protocol conformance. (4) Versioning of architectures is considered in SOFA. Compatible architectures could be rated by comparing their architecture protocols. (5) The SOFA components can be updated at run-time. An update can take a place only when a component is in a precisely defined state. The issue is to express "points of updating" in the frame or architecture protocols. (6) The conformance relation between the architecture and frame protocols, as defined in this paper, is based on separate inclusions of the provides and requires restrictions. This way, however, the interplay among the provides and requires interfaces within a frame can be lost. The issue is to find a better definition of compliance of a frame and architecture protocols overcoming the problem.

7. Related work

Probably the closest to our work is the Wright language [1]. In Wright, the behavior of components is specified as "computation" via a CSP-based notation (a system of recursive equations). In our opinion, regular-like expressions are more readable while having an expressive power strong enough to reasonably approximate the behavior of components. Components in Wright communicate by means of connectors which can be quite complex. Their behavior specification ("glue") is also CSP-based; in fact, glue is very similar to computation. In SOFA, we can simulate connectors by specialized components. In Wright, there is no black-box view of a component which contains subcomponents. In our approach, frames with frame protocols are introduced for this purpose, which we consider very important for refinement-based design of components and for component updating.

The work on interfaces and protocols [17] is quite similar to our approach in the sense that it describes communication between component interfaces. It, however, concentrates only on a behavior description related to a single pair of collaborating interfaces. The specification of a component as whole is not considered, and therefore no concepts similar to our frame and architecture protocols are present. Consequently, the protocol description in [17] can hardly be used for reasoning about component composition, replacement, etc. On the other hand, we found it interesting that the description allows for bidirectional communication on a single pair of interfaces; while not supported directly in SOFA, this can be easily modeled by our communication model. In our opinion, the way we have chosen for expressing component behavior is easier to apply. Similar approach is chosen in ROOM [14] where the communication is not limited to a pair of interfaces. Also, a protocol conformance (called role substitutability) is briefly outlined here.

Reuse contracts [15] introduce the idea of specifying the set of internally invoked methods for each method of an interface, thus capturing the invocation dependencies among methods. However, the model presented in this work is limited in the sense that since it provides description only at the object level of abstraction, it does not support the component-based approach with more cooperating interfaces. While we can describe ordering of nested method invocations, reuse contracts do not aim at expressing such information.

8. Summary

This paper introduces a novel technique for specification and bounding of component behavior via behavior protocols which take a form similar to regular expressions. The description of a component behavior by means of behavior protocols is precise enough to capture the necessary requirements in terms of describing the method calls ordering requirements. It is easy to read, and, at the same time, simple to create because the notation is easy to comprehend. Thus, the protocols meet the basic requirements for a practically useful specification. The paper presents a way of their deployment in the SOFA CDL language.

In SOFA, the three abstraction levels of protocol employment (i.e. interface, frame, and architecture) significantly support the refinement design process, allowing to reason about component behavior on different levels of information hiding. Without unduly exposing any details of the component structure, the interface protocol enhances the description of the service provided or required on an interface. The frame protocol hides the architecture details; it provides behavior information important for component design and trading and, furthermore, supports seamless component updating. The architecture protocol describes component architecture in more detail in order to provide guidelines for design and implementation purposes.

Interface, frame, and architecture protocols are tied together by the protocol conformance relationship which incorporates the idea of behavior compatibility. The verification of protocol conformance can be done statically, i.e. at design time, in many cases, allowing for reliable composition of applications. Moreover, in an implementation of a component type, it is also possible (by intercepting method invocations) to check compliance of the real component behavior with the component specification at run-time.

Acknowledgments

The authors of this paper would like to express their special thanks to Petr Tuma for his useful comments. The authors' appreciation goes also to their colleagues Marek Prochazka for drawing their attention to the nested calls problem and Dusan Balek for comments on the communication model. This work was partially supported by the Grant Agency of the Academy of Sciences of the Czech Republic (project number A2030902), the Grant Agency of the Czech Republic (project number 201/99/0244), and MLC Systeme, Ratingen, Germany.

References

[1]   Allen, R. J.: A Formal Approach to Software Architecture, Ph.D. Thesis, School of Computer Science, Carnegie Mellon University, Pittsburgh, 1997.

[2]   van den Bos, J., Laffra, C.: PROCOL: A Concurrent Object-Oriented Language with Protocols Delegation and Constraints, In Acta Informatica, Springer-Verlag, 1991, pp. 511–538.

[3]   Campbell, R. H., Habermann, A. N.: The Specification of Process Synchronization by Path Expressions, Springer LNCS, Vol. 16, 1974, pp. 89–102.

[4]   Florijn, G: Object Protocols as Functional Parsers, In Proceedings of the ECOOP '95, Springer LNCS 952, August 1995, pp. 351–373.

[5]   Hoare, C. A. R.: Communicating Sequential Processes, Prentice-Hall, 1985.

[6]   van Leeuwen, J.(ed): Formal Models and Semantics, Handbook of Theoretical CS, MIT Press, 1990.

[7]   Mencl, V.: Component Definition Language, Master Thesis, Charles University, Prague, 1998.

[8]   Milner, R.: A Calculus of Communicating Systems, Springer LNCS 92, 1980.

[9]   Nierstrasz, O.: Regular Types for Active Objects, In Proceedings of the OOPSLA '93, ACM Press, 1993, pp. 1–15.

[10] Nierstrasz, O, Meijler, T. D.: Requirements for a Composition Language, In Proceedings of the ECOOP '94, Springer Verlag, LNCS 924, 1995, pp. 147–161.

[11] Plasil, F., Balek, D., Janecek, R.: SOFA/DCUP Architecture for Component Trading and Dynamic Updating, In Proceedings of the ICCDS '98, Annapolis, IEEE CS, 1998, pp. 43–52.

[12] Plasil, F., Mikusik, D.: Inheriting Synchronization Protocols via Sound Enrichment Rules, In Proceedings of the Joint Modular Programming Languages Conference, Springer LNCS 1204, March 1997.

[13] Plasil, F., Visnovsky, S., Besta, M.: Behavior Protocols and Components, Tech. report No. 99/2, Dept. of SW Engineering, Charles University, Prague, February 1999.

[14] Selic, B.: Protocols and Ports: Reusable Inter-Object Behavior Patterns, ObjecTime Limited, Kanata.

[15] Steyaert, P., Lucas, C., Mens, K., D'Hondt, T.: Reuse Contracts: Managing the Evolution of Reusable Assets, In Proceedings of the OOPSLA '96, ACM SIGPLAN Notices, Vol. 31, No. 10, October 1996, pp. 268–285.

[16] Szyperski, C.: Component Software, Beyond Object-Oriented Programming, Addison-Wesley, 1997.

[17] Yellin, D. M., Strom, R. E.: Interfaces, Protocols, and the Semi-Automatic Construction of Software Adaptors, In Proceedings of the OOPSLA '94, ACM Press, 1994, pp. 176–190.

Towards efficient support for executing
the Object Constraint Language

Philippe Collet
collet@i3s.unice.fr

Roger Rousseau
rr@unice.fr

I3S – CNRS – University of Nice - Sophia Antipolis
Les Algorithmes, Bat. Euclide, 2000 route des Lucioles
Sophia Antipolis F-06410 Biot, France

Abstract

The Object Constraint Language (OCL) forms part of the UML notation as a language to complete graphical models by expressing precise constraints or assertions. As OCL is developed as a non-executable language, expressed properties cannot be embedded as executable assertions in the resulting implementations to provide correctness testing. Nonetheless a large part of OCL seems to be easily executable, but straightforward implementations would be inefficient and detrimental to the approach.

This paper proposes a pragmatic solution for an OCL runtime support and determines the origins of potential inefficiency. The evaluation of assertions is streamlined according to their roles and the possibility of sampling quantified assertions. The triggering of assertions is driven by a changed-based system that simplifies large-scale use while ensuring that unstable parts undergo more controls.

1: Introduction

The Object Constraint Language (OCL) [1, 2] forms part of the UML notation [3] as a language to complete graphical models by expressing precise constraints or assertions. OCL is a typed and functional language that provides support for specifying invariants on classes and types, describing pre and postconditions on operations, defining guards on transitions and specifying supplementary operations if necessary.

As the roots of OCL rest on work on formalization around object-oriented methods, it was not developed as a programming language, thus it does not provide any control flow mechanisms and does not deal with specific implementation issues. Even if OCL was not designed with full executability in mind, it is very important to dispose of specifications that can be defined during design and executed during implementation, testing the final code against specifications. Executing OCL specifications thus ensures the seamlessness of the development. Testing OCL assertions reveals design and programming mistakes, leading to corrections and improvements in the code. These corrections may result in design modifications and as the same formalism is used throughout the development, which provides a seamless and reversible approach that suits very well to an iterative and incremental process.

Moreover as OCL is part of an OMG standard, its use will surely be more extensive than any other assertion language. A large part of OCL seems to be easily executable and some assertion languages, like iContract [4] for Java, already use an OCL subset. But straightforward implementations of expensive OCL expressions would be inefficient and detrimental to the approach, especially for the large-scale development of constantly evolving applications.

In this paper, we study the main issues for executing OCL specifications and we determine the origins of potential inefficiency. We then distinguish OCL expressions that must be fully evaluated to preserve the original semantics and other expressions that can be approximated to speed up evaluations. The evaluation of assertions is then streamlined according to their roles and the possibility of sampling quantified assertions. In order to improve further the efficiency of the approach, the problem of assertions triggering is also studied. We propose a semiautomatic assistance system that helps developers by determining the assertions to be evaluated according to changes made on classes. This triggering system promotes the large-scale use of assertions as it ensures that unstable parts undergo more controls.

The remainder of the paper is organised as follows. Section 2 studies the executability of OCL and determines significant points for execution. Section 3 considers evaluation techniques for assertions. Section 4 deals with the semiautomatic triggering of assertions. Section 5 concludes with an overview of future work on efficient implementation of assertions.

2: OCL expressiveness and executability

OCL provides an expression language which is indeed more powerful and richer than classic executable assertion languages. Our work deals with OCL as a class specification language, that is, on invariants, pre and post conditions, as it is its main utilization, which directly matches with implementation languages. Our work is based on OCL from UML v1.1 and does not take into account the UML v1.3 working draft. In order to provide an efficient framework for the execution of OCL, we must determine which expressions in the language are expensive to evaluate and how to improve their execution.

We use a university management application, which is taken from [5], as a running example. We particularly focus on the registration of students in various courses, each course is made of sections and is on the responsibility of a teacher. Figure 1 shows a simplified relationship graph of the extracted classes, using the UML notation [3].

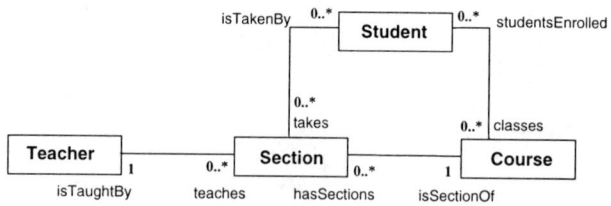

Figure 1. Simplified class diagram describing courses management.

2.1: Overview of OCL features

Recent work on the semantics of OCL [6, 7] clarified some vague points and it seems now easy to adapt most of the OCL functionalities to implementation languages. This section makes a quick overview of the OCL language, see [1, 2] for more detailed presentations.

OCL is a typed functional language, which uses many predefined types from the UML meta-model. It supports basic types : `Integer`, `Real`, `String` and `Boolean`. One can use their values and some predefined operators. In addition, OCL provides Enumeration types and every type defined in an UML model can be reused in an OCL expression. Generic collections are available as well, with `Collection` at the top of the containers hierarchy and `Set`, `Bag` and `Sequence` as heirs. Their semantics is classic and straightforward. A reification of each type as an object is also provided with `oclType` and `oclAny` represents the ancestor of every class.

One can access *properties* of an object, that is, attributes, association ends and functions (without side-effects). Accessing a property is normally made through a dot notation (`aCourse.scheduled`). Accessing a property of a collection object is distinguished by using an arrow (`hasSections->size`). OCL also supports navigation through qualified associations using square brackets for the qualifier and package naming through the package name followed by a double colon. Collections can also be described as a literal list of values between curly brackets prefixed by the collection type.

OCL provides several useful operations on collections that result in the powerful expressiveness of the language. We only deal here with the most important ones. The `select` operation correponds to the classic selective operation used in object query languages and gives the sub-collection of elements that satisfy a given condition. It uses a general canvas to pass an OCL expression as a parameter for a collection operation:

```
collection->select( var : Type | expression-with-var )
```

Shortcuts may be used, by omitting the `Type` or by passing directly an expression related to each element of the collection. Naming the bound variable is in any case useful when nesting collection operations. An example of `select` operation follows, selecting the sections taught by a given professor that belong to a particular course:

```
aProf.teaches->select( s | s.isSectionOf = aParticularCourse )
```

A `reject` operation is also provided, selecting elements that do not satisfy the given condition. A `collect` operation applies a given expression to all elements of the collection and return a new Bag containing them.

Operations `forAll` and `exists` represent the first-order logic quantifiers and use the same canvas as previous operations to deliver a boolean result. Expressing the fact that all my favourite students take the Object Technology class can be written as follows :

```
myFavouriteStudents->forAll( classes->exists( name = 'Object Technology' ) )
```

The most generic operation on OCL collections is `iterate`, which represents a traverse on a collection with the possibility of building a result using an accumulator.

The specification of the OCL language allows to define recursively operations. As far as we know, no recursive definition is used in the definition the UML notation semantics [8], which uses a great deal of OCL expressions. As evaluating recursive definitions would lead to complex solutions, we do not include them in our execution framework.

2.2: Using OCL for class specification

The different features of OCL can be combined to annotate class diagram to express class specifications, which we want to make executable. In these specifications, the instance of the current class is represented by `self` and the result of a function is `result` inside assertions. The labels `pre:` and `post:` are used to annotate operations, like the function `openForRegistration` in class `Course` that specifies if the course is still available for students registration:

<u>Course</u>
```
openForRegistration : Boolean
--  Can students still register for the course ?
post: result = ( today <= closingDate )
```

Procedures can also be described with pre and postconditions. The specification of procedure register in class Student shows both pre and postconditions. The first precondition specifies that section s really forms part of course c using the relationship between course and section. The second one checks that the student has not already registered for this section using an universal quantification. The last precondition specifies that the course must be currently open for registration so that the registration can be performed. Posconditions define the effect of the registration on the collection of courses and sections associated with the student. The first two postconditions ensure that the section s is within the set of sections takes and that this set has one element more, as the preconditions required that section s was not in takes before the registration. The second postcondition illustrates the use of the operator @pre to reference the size of set takes before the register call. In the third postcondition, it is specified that course c must form part of the set classes of courses associated with the student:

<u>Student</u>
```
register(s: Section; c: Course)
--  Registration in section  s (part of course  c)
pre: c.hasSections->includes(s)
pre: takes->forAll(sec | sec <> s )
pre: c.openForRegistration
post: takes->includes(s)
post: takes->size=takes->size@pre+1
post: classes->includes(c)
```

UML invariants are expressed through a stereotyped constraint named «invariant» but in OCL v1.1, there is no keyword distinction for invariants (a inv: keyword has been added in the 1.3 working draft). For example, the following three invariants state the mutual exclusion between the three states established on a course by using the implicit conjunction of the three assertions, where the equality operators correspond to logical equivalences:

<u>Course</u>
```
openForRegistration = ( not scheduled and not canceled )
scheduled = ( not openForRegistration and not canceled )
canceled = ( not openForRegistration and not scheduled )
```

As any OCL type can be accessed as an object, one can also access its extent, that is, the set of its instances, through the feature allInstances, and then express properties on the type itself. For example the following invariant expresses the uniqueness of card number for all students:

<u>Student</u>
```
Student.allInstances->forAll( s1,s2 | s1<>s2 implies s1.cardNb<>s2.cardNb )
```

2.3: Main principles for a runtime support

Large parts of OCL functionalities may be easily executed. Predefined basic types, enumeration types and their operations can be mapped to many implementation languages or can be emulated. Some points need a correct interpretation to provide a reliable execution framework.

The times for evaluation of the different assertions can be borrowed from other assertion approach. Preconditions are evaluated before the routine call, postconditions as well as invariants after the call. Some OCL expressions can fail to evaluate and be regarded as undefined [1, § 4.7], like wrong type-casting. The runtime support must handle undefined expressions by raising an appropriate exception for each cause of un-definition. The semantics of the @pre construction (to reference the previous object state in postcondition) enables to implement it as object cloning at the beginning of routines, like in other executable assertion languages.

UML associations used in OCL must be implemented in the runtime support and navigation through associations must be fully supported. Moreover navigation with qualified associations must also be implemented, allowing to collect instances from qualifier attributes. All these features can be supported by providing support for associations in the implementation languages. As OCL provides a reification of types, the implementation must do the same and must provide in addition an access to each type extent in a deep interpretation. A deep type extent includes all instances that are compatible (substitutable using subtyping) with this type.

The OCL collection hierarchy is very compact. If a more sophisticated hierarchy would provide a richer set of features, the current hierarchy has the advantage of being easily adaptable to collections hierarchies of many implementation languages like C++, Java or the ODMG standard for OODB. In OCL the operations available on collections are the most expensive ones, as they implies the traverse of collections. We distinguish constructive operations, like select and collect, from boolean operations like exists and forAll. The former are known to be used in query languages and one might think of using query optimisation techniques to speed up evaluations. But the analysis of query expressions is time-consuming and the use of select and collect operations is less important than the use of quantifications. This kind of optimisations would be too complex for the few benefits obtained.

On the contrary quantifications only return a boolean result and can be easily approximated. Moreover universal quantifications are used a lot in OCL specifications. They also constitute an important part in object-oriented queries [9]. Therefore assertions with quantifications are both expensive and widespread and our whole attention must be devoted to the optimisation of their evaluations.

3: Efficient evaluation of assertions

A very accurate knowledge of the entities involved is necessary to determine precisely the dependencies between classes and the most efficient techniques for triggering and evaluating assertions. We thus recommand using a reification of the different elements that compose a class, including assertion clauses and assertions themselves. Nonetheless the techniques presented in the following sections can be applied using information usually found inside CASE tools or compilers.

3.1: Using the form of assertions

Assertion categories allow us to deduce various evaluation constraints. As preconditions act as guards on computations, it is not possible to make any distinction on the intention of a precondition. Their evaluation must be systematically exhaustive, as they are the basis of the contract.

On the contrary, postconditions may express different forms of expressions, like definitions of result or state change for operations, but they may also express incomplete constraints on some attributes or some abstract operations. The OCL language does not allow to distinguish these intentions and we cannot use this information to determine the importance of an assertion according to another. Nevertheless it is possible to use approximation algorithms on postconditions and invariants in order to get some confidence in the test. This approximation is realized on some collection operations by using a sample of the collection instead of the collection in its entirety.

Using a more accurate classification of assertions, different forms of assertions could be distinguished for postconditions and invariants, and they could provide enough information to adapt more efficiently the implementation techniques. But this study is out of the scope of this paper.

To ensure a better overall efficiency of assertion evaluation, it is thus necessary on the one hand to consider assertion triggering according to the assertion categories and to the stability of a class (see section 4). On the other hand, it is necessary to minimize such expensive evaluations, like universal quantifications.

3.2: Level of confidence in a class

The evaluation strategies that we propose are inspired by experience with random generation of test sets [10] and their application to estimations of confidence in the reliability of a programme [11]. Even if tests do not reveal any error, one cannot have complete confidence in the programme, regardless of the methods used to test it. However, by using a probabilistic approach to test generation, it is possible to derive a *statistical* confidence in the programme. In our case, we use the concept of confidence in a class as an input parameter for selecting new tests to be run. The confidence in a class is then estimated using a class evolution detection tool, which is described in section 4. If a class is under development we cannot rely on its features, so testing must be more thorough. On the contrary, if a class is stable, it must have a test *history* that gives us confidence in it, and a sample of instances is then enough to check that our confidence is deserved.

3.3: Existential quantifications

Sampled evaluation strategies are only applied to universal quantifications. A simple logical manipulation can transform an existential quantification into an expression containing a universal quantification (collection->exists(x | P(x)) is equivalent to not collection->forAll(x | not P(x))). If the forAll expression is sampled, the result would be most often true, as exists expressions often mean that one element satisfies the condition. As the result is prefixed with the operator not, the result would be most often false and the test would fail although it should not. Therefore sampled evaluation strategies are not applied to existential quantifications.

3.4: Universal quantifications

There are many techniques for selecting test sets. Random methods are chosen as they are relatively simple and especially as they are inexpensive. Statistical studies have shown that these random methods appear to be as powerful as others, while statistical confidence can easily be derived from the testing [11]. Two forms of evaluation are directly applicable to OCL.

The first one is *exhaustive evaluation* and corresponds to a complete traverse of the object collection, which implies that the result of the test is certain. This evaluation is the only implementation provided by current assertion environments, but applied systematically, it absorbs a great deal of computing time. In order to reduce costs, this evaluation is reserved for very unstable classes and for preconditions.

The second one is *random sampling* and carries out a traverse on only a part of the object collection, by using the Knuth sampling algorithm [12]. This traverse has interesting properties, as the number of selected elements is chosen in advance, according to the overall number of elements. This enables regulation of the sampling by keeping the percentage traversed fixed. Moreover the algorithm ensures an equal distribution of the sample over the collection, so that all instances are tested equitably. Finally the generation of random numbers for each selection ensures that each evaluation uses a potentially different sample.

3.5: Shallow or deep evaluation

The OCL definition of the features `allInstances`, which can be apply to any type, correspond to a deep extent of the type. This semantics is certainly the most reasonable one in the OCL context, but traversing deep type extents to evaluate quantified expressions on `allInstances` is very expensive. Therefore the preceding evaluation techniques are coupled with the use of shallow or deep extents. A shallow extent includes only those instances that are directly of the specified type and thus comprises a much more restricted set of instances[1]. In addition, deep extents are systematically used to evaluate invariants on abstract types, since these have no implementation and no shallow extent, as no instance can be created.

4: Semiautomatic assertions triggering

The different evaluation and triggering techniques are complex to combine and to implement on a real-size application. This is why we developed a system of triggering assistance to automate most of this task intelligently, by using the dependencies between classes and the changes that occur. Assertion triggering is driven by an ordering of the assertions categories that creates checking levels, as for classic assertions systems based on implementation languages:

$$no < pre < post < invariant < all^2$$

Each greater level includes the next lower one; that is to say, it corresponds to the triggering of both its own clauses and the lower ones; for example, level `post` corresponds to the evaluation of clauses `post` and `pre`. The checking levels are then allotted to particular classes, sets of classes or as default triggering on the whole application. If developers make these choices through configuration files or class-by-class parameter setting [13, 4], they must revise the checking levels by hand whenever classes evolve, when they would naturally arm more assertions on unstable classes and would reduce controls on the more stable parts. Triggering management is then more complex and developers are not likely to execute the essential triggering modifications.

4.1: Change-based classes distinction

The system is partly based on research undertaken in the project IREC [14] on evolution management of classes using their complete reification. This made it possible to perceive with a high degree of accuracy the dependencies between classes and the introduced changes. The triggering system uses a detection mechanism for changes on classes, which is based on the same principles, without reifying all the *elements* of a class for efficiency purpose. Classes are then placed in one of the following four categories.

---

[1] It should be noted that shallow extents are only used with `allInstances->forAll` expressions.
[2] `all` corresponds to the triggering of all interface assertions and all assertions inside routine bodies, as assertions can also annotate routine code.

Modified classes have directly undergone a change by an editor or a programming environment since the last execution of the application. They are thus regarded as the most unstable.

Dependent suspect classes have at least a dependency link with a modified class, and this dependency is regarded as *suspect* because the change affects the dependency; for example, the modification of a routine body, whereas this routine is used in another class. In our university example, the modification of the body of the feature openForRegistration in class Course, or of its definition by assertions, makes the class Student suspect, as openForRegistration is used in the preconditions of routine register.

Dependent compatible classes also have a link of dependency, but the change in the modified class does not directly affect the current class because it does not make use of the modified service. For example, suppose that the class Section, which is related to class Course, never uses the feature Course openForRegistration, this class is then dependent-compatible if only openForRegistration is modified.

Independent classes do not have any link of dependency with the modified classes and are thus regarded as the most stable.

After the detection of all changes, each class is placed in the most *unstable* of the categories to which it could be assigned. This rule ensures a partition of the set of all classes. It is thus possible to associate an assertion checking level of appropriate strength to the category of each class, thus partly reflecting their stability and our *confidence* in them.

4.2: Using the development context

In order to refine still further the triggering process and to provide a more automated user framework, the triggering system is also parameterized by a concept of development phase, which is typically managed by the project leader. For the moment four values are provided for this parameter, reflecting four relevant contexts in the use of assertions.

The *construction* phase corresponds to the implementation of the application classes, where only a small number of classes are very unstable at a given time. As they are evolving unceasingly, these classes require the most possible controls. At this stage of the development, execution time is often less significant because only some parts of the application are tested and reliability is the first requirement. Many assertions can be evaluated on these unstable classes because the balance between the possibility of error detection and the increased cost generated by the evaluation is very advantageous.

The *improvement* phase corresponds to an application where some classes are already stable, with checks necessarily less frequent on those classes. However, tests are now also run on the whole application. Various checking levels are used through the application: greater levels on parts still to be developed, lower levels on those that are already stable.

The application at *beta-test* level is regarded as finished and relatively reliable, and is tested at its real size. But small changes are always needed to correct some errors. Most of the application is thus minimally controlled.

Maintenance is the last phase, after the integration of the application that is now in operation. No assertion is armed, even if some authors recommend leaving the preconditions active, but an operational programme does not normally evaluate any assertions, because they always indicate a programming error. The robustness controls on the environment are processed using exceptions that must organise a coherent action in the event of errors. But if the application needs to be corrected, it is necessary to begin by strongly controlling the modified classes and their dependent suspects, the remainder always being regarded as stable.

Table 1. Assertion triggering table.

Confidence → Context ↓	Explicit change	Suspect dependent	Compatible dependent	Independent
Under construction	all *exhaustive* ∀ *deep extent*	invariant *deep extent*	invariant	pre
Improvement	all *deep extent*	invariant	pre	pre
Beta-test	invariant	post	pre	no
Maintenance	all	invariant	no	no

The table 1 presents an assertions triggering table according to the class confidence level deduced from changes and the development context. Each cell indicates a set of assertion clauses to be evaluated, deduced from the predefined ordered list. The presented levels are only indicative and can be adjusted, but they reflect the concerns of the development stage. For example, during the improvement phase, any modified class evaluates all its assertions using deep type extents. Suspect classes evaluate all their assertions up to instance invariants. Compatible and independent classes only evaluate their preconditions. It should be noted that each cell may contain evaluation parameters that correspond to the use of the techniques that we have previously proposed. These parameters modify default settings that are valid for any class of the application.

Triggering levels for assertion checking are set by default to independent class levels as they do not depend on changes. Different default settings can be selected for the evaluation techniques. The traverses that implement universal quantifications can be sampled, with the sampling percentage, or remain exhaustive: table 1 assumes that the default is *sampled* ∀ *(10 %)*. Type extent traverses can be shallow or deep: *shallow extent* is the default in table 1.

4.3: Critical classes

In spite of the facilities offered by these default settings, some classes may be critical to the application, because they are provided by a somewhat unreliable external partner or because they act as interfaces with some underlying system, with existing applications or with distant systems. These classes must always be regarded as suspect. The triggering system thus lets the developer explicitly specify the classes that must always be regarded as modified or suspect, in order to place them at least in this category. The dependency manager can determine which classes are dependent early in the analysis and then position default checking levels on them according to the triggering table. The developer can thus use dependencies between classes to control some parts of the application, whatever changes are made.

5: Conclusion

In this paper we have considered the issues related to the execution support for the Object Constraint Language. Executing OCL assertions enables to test the implementation against specifications expressed during design, while providing a seamless and reversible approach. As an efficient implementation is necessary to apply the approach to large-scale applications development, we have proposed a pragmatic solution for an OCL runtime support and have determined the origins of potential inefficiency. We have thus presented a set of efficient implementation techniques for the triggering and the evaluation of OCL assertions.

The evaluation techniques rest on the possibility of sampling the traverses related to universal quantifications. The assertions triggering is controlled by a system which detects changes on classes and thus guides the triggering of more or less assertions. That reduces the number of evaluations while putting more controls on the unstable parts of an application. The proposed techniques were already partially implemented in a prototype using an equivalent assertion language, OQUAL [15], which is based on Eiffel 3 [16].

This work will be also applied through the use of an assertion system for evolution management in a persistent framework. In future work, we will study pragmatic solutions to test recursive definition, as well as new features that may appear in new versions of OCL. We also intend to work on the distinction of new assertions for the specification and modeling of concurrent systems.

References

[1] Object Management Group, "Object Constraint Language specification", Tech. Rep. version 1.1, ad/97-08-08, IBM www.software.ibm.com/ad/ocl, 1 Sept. 1997.

[2] Jos Warmer and Anneke Kleppe, The Object Constraint Language: Precise Modeling with UML, Addison-Wesley Publishing Co. (Reading, MA), 1999.

[3] Object Management Group, "UML notation guide", Tech. Rep. version 1.1, ad/97-08-05, Rational Software Corporation www.rational.com/uml, 1 Sept. 1997.

[4] Reto Kramer, "iContract - the Java Design by Contract tool", in International Conference on Technology of Object-Oriented Languages and Systems (Tools 26, USA'98), Madhu Singh, Bertrand Meyer, Joseph Gil, and Richard Mitchell, Eds. 1998, p. 513 pages, IEEE Computer Society Press (New York).

[5] R.G.G. Cattell, Douglas Barry, Dirk Bartels, Mark Berler, Jeff Eastman, Sophie Gamerman, David Jordan, Adam Springer, Henry Strickland, and Drew Wade, The Object Database Standard : ODMG 2.0, Morgan Kaufmann Publishers Inc., 1997.

[6] Mark Richters and Martin Gogolla, "On formalizing the UML Object Constraint Language OCL", in Proc. 17th Int. Conf. Conceptual Modeling (ER'98), Tok Wang Ling, Sudha Ram, and Mong Li Lee, Eds. 1998, number 1507 in Lecture Notes in Computer Science, Springer-Verlag (Berlin).

[7] A. Hamie, J. Howse, and S. Kent, "Interpreting the Object Constraint Language", in Asia Pacific Conference in Software Engineering. 1998, IEEE Computer Society Press (New York).

[8] Object Management Group, "UML semantics", Tech. Rep. version 1.1, ad/97-08-04, Rational Software Corporation www.rational.com/uml, 1 Sept. 1997.

[9] J. Claussen, A. Kemper, G. Moerkotte, and K. Peithner, "Optimizing queries with universal quantification in object-oriented and object-relational databases", in 23rd International Conference on Very Large Data Bases (VLDB 1997). 1997, Morgan Kaufmann Publishers Inc.

[10] Joe W. Duran and Simeon C. Ntafos, "An evaluation of random testing", IEEE Transactions on Software Engineering, vol. 10, no. 4, pp. 438–444, Jul. 1984.

[11] Joe W. Duran and John J. Wiorkowski, "Quantifying software validity by sampling", IEEE Transactions of Reliability, vol. 29, no. 2, pp. 141–144, Jun. 1980.

[12] Donald E. Knuth, Seminumerical Algorithms, vol. 2 of The Art of Computer Programming, Addison-Wesley Publishing Co. (Reading, MA), 1969.

[13] Bertrand Meyer, An Object-Oriented Environment: Principles and Application, The O-O series. Prentice Hall Inc. (Englewood Cliffs, NJ), 1994.

[14] Philippe Brissi and Roger Rousseau, "IREC: An object-oriented abstract representation to handle software components in a persistent framework", in Object-Oriented Technology for Database and Software Systems, Vangalur S. Alagar and Rokia Missaoui, Eds., pp. 6–21. World Scientific Publishing Co. (Singapore), 1995.

[15] Philippe Collet and Roger Rousseau, "OQUAL: An Expressive and Efficient Object Assertion Language", in Third Intern. Conf. on Object-Oriented Technology (WOON'98), Alexander V. Smolyaninov and Alexei S. Shestialtynov, Eds. St Petersburg Electrotechnical Univ., Jun. 1998, pp. 1–10, Martinus Nijhoff Intern., (Zoetermeer, The Netherlands).

[16] Bertrand Meyer, Eiffel: The Language, Object-Oriented Series. Prentice Hall Inc. (Englewood Cliffs, NJ), 1991, Second revised printing, 1992.

Tutorials

Quality

Systematic Techniques for Inspecting Critical Software

David Parnas
McMaster University, USA

Software is devilishly hard to inspect. Serious errors can hide for years. Consequently, many are hesitant to employ software in safety-critical applications and all companies are finding the cost of correcting and improving software to be an increasing burden.

This talk describes a procedure for inspecting software that consistently finds subtle errors in software that was believed to be correct. The procedure is based on four key ideas:

- All software reviewers actively use the code

- Reviewers exploit the hierarchical structure of the code rather than proceeding sequentially through the code

- Reviewers focus on small sections of code, producing precise summaries that are used when inspecting other such sections

- Reviewers proceed systematically so that no case, and no section of the program, gets overlooked

During the procedure, the inspectors produce and review precise documentation. They are able to check for complete coverage; tabular notation allows the work to proceed in small systematic steps. The procedure was originally developed and used to inspect safety-critical software in a nuclear power plant, and then improved based on that experience.

David Lorge Parnas is the NSERC/Bell Industrial Research Chair in Software Engineering in the McMaster University Faculty of Engineering's Computing and Software Department where he is Director of the Software Engineering Programme. He is also an associate member of the Department of Electrical and Computer Engineering. He has been Professor at the University of Victoria, the Technische Hochschule Darmstadt, the University of North Carolina at Chapel Hill, Carnegie Mellon University and the University of Maryland. He has also held non-academic positions advising Philips Computer Industry (Apeldoorn), the United States Naval Research Laboratory in Washington, D.C., the IBM Federal Systems Division, and the Atomic Energy Control Board of Canada.

The Development and Verification of Safety Critical Software

George Romanski
Aonix, USA

A safety critical system controlled by software relies heavily on the properties of the software, because they affect the level of trust of the system as a whole. Absolute measures of correctness do not exist for software. We rely on verification techniques to provide an acceptable level of confidence.

Simple assembly level and programs can be verified by building up the behavior of each instruction, sequences of instructions, functions, and so on until the entire program is understood. For larger systems this is impractical. When high level languages are used in control systems, several levels of abstraction contribute to the understanding of system behavior. To verify that a program does not compromise system safety, each construct must be verified as well as the transformations between abstraction levels.

A number of verification techniques exist. Information hiding, overloading, inheritance and other techniques offered in a programming language may ease program development, but they may make verification more difficult or impossible. Use of certain concurrency constructs may simplify the real-time model and our understanding of system behavior, while other constructs may make the model non-deterministic.

The relationship between programming language constructs, verification techniques and safety certification requirements will be presented.

George Romanski is the Director of Safety Critical Software at Aonix. He has specialized in the production of software development environments for the last 29 years. The work focused on compilers, cross compilers, run-time systems and tools, primarily for embedded real time applications in several languages, but focusing on Ada over the last 19 years.

Over the last seven years George Romanski has concentrated on software tools and certification materials for safety critical applications. The results of the work have been used on avionics, railway and nuclear applications at the highest levels of criticality.

Managing By Contract

Bertrand Meyer
Interactive Software Engineering, USA

To deliver on its promises, object-oriented technology must be able to produce systems that are reliable (correct and robust). Only under these conditions will the other quality factors advertized for the method, in particular the increase in reusability and extendibility, yield the expected benefits for software practitioners. It is indeed possible to use object-oriented technology to produce, almost routinely, software systems that reach a degree of reliability without any equivalent in conventional methods, languages and tools. The presentation will explain how Managing by Contract will help project managers achieve this goal.

Bertrand Meyer is president of Interactive Software Engineering and a pioneer of object technology through his books, in particular "Object-Oriented Software Construction" (whose second edition published by Prentice Hall received the Software Development Jolt Product Excellence Award 1997), "Reusable Software" and "Object Success". Active in both the business and academic scenes he has directed the development of widely used O-O tools and libraries totaling hundreds of thousands of lines, and taught O-O principles and modern software engineering worldwide. He is editor of the Object Technology column of IEEE Computer, the Eiffel column in the JOOP, the Prentice Hall O-O Series, and the Addison-Wesley Eiffel in Practice Series.

Verification and Validation of Object-Oriented Software Systems

Kasi Periyasamy

University of Manitoba, Canada

Verification and validation processes become integral part of software systems, particularly when the software systems are large and complex. The methods for verification and validation that are currently applied to procedural software development processes are not adequate for object-oriented software development. This is because some of the distinguishing characteristics of the object-oriented paradigm such as inheritance and polymorphism require additional efforts, methods and techniques for verification and validation. In this tutorial, I first motivate the participants towards the need for verification and validation of software systems and then give a brief overview of the methods for verification and validation of procedural software systems. I will then discuss in detail some methods for verification and validation of object-oriented software systems. The discussion will include a number of simple examples for each method. The tutorial will also address the limitations of these methods and current research issues in this topic. The tutorial has been designed to be more general so that project leaders, project managers and software designers can attend this tutorial.

Kasi Periyasamy is an Associate Professor in the Department of Computer Science at the University of Manitoba, Winnipeg, Manitoba, Canada. His main area of interest is the application of formal approaches to software development. He has used many formal specification techniques for various phases in software development, mainly for requirements analysis. He has developed a real-time extension to the Object-Z specification language called Real-Time Object-Z (RTOZ), in collaboration with Dr. Alagar at Concordia University, Montreal. Dr. Periyasamy is a co-author of the book "Specification of Software Systems" published by Springer-Verlag in 1998. Dr. Periyasamy was a principal member of the X3J21 Standards Committee (accredited by ANSI) on "Formal Specification Languages: VDM-SL and Z" until 1996 and continues to be a member in correspondence.

Dr. Periyasamy has taught several undergraduate and graduate courses on formal methods and object-oriented software development, both at the University of Manitoba and at Concordia University. He has taught the course on Software Verification and Validation at the graduate level. He has given short courses to industries on object-oriented analysis and design.

Verification and Validation Techniques for Object-Oriented Software Systems

K. Periyasamy
Department of Computer Science
University of Manitoba
Winnipeg, Manitoba, Canada R3T 2N2

V.S. Alagar and D. Muthiayen
Department of Computer Science
Concordia University
Montreal, Quebec, Canada H3G 1M8

Abstract

Validation entails methods to ascertain that the system built is the right one, whereas verification implies reaching a certain level of confidence in the correctness of the software system. Although there is substantial grey area in-between, validating a software system reduces to determining whether it meets the specified requirements. On the other hand, verification involves establishing that the software will work properly, both in terms of functionalities and in terms of satisfying certain properties, such as safety properties. Object-oriented software development brings about a new set of concepts, such as inheritance, polymorphism, and dynamic binding, calling for the emergence of a new set of analytical methodologies.

1: Introduction

Both verification and validation involve analysis with a view to improving the quality of the final product. We may characterize validation as the convincing demonstration of stated requirements, and verification as a more formal proof of the presence of properties in the product. Validation may be achieved through the application of test suites, investigative exploration of a model, and simulation. Verification is usually achieved through a formal proving process. In the absence of a formal framework needed for formal verification, the process is inevitably informal. It is more appropriate to conduct an informal verification procedure, such as inspection, on formal specifications, than to conduct an informal reasoning on informal documents. There is an increasing demand for the construction of provably correct software systems in strategically important areas, such as aerospace projects.

It has been observed that the most expensive mistakes are made in the early development stages of a project. Errors undetected during the requirements specification and design phases are very expensive to detect and fix in later stages. Some of the difficulties associated with a verification approach are due to the different notations used in different phases of a software life cycle. For example, requirements are usually written in a natural language, while a structured design is expressed using a combination of textual and graphical notations. In this situation, it is hard to assert that a design preserves the functionalities expressed in the requirements.

The object-oriented approach is a step towards a solution to this problem. The notions of *class* and *object* are persistent throughout the life cycle, except for minor syntactic differences in an implementation. If requirement specifications and design documents are available only in an informal medium, such as natural language descriptions and diagrams, then inspections, interviews, and structured reading tend to be barely useful for the following reasons: (i) interviews may be useful in unraveling requirements, but cannot be assumed to be a sufficient technique, (ii) there may be contradictions and misunderstandings across successive interviews, and (iii) structured reading implies tracing the presence of all object functionalities. Even if all cross-referenced object functionalities can be traced by the inspection team, it may not be possible to identify the missing functionalities. The virtues of formalization can be recognized in this situation: specification and design inspections based on formal documents yield higher levels of precision and confidence. However, inadequate training in formal specification techniques may pose difficulties to properly conduct these activities. This may be resolved with the use of tools to analyze formal documents in the specification and design stages.

This paper discusses verification and validation goals and techniques adopted by the authors for various application domains. These are broadly classified into three categories: (i) methods that use documents produced in an informal medium, such as natural languages and diagrams, (ii) methods based on graphical notations supported with formal semantics, and (iii) methods founded on formal specifications.

2: Object-Oriented Verification Techniques

The following subsections present object-oriented verification techniques based on (i) informal descriptions, (ii) graphical notations, and (iii) formal notations. Each section includes a brief introduction to the characteristics of documents, notations, and languages used for that technique, followed by the goal of verification in that context, and finally the current practice for the methods.

2.1: Verification based on Informal Descriptions

The major goal of verification in the requirements phase is to ensure whether it is feasible to develop the system as described in the requirements document, with respect to time and costs. It is also important to check for errors and inconsistencies in the requirements document. It requires an extensive analysis of the document and a thorough understanding of the application domain. Due to inherent ambiguities in natural language descriptions, consistency checks in requirements documents are hard to perform, particularly in the case of large and complex systems.

There are two approaches to produce a requirements document in an object-oriented fashion: (i) a requirements document is produced with focus on objects and their encapsulated structure and behavior, and (ii) a functional requirements document is produced to describe what the system is supposed to do, and then an object-oriented requirements document is derived from the functional requirements document. The later document describes the set of objects and their encapsulated structure and behavior. The first approach is hard to achieve and requires an expert in object-orientation. Moreover, customers often do not understand requirements written in an object-oriented style. The second approach is most commonly used in practice. Given the informal nature of the medium in which the requirements document is produced, a manual verification process, such as inspection and structured reading, is necessary. However, this may not produce the desired results in locating inconsistencies and errors.

2.2: Verification based on Graphical Notations

Most of the object-oriented analysis and design methods rely heavily on graphical notations. Among those methods that are reported in the literature, Booch's method [8], the OMT method [22], and the Use Case method [13] are the most popular ones. These have been integrated into one method, the *Unified Object-Oriented Software Development Process* [14]; the associated language is the *Unified Modeling Language* (UML) [9]. UML provides a fairly rich set of graphical notations. Each phase in a software development process may use a subset of UML notations. The UML metamodel describes its syntax and the well-formedness rules. The metamodel can be used to understand the notation and to decide when and how to use a particular kind of diagram in the development of a design. The authors of UML claim that the language can be used in all phases of the software development process by enriching the information in each phase [9].

According to Rumbaugh [22], the goal of an object-oriented analysis process is to construct a precise, understandable and correct model of the real-world. The OMT method emphasizes analysis of various models for the same problem using the same notations, prior to choosing the appropriate model that is amenable for design and implementation, and at the same time reflects the behavior of the real-world objects. Rumbaugh's view of analysis closely matches the notion of verification that implies to verify that the objects in the models behave as those in the real-world. Dennis de Champeaux [10], while agreeing with the definition of Rumbaugh on object-oriented analysis adds that the level of formality associated with the graphical notations indicates the expressive power of the notations and consequently the ability to verify consistency and correctness of the model under construction. As opposed to a logical basis for checking for consistency and completeness, de Champeaux introduces a quantitative approach based on metrics to measure consistency and correctness. Aoki and Katayama [6] argue that consistency must be checked among all models that share the same information, but do not propose a technique for achieving it.

Although consistency checking for object-oriented design models has been presented as an important activity, no corresponding method has yet been reported in the literature. This can be attributed to the fact that the semantics of the graphical notations are not well-defined, and consequently a basis for verification is hard to build. Since the graphical notations are mainly used for developing the models, designers of the graphical notations for object-oriented analysis and design methods focus more on the flexibility and ease-of-use afforded by the notations, often ignoring the need for verification. In section 3 we discuss a formal verification approach to checking consistency and completeness of object-oriented models.

2.3: Verification based on Formal Notations

A formal specification language is a notation used to describe aspects of a software system, such as requirements, design, or implementation. Formal notations are founded on mathematics. Within a formal framework, software developers have the mathematical apparatus to construct abstract models of a system, to refine the abstract models towards design and implementation, to reason about properties of the system thereby establishing correctness of the models, and to reason about the refinement of the models to establish consistency between the models. Several formal specification languages have been developed in the past decade. A survey of object-oriented formal specification languages is available in [24]. These languages are extensions of the Z notation [23]. Other object-oriented formal specification languages include VDM++ [12], TRIO+ [16], and RTOZ [5]. Most of these languages are primarily used for capturing object-oriented software requirements. The two important verification goals are: verifying that the system under development satisfies certain properties, and verifying that the requirements are consistent. In both cases, the semantics of the formal specification language is an essential requirement. PVS (Prototype Verification System) [17] and Z/EVES [15] are now used for verification of large scale industrial applications.

3: Verification using Graphical and Formal Notations

This section discusses two research projects on verification of object-oriented designs. The goal is to verify the consistency and completeness of object-oriented models.

3.1: Consistency of OMT models

We have developed a verifier [18] for object-oriented designs described in OMT notation [22]. The purpose of the verifier is to check for consistency between OMT models of an application. We specified OMT model elements in Z notation, and represented the semantics as a set of rules in a knowledge-base system. The object-oriented design to be verified is translated into a set of logical assertions; these assertions are checked for consistency with respect to the rules representing the semantics of OMT. The verification process demonstrates that the object-oriented design conforms to the principles of object-orientation. We used CLIPS [11] to develop the knowledge-base.

OMT supports the development of three models of a software product: an object model represented by class and object diagrams, a dynamic model described by a set of state transition diagrams, and a functional model described by data flow diagrams. Since the third model is based on a functional view and is not generally used in conjunction with the object and dynamic models, we do not include it in our verification technique. We check for consistency between the object and dynamic models. Table 1 shows the object-oriented features that can be checked by the verifier.

Object Model	Dynamic Model
Class structure	Events
Relationships	- Event class
- Association	- Event generalization
• roles	States
• qualifier	- Aggregation
- Generalization	- Generalization
- Aggregation	- Actions
	- Activities
	- Conditions
	Transitions
	- guarded
	- unguarded

Table 1. Object-Oriented Modeling Elements Checked by the Verifier

The verifier supports both online and off-line verification; some features such as duplicate names are verified online while other features are verified off-line. We observed that the verifier captures more errors than Rational Rose [19] that supports the Unified Modeling Language (UML) [20] and implements few primitive verification strategies. Our goal is to integrate the verifier with an object-oriented analysis and design tool, with a graphical user interface supporting the OMT models. At this stage, the conversion of an object-oriented design into a set of logical assertions is done manually. Below, we give the Z specification for inheritance relationships as implemented in the verifier, and its corresponding CLIPS code. A more detailed description of the design and implementation of the verifier appears in [7].

$$\_\,\text{inherits}\,\_ : Class \longleftrightarrow Class$$

$$
\begin{aligned}
&\forall\, c_1, c_2 : Class \bullet c_1 \text{ inherits } c_2 \Leftrightarrow \\
&\quad c_1 \neq c_2 \,\wedge \\
&\quad ExportedFeatures(c_2) \subseteq Features(c_1) \,\wedge \\
&\quad ExportedFeatures(c_2) \cap Features(c_1) \neq \varnothing \,\wedge \\
&\quad (Features(c_2) \subset Features(c_1) \,\vee \\
&\qquad ((\exists\, o_1, o_2 : Operation \bullet \\
&\qquad\qquad o_1 \in c_1.ops \,\wedge\, o_2 \in c_2.expops \,\wedge\, o_1.name = o_2.name \,\wedge \\
&\qquad\qquad (o_1.parms \neq o_2.parms \,\vee\, o_1.type \neq o_2.type) \Rightarrow o_1.body \neq o_2.body)) \,\vee \\
&\qquad (\exists\, a_1, a_2 : Attribute \bullet \\
&\qquad\qquad a_1 \in c_1.attrs \,\wedge\, a_2 \in c_2.attrs \,\wedge\, a_1.name = a_2.name \,\wedge\, a_1.type \neq a_2.type)
\end{aligned}
$$

$$
\begin{aligned}
&\forall\, c_1, c_2, c_3 : Class \bullet \\
&\quad (c_1 \text{ inherits } c_2 \,\wedge\, c_2 \text{ inherits } c_3 \Rightarrow c_1 \text{ inherits } c_3) \,\wedge \\
&\quad (c_1 \text{ inherits } c_2 \Rightarrow \neg\,(c_2 \text{ inherits } c_1))
\end{aligned}
$$

Informally, the specification for the inherits relation asserts the following: when a class c_1 inherits a class c_2,

- the classes are distinct; otherwise, inheritance is equivalent to aliasing;
- all the exported features of the superclass c_2 are inherited by the subclass c_1;
- at least one exported feature from c_2 is retained as unmodified in c_1; if everything is modified, then c_1 will not be a subclass of c_2, rather, it will be a different class altogether;
- one or more of the following three conditions must be satisfied:
  - c_1 adds more features to those inherited from c_2;
  - c_1 redefines one of the inherited operations;
  - c_1 redefines one of the inherited attributes (changes the type); at this stage, we permit changes in the type of an attribute as long as the new type is compatible with the old type; however, compatibility checks have not yet been included in the verifier.

The two global constraints assert that (i) inheritance is transitive, and (ii) cyclic inheritance is not permitted. The CLIPS template definition representing the inheritance relationship between two classes is given below:

```
(deftemplate inherits-from
     (slot sub
          (type SYMBOL)
          (default ?NONE))
     (slot super
          (type SYMBOL)
          (default ?NONE)))
```

The designer does not explicitly define the inherits relation between two classes; rather, the designer specifies a generalization which is represented by a connector symbol between one or more subclasses and one superclass. Once the connector is created, the verifier attempts to check whether the inheritance relation holds good with respect to the specification of the inherits relation. This is ascertained by the following rule:

```
(defrule generalization-good
    "A valid generalization"
    (Generalization (property ?p)
        (subclasses $?clist) (superclass ?c2))
    =>
    (progn$ (?class ?clist)
        (assert (inherits-from (sub (nth$ ?class-index ?clist))
                                (super ?c2)))))
```

The following rule ensures that a class does not inherit from itself:

```
(defrule inherits-err-class-inherits-itself
    ''A class cannot inherit from itself''
    (declare (salience -10))
    (inherits-from (sub ?c) (super ?c))
    =>
    (printout t "OODV Error: The class " ?c
        " inherits from itself." crlf))
```

Currently, we are configuring the verifier to check designs developed using the UML notation. This requires a major revision to the semantics of the graphical model elements incorporated in the verifier. One of our goals is to integrate the verifier with Rational Rose.

3.2: Consistency and Completeness of UML models

Achieving design consistency when using a notation with several interleaving components is a major issue. We have outlined a technique [2] for describing real-time reactive systems in UML. The aim of this work is to provide a graphical user interface as a front-end to a design tool for real-time reactive systems for use by industries that have adopted Rational Rose. We have provided a formal semantics and a translation mechanism from graphical models to formal notations. Although rigorous analysis is not attainable at the modeling level, visualizing entities and the configuration of a system provides insight into its overall structure and behavior. Moreover, since a formal specification of a reactive system is automatically generated from the graphical model, it alleviates the need for a user to learn and use the formal specification language.

UML uses an assortment of diagrams to capture different aspects of system design; however, several model elements occur in more than one type of diagram. Such relations among components are not brought out by the semi-formal semantics given in the UML Semantics document [21]. Consequently, it is hard to establish consistency among models of system components, to ensure the presence of requirements, and to ensure the satisfaction of properties across UML diagrams capturing system design. Inconsistencies among different components of a design may remain undetected. However, it is imperative that consistency between diagrams be established to ensure the satisfaction of system properties across the different layers. For example, the developer must be able to conclude that (i) timing constraints in statechart diagrams are consistent with timing constraints in sequence diagrams, and (ii) messages in a sequence diagram or a collaboration diagram have an effect in the corresponding dynamic model captured by the statechart diagrams.

Our approach involves transforming each design diagram into a PVS specification. A relationship R between two UML diagrams is stated in the form of a theorem in a parameterized theory T_R. The theorem in theory T_R instantiated with two actual design specifications must be proved in order to establish consistency between the designs. More formally, let d_1 and d_2 denote two design specifications in UML, and let p_1 and p_2 be their corresponding PVS specifications. Corresponding to a relationship R between designs d_1 and d_2, there exists a parameterized theory T_R. If a proof can be constructed for the theorem in the instance $T_R(p_1, p_2)$ of the theory, then we conclude that design specifications d_1 and d_2 are consistent. Checking for design consistency may not be possible without sufficient axioms capturing the properties of data types in the specifications. Consequently, consistency cannot be assumed without *completeness* of data types. A data type specification is complete if every intended property of the data type can be deduced from the axioms. Whenever a proof cannot be discharged, it is due to the incompleteness of the specifications. To remedy this situation, we need to include more properties in the data type specifications.

4: Validation and Verification based on Formal Specifications

We have been studying a formal specification method [1] tailored for object-oriented development of real-time reactive systems. This section briefly discusses rigorous techniques that we have developed to validate design against requirements, to discharge proofs for design refinements, and to verify safety properties in the design.

4.1: Animation, Prototyping, and Reasoning

Informal inspection techniques cannot be applied to validate real-time reactive systems. A reactive object encapsulates both timing constraints and functional behavior. An object responds to every stimulus received from its environment in such a way that the response synchronizes with the environment. The objects within a reactive system interact among themselves in conformance with strict time constraints stated in the requirements. Since the time dimension can be handled only during system execution, it is important to validate the system before deploying it in the environment where it operates. We use one of the conventional techniques in mathematical modeling to simulate the model and to observe the simulation scenarios.

We have designed and implemented an animation tool, whose central piece is the simulator, for a rigorous validation of real-time reactive systems built on TROM (Timed Reactive Object Model) formalism [1]. The TROM methodology formally integrates object-oriented and real-time technologies. The simulation employs the design specifications, as opposed to an implementation of the design. In order to ensure safety properties in the system, it then becomes sufficient to verify that the program implements the model. In addition, the model must be validated to be an acceptable abstraction of the system under development.

Simulation allows observing the behavior of a system; animation provides a graphic visualization of interactions. The configuration of formally specified subsystems can be validated, and timing constraints and properties can be verified during the simulation process. A simulation model should be capable of detecting faults in the design of a system. Such a model introduces *predictability* for properties that have to be maintained in the future. The history of event traces allow going backward in time, and detecting and fixing faults in the design.

An important goal of animating the simulation process is to facilitate design-time debugging. Sufficient information is required in the validation toolset to verify properties and deduce reasons for a specific behavior. Incorporating a reasoning system in the simulation environment allows using deduction to check for properties of the system under development, based on the history of computational steps. Thus, both validation and verification are integrated in one toolset. Other benefits include: (i) the system becomes more understandable while obtaining feedback on its behavior during system evolution, (ii) system validation can be performed by experts in the application domain who are not knowledgeable in the underlying formalism used in the development of the system, (iii) in addition to design errors, consequences of certain requirements and definitions come to light while simulating the system, and (iv) it increases confidence in the model constructed, and may infer that a particular conjecture is a corollary.

4.2: Equivalence and Satisfaction

For rigorous development of real-time reactive systems, we have provided three forms of *differential* or *incremental* system development. These are commonly known as *inheritance* in the object-oriented paradigm. The aim is at defining new classes using existing classes in such a way that only those properties of the new classes that differ from the properties of existing classes have to be defined explicitly; other properties are inherited from existing classes. It is our view that large systems can be maintained well if the subclass relationship is restricted to behavioral properties. In object-oriented programming the preservation of behavior ensures substitutability. But, it is not so when we combine real-time and object-oriented concepts to design embedded reactive systems. The problem of non-substitutability arises due to the fact that the occurrence of specialized signals in a reactive object of the subtype may not be possible in the context of objects of the supertype reactive class. Consequently, we need to distinguish between substitutability which preserves behavior in any context of substitution, which we call *behavioral* subtype, and substitution-preserving behavior in a specific context, which we call *polymorphic* subtype [1]. We have also studied *extensional* subtype which preserves behavior in any context, but is not substitutable.

One of the focus of verification in TROM methodology is to prove that a particular relation holds between two TROM objects. From the specification of two TROM objects and the formal definitions for *extensional*, *substitutable*, and *polymorphic* inheritance definitions [1], we can establish whether or not one of these relations hold between two TROM objects. Upon this verification, the designer gains more confidence in further refining the design towards a specific implementation. It is all the more important, when the verification fails to establish the relation, for the designer to be aware of the consequences of refining a design.

4.3: Verifying System Properties

Two important formulations of verification goals are being studied in TROMLAB: P_1, the need to express and prove temporal or time-dependent properties, and P_2, that a specific property, such as a safety property, always holds in the system. The simplest case for verification of the first kind is formulated in the form e_k *precedes* f_k, where e_k denotes the k-th occurrence of an event e. An example of a safety property is: "*there is no collision between aircrafts landing and taking-off*". A property of kind P_1 involves signals within an object or may involve signals in two different objects. A safety property concerns the whole system, and consequently is a statement involving all system objects. We have used PVS specification language to express verification requirements and conduct a formal verification of the stated requirements in PVS verification system.

The PVS specification and verification environment is being applied in the development of large-scale NASA projects. The higher-order logic of PVS, together with its rich and rigorous type system, makes it suitable for formally expressing the semantics of complex design specifications. PVS specification language is complemented with a powerful reasoning system. The theorem prover is interactive, with a comprehensive set of proof commands. These features make PVS well-suited for stating properties of the two kinds P_1 and P_2, and mechanically verifying their satisfaction in design specifications.

Verifying system properties in a design specification consists of demonstrating that a desired property is a logical consequence of the axiomatic descriptions of the design. We have developed a general theory for mechanized verification of time-dependent properties in a timed transition system [3]. We have explained some of the algorithmic steps [4] to automatically develop PVS theories from the design of the subsystem to be verified. Since a reactive system maintains an ongoing continuous interaction with its environment, in general its behavior is infinite. We focus the verification procedure on each *period*, where a period corresponds to the time interval between two successive instances of the system in its initial state. For each generic reactive class in our design, we define a higher-order function that gives the transition time corresponding to an occurrence of an event within a period for an instance of that class. From the formal specifications of the objects comprising the subsystem we derive four types of axioms: transition, time constraint, synchrony, and supplementary axioms. The property to be verified is specified as a theorem to be proved in the theory containing the axioms. The proof construction process is conducted using PVS theorem prover. Our approach has been applied to prove the safety property of the generalized railroad crossing problem, a bench-mark problem studied by researchers in the verification community.

5: Conclusion

Verification and validation methods can be applied at early stages of a software development lifecycle. For instance, detecting flaws at the design level substantially reduces development costs. This is particularly effective in cases where the set of requirements is ambiguous, incomplete, or faulty. In such cases, the requirements can be modified before defects propagate to the implementation, and become indiscernible. This paper discussed the verification and validation techniques that we have developed for a rigorous analysis of object-oriented software systems at the design stage.

Most object-oriented analysis and design methods use graphical notations for describing models of a software system. Verification of object-oriented designs involves consistency checks. Verification requires a sound semantic foundation so as to provide confidence in the correctness of software. Verification of the design becomes more effective when graphical notations are integrated with formal notations. Formal notations not only improve the preciseness of the design, but also enables formal verification at an early stage.

References

[1] V.S. Alagar, R. Achuthan, and D. Muthiayen, "TROMLAB: A software development environment for real-time reactive systems", Technical Report, Department of Computer Science, Concordia University, Montreal, Canada, July 1998. Revised February 1999.

[2] V.S. Alagar and D. Muthiayen, "A Formal Approach to UML Modeling of Complex Real-Time Reactive Systems", Journal paper submitted for publication, May 1999.

[3] V.S. Alagar and D. Muthiayen, "Mechanized Verification of Real-Time Reactive Systems in an Object-oriented Framework", Journal paper submitted for publication, May 1999.

[4] V.S. Alagar, D. Muthiayen, and F. Pompeo, "From Behavioral Specification to Axiomatic Description of Real-Time Reactive Systems", Fifth IEEE Real-Time Technology and Applications Symposium Work-in-Progress Session, RTAS'99 WIP, Vancouver, Canada, June 1999.

[5] V.S. Alagar and K. Periyasamy, "Real-Time Object-Z: A Language for the Specification and Design of Real-Time Reactive Systems", Technical Report, Department of Computer Science, Concordia University, Montreal, Canada, June 1996.

[6] T. Aoki and T. Katayama, "Unification and Consistency Verification of Object-Oriented Analysis Models", *Proceedings of the 1998 Asia Pacific Software Engineering Conference*, Taiwan, Dec 1998, pp. 296-303.

[7] W. Baluta, "Verification of Object-Oriented Designs", Masters Thesis, Department of Computer Science, University of Manitoba, Winnipeg, Manitoba, Canada, Dec 1997.

[8] G. Booch, *Object-Oriented Analysis and Design with Applications*, Benjamin Cummings Publications, 1994.

[9] G. Booch, J. Rumbauch and I. Jacobson, *The Unified Modeling Language User Guide*, Addison-Wesley Publishing Company, 1998.

[10] Dennis de Champeaux, *Object-Oriented Development Process and Metrics*, Prentice Hall, 1997.

[11] *CLIPS 6.0: Reference Manual*, NASA, Johnson Space Center, 1993.

[12] E.H. Dürr and N. PLat (Eds.), *VDM++: Language Reference Manual*, Afrodite (ESPRIT-III project number 6500) document, Cap Volmac, August 1995.

[13] I. Jacobson, *Object-Oriented Software Engineering*, Addison-Wesley Publishing Company, 1992.

[14] I. Jacobson, G. Booch and J. Rumbaugh, *The Unified Software Development Process*, Addison-Wesley Publishing Company, 1998.

[15] I. Meisels and M. Saaltink, "The Z/EVES Reference Manual", ORA Canada, Ottawa, Canada, April 1996.

[16] A. Morzenti and P. San Pierto, "Object-Oriented Logical Specification of Time Critical Systems", *ACM Transactions on Software Engineering and Methodology*, Vol. 3, No. 1, Jan 1994, pp. 56-98.

[17] S. Owre, J.M. Rushby, and N. Shankar, "PVS: a prototype verification system", Proceedings of 11th International Conference on Automated Deduction, CADE'92, volume 607 of Lecture Notes in Artificial Intelligence, pp. 748-752, Saratoga, NY, 1992.

[18] K. Periyasamy abd W. Baluta, "A Verifier for Object-Oriented Designs", *Proceedings of the Twenty-Second Annual Software Engineering Workshop*, NASA, Greenbely, MD, Dec 1997, pp. 303-328.

[19] Rational Software Corporation, *Rational Rose Version 4.0: Reference Manual*, 1997.

[20] Rational Software Corporation, *UML Notation Guide, Version 1.1*, September 1997.

[21] Rational Software Corporation, *UML Semantics, Version 1.1*, September 1997.

[22] J. Rumbaugh *et al.*, *Object-Oriented Modeling and Design*, Prentice Hall, Englewood Cliffs, NJ, 1991.

[23] J.M. Spivey, *The Z Notation: A Reference Manual*, (Second Edition) Prentice Hall International Series in Computer Science, 1992.

[24] S. Stepney, R. Barden and D. Cooper (Eds.), *Object-Orientation in Z*, Springer-Verlag, Workshops in Computing Series, 1992.

Tutorials

Language

Mastering JFC 'Look and Feel' and UI Delegation

Mitchell Goldstein
Modis Inc., USA

This is an in-depth presentation on UI (user interface) delegation in Java Foundation Classes and how JFC component classes support platform-emulation and cross-platform 'look and feels'. This talk will cover: detailed analysis of the LAF and UI management classes, discussion of the standard LAFs , customizing LAFs through multiplexing and custom schemes, and a tutorial on how to design, develop, debug and deploy a custom cross-platform 'look and feel'.

Mitch Goldstein is a consultant with over fifteen years of experience in the data processing field, specializing in object-oriented and component-based development of graphical user interfaces and enterprise distributed systems. Mitch is the author of "Comprehensive JFC", an advanced technical guide to the Java™ Foundation Classes, to be published by SIGS/Cambridge University Press in the fall of 1999. Mitch is currently working with NASDAQ/AMEX to redesign their equity trading workstation in Java/JFC.

0-7695-0278-4/99 $10.00 © 1999 IEEE

Quality Component Development: Making the Most of JavaBeans and Enterprise JavaBeans Features

Gilda Pour

San Jose State University, USA

Component-based software development (CBSD) is the rapidly emerging trend in the field of enterprise software engineering. CBSD delivers the promise of large-scale software reuse and has the potential to:

- Reduce significantly the cost and time-to-market of enterprise systems b
- Enhance the reliability of enterprise systems
- Improve the maintainability of enterprise systems
- Enhance the quality of enterprise systems

The attendees will have the opportunity to become familiar with the key features of the leading Java-Based component technologies: JavaBeans and Enterprise JavaBeans (EJB). They will also learn how to develop quality components for client-side using JavaBeans and for server-side using EJB. Major topics include:

- Java Platform for the Enterprise (JPE)
- JavaBeans Component Model
- Enterprise JavaBeans (EJB) Component Model
- Quality Component Development Using JavaBeans and EJB
- Future of JavaBeans and Enterprise JavaBeans
- Useful Resources

Gilda Pour has over eleven years of R&D and industrial experience and seven years of academic experience in object-oriented software engineering for parallel and distributed systems. Dr. Pour's current research areas lie in the field of object-oriented component-based enterprise application development including multi-tier Web-based enterprise application development. She has made significant contributions to several projects in the field while working in the R&D Laboratories of Hewlett-Packard and Software Engineering Research Center.

Dr. Pour is currently a professor of software and information engineering at San Jose State University. She has developed and taught several courses in both industry and academia. On related topics, she has given seminars and tutorials, chaired panels, and led workshops at several international conferences. She serves as Workshop and Panel Chair for the TOOLS USA '99 Conference and as Tutorial Chair for the TOOLS ASIA '99 Conference.

Java-Based Component Model for
Enterprise Application Development

Gilda Pour, Ph.D.
San Jose State University
San Jose, CA, U.S.A.
Email: gpour@email.sjsu.edu

Abstract

Component-based software development (CBSD) is viewed as the industry's best hope for building high-quality enterprise systems in a timely manner. CBSD has the potential to reduce significantly the cost and time-to-market of enterprise software systems, and improve the reliability, maintainability, and the overall quality of those systems. CBSD is based on the concept of building software systems by selecting a set of pre-engineered and pre-tested reusable software components and assembling them within appropriate software architectures. A key challenge in CBSD is the selection of the component model that fits best a project. A component model is a collection of techniques and rules that allows software developers to focus on components and their relationships rather than infrastructure and low-level systems programming issues. Two leading component models are available: (1) Java-based component model (JavaBeans for the client-side components & Enterprise JavaBeans for the server-side components), and (2) COM/DCOM-based component model (ActiveX & Microsoft Transaction Server (MTS)). The third component model will be defined by the OMG CORBA Components Specification, which is on the way. This paper provides a tutorial on Java-based component model. The paper compares Java-based component model with its competitors. It also provides the background information required for understanding the issues and technologies involved.

1. Introduction

Component-based software development (CBSD) is viewed as the industry's best hope for building high-quality enterprise systems in a timely manner. CBSD has the potential to: (1) reduce significantly the cost and time-to-market of enterprise software systems by allowing the systems to be built by assembling a set of reusable components rather than from scratch, (2) enhance the reliability of enterprise software systems by the use of pre-engineered reusable components which have gone through several review and inspection stages in the course of its original development and previous usages, and by reliance on explicitly defined architectures and interfaces, (3) improve the maintainability of enterprise software systems by allowing new (higher) quality components to replace old ones, and (4) enhance the quality of enterprise software systems by allowing application-domain experts to develop components, and software engineers specialized in component-based software development to assemble the components and build enterprise software systems [1,2,3].

CBSD is based on the concept of building software systems by selecting a set of software components and assembling them within appropriate software architectures [4]. A component is a piece of code, which has certain functionality, and is used as a high-level building block of a few different software systems. Components are at the appropriate level of granularity for being packaged, distributed as black boxes (binaries), and assembled to build applications [5]. A set of objects can be packaged to create a component at the desired level of granularity. Judith Hurwitz identifies three major characteristics of components that make them the ideal module for software development: they are large grained, self-contained, and standard-based.

A major challenge in any component-based software development project is the selection of the component model that fits best the project. A component model is a collection of techniques and rules that allows software developers to focus on components and their relationships rather than the infrastructure and low-level systems programming.

Two leading component models are currently available: (1) Java-based component model, and (2) COM/DCOM[1]-based component model. The third component model will be defined by the OMG CORBA Components Specification, which is on the way. This paper provides a tutorial on Java-based component model. More emphasis is given to the EJB server component model.

The paper is organized as follows. Section 2 introduces component models. Section 3 explains Java-based component model. Section 4 provides an overview of JavaBeans. Section 5 describes Enterprise JavaBeans. Section 6 compares Java-based component model with its competitors. Section 7 presents the final notes.

2. Component Models

A component model refers to a set of specifications that delineate the APIs, encapsulation boundaries, binding and bridging mechanisms, and such services as event handling and persistence storage that a software component should support to interoperate with other software components. A component model consists of both client and server component models.

The idea of using client-side components such as graphical user interfaces (GUIs) (i.e. spreadsheet and table components) has been around for some time. However, development of server-side components for enterprise systems has been challenging due to the complexity of server-side issues.

A server component model adds a server component environment, which is a transparent layer between client and server. This layer monitors all the client/server communications, and modifies the communications to ensure that the correct thread, security, transaction, and persistence semantics are used. Consequently, server logic does not require any transaction-specific code. In this new setting, all application developers need to do is to configure the environment to use the correct transaction rules.

Java-based component model and COM/DCOM-based component model are the two leading component models. The Object Management Group (OMG) has also been working on the CORBA Components Specification that defines the third component model. Java-based component model uses JavaBeans specification for its client component model and Enterprise JavaBeans (EJB) for its server component model. COM/DCOM-based component model is built on ActiveX for and Microsoft Transaction Server (MTS).

---

[1] COM stands for Component Object Model and DCOM for Distributed Component Object Model.

3. Java-Based Component Model

The major objectives of Java-based component models include the followings: (1) liberating software developers from systems programming (a very difficult part of traditional software development) so that they can focus on the application requirements and logics, (2) providing platform independency.

Java has many advantages including Web enablement and platform-independent deployment. Java platform independency has been the key to the extensive use of Java-based component technologies for development of client-side components of enterprise applications. In addition, the ability of Java classes to be dynamically loaded has promoted the use of Java for developing server-side components for enterprise applications. Consequently, Java provides a universal integration and enabling technology for enterprise application development.

JavaBeans specification is used for Java-based client component model and Enterprise JavaBeans (EJB) specification for Java-based server component model. JavaBeans and EJB extend all native strengths of Java including portability and security into the area of component-based software development. EJB has inherited the portability, security, and reliability features of Java. This has made EJB suitable for developing server-side components that are robust, and independent of operating systems, Web servers, and database management servers.

4. JavaBeans

JavaBeans specification, which defines Java-based client component model, has the following mission statement: "Write once, run anywhere, reuse everywhere." JavaBeans supports development of portable and reusable client-side components--called beans. A Java bean is a special kind of Java class, which can be created, reused, customized, and assembled into new feature-rich applications. A developer can use a Java builder tool to customize a bean through its property table or through customization methods. Multiple beans can be combined and interrelated to build Java applets or applications, or to create new, more comprehensive, and specialized Java beans.

5. Enterprise JavaBeans (EJB)

Enterprise JavaBeans specification defines a Java-based component architecture for the development and deployment of reusable platform and application independent sever-side business components. An enterprise bean is a specialized non-visual JavaBeans component that can run on application servers, transaction servers, and database servers.

As Java beans, enterprise beans can be assembled with other beans to create new enterprise applications. Enterprise beans are Java objects with transactional properties that run in an EJB container (Refer to section 5.1 for more information). An EJB class can be manipulated and customized through its property table and customization methods.

Enterprise beans use CORBA IIOP for the following purposes: (1) interoperating across multi-vendor servers, (2) propagating transaction and security contexts, (3) servicing multilingual clients, and (4) supporting ActiveX via DCOM/CORBA bridges.

EJB has several advantages for enterprise application development, as it provides: (1) efficient data access across heterogeneous servers, (2) faster Java client connections, transaction state management, caching, and queuing, (3) connection multiplexing, and (4) transaction load balancing across servers.

5.1. EJB Container

An enterprise bean lives inside in an EJB container. The type of container associated with an enterprise bean depends on the enterprise bean's class. This is determined at deployment. An EJB container manages the enterprise bean's life cycle; implementing the management and control services for a class of enterprise beans that live in the container. More specifically, the EJB container, on behalf of the enterprise beans that live in the container, provides various services such as transactions, transparent distribution services, security services, persistence management, concurrency, and other services for life cycle management and instance pooling (including enterprise bean creation, activation[1], passivation[2], and destruction).

An EJB container uses the EJB interfaces to manage all of its objects in the most scalable way [6]. An EJB container communicates with its enterprise beans via callback interfaces. An EJB container makes no actual service demands on the beans. An EJB container intercedes between clients calls on Remote interface and the corresponding methods in a bean to enforce transaction and security constraints. It also provides notification at the start and end of each transaction involving a bean instance. In addition, an EJB container enforces policies and restriction on bean on bean instances such as reentrance rules, security policies, and others.

5.2. EJB Server

An EJB server is the execution system for enterprise beans. An EJB server provides various facilities including threading information, resource management, and distributed transaction management service to an EJB container. An EJB server hosts an EJB container.

5.3. Enterprise Beans Types

EJB specification describes two types of enterprise beans: (1) session enterprise beans, and (2) entity enterprise beans. A session enterprise bean is a transient object; its lifetime is limited to the lifetime the Java Virtual Machine (VM) process in which the bean is created. In contrast, an entity enterprise bean is persistent.

5.3.1 Session Enterprise Beans: A session enterprise bean is developed by a client, typically, only for the client's use. Hence, a session enterprise bean is anonymous. Session enterprise beans represent application functionality, and usually exist for the duration of a single client-server session. If the server crashes, all session beans are lost. A session enterprise bean, on the behalf of its client, performs operations such as accessing and updating data in an underlying database or performing calculations.

There are two kinds of session beans: (1) stateless session beans, and (2) stateful session beans. A stateful session bean maintains conservational state across methods and transactions while a stateless session bean does not. A stateless session bean is used only by one client at a time. However, it can be used on a message-by-message basis by several clients because message calls do not share any data. In addition, the server may use pools of beans to minimize the total number of beans created.

---

[1] Activation of a bean refers to loading the bean into memory.
[2] Passivation of a bean refers to deactivating a bean.

A stateful session bean has its own state. After a client creates or finds a stateful session bean, it starts a session that uses the same bean from that point on. When a client is done, it ends the session. While the session is open, the stateful session bean may use its instance variables to store information about its interaction with the client.

5.3.2 Entity Enterprise Beans: An entity enterprise bean has a persistent object reference which generally survives the crash and restart of EJB container in which the entity bean is created. An entity enterprise bean represents the data in the database, may update shared data in an underlying database, participates in transactions, and can be accessed by multiple users simultaneously.

There are two kinds of entity beans: (1) container-managed entity beans, and (2) bean-managed entity beans. A container-managed entity bean relies on its container to make it persistent. The deployer defines and changes the persistence of a container-managed entity bean. However, a bean-managed entity bean is responsible for managing its own persistence.

5.4. EJB Interfaces

The Enterprise JavaBeans specification defines enterprise beans interfaces as a standard Java RMI[1] interface. However, the actual communication is independent of RMI. An enterprise bean has two interfaces: (1) Home interface, and (2) Remote interface. A client of an enterprise bean uses the enterprise bean's Home interface to call the bean's lifecycle services for creating, finding, and destroying the bean's instances. The Remote interface specifies the business methods provided by the enterprise bean. It lists all the methods or public interfaces of the enterprise bean that clients can call. The 'class implementation' implements the functionality defined in both Home and Remote interfaces.

5.5. EJB Specification for Enterprise Application Development

To simplify development of complex enterprise systems, EJB specification defines six roles associated with different tasks in system development. The roles are as follow: (1) implementing a platform for development and execution of distributed applications, (2) developing enterprise beans, (3) providing connection between EJB server and enterprise beans, (4) assembling application, (5) deploying application, and (6) administrating the application execution. Figure 1 illustrates all the roles explained in section 5.5.

5.5.1. EJB Infrastructure: EJB infrastructure consists of EJB Container Provider and EJB Server Provider. EJB Container Provider implements a platform, which facilitates the development of distributed applications and provides a run-time environment for those applications. An EJB Container Provider provides the connection between enterprise beans and the EJB server.

5.5.2. Enterprise Bean Provider: An enterprise bean provider implements only enterprise beans. All non-business-specific aspects of the application including bean distribution, transaction, and security are handled by the other parts of the system.

5.5.3. Application Assembler: An application assembler integrates enterprise beans (i.e. building blocks of an application) with Java applets, servlets, and GUI clients as required in

---

[1] RMI is the acronym for Remote Method Invocations. Java RMI is used for communications between Java objects.

the application. The assembly of enterprise beans is based on the enterprise beans' interfaces rather than the beans' implementations.

5.5.4. Deployer: A deployer adapts an application composing a set of enterprise beans to the target operation environment. It does it by modifying the properties of the enterprise beans. The deployer is also in charge of setting transaction and security policies by modifying the appropriate properties in the deployment descriptor[1], and integrating with enterprise management software.

5.5.5. System Administrator: A system administrator monitors the execution of the application, and takes appropriate actions in the case of abnormal behavior of the application.

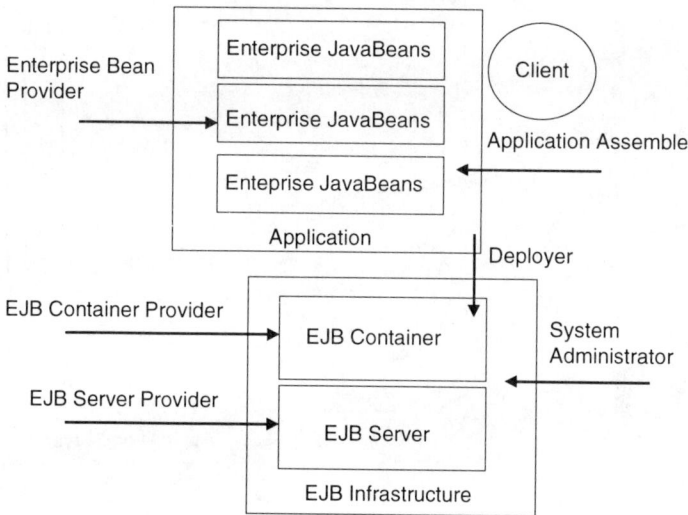

Figure 1. EJB Specification for Enterprise Application Development

5.6. Enterprise Bean Construction

A main objective of EJB specification is to make it easy for developers of enterprise applications to focus on the application business logic rather than the infrastructure and system-level issues. To achieve this objective, EJB specification saves application developers from system-level programming, and separates the development of actual bean

---

[1] An EJB deployment descriptor is a Java serialized object that extends the base deployment descriptor class. It allows the developer to specify the bean's transactional and security attributes declaratively, simplifying the process of developing transactional applications, and providing a level of abstraction that makes possibility across EJB servers.

objects from development of their clients. The client of an enterprise bean may or may not exist in the same application.

The client gets access to the enterprise bean through an object that implements an interface called EJBHome. That object serves as a factory of enterprise beans; creating the enterprise beans for the client and removing them when the client does not need those beans any more. The client can also access the enterprise bean through a Remote interface. This interface is implemented by an object that the EJB host constructs at the deployment. The interface or proxy forwards messages to the enterprise bean as needed. The object implementing the EJBHome interface works with the bean to initialize it. The EJB container provides the EJBHome and EJBObject interfaces for the enterprise bean that lives in the container. Figure 2 illustrates the communication between an enterprise bean and a client.

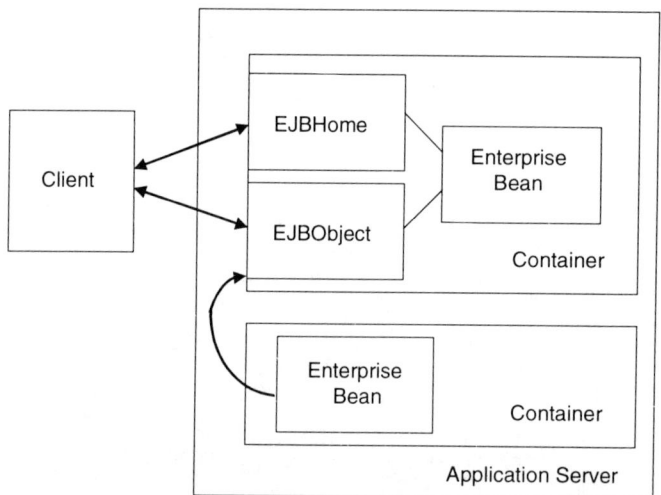

Figure 2. Communication between an Enterprise Bean and a Client

6. Component Models Evaluation

The key competing component model for Java-based component model is from Microsoft. This model uses ActiveX and Microsoft Transaction Server (MTS). Another component model is the OMG CORBA Component Specification that is expected to become available soon.

6.1. ActiveX

ActiveX from Microsoft is the competing component technology to JavaBeans. Microsoft introduced ActiveX in March 1996 as the company's main strategy for the Web, and has promoted it as a complete environment for components and distributed objects. ActiveX is based upon Component Object Model (COM) [7,8,9]. COM components are classes that advertise their services through their interfaces.

Authorized client components or programs create an object of the component class and get a pointer to the interface providing the services they need. Client components use the pointer to invoke methods on the object and access the object's services. Distributed Component Object Model (DCOM) is the ORB for ActiveX [10]. DCOM serves as a core technology for remote communications between ActiveX components.

6.2. JavaBeans versus ActiveX

Both JavaBeans and ActiveX are the component technologies designed for the Web. However, they have major differences. JavaBeans is platform-independent and language-dependent (Java-based) while ActiveX is Microsoft Windows platform-dependent and language-independent. The platform dependency of ActiveX is one of its critical weaknesses for the Internet-based enterprise application development. The Internet market share of Java and JavaBeans has been significantly expanded due to their platform independency. Furthermore, language-dependency of JavaBeans is not a problem because Java beans can run on any platform with Java VM (practically any platforms).

Another major difference between JavaBeans and ActiveX technologies lies in the approach that these two technologies have taken to address security of components. ActiveX relies only on the digital signature verification method while JavaBeans provides higher level of security through a combination of sandboxing, digital signature verification, and trusted servers. ActiveX has been roundly criticized by computer security professionals since its approach to security is seen as lacking [11,12].

JavaBeans leads ActiveX in terms of security and portability. However, ActiveX leads JavaBeans in its existing code base due to its underlying OCX technology that is widely used in the Windows software community. This may change over the next few years as JavaBeans takes off.

6.3. Microsoft Transaction Server (MTS)

Microsoft Transaction Server (MTS) was introduced in 1996. MTS provides the environment for components, which are built around COM and DCOM, to work in multi-tier architectures [13]. MTS provides components with a nurturing environment, as does EJB. However, MTS runs only on Microsoft Windows platform while JavaBeans is platform-independent.

MTS currently does not provide a good solution to the problem of load balancing. The next generation of MTS is called COM+, which is a part of Windows 2000. COM+ combines MTS, COM, and DCOM, and provides significant functionalities such as asynchronous components and an advanced event technology. Additionally, it is supposed to improve the load balancing of MTS.

6.4. EJB versus MTS and CORBA Components

Both EJB and MTS provide support for component-oriented transactions, declarative authorization, resource pooling, state management, and other related services. The OMG CORBA Components Specification (to become available soon) has the advantage of language neutrality over EJB, and the advantage of portability over MTS. However, EJB has the following attractive features:

1. EJB is portable across Java VMs and EJB servers. The EJB transaction server concept allows scalability, reliability, load balancing, and atomic transactions of enterprise applications on various platforms.

2. Application development using EJB does not involve low-level system programming such as thread-aware programming. The EJB server implementation addresses scalability requirements.

3. Application development using EJB does not involve creating and using Interface Definition Language (IDL) files, as EJB defines the interfaces between a server-side component and its container. Consequently, modification and maintenance of applications using JavaBeans and EJB are easier than those using CORBA or COM/DCOM.

4. Application development using EJB does not deal with transactional and security semantics in the bean implementation because the transaction and security rules for an EJB can be defined at the time of assembly and deployment. The transaction semantics are defined declaratively through a bean's deployment descriptor rather than programmatically. The EJB server, on the behalf of its enterprise beans, manages the start, commit, and rollback of transactions. It does so according to a transaction attribute specified in the EJB deployment descriptor.

7. Final Notes

This paper has provided a tutorial on Java-based component model where JavaBeans specification defines the client component model and EJB specification defines the server component model. The paper has also discussed major differences between JavaBeans and ActiveX; as well as those between EJB, MTS, and the OMG CORBA Components. It is important to note that the selection of a component model, which is the most suited for a project, is crucial to the success of the project. This requires a good understanding of all the leading component models and the involving technologies. Presenting the features of all the major component models is beyond the scope of this paper. In addition, all these technologies are fast evolving. Therefore, the paper should be considered as a 10-page tutorial on Java-based component model, in particular, EJB server component model.

References

[1] G. Pour, "Component-Based Software Development: New Opportunities and Challenges," *Proceedings of the International Conference on Technology of Object-Oriented Systems and Languages (TOOLS USA)*, Santa Barbara, CA, August 1998.

[2] G. Pour, "Moving Toward Component-Based Software Development Approach," *Proceedings of the International Conference on Technology of Object-Oriented Languages and Systems*, Beijing, China, September 1998.

[3] M. Griss, G. Pour and J. Favaro, "Making the Transition to Component-Based Enterprise Software Development: Overcoming the Obstacles - Patterns for success," *Proceedings of the International Conference on of Object-Oriented Languages and Systems (TOOLS USA '99)*, Santa Barbara, CA, August 1999.

[4] G. Pour, "Towards Component-Based Software Engineering," *Proceedings of the International Computer Software & Applications Conference (COMPSAC '98)*, Vienna, Austria, August 1998.

[5] G. Pour and J. Xu, "JavaBeans, Java, Java Servlets, and CORBA Revolutionizing Web-Based Enterprise Application Development," *Proceedings of the World Conference of the WWW, Internet, and Intranet (WebNet)*, Hawaii, 1999.

[6] R. Orfali and D. Harkey, *Client/Server Programming with Java and CORBA*, Wiley, 1998.

[7]   D. Platt, *Essence of COM with ActiveX*, Prentice Hall, 1998.

[8]   A. Denning, *ActiveX Controls Inside Out*, Microsoft Press, 1997.

[9]   D. Chappell, *Understanding ActiveX and OLE*, Microsoft Press, 1996.

[10] G. Pour, "Developing Web-Based Enterprise Applications with Java, JavaBeans, and CORBA," *Proceedings of the World Conference of the WWW, Internet, and Intranet (WebNet)*, Orlando, FL, Nov. 1998.

[11] G. McGraw and E. Felten, *Securing Java*, Wiley, 2nd ed., 1999.

[12] G. McGraw and E. Felten, *Java Security*, Wiley, 1997.

[13] R. Session, *COM and DCOM: Microsoft's Vision for Distributed Objects*, Wiley, 1998.

Ada and the Objects

Benjamin Brosgol

Aonix, USA

The original Ada language, designed in the early 1980s, was object-based but not fully object-oriented; it supported encapsulation and data abstraction but not inheritance, polymorphism or dynamic binding. A language revision effort culminating in ISO standardization in 1995 has filled this gap. After summarizing Ada's main features, this tutorial explores the language's approach to Object Orientation. The presentation develops an example to motivate and illustrate the key semantic and stylistic points, compares Ada with other OO languages (C++, Eiffel, Java), and explains the rationale for major language design decisions. Topics include:

- Why Ada realizes the class concept through both a data type facility and a modularization construct, and the effects of this design decision

- Implications of explicit versus implicit "pointers" for polymorphism

- Interactions between encapsulation (visibility control) and OOP

- How Ada models multiple inheritance

- How the developer can define class-specific operations for storage management and assignment

- Why object creation presents pitfalls for effective de-centralized OO style, and how to avoid these pitfalls

- How to write applets in Ada

After attending this tutorial, the student will understand Ada's OO model, but will also see the underpinnings of OOP in a way that leads to more effective OO styles with other programming languages.

Benjamin Brosgol has over 25 years of experience in the computer software industry, with a focus on programming language design and implementation (Ada in particular), software engineering, Object-Oriented technology, Information Systems, and real-time applications. He has been continually and actively involved with Ada since its inception in the mid-1970s, as a language designer, reviewer, compiler developer, user, and educator. He was a member of the team that conducted the Ada 95 language revision, where he was responsible for designing the Information Systems support. He has been conducting Ada courses since 1982, both in the U.S. and abroad, for private industry, government, and academia. Dr. Brosgol has long been active in the Ada community and is currently the chairman of ACM's SIGAda (Special Interest Group on Ada). He is presently a senior member of the Professional Services group at Aonix.

0-7695-0278-4/99 $10.00 © 1999 IEEE

Programming with C++ Exceptions

Angelika Langer
Germany

When introduced to the language, exception handling added a whole new dimension of programming techniques to C++. Despite of its indisputable advantages, it is still rarely used. This is because exception handling can be quite harmful when used in programs that are not prepared to cope with exceptions. In ANSI C++, we cannot ignore exceptions any longer because certain language constructs, such as new expressions or dynamic_cast as well as the standard library, already raise exceptions. In this lecture we explore exception safety, i.e. what we can and have to do in order to make our programs behave nicely even in presence of exceptions. Another aspect of interest is exception safety in conjunction with template libraries such as the STL. We will see which safety guarantees the STL gives and what it requires of its users. To round up our knowledge of C++ exceptions handling we eventually take a look at some of the less widely known language features such as uncaught exceptions, terminate handlers, and exception specifications.

Angelika Langer teaches C++ related topics as a freelancer in Europe and the US. She's a recognized speaker at various international conferences, among them C++ World, OOP, TOOLS Pacific. She's a columnist for C++ Report and a member of the C++ standards committee.

Behind the Beans

Michael Stal

Siemens AG, Germany

Developers are facing a very rapid evolution of new products and technologies. In addition, they have to cope with increasing customer requirements. Competitors must provide new products releases in decreasing time frames without hampering quality. Thus, the question arises how these different forces might be balanced. The right answer is: If technological evolution and requirements are changing rapidly, at least the underlying software architectures should remain stable. Architectures must be built with future changes and extensions in mind. On one hand, Multi-tier Architectures might be introduced for this purpose. This helps for a separation of concerns, but alone it is not sufficient. To design for change and evolution a component-based approach is the right choice. Components represent fundamental units of distribution and functionality. They define hooks for future change and extension. This is the reason why the Java Beans technology was introduced by JavaSoft. However, JavaBeans are a perfect solution for building desktop-centered user interfaces, but they do not help for deploying functionality on the server-side. Therefore, JavaSoft has recently provided the Enterprise JavaBeans Specification. Despite of their names, JavaBeans and Enterprise JavaBeans are different technologies addressing different tiers of multi-tier architectures. The tutorial will give an in-depth introduction of both technologies. It will also compare the technologies with the alternatives provided by Microsoft WindowsDNA.

Michael Stal is responsible for the research project Distributed Object Computing at Siemens AG. His main research areas are Object-Orientation, Distribution, Design Patterns, and Java. He is co-author of the book "Pattern-Oriented Software Architecture -A System of Patterns", Wiley & Sons, 1996. He is also editor of Java Spektrum, a German SIGS magazine on Java. Michael is member of the Object Management Group. His articles were published in magazines such as C++ Report, Objektspektrum, Java Spektrum, Object Magazine, JOOP, and i'x. He gave talks and tutorials at TOOLS '94, OOP'95, '96, '97, '98, CUC'96, '97, OOPLSA '96, '97, '98, Object Expo London '95, Object Expo New York '96, object+component forum Vienna '97, '98.

Java, Eiffel and C++: The Language Comparison

Ian Joyner

Microsoft Research Institute, Australia

This tutorial is based on my upcoming book comparing Eiffel, Java and C++. While the object models of these languages are very similar, they are very different in the ease with which software can be built. We will examine the differences between the languages, their strengths and weaknesses in a hard-headed look. The superficial syntactic differences will be looked at, but more importantly, the semantic differences and philosophical basis of each language.

We will see how these differences apply in actually developing software, as it is not just a question of theoretical niceness, but practical application, and what this means in terms of ensuring quality in software.

Ian Joyner has been involved in object-oriented programming for almost 20 years, has developed many OO systems, notably communications programs and a music publisher in MacApp, and written OO compilers. He is also interested in programming language issues and is currently writing a book comparing Java, Eiffel and C++. He has ported EiffelS to the Macintosh, and has developed the MOTEL library. He is currently employed at Macquarie University in the Microsoft Research Institute where he is involved with project Bruce to translate Eiffel to Java, and interface the Eiffel and Java libraries. He also tutors the third year database course.

Tutorials

Technology

Mastering the Windows Eiffel Library

Glenn Maughan, *Westernport Group Pty Ltd, Australia*
Raphael Simon, *Interactive Software Engineering, USA*

An object-oriented approach to building Windows software requires at least three components. These are: an object-oriented language that provides proper support for object oriented concepts, an object-oriented encapsulation of the Windows API library and a set of base or kernel classes that provide all of the necessary data structures and abstractions needed to build software. The language used in this tutorial is Eiffel. Eiffel is a pure object-oriented language designed from the ground up to support the production of quality software. The API encapsulation library is the Windows Eiffel Library (WEL) providing a complete and easy way to use encapsulation of the Windows API. And finally, the base library used is the EiffelBase library providing a myriad of standard software component abstractions. These three tools provide a surprisingly powerful way of engineering quality Windows software.

This tutorial explores the use of object technology, COM, and the WEL library for building quality Windows software. The components that the WEL library provides and how to use them are discussed incrementally through the development of a small application.

COM and the Eiffel COM interface (EiffelCOM) are used to interact with existing Windows components and to componentize the developed application.

The tutorial provides a sufficient description of using object technology, COM, and the WEL library for use in constructing complete Windows applications.

Glenn Maughan has been studying object-oriented methods and development for the past 8 years. After gaining his PhD in object-oriented architecture at Monash University (Australia) he continued to develop his experience in the field. Glenn's breadth of experience includes developing and deploying both academic and industrial systems written in Eiffel, Java and C++. He is currently a Software Consultant for the Westernport Group in Australia and, in the few hours spare each week, is co-authoring a book on Windows programming in Eiffel.

Raphael Simon a graduate of ENSEIHHT in Toulouse, France, is a software engineer at Interactive Software Engineering, where he has worked on Windows object-oriented development tools, OLE, COM, and the EiffelCOM library. He consulted on various large projects in the US and UK and gave several training courses in Canada and South Africa.

Distributed Objects from a Patterns Perspective

Michael Stal

Siemens AG, Germany

Nowadays, infrastructures for Distributed Object Computing such as COM, CORBA or RMI have become common place. When building software systems with one of these technologies it is essential to understand the fundamental concepts behind them. But what are the concepts behind these infrastructures? Actually, there is no architectural description available, neither for DCOM nor for CORBA or RMI. However, only with this knowledge it is possible to build distributed systems that adhere to functional and non-functional requirements. With patterns a new method for building and also for analyzing software systems has emerged. Patterns help to get a substantial understanding of the structure and dynamics of distributed objects systems such as DCOM or CORBA. The tutorial presents a pattern system that covers many fundamental aspects of Distributed Object Computing. A web of patterns will be presented that together reveal the architecture of distributed objects infrastructures.

Michael Stal is responsible for the research project Distributed Object Computing at Siemens AG. His main research areas are Object-Orientation, Distribution, Design Patterns, and Java. He is co-author of the book "Pattern-Oriented Software Architecture -A System of Patterns", Wiley & Sons, 1996. He is also editor of Java Spektrum, a German SIGS magazine on Java. Michael is member of the Object Management Group. His articles were published in magazines such as C++ Report, Objektspektrum, Java Spektrum, Object Magazine, JOOP, and i'x.He gave talks and tutorials at TOOLS '94, OOP'95, '96, '97, '98, CUC'96, '97, OOPLSA '96, '97, '98, Object Expo London '95, Object Expo New York '96, object+component forum Vienna '97, '98.

Building Scalable ODBMS Applications

Matt BenDaniel

Object Design, USA

Experienced application developers have concluded that an Object Database is an essential building block for OO systems that support high usage loads and gigabyte-to-terabyte-sized storage. ODBMS provide tremendous advantages compared with RBDMS, flat files or serialization, but only when the appropriate design and implementation techniques are applied. The nature and importance of these techniques can become painfully apparent during project delays due to the pitfalls that abound.

The tutorial first reviews the main aspect of ODBMS architecture and key scalability concepts. The techniques are covered with diagrams and examples. The tutorial concludes with a close look at a deployed application using these techniques.

Matt BenDaniel is Principal Consulting Engineer at Object Design, Inc. For eight years the author has provided ODBMS training, design consulting, and deployment assistance to hundreds of clients. BenDaniel has an SB from MIT in Computer Science and an SM in Management from the Sloan School at MIT.

Real-Time Object-Oriented Distributed Systems: RT CORBA and RMA

Antonios Broumas

Tri-Pacific Software, USA

CORBA stands for Common Object Request Broker Architecture and it is a set of middleware architectural specifications adopted by the OMG, the Object Management Group. One of the goals of the class is to enable the attendees to see independently why CORBA is the best middleware choice available and how to choose and configure the appropriate ORB that meets their needs. A long awaited natural extension to CORBA is Real-Time CORBA. The goal of RT CORBA is to support end-to-end predictability. In our tutorial we will explain what a "Schedulable Entity" actually is, what are its interfaces and how priorities are controlled and propagated in a CORBA real-time distributed object oriented computing environment.

Subsequently we will introduce the attendees to Real-Time analysis and design and in particular schedulability analysis using RMA, Rate Monotonic Analysis. The term "rate monotonic" originated as a name for the optimizing task priority assignment technique in which higher priorities are accorded to tasks that execute at higher rates. RMA is a simple, practical, mathematically sound way to ensure that all timing requirements will be met. Using RMA we are able to identify and eliminate unbounded priority inversion, and can guarantee that all hard deadlines will always be met. In addition toworst-case schedulability analysis, RMA can also show that average-case performance demands are satisfied.

After the tutorial the attendees would be able to have a global view of the development process of a Real-Time CORBA application environment based on a sound understanding of the underlying basic RMA concepts.

Antonios Broumas joined Tri-Pacific Software Inc. in 1998 as a senior consultant. He is a graduate of the Electrical Engineering School of the National Technical University of Athens, Greece. He received his M.S. in Electrical Engineering and his Ph.D. in Mathematics from The University of Texas at Austin. He has held positions in teaching, research, and software development at The University of Arizona at Tucson and at the Mathematical Sciences Research Institute at Berkeley, California, USA.

Tutorials

Methodology

System Design: Architectures and Archetypes

Stephen J. Mellor

Project Technology, USA

The challenges of developing high performance, high reliability, and high quality software systems are too much for ad hoc and informal engineering techniques that might have worked in the past on less demanding systems. New techniques for managing these growing complexities are required to meet today's time-to-market and productivity demands. This tutorial shows you how to:

- engineer the system-wide design to meet performance constraints;
- identify the characteristics of the problem that determine the system design;
- model the system-wide design--the software architecture;
- build archetypes that generate efficient code.

This approach produces a number of beneficial results:

- productivity: reuse is built in to the software architecture;
- error reduction: archetypes limit coding errors;
- time-to-market;
- open code generation reduces project schedules.

The tutorial will include a number of pencil and paper exercises that illustrate the concepts.

Stephen J. Mellor is best known for his contribution to the development of Object-Oriented Analysis and the Shlaer-Mellor Method. He is currently Senior Vice President of Project Technology, Inc., where he serves as co-researcher, with Sally Shlaer, for Project Technology's extensions and applications of the Shlaer-Mellor Method. Mr. Mellor and Ms. Shlaer are currently working on their third book: Shlaer-Mellor Method: Recursive Design. Mr. Mellor is also a member of the editorial board for IEEE Software.

A Short Use Case Writing Workshop

Alistair Cockburn
Humans & Technology, USA

A use case is a collector for scenarios that describe an actor interacting with a system in pursuit of a goal. The workshop starts from this definition, showing how use cases can be written, cross-connected and managed. You will work with others around you, attempting to list use cases for a system, write a main scenario, and uncover failure scenarios in an impossibly short time frame. Expect to encounter differences in writing styles and to discover that use cases are much trickier to write than they seem. Learn the degrees of variation that still permit use cases to be effective.

Alistair Cockburn, special advisor to the Central Bank of Norway for object technology and software project management, was the OO methodology designer for the IBM Consulting Group before founding Humans and Technology in 1994. His book, "Surviving OO Projects", was published in 1998. He is an expert on use cases, object-oriented design, project management, and software methodologies. He has been the technical design coach and process consultant on projects ranging in size from 3 to 90 people. Materials that support Alistair's workshops can be found at http://members.aol.com/acockburn.

Modularization Revisited: Aspects in the Design and Evolution of Software Systems

Cristina Videira Lopes

Xerox Research Center, USA

Objects have been a great success. They have improved software development by allowing us to cleanly encapsulate units of functionality of various scales - from simple data structures to GUI tools to network servers - inside of well-defined classes.

But objects don't seem to help as much in dealing with systemic concerns such as synchronization, multi-object protocols, resource sharing, distribution, memory management, replication and the like. Rather than staying well localized within a class, these concerns tend to cross-cut the system's class and module structure. Much of the complexity and brittleness in existing systems appears to stem from the way in which the implementation of these kinds of concerns ends up being intertwined throughout the code.

Aspect-oriented programming is a new technique that has been proposed specifically to address this problem. Like objects, aspects are intended to be used in both design and implementation. During design, the concept of aspect facilitates thinking about cross-cutting concerns as well-defined entities. During implementation, aspect-oriented programming languages - namely AspectJ™ - make it possible to program directly in terms of design aspects.

This tutorial shows how to design and program with aspects and how aspects can be used to improve separation of concerns in complex software systems. Particular attention will be given to how AspectJ can support the implementation of common OO design patterns.

Cristina Videira Lopes is a research scientist at the Xerox Palo Alto Research Center. Her research interests are in software engineering and programming languages. She has been developing aspect-oriented programming languages, in particular for distributed applications. She has co-organized several workshops in several conferences, namely the AOP workshops at ECOOP, and she has presented a number of tutorials at ECOOP and OOPSLA that got excellent evaluations. She has published papers in ECOOP and ICSE, and she is a member of the Program Committee for ECOOP'99.

Advanced Visual Modelling: Beyond UML

Stuart Kent, *University of Kent, UK*
Joseph Gil, *Technion, Israel*
John Howse, *University of Brighton, UK*

With the adoption of UML by the OMG and industry as the standard visual modelling notation, it is interesting to wonder what will come next in this field? This tutorial presents a vision for visual modelling beyond UML. It is based on a series of recent research papers, which have introduced some radical new notations and which have suggested the kinds of tools that could be available to support the modeller of the future. Highlights include:

- a crash course in UML, its weaknesses and strengths
- a rich visual constraint language (based on Venn diagrams), and an insight into subtle issues that arise when defining a visual language
- a series of 3D notations for providing rich visualisations of dynamic behaviour
- a vision for visual modelling tools of the future.

Stuart Kent is a Senior Lecturer in Computing at University of Kent, UK, and consultant and trainer to industry on both sides of the Atlantic. Research active in the areas of visual modelling, OOD and CBD. Dr. Kent has been on the programme committee for various workshops and conferences including UML '98/9, TOOLS USA '98/9 & EDOC '99.

Joseph (Yossi) Gil is Assistant Professor at Technion Israel. He is widely published in many journals and conferences on a broad spectrum of topics, including both the theory and practice of Computer Science. He recently spent a year with IBM Research, New York. Dr. Gil was Chair of TOOLS USA '98 and on the programme committees for numerous conferences including past & present OOPSLA's and ECOOP's. He is an experienced university teacher and trainer to industry.

John Howse is Principal Lecturer in Computing and Mathematics at University of Brighton, UK. His research focus is in the areas of semantics for OO and visual modelling languages, and, more recently, in diagrammatic reasoning. Dr Howse has many years experience in teaching.

Constraint Diagrams: A Step Beyond UML

Joseph (Yossi) Gil
Software Systems Laboratory
Faculty of Computer Science
Technion , Technion City, Haifa
32000, ISRAEL.
yogi@cs.technion.ac.il

John Howse
School of Computing &
Mathematical Sciences
University of Brighton
Brighton, UK
John.Howse@brighton.ac.uk

Stuart Kent
Computing Laboratory
University of Kent,
Canterbury, UK
S.J.H.Kent@ukc.ac.uk

Abstract

The Unified Modeling Language (UML) is a set of notations for modelling object-oriented systems. It has become the de facto standard. Most of its notations are diagrammatic. An exception to this is the Object Constraint Language (OCL) which is essentially a textual, stylised form of first order predicate logic. We describe a notation, constraint diagrams, which were introduced as a visual technique intended to be used in conjunction with the UML for object-oriented modelling. Constraint diagrams provide a diagrammatic notation for expressing constraints (e.g., invariants) that could only be expressed in UML using OCL.

Keywords

Modelling, visual formalism, object-oriented software development, formal methods.

1. Introduction

The uptake in industry of notations for designing systems visually has been accelerated with the recent standardisation of UML. But, in our opinion, UML is only the culmination of the first stage in the development of this young field. It brings together a number of informal visual notations (the possible exception being statecharts) that have proven useful to some parts of industry. It has made little progress in integrating these notations; and it certainly does not include anything that is radically different from the existing status quo (but then the goal was to consolidate not to innovate).

In this paper, we provide some insight into what lies beyond UML. We describe a notation, *constraint diagrams*, which were introduced in (Kent, 1997) as a visual technique intended to be used in conjunction with the Unified Modelling Language for object-oriented modelling. Constraint diagrams provide a diagrammatic notation for expressing constraints (invariants) that could only be expressed using the Object Constraint Language (Warmer and Kleppe, 1998), essentially a textual, stylised form of first order predicate logic which is part of the UML standard (OMG, 1997).

Constraint diagrams are a significant advance on class diagrams in UML for the visualisation of object structures. Whereas class diagrams are only able to show that

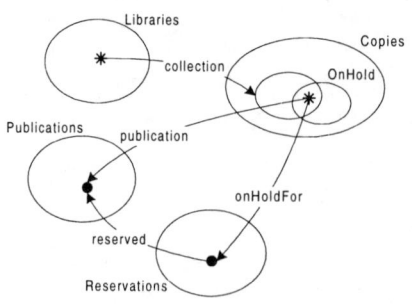

Figure 1 - A constraint diagram

there are relationships between certain kinds of object, constraint diagrams are able to visualise properties of those relationships and compositions of those relationships. Whereas class diagrams make no use of the relative positions of the diagrammatic elements (e.g. whether a class overlaps with another class or not), the relative positioning of diagrammatic elements on constraint diagrams is vital.

The constraint diagram in Figure 1 expresses (amongst other constraints) an invariant on a model of a library system: for any library object, and any copy of that library which is on hold, that copy's publication must be the same as that associated with the reservation for which it is on hold:

$$\forall x \in \textit{Libraries}, \forall y \in x.collection \cap OnHold,$$

$$onHoldFor.reserved = y.publication$$

This reading is obtained by treating the *s as wildcards, universal quantifiers over the regions which contain them, and arrows as showing the range of relations when their domain is restricted to the set or element at their source. Venn diagrams are then used to show relationships between all the sets and elements involved.

Pairs of constraint diagrams have also been used in post and contract boxes to express post conditions and pre/post contracts for actions in a visual form (Kent and Gil, 1998), which forms the basis of further work in three dimensional notations for software and systems modeling (Gil and Kent, 1998). A form of the notation has also been used in the precise, visual representation of design patterns (Lauder and Kent, 1998).

A second goal of this paper is to illustrate how hard it is to define a visual notation, and to highlight some of the issues that arise. In the work on constraint diagrams it soon became apparent that the notation was far more sophisticated than it first seemed. Specifically we started to discover examples where, although there seemed to be an intuitive reading, it was not obvious how that reading was derived in any general or systematic way. And whenever a new piece of notation was added, the impact of that notation on what was already there was not obvious.

A sub-notation of the language of constraint diagrams is the language of spider diagrams – essentially constraint diagrams without the arrows. Spider diagrams are themselves a development from Venn diagrams and Euler circles. The paper is structured in a similar manner. Section 2 overviews the work on Venn diagrams and Euler circles, and places spider diagrams in that context. Section 3 introduces and discusses the informal semantics of the notation for spider diagrams, being careful to motivate and explore the consequences of decisions made. Similarly, Section 4 introduces the notation for constraint diagrams. Section 5 summarises some of the issues still outstanding before the formal definitions of syntax and semantics can be completed.

2. Venn diagrams and Euler Circles

Circles or closed curves, which we will call contours, have been in use for the representation of classical syllogisms since at least the Middle Ages (Lull, 1517). The Swiss mathematician Leonhard Euler (1707-1783) introduced the notation we now call Euler circles (or Euler diagrams) (Euler, 1761) to illustrate relations between classes. This notation uses the topological properties of enclosure, exclusion and intersection to represent the set-theoretic notions of subset, disjoint sets, and set intersection, respectively. Table 1 illustrates the possible relationships between two contours.

456

	Contours are disjoint, meaning that the sets they denote are disjoint.
	Contours intersect, meaning that the sets they denote *may* intersect.
	One contour may be contained in another, with the corresponding relationship between the sets they denote.

Table 1: Relationships between contours

The nineteenth century logician John Venn modified this notation to represent logical propositions (Venn, 1880). In Venn diagrams all possible intersections of the closed curves must be shown and shading is used to show that a particular region represents the empty set. Figure 2 shows the standard "clover" Venn diagram of three intersecting contours.

More (1959) gives an algorithm for adding a new closed curve to a Venn diagram. In Figure 3, a new, highlighted, contour has been added to the standard clover. Note that all possible intersections between the four contours occur.

Figure 2 – Clover Diagram

In 1896, the logician Charles Peirce modified Venn diagrams by introducing *X-sequences* to introduce elements and disjunctive information into the system (Peirce, 1933). Very recently formal semantics and inference rules have been developed for Venn-Peirce diagrams (Shin, 1994) and Euler diagrams (Hammer, 1995).

In summary, Venn-Peirce diagrams are expressive, but complicated to draw because all possible intersections have to be drawn and then some regions shaded. Euler circles are intuitive and easier to draw, but not so expressive because they do not include provisions for shading and for "X-Sequences".

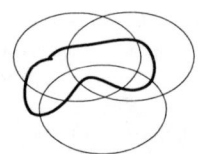

Figure 3 – Four-contour Venn diagram

3. Spider Diagrams

Spider Diagrams are Euler circles augmented as follows:
1. *Shaded Regions*, just like in Venn Diagrams.
2. *Spiders*, which are similar to X-Sequences in Venn diagrams, used to denote that an element exists in a set which is the union of one or more regions. They are different from X-sequences because a region might have more than one spider in it, e.g. to denote that a set has two or more elements. Spiders may also be connected by *strands* or *ties* in a region, to indicate that elements denoted by the spiders may or must be the same in that region.
3. *Projections*, which can be used to show the intersection of more than three closed curves in a clear and uncluttered way given the notorious difficulty of showing the intersection of more than three sets on a Venn diagram.

3.1 Contours and Regions

A *contour* is a simple closed plane curve. Contours denote sets of arbitrary size. It is convenient to draw contours as ellipses. However, this is not mandatory. Other iconic representations may be used for making a visual distinction between different kinds of contour. For example, in object-oriented modelling, rectangle contours are used to indicate that a set corresponds to a class of objects. All concepts described in this section are independent of the chosen iconic representations. In Venn diagrams, all contours must intersect. We do not require this property in spider diagrams. As with Euler circles, two contours can stand in one of the three relations listed in Table 1. A *boundary contour* is not contained in and does not intersect with any other contour. We assume that a diagram has one and only one boundary contour, which denotes the universal set for that diagram. However, most of the time we do not bother to draw the boundary contour: it is assumed to be the bounding box for the diagram, be it the edges of the drawing surface, the edges of a figure, etc.

A *basic region* is the bounded region of the plane enclosed by a contour. A *region* is defined as follows: any basic region is a region; if r and s are regions, then their union, intersection, or difference, are regions provided these are non-empty. A *minimal region* is a region having no other region contained within it. Thus a minimal region is an area enclosed by one contour or more which is not further divided by other contours, so the contours of a Spider diagram partition the plane into disjoint minimal regions. Figure 4 shows all but one (the minimal region outside the contours shown but inside the boundary contour is not depicted) of the minimal regions of a standard "clover diagram".

Regions can be generated by taking the union of any combination of the minimal regions. In a Venn diagram with c contours, there are 2^c minimal regions and $2^{2^c} - 1$ regions. Thus, in Figure 4, there are $2^8 - 1 = 255$ regions in total, which is the number of ways the 8 minimal regions (including the one not shown) may be combined. The set denoted by a minimal region is easily calculated: it is the intersection of all contours that contain it, minus the union of all contours that do not contain it.

A *contour label* is a Capitalized string of characters, appearing outside some contour. A *region label* is an underlined, Capitalized string of characters, appearing in a minimal region. Underlining the region label allows region and contour labels to be easily distinguished.

Figure 4 - minimal regions

3.2 Spiders

A *spider* is a tree with nodes (called *feet*) placed in different minimal regions; the connecting edges (called *legs*) are straight lines. A spider *touches* a minimal region if one of its feet appear in that region. A spider may only touch a minimal region once. A spider is said to *inhabit* the region which is the union of the minimal regions it touches; this region is called the *habitat* of the spider.

Spiders are used to denote elements. Two distinct spiders denote distinct elements, unless they are joined by a *tie* or by a *strand* (see below). A *spider label* is a lowercase string of characters.

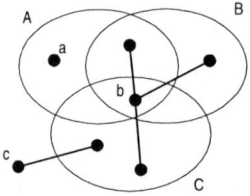

Figure 5 - Spiders

In Figure 5, the spider labelled b inhabits a region which is the union of four minimal regions. The semantics is that

$$b \in (B - C) \cup (C - A)$$
$$a \in (A - B) - C$$
$$c \in (U - A) - B$$

where U is the universal set denoted by the boundary contour. Also, all the elements are distinct, i.e., $a \neq b$, $b \neq c$, and $a \neq c$.

A *strand* is a wavy line connecting two nodes, from different spiders, placed in the same minimal region. Two spiders joined by a strand are referred to as *friends*. The *web* of spiders s and t is the union of minimal regions each containing a strand between nodes of s and t.

Strands (of a web) are used to allow spiders to denote the same elements in some circumstances. Specifically, spiders s and t may (not must) denote the same element if that element is in the set denoted by the web of s and t. In Figure 6, it is possible that if the element denoted by c happens to be in C then this may be the same as the element denoted by b. More generally, the elements denoted by s and t are distinct if they are in different minimal regions or not in the web of s and t.

A *tie* is a double, straight line (an equals sign) connecting two feet, from different spiders, placed in the same minimal region. Two spiders joined by a tie are

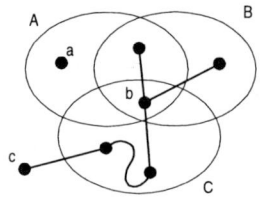

Figure 6 - strands

referred to as *mates*. The *nest* of spiders s and t is the union of minimal regions each containing a tie between feet of s and t. If both the elements denoted by spiders s and t are in the set denoted by the same minimal region in the nest of s and t, then s and t denote the same element. Two spiders s and t may (but not necessarily must) denote the same element if that element is in the set denoted by the web of s and t.

A tie is stronger than a strand in the sense that it requires s and t to denote the same element in any minimal region in which the tie appears. Thus in Figure 7, $c = b$ when both $c \in (C - A) - B$ and $b \in (C - A) - B$, otherwise $c \neq b$. Clearly, if

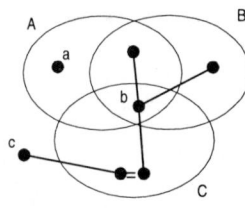

Figure 7 - ties

there is a tie between feet, then a strand between those feet is redundant. Similarly, multiple strands or ties between the same pairs of feet are redundant.

3.3 Shading and Schrödinger Spiders

Already, spiders can be used to place a lower limit on the number of elements in a set. In Figure 8, the region $A - B$ has at least two elements, and the region $B - A$ has at least one element. Clearly one can place any number of spiders in a region, hence express any lower bound.

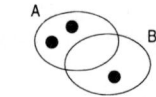

Figure 8 - cardinality with spiders

In order to place an upper bound on the cardinality of a set, we need a way of saying that a region is empty apart from those elements denoted by spiders in the region. We do this by shading. A minimal region is *shaded* if it contains a × or it is actually shaded. A region is *shaded* if each of its component minimal regions is shaded. Shading is visually appealing, but difficult to draw freehand, a × is easier to draw freehand but is, perhaps, not so visually appealing.

Figure 9 mixes both mechanisms to show that two minimal regions are empty. It is equivalent in meaning to Figure 10.

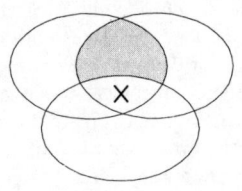

Figure 9 - shaded regions

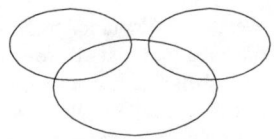

Figure 10 - alternative to shading

Figure 11 shows a case, which is difficult to show without shading. The difficulty is that all three sets within the boundary need to intersect as the intersection of all three may not be empty, but, if one is not careful, this has the effect of introducing new regions. Shading is then required to show that these new regions are empty. So the effect of shading a region and placing no spiders in that region, is to guarantee that the cardinality of the set denoted by the region is zero.

Shading a region which includes spiders has the effect of placing an upper limit on the number of elements in the set denoted by the region. In Figure 12, A contains at most 3 elements; it may contain less as the elements denoted by spiders a, b and c may be selected from other regions. B contains exactly 2 elements; the spiders in the region mean a lowerbound on its size of 2, the shading ensures that this is also an upperbound. C contains between 1 and 3 elements.

In Figure 12, the sizes of sets A and C are related: the more elements in A the less in C, and vice-versa. If we wished to avoid this, then it would be necessary to always have an element in the universal set but not in the sets represented by all other contours. In Figure 13, the same restrictions on the size of A

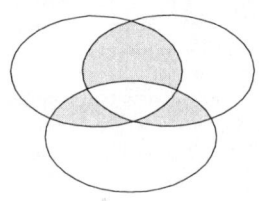

Figure 11 – Shading is essential

and C are in force, but this time if a, b and c denote elements in A this has no impact on the size of C, as the habitats of these spiders do not include C. But the price to pay is that D must contain a single element if the size of A and C both hit their lower bounds.

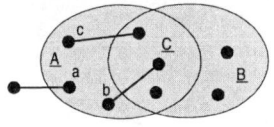

Figure 12 - Shading & spiders

We are not sure whether this has any practical significance when using spider diagrams in modelling (except perhaps that it's also awkward to draw). However, as mathematicians we feel uneasy about such a state of affairs. The fix is not difficult: a *Schrödinger Spider*.

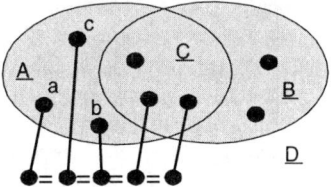

Figure 13 - Shading & spiders II

460

A *Schrödinger Spider* is represented by the symbol $\oslash$, and may appear in any region. It can be friends or mates with other spiders. A Schrödinger spider denotes a set whose size is zero or 1: rather like Schrödinger's cat one is not sure whether the element exists or not. Figure 14 is a reworking of Figure 13, this time using Schrödinger spiders. $\underline{D}$ is not forced to contain an element. The diagram is also less complicated to draw.

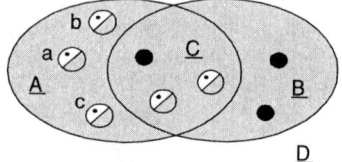

Figure 14 - Schrödinger Spiders

Obviously there is a limit to the amount we can express in this notation about the cardinality of sets. For example, we are unable to say that the size of A is the sum of the sizes of B and C. In the past, we have toyed with extending the notation to allow this kind of constraint to be expressed (Kent and Gil, 1998), but have realised that all we were really doing is adding textual annotations to the diagram. We can use labels to achieve a similar effect: for example, it is easy to write $|A| = |B| + |C|$. Thus, in general, labels allow us to combine constraints expressed visually with constraints expressed textually; diagrams can then be used for those constraints which are intuitive to express using a diagram, and do not need to be overburdened with textual annotations in an attempt to make them more expressive, but which results in them being overly complex with corresponding loss of intuitiveness.

3.4 Projections

A *projection* is a contour, which is dashed in appearance. A *projected label* is a contour or region label, written within brackets and appearing outside some projection.

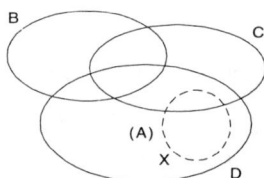

Figure 15 - Simple projection

The *region containing a contour* is the smallest region that *strictly* contains the basic region for that contour. Strictness ensures that the basic region itself is not the region containing the contour. A projection denotes the set obtained by intersecting the set denoted by its projected label with the set denoted by its containing region, which can always be calculated from the sets denoted by contours other than the projection itself.

Figure 15 shows a simple example. The dashed contour labelled X denotes the set obtained by "projecting" the set A onto the containing region $D - B$, i.e., $X = A \cap (D - B)$.

The same semantics could have been obtained by using More's algorithm (More 1959) to draw the Venn diagram with four contours, as in Figure 16, in which $X = \underline{X1} \cup \underline{X2} = A \cap (D - B)$.

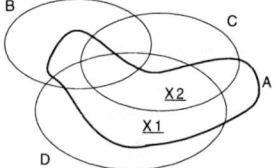

Figure 16 – Semantics of Figure 15

There are fascinating mathematical intricacies involving interacting projections.

4. Constraint Diagrams

Constraint diagrams are spider diagrams augmented by *arrows* and *wildcards*. Arrows determine relationships between sets and wildcards denote universal quantification.

4.1 Arrows

An arrow has a label, a source and a target. The source of an arrow can be a contour, a region or a spider; it is the set or element from which *navigation* (i.e., the relationship computation) begins. In figure 18 the source of arrow *f is* spider *x* and its target is contour *B*. The semantics of the navigation expression is $x.f = B$, where $x.f$ is shorthand for $\{y : f(x, y)\}$.

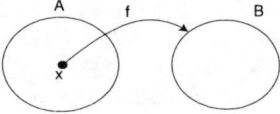

Figure 18 – One-arrow constraint diagram

In Figure 19 the source of arrow *f is* spider *x* and its target is a contour contained in *B*. In this case, we have $A.f \subseteq B$. The dot notation is overloaded; $A.f$ is shorthand for applying *f* to each element in *A* and then taking the union of the resulting sets; i.e., it is the union of sets $\{y : f(x, y)\}$ for each $x \in A$. The contour on which *f* is targeted is a *derived* set; it is defined by the arrow *f*.

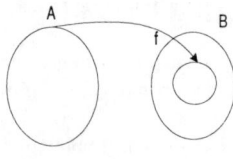

Figure 19 – Derived contour

The source of an arrow can also be a region. In Figure 20, the arrow has a double source indicating that the source of the arrow is the union of the two minimal regions denoting the sets $A - B$ and $B - A$. The target of an arrow should be a set. However, the arrow *f* in Figure 20 is targeted on a spider. This spider is treated semantically as a derived singleton set. The interpretation of the navigation expression is $((A - B) \cup (B - A)).f \in C$. We are implicitly allowing coercion between a singleton set and its element.

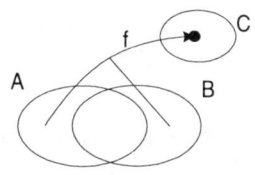

Figure 20 – Region as source and spider as target of an arrow

4.2 Quantification

Wildcards are introduced into constraint diagrams to represent universal quantification. The wildcard spider * ranges over all the elements of the set denoted by the minimal region in which it is situated.

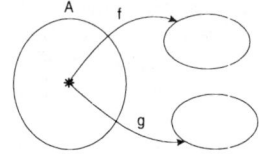

Figure 21 – Universal quantification

In Figure 21, the wildcard ranges over all elements of the set *A*. The interpretation of this diagram is that for each *x* in *A*, $x.f$ and $x.g$ are disjoint, i.e., $\forall x \in A \bullet x.f \cap x.g = \{\}$.

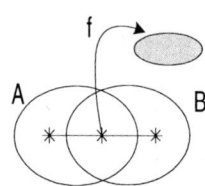

Figure 22 – Articulated wildcard spider

A wildcard can only be the source of an arrow. No arrow can be targeted on a wildcard and a wildcard that is not the source of an arrow cannot exist. A wildcard can be a foot of an articulated spider (i.e., a spider with more than one foot), in which case all feet of the spider are wildcards.

In Figure 22, the source of arrow f is an articulated, wildcard spider. The interpretation of this is that for each x in $A \cup B$, $x.f$ is empty, i.e., $\forall x \in A \cup B \bullet x.f = \{\}$.

The navigation expression in Figure 23 is existentially quantified. Its interpretation is that there exists an x in A such that $x.f$ is not empty, i.e., $\exists x \in A \bullet x.f \neq \{\}$.

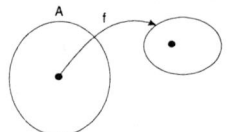

Figure 23 - Existential quantification

4.3 Navigation

So far, we have only considered single-arrow navigation expressions. In Figure 24, there is a two-arrow navigation expression $x.f.g$. This is interpreted as $\{y : g(x.f, y)\}$; we apply g to each element of the derived set $x.f$.

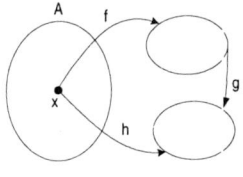

Furthermore, the set obtained by navigating from x via arrows f and g is the same as that obtained by navigating from x along h. Thus we have $x.f.g = x.h$.

In Figure 1, we had a similar expression involving a constraint on a library system. One of the key strengths of constraint diagrams is their ability to illustrate diagrammatically navigation expressions and the relationships between them.

Figure 24 - Navigation

5. Issues and Further Work

The formal semantics of spider diagrams, with the exception of projections, are given in (Gil, Howse, Kent 1999). Diagrammatic inference rules have been developed for spider diagrams along with rules for combining spider diagrams (Howse, Molina, Taylor, Kent 1999).

There are, however, some difficult issues to be considered before the formal semantics of constraint diagrams can be given fully. As mentioned earlier, there are some fascinating mathematical intricacies involving interacting projections. For example,

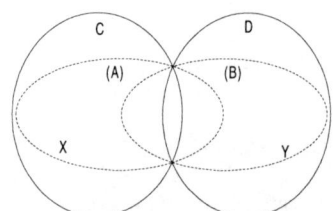

Figure 25 – Interacting projections

consider Figure 25. X and Y are the labels of the projected contours and A and B are the projected sets. How do we interpret X and Y?

By the definition of projected contours, we have two simultaneous set equations in X and Y:

$$X = A \cap (C \cup Y)$$
$$Y = B \cap (D \cup X)$$

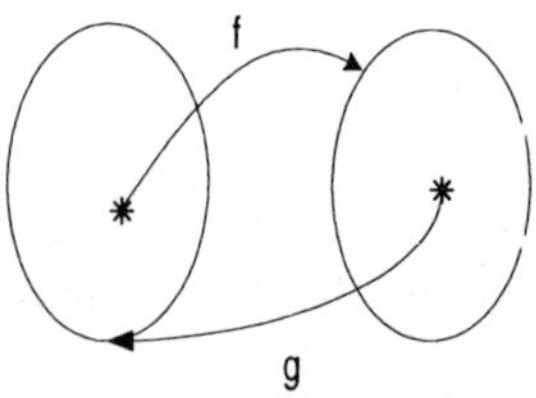

These can be solved using a form of Gaussian elimination and some results from set theory. Unfortunately, there are many possible solutions. There is, however, a unique "minimal solution" in this case:

$$X = A \cap (C \cup B)$$
$$Y = B \cap (D \cup A)$$

This is the intuitive solution. The interpretation of interacting projections in general is still being investigated.

Figure 26 - Circularity

Another difficult issue is that of circularity. Consider Figure 26. Each contour is a derived contour defined in terms of the other contour. It is very difficult to interpret this and it is doubtful whether such a situation should be allowed.

A related difficulty is that of the ordering of quantifiers. In Figure 27, there are at least two logically different interpretations: $\forall x \in A, \exists y \in B \bullet x.f = y.g$ and $\exists y \in B, \forall x \in A \bullet x.f = y.g$. These are very different. In the second interpretation, it is the same y for each x, while in the first, each x may be associated with a different y.

We are developing a very sophisticated algorithm for capturing the intuitive semantics of a constraint diagram and translating it into a logical formula. One way of tackling the problems of circularity and the ordering of quantifiers is to insist that each quantifier is at a particular unique "level", and that any diagram not satisfying this condition is deemed to be not well-formed.

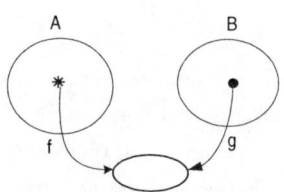

Figure 27 – Ordering of quantifiers

References

Euler, L. (1761) Lettres a Une Princesse d'Allemagne, Vol 2, Letters No. 102-108.

Gil, Y, Howse, J, Kent, S (1999) Formalizing Spider Diagrams, *Proceedings of VL99.*

Gil, Y. and Kent, S. (1998) Three Dimensional Software Modelling. *Proceedings of International Conference in Software Engineering 1998,* IEEE Computer Society Press.

Hammer, E.M. (1995) *Logic and Visual Information,* CSLI Publications.

Harel, D. (1998) On Visual Formalisms. In: Glasgow, J., Hari Narayanan, N. and Chandrasekaran, B., (Eds.) *Diagrammatic Reasoning,* pp. 235-271. MIT Press.

Howse, J, Molina, F, Taylor, J, Kent, S (1999b) Reasoning with Spider Diagrams, *Proceedings of VL99.*

Kent, S. (1997) Constraint Diagrams: Visualising Invariants in Object Oriented Models. *Proceedings of OOPSLA97,* ACM Press.

Kent, S. and Gil, Y. (1998) Visualising Action Contracts in OO Modelling. *IEE Proceedings: Software* 145.

Lauder, A. and Kent, S. (1998) Precise Visual Specification of Design Patterns. *Proceedings of ECOOP98,* Springer Verlag.

Lull, R. (1517) *Ars Magma,* Lyons.

OMG (1997) UML 1.1. Specification. *OMG Documents ad970802-ad970809.*

Peirce, C. (1933) *Collected Papers,* Harvard University Press.

Shin, S.-J. (1994) *The Logical Status of Diagrams,* CUP.

Venn, J. (1880) On the Diagrammatic and Mechanical Representation of Propositions and Reasonings. *Phil.Mag.* 123.

Warmer, J. and Kleppe, A. (1998) The Object Constraint Language: Precise Modeling with UML, Addison-Wesley.

Advanced OO Modelling:
Metamodels and Notations for the Next Millenium

Brian Henderson-Sellers

University of Technology, Sydney, Australia

Building an object-oriented model requires knowledge of process and techniques. Representing the model itself requires the use of a notation underpinned by a rigorous definition. Today this underpinning usually starts with a metamodel. Together, the metamodel and the notation are known as a "modelling language". Two modelling languages are described, discussed and compared: OML (the OPEN Modelling Language) and UML (the Unified Modeling Language). Advanced use of both languages is described particularly for concepts such as roles, for stereotypes and for aggregations, associations and other relationships.

Brian Henderson-Sellers is Director of the Centre for Object Technology Applications and Research and Professor of Information Systems at University of Technology, Sydney (UTS). He is author of eight books on object technology and is well-known for his work in OO methodologies (MOSES, COMMA and OPEN) and in OO metrics.

Brian is also Regional Editor of Object-Oriented Systems, a member of the editorial board of Object Magazine/Component Strategies and Object Expert for many years, Founder of the Object-Oriented Special Interest Group of the Australian Computer Society (NSW Branch) and Chairman of the Computerworld Object Developers' Awards committee for ObjectWorld 94 and 95 (Sydney). He is a frequent, invited speaker at international OT conferences.

Analysis by Contract:
An Introduction to Precise OO Modeling with UML and OCL

Richard Mitchell

University of Brighton, UK

It is easy to be abstract (draw bubbles). It is easy to be precise (write code). It is harder to be precise whilst remaining abstract. The tutorial aims to lay a firm foundation for being both abstract and precise, by showing how the principles of design by contract can be applied to analysis-level models.

At the heart of the UML are a number of visual modeling notations for describing classes, states, and so on. The UML also contains an Object Constraint Language, OCL, for adding precision to models. OCL can be used to add preconditions, postconditions and invariants to classes or types, allowing the precision of design by contract to be applied at any level of abstraction. The precision that this affords will be increasingly important as the software industry moves further towards component-based development.

The tutorial will introduce the key features of OCL. By means of a small case study in object-oriented analysis, it will then show how OCL can be used to add precision to analysis-level models. The case study will emphasise:

- why types are a suitable analysis-level abstraction
- how type models can provide a vocabulary for modeling
- how type models can be improved with invariants
- how state modeling can support analysis-level modeling
- how state models and type models can be cross-checked
- how behavior can be expressed using preconditions and postconditions.

Richard Mitchell is Professor of Computing at the University of Brighton, UK, where he has been teaching and researching object technology since the 1980s. His research addresses the use of contracts at all levels of software development. He is a member of the "Amsterdam group", a group of six experts on OCL. The group is formulating proposed revisions to OCL and UML, to be presented to the OMG.

Richard is a qualified instructor for Catalysis, an advanced methodology that embodies the principles of design by contract at all levels of modeling, and is targeted at component-based development. Richard is working with Jim McKim on a book about design by contract. He is a member of the recently-formed Trusted Components project, and he is Chair of the Programme Committee for TOOLS Europe 2000.

Analysis by Contract
or
UML with Attitude

Richard Mitchell

University of Brighton
Brighton BN2 4GJ, UK
<Richard.Mitchell@brighton.ac.uk>

Abstract

This paper summarises a tutorial entitled Analysis by Contract. Using fragments from a simple case study concerning a video store, the paper shows how a type model can provide the vocabulary needed to specify the behaviour of a video store system. Behaviour is modelled as events, such as the renting of a video by a member of the video store. It also shows how state models can be used to enrich the vocabulary of the type model.

The specifications of behaviour are in the form of contracts, with preconditions and postconditions. The "with attitude" part of the sub-title comes from the use of the Object Constraint Language to express the contracts, and to cross-reference the vocabulary of the state models to the vocabulary of the type models.

1. Introduction

The Unified Modeling Language—UML—provides a wide range of diagrammatic and textual notations (Booch, Jacobson and Rumbaugh 1998). It also provides a general mechanism for attaching constraints to individual elements of models. From its early days, it had placeholders for writing the kinds of constraints associated with design by contract: preconditions, postconditions and invariants (Meyer 1992). Now it has a formal notation for writing such assertions—OCL, the Object Constraint Language (Warmer and Kleppe 1998). This makes it possible to combine navigation expressions over a class diagram and constraints in OCL, in order to express properties of a model with great precision. Think of the addition of OCL to the original UML as allowing you to write 'UML with attitude.'

There are several challenges for those wishing to build precise models. One is to find and maintain a suitable level of abstraction—it is easy to be pulled downwards to the familiar world of programming languages in order to achieve precision. Another is to make sure that different kinds of modelling (static structure, behaviour specifications, state models, and so on) are cross-referenced, to ensure that they contribute to a single underlying model.

Using extracts from a small case study, this paper explores how these challenges can be met. It does not propose a method with an underlying process. Rather, it explores the technical background against which a development process could be defined. It shows how the ideas of design by contract can be applied during analysis.

The case study concerns a system to support the operation of a video store. Section 2 presents the requirements for the system. Section 3 shows a first attack on the problem of finding a level of abstraction, by showing how the problem can be divided into domains, along subject boundaries and along technical boundaries. Section 4 briefly describes the chosen approach to modelling behaviour, in which the static structure can be thought of as

0-7695-0278-4/99 $10.00 © 1999 IEEE

the vocabulary to be used to describe the behaviour. In Section 5, the approach is applied to the case study, leading to fragments of models using UML with OCL. The OCL notation is explained as it is needed. Section 6 explores how models can be connected. State models can provide extra vocabulary, and this extra vocabulary can be anchored to the static model. Then the combined vocabulary can be used to model behaviour. Section 7 briefly shows one way to remain abstract when we need to model communication between domains. Section 8 summarises the key points.

2. The case study

Here is a brief description of the operation of a video store. It is intended to provide the starting point for analysis-level modelling.

"A video store rents and sells videos. Only members can rent videos; anyone can buy videos. The store makes a rental video available for sale when it is no longer earning sufficient rental income. To become a member, you pay a fee and receive a membership card with your membership number on it in the form of a barcode.

Videos can be rented for 1 or 3 days. The daily rate for a 3-day rental is lower than for a 1-day rental. Videos returned late incur a penalty fee for each day late. This fee is set higher than the 1-day rate. Members who owe penalty fees may be forbidden to rent further videos until the fees have been paid.

Members can reserve a video that is currently not available to rent. When a video becomes available, a notice is sent to the member holding the reservation, asking him or her to collect the video within 3 days. A video not collected within 3 days is returned to the rental pool."

Before we begin modelling, we need to be reasonably clear about what we are modelling. Are we modelling the way the video store business operates now, or as we would like it to operate after we have put a computer-based system in place? Or are we modelling the computer-based system itself? To keep the example simple, we shall choose to build parts of a high-level model of a computer-based system. So, for instance, our static model will be an abstract view of the model the system is to maintain about the state of the outside world.

3. Domains

One of the principal benefits of abstraction is that it allows us to reduce the amount we need to think about at any one time. For example, we know that videos can only be rented to members. That means we must think about how people become members, how the store acquires videos to rent, and what happens when an existing member rents one of the store's videos. But we do not have to think about the details of all of these three aspects of the video store at once. We can divide the problem into a number of domains, each of which can be studied in detail separately from the other domains.

Figure 1 shows just five of the possible domains, modelled as UML packages. There are dependencies between the domains (only some of which are shown). Someone modelling the rentals aspect of the video store will know that you can only rent videos that are part of your inventory, and then only to people who are members and who make appropriate payments. But a model concerned with rentals need not be concerned with details of how people become members.

468

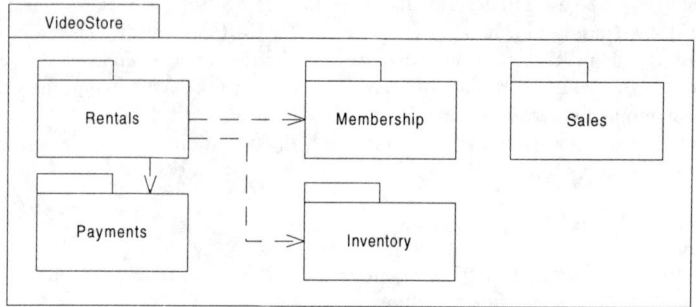

Figure 1. Five possible subject domains.

From now on, we shall call domains such as these *subject domains*, since they are concerned with different aspects of the subject matter of what we must model. There is another dimension along which we might provide different domains of modelling, which we shall call *technical domains*. Figure 2 shows a number of possible technical domains. At the heart of the system is a core domain, which might also be called the business domain. Here, we abstract away from technical issues such as user interfaces, peripheral devices and storage systems. Someone must model the components of a graphical user interface (dialog boxes, buttons, and so on). That someone might be in another company, from which we buy a GUI library. Then, in the interaction domain, we consider how users interact with the core, using GUI components (by pressing buttons, filling text fields, reading scroll lists, and so on).

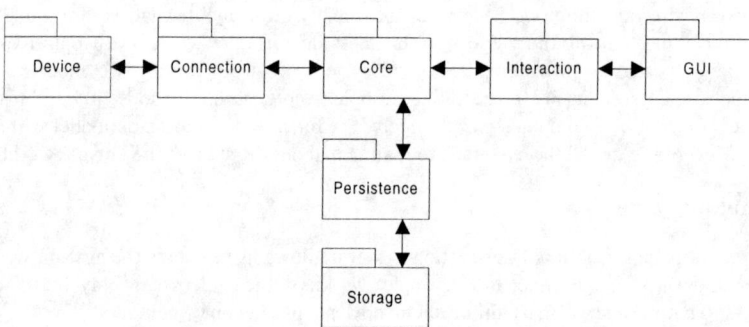

Figure 2. *Seven possible technical domains.*

Similarly, we might buy devices such as a barcode reader, complete with device drivers. Then, in the connection domain, we address the problem of mapping barcodes into core domain concepts such as members and videos. And we might choose to store objects in a relational database, which we already own. Then, in the persistence domain, we address the problem of mapping core objects to and from storage in relational tables.

The domains are not independent. But they can be treated as separate engineering problems. For example, the problem of identifying a member from a scanned barcode is a problem we can address separately from the problem of enumerating the business rules to be applied when a member wants to rent a video.

From now on, we shall concentrate on the core technical domain within the rentals subject domain. That means we shall not be concerned with barcodes, membership rules, database choices, and so on.

4. Modelling with objects and events

We can use domains to limit how much we try to model at any one moment. Now we need to decide how to model. Here is one approach. We can think of the world as made up of two kinds of things: 'things that are,' and 'things that happen.' We model 'things that are' using objects. We model 'things that happen' using events. The objects have properties (local attributes and links to other objects). The events change the properties of the objects.

Another way to think about the approach is to see the objects as giving us the vocabulary we need in order to describe what really interests us, which is behaviour. And we model behaviour as events.

Yet another way to think about the approach is in terms of an underlying model of time, such as the one described in (Jackson 1995), which is illustrated in Figure 3. This shows a timeline, with time increasing from left to right. Each vertical line represents a moment in time at which the state of the world changes. In between the vertical lines, the world remains in some state for a period of time. We model the state of the world using objects, and the changes using events. (Of course, this model of time, and hence the use of events for modelling, are not appropriate for all aspects of all systems, such as aspects of process control systems.)

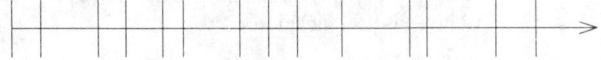

Figure 3. *A model of time.*

When we are modelling the core of a system, the events that interest us are those events happening in the world that are to affect the system. For example, suppose that we are building the system for an individual video store called LowPrice. Then we must model the core so that the event 'Kim rents copy 12 of Shakespeare In Love from LowPrice at 8.30 p.m. on August 4th, 1999, paying $4.50 in cash' is an event that changes the state of the system. But the event 'Kim borrows $5 from Heidi in order to go to LowPrice to rent Shakespeare In Love' is one that we can ignore.

We shall, of course, classify the objects and events, into types. So we shall model with object types such as *Member* and *Copy*, and event types such as *rent* and *return*.

Examples of how we model with event types and object types are coming up next, in Section 5. Section 8 discusses why we use event and object types, rather than operations and classes. But it will do no harm if you think of the object types as classes, and the event types as operations on a top-level system object.

5. A first taste of analysis by contract

In practice, we might spend some time just gathering information about our client's business and recording it informally, before attempting any modelling. For example, we could gather a list of terms used by those describing the business, and loosely classify them into 'things that are' and 'things that happen.' However, it will make the connection between object types and event types clearer if, in this paper, we build our models by a process that would not work in practice, because it records the models formally from the beginning. Strictly speaking, formal models can only be formalisations of things we understand informally.

We'll illustrate the approach by beginning to model the event type *rent*. (We'll talk about other types of event, such as *return*, *reserve* and *cancel*, but we shall not model them.) We'll begin modelling *rent* by identifying which objects we must know about for us to be able to discuss the effects of an event of this type. Whenever there is a *rent* event, we need to know in which video store it took place, who the member was, which video copy the member rented, what the time and date were, and how much money was paid. So the signature of an event of type *rent* is this:

> rent(vs : VideoStore, m : Member, c : Copy, t : Timepoint, payment : Money)
>   *-- Member m rents copy c from video store vs at time t, paying 'payment'*

We have identified that we need to talk about five types of objects (*VideoStore, Member, Copy, Timepoint* and *Money*).

Let us start work on a precondition for *rent*. Informally, we cannot rent a copy that is not part of our inventory, and we cannot rent it to someone who is not one of our members. We want to say:

> pre: *-- m is one of the members of vs*
>   vs.members -> includes(m)
>
>   and
>
>   *-- c is one of the copies in the inventory of vs*
>   vs.inventory -> includes(c)

This fragment of a precondition uses OCL syntax. Lines beginning '--' are comments. The expression "vs.members -> includes(m)" says that *m* is in the set *vs.members*. The fragment introduces new terms (*members* and *inventory*). This is because it talks about relationships between types of objects. Figure 4 shows a UML class diagram that captures the object types and their relationships that we have talked about so far. In other words, Figure 4 provides the vocabulary for the signature and precondition of the event type *rent*.

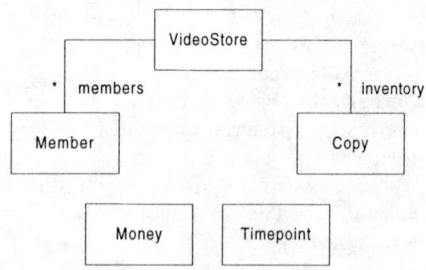

Figure 4. *An early model of object types*

The precondition is not finished. We need to say that you cannot rent a video copy that is already out on rent. The copy must be in the store. In fact, the constraint is more complicated than that. A copy could be in the store but not available to member Kim to rent because member Heidi has made a reservation. The informal requirements say that "Members can reserve a video that is currently not available to rent," but analysis has revealed that it is video *titles* that members reserve, and video *copies* that they rent. When a member holds a reservation for a title, we shall say that a copy with that title can be put *onHold* for the member. A copy that is in the store but not on hold will be *onShelf*.

These new terms we have introduced, *onHold* and *onShelf*, model different states that a copy can be in. Figure 5 shows an unfinished state model for objects of type *Copy*. The model uses some existing vocabulary: the state transitions are triggered by events of the types we listed earlier. The model also provides us with some new vocabulary: it introduces the terms *onHold*, *onShelf* and *rented*, which we can use when specifying behaviour. We now have the vocabulary to say that a member can rent a copy if the copy is on the shelf or if the copy is on hold against a reservation made by the member. In practice, the activity of constructing state models often reveals new states the objects can be in (for example, a copy can be lost).

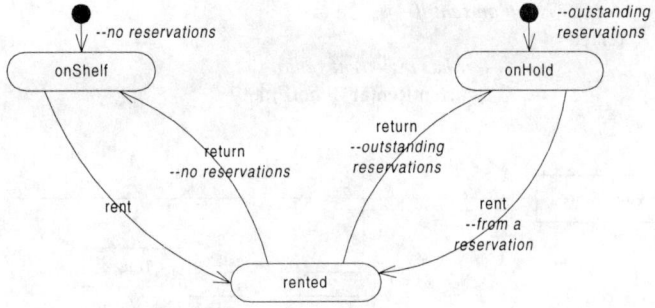

Figure 5. *An early state model for Copy.*

Standing back from the details, we see that we are modelling behaviour (by specifying event types) using a vocabulary given by types of objects and the states they can be in. To illustrate the relationships between event types, object types and object states more clearly, we are going to show some richer models resulting from more analysis, and use them to discuss cross-referencing of models.

6. Relationships amongst models

In this section, we shall see how the vocabulary of state models can be defined in terms of the type model. Then we shall see how all this vocabulary can be used to specify an event.

Figure 6 shows a richer type model, providing many more words for us to use in specifying events. (We shall not show all the state models that enrich this type model.)

In particular, the model shows us that a copy might or might not be linked to a current rental, and can be a held copy for zero or more reservations. (Reservations become fulfillable when there is a copy on hold for the member to collect. If, for example, three members hold reservations for the same title, there can be up to three copies on hold against these reservations. The model does not tie individual copies on hold to the individual reservations.) As copies pass through the states *onShelf*, *onHold* and *rented*, the values of these links must change. We can formally specify the connection between the states and the type model, as follows:

472

<u>c : Copy</u>

    -- A copy is on the shelf, available for rent if
    c.onShelf =
                  -- it does not have a current rental
                  c.currentRental -> isEmpty
                  -- and it is not on hold for a reservation
                  and c.~heldCopies -> isEmpty

and

    -- a copy is on hold for a reservation if
    c. onHold =
                  -- it does not have a current rental
                  c.currentRental -> isEmpty
                  -- but it is on hold for a reservation
                  and c.~heldCopies -> notEmpty

and

    -- a copy is out on rent if
    c.rented =
                  -- it has a current rental
                  c.currentRental -> notEmpty

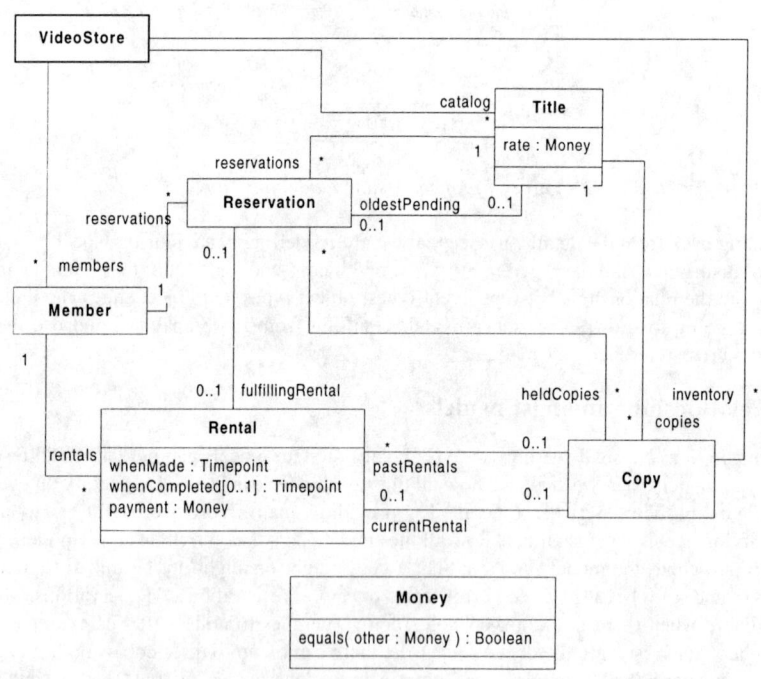

Figure 6. *A richer type model*

The left-hand sides of the three equations use terms from the state model for copies, whereas the right-hand sides use terms from the object type model. The result is that the three states of copies are now fully defined in terms of the object type model. In practice, the activity of defining states like this usually reveals that the object type model needs enriching, often with quite subtle detail, in order to be able to distinguish all states.

Now we can use the vocabulary of the object type model, augmented by the vocabulary of the state model, in order to specify an event type. Here is the specification of the *rent* event type. It uses some additional OCL operators: *select* selects a subset of elements with a given property, *exists* is the 'there exists' quantifier, and the @ operator gives us access to earlier states (especially the state in which the *pre*condition was evaluated). The specification also uses some proposed changes to OCL (the proposals come from OCL's designers): *isNew* can be used in postconditions to test whether an object is a new object in the state after an event; *let...in* is a construct for making local definitions.

rent(vs : VideoStore, m : Member, c : Copy, t : Timepoint, payment : Money)
  -- Member m rents copy c from video store vs at time t, paying 'payment'
pre:
   -- The member and the copy are known to the video store
   vs.members -> includes(m) and vs.inventory -> includes(c)
   -- and the copy is on the shelf, available for anyone to rent or
   and (c.onShelf or
       -- is on hold ...
      (c.onHold
      -- ... for member m (i.e., m has a fulfillable reservation for c)
      and c.~heldCopies -> select(fulfillable) -> exists(v | v.member = m)))
   -- and the payment is correct for this title
   and payment.equals(c.title.rate)
post:
   -- There is a new rental object
   Rental.allInstances -> includes(r : Rental | r.isNew

     -- which is a rental by member m of copy c at time t
     and r.member = m and r.~currentRental = c and r.whenMade = t
     -- for a payment of 'payment'
     and r.payment = payment
     -- and which has no 'whenCompleted' date and which is not a past rental
     and r.whenCompleted -> isEmpty and r.~pastRentals -> isEmpty

     -- and if the copy had been on hold for m against a reservation then
     and c.onHold@pre implies
       let
          -- m's (relevant) reservation is fulfilled
         fulfilledReservation =
            c.~heldCopies -> select(v | v.member = m)
       in
          -- and it is r that fulfils this reservation
         fulfilledReservation.fulfillingRental = r
     -- otherwise r has no fulfilling reservation
     and not c.onHold@pre implies r.~fulfillingReservation -> isEmpty)

Once again, in practice, the activity of defining behaviour this precisely usually reveals the need for additional vocabulary, uncovering subtleties that are very helpful to an analyst.

Before leaving this discussion of cross-referencing models, it is worth mentioning that OCL can be used to write precise invariants over object type models, which can be thought of as cross-referencing one part of a model against another. For example, invariants can:

- reduce the range of object snapshots that are allowed (for instance, an invariant can constrain every rental object to being a current rental or a past rental but not both)
- define redundant properties in terms of existing ones (for instance, the model in Figure 6 includes an *oldestPending* association between titles and reservations. This is useful in defining which reservation becomes fulfillable when a copy is returned. It can be defined in terms of other model properties such as timestamps on the reservations (not shown in Figure 6). If our client talks in terms of the 'oldest pending reservation' then so should we, in our models, and an invariant can define the term.)

7. On remaining abstract

This short section tries to show that the architectural model of domains is more than a starting point for analysis. It can support modular specification, and, if desired, a corresponding implementation. If we use domains carefully, they can help us remain appropriately abstract.

The original outline requirements said, "When a video becomes available, a notice is sent to the member holding the reservation, asking him or her to collect the video within 3 days." How should we model the sending of a notice to a member, when we are considering only the core of the system? There is a simple answer, but it illustrates an important modelling principle. The answer is that we need an object type called, say, Notice. In the postcondition of event types such as *return* we model "a notice is sent to a member" by asserting that a new object of type Notice is created, and linked to a reservation. And we say no more.

The modelling principle is that each technical domain is responsible for a certain kind of detail. The core domain is not concerned with details of printing and posting notices (or emailing them, or generating telephone call lists, or ...). Somewhere else, in a CustomerCommunication domain, perhaps, we can specify that every time a Notice object is created it is turned into a printed letter. (When we come to design the system, the CustomerCommunication domain could be built as a separate sub-system, and connected to the core using the kind of event notification that underpins the Observer pattern (Gamma, Helm, Johnson and Vlissides 1995).)

Separating different aspects of how notices are dealt with into different domains can make it difficult to show that a single requirement in a requirements document is actually being properly expressed in the models. Collins-Cope (1999) proposes separating requirements (usually expressed textually) from user interface issues, and goes on to show how both can be related to the core services of the system (which we are modelling as event types). The relationships between requirements, services and interface elements are many-to-many.

In Collins-Cope's terms, the words in quotes near the beginning of this section about sending a notice are a requirement. This requirement is related to several services. One such service is modelled by the *return* event type in the core domain, whose postcondition asserts that a new Notice is created. Another is the event that turns Notice objects into documents for printing. Somewhere else, we can show the design of a user interface that gives the user access to these services in an appropriate way.

8. Discussion

The preceding sections have shown how a model expressed using UML diagrams can be expressed more formally, and so more precisely, with the aid of OCL. The following characteristics of the approach are the important ones (the words in brackets are the way we achieved the characteristics—other choices could be equally good):

- We developed an architecture for the modelling, so that we could work on different parts of the modelling separately (we divided the problem up using subject domains and technical domains, and hinted at how inter-domain connections might be captured).
- We knew when we were defining new terms and when we were using existing terms (we defined a vocabulary in the object type model, and used it to specify behaviour by writing event specifications).
- We cross-referenced models built from different points of view (object type models present a 'panoramic view' of many object types; state models 'zoom in' on a single object type. We defined the states very precisely in terms of the object type model).

The same ideas can be used at lower levels of abstraction, nearer to the eventual code that implements the system. Indeed, it is not necessary to climb to the high levels of abstraction we have been using in order to find places to add precision to models. Eiffel programmers are very used to adding assertions to their classes and methods (Meyer 1997).

The architecture for the specification might or might not be the architecture for the implemented system. For example, we could build a system in which the subject domains became subsystems within a federated architecture, each maintaining its own version of, say, the membership list. The different versions of the list would not be identical in content: different subsystems would need different properties of members. A change notification mechanism could allow the membership subsystem to bring other subsystems up-to-date with relevant changes. Alternatively, we could treat the subject domains as divisions only within the specification, and we could combine what we learn about members from several different domains before building a system around a single membership list.

There are arguments for and against modelling using separate domains. An advantage of modelling in separate domains is that it allows modellers to focus their efforts. A danger is that the structure of the models will be taken (perhaps unconsciously) to be the subsystem structure of the implementation, even though the domains might not have been chosen to be suitable parts of an implementation. By delaying the identification of parts of the overall domain, we avoid premature decisions about system structure, but make the modelling process more difficult.

Sometimes, it is possible to decide the subsystem structure of the implementation before modelling begins, so the architecture of the specification mirrors the chosen architecture of the system. Then, we can have a more seamless process, but we begin modelling at a lower level of abstraction.

We chose to model with types of objects and types of events. The choice of object types over classes is mostly a matter of terminology. When we think about what behaviour we want from a certain kind of object, we are thinking about its type properties (types are for specifying). We write code in classes to provide those properties (classes are for implementing). The choice of events over operations is also not critical, but behind it is an important modelling choice. If we think of the types of events such as *rent* as being operations on a video store system (rather than events a video store must react to) it makes almost no difference to our models (except, perhaps, to make it harder to build models before deciding what parts of the business to automate, and to lead us towards a particular design in which a video store object is a façade in front of the other objects). However, it would be different if we added operations to any of the other types. For us, there is a design step in which we decide which type of object will do what in order to provide the behaviour of the whole system. We do not want to make design decisions of this kind whilst performing analysis.

We have deliberately avoided discussion of the difficult topic of connecting the vocabulary in models to the outside world. No matter how much precision you add to UML models, there is an informal world out there that your models are related to. There is no way to formalise that world. You do not have the choice of making the people who visit a video store into formal entities. They will always be people. There is an excellent introduction to the topic of grounding models in the world in (Jackson 1995), under the heading of designations.

The ideas expressed in this tutorial paper come from many sources. They are most directly expressed in course material from InferData Corporation (1999), which, in turn, builds on earlier work, particularly Fusion and Syntropy. The Fusion method (Coleman, Arnold, Bodoff, Dollin, Gilchrist, Hayes and Jeremaes 1994) was a significant step in the development of methods—it showed clearly that specification models could be freed from many design decisions. Syntropy (Cook and Daniels 1994) showed the power of using events to model behaviour, and showed how state models and type models could support each other. Catalysis (D'Souza and Wills 1998) makes the role of a type model as a vocabulary clear, and goes much further than previous methods in achieving precision in modelling at many levels of abstraction.

Acknowledgements

I thank Vladimir Bacvanski, Petter Graff, Benedict Heal and Ted Velkoff for their helpful comments on earlier drafts. I gratefully acknowledge support from InferData Corporation, and the Distributed Systems and Software Engineering Unit at Monash University.

References

Booch G, Jacobson I and Rumbaugh R (1998). *The Unified Modeling Language User Guide*. Addison Wesley.

Coleman D, Arnold P, Bodoff S, Dollin C, Gilchrist H, Hayes F and Jeremaes P (1994). *Object-oriented development. The Fusion method*. Prentice Hall.

Collins-Cope M (1999). *The Requirements/Service/Interface (RSI) Approach to Use Case Analysis*. In Mitchell R, Wills A, Bosch J and Meyer B (editors). Proceedings of TOOLS 29. IEEE.

Cook S and Daniels J (1994). *Designing object systems. Object-oriented modelling with Syntropy*. Prentice Hall.

D'Souza D and Wills A (1998). *Objects, Components and Frameworks with UML: The Catalysis Approach*. Addison Wesley.

Gamma E, Helm R, Johnson R and Vlissides J (1994). *Design Patterns*. Addison Wesley.

InferData Corporation (1999). *Object-Oriented Analysis and Design Course Notes*. InferData Corporation, Austin, Texas.

Jackson M (1995). *Software Requirements & Specifications: a lexicon of practice, principles and prejudices*. Addison Wesley.

Meyer B (1992). *Applying Design by Contract*. IEEE Computer, 25(10), pp40-52.

Meyer B (1997). *Object-Oriented Software Construction*. Prentice Hall (2nd edition).

Warmer J and Kleppe A (1998). *The Object Constraint Language - Precise Modeling with UML*. Addison Wesley.

Tutorials

Experience

Design of Commercial Object-Oriented Applications - The Patterns

Frieder Monninger
Object Tools GmbH, Germany

The tutorial describes the techniques used to develop a typical commercial application (just like a thousand others) - a multiuser order processing and production control package for a medium-size company, based on a relational database, with a large number of Windows clients.

The main objective was not just building this particular application but designing strategies to produce this type of application in a general way using a "object oriented cookbook". So the most important result is a collection of patterns especially targeted at this type of application, together with the associated generators; a "Toolkit for generating a business application".

Using such a cookbook it is possible to design and generate "everyday" commercial applications very fast - but still produce very general, maintainable and extendable software.

The tutorial will point out not only the final recipe but also the way it was found and the dangerous pitfalls to avoid. It will help the participants to see a familiar activity in a new light.

Frieder Monninger has 25 years experience with object oriented programming, and has presented many seminars related to OO. During the last few years he has been working on object oriented rapid prototyping. He is co-author of the Visual Eiffel environment.

Octopus/UML: An Object-Oriented Method Used in Industry

Rallis Farfarakis
Nokia Research Center, Finland

This tutorial will present the Octopus/UML method, which addresses the specific needs of software development projects for embedded real-time systems, for example, how to deal with the events issued by the external world. Moreover, the method is object-oriented because adopting object-oriented technology can help in the software development of real-time systems in a way that more naturally maps to the inherent nature of the systems being built, while providing benefits similar to those already well known and widely reported for the development of other branches of software, such as ease of maintenance and reuse.

Rallis Farfarakis works as a research engineer at Nokia Research Center. His present responsibilities include the education and promotion of object technology within Nokia. He is currently involved in projects with Nokia Telecommunications such as Base Station software development. He has also participated in projects with Rolls Royce Aerospace and Nokia Mobile Phones. His research interests include software engineering environments, object-oriented modelling and object-oriented development of telecommunication systems. He holds an M.Phil. in Software Engineering.

Octopus/UML: Combining Objects with Real-Time

Rallis Farfarakis
Nokia Research Center, P.O. Box 407,FIN-00045,
NOKIA GROUP, Helsinki, Finland.
Tel: + 358 40 5683437 Fax: + 358 9 4376 6308
E-mail: rallis.farfarakis@nokia.com

Abstract

This paper presents important concepts and the main development phases within the Octopus/UML method; an object-oriented software development method specialised for embedded real-time systems. The Octopus/UML method addresses the specific needs of software projects for embedded real-time systems. Real-time systems are widely used in industrial, commercial and military areas. Octopus/UML, as the name suggests, encompasses the Unified Modeling Language (UML) as its main supporting notation. Octopus/UML is a practical development method based on feedback received from Nokia projects using the method and research in the areas of object orientation and real-time systems.

1. Introduction

Octopus/UML is a practical object-oriented software development method for embedded real-time systems. The method is an improvement of the original Octopus method [1]. Octopus is the brainchild of Nokia Research Center, Helsinki. Since 1993, there has been constant development and refinement of the method resulting from feedback from projects and scientific research within Nokia. Several projects have applied the method, ongoing projects are currently applying it, and new projects using Octopus/UML are planned. The projects vary in length and context. Nokia is a major international telecommunications company and the projects involve mobile and fixed communications technology.

The Octopus/UML method addresses the specific needs of software projects for embedded real-time systems. Real-time systems are widely used in industrial, commercial and military areas. Characteristics of real-time software systems include embedded nature, interaction with external environment, timing constraints, real-time control and reactivity [2].

Embedded real-time software is unique because of the fact that it is tightly coupled to the physical environment. With the use of sensing and actuating devices, the control software senses and changes the state of its environment. An example of this is a computerised automobile cruise control system embedded in the automobile.

The primary focus of this paper is on the development phases that Octopus/UML proposes. It aims to present some of the core concepts of Octopus/UML that have been developed based on industrial experience gained over the past six years, continuous feedback from Nokia projects and extensive research in the specific fields of object-orientation and real-time.

2. Core concepts in Octopus/UML

In Octopus/UML, the main core concepts are an artifact, a facility, an attachment, a phase, a model and the notation.

2.1. Artifact

"An artifact describes a sensible and valuable piece of information, consisting of the aim, the semantics, the supporting notation and the template" [4].

A number of well-defined artifacts can be produced by applying Octopus/UML (see Table 1). With the help of these artifacts the designer captures, expresses and communicates essential development results in concrete terms.

Each artifact is defined for an individual purpose. However, looking at individual artifacts in isolation is not intended, since, the real value stems from using the artifacts in collaboration. The set of artifacts, the guidelines to produce one, the links from one to another and the recommended order to proceed, provides the means for an effective development progress.

To produce a certain artifact one must follow the guidelines. Each artifact uses at least one notation that must be applied to produce it. Some artifacts can be produced by applying one out of an alternative list of notations. The same notation can be used for many artifacts. Wherever feasible, the notation suggested is the UML notation [3]. There is a strict difference in Octopus/UML between the artifact and the notation applied to it.

In order to achieve a specific goal at a certain stage during development, more than one artifact may be required. The artifacts identified should be closely related to each other. The development sequence visualises this by defining phases and models that structure and manage the progress of development work based on the artifacts.

2.2. Facility

"A facility is an optional work product similar to an artifact but its content is of secondary importance" [4]. Facilities are used to help developers organise and manage more efficiently the software development (see Table 1). In cases where the information is quite complex, facilities assist in reducing ambiguities and inconsistencies.

2.3. Attachment

"An attachment is separate from the artifact, but is closely linked to it. It is used in cases where it is advisable to explain or describe some items of the artifact in more detail" [4].

Table 1. Phases, Models, Artifacts and Facilities [9].

Phase	Model	Artifact	Facility
System Requirements Specification	Use Case	Use Case Sheet.	Use Case Diagram. System Scenario.
	Context	System Context Diagram.	
System Architecture	System Architecture	System Architecture Diagram. Responsibility Sheet. Inter-Subsystem Scenario.	
Subsystem Analysis	Structural	Analysis Class Diagram. Subsystem Interface Diagram.	
	Functional	Subsystem Operation Sheet.	Subsystem Operation Diagram.
	Dynamic	Event Sheet. Statechart Diagram. Significance Table.	Event List. Event Diagram. Statechart List. Subsystem Scenario.
Subsystem Design	Refined Structural	Design Class Diagram. Class Outline.	
	Interaction	Unqualified Event Thread. Qualified Event Thread. Inter-Process Message Outline.	Inter-Process Message List.
	Process	Grouped Event Thread. Process Function Outline.	Shared Object Table.
	Concurrency	Subsystem Preemption Table.	Subsystem Inter-Process Communication Diagram. Subsystem Inter-Process Scenario.

2.4.   Phase

In Octopus/UML, each phase has an aim which relates to a stage within software development. In order to achieve this, each phase requests to build at least one model (see Table 1). If within the phase several models are developed, then, each model is assigned a segment of the aim that this phase should accomplish.

The development sequence conducts the work to proceed from one phase to the next. A phase defines a work package producing some artifacts that, in an ideal case, should be completed before work on any of the artifacts of the next phase begins. However in praxis, work on subsequent phases may overlap. Starting the next phase is acceptable only when the artifacts of the earlier phase have been developed to a mature and stable level, thus providing the necessary inputs to the artifacts of the next phase.

Every phase contains a sequence which guides the developer in organising the production of artifacts within that phase. Even though phases may be serialised, the models inside a phase must always be developed in parallel. There are exceptions where models may be developed in a sequence, and thus, completion of at least one model will depend on completion of the previous ones.

2.5. Model

A phase requests to build at least one model (see Table 1). Each model defines a specific set of artifacts. The artifacts of a model are tightly related to each other. Only when browsing the complete set of artifacts, you will understand the model. During development, the designer should work on all of them in a balanced speed.

2.6. Notation

Octopus/UML adopts the Unified Modeling Language (UML) [3], as part of its supporting notation. Six different notations are used: the class diagram, the collaboration diagram, the statechart diagram, the sequence diagram, SDL/GR process diagram and outline syntax.

3. The system development pattern of Octopus/UML

Octopus/UML does not suggest a fixed sequence that all projects must follow. Rather a pattern is given, from which, each project is invited to configure its own sequence. The System Development Pattern (see Figure 1) may act as a guide when devising such sequences. This pattern provides a standard structure, allowing flexibility when adaptation to a project's needs is advantageous.

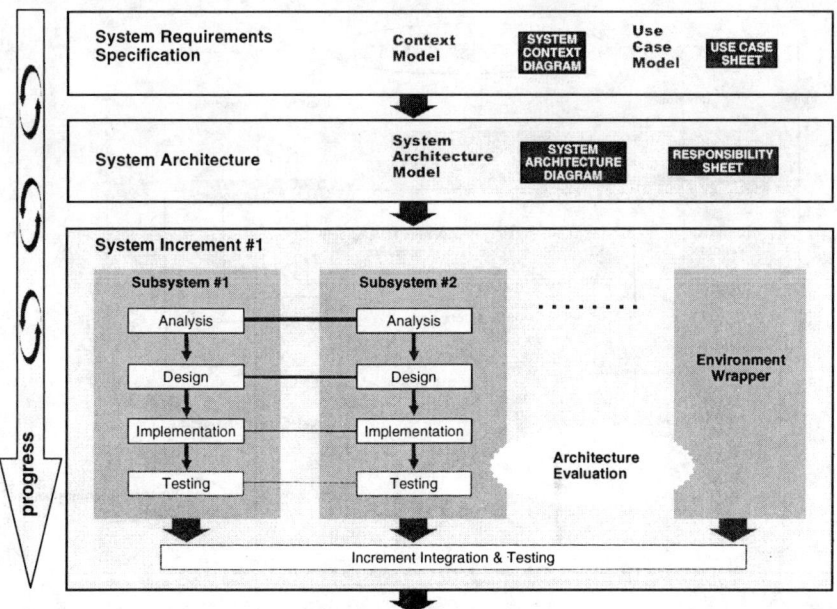

Figure 1. System Development Pattern [4].

484

4. The deployment of artifacts in phases

The way artifacts are linked and collaborate in the four distinct development phases of Octopus/UML, are presented in the following sections.

4.1. System Requirements Specification phase

In system requirements specification phase the requirements of the target software system are restructured, so that their representation supports the development of software. A number of artifacts are used to support this restructuring. The development sequence and the artifacts that can be developed, can be seen in Figure 2.

The system requirements specification phase is not intended to make the developer fully confident about all the system requirements. This phase uncovers the target software system with two limited goals in mind:

1. Product-related persons besides the software developers should be able to check if the software development is on the right track.

2. Enough information should be gathered, so that the subsequent system architecture is able to make a sensible decomposition of the system into software subsystems. Elaboration of the requirements must be achieved, starting from here till the subsystem analysis phase.

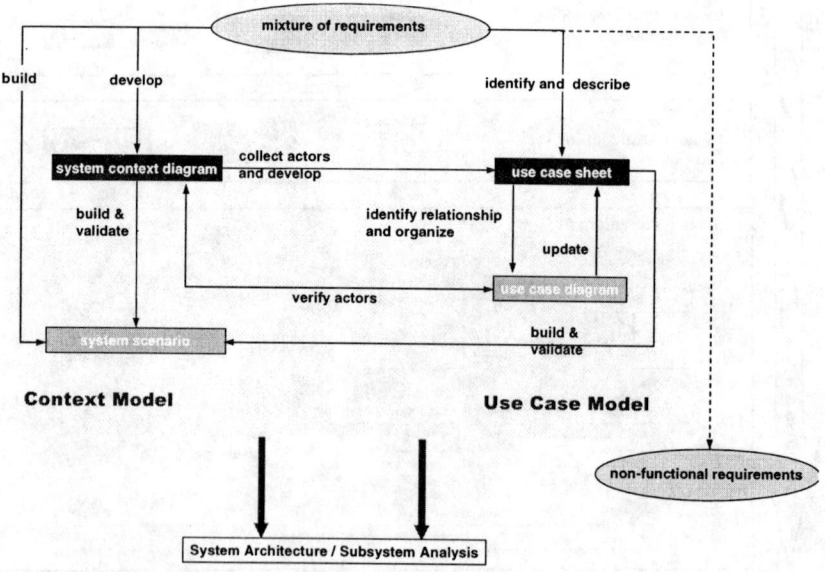

Figure 2. The System Requirements Specification Sequence [4].

4.2.   System Architecture phase

In system architecture phase, the system is decomposed into software subsystems. Each subsystem is represented as a black box and the client-server relationships between these subsystems are identified.

This work is mainly based on the knowledge gained during the system requirements specification phase. Application domains are the major decomposition criteria. A domain represents *"a separate real, hypothetical or abstract world inhabited by a distinct set of objects that behave according to the rules and policies characteristic of the domain"* [1]. Since domains are considered independent, system decomposition based on domains results in software subsystems that are loosely coupled and potentially distributed. Figure 3 presents the development sequence and the artifact interactions of this phase.

During the system architecture phase, further elaboration of the system requirements takes place. The completion of requirements definition is concentrated in the analysis phase of each software subsystem. The development within subsystems, is achieved in smaller packages at an early stage. A parallel development track is adopted and the advantages of the incremental and evolutionary models are being exploited throughout each increment. This combination of techniques outweighs the risk of making a non-optimal initial decomposition. Each system increment contains an informal architecture evaluation where corrective actions on the system architecture may be taken.

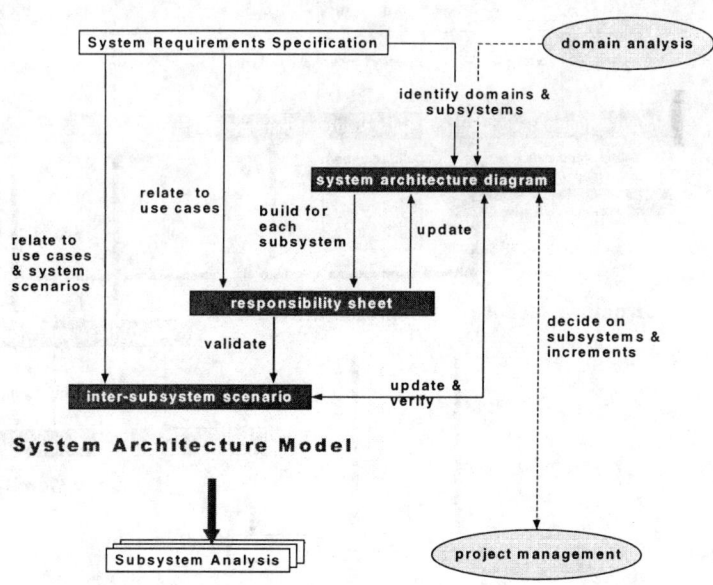

Figure 3. The System Architecture Sequence [4].

The system requirements specification phase presents the system in terms of use cases while the system architecture phase presents the system in terms of software subsystems. In order to ensure consistency and quality, system architecture demands a mapping of use cases into software subsystems and vice versa. If this mapping is difficult to achieve, or there is a one to one mapping almost everywhere, the resulting development work is questionable.

4.3.   Subsystem Analysis phase

During the subsystem analysis, the developer clarifies and documents what the subsystem is supposed to do. The artifacts to be produced, serve as a basis for a contract between the work the subsystem development team is responsible for, and the interfaces between this software subsystem and the neighbouring software subsystems. Approval of these artifacts is interpreted as a contract establishment. Thus, all other software subsystem development teams must carefully and seriously check these artifacts and vice versa.

The subsystem analysis demands to build the structural, functional and dynamic models. These models focus on what the subsystem is supposed to do, and not how it should do it. The operational internals and structure of the subsystem is deferred to the design of the subsystem, with the exception of the structural model, which defines the classes (concepts) of the subsystem and their associations.

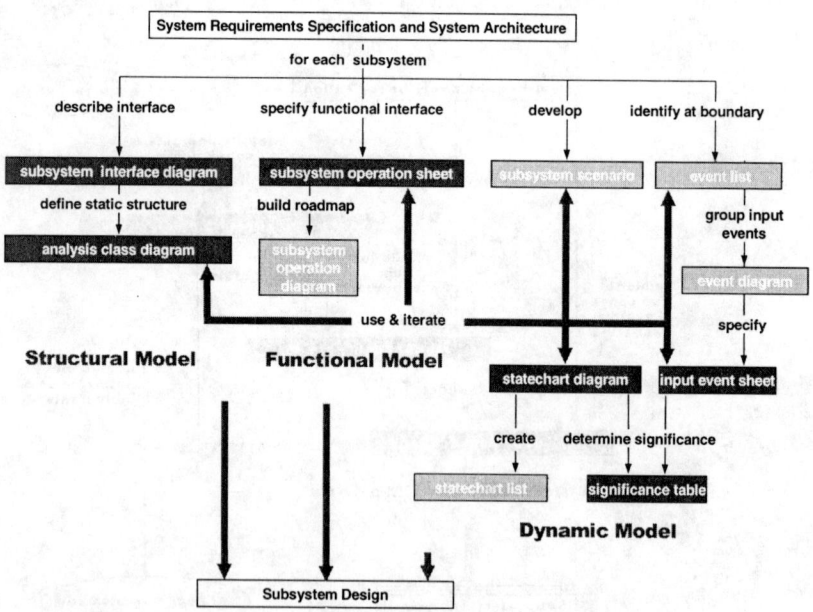

Figure 4. The Subsystem Analysis Sequence [4].

Each model defines a set of artifacts to be produced (see Figure 4). All three models are built in parallel. Nonetheless, the starting point and the order of progress should be planned and agreed on.

4.4. Subsystem Design phase

During the subsystem design phase a specification of the requirements stated in the former phases is achieved. This is the phase where the controlled transition is made from the implicit concurrency model to the explicit concurrency model [1]. Here, objects are mapped to processes of a traditional operating system.

The knowledge acquired in the previous development phases is used to construct the four models of the subsystem design phase: the refined structural model, the interaction model, the process model and the concurrency model.

All four models capture, though the artifacts, important information regarding messaging techniques (synchronous vs. asynchronous), concurrency, timing constraints, object grouping, transition from objects to processes and performance optimisation (Figure 5).

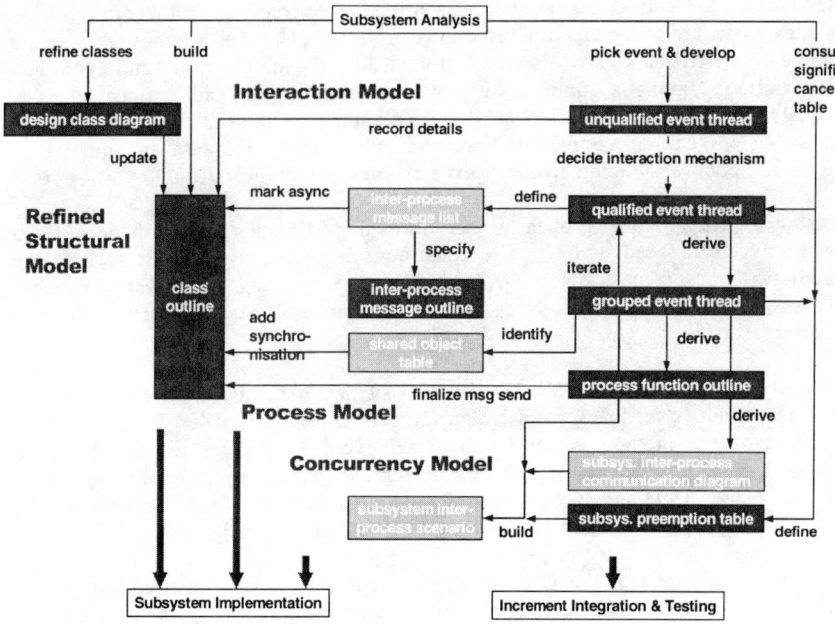

Figure 5. The Subsystem Design Sequence [4].

The objective is to produce a comprehensive software specification one level above implementation. Requirements derived from the chosen operating system and programming language should be considered but they should not drive the subsystem design.

5. Conclusion

Octopus/UML is an object-oriented software development method specialised for embedded real-time systems. A method specifies a framework in which work can be managed; identifying what should be done, when things should be done, what should be delivered and the language of deliverables. Octopus/UML follows these principles and furthermore uses objects and classes as the principal focus of attention. The purpose of the method is to create models which elaborate on issues such as:

- Which classes and objects exist.
- The structure, behaviour and purpose of those objects and classes.
- The structure and dynamics of relationships between objects.
- The structural relationships between classes.
- The smooth transition from objects and classes to tasks and processes.

Octopus/UML uses these models throughout the development phases; from requirements capture, analysis and design, implementation, to testing and maintenance. A model represents an abstraction of a problem in order to assure understanding prior to its development. Each model covers what artifacts to produce, why they exist, how they are structured in relation to each other and how they relate dynamically. Artifacts are essential for team communication and common understanding. Having a common language to communicate and criticise ideas is definitely the most important aspect of a development method. The visualisation of what a system can do, before coding, can substantially increase the quality of systems and code. Producing artifacts is the essence of Octopus/UML.

Octopus/UML applies proven object-oriented techniques and enhances them accordingly when faced with specific constraints in real-time systems, such as the unpredictable order of occurrence of external events, usage of quasi-concurrent processes provided by the underlying operating system and synchronisation of access to shared resources.

The strength of Octopus/UML lies in the fact that it has been developed within Nokia and receives feedback from Nokia projects applying it. Therefore, a realistic evaluation of the method is continuously achieved. This gives us the ability to improve and evolve Octopus/UML on a regular basis. The method has been developing since 1993 and supporting literature such as papers [5, 6,7, 8], posters [9, 10] and a book [1] which describes the method in detail are available.

Recently, Volume I of the Octopus Supplement Series, was released [4], which formally define Octopus/UML. A new volume of the Octopus Supplement Series will appear whenever mature and concrete solutions for a number of issues have been developed. If you wish to obtain a copy of Supplement Volume I, please contact the author. For further information on Octopus/UML and other activities, you can visit our web site at "http:www-nrc.nokia.com/octopus/".

6. References

[1] M. Awad, J. Kuusela and J. Ziegler, Object Oriented Technology for Real-Time Systems, Prentice Hall, 1996.

[2] H. Gomma, Software Design Methods for Concurrent and Real-Time Systems, Addison-Wesley, 1993.

[3] Unified Modeling Language, Edition 1.1, January 1997.

[4] E. Domiczi, R. Farfarakis and J. Ziegler, Octopus Supplement Volume 1, Nokia Research Center, November 1998.

[5] M. Awad and J. Ziegler, "A Practical Approach to the Design of Concurrency in Object-Oriented Systems", Software Practices and Experience, August 1997.

[6] M. Awad and J. Ziegler, "A Practical Approach to Object-Oriented State Modeling", Software Practices and Experience, March 1997.

[7] M. Awad, J. Kuusela and J. Ziegler, "Developing Object-Oriented Software for Real-Time Systems", Embedded Systems Programming, September 1996.

[8] M. Awad, J. Kuusela and J. Ziegler, "The Octopus method: Requirements Specification and Software Architecture", In Embedded Systems Programming, October 1996.

[9] E. Domiczi, "Octoguide – a graphical aid for navigating among Octopus/UML artifacts", 12th European Conference on Object-Oriented Programming (ECOOP'98), July 20-24, Brussels, Belgium, 1998.

[10] R. Farfarakis, "Octopus/UML: A pragmatic object-oriented method for real-time systems", International Conference on Object Oriented Programming Systems, Languages and Applications (OOPSLA'98), October 18-22, Vancouver, Canada, 1998.

Analysis, Design and Implementation of Distributed Java Business Frameworks Using Domain Patterns

Ali Arsanjani
IBM Enterprise Java Services, USA

The Java Business Frameworks are a convergence of OO Framework development methods, Java implementation best-practices and business system domain patterns in a distributed environment. They teach the concepts of, develop designs for and describe the step-by-step implementation of GUI patterns, Domain patterns and persistence patterns in an object-oriented framework using the Java language.

The emphasis is on designing a distributed architecture for your business, then seeing how you can build or plan to build a framework of reusable components; how to handle the analysis, design, development and deployment of CORBA/RMI-based services within the context of a business system.

Two case studies are presented and the participants are taken step by step through the issues and design decisions that make developing robust, industrial-strength application a complex process.

Ali Arsanjani has extensive expertise in distributed object computing, framework development in Java and analysis and design of business systems, teaching Object Technology for nine years in academia and industry.

Analysis, Design and Implementation of Distributed Java Business Frameworks using Domain Patterns

Ali Arsanjani
IBM Enterprise Java Services,
Maharishi University of Management
Arsanjan@us.ibm.com

Abstract

Constructing distributed object systems requires an extension to current analysis, design and implementation methods and processes. The notion of "domain pattern" is introduced as a blueprint for facilitating the construction of business frameworks. Finally, we examine lessons learned in constructing such a framework and using it in production environments.

1. Introduction

This paper describes how to construct (distributed) business frameworks using the notion of domain patterns, and very briefly covers some lessons learned in creating a framework called the *Java Business Frameworks* (JBF). It is a supplement to the tutorial given under the same name at TOOLS '99.

While mining patterns out of a number of industrial-strength applications in various domains, building generic business frameworks, and using object technology to create components, one comes across areas where many software engineering concepts tend to converge. It seems there are common issues that tend to arise in close proximity of each other. Here are some of these concepts: (reusable design constructs) patterns, pattern languages, software architectures, frameworks and components. These tend to be accompanied by general problems and issues encountered in using object-oriented programming languages. These issues include: object proliferation, object entanglement through inheritance hierarchy and direct reference to other objects, losing the picture of the whole when distributing responsibility among objects, objects having interfaces with no clear "usage rules" embedded within them, etc.

The format of this short paper is kept intentionally succinct rather than explanatory. For more elaborate explanations, please refer to the references.

Patterns generate architectures [1]. One of the most reusable architectures are application frameworks, which are typically designed to be reused through customization. In addition, patterns can be used to document frameworks [2]. Components can be considers to be small frameworks. Components bring the promise of objects into the front line of enterprise development. So *what is the intersection of the sets of activities necessary for successful framework development* and *component-based development?*

Frameworks are built by induction [10]; components are also built by iterative refinement and and induction. Components are actually mini-frameworks. They are "software Ics" (Brad Cox). Does the development of these mini-frameworks-- especially, the distributed variety-- require extensions to current software development methods and processes? Based on our experience in developing a set of distributed Java business frameworks (JBF), the answer is a definitive "yes."

In addition to requiring refinements to mainstream OOA/D methods and processes, we introduce the notion of a "domain pattern." This notion is used to describe a generic architecture that is domain-independent. It is the result of the process of taking several applications from a domain and generalizing (logicians would call this *induction*; going from the specific to the more general) the common denominator into a set of mini-frameworks (components). Then, we take the generalization up, one step further.

Let's explore an example: What is the common domain intersection (business model intersection) of a bank, a university, a franchise, a library, a software development firm, a flight reservation system? The answer is, that they are all "service providers." A Service Provider is an underlying domain pattern that was seen to span diverse industries and domains for which I had been involved in developing applications and frameworks.

This knowledge can be condensed into a "domain pattern." It can then be used to guide the creation of component-based frameworks that are amenable to distributed object design and deployment. The following will be an experience report of "gems" and "insights" we encountered along this path. They can be categorized according to various axes: OOA/D method extensions, missing links in component-based development enabling and "glue", higher level patterns, distributed framework development for business systems and other items related to our experiences in implementing the Java Business Frameworks. These include a synopsis of a pattern language for scalable design and implementation of business rules, some user-interface, persistence mapping, design and architectural patterns that were mined out of various applications and used within JBF.

2. Method Extensions to Better Support Distributed Object Design
2.1. What are some problems with objects?

2.1.1. The "uses" relationship: Objects encapsulate identity, state and behavior. They are also very "talkative"; they send messages to one another. This "uses" or "dependency" relationship creates an entirely new "bowl of spaghetti" that surpasses the old structured "bowl of spaghetti" of programming with goto's and branches to code that were not easily able to be followed. Inheritance also creates this blind-sightedness: you are trying to understand and trace some code. Does this message belong to this class or its superclass? As you go up and down the rungs of the inheritance ladder many times in tortuous but "clever" paths, you wonder about the days before structured programming: was the developer who wrote this code caught in a time-warp at about that era?

2.1.2. Objects should have manners: You can send a message "run()" to an object that simulates a person whose body parts need to be constructed first, before he can run(). An object should be able to "know" when it can run(), and when it should throw an exception. Or, try to pop() a stack object that is empty. The rules of behavior should be encoded within the object to avoid states that are invalid. This is like trying to tell a graphics framework to set resolution to 1024x680 when it has not even been initialized. The knowledge of the sequences of messages that create a valid collaborative state should be encoded within the class that reifies a collaborative role of the object.

2.2. Steps for Component and Framework Development
The following is a list of steps, extracted from a methdodology of component and framework development, that were found to be particularly successful across multiple projects:

Group use-cases into "intents"

Start with CRC cards or use cases. Group related use-cases into higher level intents of the business, or of the domain. If you are using CRC cards, create a fourth UML class compartment and put the responsibilities directly into the class model. These will turn into rules and object manners later on.

Create Job Descriptions for the domain; what are the machines, tools, materials and manpower used within the business process. (Actor, Action, Acted on; IntentScripts);

Identify Roles (Person can be Customer, a Vendor, A manager, a stockholder, a beneficiary within the same application. Or, in a university scenario a person can be a student, staff or faculty. The faculty can be full-time, adjunct, visiting. They may further play roles of advisor, lecturer, lab assistant. The staff may be full-time or part-time. [Experience tip: If you start to detail out a system in enough fine granularity, you end up with a lot of common classes and components between domains]

Job descriptions and Roles are the domain hotspots (a la Pree) which can provide future plug-points for extension. This is an accord with Meyer's Open/Closed principle that software should be open to extension but closed to modification. Using Roles in object development is not new; it has been successfully utilized on large-scale projects [11].

Identify Logical Components; these are also potential candidates for a CORBA Service, this may be different from the way they are ultimately deployed. Candidate Clusters (Components) having rules, state, serving as façade mediators.

Create a Rules Inventory ; check this with the business; cross-check with this as a single point of contact as rules change. This allows the business to be resilient to change. Rules tend to disappear within code. Maintaining this list extricates them for manipulation. Traceability to the actual detailed design and code is essential. This can be implemented by a Rule Repository and Browser.

Identify Potential Collaborations and model as collaboration diagrams; don't start with static models. Start with trying to draw the collaborations of major use-case success scenarios and one or two major alternative scenarios according to the business rules and workflow within the business domain. [here tradeoffs and decsign decisions may be made to see whether it is justifiable to create/reuse a workflow engine, a transaction processing monitor, a datawarehouse, a rules engine, or that these specialized products will be replaced by placeholder classes (this is the key to framework-based and component –driven reusability and strategic insight in retaining the ability to plug in a specialized engine in this component framework hotspot when performance, security, volume, internalization or other non-functional drivers begin to change the balance of the architectural equation]

Assign Rules to Clusters and Classes within clusters (collaborative participants); reify packages as mediator/facades. Warning: you need to balance the number of mediators with the system complexity: too few will make the system monolithic; too many will increase unnecessary complexity and levels of delegation.

Identify Contracts within Clusters. This may seem strange: aren't clusters or components supposed to expose their interfaces and thus are they not the first candidates for publishing their contracts? The Answer is yes! But, based on experience, I can say that to start with the collaboration contracts is a better starting point.

Define Class/Object Collaborations first

Instead of trying to create class diagrams with relationships first, model the major collaborations between key objects. Assign a Cluster object to each primary collaboration that will act as a Mediator. In this way, you avoid having objects refer directly to one another as much as possible.

Identify Reuse Levels

It is convenient to group objects and coarser grained constructs into the following taxonomy (called *Reuse Levels*): base class, inheritance hierarchy, aggregation hierarchy, cluster (group of collaborating objects fulfilling a business intent according to valid interaction rules), framework, patterns (the full spectrum: starting from idioms to design patterns to architectural and analysis patterns go here), generic architectures, environment interaction meta-knowledge and technology transfer knowledge[9].

Create an Architectural Model

This can be a component model or a deployment model. The emphasis is on beginning to assign clusters of collaborating objects as components or services to distributed server nodes. Use the non-functional drivers and requirements to define a development prototype. Group clusters into CORBA services.

Although the system should be designed to be independent of the implementation platform and architecture, yet going down an architectural path will lead to the discovery of high-risk issues that can then be incorporated and addressed up-front. It will impact the analysis and design in a generic and implementation-independent fashion and provide valuable feedback and validity checks that will affect the schedule and your team without necessarily being a part of the technical aspects of your business domain.

Create and Iterate an Extensible Prototype

This important step will address risks and bring out a multitude of issues that will impact the design and possibly the analysis model. The key point is to plan to create a "thin slice of functionality" that will go end-to-end, vertically exercising the system (e.g., client to web server to application servers, to back end data stores and back)

Continue the process with one of the standard software processes such as Rational Unified Process, Fractal model, Fountain model or your organization's custom process model.

3. Domain Patterns

The concept of a "domain pattern" is introduced in light of induction from several business application systems that had been created for various clients. The commonalties were factored out and generalized. This led to the creation of a framework that was designed and generated by employing only that domain pattern. This method has been subsequently tested on smaller frameworks with positive results. The key idea is to generalize a set of applications and then to introduce meta-level constructs.

The process takes UI level, persistence, architectural and business patterns and combines them into the framework generated by the domain pattern. Let's take a look at the rationale behind the Service Provider.

3.1. Service Provider[12]: A Domain Pattern
Intent

Define a domain independent and generic architecture for providing Clients with business Services and service Packages based on specific Terms of Agreement.

There are three major participants in a Service Provider (SP) scenario: a Party (Fowler [7]) that provides a set of Services (the SP), the Services (includes the notion of Product and Service) being offered and the Client Party, who is willing to pay for it. A Business exists in order to provide services or products to prospective customer populations in order to make a profit and hopefully benefit humanity in the process. So the roles in this collaboration are: [Actor] ServiceProvider Offers [Act; Process] Services [Acted On] [8]. SP is a component that contains a set of collaborating interfaces: an organization hierarchy a Location (hierarchy) with links to what Location provides what Product/Service; a set of Services (which generalizes Product and Service). The Client component will have the following set of collaborating class interfaces.

The following class diagram depicts the Service Provider's static model:

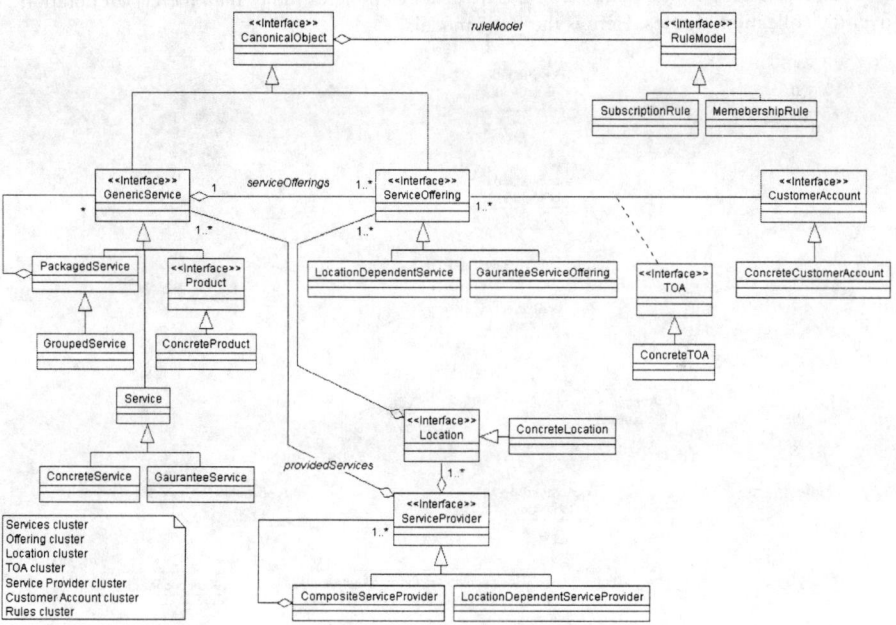

The Service Provider domain pattern uses other patterns that form a pattern language for distributed business framework development. The following is a brief synopsis of some of these patterns.

3.2. Some GUI Patterns

Objects send messages to one another in order to fulfill a collaboration. The question is: if you want to dis-associate object interactions as much as possible, therefby being able to reuse the maximum number of objects by themselves, how would you model the collaborations? The Mediator design pattern [5] offers a solution: "Encapsulate how a set of objects interact..." The essential factor here is how fine-grained should you make the mediator?

3.3. Architectural Issues and Forces

Objects send messages to one another in order to fulfill collaboration. The question is: if you want to disassociate object interactions as much as possible, thereby being able to reuse the maximum number of objects by themselves, how would you model the collaborations? The Mediator design pattern [5] offers a solution: "Encapsulate how a set of objects interact..." The essential factor here is how fine-grained should you make the mediator?

3.4. Handling Business Rules

Service Provider uses the Rule Object pattern to handle rules. Each collection of rules can also have a strategy which optimizes rules invocations policies rather than merely an iteration over the collection of rules. Here is the static model:

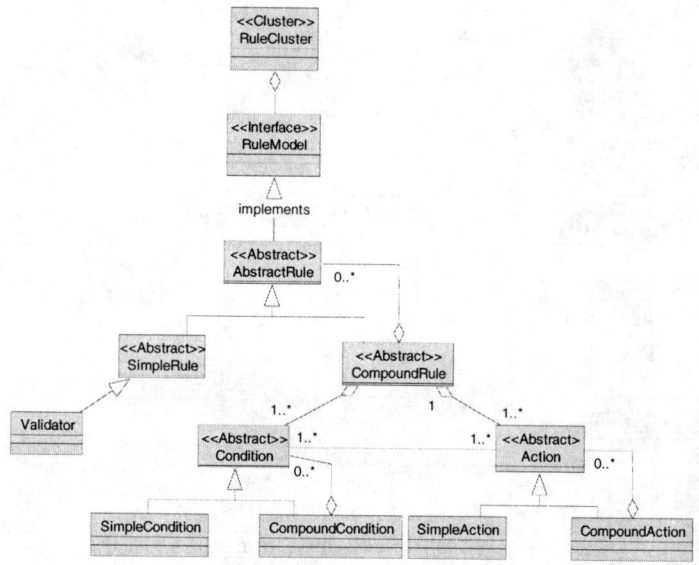

4. Component-based Development

Components have interfaces by which they are utilized within different contexts. It is essential that each component "know how to behave" within each interaction context. An interaction context in the banking domain may be loans, mortgage, accounts. IN each of these contexts, the component needs to exhibit different behavior. The ability to distinguish which type of behavior ("role") to exhibit in a given context is the component's "manners."

4.1. Components have 'manners'

Collaborations should be reified where possible. Here is a scenario. Objects send messages to one another in order to fulfill collaboration. The question is: if you want to disassociate object interactions as much as possible, there-by being able to reuse the maximum number of objects by themselves, how would you model the collaborations? The Mediator design pattern [5] offers a solution: "Encapsulate how a set of objects interact..." The essential factor here is how fine-grained should you make the mediator?

5. Scalable Rule Pattern Language

Identifying, designing how to represent rules and finally implemening them constitutes the bulk of business functionality to be implemented. The question is: what is the "best" (given various pragmatic factors as input) way to design your rules to reflect your business processes, workflow and policies is a problem all designers and developers face in terms of ease of future extension. Other factors include the need to be able to rapidly make changes as the business maneuvers itself in the market and the desire to avoid ripple effects in an application where a hierarchy of interdependent rules influence one another.

Rules may be started out as informal textual descriptions. Gradually, when the need to code arrives, they will be sprinkled throughout the application, frequently in the form of if/else blocks; to be almost inextricably dissolved within the application. Then, when the business needs to respond to demands in the market by changing the rules, programmers play a Sherlock Holmes role. They try to find clues to where the business rules have been embedded; how bad the ripple effects will be if they change this rule; what other rules are bound to this one (discover rule dependencies). No rule is an island, it is linked to other rules and is dependent upon the state of the application.

Therefore, separate the rules out into methods, as a next step in the process of sophistication in rule handling. Name the methods to display their rule functionality. Document their dependencies to other rules. As the number of rules increase and the need to reuse old rules in new contexts with slight variations arise, one is bound to encapsulate the rules.

This next step is related to a pattern I call "Rule Object" or "Rules as Objects"[4]. This means a rule will encapsulate its condition and action part [3; Taylor]. These can be embodied as Assessor [4] and Command design patterns respectively [5]. Various Strategies for rule optimization can be applied.

As the number of rules increase, the object proliferation syndrome [6] starts to become a major problem: how should I handle and maintain so many little objects that are tied to one another?

The answer lies in creating a Rule Repository as a next step. Create a repository to store rules. Trickle this down from management who is given tools to create rules to developers who will implement them in the IT organization.

The next step is to make the rules persistent and "storable". This allows modifications to be made to a database of objects through a rule browser and creation tool. Therefore, as code gets cumbersome and difficult to maintain due to fine-grained variation, turn code into data (meta-level programming).

The previous set of progressive steps represents an increasingly scalable way of designing and implementing business rules. The *last step* is to represent the object's manners (how its methods are used in concert with other collaborators) as a state chart or grammar. In this way, a component will expose its manners. Exposing manners is an additional way of increasing component reusability and maintainability. Usually, methods or operations are exposed in an interface or type definition. A class will then implement that interface or type and tie an implementation to it at runtime. The missing element is how to use the methods: "how should a client utilize the set of services provided by an interface?" Do we need some special "setup" methods to call first, to set up some state in the collaborating object at runtime? And then subsequently call methods in a special sequence in order to use those interface's services (behavior)?

As an aside, one of the highest costs in overcoming learning curves is to learn how and when to use the appropriate methods of a set of collaborating classes (or interfaces). If the knowledge of how to use the collaborations would be exposed in a component interface, then clients would have a much swifter learning period.

Also, changing the interface of a type by adding operations tends to reflect an additional specification or new feature that the type will support. For example, to implement a new business process, several collaborating types' operations are added to, some are reused and some state is added to each object in order to implement the new business process. But as soon as we hand this off to the programmer, the business process knowledge that was the underlying cause of this additional feature evolution is lost. In UML, when we define an interface or class, we can define a state machine or grammar (depending on the complexity of the behavior we are trying to design) to describe the "manners" of this new interface or class. The "manners" consists of rules of collaboration, usage rules, valid object interaction sequences and business rules.

5.1. Categories of Manners

Objects send messages to one another in order to fulfill collaboration. The question is: if you want to disassociate object interactions as much as possible, thereby being able to reuse the maximum number of objects by themselves, how would you model the collaborations? The Mediator design pattern [5] offers a solution: "Encapsulate how a set of objects interact..." The essential factor here is how fine-grained should you make the mediator?

5.1.1. Collaboration Rules: Third-order headings, as in this paragraph, are discouraged. However, if you must use them, use 11-point Times New Roman, boldface, initially capitalized, flush left, preceded by one blank line, followed by a colon and your text on the same line.

5.1.2. Usage Rules: Usage rules are for humans. They are an answer to the question: "How should I educate the new programmer on the cubicle block in using this application framework. How is the best way to mentor her and get her up to speed in using the new framework? The key is to learn the hotspots; where you should place classes and override methods that the framework will call as part of a higher level collaboration. This higher level collaboration is often implemented in an abstract class with default behavior or in a class which calls abstract (virtual) methods; to be over-ridden by sub-classing or delegation.

5.1.3. Valid Object Interaction Sequences (VOIS): Each society of collaborating classes that implement a business process or objective send messages in a certain set of sequences and not in others. In general, this is an answer to the question: " When should I send this message (m1) to this class (c1)? Should I set up some state in c1 or in other classes by invoking other methods prior to m1?"

In other words, the alternative sequences of message sends among the society of cooperating objects that will fulfill a business objective will constitute a VOIS.

5.1.4. Business Rules: Often implemented in a "middle-tier", to be used by multiple clients to verify accordance with business policies and the validity of data and the constraints on their inter-relationships, business rules are the heart of the business logic that comprises a particular

5.1.5. Manners: This helps describe the need for describing the laws of interaction with a component. It answers the question: "how can I /should I use this component?" If this (possibly scripted) specification travels along with a component's published interface, then a great deal of maintenance time can be recouped. Reuse of the component will be much more straightforward; it will decrease the time required to learn how to use a component.

Also, as component-based development increases in popularity and use, the problem of how to combine and compose component can be reduced to the problem of whether the composition in mind conforms to the interaction grammar (manners) as published by the component. A component will publish not only its interface, but a grammar representing how it has been designed to be used.

Each domain has a vocabulary and language of its own. Components designed to function within the context of the given domain will need to conform to that business domain language. A grammar naturally captures the input stream and its relation to strings of tokens that are considered to be "valid" within that language.

5.1. Grammar-Oriented Object Design

The concept of a meta domain pattern which spans multiple domains and is customizable for each domain has been dealt with in the Service Provider example and the description of the Java Business Frameworks which implement the Service Provider.

The above discussion about components having manners or "object have manners" points to using a business language definition that can then be executed. Basing object design on the manners of valid object interaction and capturing their generic collaborations as a domain-specific grammar, and producing executable business specifications in this manner, constitutes the basis for Grammar-oriented Object Design[13].

12. References

[1] Kent Beck, Ralph Johnson, "Patterns Generate Architectures", ECOOP '94, Springer-Verlag, pages 139-149, Bologna, Italy, July 1994.

[2] Ralph Johnson, "Documenting Frameworks using Patterns", OOPSLA '92 Proceedings, ACM, pages 63-76, Vancouver, British Columbia, October 1992.

[3] David Taylor, Succeeding With Objects: A Manager's Introduction, Addison-Wesley, 1993.

[4] Ali Arsanjani, "Rule Object", Whitepaper, Object-oriented Technologies, Inc., 1996. Contact author for a copy.

[5] Erich Gamma, Richard Helm, Ralph Johnson, John Vlissides, Design Patterns – elements of Reusable Object –Oriented Software , Prentice Hall, 1995.

[6] Ali Arsanjani, "The Object Proliferation Syndrome and how to Prepare for it", Whitepaper, Maharishi University of Management, June 1998.(email author for a copy: arsanjan@us.ibm.com)

[7] Martin Fowler, Analysis Patterns, Addison-Wesley, Reading, Massachussetts, 1997.

[8] Maharishi Mahesh Yogi, Lectures on Knower, Knowing and Known: The Samhitta of Rishi, Devata and Chhandas , MIU Press 1984.

[9] Ali Arsanjani, "Reuse Levels", Whitepaper, Object-Oriented Technologies, Inc., 1994.

[10] Don Roberts, Ralph Johnson, "Evolving Frameworks: A Pattern Langauge for Developing Frameworks", Addison-Wesley, Reading, Massachusetts, 1997.

[11] Dirk Riehle, Dirk Baumer, "Role Object".

[12] Ali Arsanjani, "Service Provider", Submitted for Patterns Languages of Programming '99, Monticello, Illinois, 1999.

[13] Ali Arsanjani, Hassan Miran, "Grammar-Oriented Object Design", Object-Oriented Technologies, Inc., 1990.

[14] Ali Arsanjani, "GOOD: Grammar-Oriented Object Design", Position Paper for OOPSLA Workshop on MetaData and Active Object Modeling, 1998, Vancouver, British Columbia.

Requirement Patterns

Christopher Creel
Technical Resource Connection, TRC

Few engineers in the software industry argue the profound impact of good requirement engineering on a project. Even fewer engineers can claim that they spend any tangible effort on requirements engineering. Most sheepishly smile and claim, ironically, that their management fears that requirement analysis might negatively influence the delivery schedule. This of course hints to a devil in the details.

In general, the software industry is obsessed with the "end game," or shipping the "final" product. As evidence of this obsession, witness the tools most prevalent throughout our industry. Close examination from different angles reveals a heavy slant towards the "end game." Stated plainly, ours is an industry of solution space engineers, with few tools available to us for studying the problem space.

This tutorial introduces the audience to an exciting new technique entitled Requirement Patterns that builds on the work of Ian Sommerville and Ivar Jacobsen. The first part of the tutorial on this emerging field takes the audience on a whirlwind tour of today's tools for requirement analysis. The second part introduces the audience to Requirement Patterns and highlights eight patterns successfully deployed in many industry specifications. The final part is a workshop that will focus on strengthening the existing patterns, recording the application of such patterns and looking for new patterns. Be a part of the effort as we work to expand this powerful emerging field.

Christopher Creel is a software engineer with 11 years in industry working on specifying and delivering solutions in the following problem domains:

- Forecasting the behavior of nonlinear models of weather and product demand
- Detecting negative pharmaceutical interactions
- Performance critical color imaging
- Telecommunications
- Stock option management
- Land based warfare
- Order management
- Customer care

Additionally, Chris entertains both academic and industrial audiences with his lectures on his observations of the software industry. He now works for The Technical Resource Connection, a wholly owned subsidiary of PerotSystems.

Tutorials

Management

Introduction to the OPEN Method with UML

Brian Henderson-Sellers

University of Technology, Sydney, Australia

OPEN is the premier third-generation, process-focussed, public domain OO methodology. It is documented in a number of professional-level texts. In this tutorial, a beginner's level presentation, OPEN is introduced through a number of case studies using UML as the notation.

Brian Henderson-Sellers is Director of the Centre for Object Technology Applications and Research and Professor of Information Systems at University of Technology, Sydney (UTS). He is author of eight books on object technology and is well-known for his work in OO methodologies (MOSES, COMMA and OPEN) and in OO metrics.

Brian is also Regional Editor of Object-Oriented Systems, a member of the editorial board of Object Magazine/Component Strategies and Object Expert for many years, Founder of the Object-Oriented Special Interest Group of the Australian Computer Society (NSW Branch) and Chairman of the Computerworld Object Developers' Awards committee for ObjectWorld 94 and 95 (Sydney). He is a frequent, invited speaker at international OT conferences.

Effective Strategies and Techniques for Rapid Object-Oriented Application Development

Michael P. Anton

Financial Technology Solutions, USA

This tutorial will expose some of the secrets that allow every-day developers to be incredibly effective - doing in one day what other developers may take weeks, months, or even a year to accomplish. The participants will walk-through the analysis, design, and implementation of a substantial real-world application, developed in a single week using proven Object-Oriented techniques. They will come away with the knowledge of how a software system can evolve in a very short time from concept to a fully functional system. They will learn the strategies and techniques that are used to avoid time-wasting activities. And they will see how extensibility is built in from the ground-up - to address future requirements that may or may not have been anticipated.

Michael P. Anton is a Senior Management Consultant at Sanford Bernstein, an Investment Management and Research Firm in New York City where he was Manager of Fixed Income Systems for four years. He holds a Master of Science in Engineering (Computer & Information Science) from the University of Pennsylvania and a Bachelor of Arts in Economics and Chemistry from Williams College in Massachusetts. Mr. Anton has over twenty years experience designing, building, and managing software projects. He has been involved in Object-Oriented Development for eleven years and has contributed to many dozens of projects in portfolio management & trading, molecular modeling, directional drilling, traffic control, office automation, Microwave CAD and interactive voice response.

Core: A Pattern Language for Rapid Object-Oriented Development

Michael P. Anton
Financial Technology Solutions Inc.
anton@acm.org

Abstract

Industry studies show that the most productive software developers are 20 to 200 times more effective than their least productive counterparts. No other engineering discipline shows this divergence in practitioner competency level. Although there are many factors that contribute to this productivity gap, observations suggest that the most productive developers consciously or unconsciously execute a repeatable process of applying idioms and patterns in their work. By observing and abstracting these patterns at each stage of the development lifecycle, a "Core" pattern language has evolved that provides powerful abstractions for conceptualizing, designing, and implementing computer systems in a deterministic manner. Domain experts, user interface designers, programmers, and database architects can systematically and unambiguously discuss, specify, and build computer systems using this pattern language. The "Core" language provides efficient communication among these groups, at a higher level of abstraction than possible with traditional approaches or with other pattern languages.

1. Introduction

In a field that combines art and science, its practitioners are often divided into camps – one that cares about the raw science and traditionally objective characteristics of the field and another that cares about the beauty and elegance of its creations.
                                        Richard Gabriel

This paper is not about "the next great thing". It is not about silver bullets and new tools that will solve the software crisis. It is not about the *Art of Computer Science* and how to express your creative genius by programming. It *is* about how to build great software, how to work at peak efficiency, and how to ensure the work you do today can be used with the next generations of development tools and hardware that are just a few years away.

Not long ago industry pundits published gloomy portrayals of software engineers as unproductive, overpaid producers of inferior quality systems. Those opinions now seem to be on the wane. With the same force of a glacier leveling a mountain in one location and building it in another, the software industry, moving at the speed of nanoseconds instead of milleniums, has "gone through another two generations of hardware technology... [and] witnessed the explosion of Internet, multimedia, and other technologies... [making] it possible for small teams of 3 to 5 people to accomplish what use to require 30 to 50 ... programmers." [7] But achieving extreme levels of productivity is not just about using the best tools. Rather it is more to do with *how* they are used.

Give five software developers the same problem and they will invariably come back with five different solutions. Software development is notorious for its lack of discipline. It lags so far behind other engineering fields that many argue that it is not an engineering field at all! Many areas of software development, particularly the User Interface (UI), heavily demand creative and aesthetic contributions. Other areas like databases have dozens of implementation variations. Success in system development depends greatly on the individuals on the team. If you have a different team, you will certainly get a different solution.

But is software development all art and no science? In the last decade the software industry has made a significant effort to capture current practices and experience in *patterns* and *pattern languages*. Software developers are finding and successfully applying patterns to solve problems in design [6], analysis [4], and programming [2]. Patterns have even been applied to problems in software organization structure! [3] This impressive body of published research in patterns continues to grow daily. Our intention is not to repeat or summarize these extremely useful patterns and pattern languages, but rather to demonstrate a higher level grouping of these patterns into a very practical and usable pattern language.

Over the last five years we have developed a dozen applications for the Financial Industry using a systematic application of software patterns that span the entire cycle of analysis, design, and implementation. The entire development team can use this pattern language from beginning to end to build systems at astonishing speed, particularly when supported by an appropriate framework for implementation. By sifting through the proliferation of published patterns, pattern languages, process methodologies, and best practices, and encapsulating these in a few *composite patterns* or *metapatterns*, we can deterministically generate models in the appropriate language and notation of each role on the development team. This composite pattern language is called *The Core Pattern Language* or just *"Core"*.

These higher level abstractions match the object models and patterns used in the various areas of the system. The pattern language ensures that different teams will produce consistently similar and superior results. Most of the technical details are solved, removing the *accidental complexity* of development, so that the team can focus more energy on the business problems at hand.

2. The Core Process

Models in Core are deterministic. This is the most difficult adjustment for *seasoned* developers and business systems analysts, who are used to a lot of interpretation and flexibility in models and systems they build. Unlike traditional approaches that allow a lot of room for interpretation and present non-deterministic solutions, the object models, database models, and user interface models within Core are very much intertwined. Moreover, one model is not superior to another. Although tradition dictates that we begin with an object model, develop the database model, then build the user interface, insights into the system will be gained at every step of the process. We discover limitations in the system from examining each of the models, and any changes to a model are reflected in the other models as well. For example, a change to the user interface will also be reflected in changes to the database models and object models.

There is a massive body of literature from which we abstract the *best practices* to follow. Space does not permit summarizing these, however two essential characteristics are mentioned below.

2.1. Iterative and Incremental

The process of building the system is iterative and incremental. In each iteration we plan a little, design a little, then implement and evaluate a little. It is rarely possible to get all of the requirements correct on the first pass. As the requirements articulated by the users are transformed into the implementation, the users often realize what they asked for is not what they really want, or that changes are necessary to make the system more complete or more flexible. The development continues, modifying the requirements and the subsequent models until the users have a system that meets their needs and is complete.

Participating in this process is exciting and stimulating, but reading a description of the process may put you to sleep! Imagine describing how you filled out the Sunday paper crossword puzzle last week! However, to understand how the Core patterns work and how they give insight into the business and systems problems at every stage of development, we will describe below the iterations we could go through to test and evaluate different potential solutions to a business problem.

2.2. Reuse Decisions

Over the course of developing a significant software system, thousands of decisions need to be made. Some of these are made consciously and visibly, perhaps by groups at meetings and documented in specifications. Other decisions are made quietly, most likely by one or two people, perhaps even in the middle of the night!

Sometimes the decisions are trivial, like how to capitalize and format variable names. Other times the decisions can make or break the system. In the extreme case, necessary functionality may be missing, and if the system cannot easily be extended, a rewrite may be necessary. Even seemingly trivial decisions can cause hours of frustration and unnecessary re-learning for the users, like choosing an accelerator key for the "Search" function as "Control-S" when other applications perform similar functionality with "Find" and "Control-F".

Aside from faulty decisions, *making* these decisions takes valuable time. By reaching decisions in advance, we can 1) eliminate wasting project time on trivial infrastructure decisions, 2) make the important decisions in the light of day when our minds are fresh, and 3) reuse the decisions between projects.

Core captures many of these decisions, both large and small, and removes them from the everyday process of development. This may initially appear oppressive to developers and users alike. It may appear to remove creativity and freedom from the development process. But in reality it gives developers and users new freedom to focus on the important business functionality of the system. By not arbitrarily revisiting decisions which have already been made, enormous gains in productivity can be achieved. By subsuming other patterns and pattern languages, Core eliminates the need for the application developer to study, understand, and implement many of these patterns, particularly during a demanding phase of development. Instead the Core architecture can be extended, and the knowledge of those who study pattern languages reused, without a full understanding of the deep complex patterns within.

By working at this very high level of abstraction, developers can be orders of magnitude more productive than they otherwise might. Applications are more robust, implementing generic functionality that otherwise would not be included. And users benefit from the consistency of the user interface and in the behaviors of the objects, rather than adjusting to the whims of individual developers.

When decisions in Core *are* revisited, they are done in the context of all the collective wisdom gained from building the previous applications, changes in technologies, and additional understanding from studying new patterns. When Core behavior changes, it changes consistently for all applications, easing the retraining burden on users.

3. The User Interface (UI)

To most users, the UI *is* the system. It is extremely important to get it right. On the other hand, developing the UI can be extremely time consuming.

Pattern languages have started to emerge in this area, but like most UI *frameworks* and *class libraries*, they are at the wrong level of abstraction for efficient communication and development among *all* members of the development team. Either they deal at a highly abstract level, like generic requirement specification, or they are at the level of scroll bars, buttons, and other widgets. Core focuses the discussions of the UI on the behaviors of the *business* objects, not the *GUI* objects. Most of the GUI issues have been solved within Core at an abstract level. ("Of course you'll be able to print, search, and sort the list! Now let's talk about the business functions.")

3.1. Consistency

Rather than get into philosophical debates of what the correct UI behavior should be, Core errs on the side of consistency with commercial applications popular in the user community. In very rare cases, Core behavior deviates from commercial package behavior. Only if a parallel can not be found in commercial applications will a new behavior be invented. This is an enormous time saver for the developers since they generally do not need to invent UI behavior. It is also a time saver for users, since they do not have to learn a new user interface.

3.2. Procedural User Interfaces vs. Object-Oriented User Interfaces

Because analysis (including OO analysis) focuses developers on "what the users want to do" with the system, even very experienced system designers fall into the trap of developing *procedural* UIs, rather than *object-oriented* UIs (OOUIs). A rigorous discipline is needed to avoid this peril.[1]

An OOUI does not mean using a lot of icons and bitmaps instead of words, although it does mean allowing users to work in their own way with business objects instead of executing pre-defined procedures. Since it is usually easier to draw a bitmap to represent an object (noun) than it is to represent a procedure, using pictures in the UI may focus developers more on an OOUI. However in many cases a word may be a superior representation of an object, rather than reverting to the primitive hieroglyphics common in some applications. Core uses both words and pictures to represent objects.

---

[1] Why avoid writing a procedural UI in the first place is an interesting topic, but one that is beyond the scope of this paper.

4. Example: Financial Portfolio Management System

Rather than a detailed discussion of the pattern language itself, we present here an actual use of Core to produce a functional application in hours, rather than the days or weeks or months often necessary in environments which do not have the advantage of this pattern language.

The most important concept necessary to achieve this hyper-productivity is the right level of abstraction. Only nine patterns are used and these can be grouped into three categories. Yet like the 26 characters you are reading that can represent hundreds of thousands of words, and an infinite number of concepts, these nine patterns can be used to conceptualize, discuss, specify, and build many different applications.

An important characteristic of Core is that the models are deterministic. If a model transformation is ambiguous, a decision is made and the decision itself becomes a part of the language so that it can be reused when a similar decision needs to be made in the future. Our goal is to avoid wasting time making decisions that *need* to be made, but can be made once and reused. Constantly revisiting the decisions and debating them is unproductive and often futile.

For example, when the user states, that a "portfolio contains holdings…" this translates *unambiguously* into certain database objects for the database architect, certain user interface objects for the user interface designer, and into certain business objects and business logic to be implemented by the rest of the programming team. Because these translations have been defined in advance, and the development team has agreed to use them, there is no "touchy-feely" interpretation of the requirements. We are no longer getting five solutions to one problem, rather everyone, when presented with the same problem, will come up with very similar solutions; and anyone on the development team can contribute to and continue the work of anyone else.

We have achieved some level of *science* in system building, rather than just *art*. The example below illustrates using Core to build a financial portfolio management system.

5. Iteration One: Financial Portfolio Management System

5.1. The Domain/Business Objects

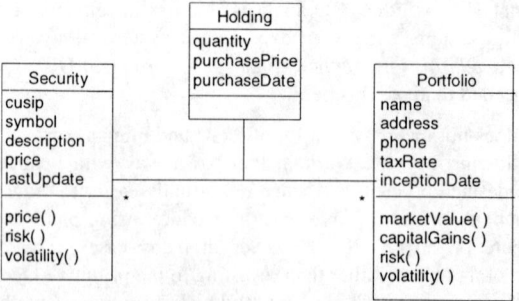

Fig. 1 - Iteration One: Object Model

A domain object (or business object) is a fundamental entity from the domain expert's vocabulary.

For example, in the case of a portfolio management system, **Security**, **Holding**, and **Portfolio** may be identified as domain objects. Through analysis with users, attributes and methods for the objects can be discovered along with their relationships. A first attempt at a model may look like Fig 1.

5.2. Object Persistence

Sufficient information is available in the object model to unambiguously specify object persistence. The persistence layer of the Core objects can be implemented in either an OODBMS or RDBMS. This example will use an RDBMS. In a relational database implementation, a table is generated for each *class* and *object identifiers* (OID) are added along with foreign keys to represent the relationships. Appropriate data types are selected for the attributes.[2]

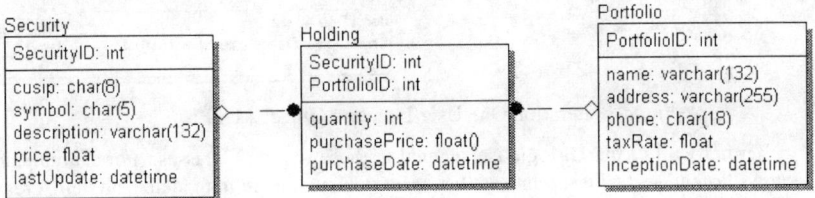

Fig. 2 - Iteration One: Database Model

5.3. User Interface Objects

A domain object is displayed in the UI in one of two ways: as a single object called an **Item** or as a collection of objects called a **List**. These are the *only* two ways an object is presented to the user. An *Item* gives access to all of the attributes and methods that should be exposed to the user.

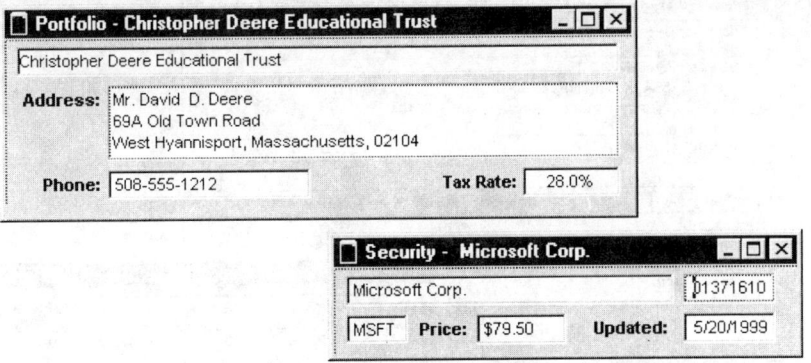

Fig. 3 - Iteration One User Interface Objects: UI Item

---

[2] An excellent discussion of mapping objects to relational databases is found in [1] along with a Portfolio Management case study. Some of the notation and style presented here was adopted from this book, although the object models differ somewhat.

A *List* also displays attributes of the domain object, usually a subset of the *Item's* attributes.

Security List		
Cusip	**Sym**	**Description**
01471006	ADPT	Adaptec Inc.
01271005	CATP	Cambridge Technology Partners Mass Inc.
01671042	CPQ	Compaq Computer Corp.
01361012	HU	Hudson Utd. Bancorp.
01771002	INPR	Inprise Corp.
01671502	KEA	Keane Inc.
01371610	MSFT	Microsoft Corp.
01671002	ORCL	Oracle Corp.
01961008	SYBS	Sybase Inc.

Portfolio List	
Name	**Date**
Angela Doe	Jun-88
Angela Doe Retirement Plan	Jan-91
John & Angela Doe JTWROS	Feb-93
Doe Enterprises Pension Plan	Mar-99
Christopher Deere	Aug-98
John Doe	Apr-77
John Doe 401K	Mar-88
Christopher Deere Educational Trust	Apr-92

Fig. 4 - Iteration One User Interface Objects: UI List

Virtually all of the UI logic is executed in these two base classes. For example, a *List* knows how to sort, filter, print as a list, print items, open an item, delete an item, create an item, change the columns displayed, change the width of columns, resize the window, drag & drop, etc. An *Item* does similar operations.

Does it make sense here to also have a Holding *List* and perhaps a Holding *Item?* No, but the user *will* need to see the holdings. This is already available in the object model and the database model. How should it appear in the UI? Whenever the multiplicity of the association between objects is more than one, the *Item List* pattern is used. *Item* is extended to present this association as a *List*, but in the context of a single object. An *Item List* on **Security** may also be used to display the portfolios that hold that security.

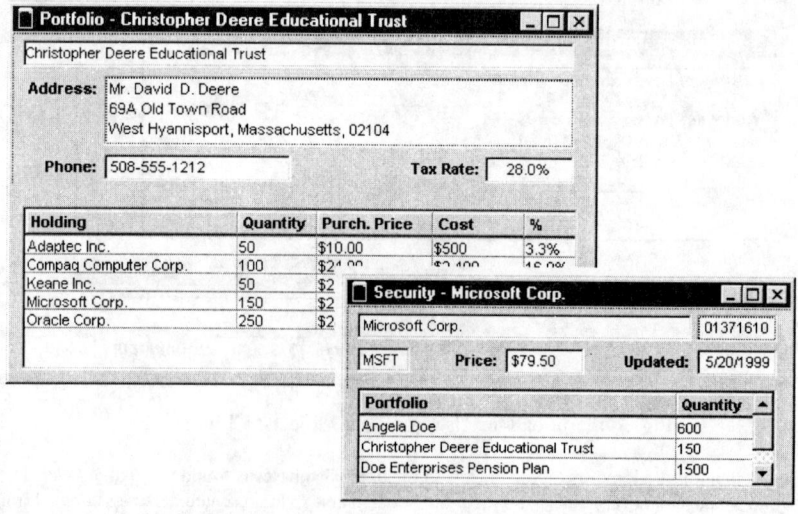

Fig. 5 - Iteration One User Interface Objects: UI Item List

An object's associations to other objects represent some of the most interesting domain logic. In the process of building the **Portfolio Item**, we also added some domain logic to calculate the cost of the holdings and the percentage of the portfolio that was invested in each asset. The *Item List* and *Reference Item* are two ways to represent relationships in the UI. A *Reference Item* will be used later.

So we have completed our first iteration! With the help of a framework supporting the Core patterns, this entire iteration can be completed in a few hours! We already have a partially useful application that can keep track of portfolio holdings and perform some rudimentary calculations.

6. Iteration Two: Financial Portfolio Management System

A problem becomes very obvious in the UI that may also be apparent in the data model or object model with sufficient study.

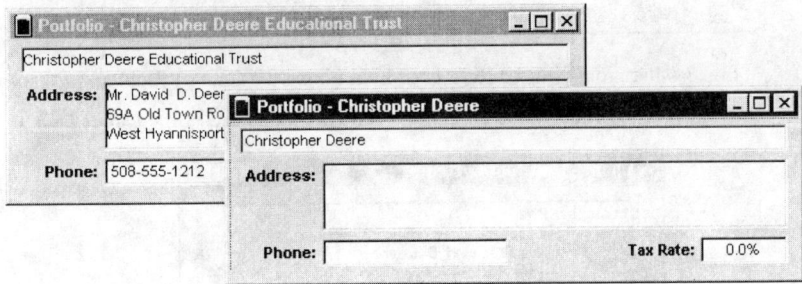

Fig. 6 - Iteration One User Interface Objects: Problem with Contact Information

Contact information needs to be entered for *each* portfolio, even if it is the same as another portfolio. The domain experts in this application may have known this was unacceptable, and a seasoned business systems analyst may have been able to anticipate this early. However, revealing the tacit assumptions and hidden requirements of a project is what good OO development is all about. We can fix this easily in the object model by adding a **Client** to hold the contact information instead of keeping it in **Portfolio**.

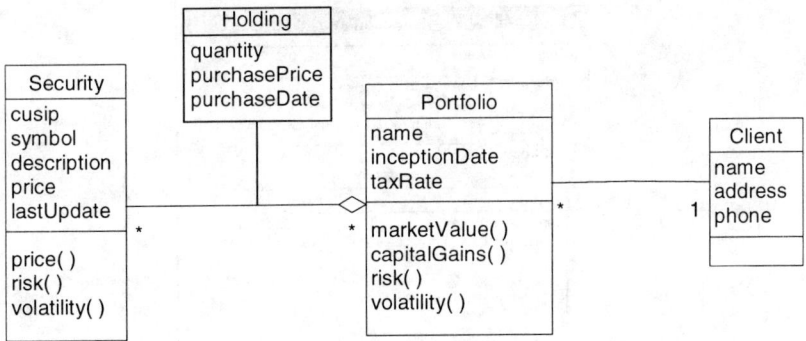

Fig. 7 – Iteration Two: Database Model Fixing the Contact Problem

How does this affect the other models? Using a *Item List* to display **Client** on the **Portfolio** would be strange, since there is only one **Client** for each **Portfolio**. Whenever the multiplicity between objects is one, the *Reference Item* is used.

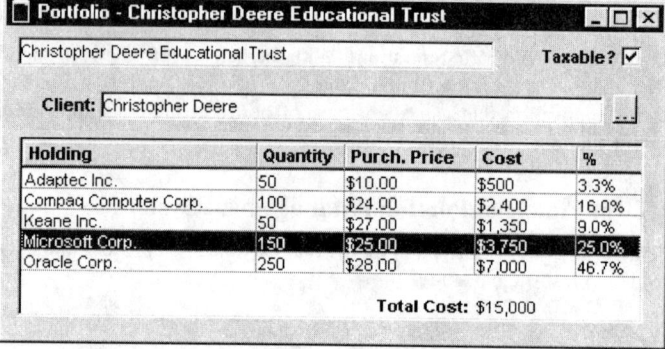

Fig. 8 – Iteration Two: UI Reference Item Fixing the Contact Problem

The *button* next to the client name on the **Portfolio** is used to access the **Client** *Item*.

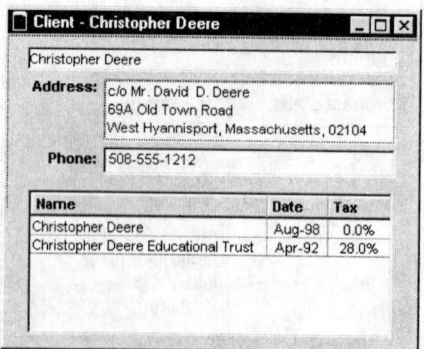

Fig. 9 – Iteration Two: Client Opened from Portfolio Reference Item

We may also like to add a **Portfolio** list to the **Client**, allowing users to see and access all of the portfolios for a particular client. We have everything we need to support this using the *Item List* pattern.

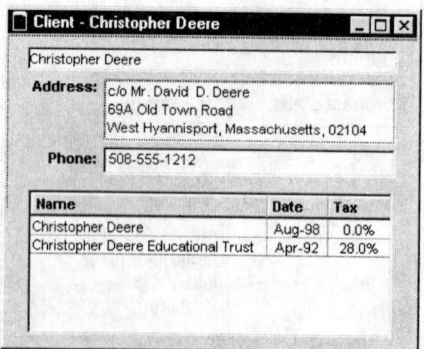

Fig. 10 – Iteration Two: UI Reference Item Fixing the Contact Problem

We have completed another iteration and once again evaluating the UI gives insight into the system and possible limitations. We may need more contact information than just a single client. In this example the "client" is actually the "trustee" for the portfolio. There may also be other people involved with the portfolio like accountants, lawyers, co-owners, and beneficiaries. If we try to articulate *all* the possible roles, it will really slow us down! Another problem in this example is that projected tax rates change, both because of legislative actions and personal circumstances. Another refinement of the model seems to be in order.

7. Iteration Three: Financial Portfolio Management System

Client could actually be considered a special type of **Contact** or a role played a contact. By adding the concept of a **Role**, we can allow additional contact roles to be added later, without taking the time to define them all now. We also can separate the concept of an **Account** to encapsulate the tax rate and possibly other information in future iterations. This model is more flexible and resilient to change than our earlier attempt.

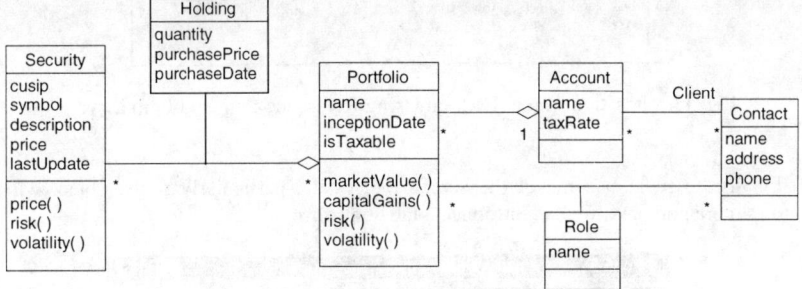

Fig. 11 – Iteration Three: More Flexible Database Model

What is the impact on the other models? These are shown in Figs 12 and 13.

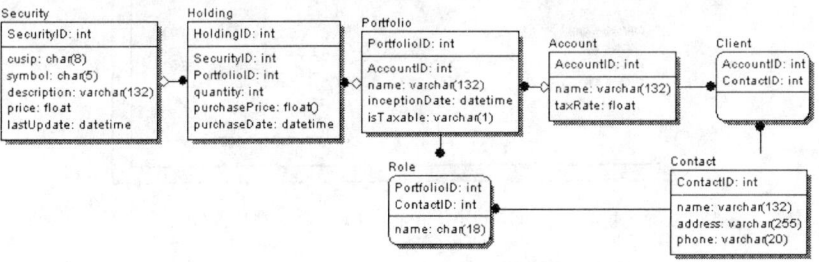

Fig. 12 – Iteration Three: More Flexible Database Model

By using RAD, characteristics of the objects and their relationships are really becoming known! In this iteration **Portfolio** was extended with additional domain logic to calculate capital gains. The UI was extended in Fig 13 to provide an interface to this logic. It is invisible to the user whether these calculations are accessing methods or attributes of the object. Note that if the model is later changed to pre-calculate and store the capital gains,

516

the user will not need to make any adjustments, in fact she may not even know! Ah, the beauty of OO encapsulation!

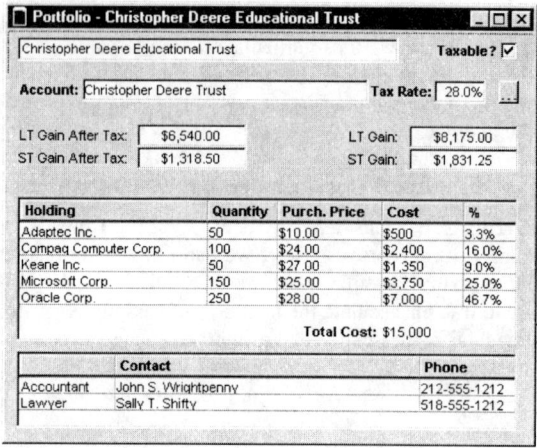

Fig. 13 – Iteration Three: UI Item Using Reference Item and Item Lists

Finally, to reclaim some of the screen real estate, particularly if the object will be getting more complex, we can introduce a tab control.

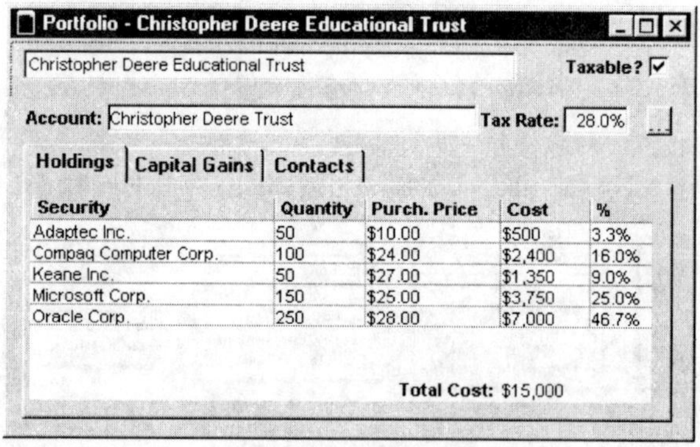

Fig. 14 – Iteration Three: UI Item Final Design

A notable achievement is that the user interface behaves consistently and is fully functional across all applications using Core. If the UI behavior is changed, it changes in *all* applications.

8. Other Patterns

Most systems can be completely designed and implemented using these basic Core patterns. The OOUI and underlying object models are very powerful and can be easily extended to new requirements, unlike a procedural UI and a traditional database schema. However, there are circumstances which may require a *process* or *procedure* to be modeled and captured: 1) if the users are inexperienced or the process is complex and error prone, users should be guided through the process or 2) the task involves a large number of domain objects making it tedious or perhaps repetitive. To address these issues, other UI patterns including **Dialogs**, **Wizards** and **Navigators** have been developed to augment the UI and business logic. Unfortunately space does not permit addressing them here.

Conclusion

The Core Pattern Language suggested above is not intended to solve problems for all applications. In fact it is just the opposite, intended to solve development complexities for a very narrow range of problems. However we are finding that Core is also applicable to a broader range of systems, typically those built by large MIS organizations. Although optimized for data-intensive applications with complex objects and object relationships, Core is also appropriate for simpler applications. It would not be appropriate to use for building a word processor, but it would be appropriate for use in building a mail reader or a web-based shopping cart application.

The results are encouraging and we believe this pattern language can be extended to other application areas. Just as Henry Ford set out to develop an approach to manufacturing automobiles that later was found to apply to a large variety of other industries, we have found that this pattern language developed for applications in the financial industry also may be applied to many other industries. Perhaps a couple dozen *metapatterns* are required for a robust and expressive language across application domains. As the language is used, like human languages, it will gradually evolve and meet the needs of future generations of developers.

Acknowledgements

Special thanks to developers and managers at Bernstein and other companies who shared our vision of "finding a better way": Keith Almeida, Bogdan Bradu, John Devlin, Kerry Foley, Vani Kadur, Soo Lee (Financial Technology), Cian O'Suilleabhain, Mark Reynolds (TechSys), Daniel Rosengarten, and Anil Yadav. Without their poignant criticism, blood, sweat, tears, and encouragement, Core would not exist.

References

[1] Blaha, Michael et. al. Object-Oriented Modeling and Design for Database Applications. Prentice Hall. Upper Saddle River, New Jersey. 1998.

[2] Coplien, James O. Advanced C++ Programming Styles and Idioms. Addison-Wesley Publishing Company. Reading MA, 1992.

[3] Coplien et. al. Pattern Languages of Program Design. Addison-Wesley Publishing Company. Reading MA, 1995: 179-237.

[4] Fowler, Martin. Analysis Patterns: Reusable Object Models. Addison-Wesley Publishing Company. Reading MA, 1997.

[5] Gabriel, Richard P. Patterns of Software: Tales From the Software Community. Oxford University Press, New York NY, 1996.

[6] Gamma et. al. Design Patterns: Elements of Reusable Object-Oriented Software. Addison-Wesley Publishing Company. Reading MA, 1995.

[7] Yourdon, Edward. Rise & Resurrection of the American Programmer. Yourdon Press Computing. Upper Saddle River, New Jersey, 1997.

Software Development "in the Zone"

Todd Lauinger
Reliastar Inc., USA

The purpose of this presentation is to have the participants of the tutorial understand common patterns of project management mistakes. Such mistakes directly cause late, over budget, poor quality software to be produced. Participants will then learn a new approach to developing software which keeps their teams on target. As long as the team operates under the new paradigm, the team is very productive and stays in "the software development zone."

The zone approach addresses risk in all activities of software development. Risk management done in this manner is one of three critical success factors that serves to keep your software staff "in the zone." The two other factors will be discussed in the presentation.

After understanding all three of the critical zone factors, participants of the presentation will have an opportunity to practice zone management on a sample requirements specification.

Todd Lauinger is an Application Consultant at Reliastart, and a published author and experienced teacher, mentor, and software architect. Todd presented a tutorial titled "Resolutions of an Object Designer" at the TOOLS USA '98 Conference in Santa Barbara. He is scheduled to give the same talk at the Smalltalk Solutions '99 Conference in New York. You may also read a new article of his in the Java Report titled "Object-Oriented Software Development in Java?" to be published in the February 1999 issue of the magazine.

Creating Social Agents with Reusable Components:
A Practitioner's Guide

Dana Moore
AT&T Labs, USA

This tutorial is aimed at practitioner-level developers and is motivated by a desire to share with other developers the potential techniques, available tools and resources, and issues of interest augmenting the desktop with software agents.

The tutorial will focus on integrating technologies for reuse, such as COM, Java, WFC, and XML to design, create, and deploy social interface agents. It covers underlying concepts (animation, character creation, speech recognition, text-to-speech) application design issues (interactions, turn taking, interruption, persistence, levels of confidence) and programming issues (IDEs , commercial agent resources, and COM integration).

The tutorial will demonstrate integration of software agents into MS Office applications, Web pages, and on the desktop. The session is primarily a 'hands-on' discussion, and presents 1) a conceptual framework and detailed design discussions for agent applications, and 2) an interactive demonstration using a standard IDE and other off-the-shelf resources to create the speech-enabled, animated social agents.

Dana Moore is a senior researcher, designer and software developer specializing in agent-based system. He holds a degree in engineering and a graduate degree in technology management, both from the University of Maryland, College Park and has written numerous articles on topics ranging from active object data bases to self-managed work teams. He is one of the architects of Autopilot, an agent-based system for complex workflows. Dana is a founding member of the Agent Society and sits on its Board, currently as the AT&T representative.

Tutorials

UML Demo

Features of UML Tools

Tony Wasserman

Software Methods and Tools, USA

Effective use of the UML notation requires automated support to make certain that UML models are complete and consistent. Automated support for UML ranges from simple drawing tools to sophisticated multiuser environments that provide code and document generation, as well as aids to project management. This tutorial surveys important requirements for UML development tools, including:

- Support for the modeling process
- Support for the UML language (syntax and semantics)
- Tool usability
- Code, schema, and document generation
- Customizability and adaptability
- Scalability for large models
- Multi-user support
- Life cycle support

The tutorial is accompanied by live demonstrations of several UML products as a way to illustrate some of the characteristics of various tools. These UML products cover the range of available products in price, scalability, and target market.

Anthony I. Wasserman is Principal of Software Methods & Tools, which offers consulting services on software development. He was previously Founder and Chairman of IDE, which built the Software through Pictures modeling environment. Prior to that, Dr. Wasserman was a University of California professor, and made numerous contributions to software engineering research. He is one of a handful of people to be elected as a Fellow of both ACM and IEEE.

Workshops

Project Management of Object-Oriented Developed Systems

Guy Carter

School of Computing, Information Systems and Mathematic
South Bank University, London, England.
guyc@sbu.ac.uk
Dilip Patel
Head of the Centre for Information and Organisation Studie
School of Computing, Information Systems and Mathematics
South Bank University, London, England.
dilip@sbu.ac.uk

Abstract

Quality system developmen can only occur with a co-ordinated strategy of planning and management. This paper considers the Project Management (PM) requirements of object-oriented(O-O) system development and addresses the need for an integration of these PM requirements to form one complete strategy for thPM of O-O developed systems.

1. Introduction

The potential for delivering quality software can only exist with quality investigation, analysis and design. The potential for a quality, systems development, life cycle (however brief) can only exist with a co-ordinated strategy of planning and management.
Traditionally the development of Information Systems does not run to plan. It is not uncommon for an IS project to overrun by 100-200% both in cost and time. In fact 15% of IS projects never deliver, i.e. never reach their goals [1].
Whilst subsequent development methods purport to improve the IS development process, by producing methodologies for the practitioners to follow, the management of this development is sadly neglected. Management of IS development is either ignored completely or at best traditional engineering project management techniques are wheeled out yet again. As Carter, Clare and Thorogood (1987) [2] noted these techniques are far from effective - presenting 'time-boxes', milestones, walkthrus etc. but not giving effective estimates of how to set the time scales for these, nor how to manage these aspects of the life cycle.
The evolution of Object-oriented (O-O) development in recent years has resulted in a number of methodologies focused on model building, however as a paper by Henderson-Sellers et al (1995) [3] pointed out Project management (PM) has, in general, been notable by its absence.

Ian Graham (1994) [4] paraphrases the theories of the military tactician Carl von Clausewitz as:
a. Tactics - the method of organising teams to carry out particular activities, tasks or processes.
b. Strategy - the method by which these activities, tasks or processes are combined to achieve a firms objectives.
Graham also suggests that Clausewitz's view - that it is easier to make a theory for tactics than for strategy - is the reason for the lack of strategic modelling in most O-O methods.
In order to be successful IS development projects must be strictly controlled. Control entails measurement; measuring performance against pre-set plans and management.

2. PM Requirements

Thus Project Management has three major areas of concern - not just the management of a project but also its planning and control throughout its life cycle
Planning
> Plans must be set for the complete life cycle of the IS development. Plans that define the time scale and cost for each elemental stage of the project.

Control
> There must exist a capability to control the progress of the project. That is to manage the project so development performance is equal to

or greater than some set of standards - the plans. Also to ensure that expectations are not greater than what is possible. To do this some facility must be in place to measure progress against the plans that have been set - and allow for adjustment of the plans where necessary.

Management

The process of management requires:
- commitment to the project by the management of the organisation;
- strong project team motivation;
- a clear understanding of the issues involved in each project;
- a grasp of the relevant technologies;
- capability in the political sphere in which the IS is to be developed;
- an understanding of the work flow in the organisation undertaking the development project.

It is apparent from these management requirements that the investigation of PM must address both the hard and soft aspects of each stage of a project. Soft components typically being those involving people management and hard aspects those that are either measurable or specifiable. It is also apparent that these PM requirements are applicable to all projects - regardless of discipline or method.

Whilst the management of the soft aspects of system development must obviously be included in a complete PM strategy this paper is concerned specifically with the hard aspects of systems development and even more specifically with development by O-O techniques. (It should be noted that a great deal of research has been carried out into the soft side of PM, people management and education, by De Marco and Lister [1, 5, 6] and Dooley [7,8] and this will be included in the final version of the overall strategy).

Recent developers of O-O techniques have recognised the need for PM in O-O development.

In his text on managing the O-O project Grady Booch [9] points out that O-O design presents the same problems as more traditional methodologies but apart from proposing that PM needs both strategic and tactical decision making regarding the final IT product, does not give any further insight into managing a project. He does however confirm the importance of control, hence the need to set milestones and deliverables, to ensure that there exists a flexibility that allows change if constraints are not met.

Work by Henderson-Sellers [3] recognises the lack of PM support even though O-O development has three business-focused stages - business planning, building and delivery - all needing management. He also suggests that the reuse of O-O code packages, together with O-O SW metrics must be incorporated into any project planning.

In a more recent paper [10] Henderson-Sellers and Due propose a management strategy for OPEN - a third generation O-O methodology that contains a tailorable process life cycle model. They describe the tasks of the project manager as having to deal with the variables of time, money, people, scope, tools, techniques and quality in a new environment of iterative development, incremental delivery and rapid prototyping. However we are still presented with a model which only addresses the physical aspects of one development methodology - but it does suggest that traditional PM tools have value.

A similar concept, PM for a new development technique, is explored by Daniels [11]. Although not aimed at one particular methodology, he addresses the concept of project life cycles being addressed in terms of Cycles. This approach provides a possible way forward in the initial stages of PM planning but no real advance in a method for implementing management in each of the life cycle Cycles.

Poo and Lee [12] also recognise the possibilities of using PM techniques developed for structured development methods - inherent in their paper proposing an O-O system modelling method based on a traditional structured methodology.

Although Henderson-Sellers and Daniels indicate that PM techniques used in traditional IS development methodologies should also suit O-O developments this belief is not shared by all. For example O'Callaghan [13] states that O-O models differ completely to structured models. So to use a PM strategy developed for structured models as a common platform for PM is not realistic.

Prototyping and Rapid Application Development (RAD) development techniques present a new set of problems to the project manager. The basic premise of these techniques is that complete system requirements are not known at the commencement of a project. So how is it possible to manage and control where the progress toward a goal, the very thing to be controlled, is not quantifiable?

A similar approach to RAD, in system development, is proposed by Tom Gilb's paper [14]. Gilb promotes Evolutionary Object management (Evo) which addresses the inherent problems of engineering type PM techniques when applied to IS type projects. Evo approaches the IS development cycle from a different angle - suggesting that PM should be based upon the premise that, at the outset, one cannot be precise about the requirements, and thus the planning, for the project. Whilst this may seem to be a rather controversial approach it does fully recognise the need for quality and quantifiable assessment.

Whatever the development methodology to be used there would appear to be agreement that PM is of paramount importance. The argument regarding the similarities, or lack of, between managing an O-O project and one using some other technique is largely irrelevant - due to the lack of a complete PM strategy for any development methodology.

3. PM Strategy Requirements

A PM strategy for O-O systems development must address:

    a. People management - all those involved in the development of the system - at all stages of the IS development life cycle.

    b. Techniques for planning, controlling and managing the physical, hard aspects of the system development.

    c. Business procedures that effect IS development (risk, bottlenecks, technology etc.).

Disregarding, for the purpose of this investigation, the soft issues a model of management must be built which addresses the contents of each of the basic building blocks of system development Business Planning, Building and Delivery. These will exist, in some form, for any of the O-O methodologies.

Business Planning

Business procedures - factors within an organisation that affect and may constrain the project development, strategic modelling and business process re-engineering.

Risk assessment - risk analysis, risk management and risk sensitivity, any probability of risk occurrence and jeopardising the project , or some key aspect.

Co-ordination - other projects running concurrently and their likely effect on the project.

Available tools.

Building

Measurement, including SW metrics, estimating and assessing elemental development module time scales.

Reuse - assembling the project from existing components.

Delivering

Testing and Evaluation - how are user expectations matched? (with a complete PM strategy this should be formality!)

The requirements are a PM strategy that will manage and control all factors of the areas of concern listed in the above model. Management techniques for each of these factors will need to be addressed as individual entities with the overriding constraint of holistic development to create one encompassing strategy.

References

1.   DeMarco, T. (1982). Controlling SW Projects. *Yourdon Press*

2.   Carter, G. D., Clare, C. P., Thorogood, D. (Jan 1987). Engineering Project Management Techniques and Their Application to Computer Projects. *Software Engineering,*.

3.   Henderson-Sellers, B., Graham, I. M., Swatman, P., Winder, R., Reenskaug, T. (1995). Using Object-oriented Techniques to Model the Life Cycle for O-O Software Development.

4.   Graham, I. (1994). Migrating to Object Technology. *Addison-Wesley Press.*

5.   DeMarco, T. & Lister, T. (1990). Software State of the Art - Selected Papers. *Dorset Hse Press*

6.   DeMarco, T. & Lister, T. Peopleware productive projects and teams

7.   Dooley, A. (March 1998). Is Training killing Project Management? *IT Training*, 7(3), 25-27.

8.   Dooley, A. (Feb 1998). The Real Causes of Success and Failure. *Project Manager Today*, 10(2), 12-14.

9.   Booch, G. (1996). Object Solutions: Managing the Object Oriented Project. *Addison-Wesley Press*

10.   Henderson-Sellers, B., Due, R. (Jan- Feb 1997). Open Project Management. *Object Expert*, 2(1), 30-35.

11.   Daniels, J. (Jan- Feb 1997). Object Method: Beyond the Notation. *Object Expert.*

12.   Poo, D., Lee, S-Y. (1994). An Object Oriented Systems Modelling Method based on the Jackson Approach.

13.   O'Callaghan, A. (1996). A Process Model for the Migration Phase. *Object Expert*, 1(6), 48-51.

14.   Gilb, T. (Jan- Feb 1997). Evolutionary Object Management. *Object Expert.*

Making the Transition to
Component-Based Enterprise Software Development
Overcoming the Obstacles - Patterns for success

Workshop Organizers

Martin Griss, Ph.D.	Gilda Pour, Ph.D.	John Favaro
Hewlett-Packard Laboratories	*San Jose State University*	*Intecs Sistemi*
Palo Alto, CA	*San Jose, CA*	*Pisa, Italy*
Email:	*Email:*	*Email:*
griss@hpl.hp.com	*gpour@email.sjsu.edu*	*favaro@pisa.intecs.it*
Tel.: (650) 857-8715	*Tel.: (408) 924-4145*	*Tel: +39-50-545111*

Abstract

This workshop addresses the critical success factors facing practitioners engaged in component-based enterprise software development (CBESD). Component-based software development is based on the concept of developing software systems by selecting previously developed or purchased reusable software components and assembling them within appropriate software architectures. Workshop participants will describe their experiences (successful or otherwise) in establishing CBESD programs, and will work together to captures the leanings in the form of "CBESD adoption patterns," detailing process, organizational, management and technical guidelines for success.

1. Introduction

All major IT market research firms have identified component-based enterprise software development (CBESD) as the rapidly emerging trend in the software engineering. Component-based software development is based on the concept of developing software systems by selecting reusable software components and assembling them within appropriate software architectures [1]. By promoting the use of software components built by commercial vendors or in-house developers, the component-based software development approach delivers the promise of large-scale software reuse. Component-based enterprise software development has the potential to:

- Reduce significantly the cost and time-to-market of enterprise software systems by allowing the systems to be built by assembling a set of reusable components rather than from scratch.

- Enhance the reliability of enterprise software systems because each reusable component has gone through several review and inspection stages in the course of its original development and previous usages, and because CBESD relies on explicitly defined architectures and interfaces.

- Improve the maintainability of enterprise software systems by allowing new (higher) quality components to replace old ones.

- Enhance the quality of enterprise software systems by allowing application-domain experts to develop components, and software engineers specialized in component-based software development to assemble the components and build enterprise software systems [2,3].

Over the past few years, IT and business organizations have been engaged in an informal kind of reuse through code sharing, design patterns, etc. However, the systematic reuse of software components across multiple applications and projects is in its infancy.

The reason is that a wide variety of obstacles are faced in making the transition from the traditional software development approach to component-based enterprise software development [4]. To overcome those obstacles, several engineering, process-related, organizational, and business-oriented issues should be addressed [5].

The following obstacles are typically cited:

- Business-oriented issues concerning how component development and support should be funded, lack of funding for education, training, access to vendor-supplied components, lack of a convincing business case and economic model for long term investment [6], unclear definition of product-line model and features [7], etc.

- Process-related issues due to low process maturity of the organization, ill-defined or unfamiliar reuse-oriented methods and processes, new inter-group coordination and management needs, well tested and documented methods and models to relate features to component sets and variability, etc.

- Organizational issues due to the lack of a systematic practice for reuse activities and enterprise component development, lack of management expertise and support, etc.

- Engineering issues mainly due to the lack of adequate techniques and tools for identifying, designing, documenting, testing, packaging, categorizing reusable software components, too few and poorly understood standard patterns and architectures, etc.

- Infrastructure issues due to the lack of widespread use of a standardized design notation such as the UML, common tools, base components, different programming languages and environments, support for multi-group configuration management, etc.

2. Workshop description

This workshop provides a forum for researchers and practitioners to meet and discuss the major challenges involved in the transition to component-based enterprise software development. The workshop builds on related reuse-oriented architecture (ROA) and CBESD workshops at TOOLS EUROPE '99 [8] and the CBSE Handbook workshop at ICSE'99 [9], which together mark the beginning of an international collaborative effort that aims at developing a consensus on the dominant obstacles and their best practice solution(s).

We will build our next workshop at OOPSLA '99 on the results of this workshop. We will also establish a repository of patterns of reuse success [10], and set up a special web page for this purpose. Our results will also be fed back to the CBSE Handbook project, focusing on adoption issues and critical success factors.

All IT and software professionals who have actively participated in making such transitions in their organizations are invited to participate in the workshop and share their experiences and their patterns of reuse success with workshop attendees. It would be most beneficial if participants describe how the approach taken by their organizations has integrated different elements such as business-case analysis, domain engineering, product line architecting, people and process management, and lifecycle software asset management.

Each workshop participant will give a short presentation (about 5-8 minutes) on his/her organization's experience of the transition and the lessons learned from that experience. Workshop attendees will participate in making and prioritizing a list of the obstacles that they find important and relevant to the workshop theme. Focus groups will then discuss and brainstorm a number of the obstacles, and identify the best approaches to overcome those obstacles, ideally documented in the form of patterns. Each group will report on the results of their discussion and brainstorming. The collection of discussions, comments and their suggested solutions (patterns) will be merged and refined to provide a prioritized list with suggested practical remedies.

3. Workshop Web Site

The workshop output will be made available on the workshop web site at http://www.hpl.hp.com/reuse/cbesd. This site will contain copies of the 3-5 page position papers of participants, workshop notes, a summary of the key issues facing CBSED adoption, and success patterns. There will also be links to other CBESD or CBSE sites.

References

[1] G. Pour, "Towards Component-Based Software Engineering," Proceedings of the 22nd International Computer Software & Applications Conference (COMPSAC'98), Vienna, Austria, August 1998.

[2] G. Pour, "Component-Based Software Development: New Opportunities and Challenges," Proceedings of the 26th International Conference on Technology of Object-Oriented Systems and Languages (TOOLS USA''98), Santa Barbara, CA, August 1998.

[3] G. Pour, "Moving Toward Component-Based Software Development Approach," Proceedings of the 27th International Conference on Technology of Object-Oriented Languages and Systems, Beijing, China, September 1998.

[4] W.B. Frakes and S. Isoda, "Success factors of systematic reuse." IEEE Software, 11(5): 15-19, September 1994.

[5] I. Jacobson, M. L. Griss and P. Jonsson, Software Reuse: Architecture, Process and Organization for Business Success, Addison-Wesley-Longman, 1997

[6] J. Favaro, K. Favaro, and P. Favaro "Value Based Software Reuse Investment," Annals of Software Engineering (5) 1998.

[7] M.L. Griss, J. Favaro and d'Alessandro, "Integrating Feature Modeling with the RSEB." Proceedings of 5th International Conference on Software Reuse, Victoria, Canada, June 1998, IEEE, pp. 76-85.

[8] J. Bosch, Joint workshop, "Designing Reusable Object-Oriented Architectures - Challenges, Methods & Tools" and "Making the Transition to Component-Based Enterprise Software Development: Overcoming the Obstacles - Patterns for Success ," TOOLS'99 Europe, Nancy, France, June 7-10, 1999. (See http://www.cs.tut.fi/~kk//ToolsEurope99WSProp.htm)

[9] A. Brown, et al, workshop on "Developing a Handbook for Component-Based Software Engineering," ICSE99 Los Angeles, May 17-18, 1999. (See http://www.sei.cmu.edu/cbs/icse99/cbsewkshp.html)

[10] M.L. Griss, "Reuse Strategies - Models and Patterns of Success." Component Strategies, SIGS, Oct. 1998.

Biographies

Martin L. Griss is a Principal Laboratory Scientist at Hewlett-Packard Laboratories, Palo Alto, California, where for the last 17 years he has researched software engineering processes and systems, systematic software reuse, object-oriented development and component-based software engineering. He is currently working on model-driven, agent-based application management systems. He created and led the first HP corporate reuse program and participated in the development and execution of the HP corporate software initiative. He led HP efforts to standardize UML for the OMG, and is a member of the OMG UML revision taskforce. He was previously director of the Software Technology Laboratory at HP Laboratories, and spent 9 years as an Associate Professor of Computer Science at the University of Utah. He is co-author of the influential book "Software Reuse: Architecture, Process and Organization for Business Success" (with Ivar Jacobson and Patrik Jonsson), which holistically addresses technology, people and process issues in a UML framework. He has written numerous articles on software engineering and a reuse column for the "Object Magazine/Component Strategies". He lectures widely on systematic reuse and software process improvement, and is a frequent keynote speaker and panelist. Dr. Griss received a Ph.D. in Physics from the University of Illinois. He has over 30 years of experience in software development, education and research. He is an adjunct professor at the University of Utah. He is a member of the ACM SIGSOFT Executive Committee, and of the joint IEEE/ACM committee on software engineering education and accreditation. He is a member of the SSR steering committee, the ICSE99, UML99, OOPSLA99 and TOOLS99 program committees, and the ICSE2002 organizing committee.

Gilda Pour has twelve years of R&D and industrial experience and seven years of academic experience in object-oriented software engineering for parallel and distributed systems. Her current research projects, funded by NASA and industry, are in the field of object-oriented component-based enterprise application development including multi-tier Web-based enterprise application development. She contributed to several projects in the fields of distributed enterprise object computing and Internet technology when she worked in the R&D Laboratories of Hewlett-Packard Company and Software Engineering Research Center. She has also made significant contribution to several research projects funded by Rome Laboratory/Air Force and industry. Dr. Pour is currently a professor of software and information engineering at San Jose State University. She has developed and taught several courses in the fields of component-based software engineering, component technologies, and distributed object computing in both industry and academia. On related topics, she has given seminars and tutorials, chaired panels, and led workshops at international conferences including TOOLS Conference Series, Computer Software and Applications Conference (COMPSAC), and the World Conference of the WWW, Internet, and Intranet (WebNet). Dr. Pour serves as the Workshops and Panes Chair for the TOOLS USA '99 Conference and the Tutorials Chair for the TOOLS ASIA '99 Conference. Gilda Pour holds a doctoral degree in Computer Science/Software Engineering from University of Massachusetts, an Engineer's degree in Computer & Information Sciences and Engineering/Software Engineering from University of Florida, a M.S. degree in Electrical Engineering/Systems, and a B.S. degree in Electrical and Computer Engineering.

John Favaro has more than twenty years of experience in the information technology field. After spending several years at CIT-Alcatel in Paris and Siemens AG in Germany working in the area of software engineering environments and telecommunications, he joined Intecs Sistemi in Pisa, Italy as project leader for the European Space Software Engineering Environment. He now leads the information systems methodologies initiative at Intecs. Mr. Favaro has published widely in the areas of software reuse and object oriented domain analysis. He is European Co-Chair of the IEEE Technical Subcommittee on Software Reuse, and was

European Chair for the 1998 International Conference on Software Reuse. Recently he has launched an initiative to apply principles from Value Based Management to information technology investment, and is a co-organizer of the first workshop on Economics-Driven Software Engineering Research (EDSER-1) in May 1999. His most recent publications include "Value Based Software Reuse Investment," and "Strategic Analysis of Application Framework Investments" in the John Wiley & Co. series on object technology. Mr. Favaro has a B.S. in Computer Science and Mathematics from Yale University and a M.S. in Electrical Engineering and Computer Science from the University of California at Berkeley.

Workshop on Component-Based Software Engineering Processes

Kingsley C. Nwosu
Lucent Technologies, Inc.
600-700 Mountain Ave
Room 3D-435
Murray Hill, NJ 07974
+1 908-582-7131

Robert C. Seacord
Software Engineering Institute
Carnegie Mellon University
Pittsburgh, PA 15213 USA
+1 412-268-3265

Abstract

Component-based software engineering (CBSE) spans a range of technologies and engineering practices. Engineering practices for component-based systems (e.g., design, integrate, test, deploy and sustain) are emerging, but in isolated settings rather than at a community level. The goal of this workshop is to provide a baseline understanding of the broad aspects of CBSE processes.

1 Introduction

Over the years, it has been the ambition and goal of the Software Engineering committee to have the ability to quickly assemble or build a software system from compatible and cooperating entities or components. At last, the long cherished ambition of Software System Developers and Integrators is coming to fruition. This has been largely motivated by similar abilities in the companion hardware areas and also by the other foreseeable by products such as shortened time to market and increased productivity.

The Component-Based Software Engineering (CBSE) process departs drastically from the conventional software development process in that it's integration-centric as opposed to development-centric. And a true CBSE depends mostly on selection, acquisition, and integration of components from external vendors, which raises a lot of issues and problems. There are numerous issues, questions, and risks involved in component selection, acquisition, and integration that must be adequately addressed and resolved in a CBSE project. And all these, and other necessary tasks, such as requirements engineering, domain engineering, etc., must be addressed in the context of a formal Component-Based Software System Development (CBSE) Process.

0-7695-0278-4/99 $10.00 © 1999 IEEE

2 Workshop goals

The goal of this workshop is to address issues involved and surrounding the development of Component-Based Software System Development (CBSE) processes. As a result, this workshop will target research and industrial works and experiences that deal with the issues as they related to CBSE:

Requirements engineering and analysis

Inadequate, incomplete, erroneous, and ambiguous system and software requirements are a major and ongoing source of problems in systems development. These problems manifest themselves in missed schedules, budget excesses, and systems that are to varying degrees unresponsive to the true needs of the sponsor. These difficulties are often attributed to the poorly defined and ill-understood processes used to elicit, specify, analyze, and validate requirements [2].

Domain engineering and analysis

Domain engineering is the process of defining the scope (i.e., domain definition) analyzing the domain (i.e., domain analysis) specifying the structure (i.e., domain architecture development) building the components (e.g., requirements, designs, software code, documentation) for a class of subsystems that will support reuse. Domain analysis focuses on supporting systematic and large-scale reuse (as opposed to opportunistic reuse, which suffers from the difficulty of adapting assets to fit new contexts) by capturing both the commonalties and the variabilities of systems within a domain to improve the efficiency of development and maintenance of those systems. The results of the analysis, collectively referred to as a domain model, are captured for reuse in future development of similar systems and in maintenance planning of legacy systems (i.e., migration strategy) [1]

Interface specification languages and tools

Interface languages are used to specify the interfaces between program components. Each specification provides the information needed to use an interface. A critical part of each interface is how components communicate across the interface. Communication mechanisms differ from programming language to programming language. For example, some languages have mechanisms for signaling exceptional conditions, other do not. More subtle differences arise from the various parameter passing and storage allocation mechanisms used by different languages.

Product and technology evaluation

To ensure that systems meet immediate user requirements, component qualification practices must be developed. Typically, we describe products in terms of interfaces that provide access to functionality. Here, standards may provide a frame of reference for comparing the product to generally accepted capabilities. Various approaches have been developed for evaluating products in terms of their interfaces. For example, [5] describes a rigorous process for selecting between competing COTS products.

However, a broader interpretation of the interface to a product includes far more than its functionality. To make use of a product one must also understand aspects of performance, reliability, flexibility, etc., as well as the implicit assumptions made by the product about the operating environment. For example, while examination of the published interface of a product may suggest that it can interoperate with a second product, interoperation may be limited by each product's assumption that it has primary responsibility for handling incoming events. Much of this sort of information is not addressed by standards and is unavailable from product suppliers. Thus, hands-on evaluation to identify such mismatches (alternately called architectural mismatches [6], and interface mismatches by [7]) must be a primary option.

Integration

In CBSD, the notion of building a system by writing code has been replaced with building a system by assembling and integrating existing software components. In contrast to traditional development, where system integration is often the tail end of an implementation effort, component integration is the centerpiece of the approach; thus, implementation has given way to integration as the focus of system construction. Because of this, integrability is a key consideration in the decision whether to acquire, reuse, or build the components.

Modeling

A model is a representation of a system whose representations are used to answer questions about the system. The reason for creating a model, rather than examining the system as a whole is that the model can abstract away from unimportant details and allow us to more easily investigate the relevant questions.

Software models are created to examine the function, performance, safety, security, and availability of a system or a component. Functional models are created to ensure that a system will behave as expected.

System behavior can be predicted by creating situations and using the model to test them. If the model's behavior is satisfactory we gain some confidence that in the same situation the system will perform as desired. One reason for modeling is that we expect the creation of a model to be cheaper than the creation of a system. In such cases, the model is a predictor of the future system and development requires that the system conform to the model. Sometimes we model a system or component after the fact, we may already have the component and, through testing or other investigative techniques we uncover facts about the component which we build into our model. Again, we use the model to predict the behavior of the component when placed in certain situations. We might choose this approach if we wish to create a system using a particular component where the failure of the component could cause catastrophic failure of the system. Safety or security related systems might take this approach.

Design and development

A fundamental change necessary in developing component-based systems is the simultaneous definition and tradeoffs among the system context, the architecture and design, and the availability of products in the marketplace, as shown in Figure 1 Component-based development

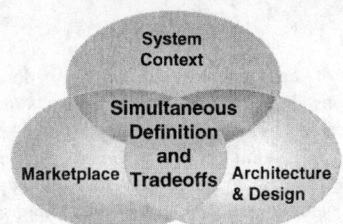

Figure 1 Component-based development

Risk analysis and management

Risk management is a practice with processes, methods, and tools for managing risks in a project. It provides a disciplined environment for proactive decision making to assess continuously what could go wrong (risks) determine which risks are important to deal with and implement strategies to deal with those risks.

Process models

A process model is a relatively detailed, formal or semi-formal representation of a process. The primary users of process models are process engineers, who analyze, assess, design and monitor processes for continuous process improvement and process automation, and process participants, who perform the processes or are interested in their performance (e.g., project managers). Process models can support a wide range of uses, and some of the most common are:

♦ as a mechanism to help people understand and visualize a process (especially graphical models),
♦ as a basis for engineering (i.e., developing, evaluating, improving, etc.) a process, and
♦ as the means of formalizing a process for machine-assisted enactment by a process-centered software
♦ engineering environment, workflow engine, or the like.

Numerous process-modeling notations have been proposed and applied in practice. Process models have been used to describe existing (as-is) processes and prescribed processes (e.g., standards, regulations), evaluate them for desirable characteristics and improvement opportunities, and develop and analyze new (to-be) processes. They have also been used to quantitatively simulate and analyze processes in support of management planning and control, and process improvement [3].

System frameworks and architectures

Components implement two kinds of interface: a functional interface that reflects the role of a component in the system, and another extra-functional interface that reflects the component model imposed by some underlying system framework [8]. These extra-functional interfaces express the architectural constraints that enable composeability and other desirable properties of component-based systems. Therefore, our understanding of what makes a component a component is inextricably linked to our understanding of the architectural constraints imposed on components by a system framework.

System maintenance

The one constant aspect of component-based software development is change [4]. Constituent components are constantly evolving – new products are emerging while existing products become dated or obsolete. Keeping existing systems "current" is a difficult but necessary maintenance task. In maintaining a best-of-breed solution, the maintainer needs to continually monitor the marketplace to evaluate new technologies, new products and new releases of component products and upgrade the system when appropriate. These skills are not very different from the skills required to initially develop these systems.

Repository management

The benefits of developing an effective component library are readily apparent: by allowing system integrators to fabricate software systems from pre-existing components rather than laboriously develop each system from scratch, enormous time and energy can be saved in the development of new software systems.

However beneficial a component library might be, a useful and effective repository has turned out to be an elusive goal. Traditional software libraries have been conceived as large central databases containing information about components and, often, the components themselves. Examples of such systems include the Center for Computer Systems Engineering's Defense System Repository, the JavaBeans Directory, and the Gamelan Java directory.

While the JavaBeans and Gamelan directories are still going concerns, similar systems have failed in the past largely as a result of their conception as centralized systems. Problems with this approach include limited accessibility and scalability of the repository, exclusive control over cataloged components, oppressive bureaucracy, and poor economy of scale (few users, low per-user benefits, and high cost of repository mechanisms and operations).

3   Publishing workshop results

A workshop summary will be published on the WWW via the workshop homepage www.sei.cmu.edu/cbs/tools99.

References

1.   Foreman, John. Product Line Based Software Development- Significant Results, Future Challenges. Software Technology Conference, Salt Lake City, UT, April 23, 1996.
2.   Requirements Engineering and Analysis Workshop Proceedings, CMU/SEI-91-TR-030, December 1991.
3.   Marc I. Kellner, Ulrike Becker-Kornstaedt, William E. Riddle, Jennifer Tomal, Martin Verlage, Process Guides: Effective Guidance for Process Participants, Published in the Proceedings of the 5th International Conference on the Software Process: Computer Supported Organizational Work, International Software Process Association, New Jersey, 1998.
4.   Robert C. Seacord, Kurt Wallnau, John Robert, Santiago Comella Dorda, Scott A. Hissam, Custom vs. Vendor-Integrated COTS Software, CMU/SEI-99-TN-003, May 1999.
5.   Kontio, J., "A Case Study in Applying a Systematic Method for COTS Selection," Proceedings of the International Conference on Software Engineering, Berlin, 1996.
6.   Garlan, D., Allen, R. and Ockerbloom, J., "Architectural Mismatch: or Why It's Hard to Build Systems Out of Existing Parts," Proceedings of the International Conference on Software Engineering, Seattle, 1995.
7.   Wallnau, K., Clements, P. and Zaremski, A. "Correcting, Identifying, and Avoiding Interface Mismatch: Theory and Practice", Draft Paper, Software Engineering Institute, Carnegie Mellon University.
8.   Alan Brown, Kurt Wallnau, The Current State of Component-Based Software Engineering (CBSE) IEEE Software, September 1998, pg. 37-47.

Life Cycle Activity Areas for
Component-Based Software Engineering Processes

Robert C. Seacord
Software Engineering Institute
Carnegie Mellon University
Pittsburgh, PA 15213 USA
+1 412-268-3265

Kingsley C. Nwosu
Lucent Technologies, Inc.
600-700 Mountain Ave
Room 3D-435
Murray Hill, NJ 07974
+1 908-582-7131

Abstract

Although traditional software engineering focuses on development Component-based software engineering (CBSE) processes must focus on integration. In this paper, we elaborate on this focus into a process framework for CBSE consisting of four major activity areas: engineering, business, management, and overarching. We show how these activities are concurrent with respect to an iterative and incremental development model. Detailed discussions are also presented on the consequent issues, concerns, problems, and recommended solutions.

Introduction

Over the years, it has been the ambition and goal of the Software Engineering community to quickly build a software system from components that have been developed outside of the development organization. This has been motivated by similar abilities in the companion hardware areas resulting in associated benefits such as shortened time to market and increased productivity. Due to developments in several areas of the industry and technology, that long cherished ambition is coming to fruition. Today, there are commercial off-the-shelf (COTS) products that perform functions that previously required custom-built software components.

Component-Based Software Engineering (CBSE) process departs from the conventional software development process in that it is integration-centric as opposed to development-centric. A true CBSE process depends largely on selection, acquisition, and integration of components obtained from external vendors. While this is a positive trend, there are numerous issues, questions, and risks involved in component selection, acquisition, and integration that must be adequately addressed and resolved in a CBSE project.

Multiple process models exist today, primarily focused on the building of custom systems. The exact nature of the relationships between traditional build process models and process models that incorporate the differences imposed by CBSE are unknown. There is an increasing belief that existing process models are inadequate to address the unique CBSE concerns of development as primarily an integration effort as opposed to a custom development. Some of the issues to be determined include what the appropriate process model for CBSE should look like.

In [Oberndorf 98a], Oberndorf, Sledge, Brownsword developed a *process framework* that defines the activity areas that cover the development and evolution of COTS-based systems for government programs. In this paper we adopt the broad outlines of this process framework and discuss the needs of component-based systems within this context. The exact nature of activity areas described in this paper differs in some regards from the COTS-based systems process framework defined in [Oberndorf 98a].

In our discussion of the process framework, we first present an overview of the integrated relationship between the different activity areas within the development life cycle. Secondly, we discuss the different activity areas, and the issues within each activity area, followed by our conclusions.

Development life cycle overview

The CBSE process framework consists of four system activity areas: engineering, business and management, and overarching. The *engineering activity area* covers activities associated with the technical conceptualization, construction, and sustaining of a system (hardware, software, and people). The *business activity area* includes activities associated with developing a business case for a component-based system, determining business process implications, and developing cost estimates. The *management activity area* covers activities that a project manager is directly responsible for such as cultural transition, information sharing, and CBSE policies. The overarching activity area covers organizational activities, or activities that may be common to several projects and are accordingly better addressed at an organizational level. Figure 1 shows the relationship of the major activity areas with respect to each other.

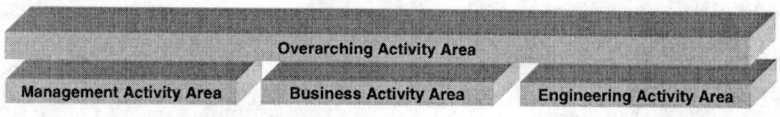

Figure 1. Activity areas

The activity areas are not an ordered sequence of phases, rather they involve iterative and incremental development activities that usually characterize and are often needed to accommodate the uncertainty that exists with most CBSE projects.

Incremental development consists of a series of iterations involving activities from one or more activity areas, the successful completion of which results in the delivery of a final system. To elaborate these incremental life cycle activities, we adopt the Rational Objectory Process model [Quantrani 97] that structures the development process along two dimensions - division of the life cycle into phases and iterations (time) and production of a specific set of artifacts with well-defined activities (process components). The time dimension consists of the inception, elaboration, construction, and transition phases. The inception phase specifies the project vision; the elaboration phase defines the planning and architecture specification and design. The construction phase builds the product incrementally, while the transition phase does the manufacturing, delivering, and training. In our case, we use the same time phases, but the process components are the activity areas identified above. As a result, Figure 2 shows the application of the Rational Objectory Process model on the proposed framework development process.

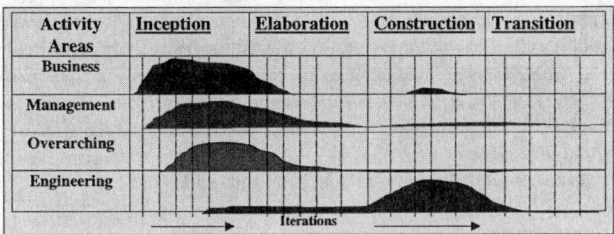

Figure 2. Development life cycle phases and iterations

As shown in Figure 2, successive iterations are required to complete each development life cycle phase. The inception phase, for example, comprises successive iterations of activities in the business, management and overarching activity areas. Specifically, these include business case analysis, cost estimations, addressing cultural issues, defining policies, and risk management. During the construction phase, these iterations are principally of activities in the engineering area.

Activity areas

The activity areas should be considered as a notional model that would be used to guide the detailed planning of a specific development project. Depending on the particular needs of a project, some activity areas would have greater emphasis than other areas.

Overarching activity area

The overarching activity area covers organizational activities, or activities that may be common to several projects and are accordingly better addressed at an organizational level such as managing vendor relationships. Examples of overarching activities include training, knowledge sharing and licensing. Although many of these activities correspond to activities within individual projects, they are on a significantly different level and have a different focus. For example, the licensing of a component or components at an organizational level may have a significant impact on the organization. Often an organization can negotiate a significantly better price on a component or component-line. This can assist projects in providing a core set of components they can use at a reduced cost. However, this approach may also have a negative impact by leading projects to select components that may not be the best fit for the particular needs of the project. Components may be selected because they are available at a reduced cost, particularly if project allowances for licensing components are cut as a consequence of spending at the organizational level.

The most important activity in the overarching activity area is the establishment of an effective component-based strategy. This strategy can be represented in very broad terms or in very specific guidelines. Each approach has risks and benefits. In the Clinger-Cohen act, the federal government strongly encouraged the use of COTS in government acquisitions [Oberndorf 98b]. This has been interpreted in many different ways, often with adverse effect to the programs involved. This is illustrative of the risks involved in defining strategy in broad terms.

An alternate approach is to provide very specific guidelines. For example, an organization may go as far as to select a specific component model or framework and require projects to adhere to this framework. An organization may make a strategic decision, for example, to use only Microsoft COM components. This decision may have advantages in providing common components that can be re-used in different projects throughout the organization, and in having a common knowledge base that can be shared between development groups. The disadvantages, again, comes from encouraging projects to adopt technologies that may not be appropriate to the particular needs of the project. Strategic decisions are often made for reasons that have little or nothing to do with technology issues. However, it is important that the technical consequences of these decisions are understood.

Engineering activity area

The engineering activity area covers activities associated with the technical conceptualization, construction and sustainment of a system. CBSE has significantly different characteristics from traditional, custom system development. In particular, the use of system architectures and frameworks take on additional importance in a CBSE process. In fact, with the advent of Enterprise JavaBeans and the continued evolution of CORBA architectures can be viewed as components and be selected through an evaluation process. The characteristics of the architecture vary between domains, but in general the architecture attempts to ensure system characteristics that need to be handled in a common manner over multiple components. One example of this can be distributed transaction processing, where multiple components may implement operations that are part of a larger transaction that may need to be completed or rolled back as a whole. Problems such as these are intractable without a consistent architecture.

Mismatches between an architecture and components often need to be addressed before a component can be successfully integrated. Architectural mismatch [Garlan 95] can often be addressed by implementing a wrapper, bridge or adapter for the mismatched component. Rarely should the architecture be altered to suit the needs of a specific component, unless this change can then be generalized and consistently applied to all components that comprise the system.

Business activity area

The business activity area includes activities associated with developing a business case for a component-based system, determining business process implications, and developing cost estimates. A component-based software engineering effort often introduces new concerns that are not at issue in more traditional custom development approaches. Software licensing issues, for example, often dictate the system design, as certain configurations may be prohibitively priced.

Management activity area

The management activity area covers activities a project manager is directly responsible for such as budgeting and risk management.

In a component-based development effort, the budget is distributed between human resources and the purchase of licenses for software components. In a custom development effort, the development effort can be sized and an appropriate development team can be staffed for the necessary period to complete the project. In CBSE, a tradeoff exists between purchasing and integrating commercially available components and the development of custom components. It is often impossible to determine in advance the requirements in each of these areas until the process is sufficiently advanced. For example, it is normally impossible to determine if a particular component can be used to provide a required capability until that component has been evaluated. In this case, it is impossible to determine if funds should be allocated for the purchase of the component or for a development effort to create a custom component until the evaluation is completed. An advanced CBSE process in this area will provide for maximum flexibility in exchanging development and licensing resources.

Risk management exists in both a custom development effort and in a component-based software engineering effort, although the nature of the risks is often significantly different and must be understood and accounted for in a risk mitigation plan. CBSE must provide for continued evaluation of products so that the integration team can understand how market changes may affect their efforts.

Conclusions

In this paper, we have discussed a number of activity areas that form a process framework for component-based software development. We presented the concurrency between the activities of these activity areas with respect to an iterative and incremental development model. Detailed discussions are also presented on the issues, concerns, problems, and recommended solutions to the different major activity areas. As alluded to in several places in this paper, a true realization of a CBSE project involves addressing and solving numerous issues, many of them presented here, that are novel to component-based software engineering. All the issues presented here do not necessarily apply to every CBSE project, however, every CBSE project will be faced with many of these issues.

References

1. Garlan, D., Allen, R., and Ockerbloom, J.: Architectural Mismatch or Why It's Hard to Build Systems Out of Existing Parts, Proceedings of the International Conferences on Software Engineering, Seattle (1995)
2. Oberndorf, P., Sledge, C., Brownsword, L., COTS-Based Systems for Program Managers, Software Engineering Institute, Carnegie Mellon University, briefing.
3. Oberndorf, P., A Clarification of DoD COTS-Related Policies," , Software Engineering Institute, Carnegie Mellon University, briefing. Available WWW: URL:
   http://www-preview.sei.cmu.edu/cbs/cbs_slides/index.html
4. Visual Modeling with Rational Rose and UML, Terry Quantrani, Addison-Wesley, 1997, ISBN:0-201-31016-3.

The use of Mediators for Component Retrieval in a Reuse Environment

Regina M. M. Braga   Marta Mattoso   Cláudia M. L. Werner

COPPE/UFRJ - Computer Science Department
Caixa Postal 68511 – CEP 21945-970
Rio de Janeiro – Brazil
{regina, marta, werner}@cos.ufrj.br

Abstract

CBD (Component Based Development) aims at constructing software through the inter-relationship between preexisting components. However, these components must be connected to a specific domain of application in order to reuse components effectively. In general, reusable components are stored in a great variety of data sources. Thus, a possible solution for accessing domain information is to use a software layer that permits the integration of different component sources. In this paper, we present the use of the HIMPAR integration data layer, based on the use of mediators, which was modified to support a reuse environment. Through mediators, domain ontologies are used as a tool/mechanism for specifying the ontological commitments or agreements between component users and providers.

1. Introduction

Component Based Development (CBD) [1] aims at constructing software through the inter-relationship between preexisting components, thus reducing the complexity, as well as costs of software development, through the reuse of exhaustively tested components. According to Jacobson, Griss and Jonsson [1], the effectiveness of component reuse depends on the connectiveness among them and the specific application domain. Therefore, reuse possibilities increase when components are binded to domain concepts. We propose the search for reusable components at the level of its relevant semantic concepts.

Apart from the component integration difficulty, a reuse environment has to deal with interoperability issues between component repositories. Reusable domain components (in all abstractions levels) can be stored in a great variety of data sources, using the most different data models, access mechanisms and platforms. Moreover, domain components can be geographically distant, incurring in complex manipulations.

Therefore, the effectiveness of a reuse environment is associated to its capacity to handle the following three characteristics: (i) distribution and heterogeneity- domain information can be distributed [2] and uses different kinds of storage; (ii) Domain Ontology- to organize component repositories; (iii) Domain information evolution – to insert new information (including legacy information).

In order to address these three issues, a reuse environment must organize component repositories within a domain ontology while preserving its original characteristics of distribution and heterogeneity, all in a flexible way. This organization can be accomplished through a software layer that provides the integration of different domain repositories (distributed and/or heterogeneous). This software layer can be seen as a particular case of Heterogeneous and Distributed Data Base Systems (HDDS) [4]. One solution in HDDS is the use of the mediation technique [2].

In this paper, we present the adaptation of an integration data layer, based on mediators, to support reuse environments, particularly the Odyssey environment [5]. The main objective of this layer is to integrate information from several domains stored in distributed data sources, in a way that users have transparent and uniform access to these domains while preserving their autonomy. This layer also stores a description of components repositories providing metadata services such as queries on the available components.

2. Mapping a Mediation Architecture into a Reuse Environment

According to Wiederhold [2], mediators are modules that encompass layers of mediation services, connecting bases of heterogeneous and distributed data (producers) to information systems (consumers). As new sources of information are aggregated to the mediation structure, the amount of information to be modeled increases, frequently generating inconsistencies, ambiguities and conflicts in the represented information on the mediation structure.

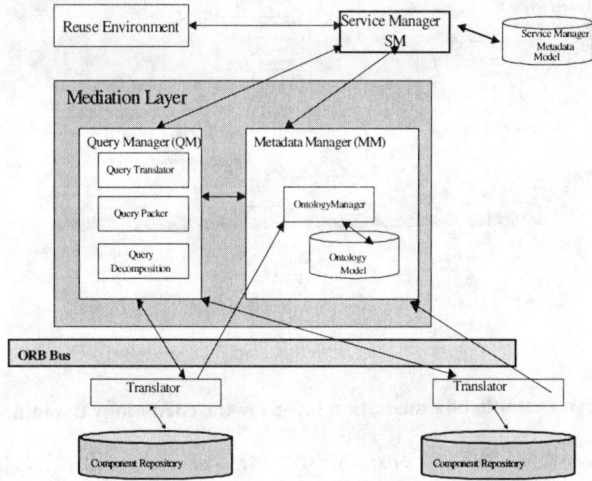

Figure 1- Architecture of the Odyssey Mediation Layer

The description of each domain (Mediator) is stored on a metadata repository. The metadata represents the domain ontology as well as the description of the components provided by the mediator. Each mediator provides a uniform view of the available components through their representation within a global model. Also, each mediator is responsible for the mapping between the description of the component within the domain and the component itself as stored in the component repository. To handle different formats and representations, the architecture provides a translator module that maps the local description into the global component description model.

Figure 1 presents the Odyssey Mediation Layer that comprises four levels: Interface, Mediation Layer, ORB bus and Translators, which were derived from the mediation model of the HIMPAR architecture [3]. The Interface level is implemented by the Service Manager (SM) which creates and modifies the mediation layer. The Mediation Layer provides the management of each mediator through the Metadata Manager (MM) and also provides the access to mediators though the Query Manager. At the ORB level, communication between the mediation layer and translators is established through the CORBA standard services. Finally, the Translator level provides one translator for each component repository so that it can participate in the Mediation Layer integration model.

Figure 2 presents an example of a mediation layer for a specific application domain, i.e. The Cardiology Domain. Several mediators are presented as sub-domains, such as Cardiology and Hospital Administration domains. There are several mediators responsible for managing specific domains; for example, the Cardiology domain mediator is specialized (P2) in a mediator that provides detailed information about a cardiology sub-domain, the domain of Heart attack. The Hospital Administration Mediator is aggregated (P1) to the Cardiology mediator, generating a more generic mediator that combines the two domains. The latter can be used in cases where information concerning the two domains is necessary. Each mediator is connected to data sources that contain reuse components related to its domain.

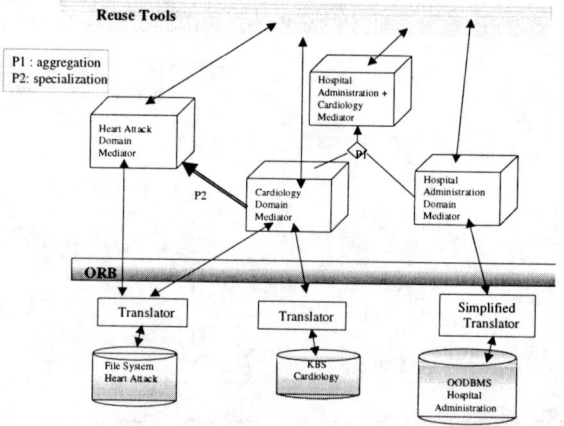

Figure 2 - An example of a mediation layer for the cardiology domain

The KBS data source has the class *Therapy,* whose extension is called *Therapies,* and the File System data source has the class *Clinical-Treatment,* whose extension is called *Treatment*, as shown in the ODL definition below. Both data sources store components that have the ability to, given some patient symptoms, provide a clinical therapy for treating the patient symptoms, and thus were mapped to the Cardiology Domain Mediator.

`Class Therapy`
`(extent Therapies)`
`{attribute String`
`ComponentDescription;`
`attribute Byte Bytecode;`
`attribute String`
`InterfaceDescription;`
`attribute String sourcecode;`
`attribute String TypeofRequiredInput;`
`attribute String TypeofRequiredOutput;}`
	`Class Clinical_Treatment`
	`(extent Treatment)`
	`{ attribute Byte ComponentCode;`
	`attribute String Description;`
	`attribute String InputDescription;`
	`attribute String OutputDescription;`
	`attribute String`
	`ImplementationLanguage;}`

For the integration of these information, an association class (the Clinical_Therapy Class) has to be defined in the MM, and stored in the Ontology Model Repository corresponding to the data types from each data source:

```
Class Clinical_Therapy
{ attribute Byte Component;
  attribute String ComponentDescription;
  attribute String DescriptInterfaceIn;
  attribute String DescriptInterfaceOut;}
```

The service structure for the class creation in the MM is:

```
MM->NewTypeCreation (
"Cardiology Domain Mediator",
"ClinicalTherapy", "attribute..." )
```

where the three parameters of the service correspond to `char* MediatorName, char* ClassName,` and `char* Structure`.

To add the data sources KBS and File System to the mediation layer, objects of SM model must be instantiated. The syntax for this service for the KBS source is:

```
SM->ComponentCreation(char* HimparObjectName; char* StructureOfHimparObject);

SM->ComponentCreation("Container", "name = ContainerKBS; Owner = SUS Hospital;
Structures = {{Therapy, Component = Bytecode} , {Therapy, ComponentDescription =
ComponentDescription}, {Therapy, DescriptionofInterfaceInput =
TypeofRequiredInput}, {Therapy, DescriptionofInterfaceOutput =
TypeofRequiredOutput}},Implementational");

SM-> ComponentCreation("Translator", "name = TranslatorKBS; Translator that deals
with Knowledge Based Systems; KBS;{ContainerKBS}");
```

where `HimparObjectName` identifies which SM type is being created, i.e., a Mediator, a Translator, or a Container. The `StructureOfHimparObject` provides the object values. It is important to notice that the field `Structures`, specific of the Container class, provides a one-to-one mapping between the source attributes and the mediator attributes of a specific class. In the case of ContainerKBS, the class is named Therapy. Corresponding objects must also be instantiated for File System container.

Finally, in order to associate the Mediator Clinical_Therapy class with the Therapy (KBS) and ClinicalTreatment (File System) container's classes, the following service is provided:

```
SM->ClassAssociation( "Cardiology Domain Mediator", "ClinicalTherapy",
"{ContainerKBS, Therapy},{ContainerFileSystem, ClinicalTherapy}");
```

where the three parameters correspond to: `char* MediatorName, char* MediatorClassName,` and `char* ContainerClassName`.

The following query retrieves information about all containers associated with Clinical_Therapy class:

```
Select X.component from X in ClinicalTherapy
where "Cardiac Problems" in X.ComponentDescription;
```

Therefore, this query provides access to KBS and File System data sources producing the desired results, i.e., all binary code from components that deals with clinical therapies for cardiac problems. Such modeling enables the management of data sources insertions and deletions. Therefore, a large number of data sources can be integrated to the system without modifications in the Cardiology Domain Mediator. Through the mediation structure, Odyssey users can search for components in a transparent and uniform way. In the above example, the users of reuse tools do not have to know where the components are stored. Moreover, users do not have to query all components repositories, using the repository query language format (when a query language exists) to know where the needed components are stored. They do not have do know either how to access the KBS and File system repositories.

All the complexity for dealing with these heterogeneous repositories is treated by the mediation layer. Without the layer, Odyssey reuse tools would have to handle these repositories, increasing the complexity of the Odyssey Environment. Using mediators, reuse tools can query specifically the mediation metadata, using one single model. The mappings between mediators metadata and translators redirect and decompose the query

546

to KBS and File System repositories respectively. Also, the identification of components of the same domain that are in different repositories, as it is the case of objects from Therapy and Clinical_Treatment classes, was detected at the time of the registration of components in the mediation layer. Afterwards this is all transparent to reuse tools.

3. Conclusions

This work addresses the interoperability problem between component repositories in a reuse environment. An integration layer was developed to help the search and identification of suitable reuse components in the Odyssey environment. This layer is based on mediators and ontology to provide the binding of different components to their domain concepts. To assist the identification of related components and their appropriated domain organization, each mediator represents a domain ontology and provides the mapping to their respective components repository.

Mediators provide a uniform view of the available components organized in a domain taxonomy. Domain ontologies are used to help the search for reusable components through the representation of domain semantic concepts. Therefore, this mediation layer promotes domain integration and mechanisms to translate component requests across ontologies. The innovative aspect of our proposal is the use of domain ontologies, for reusable component retrieval, allowing users to express component requests at a higher level of abstraction when compared to keyword based access or component interface based access.

Using this mediation layer, the structure of the reuse environment becomes more flexible, since the existing domain information/component can be easily added to the environment, without conversions from the original information format (format of the information source) to the reuse environment format. Without the mediation layer, the Odyssey reuse tools would have to access directly the repositories, dealing with specific characteristics of each repository. Moreover, when a new repository has to be used, all reuse tools have to be updated for dealing with this new one.

Therefore, the main contribution of this paper is to show the potential of the technology of mediators, together with ontology models, for dealing with components repositories complexities, organizing the manipulation of different components within a domain ontology. Although, the mediation technology is quite popular within HDDS, its adaptation, using domain ontologies for component retrieval in a reuse environment is innovative. Currently we have an operational interoperability architecture based on the use of mediators, translators and a CORBA communication protocol, which is responsible for the connection among translators and mediators in a distributed and heterogeneous environment.

References

[1] Jacobson, I.; Griss, M.; Jonsson, P. ; "Software Reuse: Architecture, Process and Organization for Business Success"; Addison Wesley Longman, May, 1997.
[2] Wiederhold, G.; Genesereth, M.; "The Conceptual Basis for Mediation Services"; IEEE Expert, Vol.12 No.5, Sep-Oct,1997.
[3] Pires, P.; Mattoso, M.; "A CORBA based architecture for heterogeneous information source interoperability"; Proceedings of Technology of Object-Oriented Languages and Systems - TOOLS'25, IEEE CS Press, Melbourne Australia, November, 1997, pp.33-49.
[4] Ram, S.; "Guest Editor's Introduction: Heterogeneous Distributed Database Systems,"; IEEE Computer, Vol. 24 No.12, December, 1991.
[5] Braga, R.; Werner, C.; Mattoso, M.; " - Odyssey: A Reuse Environment based on Domain Models"; Proceedings of IEEE Symposium on Application-Specific Systems and Software Engineering Technology (ASSET'99), Richardson, Texas, March 24-27, 1999, pp. 49-57.

A Generic Process and Terminology
for Evaluating COTS Software

Wilfred J. Hansen
Software Engineering Institute
Carnegie Mellon University
wjh@sei.cmu.edu

Abstract

Papers on evaluation of COTS (Commercial-Off-The-Shelf) software fail to agree on a universal terminology. What exactly is an attribute? a criterion? a feature? a characteristic? ... In writing a tutorial, we arrived at answers that made sense to us and found that they implied a process for evaluation. After defining a goal and identifying candidate entities, the evaluation process, named "QESTA," proceeds through Quantification of qualities into metrics, Examination of the entities to find their values for those metrics, Specification of transforms based on the metrics, Transformation of those values according to the transforms to produce factors, and Aggregation of the factors to generate decision data. This process and terminology are shown to be consistent with, and an extension of, ISO 9126.

Keywords: evaluation, COTS software, QESTA, selection, aggregation, MAUT, attribute, criterion, ISO 9126, quantification, metrics

Development of systems incorporating COTS (Commercial Off-The-Shelf) software inevitably entails evaluation of alternative products in order to choose among them. Since the required evaluation process is correspondingly more central to the software development process, we at the Software Engineering Institute have been developing a tutorial on evaluation. In the course of this work, we have encountered numerous disparate processes and terminologies for evaluation and its data artifacts. To focus the tutorial on a single set of terms, we developed the terminology and process reported here.

The need for a single terminology is apparent when various authors utilize almost-but-not-quite interchangeable terms like attribute, characteristic, condition, criterion, property, quality, and so on. For instance, ISO 9126 [8] defines several terms as follows:

Assessment - "action of applying specific documented assessment criteria"

Features - "identified properties ... related to the quality characteristics"

Quality - "the totality of features and characteristics [that bear on ability] to satisfy stated or implied needs"

Software quality assessment criteria - "rules and conditions which are used to decide whether the total quality ... is acceptable"

Software quality characteristics - "set of attributes [by which] quality is described and evaluated"

Despite their length, these definitions are rootless since ISO 9126 nowhere defines precisely what is meant by *attributes*, *characteristics*, *conditions*, *properties*, or *rules*. Because of their ambiguity, we avoid altogether these terms and the additional term *criteria*. Instead we use the terms *metrics* and *transforms*, defining them as functions producing numeric values of specific sorts.

In this paper we are concerned with the actual process of evaluation, excluding such phases as developing a plan and choosing the alternative *entities* to be evaluated. However, we do insist that preparatory work will have arrived at a *context* for the evaluation [2]; that is, a description of the target system and the environment into which it will be deployed. If I am buying a car, the context is my situation--financial resources, driving patterns, aesthetic tastes. For an organization, the context includes the organization's mission, its structure, and its existing procedures for the tasks that will be affected by the target system. From the context the project personnel will adduce various—possibly ill-defined—*qualities* which the target system should exhibit.

Various sources describe appropriate *Qualities*. ISO 9126 prescribes some general Qualities for software. For evaluating vendors, [6] notes the traditional metrics and goes on to define new ones suitable for startup vendors not yet having a corporate track record. Estimation of costs is well covered by COCOMO [1]. Estimation of error propagation is covered in [13]. When substantial amounts of addition code is needed to integrate COTS software, the costs can be estimated with the function-point based work described in [4].

The heart of the evaluation process is shown in Table 1 and is called "QESTA" from the names of the constituent operations. Each of the five bracketed processes in Table 1 operates on data of the type or types shown to the left and produces data of the type shown to its right. The overall inputs are the entities to be evaluated and the desired qualities, as derived from the context; the eventual outcome is *Decision Data*.

Context, Qualities --> [**Quantification**] --> *Metrics*
Entities, Metrics --> [**Examination**] --> *Values*
Metrics --> [**Specification**] --> *Transforms*
Transforms, Values --> [**Transformation**] --> *Factors*
Factors --> [**Aggregation**] --> *Decision Data*

Table 1. Schematic of QESTA Evaluation Process. Operations are in bold and inside square brackets. Data types in italic on the outsides of the arrows serve as inputs and outputs.

Quantification: Usually the qualities of the desired system are not directly measurable but are instead vague statements about like "acceptable performance," "small size," and "high reliability." (These particular qualities apply to both cars and computer systems!) The Quantification step defines for each desired quality one or more *Metrics*, where a metric is a procedure for examining an entity to produce a single datum, either a symbol or a number. For a car, typical metrics might be color and price. (That is, the metrics will be measurement procedures that yield color or price values. By convention we use the type of the value returned as a shorthand for the procedure that produces that value.)

Examination: Most of the tedious effort of an evaluation comes in the Examination step wherein the selected candidate entities are each measured against the metrics identified in the Quantification step. The result of the Examination is a set of *Values*, one for each combination of entity and metric. A typical result is shown in Table 2 where the first two metrics have yes-or-no values, the third yields a set of symbols, and the last a number. Many errors can distort examinations; see for instance, the criticisms in [9].

Product:	A	B	C	X
Metric a:	-	-	Y	Y
Metric b:	-	Y	-	Y
Metric c:	X	+	#	+
Metric d:	1.5	2.1	0.1	5.2

Table 2. Sample results of an Examination

Specification: Once the metrics are defined, the stakeholders and decision makers must be consulted as to their judgmental interpretation of the values resulting from each metric. Does a "yes" mean the entity is acceptable? or not acceptable? Does a "no" disqualify the entity altogether? Are higher numeric values more meritorious than low? or is there a threshold? Based on these judgments, a *transform* is defined for each metric such that the value reported is converted to a value suitable for Aggregation. For a car, the transform for color might convert red to 1 and any other color to 0 while the transform for price divides by some price deemed most desirable, say $20,000. For a computer system, disk occupancy could be similarly transformed into either a Boolean or ratio value. Many transformation tools and other useful evaluation strategies are covered in [10].

Transformation: In this step the transforms developed in the Specification step are applied to the values from the Examination step to produce *factors*. Given the car transforms described above, a $13,000 red car would have the values yes and $13,000 which would be transformed into factors of 1 and 0.65. One purpose in introducing transformations is to align all values in comparable ranges, say -1 to 1. More important are those transforms which simply reject an entity because of a failure to have an appropriate value for some metric.

Aggregation: There are many aggregation methods of varying mathematical formality; [3, 7, 11, 12]. One common method is to assign weights to the factors. For the example in Table 2, the values could have been transformed with one/zero for yes/no and 0/1/-1 for X/+/#. By weighting the four metrics at .2, .2, .3, and .5, a final decision datum for each product could be computed as a cross product:

$$\text{Product A:} \quad 0*0.2 + 0*0.2 + 0*0.3 + 1.5* 0.1 = 0.15$$
$$\text{Product B:} \quad 0*0.2 + 1*0.2 + 1*0.3 + 2.1* 0.1 = 0.71$$
$$\text{Product C:} \quad 1*0.2 + 0*0.2 - 1*0.3 + 0.1* 0.1 = -.09$$
$$\text{Product X:} \quad 1*0.2 + 1*0.2 + 1*0.3 + 5.2* 0.1 = 1.22$$

In this case, it might be suitable to choose Product X. However, such ad hoc weightings are usually erroneous, as pointed out strongly in [5] and [11].

A more modern Aggregation method is the Analytical Hierarchy Process (AHP) implemented in Expert Choice [5]. In this system, stakeholders do a pairwise rank ordering of alternatives and the system computes an overall figure-of-merit for each entity. In this and other Aggregation methods, the step concludes by trying a variety of weightings to explore the sensitivity of the derived entity rank ordering to the particular weighting values chosen.

The metrics and transforms need not be "pure" functions—they may have side effects. We can consider examples of side effects by way of illustrating not only those effects, but also the flexibility of the QESTA evaluation approach. Our illustrations come from the class of techniques we call "formative evaluation," so called because the main focus of the evaluation is on understanding the nature of the entity and what qualities and metrics are important for evaluating it and its peers. The process is akin to house hunting where prospects are unsure of their desires and hone their metrics and transforms by looking at available houses.

The "model problem" technique creates a working system that focuses on differences in systems that may arise due to new technologies and how they can be factored together given existing implementations. Model problem construction is the Examination step, but the values produced are often not numeric but instead new ideas for metrics. The Specification step considers each new metric and may cause a change in the evaluation plan, or as a model for deriving metrics for products that meet the technologies.

The "risk/misfit" technique examines how well an entity meets the requirements of the context and what "repairs" may be needed to use the entity in the new system. In particular, some COTS products may embody task procedures that differ from those currently in use. Thus this step may lead to re-engineering the organization's procedures to take maximum advantage of a COTS technology or product. For risk/misfit, the result of Examination may include an altered context for each entity. It is common in such cases to utilize transforms that convert all necessary changes and development into costs so these can be combined in the aggregation step.

Requirement definition phase
Stated or implied needs --> [Quality Requirement Definition]
          --> Quality requirement specification
Preparation phase
Qual. req. spec. --> [Metric Selection] --> Metrics
Qual. req. spec. --> [Rating Level Definition] --> Rating levels
Qual. req. spec. --> [Assessment Criteria Definition]
          --> Assessment criteria
Evaluation phase
Product, Metrics --> [Measurement] -> Measured values
Measured values, Rating levels --> [Rating] --> Rated level
Rated level, Assessment Criteria --> [Assessment] --> Result

Table 3. The ISO 9126 Process.

The steps of QESTA are not in discord of the corresponding part of ISO 9126, which, as shown in Table 3, has eight steps in three phases. The first step of Quality Requirement Definition is roughly equivalent to the setting of the context in QESTA; both influence all remaining steps. The Metric Selection step is QESTA's Quantification, wherein the desired qualities are operationalized into measurable metrics. The Rating Level Definition step is a special case of QESTA's more general specification step during which the attitudes of stakeholders concerning desirable metric values are elucidated to determine appropriate transforms. QESTA does not have an explicit Assessment Criteria Definition step, but this is implied in the choice of an Aggregation method. QESTA's Examination, Transformation, and Aggregation steps are the same operations as the ISO 9126 Measurement, Rating, and Assessment steps.

One major difference between QESTA and ISO 9126 is in the form of transformed values, that is, the values QESTA calls factors and ISO 9126 calls Rated levels. The latter are described as being measured in four levels--excellent, good, fair, poor--while QESTA admits to any form of value suitable to the chosen Aggregation method. (See ISO 9126-2.)

The close alignment of our terminology with that of ISO 9126 validates our choice of steps; we have gone beyond ISO 9126 in more precisely defining both the terms used to refer to the data artifacts generated in each step. We expect to be able to demonstrate in the completed tutorial that these terms can be readily adapted to the description of all the many forms of evaluation encountered in developing COTS systems.

References

[1] Boehm, B., B. Clark, E. Horowitz, C. Westland, R. Madachy, R. Selby, *"Cost models for future software life cycle processes: COCOMO 2.0,"* **Annals of Software Eng., V. 1,** Baltzer (Amsterdam, 1995) pp. 57-94.

[2] Carney, David J. and Kurt C. Wallnau, *"A basis for evaluation of commercial software,"* **Information and Software Technology 40** (1998) 851-860.

[3] Dyer, James, *"Remarks on the Analytic Hierarchy Process,"* **Management Science, Vol. 36,** No. 3, pg. 249-275, March 1990. Also: Saaty, T., *"An Exposition of the AHP In Reply to the Paper 'Remarks on the Analytic Hierarchy Process'"* and: Harker, P. and Vargas, L., *"Reply to 'Remarks on the Analytic Hierarchy Process'"* in the same issue.

[4] Ellis, Tim, *"COTS integration in software solutions: A cost model,"* **Systems Engineering in the Global Marketplace, Proceedings of the 5th International Symposium on NCOSE, Vol. 1,** (1995) pp. 171-177.

[5] Expert Choice, Inc., Battelle Memorial Institute, *"Protest Proof Source Selection,"* (October, 1998). (http://www.expertchoice.com/selection/)

[6] Herschel, D., *"Techniques for selecting a start-up vendor,"* Gartner Group, #TG-06-0532, 1998, 3 pp.

[7] Hwang, Ching-Lai, Kwangsun Yoon, **Multiple attribute decision making : methods and applications : a state-of-the-art survey,** #186 Springer-Verlag (Berlin, 1981).

[8] ISO/IEC. *"Information Technology – Software Product Evaluation,"* ISO/IEC 9126 (1991-12-15).

[9] Kitchenham, B. A., S. G. Linkman, D. T. Law, *"Critical Review of Quantitative Assessment,"* **Software Engineering Journal, vol.9,** no.2 (Mar 1994) p. 43-53.

[10] Kontio, Jyrki, *"OTSO: A Systematic Process for Reusable Software Component Selection,"* Technical Report CS-TR-3378, UMIACS-TR-95-63, University of Maryland College Park, MD 20742, Dec. 1995.

[11] Morisio, M., and Tsoukiàs, A., *"IusWare: a methodology for the evaluation and selection of software products,"* **IEEE Proceedings of Software Engineering, Vol. 144,** No. 3. (June, 1997) pp. 162-174.

[12] Roy, Bernard, *"The Outranking Approach and the Foundations of ELECTRE Methods,"* in **Theory and Decision, Vol. 31,** pg. 49-73, 1991, Kluwer Academic Publishers, Netherlands.

[13] Voas, J., *"Error propagation analysis for COTS systems,"* **Computing & Control Engineering Journal, vol.8,** no.6 (Dec, 1997) pp. 269-272.

A Component Selection Methodology with Application to the Internet Telephony Domain

Indira Kuruganti
Software Technology Center
Lucent Technologies, Inc.
600 Mountain Ave. Rm 3D-435
Murray Hill, NJ 07974-0636
indira@lucent.com

Abstract

In this paper, a simple 3-part methodology for component selection is described. The motivation for this methodology came from an empirical study on the selection criteria employed and tasks performed by software development groups in our company when considering certain types of components. The iterative methodology outlined here describes activities and roles for selecting components and provides a list of concerns and vendor selection criteria for consideration by component users when executing each of these activities. It is expected that the proposed methodology will be of pragmatic value to practitioners of the component-based software-engineering (CBSE) paradigm, especially to those operating in immature problem domains where the requirements are subject to frequent and rapid changes. To illustrate this methodology, we will present examples from one such domain, namely the Internet telephony domain.

Keywords: CBSE, Component Selection, Internet Telephony, selection criteria, protocol stacks.

1. Introduction

The ability to effectively select a component that meets the needs of a given system development activity is fundamental to achieving the anticipated benefits from the use of the component based software engineering (CBSE) paradigm. However, the selection criteria and evaluation methodology to be used are not very well understood at this time. Software development projects therefore run the risk of incurring higher costs and longer lead times in the final product due to poor component selections or avoiding the component selection problem altogether.

This led us to recently conduct a study of groups involved in evaluating or selecting certain components for use in the Internet telephony domain. The focus was on understanding how the component selection problem was approached, compiling the criteria used when evaluating components in each category, and, capturing retrospective insights into the component selection process.

In this paper, we describe a simple 3-stage methodology to select components that is partially motivated by our findings from this study. The 3 stages here are screening, evaluation and decision-making. Accordingly, we describe steps, roles and selection criteria when performing each of these activities. In particular, we separate the selection criteria for a component along 3 dimensions:

- functional specifications (what does the component do),
- operational or performance attributes (how well does it perform), and,
- deployment factors (when and where can the component be used).

In addition we also list vendor selection criteria to be employed at each stage.

Finally, to illustrate this methodology, we will briefly discuss components (speech coders and protocol stacks) used in Voice over IP applications.

2. Motivation

Component selection, from the perspective of a component user, is focussed on understanding the needs that must be met by a particular component and evaluating available vendors and their offerings to identify the best-fit solution. This is often a difficult problem because of the following reasons:

- Lack of understanding on what constitutes a component and how to evolve a component-based architecture and framework
- Incomplete understanding of the functional specifications, performance attributes and deployment constraints that must be met
- Non-uniformity in vendor offerings with respect to packaging of functionality into components

We elaborate below on the above points.

Component selection is often interpreted as an activity for finding assets (pieces) that best fit into an underlying (jigsaw puzzle) context. But it is not often clear how to evolve such an architectural and framework context for the problem at hand. This is especially true for new and evolving problem domains (e.g., internet telephony) wherein not enough domain expertise is available to apply available domain engineering techniques.

Moreover, we have found (in an internal study) that individuals faced with the task of component selection (especially in the context of new development in a new domain) undertake this in the requirements definition and/or architecture phases. So, comprehensive component specifications with well-defined and documented interfaces are hardly likely to be available at the beginning of the selection task. Indeed information gathered during the component selection activity is often employed to refine the component specifications and its interfaces [1]. In some cases, if the component being selected is deemed to have profound impact on the achievement of the project's technical and budgetary goals then the architecture of the system is adapted to accommodate an existing component rather than the other way around!

Finally, the component consumer has to contend with vendors marketing products at several layers: from basic building-block type components to platform and sub-assemblies to complete applications [3]. But as components become more complex and better differentiated, the component selection problem becomes more difficult. Also, the consumer has typically little control on how different components will be "bundled" for marketing purposes, the consumer is often faced with the prospect of comparing "apples" with "oranges" and making a decision on which best fits current needs!

Our goal in this paper therefore is to provide some guidance to CBSE practitioners faced with this difficult yet essential task. Our approach here is to design a methodology that focuses on the activities most likely to be performed and providing information on how best to use available information to execute these activities. We also indicate which selection criteria and roles to employ at each stage.

3. Methodology for Component Selection

The 3 activities in our methodology are Screening, Evaluation and Decision-Making. These activities can be viewed as 3 iterations of the component selection task which investigate with increasing detail the "fit" of the component to the functional needs, operational/performance constraints and deployment factors at hand. Our approach thus includes facets of the 3 different component selection and evaluation strategies described in [2].

Each of the activities in our methodology is decomposed into steps, involves several roles and employs a checklist of selection criteria and concerns. The checklist in each case is separated along 3 dimensions:

- functional specifications (what does the component do),

- operational/performance attributes (how well does it perform),
- deployment factors (when and where can the component be deployed).

Accordingly, our methodology addresses component specification, selection criteria and evaluation tasks along all these 3 dimensions. Vendor selection criteria are also explicitly addressed.

3.1 Screening

The primary goal of this activity is to identify existing vendors and components, filter these to a candidate set and simultaneously clarify the specifications that the component must meet. Accordingly, inputs to this activity include:

- (draft) specifications including list of must-have features, interface characteristics and technical standards
- available information on performance requirements & operational constraints that must be met
- desired development and target environments (hardware, OS, tools etc.) and
- expectations from vendor with regards to business alignment & market share.

Outputs of the screening activity are:

- a ranked list of screened components (and implicitly, a list of components and vendors that failed the screening),
- revised product requirements & architecture
- (refined) component specifications (with additional information on functional & performance specs., operational constraints, and nice-to-have features)

Primary roles involved here include system architects and software designers with appropriate input obtained as desired from systems engineers, software developers and product managers.

Screening involves the following steps:

- Gather information on candidate components (e.g., by attending vendor briefings and examining available marketing literature)
- Identify list of candidate components

- Gather preliminary cost information on the candidates
- Roughly assess the components and vendors using a checklist of selection criteria and concerns

An illustrative list of selection criteria and concerns are provided under 3 separate categories here:

Functional Specifications
- Includes all must-have features?
- Satisfies relevant technical standards?
- Does vendor documentation on component interfaces match the necessary interface requirements?

Operational /Performance Attributes
- Component meets known minimal performance requirements?
- Any violation of required operational constraints in vendor documentation?

Deployment Factors
- Availability of implementations on development and target hardware/OS platforms
- Support of multiple hardware/OS implementations by vendor
- Platform and OS independent

Vendor Selection Criteria:
- Alignment of vendor organization with component user business goals
- Market share as an indicator of market acceptance of the vendor solution
- Existing in-house customer base for vendor and previous experiences (if any) with the vendor
- Vendor Commitment to the component (product) in terms of current & projected R&D investment and level of marketing support

For components that are expected to have low technical impact on product architecture and low economic impact on product development cost, the user can simply select the component (and vendor) that heads the ranked list of candidates.

For instance, the speech codec to be used when building IP Telephony gateways may be considered to be an example of such a component. Selection criteria applicable for speech codecs include: compliance with H.323 standards for audio coding and compression (e.g., G.711 - mandatory; G.723.1, G.729.A - recommended); vendor claims on coder delay, frame size, processing requirements and compatibility with target deployment platform. Duration of operation by the vendor in the speech codec business may also be very relevant.

3.2 Evaluation

Here, the emphasis is on verifying component functionality and performance against vendor claims as well as validating these against relevant technical standards and refined component specifications. This verification must be done in the context of the component user's particular application domain and development/deployment environments. Accordingly, inputs to this activity include:

- the subset of screened components to be evaluated,
- refined component specifications (from the screening activity)
- development and target environments (hardware, OS, tools etc.) in which the component is to be evaluated
- initial price quote from the vendors for licensing, training and support

Outputs of the evaluation activity are:

- evaluation results for each candidate component
- revised component specifications and system architecture
- ranking of vendors and component.

Since the components must be evaluated in the context of the actual application and deployment, software developers, designers and systems engineers play the pivotal role in the evaluation activity with appropriate inputs from the secondary roles of product management and system architecture.

Evaluation involves the following steps:

- Generate a compliance matrix for features and performance requirements
- Execute vendor-provided examples and test applications and summarize results for each candidate component in the compliance matrix
- Obtain comparative benchmark data from an independent agency [optional]

- Develop context-specific examples, test applications and tools to verify functionality and performance on target platform
- Document the results of the component evaluation and experiences in dealing with the vendor during the evaluation
- Rank the candidate components and vendors using a checklist of selection criteria and concerns (as below)

Some selection criteria and concerns that may be applicable here are:

Functional Specifications
- Satisfies all mandatory requirements from relevant technical standards?
- Can handle all operational scenarios in component specifications?
- Component interfaces behave as advertised by the vendor and as required by component specifications?
- Any duplication of functionality between the existing system architecture and the candidate component?

Operational /Performance Attributes
- Meets the scalability demands at hand?
- Meets known requirements for performance, reliability & robustness?
- Compatible with development tools?
- Complies with existing architectural principles and strategies (e.g. open system principles or distributed object strategies)
- Do the architectural model and/or interface definitions of the candidate impose any constraints on the system?

Deployment Factors
- Ready to use out-of-the-box?
- Interoperable with products (in use or likely to be used) from other vendors?
- Can be used individually and/or optionally?
- Does the selection of candidate component constrain the selection of other needed components?
- Comprehensive and Easy to understand documentation which is supportive of trouble-shooting?

Vendor Selection Criteria:
- Quality of support and training

- Responsiveness to user's concerns and custom needs
- Involvement in standards bodies
- Maturity with the candidate component (i.e. frequency of upgrades/releases)
- Leverage i.e. opportunity to influence future product direction

For components that are a cornerstone of the system architecture, the evaluation activity should be conducted with great diligence and attention to detail. In the Internet telephony domain, the H.323 protocol stack used in Gateway applications is an example of such a cornerstone component because it has a profound impact on the rest of the system architecture. Some selection criteria that may be useful in evaluating protocol stacks include: compliance with the standard, complexity of the API, interoperability with different vendors' products, compatibility with the target platform, and performance measures such as memory footprint, number of concurrent threads supported and customizability of the threading performance. In addition, vendor leadership in standards bodies and the ability to influence future product direction are very important selection criteria.

At the end of evaluation, the team should discuss the results and identify the top-ranking vendors and their offerings. If a particular component (and vendor) clearly dominates the others, the selection task can be terminated at this point. If not, the team should proceed to the next activity.

3.3 Decision-Making

The purpose of this activity is to analyze the complex trade-off factors that impact the component selection decision. The premise here is that no single component and vendor could be identified at end of the previous 2 activities either because none of candidates met all requirements or because there is a lack of consensus on "best-fit".

Inputs to this activity include the all outputs from the previous 2 activities. Outputs include a decision on the "make vs. buy" question and in case of a decision

to buy, the alternative that offers the best compromise. In addition, a list of risks and associated with the selection decision and a mitigation plan can be optionally generated.

Primary roles involved in the decision-making activity are technical and product managers and system architects. The key steps involved here are:

- Compile a list of critical component and vendor selection criteria
- Discuss trade-off factors and risks
- Elicit each individual's assessment of the candidate components
- Normalize and aggregate individual scores to arrive at overall score.

Some of the trade-off aspects that should be considered here include:

- Necessary vs. Sufficient Requirements for functionality and performance
- Current Concerns vs. Future Needs (relating to interoperability, multiple target platform support and scalability)
- Cost vs. Benefit Analysis (including current and lifecycle costs)

Also relevant are the vendor's experience in multiple market domains and opportunities for partnership in the areas of marketing and customer support.

4. Conclusions

Our experience indicates that there is often a lack of adequate time and resources for performing component selection. We have described here a methodology that we hope will aid practitioners of CBSE especially in new problem domains such as the internet telephony domain.

REFERENCES
1. Nwosu, K., "Component Based Software Development Process Reference Guide," http://www.stc.lucent.com/~knwosu/, May 1999.
2. Oberndorf, P., Brownsword L, Morris E., and Sledge, C. (editors), *Workshop on COTS-Based Systems*, CMU/SEI-97-SR-019, Nov.1997, pp
3. Welke, R. J., "The Shifting Software Development Paradigm," *Database*, Vol 25 No. 4, November 1994, pg. 9-16.

Panels

Agents and Workflow -- An Intimate Connection, or Just Friends?

Martin L. Griss (*moderator*)
Hewlett-Packard Laboratories,
Palo Alto, CA
griss@hpl.hp.com

Gregory A. Bolcer
Endeavors Technology Incorporated,
Irvine, CA
gbolcer@ics.uci.edu

Quiming Chen
Hewlett-Packard Laboratories,
Palo Alto, CA
qchen@hpl.hp.com

Robert R. Kessler
Department of Computer Science,
University of Utah, Salt Lake City, UT
kessler@cs.utah.edu

Leon J. Osterweil
Computer Science Department,
University of Massachusetts, Amherst, MASS
ljo@freya.cs.umass.edu

Abstract

This panel addresses the perspective that agents and workflow can be seen as an evolution of components and scripting. There are several ways in which agents can be used to perform or support a workflow, and several ways in which workflow can be used to orchestrate or control the interactions between agents. The panelists explore several of these connections and various applications of agents and workflow. They discuss some of these relationships between agents and workflow, and propose opportunities for research and practice.

1. Introduction: Components, Scripting, Agents and Workflow *(Griss)*

While there are many definitions of software agents[1,2,3], they can be usefully viewed as an evolution or combination of distributed objects[4], business objects[5] and scriptable components. Agents are components, sometimes mobile, that expose specialized interfaces, are usually driven by goals and plans (rather than procedural code), have "business" or "domain" knowledge, operate autonomously, and quite often interact using a specialized, declarative agent communication language (ACL), such as KQML (rather than direct method invocation). While agents often are used individually (e.g., internet information mining), things become much more interesting when a group or society of agents collaborate together to perform some task (e.g., auctions, or telecommunications provisioning). A number of different agent systems have been developed (e.g., Agent-TCL, Aglets, Voyager, ...), focusing on different mixes of mobility, adaptability, intelligence, ACL and multi-language support.

Workflow is a method and mechanism to allow the explicit definition and control of a group of participants in enacting a process of some sort. A variety of different workflow languages and systems have been developed (e.g., HP ChangeEngine[6], Endeavors[7,8], Little-JIL[9,10]), many of which involve a graphical interface to describe allowed connections between participants, desired and exceptional processing conditions, the assignment of roles, and the request and allocation of resources.

Scripting is an increasingly popular way of gluing components into complete solutions. Scripting languages are typically small, interpretive languages that have good access to the underlying component model (e.g. VB Script or VBA for COM components, Java or Java Script Java for JavaBeans, and TCL or Python). Developers and end-users can create applications by using scripting to combine, control or modify robust components created by domain experts; this is a key strategy that underlies the great appeal of Visual Basic in the enterprise.

Several researchers and practitioners have noticed several interesting connections between agents and workflow. On the one hand, an interesting way of creating a workflow system is to have agents represent the participants and resources, and to have the society of agents collaborate to enact the workflow. In some workflow systems, the participants (human or machine) are in fact referred to as agents. On the other hand, a convenient way of choreographing the interaction between collaborating agents in a multi-agent society is to use workflow as a form of next generation scripting language[11]. Either a new workflow/scripting language will be developed, or workflow primitives will be added to an existing scripting language, such as TCL, VB Script or Java Script.

This panel will discuss these and other relationships between agents and workflow, and propose some opportunities for research and practice.

2. Process Programming Languages As Agent Coordination Specification Vehicles *(Osterweil)*

We consider the definition or specification of a process to be an effective basis for the specification of agent coordination as well. Our view is that a process that is to be executed by the coordinated actions of a variety of agents can and should be specified in such a way that the individual steps of the process can be seen as being allocatable to the different agents. The Little-JIL process programming language demonstrates this[9,10]. In Little-JIL a process is specified as a hierarchical decomposition into steps and substeps. Each step is defined in terms of a variety of characteristics and attributes. But one of the most important of these definition elements is a specification of the type of agent that is to be employed to take responsibility for the execution of the step. In Little-JIL a runtime system is used to determine dynamically the specific agent that meets the specification associated with the step, and to bind that agent to execute the step. In this way, the Little-JIL process specification is also a specification of the way in which the available agents are to be coordinated to execute the defined process.

We have also related our Little-JIL process specifications to an established multiagent scheduling system, called GPGP, developed by the Multiagent Systems Laboratory at the University of Massachusetts. Using Little-JIL and its execution environment we are able to tentatively assign specific agents to the execution of specific steps. This is expected to cause many agents to each have several steps to execute. Because of this it will be useful to provide these agents with guidance about the order in which each should execute its assigned steps. In our work we have devised translation systems that convert Little-JIL process programs into representations in the TAEMS system, which is used as input to GPGP. The result is a set of specifications of the way in which each agent participating in the process is to execute the steps it has been assigned from the overall process. This serves to further confirm our view that process specifications can be most effective bases for the determination of the ways in which agents should be coordinated.

We are in the process of evaluating these ideas in the context of a larger robot team coordination project, called SAFER, sponsored by DARPA.

3. Intelligent Agents Augment Flexible Workflow *(Bolcer)*

Data agents are small, autonomous software modules that automatically perform a localized task. Intelligent agents, in addition, have the ability to reason about the input data and manipulate it in such a way that it can work in conjunction with other agents without violating any global constraints. Examples of activities that data agents perform range from simple to complex. An agent's activities may include automatic notification via email of the availability of a report, sending a reminder of a scheduled meeting, advising a user of alternate meeting times as the result of a scheduling conflict, or even actively going out and doing research based on some specified criteria. Agent's activities, from the viewpoint of the workflow system, should allow the activity to be accomplished by either a human or non-human agent or both[7]. By allowing the mix of both human and non-human activities, the availability of more intelligent agents allows for the incremental automation of certain activities.

The people participating in the workflow should be allowed to hand off or delegate activities to an agent or take ownership of the activity back from one[8]. Similarly, agents should be allowed to delegate tasks to sub-agents or request the help of human participants as needed. The management of multiple agents allows end-users to accomplish tedious or repetitive tasks with minimal effort and avoids the "keep checking back" syndrome. Agents should allow customization by individuals with or without technical programming knowledge, notification based on existence and changes, constraints on values and appropriate strategies for resolution, and significant event filtering and topic interest registration. At some level of abstraction, an agent and an automated workflow process are interchangeable. Agents historically have been focussed on non-human involved, small-scale coordination activities.

4. Scriptable Agents for Distributed Measurement *(Kessler)*

Much of our work on distributed measurement involves the use of non-mobile agents deployed at startup to the measurement site[12]. These agents, implemented as COM or OCX components in the CWave system, utilize a publish/subscribe bus for communication between agents[13]. As part of this infrastructure, the agents include standard libraries of measurement objects and methods in support of the task at hand; in particular, support for loading and running multi-threaded scripts in VBScript, JavaScript or Perl. Measurements are then initiated, changed, and updated by dynamically sending scripts which are evaluated in the context of the local agent. The script is responsible for performing the measurements and providing any necessary actuation/control of the attached devices. Agents may be logically grouped together to provide a higher-level functionality, which is undertaken via communication and negotiation amongst the agents within the group.

The group communication and coordination in our measurement domain is very similar in style to workflow. We are considering extending our libraries and scripts with workflow primitives. In addition, currently all communication is directly "programmed" in compatible scripts with publishers and subscribers programmatically agreeing on what will be communicated. This is a different style as compared with agent communication languages that explicitly indicate steps, allocate tasks to agent roles, and negotiate specific tasks and goals. We are exploring how to integrate both workflow primitives and agent communication performatives as an extension of our scripting language. These extensions could lead to an environment in which it in would be easier to set up workflow style collaborations using our scriptable agent technology.

5. Dynamic Agents for Dynamic Workflow Service Provisioning *(Chen)*

We claim that a dynamic-agent infrastructure can provide a shift from static distributed computing to dynamic distributed computing, and we have developed such an infrastructure to realize such a shift[14]. We shall show its impact on software engineering through a comparison with other distributed object-oriented systems such as CORBA and DCOM, and demonstrate its value in highly dynamic workflow system integration and service provisioning.

The infrastructure is Java-based, light-weight, and extensible. It differs from other agent platforms and client/server infrastructures in its support of dynamic behavior modification of agents. A dynamic-agent is not designed to have a fixed set of predefined functions but instead, to carry application-specific actions, which can be loaded and modified on the fly. This allows a dynamic-agent to adjust its capability for accommodating environment and requirement changes, and play different roles across multiple applications.

The above features are supported by the light-weight, built-in management facilities of dynamic-agents, which can be commonly used by the "carried" application programs to communicate, manage resources and modify their problem-solving capabilities. Therefore, the proposed infrastructure allows application-specific multi-agent systems to be developed easily on top of it, provides "nuts and bolts" for run-time system integration, and supports dynamic service construction, modification and movement. A prototype has been developed at HP Labs and made available to several external research groups.

References

[1]   M.R. Genesereth, and S.P. Ketchpel: "Software Agents", Communications of the Association for Computing Machinery, July 1994, pp 48-53.

[2]   M.N. Huhns and M.P. Singh, "Readings in Agents", Morgan-Kaufman, 1998.

[3]   N.R. Jennings and M.J. Wooldridge, "Agent Technology," Springer, 1998.

[4]   J. Odell, "Tutorial, Beyond Objects: Agents", OOPSLA98.

[5]   O. Sims, Business Objects, McGraw-Hill, London, 1994.

[6]   HP Changengine - an Enterprise Process Flow System. (See http://www.ebizsoftware.hp.com/main1.html).

[7]   G. Bolcer and R. Taylor, "Endeavors: A Process System Integration Infrastructure," International Conference on Software Process (ICSP4), December, 2-6, 1996, Brighton, U.K. (See http://www.ics.uci.edu/pub/endeavors/endeavors.html).

[8]   G. Bolcer and R. Taylor, "Advanced Workflow Management Technologies," Software Process: Improvement and Practice, Dewayne E. Perry and Wilhelm Schaefer, Co-Editors-in-Chief, John Wiley & Sons, Baffins Lane, Chichester, West Sussex, PO19 1UD, UK. http://www.wiley.com/journals/spip/ 1999 (to appear) .

[9]   S.S. Sutton Jr. and L.J. Osterweil, "The design of a next generation process programming language," Proceedings of ESAC-6 and FSE-5, Springer Verlag, 1997, pp. 142-158.

[10] A. Wise, "Little-JIL 1.0 Language Report," Technical Report 98-24, University of Massachusetts at Amherst, Sept. 1998.

[11] M.L. Griss, "From components and scripts to agents and workflow," Technical report, HP Laboratories, June 1999 (in preparation).

[12] M.L. Griss and R.R. Kessler, "Building Object-Oriented Instrument Kits," Object Magazine, Apr 1996.

[13] C. Mueller-Planitz, CWave, a Visual Workbench for Distributed Measurement Agents, Ph.D. Dissertation, Computer Science Department, University of Utah 1999 (in preparation).

[14] Q Chen, P Chundi, U Dayal, and M Hsu, "Dynamic Agents for Dynamic Service Provisioning," accepted for publication, Intl. Conf. on Cooperative Information Systems, August 1998.

Biographies

Greg Bolcer received his Ph.D. in Information and Computer Science at the University of California, Irvine (UCI) in 1998, M.S. in Computer Science at the University of Southern California (USC) in 1993, and B.S. in Information and Computer Science at UCI in 1989. He is the CEO and Founder of Endeavors Technology Incorporated, a small California Internet startup dedicated to building tools supporting Web-based workflow, Web-based information systems, and e-business processes. Prior to founding ETI, Bolcer was the project leader for the DARPA funded Endeavors workflow research prototype. He is also one of the key working group participants for the Simple Workflow Access Protocol (SWAP) extensions to HTTP/1.1 and WebDAV. His current research interests include automating business-to-business electronic commerce processes and Internet-scale event notification.

Qiming Chen is a senior computer scientist in Software Technology Lab, HP Labs. He joined HP Labs in 1992, and since then he has conducted research in database, workflow, agent framework and data mining. He designed and developed a Java based workflow system and a dynamic agent infrastructure in HP labs. He was appointed to 13 international technical committees in USA, Europe and Japan, including program committees of 1986, 1989, 1990, 1991, 1992 International Conference on Very Large Databases (VLDB), and editorial committees of international journals and book series. He has authored over 70 technical publications in journals, books and international conferences on databases, knowledge bases and software engineering.

Martin L. Griss is a Principal Laboratory Scientist at Hewlett-Packard Laboratories, Palo Alto, California. At HP since 1982, he has researched software engineering processes and systems, systematic software reuse, object-oriented development and component-based software engineering. He is currently working on model-driven, agent-based application management systems. He created the first HP corporate reuse program, and led HP efforts to standardize UML for the OMG. He was previously director of the Software Technology Laboratory at HP Laboratories, and an Associate Professor of Computer Science at the University of Utah. He is co-author of the book "Software Reuse: Architecture, Process and Organization for Business Success". He has written numerous articles on software engineering and reuse, and lectures widely on systematic reuse and software process improvement. He is a member of the ACM SIGSOFT Executive Committee, and of the joint IEEE/ACM software engineering education project. He is a member of the SSR steering committee, the ICSE99, UML99, OOPSLA99 and TOOLS99 program committees, and the ICSE2002 organizing committee.

Robert R. Kessler is currently a professor and chairman of the Department of Computer Science at the University of Utah. In the early 90's, he founded the Center for Software Science, a state of Utah Center of Excellence. He has also founded several startup companies and is currently involved with an Internet startup company, emWare, as a member of the board. He has served as member-at-large of ACM SIGPLAN and is currently Vice Chairman for Conferences for SIGPLAN. He recently completed a seven year assignment as co-editor-in-chief of the International Journal of Lisp and Symbolic Computation. His current research interests are in agents, software engineering, distributed systems, and visual programming.

Leon J. Osterweil is currently a professor in the Department of Computer Science at the University of Massachusetts, Amherst. Previously he had been a Professor in, and Chair of, Computer Science Departments at both the University of California, Irvine, and University of Colorado, Boulder. He was the founding Director of the Irvine Research Unit in Software (IRUS) and the Southern California SPIN. He has been Program Committee Chair of ICSE 16, TAV 2, ISPW4, and SDE2, and General Chair of FSE 6. He has also presented keynote talks at such meetings as CASE 92 in Montreal, Quality Week 96 in San Francisco, the Inaugural Symposium of JAIST (the Japan Advanced Institute for Software Technology) in Kanazawa, Japan, and ICSE 9 (the Ninth International Conference on Software Engineering) where he introduced the concept of Process Programming. His ICSE 9 paper has been awarded a prize as the most influential paper of ICSE 9, awarded as a 10-year retrospective. He has consulted for such organizations as IBM, Bell Laboratories, SAIC, MCC, and TRW, and SEI's Process Program Advisory Board. Prof. Osterweil is a Fellow of the Association for Computing Machinery.

High level Modelling Languages, Adaptable Process Models and Software Generation: Drivers for Quality and Productivity

Moderator:
Ulrich Frank, Universität Koblenz, Germany
Panelists:
Don Batory, University of Texas at Austin, USA
Jean Bézivin, LRSG, Université de Nantes, France
Brian Henderson-Sellers, University of Technology, Sydney, Australia
Houman Younessi, Rensselaer at Hartford, USA

Summary

It is widely accepted that conceptual models are a prerequisite for successfully planning and designing complex software systems. They are a medium to foster communication with prospective users and they (should) define a sound basis for system implementation. By providing common domain level concepts they also support the integration of applications and foster the convenient reuse of high level artifacts. However, despite these advantages, conceptual modeling comes with a number of challenges. Recent object-oriented modeling languages (like [OMG97], [FiHe97]) offer a wide range of different diagrams. While the views they allow for complement each other more or less, it is not always clear which abstraction to use for a particular modeling purpose. During the last years, a few approaches have emerged that recommend concepts and abstractions other than objects - like patterns, components or frameworks. While they all claim to contribute to software quality, it is not evident how they can be integrated with object-oriented models in a consistent and intuitive way.

Describing systems on a high level of abstraction does not only serve to improve communication between various stakeholders. At the same time it serves to increase the productivity of software development - mainly through reuse of high level artifacts and the generation of code from domain level specifications. Despite the obvious benefits of this vision, it imposes a number of questions. What are appropriate concepts to specify application level artifacts that can be reused and adapted to individual needs in a convenient and save way? Does software generation recommend any special concepts for modeling languages? It also relates to the coupling of modeling languages and implementation languages (database or programming language). On the one hand it is desirable to abstract from the peculiarities of a particular implementation language in order to facilitate the change of implementation languages over time or to use more than one implementation language. On the other hand a tight coupling of modeling and implementation language fosters a seamless transformation of design models into code and improves the chances for traceability as well.

From a managerial point of view, providing modeling languages and reusable artifacts is not sufficient: There is need to support the process of software development. Adaptable process models and specialized project management concepts are promising help. However, it remains difficult to specify them on an appropriate level of detail and rigor. This is also the case for the design of software to support the development process, such as specialized workflow management systems. Furthermore, it is not trivial to decide to what degree a process model can be independent from the modeling languages used within a project.

While we tend to assume that object-oriented modeling is based on "natural" abstractions, many people do not find object-oriented concepts to be intuitive. Moreover, even for those who have understood the basic concepts, the design of object-oriented models is a huge intellectual challenge. As a result, the quality of conceptual models is often poor. For this reason, there is need for effective training. The way in which we perceive, understand and represent the world through language has been a subject of many disciplines for long. Corresponding research results, especially from cognitive psychology, can be used for the specification of modeling languages (semantics and notation) and the training of modellers - for instance metaphors/abstractions that have proved to foster an intuitive access to a domain of interest.

Against this background, the panel serves to discuss - among other things - the following aspects and questions:
- relevance of modeling for object-oriented software development
- shortcomings of existing modeling languages
- do we need formal modeling languages?
- evaluation of object-oriented models
- is the state of the art mature enough to define a standard modeling language?
- Features of a "good" process model for software development
- conceptual integration of modeling and programming
- what do we need to accomplish "plug&play" of domain level components?
- what are the abstractions that are most promising for the future of software engineering?

References
[FiHe97] Firesmith, D.; Henderson-Sellers, B.; Graham, I.; Page-Jones, M.: OPEN Modeling Language (OML). Reference Manual. SIGS Books, New York 1997

[OMG97] OMG: UML Semantics, Version 1.1, 15 September 1997, OMG document ad/97-08-04 (unpubl.)

Software Quality, Components, and Automation

Don Batory
Department of Computer Sciences
University of Texas at Austin, USA

Central problems in software engineering stem from one fact - that software is written by hand. Once this is understood, it is easy to see why users complain about the lack of software quality, performance, reliability, the cost of maintenance, and difficulty of application evolution. The core of all the complaints is software quality, which is largely a function of two things: the quality of an application's design and the quality of the programming staff. Everyone knows that software design is hard. It often takes several iterations, coupled with major implementation efforts, to get the design "right". The quality of the programming staff also has a major impact on software quality. Really good system implementors are hard to find, while average or below average programmers are more than plentiful. With the variability of both quality designs and quality programmers, many of the problems we face today in software development seem unavoidable.

How can we do better? How can we better exploit our experiences in designing software and improving the quality of our programmers? The answer lies in automation. That is, the future of software engineering lies in the automated production of well-understood software. Machines can do the tasks of rote software development far better, more efficiently, and with greater cost-effectiveness than people.

Our research over the last 15 years has led to the development of practical tools and methodologies for automating the assembly of customized applications - or more accurately, application product-lines - by composing reusable components. We have created product-lines for many different domains from avionics to extensible Java compilers, and our ideas are being used in industry and research institutions to develop their own product-lines. The elements of automation that we have brought to the software development process is a simple and declarative way in which applications are specified through component compositions; compositions are validated automatically (or errors are reported along with suggestions on how to repair the errors); and tools can be developed that automatically critique designs as well as suggest improvements to an application's design (as a composition of components) given a declarative, high-level specification of its workload. All of this is possible because the target domain is well-understood and what we are automating are rote procedures that are manually performed by domain experts.

[1] D. Batory, Product-Line Architectures, Invited presentation, Smalltalk und Java in Industrie and Ausbildung, Erfurt, Germany, October 1998.
[2] D. Batory, et al., "Web-Advertised Generators and Design Wizards", 5th International Conference on Software Reuse, Victoria, Canada, June 1998.

On The Interplay Between Models, Components And Software Processes

Jean Bézivin

LRSG, Université de Nantes, Frances

The arrival to maturity of object technologies has allowed the idea of model-based software development to find its way to practicality. The OMG (Object Management Group) is now centering its activities not only on one interoperability bus, but on two different ones: the classical CORBA software bus (for code interoperability) and the emerging MOF (Meta-Object Facility) knowledge bus (for model interoperability). The consensus on UML (Unified Modeling Language) has been instrumental in this transition from code-based to model-based software production techniques. An essential role is now played by the concept of meta-model in new software organizations like the OMG meta-model stack architecture or the corresponding Microsoft OIM (Object Information Model). The concept of a MOF (Meta-Object Facility) has progressively emerged in the last ten years from the work of different communities like CDIF, IRDS, etc.

Some have predicted the end of object technology per se, and the beginning of component technology, based on the increasing importance of so-called "development-time" objects such as use cases, patterns, packages, business objects, beans, enterprise beans, etc. versus classical "execution-time" objects. The definition in December 1997 of the Unified Modeling Language at OMG, the acceptance of the MOF at the same meeting and more recently of the XMI (XML Meta-data Interchange) in January 1999, clearly opens the debate on the key contribution of modeling and knowledge representation techniques in this new deployment period of component technology. Various benefits may be reaped from the move to model-based architecture. It is anticipated that many tools applicable to model-based software development will shortly become available (mainly XML related tools). The associated meta-data techniques will narrow the gap between application development and enterprise repositories.

Component technology is mainly dealing with "development-time" objects, a matter much more complex than single "execution-time" objects. Many new attributes are being considered for components like those related to use-cases, to patterns, to organization packages or clusters, to behavior, architecture or deployment consideration to name just a few. The code model remains just one among several models and may no more be considered as central, as it was in the previous period. By having separate models, we shall be in a position to deal explicitly with quality attributes of components, applications and systems. Not only assertions and contracts may already be expressed in today's models, but other properties like performance or quality of service will be part of non-functional models, alongside the test model, the requirement model, the architecture model, etc. Therefore, moving to model-based software production will contribute to increase the quality of the delivered software.

The Importance of OO Processes

Brian Henderson-Sellers
University of Technology, Sydney (UTS), Australia

In object-oriented methods (or methodologies) which were created, published and used in the early 1990s, the advice given by them on modelling was qualitative, based on experience and often imprecisely described. Little attention was paid to consistency, formality or ways of ensuring that the techniques proposed produced a quality outcome. While these proponents of object technology firmly believed the use of object technology to be a key to increased software quality, these claims were difficult to prove scientifically. Indeed, in the hands of an unskilled software developer, poor use of object technology is likely to lead to *decreased* software quality. This is a result of the higher degree of sophistication and complexity implicit in object-oriented modelling techniques.

One move towards more formality was the investigation of the ideas of creating metamodels of the existing OO techniques and the (usually incomplete) methodologies. The COMMA project of 1995 and the creation of the two modelling languages of UML and OML all focused on the idea of formalizing existing concepts and models by the use of metamodelling techniques. In doing so, many anomalies and inconsistencies were identified and fixed (although some still remain!). The use of OCL in UML has added another level of formality although sceptics suggest it is more useful in fixing bugs in the metamodel rather than enhancing a supposedly correct metamodel. This has led to the formation in Europe of the pUML group, a group of industry and academic experts who find UML to have "a semantics that is informal and full of gaps and inconsistencies".

Quality can be enhanced if the semantics of the modelling language, largely through the use of a metamodel and possibly a constraint language, are clear and unambiguous - the higher the quality of the modelling language used, the potentially higher the quality of the software produced. Documenting the design decisions is done using the second part of a modelling language: a notation. Notations are more likely to lead to quality designs if, again, they are clear, unambiguous, simple and user-friendly. For example, semiotic theories have been used in the creation of the OPEN Modelling Language (OML) in order to ensure quality of notational elements. The underpinning idea here is that any sign or symbol should be intuitively suggestive of its meaning rather than something that has to be learned by rote (like OMT notation).

However, despite the apparent enthusiasm for UML as a manifestation of some degree of agreement and convergence in metamodel and notation, *a notation is not enough* to build software. The notation merely documents the deliverables from a process. In addition, the deliverables themselves need to provide multiple views on *a single model* - expressible in terms of the way the diagrams link together synergistically. But even diagram suites are not enough. What is needed is a full process and a technically focused development method. The key elements of such a Software Engineering Process (SEP) are (i) methodology (which in turn consists of lifecycle process, techniques and a modelling language such as UML or OML); together with (ii) people and organizational culture; and (iii) tools and available technology.

We are now moving to so-called "third generation OO methodologies" which are defined as those which are supported collaboratively (no longer the purview of a single methodologist) and which contain process. The current candidates would appear to be OPEN and Objectory/Rational Unified Process. These newer OO methodologies have a more evident process focus and, in principle, can use any good quality notation. However, if the process chosen produces deliverables that need documenting using concepts not recognized by the notational set, then there is a poor match. Users of the process should thus be circumspect in adopting a notation that is incomplete (for their purposes). Similarly dangerous is the common view that a process should be built on top of a notation - if a notational element has been accidentally omitted, then the resultant process is unlikely to be of the highest quality achievable.

Link Between the Quality of the Modelling Process And the Quality of the Product

Houman Younessi
Rensselaer at Hartford

The "axiom of software engineering" [1] states that "product quality is underpinned by process quality". If process matters however, then it is worth examining the quality of the process every time the quality of a product goes under question. This panel deals with the question: "how does the quality of the modelling process impact the quality of the software artefact"? Important as this question is, I feel there is still a more important one in this context that we must ask first. " Is modelling at all necessary as a process or process component in creating software?" Can we save ourselves lots of time and dispense with all this silly diagram drawing? I say we mustn't. In fact I assert that we can't!

A program (a software product) is in itself a model. When we build software, we are doing modelling. Our issue however is whether we need to build any "intermediate" models between our initial cognitive concept (mental model) and the final "simulation" of it. Intermediate models only make sense if they can improve the process by which the final product is arrived at. Intermediate modeling stages, I assert, assist with handling of complexity; capturing of all that is relevant, and; capturing of only what is relevant. They assist in handling complexity in that they allow us to focus on specific modules and permit use of abstraction. If we could not achieve this, then our process will not be efficacious nor our product will be built effectively. They help with capturing of all that is relevant in that they permit us to focus on the requirements. If we could not achieve this, then our product will score low on effectiveness. It can be argued that efficiency and efficacy would also suffer. Finally they assist in capturing only what is relevant and not more. If this was not achieved, then there will be extra unnecessary "baggage" that our product would carry. Obviously this will violate the concept of efficiency. More subtly, it also violates the concepts of effectiveness and efficacy. Therefore, as in order to build models, we cognitively translate what we see as relevant from one environment into another, given a particular purpose and abstraction level, modelling allows us to largely concentrate on what is deemed relevant and thus simplify the development task enormously by excluding what need not be considered. Also to give us the capability to abstract. The next question is: "what characteristics should such a modelling system possess?" I shall assert that there is a general "best" way to do this; at least in the context of the state of practice, and as it pertains to the development of deterministic models.

It has been observed throughout the centuries [2, 3, 4] that knowledge of structures, processes and sequences in which events occur are all necessary for comprehending the real world, which is in turn a prerequisite for modeling some aspect of it. The Plutonian view of the world refers to the world of "Being", that of structure. The Aristotelian view considers, the world of "Becoming" in addition to that of "Being", the former being the concept of transformation. The Cartesian world-view talks of "Cause and Effect", thus advocating in addition to the other views that of causality, sequence and if on an absolute scale, that of temporality. In other words, it can be argued that in order to capture the essence of any situation that is deterministic, we need to address these three dimensions (those of structure, transformation, and causality). This is particularly of relevance when there is an absence of a priori knowledge in terms of the future utility of the model to be constructed. This is usually the case when software is developed, and the fact that in software systems usually all three aspects are sufficiently if not equally important, the modeller has no choice but to provide all three models and clear evidence of their inter-relation. In fact, in addition to seamlessness, this ability to provide such a rich model that does not depend on any specific modelling view is one of the greatest strengths of object orientation.

Thus I declare that, given the two primary characteristics of object oriented models (i.e. seamlessness and comprehensiveness), the opportunity to capture and communicate what and only what is necessary is increased whilst the chances of mistakes being injected are reduced. This allows for at least a "practically" (as distinct from "Formally") robust, necessary and sufficient basis for further development work, whether it be design, coding or defect management thus positively impacting the final product quality.

References
1. N. Fenton. Software Metrics: A Rigorous Approach (Chapman-Hall, UK, 1991)
2. Plato. The Republic. Trans. G.M.A. Grube (Hackett, IN, 1974)
3. Aristotle. Metaphysics. Trans. W.D. Ross (Oxford University Press, Oxford, 1924)
4. R. Descartes. Discourse on Method. in The Philosophical Works of Descartes, Trans. E. Haldane, and G.R.T Ross (Cambridge University Press, Cambridge, 1911).

The Great Language Debate

Moderator: Richard Riehle,
Adaworks, USA

Abstract

The Great Language Debate will explore the benefits of some of the currently in-use object-oriented programming languages. Languages will include Ada, Eiffel, Java, C++, and Smalltalk, and possibly others. This is a moderated panel. The moderator will be someone who is as unbiased as possible. Each language will be represented by an advocate who will share a short presentation about a favorite language. Members of the panel will pose questions to each other. Those in the audience will be free to ask questions of the panelists.

This is a regular feature of the TOOLS USA conference. It is usually spirited — sometimes slightly irreverent as panelist and audience members identify their own prejudices about the languages represented.

We hope that, as the participants frankly reveal their own views, and hear intelligent rebuttals, that everyone will learn something new about the languages we use for object-oriented software construction. Although no one can possible learn each language in depth from this panel discussion, participants might be encouraged to pursue more in-depth study of some language that might have eluded their interest in the past.

Eiffel Summit '99

Direct Mapping and User Interface

Rex Fowler

Fowler Software Design LLC

rfowler@fowlersoftware.com

Abstract

Direct Mapping is the rule that there should be a direct correspondence between object types in the problem domain and in the software solution. But once direct mapping has been achieved, how should user interface object types be designed to work with the behavioral object types? This paper answers that question and presents some design patterns which were employed by Fowler Software Design in a recent Eiffel software project.

1. Introduction

Bertrand Meyer [1] states the Direct Mapping Rule as follows:

"The modular structure devised in the process of building a software system should remain compatible with any modular structure devised in the process of modeling the problem domain."

So if we have a model of a problem domain which, for example, involves pipes, fluids, and meters that measure flow and fluid characteristics, we should end up with software modules such as the following:

PIPE	**METER**
FLUID	**FLOW_RATE_METER**
WATER_FLUID	**TEMPERATURE_METER**
AIR_FLUID	**PRESSURE_METER**
OTHER_LIQUID_FLUID	
OTHER_GAS_FLUID	

But how should these modules, which map back to the problem domain, relate to other modules which present a user interface for the operator? This paper outlines how we solved this in a recent windows application (which does processes data for pipes and fluids).

2. Business classes and presentation classes

Those Eiffel classes, such as those listed above, which map back to items in the problem domain, we called "business classes". All of our solutions are for business, so for us the problem domain is always the domain of a business problem. A more general name might have been "behavioral classes".

Our first requirement on the software solution was that the business classes must be kept separate from the presentation classes -- those involved in the user interface. There should be few interfaces between the categories of classes, and the interfaces should be both small and explicit [1].

On the presentation side, we have a selection of WINDOW classes which present information to the operator and accept operator input.

2.1 Many-to-many relationship

We noted that there is a many-to-many relationship between WINDOW classes and business classes. Any one window may present data from several different business classes; any one business class may have its data represented on several different windows.

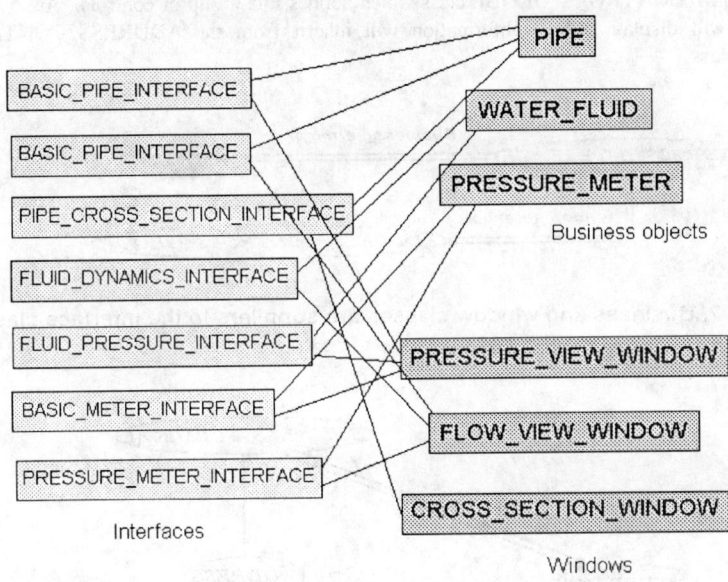

Figure 1. Business, window, and interface objects

A student of relational database design learns that a many-to-many relationship between entities is resolved by introducing an association entity to represent the connection. This results in two one-to-many relationships with the association entity now in the middle. This same technique works to resolve the many-to-many relationship between business classes and window classes.

2.2 The INTERFACE class

We decided to call the association class in this case an "INTERFACE". Figure 1 illustrates an example of the resulting object relationship. Three business objects present their data on three windows of different types in various combinations. The INTERFACE objects provide the connections between the business objects and the WINDOW objects. (The specific interface classes all inherit from INTERFACE and the specific window classes all inherit from WINDOW.)

2.3 Control groups

But early in the development project we discovered that the INTERFACE only connects to part of a window. Specifically, it connects to that group of controls on the window that relate to the INTERFACE. One early example brought this home clearly. We have a CUSTOMER class which has an ADDRESS attribute. The ADDRESS_INTERFACE class is reusable. An ADDRESS_INTERFACE object connects an ADDRESS object to various address controls on a window. The controls are the same every time regardless of the window. So of course there is an ADDRESS_CONTROLS_GROUP class which defines this group of controls. Any window class that will display address information will inherit from the ADDRESS_CONTROLS_GROUP class.

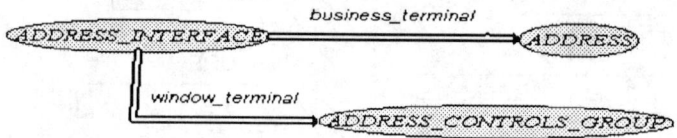

Figure 2. Business and window classes are suppliers to the interface class

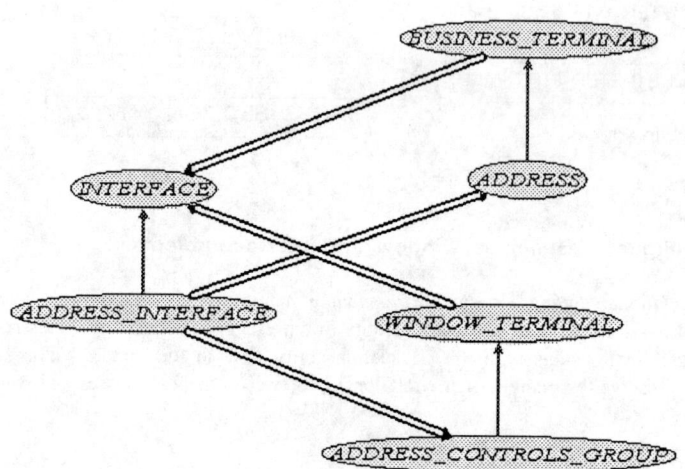

Figure 3. Business, interface, and window relationships

The INTERFACE abstract data type can be thought of as a communication line strung between two points. The line has two "terminals" -- its two ends. We called one the BUSINESS_TERMINAL and the other the WINDOW_TERMINAL.

So we now have all business classes that can present their data on a user interface inheriting from the BUSINESS_TERMINAL class and we have all window and controls-group classes that can present business data inheriting from WINDOW_TERMINAL.

Figure 2 shows that an INTERFACE has one BUSINESS_TERMINAL and one WINDOW_TERMINAL.

The references are mutual, but the strongest relationships are INTERFACE as client and BUSINESS_TERMINAL and WINDOW_TERMINAL as suppliers. As shown in figure 3, the specific INTERFACE class will know the exact types of its associated business and window terminals, but the business and window terminals will know all their interfaces only as objects of type INTERFACE (the ancestor class).

With this pattern, we have accomplished an effective independence between the business side and the presentation side. Both are suppliers to the INTERFACE classes.

3. The BRIDGE class

An INTERFACE is not just one communication line. It is a bundle of communication lines -- like a cable containing many wires.

Given a single interface, on the business side, we have many sources of data; on the window side, we have many controls to present those sources of data. We rejected class names like "WIRE", "CABLE", and obviously "STRING" as straining the analogy too much. We decided on "BRIDGE" as a word that suggests the concept sufficiently and could be redefined from its usual meanings without creating ambiguity. So, as illustrated in figure 4, an interface consists of many bridges.

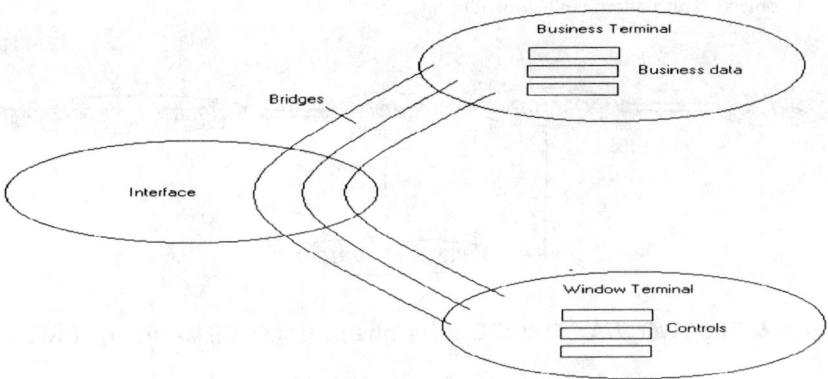

Figure 4. An interface consists of a series of bridge objects

On the window end of each BRIDGE, we have a single control, usually a text box or a drop-down list box. Sometimes, it's a single cell in a grid, but we will have to save the subject of grids for a subsequent paper. There is much more to be said about grids than can be said in this present paper.

What functionality will we require of bridge objects? Some will be display-only bridges. They will just copy the business data to the window control for display. Some bridges will move data in both directions, copying it to the control for display and updating the business data when the operator changes what is in the control.

We want bridges to be alerted automatically whenever the business data changes so the change can be displayed in the window control.

If the business terminal has validation rules which must be satisfied prior to an update, we want the bridge to check the validation rules before attempting to update the business data. If the change is not valid, we want to inform the operator using a standard message window.

The Eiffel presentation libraries contain the concept of a COMMAND. A COMMAND is something that is registered with a control on a window. Then, when there is a windows event like a mouse click or a lost focus or a selection from a list, the control tells the COMMAND to execute.

3.1   The TWO_WAY_BRIDGE class inherits from COMMAND

We found that it was very natural to have our TWO_WAY_BRIDGE class inherit from the COMMAND class. TWO_WAY_BRIDGE is the bridge that both displays business data in the window control and updates business data from the window control. Data flows both ways. The ancestor BRIDGE class does not have to inherit from COMMAND since windows events are ignored for display-only controls.

So moving data across from the window side to the business side is easy. The operator enters changed data or causes a windows event like a click or a selection using the mouse. This fires the execute feature of the COMMAND class which tells the TWO_WAY_BRIDGE to attempt to update the business data. The bridge checks for a valid update by executing a query on the business object. If the update is valid, the bridge executes the proper update command on the business object. This pattern is illustrated in figure 5.

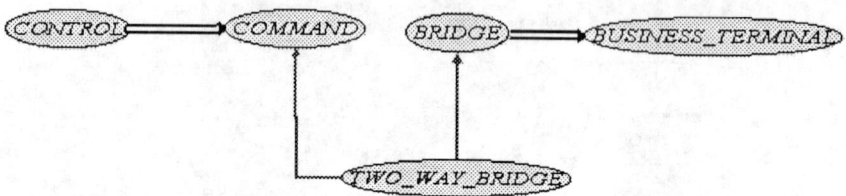

Figure 5. The TWO_WAY_BRIDGE class inherits from COMMAND and BRIDGE

Surprisingly, getting data from the business side to the window control was a little more difficult. The problem to solve here is the problem of the business data update event. On the window side, we had a windows event and we had a mechanism already built into the library classes for calling an execute command whenever there is an expected windows event.

There is an analogous event over on the business side. Whenever business data is updated, by whatever means, we can say there is an update event. We want our BRIDGE object to respond by displaying the updated data in the control in the window.

The operator can change data in one window and it may affect other data in the same window as well as affecting other data in other active windows. But note that updates from window controls are not the only updates that occur for business data. Business data can also be updated by loading from disk storage, by a calculation done in some business process, and by a consistency algorithm triggered by another update.

We have to (1) recognize whenever a change has been made to any business data and (2) notify all BRIDGE objects connected with the changed data. (Many bridge objects can be connected to one business datum. For example, a phone number on the business side may be displayed in three different active windows. In that case, three BRIDGE objects would be connected to the one phone number business datum.)

4. Managing business datum updates

We created a DATA_DISPATCHER class which yields instances which require very little memory. Its purpose is to pass an update notification on to any number of other objects which inherit from the class NOTIFIABLE. The Eiffel texts for both the DATA_DISPATCHER and the NOTIFIABLE classes are included at the end of this paper.

4.1 BRIDGE inherits from NOTIFIABLE

The BRIDGE class inherits from NOTIFIABLE. (We found that other classes besides BRIDGE also needed notification from time to time when some business update occured, so we factored the NOTIFIABLE concept out of the BRIDGE class.)

DATA_DISPATCHER objects are like the little seeds on the outside of a strawberry. They are small and exposed publicly. You get them with the business class and they are essential to its proper operation, but they are not why you bought the business class.

The designer of any business class will either employ business datum classes like BUSINESS_STRING and PUBLIC_OPTION that have their own DATA_DISPATCHER objects built in, or he/she will supply a DATA_DISPATCHER attribute, maybe just exported to {BRIDGE, INTERFACE}, for each business datum in the business class.

Here is an example of that last. Our PIPE class includes the following attributes:

```
feature {INTERFACE, BRIDGE} -- Bridge features

        nominal_size_dispatcher: DATA_DISPATCHER
                        -- To notify other objects when the pipe
                        -- nominal size changes.

        inside_diameter_value_dispatcher: DATA_DISPATCHER
                        -- To notify other objects when the value
                        -- of the pipe's inside diameter changes.

        inside_diameter_unit_dispatcher: DATA_DISPATCHER
                        -- To notify other objects when the unit
                        -- of measure (inches, mm, etc.) of the
                        -- pipe's inside diameter changes.
```

Whenever the value of the pipe's inside diameter changes, whether by operator input, loading from disk, or by lookup due to a change in pipe nominal size,

```
        inside_diameter_value_dispatcher.notify
```

is executed by the routine that made the change and the DATA_DISPATCHER then passes the notification on to any NOTIFIABLE object connected to the DATA_DISPATCHER.

To set this up, it is usually sufficient for the interface to give a reference to the proper DATA_DISPATCHER object to the bridge object when the bridge is first created. The bridge then manages connection to and disconnection from the DATA_DISPATCHER. Figure 6 illustrates this design pattern.

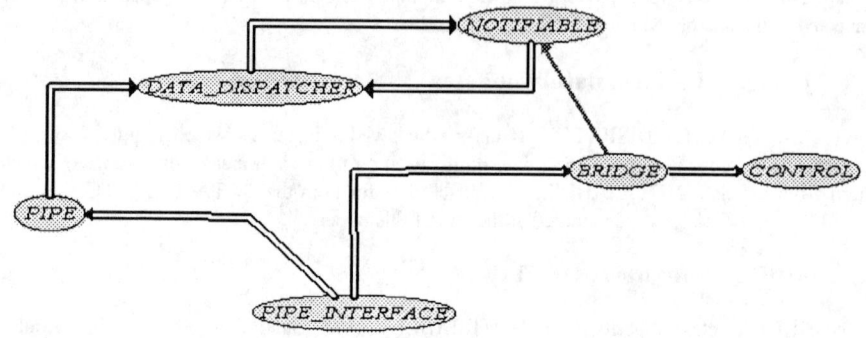

Figure 6. Notification of the BRIDGE object

4.2   Reusing BRIDGE classes

The only remaining problem to solve is the proliferation of bridge classes. This is a problem because, in general, the bridge has to know four things about the business datum to which it is connected:

(1) The bridge has to have a reference to the proper DATA_DISPATCHER object.

(2) The bridge needs to be able to execute the proper query to get the value of the business datum for display purposes.

(3) The bridge needs to be able to execute the proper validation query to determine if a proposed update should be attemped.

And (4) the bridge needs to be able to execute the proper update command once validation is successful.

Of these, the first is relatively easy. The interface object gives a reference to the DATA_DISPATCHER object to the bridge when the bridge is created.

The other three cause the problem. For each business datum (of which there may be many per business class) there may be several different queries giving display values in different forms. And there may also be several update commands -- different ways to update the same business datum. How many different bridge classes do we have to write? Several different classes for EACH business datum? That's too many bridge classes.

4.3 Active objects to the rescue

Active Objects is a new feature of Eiffel 4.3 that permits the creation of an object to represent either a FUNCTION or a PROCEDURE. The active object can be created by the interface object just prior to the creation of a bridge object, it can be handed over to the bridge object, and then, at a later time, the bridge object can have the active object actually execute the corresponding function or procedure.

This cuts down substantially on the number of different bridge classes that have to be written. The bridge classes can now be relatively ignorant of the exact business feature to be executed. The bridge simply knows to execute the proper FUNCTION or PROCEDURE and to act on the results.

5. Conclusion

In the end, after constructing the contract pattern outlined in this paper, we have a set of library classes which take much of the work of coordinating between business classes and window controls out of the application programmer's hands. The application programmer is now left with the following tasks.

1. Write the business classes and include a DATA_DISPATCHER attribute for each business datum which may show up on a window.

2. Construct the windows and the controls on the windows.

3. Write interface classes that set up bridges between the business data and the window controls.

Each of these tasks has its own easily-recognizable sphere of software maintenance. The software development and software maintenance teams now have the software nicely separated into segments that can be addressed more easily and more effectively over the lifetime of the application software.

6. Class text for the DATA_DISPATCHER class

```
indexing
        description: "Informs all NOTIFIABLE objects when business data has %
                % changed.";
        date: "$Date: 11 February 1999$";
        author: "Rex Fowler"
class
        DATA_DISPATCHER
creation
        make
feature {NONE} -- Initialization
        make is
                        -- Initialize a new DATA_DISPATCHER object.
                do
                        !! notifiable_array.make (initial_count)
                end
feature -- Status report
        is_connected_to (a_notifiable: NOTIFIABLE): BOOLEAN is
                        -- True if this current DATA_DISPATCHER is
                        -- connected to the argument NOTIFIABLE.
                require
                        good_argument: a_notifiable /= Void
```

```
                    do
                                Result := notifiable_array.has (a_notifiable)
                    end
        feature -- Action
                notify is
                                -- Notify all connected notifiables that there
                                -- has been some change to the business data.
                    do
                                if not notifiable_array.empty then
                                        from
                                                notifiable_array.start
                                        until
                                                notifiable_array.off
                                        loop
                                                notifiable_array.item.notify
                                                notifiable_array.forth
                                        end
                                end
                    end
        feature {NOTIFIABLE} -- Private access
                connect (a_notifiable: NOTIFIABLE) is
                                -- A NOTIFIABLE object connects itself to the business
                                -- data object.
                        require
                                good_notifiable: a_notifiable /= Void
                                not_connected: not is_connected_to (a_notifiable)
                        do
                                notifiable_array.extend (a_notifiable)
                        ensure
                                connected: is_connected_to (a_notifiable)
                        end
                disconnect (a_notifiable: NOTIFIABLE) is
                                -- A NOTIFIABLE object disconnects itself from the
                                -- business data object.
                        require
                                good_notifiable: a_notifiable /= Void
                        do
                                notifiable_array.prune_all (a_notifiable)
                        ensure
                                not_connected: not is_connected_to (a_notifiable)
                        end
        feature {NONE} -- Implementation
                notifiable_array: ARRAYED_LIST [NOTIFIABLE]
                                -- List of NOTIFIABLE objects connected to this business
                                -- data object.
                initial_count: INTEGER is 2
                                -- Size of the array at creation.
        invariant
                good_array: notifiable_array /= Void
        end -- class DATA_DISPATCHER
```

7.   Class text for the NOTIFIABLE class

```
indexing
        description: "Objects that accept notifications from a %
                % DATA_DISPATCHER object."
        author: "Rex Fowler"
        date: "$Date: 19 March 1999$"
deferred class
        NOTIFIABLE
feature {NONE} -- Initialization
        make_notifiable (a_dispatcher: DATA_DISPATCHER) is
                        -- Initialize the NOTIFIABLE object by saving
                        -- a reference to the dispatcher that will
                        -- give notifications.
                require
                        good_dispatcher: a_dispatcher /= Void
                        not_connected: not a_dispatcher.is_connected_to (Current)
                do
                        dispatcher := a_dispatcher
```

```
                        dispatcher.connect (Current)
            ensure
                        dispatcher_set: dispatcher = a_dispatcher
                        dispatcher_connected: is_connected
            end
feature -- Access
        dispatcher: DATA_DISPATCHER
                        -- Reference to the DATA_DISPATCHER object which
                        -- will notify this NOTIFIABLE when there has been
                        -- any change to the business data.
feature -- Shut down
        disconnect is
                        -- Disconnect from the DATA_DISPATCHER.
            require
                        connected: is_connected
            do
                        dispatcher.disconnect (Current)
                        dispatcher := Void
            ensure
                        not_connected: not is_connected
            end
feature -- Status report
        is_connected: BOOLEAN is
                        -- True if this NOTIFIABLE is connected to the
                        -- DATA_DISPATCHER.
            do
                        Result := ((dispatcher /= Void and then
                                dispatcher.is_connected_to (Current)))
            end
feature -- Transformation
        change_dispatcher (a_dispatcher: DATA_DISPATCHER) is
                        -- Sometimes the business data is so volatile,
                        -- we have to disconnect from one dispatcher and
                        -- connect to a new one.
            require
                        good_argument: a_dispatcher /= Void
                        connected: is_connected
                        different: a_dispatcher /= dispatcher
                        not_connected: not a_dispatcher.is_connected_to (Current)
            do
                        disconnect
                        dispatcher := a_dispatcher
                        dispatcher.connect (Current)
            ensure
                        dispatcher_set: dispatcher = a_dispatcher
                        dispatcher_connected: is_connected
            end
feature {DATA_DISPATCHER} -- Data Dispatcher Action
        notify is
                        -- The DATA_DISPATCHER is now notifying
                        -- this object that a change was made
                        -- to the business data.
            require
                        connected: is_connected
            deferred
            end
invariant
end -- class NOTIFIABLE
```

References

[1] Bertrand Meyer, Object-Oriented Software Construction, Second Edition, January 1997.

Experiences teaching Eiffel as a first programming language to Economy students

Prof. Dr. Guido Dedene
Katholieke Universiteit Leuven
Faculty of Economics and Applied Economics
Business Information Systems Group
Naamsestraat, 69
B-3000 Leuven

E-mail: guido.dedene@econ.kuleuven.ac.be

Introduction

About 25 year ago Catholic University of Leuven (K.U.Leuven) inserted information systems studies in its academic curriculum. The implementation involved the Faculties of Science and Applied Science for the topics oriented towards Computer Science while the Business Information Systems topics were assigned to the Faculty of Economics and Applied Economics. Research in this group addresses today the main topics of commercial information processing, including:

- The development of Software Applications, including Systems Analysis and Design.
- Database Management Systems, Data Mining and Data Warehousing.
- Knowledge Based Systems, including Decision Tables and Fuzzy Logic.
- Groupware, Office Systems and Workflow Management.
- Economics of Information Systems, and Systems Management

Apart from special studies, such a Business Engineering in Information Systems, some compulsory computer courses for all Economy students were inserted. One such course is the "Introduction to Information Systems", a 60-hours course which shares two major goals:

- After the course, the student should have gained insight in the current state-of-art of Information and Communication Technology (I.C.T.), sufficient to judge the possibilities (as well as restrictions) of that technology for business applications. Hence one half of the course is devoted to Information and Communication Technology subjects, including computer platforms (hardware trends, operating systems) and networking.

- Furthermore the student should learn the basic mechanisms to understand and construct computer applications. The ambition level is a first contact with software construction, illustrated with simple systems examples. The Applied Economics curriculum has two more 60-hours courses addressing more complex systems based on databases and office software.

The majority of the participants to this course had no programming experience so far. None of them will really become a programmer in a later life. It is hence quite challenging to build a course content that is interesting and appealing enough for 19-year-old youngsters.

0-7695-0278-4/99 $10.00 © 1999 IEEE

The software part

The application software part of the course was initially using BASIC. Although this was subject to criticism, one major argument to use this language was that gaining insight in software construction principles (such as structured programming) was dominant over the choice of technology. Programming exercises could be done in Waterloo Basic on a central VM-mainframe, or using various BASIC-implementations on personal computers. The main examples were commercially oriented, including a simple shop cash register management system, and an order and invoice handling system. All examples are based on character-based user interfaces. Persistent information was kept in simple files.

In the late eighties, the programming language PASCAL replaced BASIC. The students could use Waterloo Pascal on the VM-mainframe, Delphi Pascal on personal computers and Sun Pascal for Solaris at one Campus location. All the examples were translated in PASCAL, using its rich typing mechanisms and its enforcement to use structured programming constructs.

In the mid nineties, some new challenges did arise. Indeed, if any students already had programming experience, it would have been with Pascal. For them, the course was percieved as "just another Pascal programming course". Nevertheless, at the final examen it became painfully clear how some of these experienced programmers were not exactly experts in structured program development. It became also increasingly difficult to maintain a course text with different Pascal implementations (e.g. file system manipulations).

Next, students felt unhappy with the fact that they were required to write complete Pascal programs from scratch. It gave them the feeling that in the course they were learning and doing things they would never do again in their life. Finally, there was an increased interest in objects and components, with the arrival of Java and E-Commerce. Moreover, important research activities were developed in software development using object-oriented business models, using the Eiffel notation (the MERODE project (Snoeck 1998)). Whenever software was developed in our research, there was a strong commitment for object-orientation. Development activities were majorly done in Delphi, Pascal and Eiffel.

The course was split over three groups, one group being located in KULAK, a remote campus of K.U.Leuven. Three years ago, we made the decision to switch to a strict object-oriented approach with an emphasis on software components and design principles. At the final evaluation it should be possible to assess how a student gained the ability to understand and customize existing class definitions for simple software systems.

The choice of the language

Of course, one of the first questions was the choice of the programming language for the software part of the course. Realizing that for some people this is close to religious war, and remembering that the choice was made three years ago, it may be instructive to start from some of the requirements for the language:

- The syntax should be clear, unambiguous and orthogonal.
- The language should enforce the discipline of structured and object-oriented programming.
- Technology to teach the language should be available on a variety of platforms, including various personal computer Windows versions, Windows NT, Unix and Linux. The KULAK Campus is using UNIX as well as Windows NT servers.
- The availability of shareware for student practice. In principle all exercises should be possible based on "paper and pencil" since the final exam is not using computers.
- The language should preferably not be bound to one commercial organization, or one special tool.

The following gives a transcript of the discussions on the language choice. It should be realized that the arguments that are presented are bound to the didactical context sketched before. They may not apply at all, and be complemented by other arguments in a different application context.

A first and obvious choice was object-oriented Pascal. The followings are some arguments against the choice for Object-Pascal (although many of them also apply to other languages)

- There is no general accepted Object-Pascal standard with implementations. Of course there is the de facto standard Delphi-environment, which is bound to Windows platforms. It should be noted that the Delphi-development environment was felt to be one of the friendliest development environments at the moment of the choice.
- Object-Pascal makes the distinction between the (proto-)type and the implementation, the actual class definition for the objects. It was felt that this "double" definition is confusing for students, although integrated development environments may provide support for consistency checking.
- Object-Pascal is a hybrid language. Hence it does not enforce the principles of object orientation very strictly.
- Object-Pascal uses single inheritance, which restricts class libraries to a hierarchical structure and makes it difficult to combine libraries from different vendors.
- Some constructs are very difficult to explain to students whose primary interest is not in computer technology. One obvious example is the need for "Void" as a specification element.

Another very obvious choice was Java, given the market attention developed the last years. Moreover, the Computer Science department in the Faculties of Sciences and Applied Sciences made the decision to change their first-year courses to Java as a replacement for Pascal. Although it was felt that the Java Technology, and in particular the Java Platform, is a very important development, the Java Language was rejected for the following reasons.

- The Java syntax is unnecessarily complex, as inherited from C++. One obvious example is the addressing scheme in arrays, starting at 0. Another one is the manipulation of strings...
- Making attributes public violates the principle of encapsulation in object orientation.
- The Java technology is extremely rich and complex, so that a relevant subset needs to be defined for the students.
- The previous arguments about single inheritance still apply (as exemplified by the current discussion between Sun and Microsoft).

Clearly C++ was too complex for this student profile. An apart alternative could be Smalltalk, which has been so important to the initial didactics of object-orientation. Although Smalltalk is also a strict object-oriented language, and has clear merits, its major drawbacks were the following.

- The Smalltalk syntax was found to be quite difficult.
- The absence of strong typing can make it difficult to point students to specification inconsistencies without debugging.
- The distinction between class versus instance features may induce unneeded complexity in systems.
- Single inheritance binds Smalltalk implementations tightly to one vendor.

Another possible choice could have been object-oriented Cobol. Major drawbacks include the lack of an agreed standard and the language syntax. Moreover, Cobol is addressed in another course for students that wish to explore that technology.

Finally the decision was made to go for Eiffel. The major reasons for this choice were the following.

- The syntax is particularly simple and very much like Pascal (enforcing structured programming).
- The language is "owned" by a nonprofit consortium (NICE).
- The language implements in a very strict fashion object-orientation, including multiple inheritance and strong typing.
- Many shareware implementations are available. Currently, the base library, which is sufficient for the majority of the course content, is declared open source.
- Eiffel can be used as a Java-generator, in case this is needed.

The major argument against the choice for Eiffel was the slow market acceptance, or rather, the absence of marketing hype around the language. Today, increasingly it is found that commercial applications of Eiffel appear where other technologies failed. Typical examples are financial institutes and social security applications, both involving complex legislation and business rules.

Maybe the ultimate alternative could be the development of a new didactical language, such as Blue at Monash University (Kölling 1996). However, as we are not a computer science department, we lack the resources and rather like to rely on a commercially supported implementation, if possible.

The new course

The course is now running for three years, with the following (reasonably stable) structure.

Chapter 1   ***Introduction to object-oriented programming.***
    1.1 What is programming ?
    1.2 Programming by class definitions for objects.
    1.3 Classes, types and interfaces (features).

1.4 A simple "hello"-system.

The introduction gives an intuitive explanation of what is required to develop working software systems. Basic notions of class definitions, as well as strong typing are discussed. The chapter ends with everybody's first programming example: "hello world"...

Chapter 2 **Class definitions in detail.**
2.1 A simple "echo"-system.
2.2 Expansion and reference types.
2.3 Encapsulation in practice.
2.4 A simple student administration system.

This chapter explains the basic syntax for class definitions. Particular attention is devoted to the distinction between expansion type objects ("the elementary particles") versus reference type objects. After emphasizing the importance of encapsulation for software integrity (explaining briefly some of the notions of design by contract on features), all the material covered so far is illustrated in a simple student administration system. This last system is the first that is not using a "make = run" structure, which is only acceptable for very small applications...As fast as possible the students are encouraged to distribute the work coherently over different cooperative classes.

Chapter 3 **Structures in methods.**
3.1 What is "structured" programming ?
3.2 Selection structures in methods.
3.3 Iteration structures in methods.
3.4 Combining selection and iteration in menu-structures.
3.5 The student administration system with menu-structures.

This chapter deals with structured programming aspects. The basis structure primitives (sequence, selection and iteration) are clearly defined, and the orthogonality of the language that is used becomes rapidly evident. In particular the uniform expression for the iteration works very well. Recursion is mentioned, but not encouraged. Templates for menu-structures and character based user interfaces are illustrated with examples.

Chapter 4 **Object-structures.**
4.1 Why object structures ?
4.2 Arrays of objects.
4.3 Linked-lists of objects.
4.4 Relation-based structures.

Objects are combined into arrays and linked lists in this chapter. The classical tradeoff between storage-occupation and query-execution-length is discussed as an example of file organization in general. Students learn how to manipulate object structures. Various search- and sort-mechanisms are illustrated with examples, such as a small lottery-program.

The principles of inheritance for class definitions are unveiled in this chapter. Students learn how to reuse other class specifications in a disciplined way. The major application in this chapter is persistency of objects. Misuses of inheritance are discussed in detail, following the discussion in (Meyer 1997).

This is the chapter where the economics-oriented students see some realistic information systems in action. All the material from the previous chapters is combined into recognizable business software applications. The chapter reviews the system against software quality criteria and a major consistency guarding approach for software construction: design by contract.

Graphical user interfaces are not only fashionable, but difficult to handle consistently. This is the message explained in this chapter. Rather than exploring a complete user interface library, the interfacing is illustrated with a generic pre-compiled component, with facilitates a default graphical user-interface with parametrizable text-windows and buttons. This allows adding a simple GUI-front-end to the above examples. The precompiled component is based on the ISE EiffelVision library.

The Internet is a dominant worldwide global I.C.T.-infrastructure today. Web-enabled User Interfaces (WUI) are discussed with their advantages and drawbacks. A generic component for HTML/CGI-interaction is briefly illustrated. This precompiled component is based on the ISE EiffelWeb library. The examples run on the Internet Server from Microsoft.

Appendix B   Solutions to the exercises.
Appendix C   Eiffel Bibliography and WWW-references.

The roadmap of examples that are developed in the course is interesting to observe.

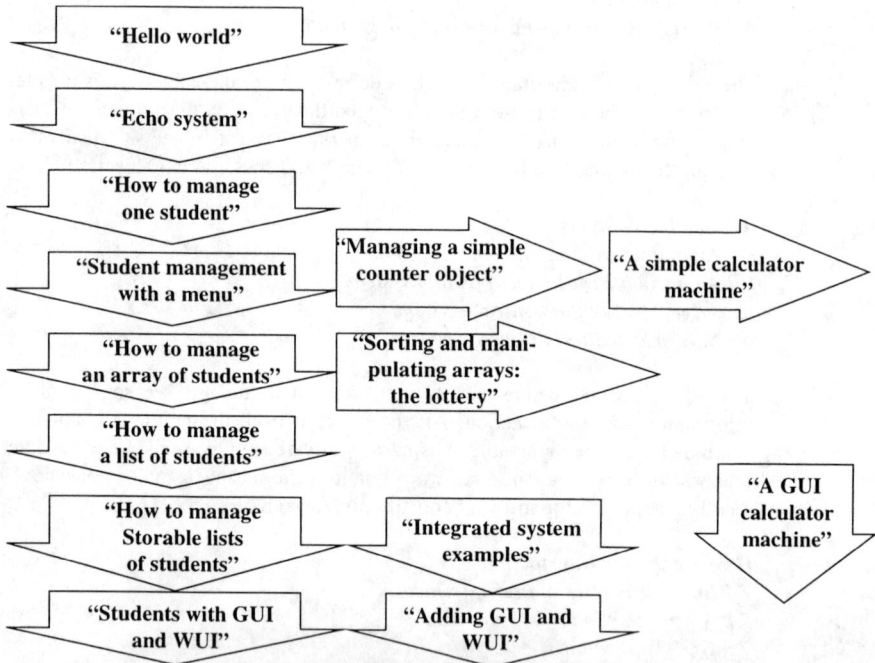

The reason that student systems are taken as leading examples is straightforward: it confronts students with their own realities, and ways to administer themselves.

Early experiences

The exam at the end of the year evaluates the students using two instruments. On one hand the students are confronted with a system in which some components are not completed. The system is of the same degree of difficulty as the elaborated systems in chapter 6. Indeed, chapter 7 and 8 are not explicit examination material.

Typically students are required to complete features in class definitions, or to complete the signatures for feature definitions. On the other hand, students get some simple multi-choice questions, confronting them with compact code fragments and asking them for the results of the code fragments. The following is an example of a multi-choice question.

```
class TEST98S2
creation make
feature a,b,c : INTEGER
feature make is
        do
                from a := 1
                until a = 10
                loop
                    b := a
                    from a := -5
                    until a = 0
                    loop
                            c := b + a
                            a := a + 1
                    end -- loop
                    a := b
                    a := a + 1
                end -- loop
            io.putint(c)
            io.readline
            end -- make
end -- class TEST98S2
```

a. Execution shows "8"

b. Invalid because control variable is changed inside iteration

c. Execution shows "10"

d. Infinite loop

GOAL: test understanding of iteration structure, control and stop conditions...

The major aim is to evaluate the student's abilities to understand a system structure and to modify, complete or modify some classes in a system. Before the actual exam, the students have two trial exams during the academic year (one after chapter 3, the second after chapter 6).

The above material is covered in 30 hours of teaching, including 5 computer-practice sessions with a duration of one afternoon. Typically, the majority of the students really catches up after the third practice session. The students have access to ISE Eiffel under a campus license for KULAK, using 20 Windows-workstations. Only the melting-compilation mode is used for the students. All appropriate components are precompiled on before by the teacher. Of course the students are free to use WWW-shareware as they feel appropriate, and some take actually a personal Eiffel license.

The student's reactions are majorly enthusiastic: they welcome the choice of Eiffel as a choice for clean, modern and hype-free technology. They have in the beginning major difficulties with the abstraction level that is required. It is interesting to see that students, initially only going for the technology part of the introductory course, get very enthusiastic about the software part. Moreover, students with previous programming experience (typically Basic or Pascal), don't really have an advantage, due to the fact that they have to think in class definitions before starting to program.

An interesting point is the following: due to the static typing, many errors are intercepted in the melting. The debugging facilities are shown at one point in the course, but students are hardly confronted with debugging, and the practice sessions never use the debugger. They feel they really have to think clearly before they can start to write down the class definitions for the objects. We can acknowledge that Eiffel forces the students really to think before they are able at all to program. A side-result of this is the fact that students get increasingly an admiration for good program designers, and some of their colleague students do indeed very well.

A weak point in the current course is that the present content doesn't discuss assertions very much in detail. Assertions are used in the examples in chapter 6, and the components in chapters 7 & 8, in conjunction with the design by contract approach. This aspect may get more attention in future versions.

After all, a relevant subset of Eiffel had to be choosen so that it was feasible to teach it to Economics students. For sure, a computer science audience can go much deeper in this material.

Currently, a project is submitted to build a didactical infrastructure based on the K.U.Leuven intranet (the Campus Wide Information System CWIS). This infrastructure should allow students to submit examples, get them compiled and running and get comments, generated as automatic as possible. The Nottingham University Ceilidh system is a major source for inspiration (Ceilidh). The student time that is gained when such an infrastructure becomes available can indeed be reinvested in explaining software quality aspects more fundamentally.

References

Kölling 1996   Kölling, M., Rosenberg, J., "An Object-oriented Program Development Environment for the First Programming Course", *Proceedings of the 27th SIGCSE Technical Symposium on Computer Science Education*, 1996.

Meyer 1997   Meyer, B., "Object-oriented software construction" Second Edition, *Prentice-Hall, Inc.*, 1997.

Snoeck 1998   Snoeck, M., Dedene, G., "Existence Dependency: the key to semantic integrity between structural and behavioural aspects of object types", *IEEE Transactions on Software Engineering*, Vol. 24 (4), 1998.

Ceilidh   http://www.cs.nott.ac.uk/ ~ceilidh

Author Index

ABOUT THE TOOLS CONFERENCE SERIES

The mission of the TOOLS Conference Series is...

- To provide quality training and education on component and object technology and other modern software development approaches.
- To offer a meeting place for experts and practitioners from all over the world.
- To foster the development of software technology, with special emphasis on software quality and productivity.

TOOLS — Technology of Object-Oriented Languages and Systems — is the major series of international conferences and exhibition entirely devoted to the applications of component and object technology. Its emphasis is on the practice of object technology and its applications in industrial environments, complementing the more academically-oriented perspective of traditional conferences. TOOLS provides a balanced coverage of the wealth of approaches, trends and variants in the object-oriented community. For anyone interested in object technology, the TOOLS Conferences are the best places to learn from the experts and compare experiences with other O-O practitioners.

Reflecting the international nature of interest and contributions to object-oriented development, the conferences are now held fives times per year on four different continents: TOOLS USA (California), TOOLS Europe (France), TOOLS PACIFIC (Australia), TOOLS ASIA (China), and TOOLS EASTERN EUROPE (Bulgaria).

Initiated in 1989, the TOOLS Conference Series now enters its second decade of international presence and continues its commitment to excellence demonstrated by earlier conferences.

Each one the TOOLS conference is a week-full of intense object technology updates including the following components:

- Keynote presentations by some of the most renowned innovators in the field;
- Hands-on tutorials by recognized experts on topics extending over the whole range of object-oriented concepts;
- Solid technical program, based on a strict refereeing process, conducted by an international program committee;
- Interactive workshops and lively panel discussions on the most exciting issues of the moment;
- An exhibition of the latest products and services by the major vendors in the field;
- Complementary events such as user group meetings, symposiums, working group discussions, BOFs etc.;
- And of course an attractive social program in the superb locations selected by TOOLS.

Proceedings of previous TOOLS Conferences are available worldwide and from the conference organization at the address below:

TOOLS Conferences
270 Storke Rd., Suite 7
Santa Barbara, CA 93117, USA
Phone: (805) 685-1006, Fax: (805) 685-6869
Email: tools@tools.com
URL: http://www.tools.com

Notes

Press Activities Board

IEEE Computer Society Publications

The world-renowned IEEE Computer Society publishes, promotes, and distributes a wide variety of authoritative computer science and engineering texts. These books are available from most retail outlets. Visit the Online Catalog, *http://computer.org*, for a list of products.

IEEE Computer Society Proceedings

The IEEE Computer Society also produces and actively promotes the proceedings of more than 141 acclaimed international conferences each year in multimedia formats that include hard and softcover books, CD-ROMs, videos, and on-line publications.

For information on the IEEE Computer Society proceedings, send e-mail to cs.books@computer.org or write to Proceedings, IEEE Computer Society, P.O. Box 3014, 10662 Los Vaqueros Circle, Los Alamitos, CA 90720-1314. Telephone +1 714-821-8380. FAX +1 714-761-1784.

Additional information regarding the Computer Society, conferences and proceedings, CD-ROMs, videos, and books can also be accessed from our web site at *http://computer.org/cspress*